# Contents

## Maps



## Northwest



## MAP SYMBOLS

### TRANSPORTATION

CONTROLLED ACCESS HIGHWAYS
- Freeway
- Tollway
- Under Construction
- Interchange and Exit Number

OTHER HIGHWAYS
- Primary Highway
- Secondary Highway
- Divided Highway
- Other Paved Road
- Unpaved Road (Check conditions locally)

HIGHWAY MARKERS
- Interstate Route
- U.S. Route
- State or Provincial Route
- County or Other Route
- Trans-Canada Highway
- Canadian Provincial Autoroute
- Mexican Federal Route

OTHER SYMBOLS
- Distances along Major Highways (Miles in U.S., kilometers in Canada and Mexico)
- Tunnel; Pass
- Auto Ferry; Passenger Ferry

### OTHER MAP FEATURES
- Time Zone Boundary
- Mountain Peak; Elevation (in Feet) — Mt. Olympus 7,965
- Perennial; Intermittent River

### RECREATION
- National Park
- National Forest; National Grassland
- Other Large Park or Recreation Area
- Small State Park with and without Camping
- Military Lands
- Indian Reservation
- Trail
- Ski Area
- Point of Interest

### CITIES AND TOWNS
- National Capital
- State or Provincial Capital
- Cities, Towns, and Populated Places (Type size indicates relative importance)
- Urban Area (State and province maps only)
- Large Incorporated Cities (City maps only)

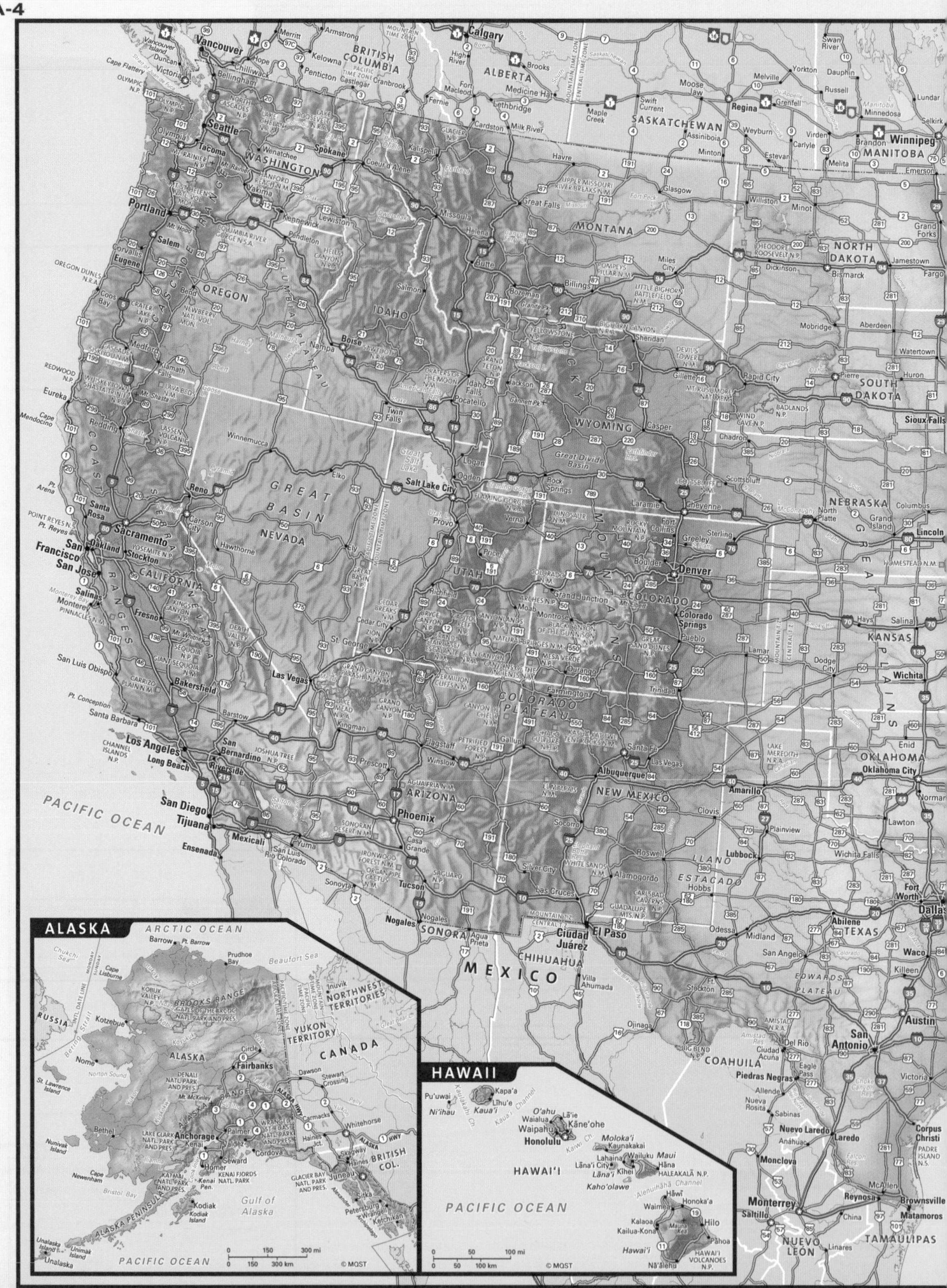
BRITISH COLUMBIA
ALBERTA
SASKATCHEWAN
MANITOBA
WASHINGTON
OREGON
IDAHO
MONTANA
NORTH DAKOTA
SOUTH DAKOTA
WYOMING
NEBRASKA
NEVADA
UTAH
COLORADO
KANSAS
CALIFORNIA
ARIZONA
NEW MEXICO
OKLAHOMA
TEXAS
MEXICO
SONORA
CHIHUAHUA
COAHUILA
NUEVO LEÓN
TAMAULIPAS
PACIFIC OCEAN
GREAT BASIN
COLORADO PLATEAU
COLUMBIA PLATEAU
LLANO ESTACADO
EDWARDS PLATEAU
Vancouver
Calgary
Regina
Winnipeg
Seattle
Spokane
Portland
Salem
Boise
Helena
Great Falls
Billings
Bismarck
Pierre
Cheyenne
Salt Lake City
Reno
Sacramento
San Francisco
Oakland
San Jose
Fresno
Las Vegas
Los Angeles
San Diego
Tijuana
Phoenix
Tucson
Albuquerque
Santa Fe
Denver
Colorado Springs
El Paso
Ciudad Juárez
Lincoln
Wichita
Oklahoma City
Amarillo
Lubbock
Dallas
Austin
San Antonio
Monterrey
ALASKA
ARCTIC OCEAN
Beaufort Sea
BROOKS RANGE
NORTHWEST TERRITORIES
YUKON TERRITORY
CANADA
RUSSIA
Fairbanks
Anchorage
Juneau
Gulf of Alaska
BRITISH COL.
HAWAII
Kaua'i
O'ahu
Honolulu
Moloka'i
Maui
Lāna'i
Kaho'olawe
Hawai'i
HAWAI'I
Hilo
© MQST

CANADA
ONTARIO
QUÉBEC
NEW BRUNSWICK
MAINE
N.H.
VT.
MASS.
R.I.
CT.
NEW YORK
PENNSYLVANIA
NEW JERSEY
MD.
DE.
WEST VIRGINIA
VIRGINIA
NORTH CAROLINA
SOUTH CAROLINA
GEORGIA
FLORIDA
ALABAMA
MISSISSIPPI
LOUISIANA
ARKANSAS
TENNESSEE
KENTUCKY
OHIO
INDIANA
ILLINOIS
MICHIGAN
WISCONSIN
MINNESOTA
IOWA
MISSOURI
OZARK PLATEAU
APPALACHIAN MOUNTAINS
Lake Superior
Lake Michigan
Lake Huron
Lake Erie
Lake Ontario
ATLANTIC OCEAN
GULF OF MEXICO
BAHAMAS
Thunder Bay
Sault Ste. Marie
Sudbury
Ottawa
Montréal
Québec
Toronto
Hamilton
London
Windsor
Minneapolis
St. Paul
Duluth
Milwaukee
Madison
Green Bay
Chicago
Detroit
Grand Rapids
Lansing
Cleveland
Toledo
Columbus
Cincinnati
Indianapolis
Pittsburgh
Buffalo
Rochester
Syracuse
Albany
Boston
Providence
Hartford
New Haven
New York
Newark
Philadelphia
Trenton
Baltimore
Washington, DC
Richmond
Norfolk
Virginia Beach
Raleigh
Durham
Greensboro
Winston-Salem
Charlotte
Columbia
Charleston
Savannah
Atlanta
Macon
Jacksonville
Orlando
Tampa
St. Petersburg
Miami
Fort Lauderdale
West Palm Beach
Key West
Birmingham
Montgomery
Mobile
New Orleans
Baton Rouge
Jackson
Memphis
Nashville
Knoxville
Chattanooga
Louisville
Lexington
St. Louis
Kansas City
Des Moines
Omaha
Topeka
Tulsa
Little Rock
Shreveport
Houston
Beaumont
Galveston
Nassau
Portland
Bangor
Augusta
Concord
Montpelier
Burlington
© MAPQUEST
0 150 300 mi
0 150 300 km

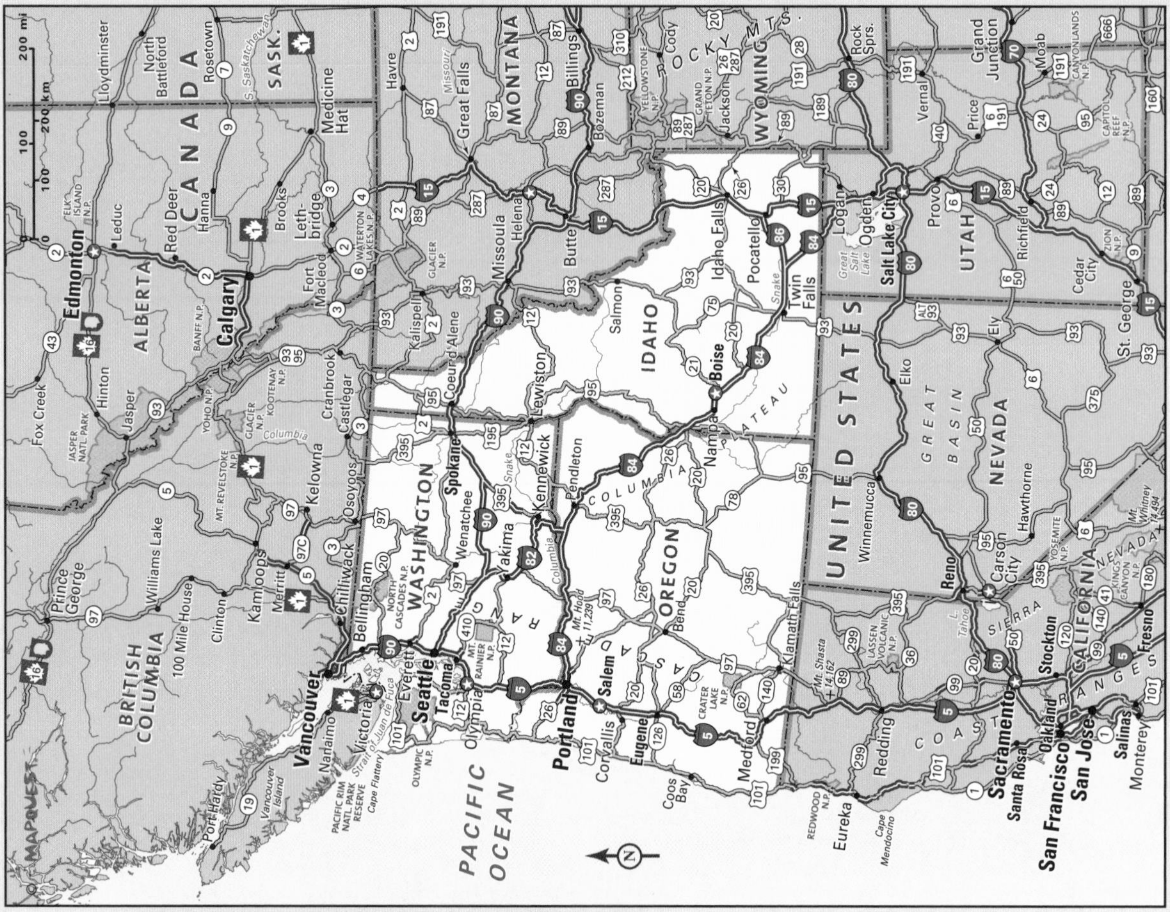

CANADA
BRITISH COLUMBIA
ALBERTA
SASK.
UNITED STATES
WASHINGTON
OREGON
IDAHO
MONTANA
WYOMING
NEVADA
UTAH
CALIFORNIA
PACIFIC OCEAN
GREAT BASIN
COLUMBIA PLATEAU
CASCADE RANGE
COAST RANGES
SIERRA NEVADA
Edmonton
Calgary
Red Deer
Medicine Hat
Lethbridge
Vancouver
Victoria
Kamloops
Kelowna
Prince George
Seattle
Tacoma
Everett
Olympia
Bellingham
Spokane
Yakima
Wenatchee
Kennewick
Portland
Salem
Eugene
Medford
Bend
Klamath Falls
Boise
Nampa
Twin Falls
Pocatello
Idaho Falls
Lewiston
Missoula
Helena
Butte
Great Falls
Billings
Bozeman
Salt Lake City
Ogden
Provo
Reno
Carson City
Winnemucca
Elko
Sacramento
San Francisco
Oakland
San Jose
Stockton
Fresno
Redding
Eureka
Salinas
Monterey
Santa Rosa
200 mi
200 km
MAPQUEST


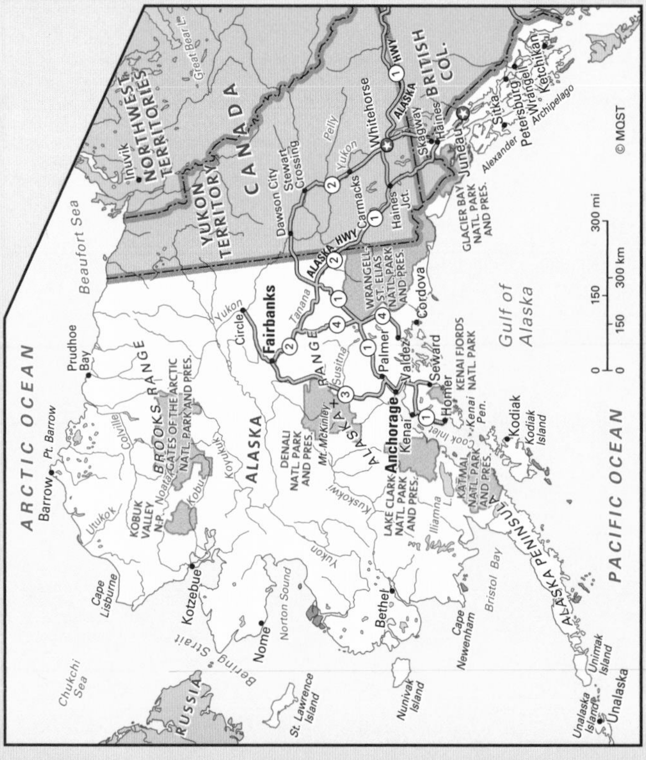

ARCTIC OCEAN
PACIFIC OCEAN
Beaufort Sea
Gulf of Alaska
Bristol Bay
Bering Strait
Chukchi Sea
ALASKA
CANADA
YUKON TERRITORY
NORTHWEST TERRITORIES
BRITISH COL.
RUSSIA
BROOKS RANGE
ALASKA PENINSULA
Barrow
Prudhoe Bay
Fairbanks
Anchorage
Juneau
Nome
Kotzebue
Bethel
Kodiak
Valdez
Seward
Homer
Whitehorse
Dawson City
Ketchikan
Sitka
Unalaska
300 mi
300 km
© MOST

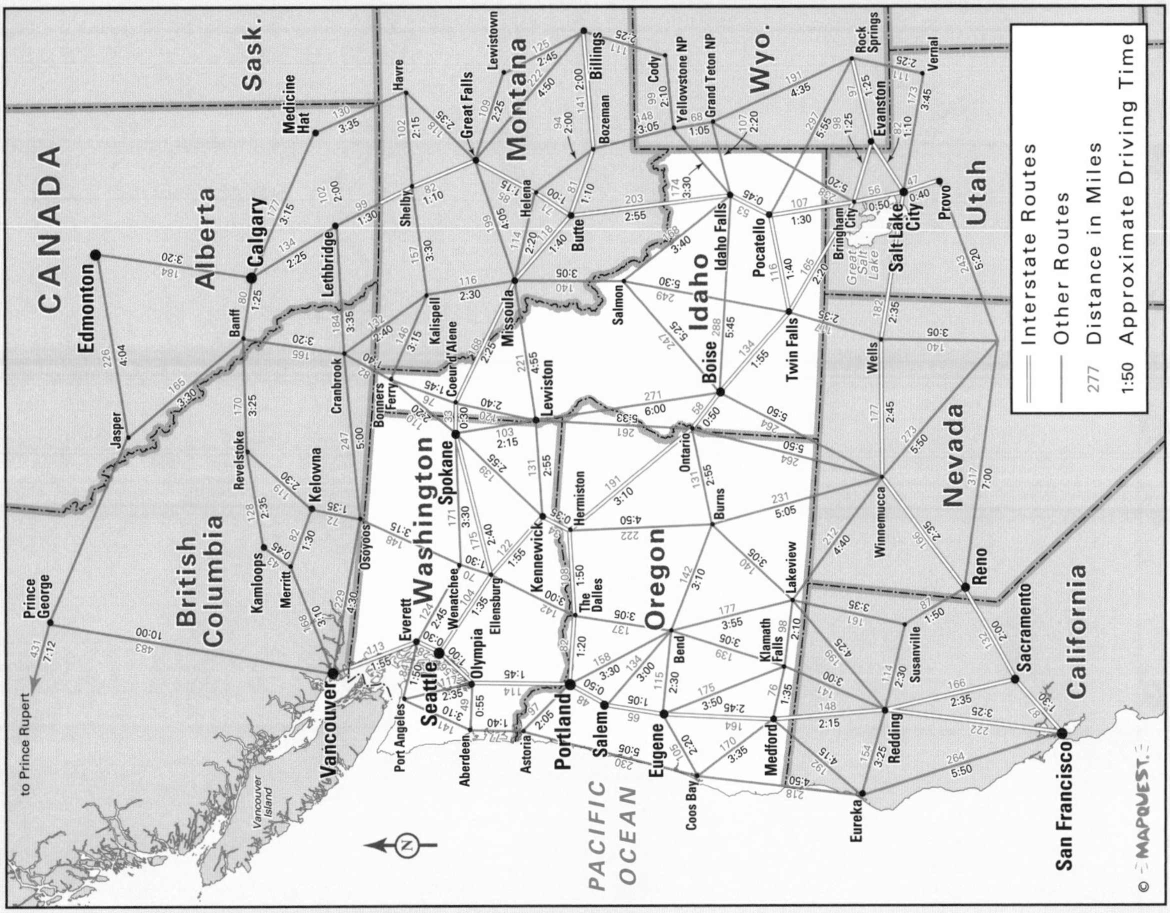

CANADA
Alberta
British Columbia
Sask.
Washington
Oregon
Idaho
Montana
Wyo.
Nevada
Utah
California
PACIFIC OCEAN

Interstate Routes
Other Routes
277 Distance in Miles
1:50 Approximate Driving Time



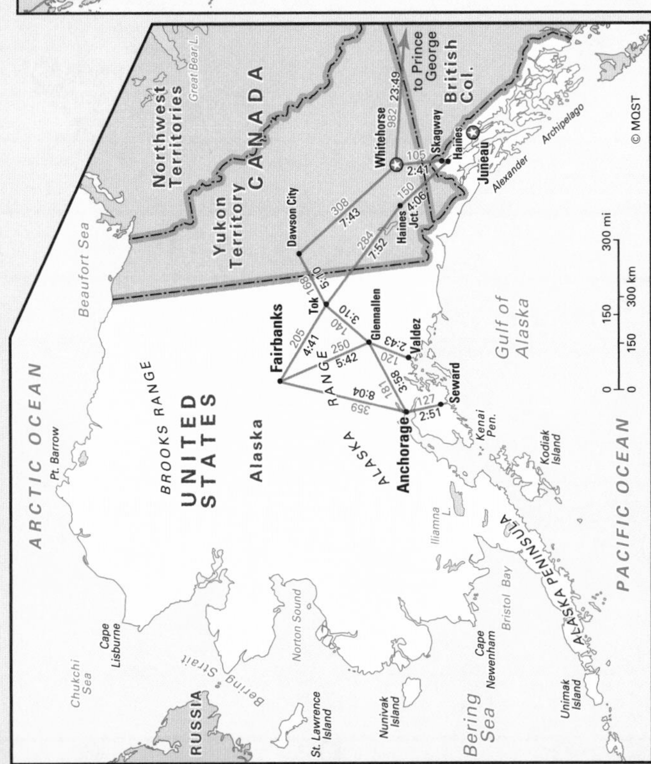

# Alaska

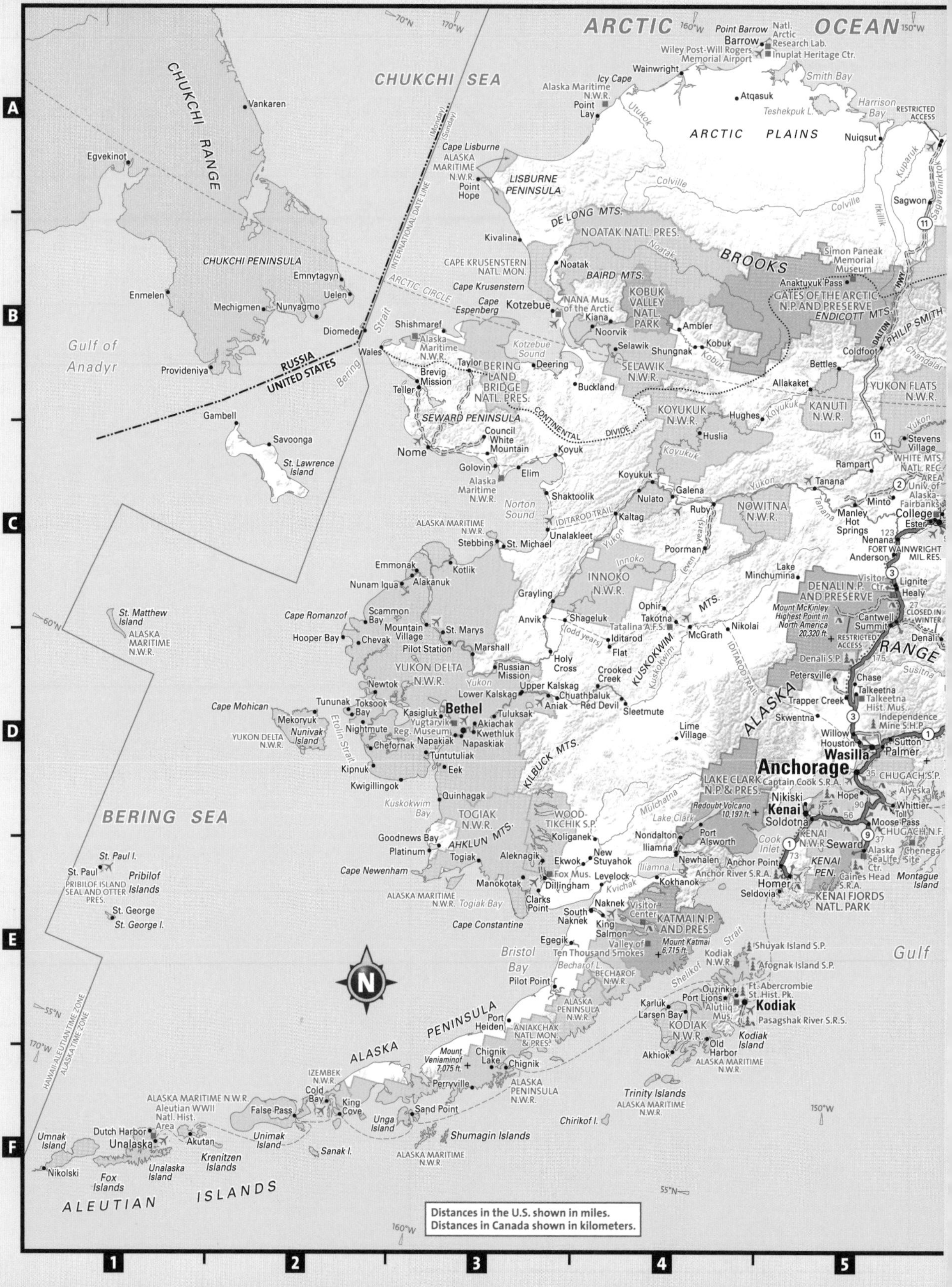

Distances in the U.S. shown in miles.
Distances in Canada shown in kilometers.

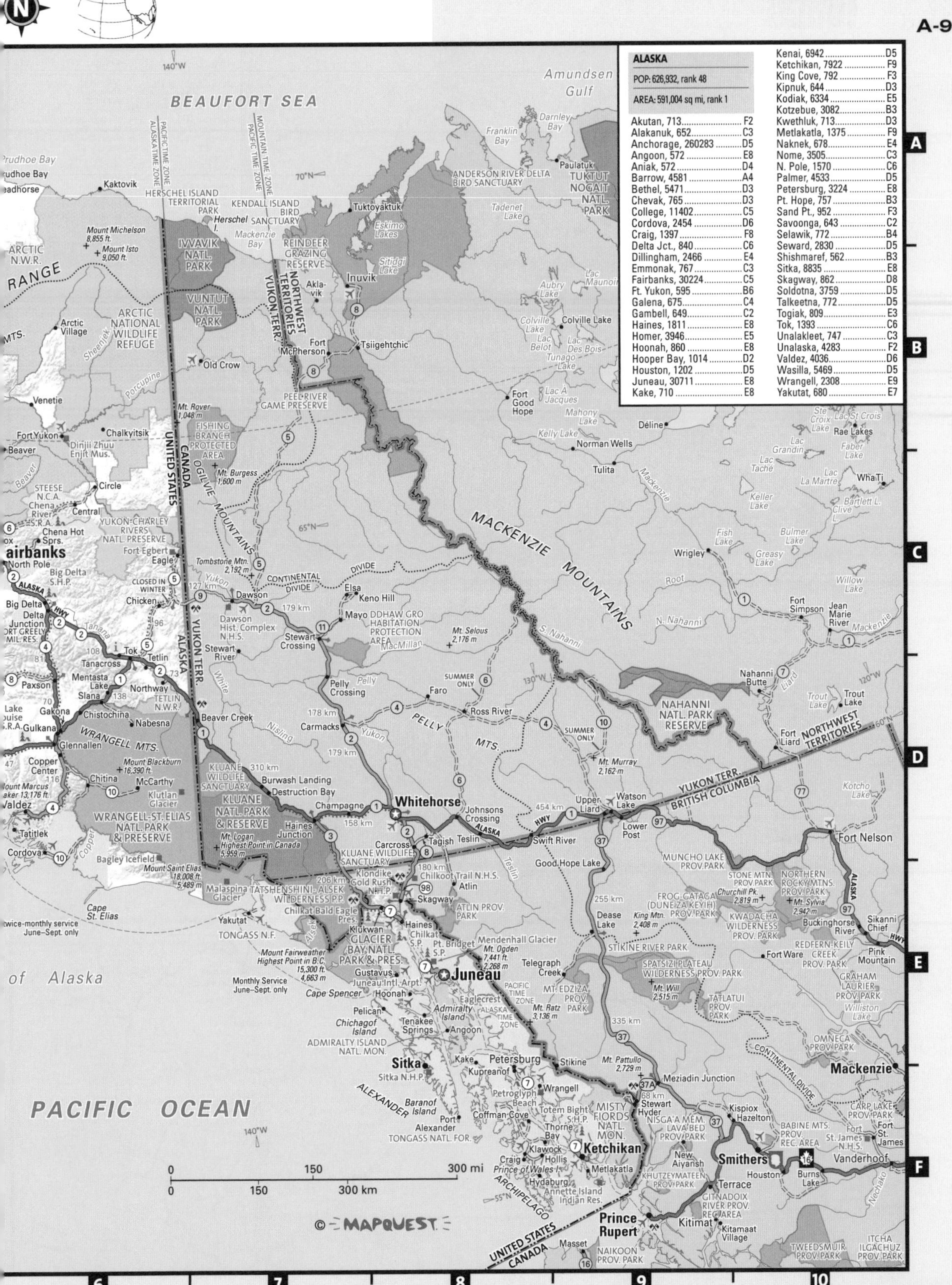

**ALASKA**

POP: 626,932, rank 48

AREA: 591,004 sq mi, rank 1

| Place | Grid | Place | Grid |
|---|---|---|---|
| Akutan, 713 | F2 | Kenai, 6942 | D5 |
| Alakanuk, 652 | C3 | Ketchikan, 7922 | F9 |
| Anchorage, 260283 | D5 | King Cove, 792 | F3 |
| Angoon, 572 | E8 | Kipnuk, 644 | D3 |
| Aniak, 572 | D4 | Kodiak, 6334 | E5 |
| Barrow, 4581 | A4 | Kotzebue, 3082 | B3 |
| Bethel, 5471 | D3 | Kwethluk, 713 | D3 |
| Chevak, 765 | D3 | Metlakatla, 1375 | F9 |
| College, 11402 | C5 | Naknek, 678 | E4 |
| Cordova, 2454 | D6 | Nome, 3505 | C3 |
| Craig, 1397 | F8 | N. Pole, 1570 | C6 |
| Delta Jct., 840 | C6 | Palmer, 4533 | D5 |
| Dillingham, 2466 | E4 | Petersburg, 3224 | E8 |
| Emmonak, 767 | C3 | Pt. Hope, 757 | B3 |
| Fairbanks, 30224 | C5 | Sand Pt., 952 | F3 |
| Ft. Yukon, 595 | B6 | Savoonga, 643 | C2 |
| Galena, 675 | C4 | Selawik, 772 | B4 |
| Gambell, 649 | C2 | Seward, 2830 | D5 |
| Haines, 1811 | E8 | Shishmaref, 562 | B3 |
| Homer, 3946 | E5 | Sitka, 8835 | E8 |
| Hoonah, 860 | E8 | Skagway, 862 | D8 |
| Hooper Bay, 1014 | D2 | Soldotna, 3759 | D5 |
| Houston, 1202 | D5 | Talkeetna, 772 | D5 |
| Juneau, 30711 | E8 | Togiak, 809 | E3 |
| Kake, 710 | E8 | Tok, 1393 | C6 |
| | | Unalakleet, 747 | C3 |
| | | Unalaska, 4283 | F2 |
| | | Valdez, 4036 | D6 |
| | | Wasilla, 5469 | D5 |
| | | Wrangell, 2308 | E9 |
| | | Yakutat, 680 | E7 |

# Idaho

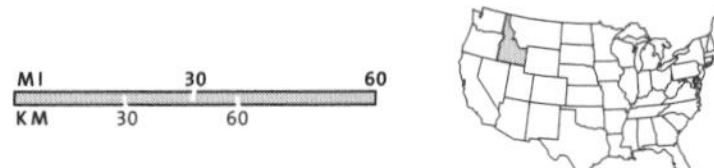

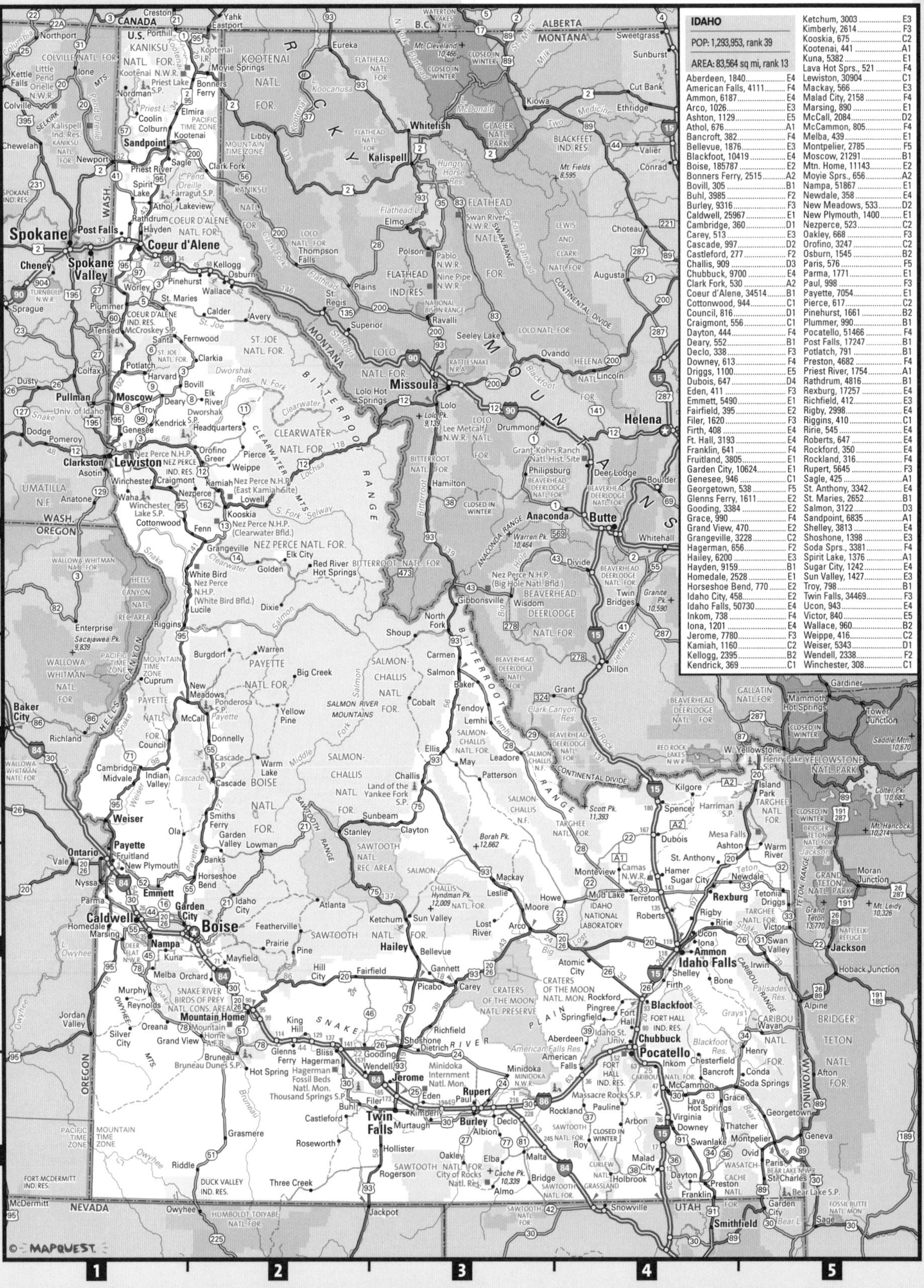

**IDAHO**

POP: 1,293,953, rank 39

AREA: 83,564 sq mi, rank 13

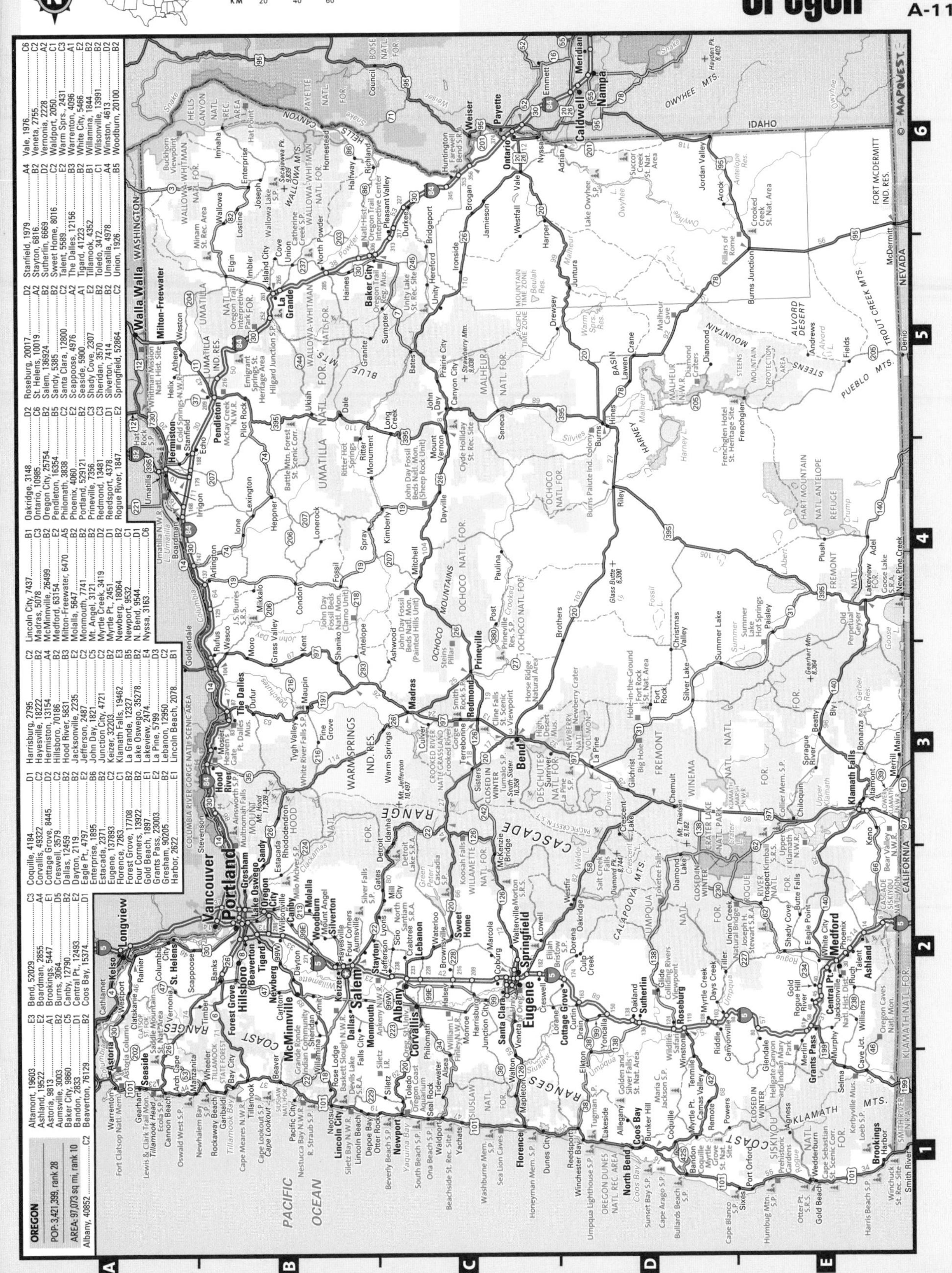

MI 20 40 60
KM 20 40 60
OREGON
POP: 3,421,399, rank 28
AREA: 97,073 sq mi, rank 10
PACIFIC OCEAN
WASHINGTON
IDAHO
NEVADA
CALIFORNIA
Portland
Salem
Eugene
Medford
Bend

# Washington

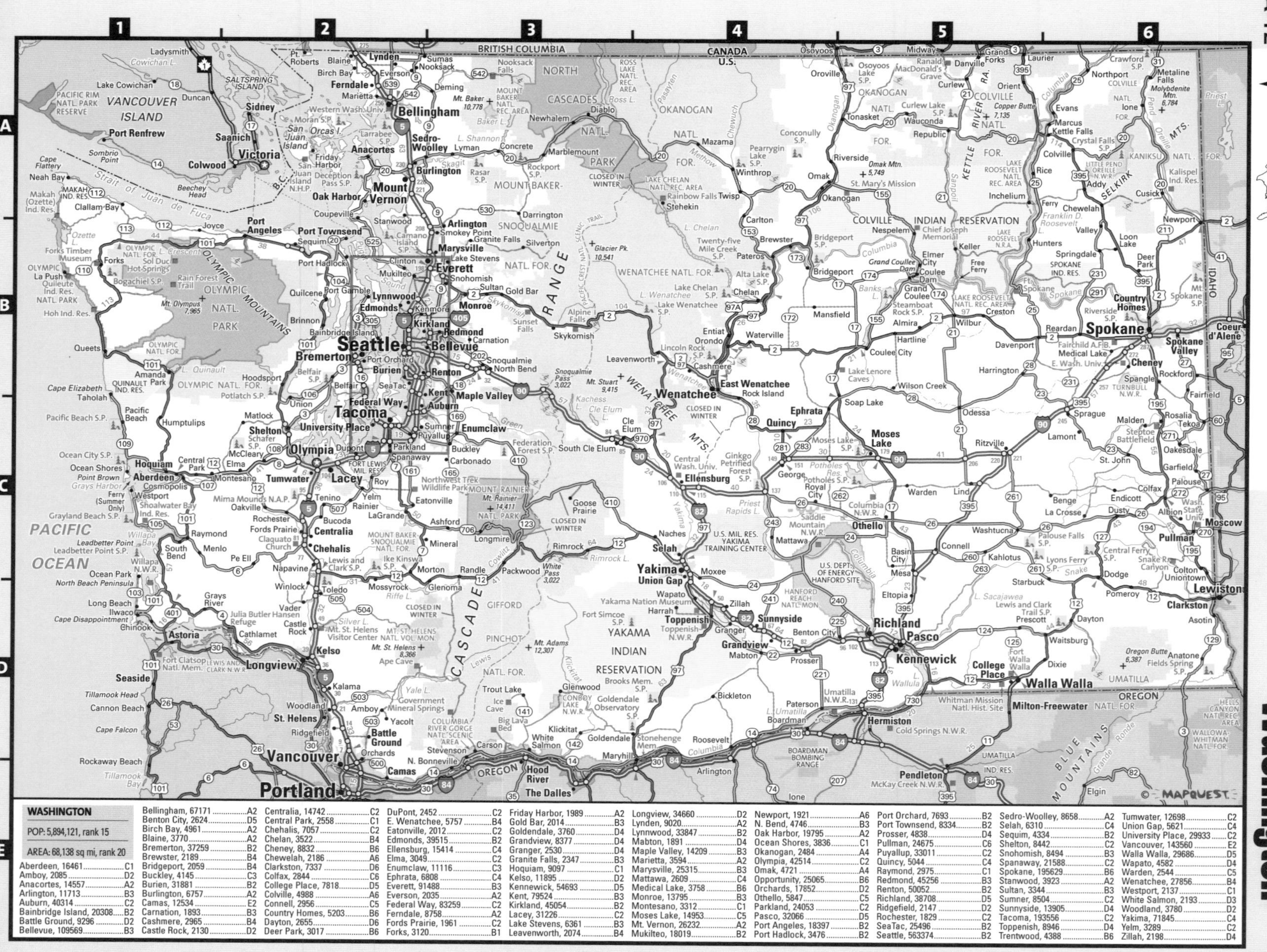

**WASHINGTON**

POP: 5,894,121, rank 15

AREA: 68,138 sq mi, rank 20

Aberdeen, 16461 ........ C1
Amboy, 2085 ........ D2
Anacortes, 14557 ........ A2
Arlington, 11713 ........ B3
Auburn, 40314 ........ C2
Bainbridge Island, 20308 ........ B2
Battle Ground, 9296 ........ D2
Bellevue, 109569 ........ B3
Bellingham, 67171 ........ A2
Benton City, 2624 ........ D5
Birch Bay, 4961 ........ A2
Blaine, 3770 ........ A2
Bremerton, 37259 ........ B2
Brewster, 2189 ........ B4
Bridgeport, 2059 ........ B4
Buckley, 4145 ........ C3
Burien, 31881 ........ B2
Burlington, 6757 ........ A2
Camas, 12534 ........ E2
Carnation, 1893 ........ B3
Cashmere, 2965 ........ B4
Castle Rock, 2130 ........ D2
Centralia, 14742 ........ C2
Central Park, 2558 ........ C1
Chehalis, 7057 ........ C2
Chelan, 3522 ........ B4
Cheney, 8832 ........ B6
Chewelah, 2186 ........ A6
Clarkston, 7337 ........ D6
Colfax, 2844 ........ C6
College Place, 7818 ........ D5
Colville, 4988 ........ A6
Connell, 2956 ........ C5
Country Homes, 5203 ........ B6
Dayton, 2655 ........ D6
Deer Park, 3017 ........ B6
DuPont, 2452 ........ C2
E. Wenatchee, 5757 ........ B4
Eatonville, 2012 ........ C2
Edmonds, 39515 ........ B2
Ellensburg, 15414 ........ C4
Elma, 3049 ........ C2
Enumclaw, 11116 ........ C3
Ephrata, 6808 ........ C4
Everett, 91488 ........ B3
Everson, 2035 ........ A2
Federal Way, 83259 ........ C2
Ferndale, 8758 ........ A2
Fords Prairie, 1961 ........ C2
Forks, 3120 ........ B1
Friday Harbor, 1989 ........ A2
Gold Bar, 2014 ........ B3
Goldendale, 3760 ........ D4
Grandview, 8377 ........ D4
Granger, 2530 ........ D4
Granite Falls, 2347 ........ B3
Hoquiam, 9097 ........ C1
Kelso, 11895 ........ D2
Kennewick, 54693 ........ D5
Kent, 79524 ........ B3
Kirkland, 45054 ........ B2
Lacey, 31226 ........ C2
Lake Stevens, 6361 ........ B3
Leavenworth, 2074 ........ B4
Longview, 34660 ........ D2
Lynden, 9020 ........ A2
Lynnwood, 33847 ........ B2
Mabton, 1891 ........ D4
Maple Valley, 14209 ........ B3
Marietta, 3594 ........ A2
Marysville, 25315 ........ B3
Mattawa, 2609 ........ C4
Medical Lake, 3758 ........ B6
Monroe, 13795 ........ B3
Montesano, 3312 ........ C1
Moses Lake, 14953 ........ C5
Mt. Vernon, 26232 ........ A2
Mukilteo, 18019 ........ B2
Newport, 1921 ........ A6
N. Bend, 4746 ........ B3
Oak Harbor, 19795 ........ A2
Ocean Shores, 3836 ........ C1
Okanogan, 2484 ........ A4
Olympia, 42514 ........ C2
Omak, 4721 ........ A4
Opportunity, 25065 ........ B6
Orchards, 17852 ........ D2
Othello, 5847 ........ C5
Parkland, 24053 ........ C2
Pasco, 32066 ........ D5
Port Angeles, 18397 ........ B2
Port Hadlock, 3476 ........ B2
Port Orchard, 7693 ........ B2
Port Townsend, 8334 ........ B2
Prosser, 4838 ........ D4
Pullman, 24675 ........ C6
Puyallup, 33011 ........ C2
Quincy, 5044 ........ C4
Raymond, 2975 ........ C1
Redmond, 45256 ........ B3
Renton, 50052 ........ B2
Richland, 38708 ........ D5
Ridgefield, 2147 ........ D2
Rochester, 1829 ........ C2
SeaTac, 25496 ........ B2
Seattle, 563374 ........ B2
Sedro-Woolley, 8658 ........ A2
Selah, 6310 ........ C4
Sequim, 4334 ........ B2
Shelton, 8442 ........ C2
Snohomish, 8494 ........ B3
Spanaway, 21588 ........ C2
Spokane, 195629 ........ B6
Stanwood, 3923 ........ A2
Sultan, 3344 ........ B3
Sumner, 8504 ........ C2
Sunnyside, 13905 ........ D4
Tacoma, 193556 ........ C2
Toppenish, 8946 ........ D4
Trentwood, 4388 ........ B6
Tumwater, 12698 ........ C2
Union Gap, 5621 ........ C4
University Place, 29933 ........ C2
Vancouver, 143560 ........ E2
Walla Walla, 29686 ........ D5
Wapato, 4582 ........ D4
Warden, 2544 ........ C5
Wenatchee, 27856 ........ B4
Westport, 2137 ........ C1
White Salmon, 2193 ........ D3
Woodland, 3780 ........ D2
Yakima, 71845 ........ C4
Yelm, 3289 ........ C2
Zillah, 2198 ........ D4

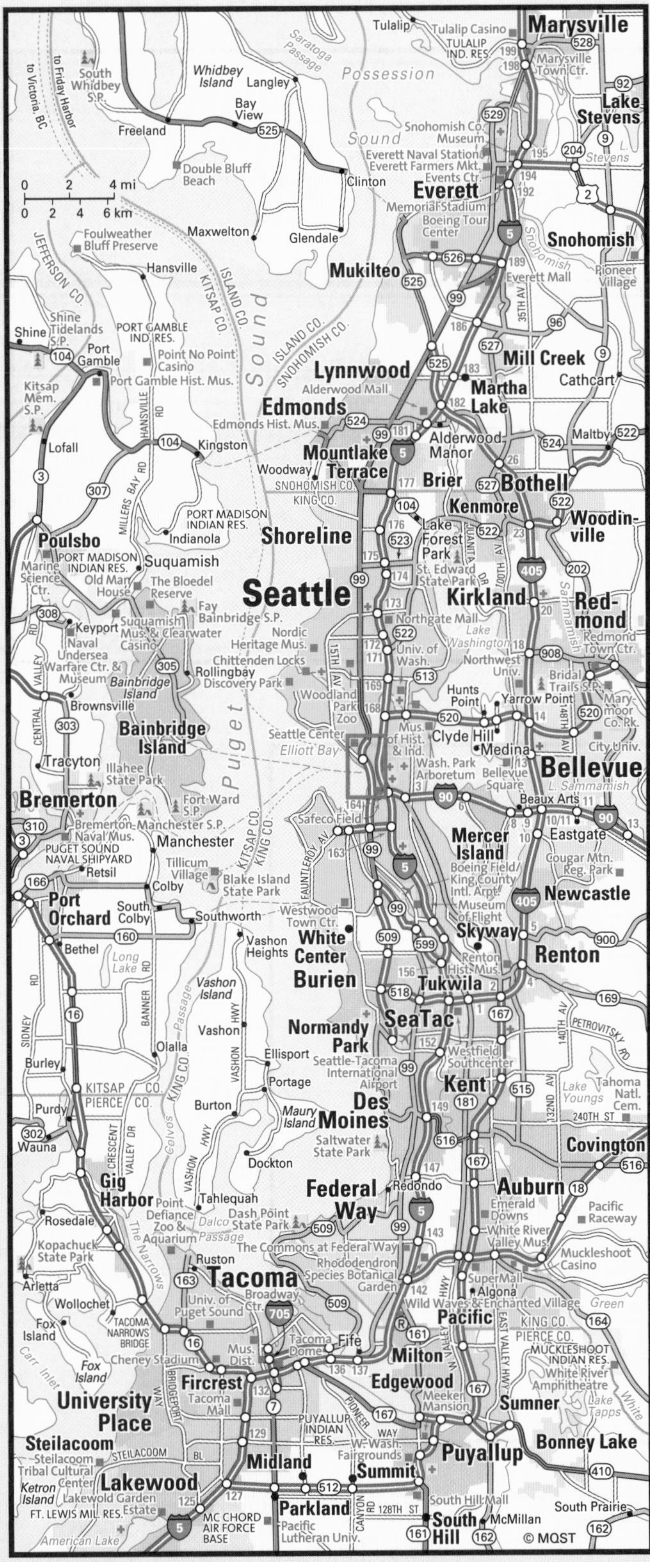

Marysville
Lake Stevens
Everett
Snohomish
Mukilteo
Mill Creek
Lynnwood
Martha Lake
Edmonds
Mountlake Terrace
Brier
Bothell
Woodinville
Kenmore
Shoreline
Lake Forest Park
Seattle
Kirkland
Redmond
Bellevue
Clyde Hill
Medina
Mercer Island
Newcastle
Renton
Skyway
White Center
Burien
Tukwila
SeaTac
Normandy Park
Kent
Des Moines
Covington
Federal Way
Auburn
Pacific
Milton
Edgewood
Sumner
Puyallup
Bonney Lake
Tacoma
Fircrest
University Place
Steilacoom
Lakewood
Parkland
Midland
Summit
South Hill
Gig Harbor
Port Orchard
Bremerton
Bainbridge Island
Poulsbo
Kingston
Possession Sound
Puget Sound
Elliott Bay
0 2 4 mi
0 2 4 6 km
© MQST

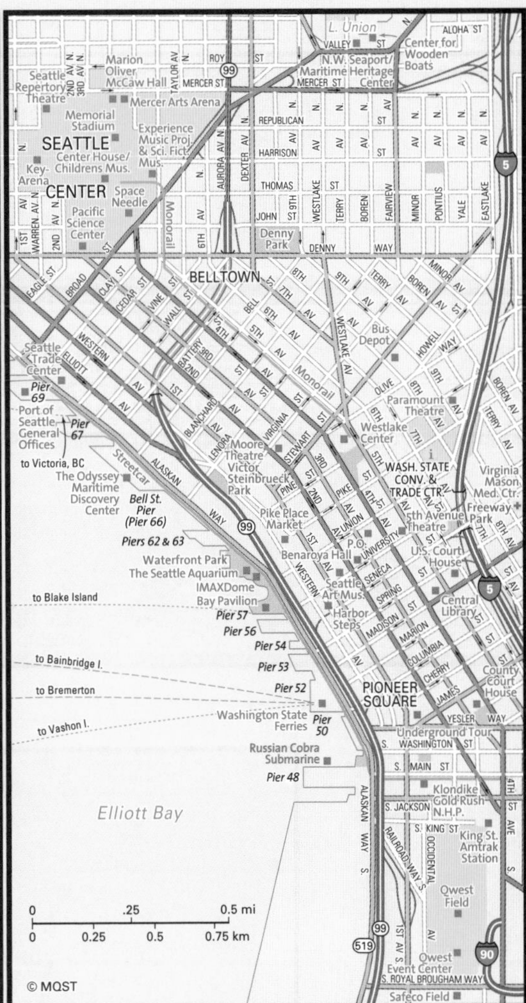

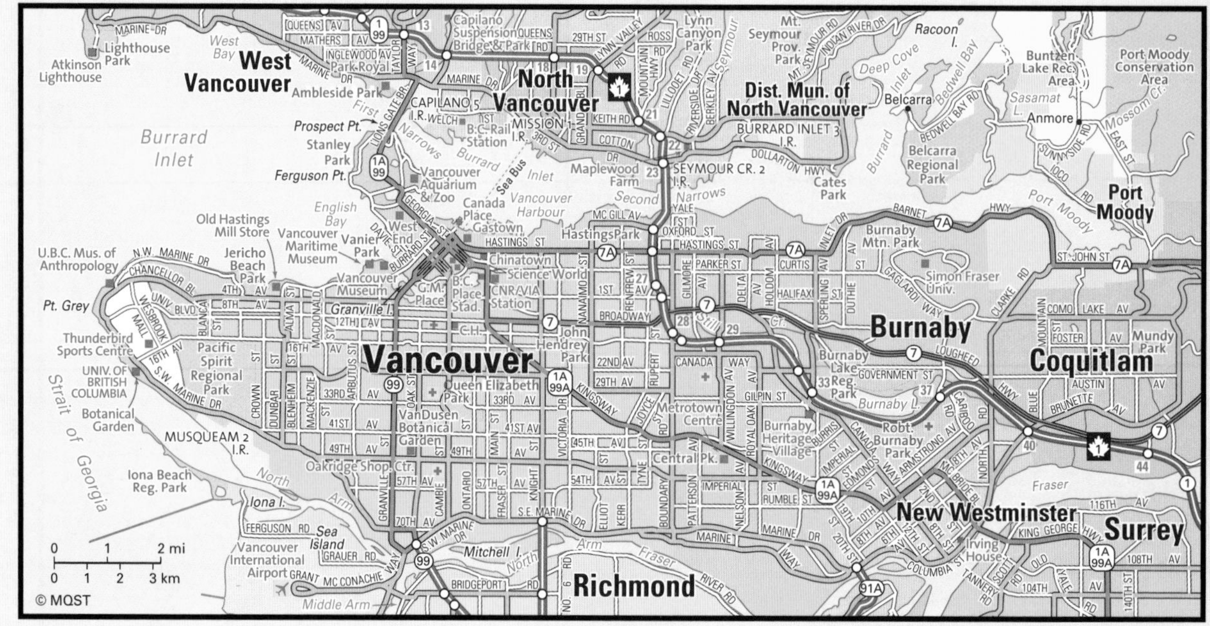

West Vancouver
North Vancouver
Dist. Mun. of North Vancouver
Burrard Inlet
Vancouver
Burnaby
Coquitlam
Port Moody
New Westminster
Surrey
Richmond
Strait of Georgia
Stanley Park
Lighthouse Park
Atkinson Lighthouse
Capilano Suspension Bridge & Park
Lynn Canyon Park
Mt. Seymour Prov. Park
Belcarra Regional Park
Buntzen Lake Rec. Area
Port Moody Conservation Area
Anmore
Simon Fraser Univ.
Burnaby Lake Reg. Park
Pacific Spirit Regional Park
Queen Elizabeth Park
VanDusen Botanical Garden
Vancouver International Airport
Iona Beach Reg. Park
UNIV. OF BRITISH COLUMBIA
Metrotown Centre
Central Pk.
© MQST


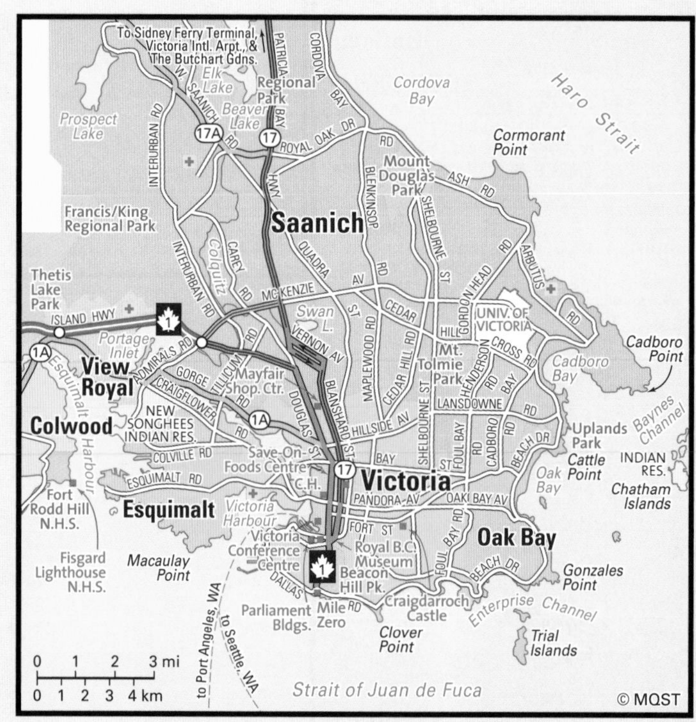

To Sidney Ferry Terminal, Victoria Intl. Arpt., & The Butchart Gdns.
Saanich
Victoria
Esquimalt
Oak Bay
View Royal
Colwood
Haro Strait
Cordova Bay
Cormorant Point
Mount Douglas Park
Francis/King Regional Park
Thetis Lake Park
Elk Lake
Beaver Lake
Prospect Lake
UNIV. OF VICTORIA
Mt. Tolmie Park
Cadboro Bay
Cadboro Point
Uplands Park
Cattle Point
Chatham Islands
Gonzales Point
Trial Islands
Enterprise Channel
Clover Point
Craigdarroch Castle
Beacon Hill Pk.
Royal B.C. Museum
Parliament Bldgs.
Mile Zero
Victoria Conference Centre
Victoria Harbour
Macaulay Point
Fisgard Lighthouse N.H.S.
Fort Rodd Hill N.H.S.
NEW SONGHEES INDIAN RES.
Mayfair Shop. Ctr.
Save-On-Foods Centre
to Port Angeles, WA
to Seattle, WA
Strait of Juan de Fuca
© MQST

Distances in chart are in miles. To convert miles to kilometers, multiply the distance in miles by 1.609

Example:
New York, NY to Boston, MA
= 215 miles or 346 kilometers
(215 x 1.609)

| | ALBUQUERQUE, NM | ATLANTA, GA | BALTIMORE, MD | BILLINGS, MT | BIRMINGHAM, AL | BISMARCK, ND | BOISE, ID | BOSTON, MA | BUFFALO, NY | BURLINGTON, VT | CHARLESTON, SC | CHARLESTON, WV | CHARLOTTE, NC | CHEYENNE, WY | CHICAGO, IL | CINCINNATI, OH | CLEVELAND, OH | DALLAS, TX | DENVER, CO | DES MOINES, IA | DETROIT, MI | EL PASO, TX | HOUSTON, TX | INDIANAPOLIS, IN | JACKSON, MS | KANSAS CITY, MO | LAS VEGAS, NV | LITTLE ROCK, AR | LOS ANGELES, CA | LOUISVILLE, KY | MEMPHIS, TN | MIAMI, FL | MILWAUKEE, WI | MINNEAPOLIS, MN | MONTRÉAL, QC | NASHVILLE, TN | NEW ORLEANS, LA | NEW YORK, NY | OKLAHOMA CITY, OK | OMAHA, NE | ORLANDO, FL | PHILADELPHIA, PA | PHOENIX, AZ | PITTSBURGH, PA | PORTLAND, ME | PORTLAND, OR | RAPID CITY, SD | RENO, NV | RICHMOND, VA | ST. LOUIS, MO | SALT LAKE CITY, UT | SAN ANTONIO, TX | SAN DIEGO, CA | SAN FRANCISCO, CA | SEATTLE, WA | TAMPA, FL | TORONTO, ON | VANCOUVER, BC | WASHINGTON,DC | WICHITA, KS |
|---|---|---|---|---|---|---|---|---|---|---|---|---|---|---|---|---|---|---|---|---|---|---|---|---|---|---|---|---|---|---|---|---|---|---|---|---|---|---|---|---|---|---|---|---|---|---|---|---|---|---|---|---|---|---|---|---|---|---|---|---|
| ALBUQUERQUE, NM | | 1490 | 1902 | 991 | 1274 | 1333 | 966 | 2240 | 1808 | 2178 | 1793 | 1568 | 1649 | 538 | 1352 | 1409 | 1619 | 754 | 438 | 1091 | 1608 | 263 | 994 | 1298 | 1157 | 894 | 578 | 900 | 806 | 1320 | 1033 | 2155 | 1426 | 1339 | 2172 | 1248 | 1276 | 2015 | 546 | 973 | 1934 | 1954 | 466 | 1670 | 2338 | 1395 | 841 | 1020 | 1876 | 1051 | 624 | 818 | 825 | 1111 | 1463 | 1949 | 1841 | 1597 | 1896 | 707 |
| ATLANTA, GA | 1490 | | 679 | 1889 | 150 | 1559 | 2218 | 1100 | 910 | 1158 | 317 | 503 | 238 | 1482 | 717 | 476 | 726 | 792 | 1403 | 967 | 735 | 1437 | 800 | 531 | 386 | 801 | 2067 | 528 | 2237 | 419 | 389 | 661 | 813 | 1129 | 1241 | 242 | 473 | 869 | 944 | 989 | 440 | 782 | 1868 | 676 | 1197 | 2647 | 1511 | 2440 | 527 | 549 | 1916 | 1000 | 2166 | 2618 | 2705 | 455 | 958 | 2838 | 636 | 989 |
| BALTIMORE, MD | 1902 | 679 | | 1959 | 795 | 1551 | 2401 | 422 | 370 | 481 | 583 | 352 | 441 | 1665 | 708 | 521 | 377 | 1399 | 1690 | 1031 | 532 | 2045 | 1470 | 600 | 1032 | 1087 | 2445 | 1072 | 2705 | 602 | 933 | 1109 | 805 | 1121 | 564 | 716 | 1142 | 192 | 1354 | 1168 | 904 | 104 | 2366 | 246 | 520 | 2830 | 1626 | 2623 | 152 | 841 | 2100 | 1671 | 2724 | 2840 | 2775 | 960 | 565 | 2908 | 38 | 1276 |
| BILLINGS, MT | 991 | 1889 | 1959 | | 1839 | 413 | 626 | 2254 | 1796 | 2181 | 2157 | 1755 | 2012 | 455 | 1246 | 1552 | 1597 | 1433 | 554 | 1007 | 1534 | 1255 | 1673 | 1432 | 1836 | 1088 | 965 | 1530 | 1239 | 1547 | 1625 | 2554 | 1175 | 839 | 2093 | 1648 | 1955 | 2049 | 1227 | 904 | 2333 | 2019 | 1199 | 1719 | 2352 | 889 | 379 | 960 | 2053 | 1341 | 548 | 1500 | 1302 | 1176 | 816 | 2348 | 1762 | 949 | 1953 | 1067 |
| BIRMINGHAM, AL | 1274 | 150 | 795 | 1839 | | 1509 | 2170 | 1215 | 909 | 1241 | 466 | 578 | 389 | 1434 | 667 | 475 | 725 | 647 | 1356 | 919 | 734 | 1292 | 678 | 481 | 241 | 753 | 1852 | 381 | 2092 | 369 | 241 | 812 | 763 | 1079 | 1289 | 194 | 351 | 985 | 729 | 941 | 591 | 897 | 1723 | 763 | 1313 | 2599 | 1463 | 2392 | 678 | 501 | 1868 | 878 | 2021 | 2472 | 2657 | 606 | 958 | 2791 | 758 | 838 |
| BISMARCK, ND | 1333 | 1559 | 1551 | 413 | 1509 | | 1039 | 1846 | 1388 | 1773 | 1749 | 1347 | 1604 | 594 | 838 | 1144 | 1189 | 1342 | 693 | 675 | 1126 | 1597 | 1582 | 1024 | 1548 | 801 | 1378 | 1183 | 1702 | 1139 | 1337 | 2224 | 767 | 431 | 1685 | 1315 | 1734 | 1641 | 1136 | 616 | 2003 | 1611 | 1662 | 1311 | 1944 | 1301 | 320 | 1372 | 1645 | 1053 | 960 | 1599 | 1765 | 1749 | 1229 | 2018 | 1354 | 1362 | 1545 | 934 |
| BOISE, ID | 966 | 2218 | 2401 | 626 | 2170 | 1039 | | 2697 | 2239 | 2624 | 2520 | 2182 | 2375 | 737 | 1708 | 1969 | 2040 | 1711 | 833 | 1369 | 1977 | 1206 | 1952 | 1852 | 2115 | 1376 | 760 | 1808 | 1033 | 1933 | 1954 | 2883 | 1748 | 1465 | 2535 | 1976 | 2234 | 2491 | 1506 | 1234 | 2662 | 2462 | 993 | 2161 | 2795 | 432 | 930 | 430 | 2496 | 1628 | 342 | 1761 | 1096 | 646 | 500 | 2677 | 2204 | 633 | 2395 | 1346 |
| BOSTON, MA | 2240 | 1100 | 422 | 2254 | 1215 | 1846 | 2697 | | 462 | 214 | 1003 | 741 | 861 | 1961 | 1003 | 862 | 654 | 1819 | 2004 | 1326 | 741 | 2465 | 1890 | 940 | 1453 | 1427 | 2757 | 1493 | 3046 | 964 | 1353 | 1529 | 1100 | 1417 | 313 | 1136 | 1563 | 215 | 1694 | 1463 | 1324 | 321 | 2706 | 592 | 107 | 3126 | 1921 | 2919 | 572 | 1181 | 2395 | 2092 | 3065 | 3135 | 3070 | 1380 | 570 | 3204 | 458 | 1616 |
| BUFFALO, NY | 1808 | 910 | 370 | 1796 | 909 | 1388 | 2239 | 462 | | 375 | 899 | 431 | 695 | 1502 | 545 | 442 | 197 | 1393 | 1546 | 868 | 277 | 2039 | 1513 | 508 | 1134 | 995 | 2299 | 1066 | 2572 | 545 | 927 | 1425 | 642 | 958 | 397 | 716 | 1254 | 400 | 1262 | 1005 | 1221 | 414 | 2274 | 217 | 560 | 2667 | 1463 | 2460 | 485 | 749 | 1936 | 1665 | 2632 | 2677 | 2612 | 1276 | 106 | 2745 | 384 | 1184 |
| BURLINGTON, VT | 2178 | 1158 | 481 | 2181 | 1241 | 1773 | 2624 | 214 | 375 | | 1061 | 782 | 919 | 1887 | 930 | 817 | 567 | 1763 | 1931 | 1253 | 652 | 2409 | 1916 | 878 | 1479 | 1366 | 2684 | 1437 | 2957 | 915 | 1297 | 1587 | 1027 | 1343 | 92 | 1086 | 1588 | 299 | 1632 | 1390 | 1383 | 371 | 2644 | 587 | 233 | 3052 | 1848 | 2845 | 630 | 1119 | 2322 | 2036 | 3020 | 3062 | 2997 | 1438 | 419 | 3130 | 517 | 1554 |
| CHARLESTON, SC | 1793 | 317 | 583 | 2157 | 466 | 1749 | 2520 | 1003 | 899 | 1061 | | 468 | 204 | 1783 | 907 | 622 | 724 | 1109 | 1705 | 1204 | 879 | 1754 | 1110 | 721 | 703 | 1102 | 2371 | 900 | 2554 | 610 | 760 | 583 | 1003 | 1319 | 1145 | 543 | 783 | 773 | 1248 | 1290 | 379 | 685 | 2184 | 642 | 1101 | 2948 | 1824 | 2741 | 428 | 850 | 2218 | 1310 | 2483 | 2934 | 2973 | 434 | 1006 | 3106 | 539 | 1291 |
| CHARLESTON, WV | 1568 | 503 | 352 | 1755 | 578 | 1347 | 2182 | 741 | 431 | 782 | 468 | | 265 | 1445 | 506 | 209 | 255 | 1072 | 1367 | 802 | 410 | 1718 | 1192 | 320 | 816 | 764 | 2122 | 745 | 2374 | 251 | 606 | 994 | 601 | 918 | 822 | 395 | 926 | 515 | 1022 | 952 | 790 | 454 | 2035 | 217 | 839 | 2610 | 1422 | 2403 | 322 | 512 | 1880 | 1344 | 2393 | 2620 | 2571 | 845 | 537 | 2705 | 346 | 953 |
| CHARLOTTE, NC | 1649 | 238 | 441 | 2012 | 389 | 1604 | 2375 | 861 | 695 | 919 | 204 | 265 | | 1637 | 761 | 476 | 520 | 1031 | 1559 | 1057 | 675 | 1677 | 1041 | 575 | 625 | 956 | 2225 | 754 | 2453 | 464 | 614 | 730 | 857 | 1173 | 1003 | 397 | 713 | 631 | 1102 | 1144 | 525 | 543 | 2107 | 438 | 959 | 2802 | 1678 | 2595 | 289 | 704 | 2072 | 1241 | 2405 | 2759 | 2827 | 581 | 802 | 2960 | 397 | 1145 |
| CHEYENNE, WY | 538 | 1482 | 1665 | 455 | 1434 | 594 | 737 | 1961 | 1502 | 1887 | 1783 | 1445 | 1637 | | 972 | 1233 | 1304 | 979 | 100 | 633 | 1241 | 801 | 1220 | 1115 | 1382 | 640 | 843 | 1076 | 1116 | 1197 | 1217 | 2147 | 1012 | 881 | 1799 | 1240 | 1502 | 1755 | 773 | 497 | 1926 | 1725 | 1004 | 1425 | 2059 | 1166 | 305 | 959 | 1760 | 892 | 436 | 1046 | 1179 | 1176 | 1234 | 1941 | 1468 | 1368 | 1659 | 613 |
| CHICAGO, IL | 1352 | 717 | 708 | 1246 | 667 | 838 | 1708 | 1003 | 545 | 930 | 907 | 506 | 761 | 972 | | 302 | 346 | 936 | 1015 | 337 | 283 | 1543 | 1108 | 184 | 750 | 532 | 1768 | 662 | 2042 | 299 | 539 | 1382 | 89 | 409 | 841 | 474 | 935 | 797 | 807 | 474 | 1161 | 768 | 1819 | 467 | 1101 | 2137 | 913 | 1930 | 802 | 294 | 1406 | 1270 | 2105 | 2146 | 2062 | 1176 | 510 | 2196 | 701 | 728 |
| CINCINNATI, OH | 1409 | 476 | 521 | 1552 | 475 | 1144 | 1969 | 862 | 442 | 817 | 622 | 209 | 476 | 1233 | 302 | | 253 | 958 | 1200 | 599 | 261 | 1605 | 1079 | 116 | 700 | 597 | 1955 | 632 | 2215 | 106 | 493 | 1141 | 398 | 714 | 815 | 281 | 820 | 636 | 863 | 736 | 920 | 576 | 1876 | 292 | 960 | 2398 | 1219 | 2191 | 530 | 350 | 1667 | 1231 | 2234 | 2407 | 2368 | 935 | 484 | 2501 | 517 | 785 |
| CLEVELAND, OH | 1619 | 726 | 377 | 1597 | 725 | 1189 | 2040 | 654 | 197 | 567 | 724 | 255 | 520 | 1304 | 346 | 253 | | 1208 | 1347 | 669 | 171 | 1854 | 1328 | 319 | 950 | 806 | 2100 | 882 | 2374 | 356 | 742 | 1250 | 443 | 760 | 588 | 531 | 1070 | 466 | 1073 | 806 | 1045 | 437 | 2085 | 136 | 751 | 2469 | 1264 | 2262 | 471 | 560 | 1738 | 1481 | 2437 | 2478 | 2413 | 1101 | 303 | 2547 | 370 | 995 |
| DALLAS, TX | 754 | 792 | 1399 | 1433 | 647 | 1342 | 1711 | 1819 | 1393 | 1763 | 1109 | 1072 | 1031 | 979 | 936 | 958 | 1208 | | 887 | 752 | 1218 | 647 | 241 | 913 | 406 | 554 | 1331 | 327 | 1446 | 852 | 466 | 1367 | 1010 | 999 | 1772 | 681 | 525 | 1589 | 209 | 669 | 1146 | 1501 | 1077 | 1246 | 1917 | 2140 | 1077 | 1933 | 1309 | 635 | 1410 | 271 | 1375 | 1827 | 2208 | 1161 | 1441 | 2342 | 1362 | 367 |
| DENVER, CO | 438 | 1403 | 1690 | 554 | 1356 | 693 | 833 | 2004 | 1546 | 1931 | 1705 | 1367 | 1559 | 100 | 1015 | 1200 | 1347 | 887 | | 676 | 1284 | 701 | 1127 | 1088 | 1290 | 603 | 756 | 984 | 1029 | 1118 | 1116 | 2069 | 1055 | 924 | 1843 | 1162 | 1409 | 1799 | 681 | 541 | 1847 | 1744 | 904 | 1460 | 2102 | 1261 | 404 | 1054 | 1688 | 855 | 531 | 946 | 1092 | 1271 | 1329 | 1862 | 1512 | 1463 | 1686 | 521 |
| DES MOINES, IA | 1091 | 967 | 1031 | 1007 | 919 | 675 | 1369 | 1326 | 868 | 1253 | 1204 | 802 | 1057 | 633 | 337 | 599 | 669 | 752 | 676 | | 606 | 1283 | 992 | 481 | 931 | 194 | 1429 | 567 | 1703 | 595 | 720 | 1632 | 378 | 246 | 1165 | 725 | 1117 | 1121 | 546 | 136 | 1411 | 1091 | 1558 | 791 | 1424 | 1798 | 629 | 1591 | 1126 | 436 | 1067 | 1009 | 1766 | 1807 | 1822 | 1426 | 834 | 1956 | 1025 | 390 |
| DETROIT, MI | 1608 | 735 | 532 | 1534 | 734 | 1126 | 1977 | 741 | 277 | 652 | 879 | 410 | 675 | 1241 | 283 | 261 | 171 | 1218 | 1284 | 606 | | 1799 | 1338 | 318 | 960 | 795 | 2037 | 891 | 2310 | 366 | 752 | 1401 | 380 | 697 | 564 | 541 | 1079 | 622 | 1062 | 743 | 1180 | 592 | 2074 | 292 | 838 | 2405 | 1201 | 2198 | 627 | 549 | 1675 | 1490 | 2373 | 2415 | 2350 | 1194 | 233 | 2483 | 526 | 984 |
| EL PASO, TX | 263 | 1437 | 2045 | 1255 | 1292 | 1597 | 1206 | 2465 | 2039 | 2409 | 1754 | 1718 | 1677 | 801 | 1543 | 1605 | 1854 | 647 | 701 | 1283 | 1799 | | 758 | 1489 | 1051 | 1085 | 717 | 974 | 801 | 1499 | 1112 | 1959 | 1617 | 1530 | 2363 | 1328 | 1118 | 2235 | 737 | 1236 | 1738 | 2147 | 432 | 1893 | 2563 | 1767 | 1105 | 1315 | 1955 | 1242 | 864 | 556 | 730 | 1181 | 1944 | 1753 | 2032 | 2087 | 2008 | 898 |
| HOUSTON, TX | 994 | 800 | 1470 | 1673 | 678 | 1582 | 1952 | 1890 | 1513 | 1916 | 1110 | 1192 | 1041 | 1220 | 1108 | 1079 | 1328 | 241 | 1127 | 992 | 1338 | 758 | | 1033 | 445 | 795 | 1474 | 447 | 1558 | 972 | 586 | 1201 | 1193 | 1240 | 1892 | 801 | 360 | 1660 | 449 | 910 | 980 | 1572 | 1188 | 1366 | 1988 | 2381 | 1318 | 2072 | 1330 | 863 | 1650 | 200 | 1487 | 1938 | 2449 | 995 | 1561 | 2583 | 1433 | 608 |
| INDIANAPOLIS, IN | 1298 | 531 | 600 | 1432 | 481 | 1024 | 1852 | 940 | 508 | 878 | 721 | 320 | 575 | 1115 | 184 | 116 | 319 | 913 | 1088 | 481 | 318 | 1489 | 1033 | | 675 | 485 | 1843 | 587 | 2104 | 112 | 464 | 1196 | 279 | 596 | 872 | 287 | 826 | 715 | 752 | 618 | 975 | 655 | 1764 | 370 | 1038 | 2280 | 1101 | 2073 | 641 | 239 | 1549 | 1186 | 2122 | 2290 | 2249 | 990 | 541 | 2383 | 596 | 674 |
| JACKSON, MS | 1157 | 386 | 1032 | 1836 | 241 | 1548 | 2115 | 1453 | 1134 | 1479 | 703 | 816 | 625 | 1382 | 750 | 700 | 950 | 406 | 1290 | 931 | 960 | 1051 | 445 | 675 | | 747 | 1735 | 269 | 1851 | 594 | 211 | 915 | 835 | 1151 | 1514 | 423 | 185 | 1223 | 612 | 935 | 694 | 1135 | 1482 | 988 | 1550 | 2544 | 1458 | 2337 | 914 | 505 | 1813 | 644 | 1780 | 2232 | 2612 | 709 | 1183 | 2746 | 996 | 771 |
| KANSAS CITY, MO | 894 | 801 | 1087 | 1088 | 753 | 801 | 1376 | 1427 | 995 | 1366 | 1102 | 764 | 956 | 640 | 532 | 597 | 806 | 554 | 603 | 194 | 795 | 1085 | 795 | 485 | 747 | | 1358 | 382 | 1632 | 516 | 536 | 1466 | 573 | 441 | 1359 | 559 | 932 | 1202 | 348 | 188 | 1245 | 1141 | 1360 | 857 | 1525 | 1805 | 710 | 1598 | 1085 | 252 | 1074 | 812 | 1695 | 1814 | 1872 | 1259 | 1028 | 2007 | 1083 | 192 |
| LAS VEGAS, NV | 578 | 2067 | 2445 | 965 | 1852 | 1378 | 760 | 2757 | 2299 | 2684 | 2371 | 2122 | 2225 | 843 | 1768 | 1955 | 2100 | 1331 | 756 | 1429 | 2037 | 717 | 1474 | 1843 | 1735 | 1358 | | 1478 | 274 | 1874 | 1611 | 2733 | 1808 | 1677 | 2596 | 1826 | 1854 | 2552 | 1124 | 1294 | 2512 | 2500 | 285 | 2215 | 2855 | 1188 | 1035 | 442 | 2444 | 1610 | 417 | 1272 | 337 | 575 | 1256 | 2526 | 2265 | 1390 | 2441 | 1276 |
| LITTLE ROCK, AR | 900 | 528 | 1072 | 1530 | 381 | 1183 | 1808 | 1493 | 1066 | 1437 | 900 | 745 | 754 | 1076 | 662 | 632 | 882 | 327 | 984 | 567 | 891 | 974 | 447 | 587 | 269 | 382 | 1478 | | 1706 | 526 | 140 | 1190 | 747 | 814 | 1446 | 355 | 455 | 1262 | 355 | 570 | 969 | 1175 | 1367 | 920 | 1590 | 2237 | 1093 | 2030 | 983 | 416 | 1507 | 600 | 1703 | 2012 | 2305 | 984 | 1115 | 2439 | 1036 | 464 |
| LOS ANGELES, CA | 806 | 2237 | 2705 | 1239 | 2092 | 1702 | 1033 | 3046 | 2572 | 2957 | 2554 | 2374 | 2453 | 1116 | 2042 | 2215 | 2374 | 1446 | 1029 | 1703 | 2310 | 801 | 1558 | 2104 | 1851 | 1632 | 274 | 1706 | | 2126 | 1839 | 2759 | 2082 | 1951 | 2869 | 2054 | 1917 | 2820 | 1352 | 1567 | 2538 | 2760 | 369 | 2476 | 3144 | 971 | 1309 | 519 | 2682 | 1856 | 691 | 1356 | 124 | 385 | 1148 | 2553 | 2538 | 1291 | 2702 | 1513 |
| LOUISVILLE, KY | 1320 | 419 | 602 | 1547 | 369 | 1139 | 1933 | 964 | 545 | 915 | 610 | 251 | 464 | 1197 | 299 | 106 | 356 | 852 | 1118 | 595 | 366 | 1499 | 972 | 112 | 594 | 516 | 1874 | 526 | 2126 | | 386 | 1084 | 394 | 711 | 920 | 175 | 714 | 739 | 774 | 704 | 863 | 678 | 1786 | 394 | 1062 | 2362 | 1215 | 2155 | 572 | 264 | 1631 | 1125 | 2144 | 2372 | 2364 | 878 | 589 | 2497 | 596 | 705 |
| MEMPHIS, TN | 1033 | 389 | 933 | 1625 | 241 | 1337 | 1954 | 1353 | 927 | 1297 | 760 | 606 | 614 | 1217 | 539 | 493 | 742 | 466 | 1116 | 720 | 752 | 1112 | 586 | 464 | 211 | 536 | 1611 | 140 | 1839 | 386 | | 1051 | 624 | 940 | 1306 | 215 | 396 | 1123 | 487 | 724 | 830 | 1035 | 1500 | 780 | 1451 | 2382 | 1247 | 2175 | 843 | 294 | 1652 | 739 | 1841 | 2144 | 2440 | 845 | 975 | 2574 | 896 | 597 |
| MIAMI, FL | 2155 | 661 | 1109 | 2554 | 812 | 2224 | 2883 | 1529 | 1425 | 1587 | 583 | 994 | 730 | 2147 | 1382 | 1141 | 1250 | 1367 | 2069 | 1632 | 1401 | 1959 | 1201 | 1196 | 915 | 1466 | 2733 | 1190 | 2759 | 1084 | 1051 | | 1478 | 1794 | 1671 | 907 | 874 | 1299 | 1609 | 1654 | 232 | 1211 | 2390 | 1167 | 1627 | 3312 | 2176 | 3105 | 954 | 1214 | 2581 | 1401 | 2688 | 3140 | 3370 | 274 | 1532 | 3504 | 1065 | 1655 |
| MILWAUKEE, WI | 1426 | 813 | 805 | 1175 | 763 | 767 | 1748 | 1100 | 642 | 1027 | 1003 | 601 | 857 | 1012 | 89 | 398 | 443 | 1010 | 1055 | 378 | 380 | 1617 | 1193 | 279 | 835 | 573 | 1808 | 747 | 2082 | 394 | 624 | 1478 | | 337 | 939 | 569 | 1020 | 894 | 880 | 514 | 1257 | 865 | 1892 | 564 | 1198 | 2063 | 842 | 1970 | 899 | 367 | 1446 | 1343 | 2145 | 2186 | 1991 | 1272 | 607 | 2124 | 799 | 769 |
| MINNEAPOLIS, MN | 1339 | 1129 | 1121 | 839 | 1079 | 431 | 1465 | 1417 | 958 | 1343 | 1319 | 918 | 1173 | 881 | 409 | 714 | 760 | 999 | 924 | 246 | 697 | 1530 | 1240 | 596 | 1151 | 441 | 1677 | 814 | 1951 | 711 | 940 | 1794 | 337 | | 1255 | 886 | 1337 | 1211 | 793 | 383 | 1573 | 1181 | 1805 | 881 | 1515 | 1727 | 606 | 1839 | 1216 | 621 | 1315 | 1257 | 2014 | 2055 | 1654 | 1588 | 924 | 1788 | 1115 | 637 |
| MONTRÉAL, QC | 2172 | 1241 | 564 | 2093 | 1289 | 1685 | 2535 | 313 | 397 | 92 | 1145 | 822 | 1003 | 1799 | 841 | 815 | 588 | 1772 | 1843 | 1165 | 564 | 2363 | 1892 | 872 | 1514 | 1359 | 2596 | 1446 | 2869 | 920 | 1306 | 1671 | 939 | 1255 | | 1094 | 1632 | 383 | 1625 | 1300 | 1466 | 454 | 2637 | 607 | 282 | 2963 | 1758 | 2756 | 714 | 1112 | 2232 | 2043 | 2931 | 2972 | 2907 | 1522 | 330 | 3041 | 600 | 1547 |
| NASHVILLE, TN | 1248 | 242 | 716 | 1648 | 194 | 1315 | 1976 | 1136 | 716 | 1086 | 543 | 395 | 397 | 1240 | 474 | 281 | 531 | 681 | 1162 | 725 | 541 | 1328 | 801 | 287 | 423 | 559 | 1826 | 355 | 2054 | 175 | 215 | 907 | 569 | 886 | 1094 | | 539 | 906 | 703 | 747 | 686 | 818 | 1715 | 569 | 1234 | 2405 | 1269 | 2198 | 626 | 307 | 1675 | 954 | 2056 | 2360 | 2463 | 701 | 764 | 2597 | 679 | 748 |
| NEW ORLEANS, LA | 1276 | 473 | 1142 | 1955 | 351 | 1734 | 2234 | 1563 | 1254 | 1588 | 783 | 926 | 713 | 1502 | 935 | 820 | 1070 | 525 | 1409 | 1117 | 1079 | 1118 | 360 | 826 | 185 | 932 | 1854 | 455 | 1917 | 714 | 396 | 874 | 1020 | 1337 | 1632 | 539 | | 1332 | 731 | 1121 | 653 | 1245 | 1548 | 1108 | 1660 | 2663 | 1643 | 2431 | 1002 | 690 | 1932 | 560 | 1846 | 2298 | 2731 | 668 | 1302 | 2865 | 1106 | 890 |
| NEW YORK, NY | 2015 | 869 | 192 | 2049 | 985 | 1641 | 2491 | 215 | 400 | 299 | 773 | 515 | 631 | 1755 | 797 | 636 | 466 | 1589 | 1799 | 1121 | 622 | 2235 | 1660 | 715 | 1223 | 1202 | 2552 | 1262 | 2820 | 739 | 1123 | 1299 | 894 | 1211 | 383 | 906 | 1332 | | 1469 | 1258 | 1094 | 91 | 2481 | 367 | 313 | 2920 | 1716 | 2713 | 342 | 956 | 2189 | 1861 | 2839 | 2929 | 2864 | 1150 | 507 | 2998 | 228 | 1391 |
| OKLAHOMA CITY, OK | 546 | 944 | 1354 | 1227 | 729 | 1136 | 1506 | 1694 | 1262 | 1632 | 1248 | 1022 | 1102 | 773 | 807 | 863 | 1073 | 209 | 681 | 546 | 1062 | 737 | 449 | 752 | 612 | 348 | 1124 | 355 | 1352 | 774 | 487 | 1609 | 880 | 793 | 1625 | 703 | 731 | 1469 | | 463 | 1388 | 1408 | 1012 | 1124 | 1792 | 1934 | 871 | 1727 | 1331 | 505 | 1204 | 466 | 1370 | 1657 | 2002 | 1403 | 1295 | 2136 | 1350 | 161 |
| OMAHA, NE | 973 | 989 | 1168 | 904 | 941 | 616 | 1234 | 1463 | 1005 | 1390 | 1290 | 952 | 1144 | 497 | 474 | 736 | 806 | 669 | 541 | 136 | 743 | 1236 | 910 | 618 | 935 | 188 | 1294 | 570 | 1567 | 704 | 724 | 1654 | 514 | 383 | 1300 | 747 | 1121 | 1258 | 463 | | 1433 | 1228 | 1440 | 928 | 1561 | 1662 | 525 | 1455 | 1263 | 440 | 932 | 927 | 1630 | 1672 | 1719 | 1448 | 971 | 1853 | 1162 | 307 |
| ORLANDO, FL | 1934 | 440 | 904 | 2333 | 591 | 2003 | 2662 | 1324 | 1221 | 1383 | 379 | 790 | 525 | 1926 | 1161 | 920 | 1045 | 1146 | 1847 | 1411 | 1180 | 1738 | 980 | 975 | 694 | 1245 | 2512 | 969 | 2538 | 863 | 830 | 232 | 1257 | 1573 | 1466 | 686 | 653 | 1094 | 1388 | 1433 | | 1006 | 2169 | 963 | 1422 | 3091 | 1955 | 2884 | 750 | 993 | 2360 | 1180 | 2467 | 2918 | 3149 | 82 | 1327 | 3283 | 860 | 1434 |
| PHILADELPHIA, PA | 1954 | 782 | 104 | 2019 | 897 | 1611 | 2462 | 321 | 414 | 371 | 685 | 454 | 543 | 1725 | 768 | 576 | 437 | 1501 | 1744 | 1091 | 592 | 2147 | 1572 | 655 | 1135 | 1141 | 2500 | 1175 | 2760 | 678 | 1035 | 1211 | 865 | 1181 | 454 | 818 | 1245 | 91 | 1408 | 1228 | 1006 | | 2420 | 306 | 419 | 2890 | 1686 | 2683 | 254 | 895 | 2160 | 1774 | 2779 | 2900 | 2835 | 1062 | 522 | 2968 | 140 | 1330 |
| PHOENIX, AZ | 466 | 1868 | 2366 | 1199 | 1723 | 1662 | 993 | 2706 | 2274 | 2644 | 2184 | 2035 | 2107 | 1004 | 1819 | 1876 | 2085 | 1077 | 904 | 1558 | 2074 | 432 | 1188 | 1764 | 1482 | 1360 | 285 | 1367 | 369 | 1786 | 1500 | 2390 | 1892 | 1805 | 2637 | 1715 | 1548 | 2481 | 1012 | 1440 | 2169 | 2420 | | 2136 | 2804 | 1335 | 1308 | 883 | 2343 | 1517 | 651 | 987 | 358 | 750 | 1513 | 2184 | 2307 | 1655 | 2362 | 1173 |
| PITTSBURGH, PA | 1670 | 676 | 246 | 1719 | 763 | 1311 | 2161 | 592 | 217 | 587 | 642 | 217 | 438 | 1425 | 467 | 292 | 136 | 1246 | 1460 | 791 | 292 | 1893 | 1366 | 370 | 988 | 857 | 2215 | 920 | 2476 | 394 | 780 | 1167 | 564 | 881 | 607 | 569 | 1108 | 367 | 1124 | 928 | 963 | 306 | 2136 | | 690 | 2590 | 1386 | 2383 | 341 | 611 | 1859 | 1519 | 2494 | 2599 | 2534 | 1019 | 321 | 2668 | 240 | 1046 |
| PORTLAND, ME | 2338 | 1197 | 520 | 2352 | 1313 | 1944 | 2795 | 107 | 560 | 233 | 1101 | 839 | 959 | 2059 | 1101 | 960 | 751 | 1917 | 2102 | 1424 | 838 | 2563 | 1988 | 1038 | 1550 | 1525 | 2855 | 1590 | 3144 | 1062 | 1451 | 1627 | 1198 | 1515 | 282 | 1234 | 1660 | 313 | 1792 | 1561 | 1422 | 419 | 2804 | 690 | | 3223 | 2019 | 3016 | 670 | 1279 | 2493 | 2189 | 3162 | 3233 | 3168 | 1478 | 668 | 3301 | 556 | 1714 |
| PORTLAND, OR | 1395 | 2647 | 2830 | 889 | 2599 | 1301 | 432 | 3126 | 2667 | 3052 | 2948 | 2610 | 2802 | 1166 | 2137 | 2398 | 2469 | 2140 | 1261 | 1798 | 2405 | 1767 | 2381 | 2280 | 2544 | 1805 | 1188 | 2237 | 971 | 2362 | 2382 | 3312 | 2063 | 1727 | 2963 | 2405 | 2663 | 2920 | 1934 | 1662 | 3091 | 2890 | 1335 | 2590 | 3223 | | 1268 | 578 | 2925 | 2057 | 771 | 2322 | 1093 | 638 | 170 | 3106 | 2633 | 313 | 2824 | 1775 |
| RAPID CITY, SD | 841 | 1511 | 1626 | 379 | 1463 | 320 | 930 | 1921 | 1463 | 1848 | 1824 | 1422 | 1678 | 305 | 913 | 1219 | 1264 | 1077 | 404 | 629 | 1201 | 1105 | 1318 | 1101 | 1458 | 710 | 1035 | 1093 | 1309 | 1215 | 1247 | 2176 | 842 | 606 | 1758 | 1269 | 1643 | 1716 | 871 | 525 | 1955 | 1686 | 1308 | 1386 | 2019 | 1268 | | 1151 | 1720 | 963 | 628 | 1335 | 1372 | 1368 | 1195 | 1970 | 1429 | 1328 | 1620 | 712 |
| RENO, NV | 1020 | 2440 | 2623 | 960 | 2392 | 1372 | 430 | 2919 | 2460 | 2845 | 2741 | 2403 | 2595 | 959 | 1930 | 2191 | 2262 | 1933 | 1054 | 1591 | 2198 | 1315 | 2072 | 2073 | 2337 | 1598 | 442 | 2030 | 519 | 2155 | 2175 | 3105 | 1970 | 1839 | 2756 | 2198 | 2431 | 2713 | 1727 | 1455 | 2884 | 2683 | 883 | 2383 | 3016 | 578 | 1151 | | 2718 | 1850 | 524 | 1870 | 642 | 217 | 755 | 2899 | 2426 | 898 | 2617 | 1568 |
| RICHMOND, VA | 1876 | 527 | 152 | 2053 | 678 | 1645 | 2496 | 572 | 485 | 630 | 428 | 322 | 289 | 1760 | 802 | 530 | 471 | 1309 | 1688 | 1126 | 627 | 1955 | 1330 | 641 | 914 | 1085 | 2444 | 983 | 2682 | 572 | 843 | 954 | 899 | 1216 | 714 | 626 | 1002 | 342 | 1331 | 1263 | 750 | 254 | 2343 | 341 | 670 | 2925 | 1720 | 2718 | | 834 | 2194 | 1530 | 2684 | 2934 | 2869 | 805 | 660 | 3003 | 108 | 1274 |
| ST. LOUIS, MO | 1051 | 549 | 841 | 1341 | 501 | 1053 | 1628 | 1181 | 749 | 1119 | 850 | 512 | 704 | 892 | 294 | 350 | 560 | 635 | 855 | 436 | 549 | 1242 | 863 | 239 | 505 | 252 | 1610 | 416 | 1856 | 264 | 294 | 1214 | 367 | 621 | 1112 | 307 | 690 | 956 | 505 | 440 | 993 | 895 | 1517 | 611 | 1279 | 2057 | 963 | 1850 | 834 | | 1326 | 968 | 1875 | 2066 | 2125 | 1008 | 782 | 2259 | 837 | 441 |
| SALT LAKE CITY, UT | 624 | 1916 | 2100 | 548 | 1868 | 960 | 342 | 2395 | 1936 | 2322 | 2218 | 1880 | 2072 | 436 | 1406 | 1667 | 1738 | 1410 | 531 | 1067 | 1675 | 864 | 1650 | 1549 | 1813 | 1074 | 417 | 1507 | 691 | 1631 | 1652 | 2581 | 1446 | 1315 | 2232 | 1675 | 1932 | 2189 | 1204 | 932 | 2360 | 2160 | 651 | 1859 | 2493 | 771 | 628 | 524 | 2194 | 1326 | | 1419 | 754 | 740 | 839 | 2375 | 1902 | 973 | 2094 | 1044 |
| SAN ANTONIO, TX | 818 | 1000 | 1671 | 1500 | 878 | 1599 | 1761 | 2092 | 1665 | 2036 | 1310 | 1344 | 1241 | 1046 | 1270 | 1231 | 1481 | 271 | 946 | 1009 | 1490 | 556 | 200 | 1186 | 644 | 812 | 1272 | 600 | 1356 | 1125 | 739 | 1401 | 1343 | 1257 | 2043 | 954 | 560 | 1861 | 466 | 927 | 1180 | 1774 | 987 | 1519 | 2189 | 2322 | 1335 | 1870 | 1530 | 968 | 1419 | | 1285 | 1737 | 2275 | 1195 | 1714 | 2410 | 1635 | 624 |
| SAN DIEGO, CA | 825 | 2166 | 2724 | 1302 | 2021 | 1765 | 1096 | 3065 | 2632 | 3020 | 2483 | 2393 | 2405 | 1179 | 2105 | 2234 | 2437 | 1375 | 1092 | 1766 | 2373 | 730 | 1487 | 2122 | 1780 | 1695 | 337 | 1703 | 124 | 2144 | 1841 | 2688 | 2145 | 2014 | 2931 | 2056 | 1846 | 2839 | 1370 | 1630 | 2467 | 2779 | 358 | 2494 | 3162 | 1093 | 1372 | 642 | 2684 | 1875 | 754 | 1285 | | 508 | 1271 | 2481 | 2601 | 1414 | 2720 | 1531 |
| SAN FRANCISCO, CA | 1111 | 2618 | 2840 | 1176 | 2472 | 1749 | 646 | 3135 | 2677 | 3062 | 2934 | 2620 | 2759 | 1176 | 2146 | 2407 | 2478 | 1827 | 1271 | 1807 | 2415 | 1181 | 1938 | 2290 | 2232 | 1814 | 575 | 2012 | 385 | 2372 | 2144 | 3140 | 2186 | 2055 | 2972 | 2360 | 2298 | 2929 | 1657 | 1672 | 2918 | 2900 | 750 | 2599 | 3233 | 638 | 1368 | 217 | 2934 | 2066 | 740 | 1737 | 508 | | 816 | 2933 | 2643 | 958 | 2834 | 1784 |
| SEATTLE, WA | 1463 | 2705 | 2775 | 816 | 2657 | 1229 | 500 | 3070 | 2612 | 2997 | 2973 | 2571 | 2827 | 1234 | 2062 | 2368 | 2413 | 2208 | 1329 | 1822 | 2350 | 1944 | 2449 | 2249 | 2612 | 1872 | 1256 | 2305 | 1148 | 2364 | 2440 | 3370 | 1991 | 1654 | 2907 | 2463 | 2731 | 2864 | 2002 | 1719 | 3149 | 2835 | 1513 | 2534 | 3168 | 170 | 1195 | 755 | 2869 | 2125 | 839 | 2275 | 1271 | 816 | | 3164 | 2577 | 140 | 2769 | 1843 |
| TAMPA, FL | 1949 | 455 | 960 | 2348 | 606 | 2018 | 2677 | 1380 | 1276 | 1438 | 434 | 845 | 581 | 1941 | 1176 | 935 | 1101 | 1161 | 1862 | 1426 | 1194 | 1753 | 995 | 990 | 709 | 1259 | 2526 | 984 | 2553 | 878 | 845 | 274 | 1272 | 1588 | 1522 | 701 | 668 | 1150 | 1403 | 1448 | 82 | 1062 | 2184 | 1019 | 1478 | 3106 | 1970 | 2899 | 805 | 1008 | 2375 | 1195 | 2481 | 2933 | 3164 | | 1383 | 3297 | 916 | 1448 |
| TORONTO, ON | 1841 | 958 | 565 | 1762 | 958 | 1354 | 2204 | 570 | 106 | 419 | 1006 | 537 | 802 | 1468 | 510 | 484 | 303 | 1441 | 1512 | 834 | 233 | 2032 | 1561 | 541 | 1183 | 1028 | 2265 | 1115 | 2538 | 589 | 975 | 1532 | 607 | 924 | 330 | 764 | 1302 | 507 | 1295 | 971 | 1327 | 522 | 2307 | 321 | 668 | 2633 | 1429 | 2426 | 660 | 782 | 1902 | 1714 | 2601 | 2643 | 2577 | 1383 | | 2711 | 563 | 1217 |
| VANCOUVER, BC | 1597 | 2838 | 2908 | 949 | 2791 | 1362 | 633 | 3204 | 2745 | 3130 | 3106 | 2705 | 2960 | 1368 | 2196 | 2501 | 2547 | 2342 | 1463 | 1956 | 2483 | 2087 | 2583 | 2383 | 2746 | 2007 | 1390 | 2439 | 1291 | 2497 | 2574 | 3504 | 2124 | 1788 | 3041 | 2597 | 2865 | 2998 | 2136 | 1853 | 3283 | 2968 | 1655 | 2668 | 3301 | 313 | 1328 | 898 | 3003 | 2259 | 973 | 2410 | 1414 | 958 | 140 | 3297 | 2711 | | 2902 | 1977 |
| WASHINGTON, DC | 1896 | 636 | 38 | 1953 | 758 | 1545 | 2395 | 458 | 384 | 517 | 539 | 346 | 397 | 1659 | 701 | 517 | 370 | 1362 | 1686 | 1025 | 526 | 2008 | 1433 | 596 | 996 | 1083 | 2441 | 1036 | 2702 | 596 | 896 | 1065 | 799 | 1115 | 600 | 679 | 1106 | 228 | 1350 | 1162 | 860 | 140 | 2362 | 240 | 556 | 2824 | 1620 | 2617 | 108 | 837 | 2094 | 1635 | 2720 | 2834 | 2769 | 916 | 563 | 2902 | | 1272 |
| WICHITA, KS | 707 | 989 | 1276 | 1067 | 838 | 934 | 1346 | 1616 | 1184 | 1554 | 1291 | 953 | 1145 | 613 | 728 | 785 | 995 | 367 | 521 | 390 | 984 | 898 | 608 | 674 | 771 | 192 | 1276 | 464 | 1513 | 705 | 597 | 1655 | 769 | 637 | 1547 | 748 | 890 | 1391 | 161 | 307 | 1434 | 1330 | 1173 | 1046 | 1714 | 1775 | 712 | 1568 | 1274 | 441 | 1044 | 624 | 1531 | 1784 | 1843 | 1448 | 1217 | 1977 | 1272 | |

# A Word to Our Readers

Travelers are on the roads in great numbers these days. They're exploring the country on day trips, weekend getaways, business trips, and extended family vacations, visiting major cities and small towns along the way. Because time is precious and the travel industry is ever-changing, having accurate, reliable travel information at your fingertips is critical. Mobil Travel Guide has been providing invaluable insight to travelers for more than 45 years, and we are committed to continuing this service well into the future.

The Mobil Corporation (known as Exxon Mobil Corporation since a 1999 merger) began producing the Mobil Travel Guide books in 1958, following the introduction of the US interstate highway system in 1956. The first edition covered only five Southwestern states. Since then, our books have become the premier travel guides in North America, covering all 50 states and Canada.

Since its founding, Mobil Travel Guide has served as an advocate for travelers seeking knowledge about hotels, restaurants, and places to visit. Based on an objective process, we make recommendations to our customers that we believe will enhance the quality and value of their travel experiences. Our trusted Mobil One- to Five-Star rating system is the oldest and most respected lodging and restaurant inspection and rating program in North America. Most hoteliers, restaurateurs, and industry observers favorably regard the rigor of our inspection program and understand the prestige and benefits that come with receiving a Mobil Star rating.

The Mobil Travel Guide process of rating each establishment includes:

- Unannounced facility inspections
- Incognito service evaluations for Mobil Four-Star and Mobil Five-Star properties
- A review of unsolicited comments from the general public
- Senior management oversight

For each property, more than 450 attributes, including cleanliness, physical facilities, and employee attitude and courtesy, are measured and evaluated to produce a mathematically derived score, which is then blended with the other elements to form an overall score. These quantifiable scores allow comparative analysis among properties and form the basis that we use to assign our Mobil One- to Five-Star ratings.

This process focuses largely on guest expectations, guest experience, and consistency of service, not just physical facilities and amenities. It is fundamentally a relative rating system that rewards those properties that continually strive for and achieve excellence each year. Indeed, the very best properties are consistently raising the bar for those that wish to compete with them. These properties proactively respond to consumers' needs even in today's uncertain times.

Only facilities that meet Mobil Travel Guide's standards earn the privilege of being listed in the guide. Deteriorating, poorly managed establishments are deleted. A Mobil Travel Guide listing constitutes a positive quality recommendation; every listing is an accolade, a recognition of achievement. Our Mobil One- to Five-Star rating system highlights its level of service. Extensive in-house research is constantly underway to determine new additions to our lists.

- The Mobil Five-Star Award indicates that a property is one of the very best in the country and consistently provides gracious and courteous service, superlative quality in its facility, and a unique ambience. The lodgings and restaurants at the Mobil Five-Star level consistently and proactively respond to consumers' needs and continue their commitment to excellence, doing so with grace and perseverance.
- Also highly regarded is the Mobil Four-Star Award, which honors properties for outstanding achievement in overall facility and for providing very strong service levels in all areas. These

award winners provide a distinctive experience for the ever-demanding and sophisticated consumer.

- The Mobil Three-Star Award recognizes an excellent property that provides full services and amenities. This category ranges from exceptional hotels with limited services to elegant restaurants with a less-formal atmosphere.
- A Mobil Two-Star property is a clean and comfortable establishment that has expanded amenities or a distinctive environment. A Mobil Two-Star property is an excellent place to stay or dine.
- A Mobil One-Star property is limited in its amenities and services but focuses on providing a value experience while meeting travelers' expectations. The property can be expected to be clean, comfortable, and convenient.

Allow us to emphasize that we do not charge establishments for inclusion in our guides. We have no relationship with any of the businesses and attractions we list and act only as a consumer advocate. In essence, we do the investigative legwork so that you won't have to.

Keep in mind, too, that the hospitality business is ever-changing. Restaurants and lodgings—particularly small chains and stand-alone establishments—change management or even go out of business with surprising quickness. Although we make every effort to double-check information during our annual updates, we nevertheless recommend that you call ahead to make sure the place you've selected is still open and offers all the amenities you're looking for. We've provided phone numbers; when available, we also list fax numbers and Web site addresses.

We hope that your travels are enjoyable and relaxing and that our books help you get the most out of every trip you take. If any aspect of your accommodation, dining, or sightseeing experience motivates you to comment, please drop us a line. We depend a great deal on our readers' remarks, so you can be assured that we will read your comments and assimilate them into our research. General comments about our books are also welcome. You can write to us at Mobil Travel Guide, 7373 N Cicero Ave, Lincolnwood, IL 60712, or send an e-mail to info@mobiltravelguide.com.

Take your Mobil Travel Guide books along on every trip you take. We're confident that you'll be pleased with their convenience, ease of use, and breadth of dependable coverage.

Happy travels!

# How to Use This Book

The Mobil Travel Guide Regional Travel Planners are designed for ease of use. Each state has its own chapter, beginning with a general introduction that provides a geographical and historical orientation to the state and gives basic statewide tourist information, from climate to calendar highlights to seatbelt laws. The remainder of each chapter is devoted to travel destinations within the state—mainly cities and towns, but also national parks and tourist areas—which, like the states, are arranged in alphabetical order.

The following sections explain the wealth of information you'll find about those travel destinations: information about the area, things to see and do there, and where to stay and eat.

## Maps and Map Coordinates

At the front of this book in the full-color section, we have provided state maps as well as maps of selected larger cities to help you find your way around once you leave the highway. You'll find a key to the map symbols on the Contents page at the beginning of the map section.

Next to most cities and towns throughout the book, you'll find a set of map coordinates, such as C-2. These coordinates reference the maps at the front of this book and help you find the location you're looking for quickly and easily.

## Destination Information

Because many travel destinations are close to other cities and towns where travelers might find additional attractions, accommodations, and restaurants, we've included cross-references to those cities and towns when it makes sense to do so. We also list addresses, phone numbers, and Web sites for travel information resources—usually the local chamber of commerce or office of tourism—as well as pertinent statistics and, in many cases, a brief introduction to the area. Information about airports, ground transportation, and suburbs is included for large cities.

## Driving Tours and Walking Tours

The driving tours that we include for many states are usually day trips that make for interesting side excursions, although they can be longer. They offer you a way to get off the beaten path and visit an area that travelers often overlook. These trips frequently cover areas of natural beauty or historical significance.

Each walking tour focuses on a particularly interesting area of a city or town. Again, these tours can provide a break from everyday tourist attractions. The tours often include places to stop for meals or snacks.

## What to See and Do

Mobil Travel Guide offers information about nearly 20,000 museums, art galleries, amusement parks, historic sites, national and state parks, ski areas, and many other types of attractions. A white star on a black background ★ signals that the attraction is a must-see—one of the best in the area. Because municipal parks, public tennis courts, swimming pools, and small educational institutions are common to most towns, they generally are not mentioned.

Following an attraction's description, you'll find the months, days, and, in some cases, hours of operation; the address/directions, telephone number, and Web site (if there is one); and the admission price category. The following are the ranges we use for admission fees, based on one adult:

- **FREE**
- **$** = Up to $5
- **$$** = $5.01-$10
- **$$$** = $10.01-$15
- **$$$$** = Over $15

## Special Events

Special events are either annual events that last only a short time, such as festivals and fairs, or longer, seasonal events such as horse racing, theater, and summer concerts. Our Special Events listings also include infrequently occurring occasions that mark certain dates or events, such as a centennial or other commemorative celebration.

## Listings

Lodgings, spas, and restaurants are usually listed under the city or town in which they're located. Make sure to check the related cities and towns that appear right beneath a city's heading for additional options, especially if you're traveling to a major metropolitan area that includes many suburbs. If a property is located in a town that doesn't have its own heading, the listing appears under the town nearest it, with the address and town given immediately after the establishment's name. In large cities, lodgings located within 5 miles of major commercial airports may be listed under a separate "Airport Area" heading that follows the city section.

### LODGINGS

Travelers have different wants and needs when it comes to accommodations. To help you pinpoint properties that meet your particular needs, Mobil Travel Guide classifies each lodging by type according to the following characteristics.

#### Mobil Rated Lodgings

- **Limited-Service Hotel.** A limited-service hotel is traditionally a Mobil One-Star or Mobil Two-Star property. At a Mobil One-Star hotel, guests can expect to find a clean, comfortable property that commonly serves a complimentary continental breakfast. A Mobil Two-Star hotel is also clean and comfortable but has expanded amenities, such as a full-service restaurant, business center, and fitness center. These services may have limited staffing and/or restricted hours of use.
- **Full-Service Hotel.** A full-service hotel traditionally enjoys a Mobil Three-Star, Mobil Four-Star, or Mobil Five-Star rating. Guests can expect these hotels to offer at least one full-service restaurant in addition to amenities such as valet parking, luggage assistance, 24-hour room service, concierge service, laundry and/or dry-cleaning services, and turndown service.
- **Full-Service Resort.** A resort is traditionally a full-service hotel that is geared toward recreation and represents a vacation and holiday destination. A resort's guest rooms are typically furnished to accommodate longer stays. The property may offer a full-service spa, golf, tennis, and fitness facilities or other leisure activities. Resorts are expected to offer a full-service restaurant and expanded amenities, such as luggage assistance, room service, meal plans, concierge service, and turndown service.
- **Full-Service Inn.** An inn is traditionally a Mobil Three-Star, Mobil Four-Star, or Mobil Five-Star property. Inns are similar to bed-and-breakfasts (see below) but offer a wider range of services, most significantly a full-service restaurant that serves at least breakfast and dinner.

#### Specialty Lodgings

Mobil Travel Guide recognizes the unique and individualized nature of many different types of lodging establishments, including bed-and-breakfasts, limited-service inns, and guest ranches. For that reason, we have chosen to place our stamp of approval on the properties that fall into these two categories in lieu of applying our traditional Mobil Star ratings.

- **B&B/Limited-Service Inn.** A bed-and-breakfast (B&B) or limited-service inn is traditionally an owner-occupied home or residence found in a residential area or vacation destination. It may be a structure of historic significance. Rooms are often individually decorated, but telephones, televisions, and private bathrooms may not be available in every room. A B&B typically serves only breakfast to its overnight guests, which is included in the room rate. Cocktails and refreshments may be served in the late afternoon or evening.
- **Guest Ranch.** A guest ranch is traditionally a rustic, Western-themed property that specializes in stays of three or more days. Horseback riding is often a feature, with stables and trails found on the property. Facilities can range from clean, comfortable establishments to more luxurious facilities.

#### Mobil Star Rating Definitions for Lodgings

- ★★★★★: A Mobil Five-Star lodging provides consistently superlative service in an exceptionally distinctive luxury environment, with expanded services. Attention to detail is evident throughout the hotel, resort, or inn, from bed linens to staff uniforms.

- ★★★★ : A Mobil Four-Star lodging provides a luxury experience with expanded amenities in a distinctive environment. Services may include, but are not limited to, automatic turndown service, 24-hour room service, and valet parking.
- ★★★ : A Mobil Three-Star lodging is well appointed, with a full-service restaurant and expanded amenities, such as a fitness center, golf course, tennis courts, 24-hour room service, and optional turndown service.
- ★★ : A Mobil Two-Star lodging is considered a clean, comfortable, and reliable establishment that has expanded amenities, such as a full-service restaurant on the premises.
- ★ : A Mobil One-Star lodging is a limited-service hotel, motel, or inn that is considered a clean, comfortable, and reliable establishment.

### Information Found in the Lodging Listings

Each lodging listing gives the name, address/location (when no street address is available), neighborhood and/or directions from downtown (in major cities), phone number(s), fax number, total number of guest rooms, and seasons open (if not year-round). Also included are details on business, luxury, recreational, and dining facilities at the property or nearby. A key to the symbols at the end of each listing can be found on the page following the "A Word to Our Readers" section.

For every property, we also provide pricing information. Because lodging rates change frequently, we list a pricing category rather than specific prices. The pricing categories break down as follows:

- **$** = Up to $150
- **$$** = $151-$250
- **$$$** = $251-$350
- **$$$$** = $351 and up

All prices quoted are in effect at the time of publication; however, prices cannot be guaranteed. In some locations, short-term price variations may exist because of special events, holidays, or seasonality. Certain resorts have complicated rate structures that vary with the time of year; always confirm rates when making your plans.

Because most lodgings offer the following features and services, information about them does not appear in the listings:

- Year-round operation
- Bathroom with tub and/or shower in each room
- Cable television in each room
- In-room telephones
- Cots and cribs available
- Daily maid service
- Elevators
- Major credit cards accepted

## SPAS

Mobil Travel Guide is pleased to announce its newest category: hotel and resort spas. Until now, hotel and resort spas have not been formally rated or inspected by any organization. Every spa selected for inclusion in this book underwent a rigorous inspection process similar to the one Mobil Travel Guide has been applying to lodgings and restaurants for more than four decades. After spending a year and a half researching more than 300 spas and performing exhaustive incognito inspections of more than 200 properties, we narrowed our list to the 48 best spas in the United States and Canada.

Mobil Travel Guide's spa ratings are based on objective evaluations of more than 450 attributes. Approximately half of these criteria assess basic expectations, such as staff courtesy, the technical proficiency and skill of the employees, and whether the facility is maintained properly and hygienically. Several standards address issues that impact a guest's physical comfort and convenience, as well as the staff's ability to impart a sense of personalized service and anticipate clients' needs. Additional criteria measure the spa's ability to create a completely calming ambience.

The Mobil Star ratings focus on much more than the facilities available at a spa and the treatments it offers. Each Mobil Star rating is a cumulative score achieved from multiple inspections that reflects the spa management's attention to detail and commitment to consumers' needs.

### Mobil Star Rating Definitions for Spas

- ★★★★★ : A Mobil Five-Star spa provides consistently superlative service in an exceptionally distinctive luxury environment with extensive amenities. The staff at a Mobil Five-Star spa provides extraordinary service above and beyond the traditional spa experience, allowing guests to achieve the highest level of relaxation and pampering. A Mobil Five-Star spa offers an extensive array of treatments, often incorporating international themes and products. Attention to detail is evident throughout the spa, from arrival to departure.
- ★★★★ : A Mobil Four-Star spa provides a luxurious experience with expanded amenities in an elegant and serene environment. Throughout the spa facility, guests experience personalized service. Amenities might include, but are not limited to, single-sex relaxation rooms where guests wait for their treatments, plunge pools and whirlpools in both men's and women's locker rooms, and an array of treatments, including at a minimum a selection of massages, body therapies, facials, and a variety of salon services.
- ★★★ : A Mobil Three-Star spa is physically well appointed and has a full complement of staff to ensure that guests' needs are met. It has some expanded amenities, such as, but not limited to, a well-equipped fitness center, separate men's and women's locker rooms, a sauna or steam room, and a designated relaxation area. It also offers a menu of services that at a minimum includes massages, facial treatments, and at least one other type of body treatment, such as scrubs or wraps.

## RESTAURANTS

All Mobil Star rated dining establishments listed in this book have a full kitchen and offer seating at tables; most offer table service.

### Mobil Star Rating Definitions for Restaurants

- ★★★★★ : A Mobil Five-Star restaurant offers one of few flawless dining experiences in the country. These establishments consistently provide their guests with exceptional food, superlative service, elegant décor, and exquisite presentations of each detail surrounding a meal.
- ★★★★ : A Mobil Four-Star restaurant provides professional service, distinctive presentations, and wonderful food.
- ★★★ : A Mobil Three-Star restaurant has good food, warm and skillful service, and enjoyable décor.
- ★★ : A Mobil Two-Star restaurant serves fresh food in a clean setting with efficient service. Value is considered in this category, as is family friendliness.
- ★ : A Mobil One-Star restaurant provides a distinctive experience through culinary specialty, local flair, or individual atmosphere.

### Information Found in the Restaurant Listings

Each restaurant listing gives the cuisine type, street address (or directions if no address is available), phone and fax numbers, Web site (if available), meals served, days of operation (if not open daily year-round), and pricing category. Information about appropriate attire is provided, although it's always a good idea to call ahead and ask if you're unsure; the meaning of "casual" or "business casual" varies widely in different parts of the country. We also indicate whether the restaurant has a bar, whether a children's menu is offered, and whether outdoor seating is available. If reservations are recommended, we note that fact in the listing. When valet parking is available, it is noted in the description. In many cases, self-parking is available at the restaurant or nearby.

Because menu prices can fluctuate, we list a pricing category rather than specific prices. The pricing categories are defined as follows, per diner, and assume that you order an appetizer or dessert, an entrée, and one drink:

- **$** = $15 and under
- **$$** = $16-$35
- **$$$** = $36-$85
- **$$$$** = $86 and up

Again, all prices quoted are in effect at the time of publication, but prices cannot be guaranteed.

## SPECIAL INFORMATION FOR TRAVELERS WITH DISABILITIES

The Mobil Travel Guide [D] symbol indicates that an establishment is not at least partially accessible to people with mobility problems. When the [D] symbol follows a listing, the establishment is not equipped with facilities to accommodate people using wheelchairs or crutches or otherwise needing easy access to doorways and rest rooms. Travelers with severe mobility problems or with hearing or visual impairments may or may not find the facilities they need. Always phone ahead to make sure hat an establishment can meet your needs.

# Understanding the Symbols

**What to See and Do**

| | | |
|---|---|---|
| ★ (boxed) | = | One of the top attractions in the area |
| **$** | = | Up to $5 |
| **$$** | = | $5.01 to $10 |
| **$$$** | = | $10.01 to $15 |
| **$$$$** | = | Over $15 |

**Lodgings**

| | | |
|---|---|---|
| **$** | = | Up to $150 |
| **$$** | = | $151 to $250 |
| **$$$** | = | $251 to $350 |
| **$$$$** | = | Over $350 |

**Restaurants**

| | | |
|---|---|---|
| **$** | = | Up to $15 |
| **$$** | = | $16 to $35 |
| **$$$** | = | $36 to $85 |
| **$$$$** | = | Over $85 |

**Lodging Star Definitions**

★★★★★ A Mobil Five-Star lodging establishment provides consistently superlative service in an exceptionally distinctive luxury environment with expanded services. Attention to detail is evident throughout the hotel/resort/inn from the bed linens to the staff uniforms.

★★★★ A Mobil Four-Star lodging establishment is a hotel/resort/inn that provides a luxury experience with expanded amenities in a distinctive environment. Services may include, but are not limited to, automatic turndown service, 24-hour room service, and valet parking.

★★★ A Mobil Three-Star lodging establishment is a hotel/resort/inn that is well appointed, with a full-service restaurant and expanded amenities, such as, but not limited to, a fitness center, golf course, tennis courts, 24-hour room service, and optional turndown service.

★★ A Mobil Two-Star lodging establishment is a hotel/resort/inn that is considered a clean, comfortable, and reliable establishment, but also has expanded amenities, such as a full-service restaurant on the premises.

★ A Mobil One-Star lodging establishment is a limited-service hotel or inn that is considered a clean, comfortable, and reliable establishment.

**Restaurant Star Definitions**

★★★★★ A Mobil Five-Star restaurant is one of few flawless dining experiences in the country. These restaurants consistently provide their guests with exceptional food, superlative service, elegant décor, and exquisite presentations of each detail surrounding the meal.

★★★★ A Mobil Four-Star restaurant provides professional service, distinctive presentations, and wonderful food.

★★★ A Mobil Three-Star restaurant has good food, warm and skillful service, and enjoyable décor.

★★ A Mobil Two-Star restaurant serves fresh food in a clean setting with efficient service. Value is considered in this category, as is family friendliness.

★ A Mobil One-Star restaurant provides a distinctive experience through culinary specialty, local flair, or individual atmosphere.

**Symbols at End of Listings**

- Facilities for people with disabilities not available
- Pets allowed
- Ski in/ski out access
- Golf on premises
- Tennis court(s) on premises
- Indoor or outdoor pool
- Fitness room
- Major commercial airport within 5 miles
- Business center

# Making the Most of Your Trip

A few hardy souls might look back with fondness on a trip during which the car broke down, leaving them stranded for three days, or a vacation that cost twice what it was supposed to. For most travelers, though, the best trips are those that are safe, smooth, and within budget. To help you make your trip the best it can be, we've assembled a few tips and resources.

## Saving Money

### ON LODGING

Many hotels and motels offer discounts—for senior citizens, business travelers, families, you name it. It never hurts to ask—politely, that is. Sometimes, especially in the late afternoon, desk clerks are instructed to fill beds, and you might be offered a lower rate or a nicer room to entice you to stay. Simply ask the reservation agent for the best rate available. Also, make sure to try both the toll-free number and the local number. You may be able to get a lower rate from one than from the other.

Timing your trip right can cut your lodging costs as well. Look for bargains on stays over multiple nights, in the off-season, and on weekdays or weekends, depending on the location. Many hotels in major metropolitan areas, for example, have special weekend packages that offer leisure travelers considerable savings on rooms; they may include breakfast, cocktails, and/or dinner discounts.

Another way to save money is to choose accommodations that give you more than just a standard room. Rooms with kitchen facilities enable you to cook some meals yourself, reducing your restaurant costs. A suite might save money for two couples traveling together. Even hotel luxury levels can provide good value, as many include breakfast or cocktails in the price of a room.

State and city taxes, as well as special room taxes, can increase your room rate by as much as 25 percent per day. We are unable to include information about taxes in our listings, but we strongly urge you to ask about taxes when making reservations so that you understand the total cost of your lodgings before you book them.

Watch out for telephone-usage charges that hotels frequently impose on long-distance, credit-card, and other calls. Before phoning from your room, read the information given to you at check-in, and then be sure to review your bill carefully when checking out. You won't be expected to pay for charges that the hotel didn't spell out. Consider using your cell phone if you have one; or, if public telephones are available in the hotel lobby, your cost savings may outweigh the inconvenience of using them.

Here are some additional ways to save on lodgings:

- Stay in B&B accommodations. They're generally less expensive than standard hotel rooms, and the complimentary breakfast cuts down on food costs.
- If you're traveling with children, find lodgings at which kids stay free.
- When visiting a major city, stay just outside the city limits; these rooms are usually less expensive than those in downtown locations.
- Consider visiting national parks during the low season, when prices of lodgings near the parks drop by 25 percent or more.
- When calling a hotel, ask whether it is running any special promotions or if any discounts are available; many times reservationists are told not to volunteer these deals unless they're specifically asked about them.
- Check for hotel packages; some offer nightly rates that include a rental car or discounts on major attractions.

### ON DINING

There are several ways to get a less expensive meal at an expensive restaurant. Early-bird dinners are popular in many parts of the country and offer considerable savings. If you're interested in visiting a Mobil Four- or Five-Star establishment, consider going at lunchtime. Although the prices are probably still relatively high at midday, they may be half of those at dinner, and you'll experience the same ambience, service, and cuisine.

### ON ENTERTAINMENT

Although many national parks, monuments, seashores, historic sites, and recreation areas may be visited free of charge, others charge an entrance fee and/or a usage fee for special services and facilities. If you plan to make several visits to national recreation areas, consider one of the following money-saving programs offered by the National Park Service:

- **National Parks Pass.** This annual pass is good for entrance to any national park that charges an entrance fee. If the park charges a per-vehicle fee, the pass holder and any accompanying passengers in a private noncommercial vehicle may enter. If the park charges a per-person fee, the pass applies to the holder's spouse, children, and parents as well as the holder. It is valid for entrance fees only; it does not cover parking, camping, or other fees. You can purchase a National Parks Pass in person at any national park where an entrance fee is charged; by mail from the National Park Foundation, PO Box 34108, Washington, DC 20043-4108; by calling toll-free 888/467-2757; or at www.nationalparks.org. The cost is $50.
- **Golden Eagle Sticker.** When affixed to a National Parks Pass, this hologram sticker, available to people who are between 17 and 61 years of age, extends coverage to sites managed by the US Fish and Wildlife Service, the US Forest Service, and the Bureau of Land Management. It is good until the National Parks Pass to which it is affixed expires and does not cover usage fees. You can purchase one at the National Park Service, the Fish and Wildlife Service, or the Bureau of Land Management fee stations. The cost is $15.
- **Golden Age Passport.** Available to citizens and permanent US residents 62 and older, this passport is a lifetime entrance permit to fee-charging national recreation areas. The fee exemption extends to those accompanying the permit holder in a private noncommercial vehicle or, in the case of walk-in facilities, to the holder's spouse and children. The passport also entitles the holder to a 50 percent discount on federal usage fees charged in park areas, but not on concessions. Golden Age Passports must be obtained in person and are available at most National Park Service units that charge an entrance fee. The applicant must show proof of age, such as a driver's license or birth certificate (Medicare cards are not acceptable proof). The cost is $10.
- **Golden Access Passport.** Issued to citizens and permanent US residents who are physically disabled or visually impaired, this passport is a free lifetime entrance permit to fee-charging national recreation areas. The fee exemption extends to those accompanying the permit holder in a private noncommercial vehicle or, in the case of walk-in facilities, to the holder's spouse and children. The passport also entitles the holder to a 50 percent discount on usage fees charged in park areas, but not on concessions. Golden Access Passports must be obtained in person and are available at most National Park Service units that charge an entrance fee. Proof of eligibility to receive federal benefits (under programs such as Disability Retirement, Compensation for Military Service-Connected Disability, and the Coal Mine Safety and Health Act) is required, or an affidavit must be signed attesting to eligibility.

A money-saving move in several large cities is to purchase a **CityPass.** If you plan to visit several museums and other major attractions, CityPass is a terrific option because it gets you into several sites for one substantially reduced price. Currently, CityPass is available in Boston, Chicago, Hollywood, New York, Philadelphia, San Francisco, Seattle, southern California (which includes Disneyland, SeaWorld, and the San Diego Zoo), and Toronto. For more information or to buy one, call toll-free 888/330-5008 or visit www.citypass.net. You can also buy a CityPass from any participating CityPass attraction.

Here are some additional ways to save on entertainment and shopping:

- Check with your hotel's concierge for various coupons and special offers; they often have two-for-one tickets for area attractions and coupons for discounts at area stores and restaurants.
- Purchase same-day concert or theater tickets for half-price through the local cheap-tickets outlet, such as TKTS in New York or Hot Tix in Chicago.

- Visit museums on their free or "by donation" days, when you can pay what you wish rather than a specific admission fee.
- Save receipts from purchases in Canada; visitors to Canada can get a rebate on federal taxes and some provincial sales taxes.

### ON TRANSPORTATION

Transportation is a big part of any vacation budget. Here are some ways to reduce your costs:

- If you're renting a car, shop early over the Internet; you can book a car during the low season for less, even if you'll be using it in the high season.
- Rental car discounts are often available if you rent for one week or longer and reserve in advance.
- Get the best gas mileage out of your vehicle by making sure that it's properly tuned up and keeping your tires properly inflated.
- Travel at moderate speeds on the open road; higher speeds require more gasoline.
- Fill the tank before you return your rental car; rental companies charge to refill the tank and do so at prices of up to 50 percent more than at local gas stations.
- Make a checklist of travel essentials and purchase them before you leave; don't get stuck buying expensive sunscreen at your hotel or overpriced film at the airport.

### FOR SENIOR CITIZENS

Always call ahead to ask if a discount is being offered, and be sure to carry proof of age. Additional information for mature travelers is available from the American Association of Retired Persons (AARP), 601 E St NW, Washington, DC 20049; phone 202/434-2277; www.aarp.org.

## Tipping

Tips are expressions of appreciation for good service. However, you are never obligated to tip if you receive poor service.

### IN HOTELS

- Door attendants usually get $1 for hailing a cab.
- Bell staff expect $2 per bag.
- Concierges are tipped according to the service they perform. Tipping is not mandatory when you've asked for suggestions on sightseeing or restaurants or for help in making dining reservations. However, a tip of $5 is appropriate when a concierge books you a table at a restaurant known to be difficult to get into. For obtaining theater or sporting event tickets, $5 to $10 is expected.
- Maids should be tipped $1 to $2 per day. Hand your tip directly to the maid, or leave it with a note saying that the money has been left expressly for the maid.

### IN RESTAURANTS

Before tipping, carefully review your check for any gratuity or service charge that is already included in your bill. If you're in doubt, ask your server.

- Coffee shop and counter service waitstaff usually receive 15 percent of the bill, before sales tax.
- In full-service restaurants, tip 18 percent of the bill, before sales tax.
- In fine restaurants, where gratuities are shared among a larger staff, 18 to 20 percent is appropriate.
- In most cases, the maitre d' is tipped only if the service has been extraordinary, and only on the way out. At upscale properties in major metropolitan areas, $20 is the minimum.
- If there is a wine steward, tip $20 for exemplary service and beyond, or more if the wine was decanted or the bottle was very expensive.
- Tip $1 to $2 per coat at the coat check.

### AT AIRPORTS

Curbside luggage handlers expect $1 per bag. Car-rental shuttle drivers who help with your luggage appreciate a $1 or $2 tip.

## Staying Safe

The best way to deal with emergencies is to avoid them in the first place. However, unforeseen situations do happen, so you should be prepared for them.

### IN YOUR CAR

Before you head out on a road trip, make sure that your car has been serviced and is in good working order. Change the oil, check the battery and belts, make sure that your windshield washer fluid is full and your tires are properly inflated (which can also improve your gas mileage). Other inspections recommended by the vehicle's manufacturer should also be made.

Next, be sure you have the tools and equipment needed to deal with a routine breakdown:

- Jack
- Spare tire
- Lug wrench
- Repair kit
- Emergency tools
- Jumper cables
- Spare fan belt
- Fuses
- Flares and/or reflectors
- Flashlight
- First-aid kit
- In winter, a windshield scraper and snow shovel

Many emergency supplies are sold in special packages that include the essentials you need to stay safe in the event of a breakdown.

Also bring all appropriate and up-to-date documentation—licenses, registration, and insurance cards—and know what your insurance covers. Bring an extra set of keys, too, just in case.

En route, always buckle up! In most states, wearing a seatbelt is required by law.

If your car does break down, do the following:

- Get out of traffic as soon as possible—pull well off the road.
- Raise the hood and turn on your emergency flashers or tie a white cloth to the roadside door handle or antenna.
- Stay in your car.
- Use flares or reflectors to keep your vehicle from being hit.

### IN YOUR HOTEL

Chances are slim that you will encounter a hotel or motel fire, but you can protect yourself by doing the following:

- Once you've checked in, make sure that the smoke detector in your room is working properly.
- Find the property's fire safety instructions, usually posted on the inside of the room door.
- Locate the fire extinguishers and at least two fire exits.
- Never use an elevator in a fire.

For personal security, use the peephole in your room door and make sure that anyone claiming to be a hotel employee can show proper identification. Call the front desk if you feel threatened at any time.

### PROTECTING AGAINST THEFT

To guard against theft wherever you go:

- Don't bring anything of more value than you need.
- If you do bring valuables, leave them at your hotel rather than in your car.
- If you bring something very expensive, lock it in a safe. Many hotels put one in each room; others will store your valuables in the hotel's safe.
- Don't carry more money than you need. Use traveler's checks and credit cards or visit cash machines to withdraw more cash when you run out.

## For Travelers with Disabilities

To get the kind of service you need and have a right to expect, don't hesitate when making a reservation to question the management about the availability of accessible rooms, parking, entrances, restaurants, lounges, or any other facilities that are important to you, and confirm what is meant by "accessible."

The Mobil Travel Guide [D] symbol indicates establishments that are not at least partially accessible to people with special mobility needs (people using wheelchairs or crutches or otherwise needing easy access to buildings and rooms). Further information about these criteria can be found in the earlier section "How to Use This Book."

A thorough listing of published material for travelers with disabilities is available from the Disability Bookshop, Twin Peaks Press, Box 129, Vancouver, WA 98666; phone 360/694-2462; disabilitybookshop.virtualave.net. Another reliable organization is the Society for Accessible Travel & Hospitality (SATH), 347 Fifth Ave, Suite 610, New York, NY 10016; phone 212/447-7284; www.sath.org.

# Important Toll-Free Numbers and Online Information

## Hotels

**Adams Mark** .......... 800/444-2326
*www.adamsmark.com*
**America's Best Value Inn** .......... 888/315-2378
*www.americasbestvalueinn.com*
**AmericInn** .......... 800/634-3444
*www.americinn.com*
**AmeriHost Inn** .......... 800/434-5800
*www.amerihostinn.com*
**Amerisuites** .......... 800/833-1516
*www.amerisuites.com*
**Baymont Inns** .......... 800/621-1429
*www.baymontinns.com*
**Best Inns & Suites** .......... 800/237-8466
*www.bestinn.com*
**Best Western** .......... 800/780-7234
*www.bestwestern.com*
**Budget Host Inn** .......... 800/283-4678
*www.budgethost.com*
**Candlewood Suites** .......... 888/226-3539
*www.candlewoodsuites.com*
**Clarion Hotels** .......... 800/252-7466
*www.choicehotels.com*
**Comfort Inns and Suites** .......... 800/252-7466
*www.comfortinn.com*
**Country Hearth Inns** .......... 800/848-5767
*www.countryhearth.com*
**Country Inns & Suites** .......... 800/456-4000
*www.countryinns.com*
**Courtyard by Marriott** .......... 800/321-2211
*www.courtyard.com*
**Crowne Plaza Hotels and Resorts** .......... 800/227-6963
*www.crowneplaza.com*
**Days Inn** .......... 800/544-8313
*www.daysinn.com*
**Delta Hotels** .......... 800/268-1133
*www.deltahotels.com*
**Destination Hotels & Resorts** .......... 800/434-7347
*www.destinationhotels.com*
**Doubletree Hotels** .......... 800/222-8733
*www.doubletree.com*
**Drury Inn** .......... 800/378-7946
*www.druryhotels.com*
**Econolodge** .......... 800/553-2666
*www.econolodge.com*
**Embassy Suites** .......... 800/362-2779
*www.embassysuites.com*
**ExelInns of America** .......... 800/367-3935
*www.exelinns.com*
**Extended StayAmerica** .......... 800/398-7829
*www.extendedstayhotels.com*
**Fairfield Inn by Marriott** .......... 800/228-2800
*www.fairfieldinn.com*
**Fairmont Hotels** .......... 800/441-1414
*www.fairmont.com*
**Four Points by Sheraton** .......... 888/625-5144
*www.fourpoints.com*
**Four Seasons** .......... 800/819-5053
*www.fourseasons.com*
**Hampton Inn** .......... 800/426-7866
*www.hamptoninn.com*
**Hard Rock Hotels, Resorts, and Casinos** .......... 800/473-7625
*www.hardrockhotel.com*
**Harrah's Entertainment** .......... 800/427-7247
*www.harrahs.com*
**Hawthorn Suites** .......... 800/527-1133
*www.hawthorn.com*
**Hilton Hotels and Resorts (US)** .......... 800/774-1500
*www.hilton.com*
**Holiday Inn Express** .......... 800/465-4329
*www.hiexpress.com*
**Holiday Inn Hotels and Resorts** .......... 800/465-4329
*www.holiday-inn.com*
**Homestead Studio Suites** .......... 888/782-9473
*www.extendedstayhotels.com*
**Homewood Suites** .......... 800/225-5466
*www.homewoodsuites.com*
**Howard Johnson** .......... 800/406-1411
*www.hojo.com*
**Hyatt** .......... 800/633-7313
*www.hyatt.com*
**Inns of America** .......... 800/826-0778
*www.innsofamerica.com*
**InterContinental** .......... 888/424-6835
*www.intercontinental.com*
**Joie de Vivre** .......... 800/738-7477
*www.jdvhospitality.com*
**Kimpton Hotels** .......... 888/546-7866
*www.kimptonhotels.com*
**Knights Inn** .......... 800/843-5644
*www.knightsinn.com*
**La Quinta** .......... 800/531-5900
*www.lq.com*

**Le Meridien** .................................800/543-4300
*www.lemeridien.com*
**Leading Hotels of the World** .................800/223-6800
*www.lhw.com*
**Loews Hotels** ...............................800/235-6397
*www.loewshotels.com*
**MainStay Suites** ............................800/660-6246
*www.mainstaysuites.com*
**Mandarin Oriental** ..........................800/526-6566
*www.mandarinoriental.com*
**Marriott Hotels, Resorts, and Suites** ...... 800/228-9290
*www.marriott.com*
**Microtel Inns & Suites** ......................800/771-7171
*www.microtelinn.com*
**Millennium & Copthorne Hotels** .......... 866/866-8086
*www.millenniumhotels.com*
**Motel 6** ....................................800/466-8356
*www.motel6.com*
**Omni Hotels** ...............................800/843-6664
*www.omnihotels.com*
**Pan Pacific Hotels and Resorts** ..............800/327-8585
*www.panpacific.com*
**Park Inn & Park Plaza** ................. 888/201-1801
*www.parkinn.com*
**The Peninsula Group** ........... Contact individual hotel
*www.peninsula.com*
**Preferred Hotels & Resorts Worldwide** .......800/323-7500
*www.preferredhotels.com*
**Quality Inn** .................................800/228-5151
*www.qualityinn.com*
**Radisson Hotels** ............................800/333-3333
*www.radisson.com*
**Raffles International Hotels and Resorts** .....800/637-9477
*www.raffles.com*
**Ramada Plazas, Limiteds, and Inns** ..........800/272-6232
*www.ramada.com*
**Red Lion Inns** ...............................800/733-5466
*www.redlion.com*
**Red Roof Inns** ...............................800/733-7663
*www.redroof.com*
**Regent International** ........................800/545-4000
*www.regenthotels.com*
**Relais & Chateaux** ..........................800/735-2478
*www.relaischateaux.com*
**Renaissance Hotels** .................. 888/236-2427
*www.renaissancehotels.com*
**Residence Inn** ...................... 800/331-3131
*www.residenceinn.com*
**Ritz-Carlton** ................................800/241-3333
*www.ritzcarlton.com*
**RockResorts** ......................... 888/367-7625
*www.rockresorts.com*
**Rodeway Inn** ...............................800/228-2000
*www.rodeway.com*
**Rosewood Hotels & Resorts** ............ 888/767-3966
*www.rosewoodhotels.com*
**Select Inn** ..................................800/641-1000
*www.selectinn.com*
**Sheraton** ........................... 888/625-5144
*www.sheraton.com*
**Shilo Inns** ..................................800/222-2244
*www.shiloinns.com*
**Shoney's Inn** ...............................800/552-4667
*www.shoneysinn.com*
**Signature/Jameson Inns** .....................800/822-5252
*www.jamesoninns.com*
**Sleep Inn** ...................................877/424-6423
*www.sleepinn.com*
**Small Luxury Hotels of the World** ............800/525-4800
*www.slh.com*
**Sofitel** ......................................800/763-4835
*www.sofitel.com*
**SpringHill Suites** .................... 888/236-2427
*www.springhillsuites.com*
**St. Regis Luxury Collection** ............. 888/625-5144
*www.stregis.com*
**Staybridge Suites** ..........................800/238-8000
*www.staybridge.com*
**Summit International** .......................800/457-4000
*www.summithotelsandresorts.com*
**Super 8 Motels** .............................800/800-8000
*www.super8.com*
**The Sutton Place Hotels** ................ 866/378-8866
*www.suttonplace.com*
**Swissôtel** ...................................800/637-9477
*www.swissotels.com*
**TownePlace Suites** .................... 888/236-2427
*www.towneplace.com*
**Travelodge** ..................................800/578-7878
*www.travelodge.com*
**Vagabond Inns** ..............................800/522-1555
*www.vagabondinn.com*
**W Hotels** ........................... 888/625-5144
*www.whotels.com*
**Wellesley Inn and Suites** ....................800/444-8888
*www.wellesleyinnandsuites.com*

**WestCoast Hotels** . . . . . . . . 800/325-4000
*www.westcoasthotels.com*
**Westin Hotels & Resorts** . . . . . . . . 800/937-8461
*www.westinhotels.com*
**Wingate Inns** . . . . . . . . 800/228-1000
*www.thewingateinns.com*
**Woodfin Suite Hotels** . . . . . . . . 800/966-3346
*www.woodfinsuitehotels.com*
**WorldHotels** . . . . . . . . 800/223-5652
*www.worldhotels.com*
**Wyndham Hotels & Resorts** . . . . . . . . 800/996-3426
*www.wyndham.com*

## Airlines

**Air Canada** . . . . . . . . 888/247-2262
*www.aircanada.com*
**AirTran** . . . . . . . . 800/247-8726
*www.airtran.com*
**Alaska Airlines** . . . . . . . . 800/252-7522
*www.alaskaair.com*
**American Airlines** . . . . . . . . 800/433-7300
*www.aa.com*
**ATA** . . . . . . . . 800/435-9282
*www.ata.com*
**Continental Airlines** . . . . . . . . 800/523-3273
*www.continental.com*
**Delta Air Lines** . . . . . . . . 800/221-1212
*www.delta.com*
**Frontier Airlines** . . . . . . . . 800/432-1359
*www.frontierairlines.com*
**Hawaiian Airlines** . . . . . . . . 800/367-5320
*www.hawaiianairlines.com*
**Jet Blue Airlines** . . . . . . . . 800/538-2583
*www.jetblue.com*
**Midwest Airlines** . . . . . . . . 800/452-2022
*www.midwestairlines.com*
**Northwest Airlines** . . . . . . . . 800/225-2525
*www.nwa.com*
**Southwest Airlines** . . . . . . . . 800/435-9792
*www.southwest.com*
**Spirit Airlines** . . . . . . . . 800/772-7117
*www.spiritair.com*
**United Airlines** . . . . . . . . 800/241-6522
*www.united.com*
**US Airways** . . . . . . . . 800/428-4322
*www.usairways.com*

## Car Rentals

**Advantage** . . . . . . . . 800/777-5500
*www.arac.com*
**Alamo** . . . . . . . . 800/327-9633
*www.alamo.com*
**Avis** . . . . . . . . 800/831-2847
*www.avis.com*
**Budget** . . . . . . . . 800/527-0700
*www.budget.com*
**Dollar** . . . . . . . . 800/800-4000
*www.dollar.com*
**Enterprise** . . . . . . . . 800/325-8007
*www.enterprise.com*
**Hertz** . . . . . . . . 800/654-3131
*www.hertz.com*
**National** . . . . . . . . 800/227-7368
*www.nationalcar.com*
**Payless** . . . . . . . . 800/729-5377
*www.paylesscarrental.com*
**Rent-A-Wreck.com** . . . . . . . . 800/535-1391
*www.rentawreck.com*
**Thrifty** . . . . . . . . 800/847-4389
*www.thrifty.com*

# *Mobil Travel Guide 2007 **Five-Star** Award Winners*

**CALIFORNIA**

Lodgings

The Beverly Hills Hotel, *Beverly Hills*
Chateau du Sureau, *Oakhurst*
Four Seasons Hotel San Francisco, *San Francisco*
Hotel Bel-Air, *Los Angeles*
The Peninsula Beverly Hills, *Beverly Hills*
Raffles L'Ermitage Beverly Hills, *Beverly Hills*
St. Regis Monarch Beach Resort & Spa, *Dana Point*
St. Regis San Francisco, *San Francisco*
The Ritz-Carlton, San Francisco, *San Francisco*

Restaurants

The Dining Room, *San Francisco*
The French Laundry, *Yountville*

**COLORADO**

Lodgings

The Broadmoor, *Colorado Springs*
The Little Nell, *Aspen*

**CONNECTICUT**

Lodging

The Mayflower Inn, *Washington*

**DISTRICT OF COLUMBIA**

Lodging

Four Seasons Hotel Washington, DC *Washington*

**FLORIDA**

Lodgings

Four Seasons Resort Palm Beach, *Palm Beach*
The Ritz-Carlton Naples, *Naples*
The Ritz-Carlton, Palm Beach, *Manalapan*

**GEORGIA**

Lodgings

Four Seasons Hotel Atlanta, *Atlanta*
The Lodge at Sea Island Golf Club, *St. Simons Island*

Restaurants

The Dining Room, *Atlanta*
Seeger's, *Atlanta*

**HAWAII**

Lodging

Four Seasons Resort Maui, *Wailea, Maui*

**ILLINOIS**

Lodgings

Four Seasons Hotel Chicago, *Chicago*
The Peninsula Chicago, *Chicago*
The Ritz-Carlton, A Four Seasons Hotel, *Chicago*

Restaurants

Alinea, *Chicago*
Charlie Trotter's, *Chicago*

**MAINE**

Restaurant

The White Barn Inn, *Kennebunkport*

**MASSACHUSETTS**

Lodgings

Blantyre, *Lenox*
Four Seasons Hotel Boston, *Boston*

**NEVADA**

Lodging

Tower Suites at Wynn, *Las Vegas*

Restaurants

Alex, *Las Vegas*
Joel Robuchon at the Mansion, *Las Vegas*

**NEW YORK**

Lodgings

Four Seasons, Hotel New York, *New York*
Mandarin Oriental, *New York*
The Point, *Saranac Lake*
The Ritz-Carlton New York, Central Park, *New York*
The St. Regis, *New York*

Restaurants

Alain Ducasse, *New York*
Jean Georges, *New York*
Masa, *New York*
per se, *New York*

**NORTH CAROLINA**

Lodging

The Fearrington House Country Inn, *Pittsboro*

**PENNSYLVANIA**

Restaurant

Le Bec-Fin, *Philadelphia*

**SOUTH CAROLINA**

Lodging

Woodlands Resort & Inn, *Summerville*

Restaurant

Dining Room at the Woodlands, *Summerville*

**TENNESSEE**

Lodging

The Hermitage, *Nashville*

**TEXAS**

Lodging

The Mansion on Turtle Creek, *Dallas*

**VERMONT**

Lodging

Twin Farms, *Barnard*

**VIRGINIA**

Lodgings

The Inn at Little Washington, *Washington*
The Jefferson Hotel, *Richmond*

Restaurant

The Inn at Little Washington, *Washington*

Mobil Travel Guide has been rating establishments with its Mobil One- to Five-Star system since 1958. Each establishment awarded the Mobil Five-Star rating is one of the best in the country. Detailed information on each award winner can be found in the corresponding regional edition listed on the back cover of this book.

# Four- and Five-Star Establishments in the Northwest

## Washington

### ★★★★ Lodging

The Fairmont Olympic Hotel, *Seattle*

### ★★★★ Restaurants

The Georgian, *Seattle*
The Herbfarm, *Woodinville*
Lampreia Restaurant, *Seattle*
Rover's, *Seattle*

# Alaska

The breathtaking beauty of million-year-old glaciers, a rugged landscape, and exotic wildlife make Alaska a paradise for nature lov-ers. Its national forests and parks are America's largest, and the abundant coastal waters provide some of the best salmon and halibut fishing in the world. Veteran rock and ice climbers routinely assault Mount McKinley, the highest peak in North America at 20,320 feet, and the truly intrepid compete in the annual Iditarod sled dog race. Surprisingly cosmopolitan and comfortable, Anchorage is home to about half of the state's population and offers first-class restaurants, nightclubs, and entertainment.

The great Yukon River cuts the Alaskan interior almost in half, carving tremendous valleys along the way as it makes its 1, 265-mile journey from the state's border to the Bering Sea. The mazelike convergence of land and water in the famed Inside Passage of the panhandle was sculpted into its present form by thousands of years of glacial ice scoring itsway toward the sea and eventually melting.

**Population:** 626,932
**Area:** 586,412 square miles
**Elevation:** 0-20,320 feet
**Peak:** Mount McKinley
**Entered Union:** January 3, 1959 (49th state)
**Capital:** Juneau
**Motto:** North to the Future
**Nickname:** The Last Frontier
**Flower:** Forget-Me-Not
**Bird:** Willow Ptarmigan
**Tree:** Sitka Spruce
**Fair:** August in Palmer
**Time Zone:** Alaska, Hawaii-Aleutian
**Information:** Alaska Travel Industry Association, 2600 Cordova St, Suite 201, Anchorage, 99503: phone toll free 800/3279372
**Web Site:** www.travelalaska.com
**Fun Fact:**
- Alaska's state gem is jade. An entire mountain of jade is located on the Seward Peninsula.

## When to Go/Climate

Befitting its vastness, Alaska experiences a huge range of temperatures throughout the year. In the far north, average daily high temperatures never reach 50 degrees, even in summer, while southeastern Alaska enjoys temperatures in the 60s and higher between June and August. Obviously, summer is peak travel season, with hours of sunlight nearing 20 hours per day. Only a few hardy souls venture here in the colder, darker months.

### AVERAGE HIGH/LOW TEMPERATURES (°F)

**Anchorage**

| | | |
|---|---|---|
| **Jan** 22/9 | **May** 55/39 | **Sep** 55/41 |
| **Feb** 26/12 | **Jun** 62/47 | **Oct** 40/28 |
| **Mar** 34/18 | **Jul** 65/52 | **Nov** 28/16 |
| **Apr** 44/29 | **Aug** 63/49 | **Dec** 24/11 |

**Juneau**

| | | |
|---|---|---|
| **Jan** 31/21 | **May** 56/40 | **Sep** 56/44 |
| **Feb** 34/24 | **Jun** 62/46 | **Oct** 47/38 |
| **Mar** 39/28 | **Jul** 64/49 | **Nov** 38/29 |
| **Apr** 48/33 | **Aug** 63/48 | **Dec** 33/24 |

## Parks and Recreation

Alaska's state parks are concentrated in the southern half of the state, with a large number on the Kenai Peninsula. Water-related activities, hiking, camping, and picnicking are available in many of Alaska's state parks on a seasonal basis. Daily parking fees are $3-$5 per vehicle, while camping fees range from $10-$15 a night. Cabins are available at more than 15 parks. The Alaska Trails System,

## Calendar Highlights

### FEBRUARY

**Fur Rendezvous** *(Anchorage). Phone 907/274-1177. www.furrondy.net.* Winter festival and carnival that leads into the Iditarod.

### MARCH

**Iditarod and Sled Dog Races** *(Anchorage). Phone 907/376-5155. www.iditarod.com.* The sled dog races are short-distance events beginning downtown. The Iditarod, a separate event run by a different group, caps off the week. This famous dogsled race covers more than 1,150 miles from Anchorage to Nome and usually takes 9 to 12 days.

### MAY

**Kachemak Bay Shorebird Festival** *(Homer). Contact the Chamber of Commerce, phone 907/235-7740. www.homeralaska.org/shorebird.htm.* A popular festival celebrating the arrival of hundreds of thousands of migratory birds each spring.

### JUNE

**Copper River Wild! Salmon Festival** *(Cordova). Contact the Chamber of Commerce, phone 907/424-7260.* Celebrates the annual arrival of Copper River Reds (red salmon)a major Alaskan export.

**Last Frontier Theatre Conference** *(Valdez).* One of the largest theatric conferences in America, with 400 to 800 participants, depending on which famous people agree to take part. Features playwrights, authors, actors, and wannabes. The honorary founder is playwright Edward Albee.

**Summer Solstice Festival** *(Fairbanks).* Considered the biggest and best in a state in which nearly every town celebrates the summer solstice.

### JULY

**Fourth of July Festival and Mount Marathon Race** *(Seward). Contact the Chamber of Commerce, phone 907/224-8051.* Considered by many to be the best Independence Day festival in Alaska. Thousands of people flood into town for parades, food booths, music, and craft fairs. The festival is capped off by the Mount Marathon Race, one of the oldest and toughest footraces in America (a 3.25-mile run from just above sea level to the top of Mount Marathon3,020 feetand crashing back down again).

**Moose Dropping Festival** *(Talkeetna). Phone 907/733-2487.* This festival ranks high in terms of small-town charm: food and craft booths, slow-pitch softball tournaments, a mini parade, a foot-race, pancake breakfasts, and the Mountain Mother Contests, where local women compete for the title of Mountain Mother (crossing a "stream" with a baby doll on their backs, shooting an arrow, casting a fishing pole, cutting firewood, etc.).

### AUGUST

**Alaska State Fair** *(Palmer). Phone 907/745-4827.* www.alaskastatefair.org. Giant veggies, including cabbages the size of beanbag chairs, lots of farm animals, and rides all in the beautiful setting of the Matanuska Valley, 40 minutes north of Anchorage.

### NOVEMBER

**Haines Bald Eagle Festival** *(Haines).* Phone 907/766-3094. baldeagles.org/festival.html. Tens of thousands of bald eagles descend on Haines for the late salmon run.

established in 2001, includes 41 land- and water-based trails notable for their scenic, historic, and recreational value, such as the Iditarod National Historic Trail. For more information or to reserve a cabin, contact the Alaska Department of Natural Resources, Division of Parks and Outdoor Recreation, at 550 W 7th Ave, Suite 1260, Anchorage, 99501 (phone 907/269-8400) or 3700 Airport Way, Fairbanks, 99709 (phone 907/451-2705); or visit the Web site www.dnr.state.ak.us/parks.

## FISHING AND HUNTING

Fishing and hunting in Alaska are legendary. From salmon to moose to brown and black bears, the state's wildlife is plentiful and thriving. Because hunting here is so different than in other states,

## ALASKA'S 92-YEAR JOURNEY TO STATEHOOD

Americans today regard Alaska as a national treasure, endowed with spectacular scenery, abundant wildlife, and valuable natural resources. Its ironic to note, then, that Alaska once was viewed by Americans as a "white elephant" and that its procession to statehood, like the glaciers that carved out its magnificent mountains and valleys, moved at a slow pace.

Secretary of State William Seward negotiated a treaty for the purchase of the Alaska territory from Russia in 1867. The US Senate approved the treaty by one vote. Financially devastated by the Crimean War, Russia received a much-needed $7.2 million for the territory, a mere 2 cents per acre but still a considerable sum of money at the time, prompting skeptical Americans to refer to Alaska–thought by many to be a frozen wasteland, devoid of valueas "Sewards Folly."

Over the next 30 years, criticism of the acquisition appeared to be well founded, as the US government made little use of the territory. But Alaska's fortunes improved dramatically at the close of the 19th century with the discovery of gold in Canada's Yukon Territory. Thousands of prospectors descended on the town of Skagway in southeastern Alaska, where they prepared for the arduous trek to the Yukon gold fields. Subsequent gold strikes within the territory itself brought prospectors to towns such as Nome and Fairbanks, providing a boost to the economies in these and other communities-and helping to improve the territory's image in the contiguous states to the south.

The US Congress granted Alaska official territorial status on August 24, 1912. By this time, the heady gold rush days had fizzled, and the territory saw its population decline in the three decades that followed. The territory rebounded during World War II, buoyed by the construction of bases and an influx of military personnel. And at the dawn of the Cold War, Alaska, sitting just across the Bering Strait from Russia, occupied a critical strategic location, and the US military continued to provide a significant boost to the territory's economy.

In July 1958, President Eisenhower inked the Alaska Statehood Act. Six months later, on January 3, 1959–92 years after the US acquired the land from Russia–Alaska was officially proclaimed the nations 49th state. In retrospect, Seward's purchase–far from being a "folly"–looks like a stroke of genius. Each year, on the last Monday in March, the state celebrates Seward's Day in honor of the man who, many years ago, possessed the foresight to recognize Alaska's tremendous value.

## CRUISING SOUTHEASTERN ALASKA

Alaska is at its most beautiful along the state's pristine southeastern coast, a spectacular stretch of densely forested islands, snowcapped mountains, ancient glaciers, and abundant wildlife. Aside from a few historic port towns, the region is undeveloped, and as such it cannot be navigated by car. The coastal area can be explored by watercraft, however, sheltered by the thousand-plus islands just off the mainland, most notably those of the Alexander Archipelago. The straits and channels between the islands enable boats of all sizes to weave their way through the Northwest's Inside Passage, protected from the open, choppy seas of the Pacific Ocean. Cruises have become a popular way to experience the splendor of Alaska's southeastern coast.

For those seeking a luxurious voyage, **Princess Cruises** offers Alaska vacations aboard ships with such amenities as swimming pools, day spas, movie theaters, casinos, and art galleries. The Voyage of the Glaciers Cruise travels between Vancouver, British Columbia, and Whittier, Alaska. The seven-day journey includes stops in scenic Glacier Bay and College Fjord, as well as the gold-rush town of Skagway and the state capital, Juneau. For more information, contact Princess Cruises toll-free at 800/774-6237 or visit www.princess.com. **Holland America** features cruises coupled with land tours, a great choice for travelers who want the conveniences of a cruise but still want to experience the magnificence and enormity of Alaska's Interior. The 14-day Alyeska Denali Adventure involves varied means of travel, including seven days of ship-based exploration within the Inside Passage, a drive up the Seward Highway for a two-night stay at the Alyeska Prince Hotel overlooking Glacier Valley, a train ride between Anchorage and Fairbanks aboard a domed railcar, and a tundra wilderness tour in Denali National Park. Call Holland America toll-free at 877/724-5425 or visit www.hollandamerica.com for details.

The elegant sternwheeler*Empress of the North* (www.empressofthenorth.com) harkens back to the 19th century, when paddlewheel riverboats plied the waterways of the Northwest. The 112-stateroom *Empress* is smaller than most cruise ships, enabling it to sail closer to shore and pass through narrow inlets and fjords. The 11-night Inside Passage Cruise travels between Seattle to the south and Sitka to the north, with ports of call in Victoria, Ketchikan, and Glacier Bay National Park. The cruise is offered by the **American West Steamboat Company**, which can be reached toll-free at 800/434-1232.

Budget-minded travelers should consider booking a trip with the **Alaska Marine Highway System** (www.dot.state.ak.us/amhs), which travels between Skagway and Bellingham, Washington, on its Inside Passage route. While not nearly as posh as the major cruise lines, the vessels in Alaska's fleet have cafeterias, recliner lounges, solariums, and private cabins with bathroom facilities. More adventurous travelers choose to pitch tents on the ship's exposed upper deck. Perhaps the main advantage of using the Marine Highway System is that each vessel has a deck for the storage of passenger cars, bikes, and kayaksperfect for travelers who want to continue their adventures when the ship comes ashore.

nonresidents must be accompanied by a registered Alaskan guide or by close relatives who are residents. Conditions are rugged and excursions are expensive, so casual hunters may want to opt for wildlife viewing instead. A nonresident hunting license costs $85, a small game license costs $20, and a state waterfowl stamp is $5. For more information, contact the Division of Wildlife Conservation, PO Box 25526, Juneau, 99802; phone 907/465-4190.

Saltwater and freshwater fishing charters can be arranged throughout the state; you can find a list of registered businesses on the Web at www.sf.adfg.state.ak.us. An annual nonresident sport fishing license costs $100, while a seven-day license runs $50, a three-day license is $20, and a one-day license is $10. A one-day king salmon stamp costs $10. For more information, contact the Division of Sport Fish headquarters, 1255 W 8th St, Juneau, 99801; phone 907/465-4180.

A combination nonresident hunting and seven-day sport fishing license can be obtained for $115. For more information about fishing, hunting, and wildlife viewing in Alaska, contact the Alaska Department of Fish and Game, PO Box 25526, Juneau, 99802; phone 907/465-4100; www.wildlife.alaska.gov.

## Driving Information

Travelers should note that most rental car agencies do not permit their vehicles to be driven on unpaved roads in Alaska, including, but not limited to, the Dalton, Denali, Elliott, Steese, and Taylor highways and the road from Chitina to McCarthy inside Wrangell-St. Elias National Park & Preserve.

## Additional Visitor Information

*Coast Magazine*, which focuses on outdoor recreation, is published monthly and distributed free throughout the state. Visit their Web site at www.coast-magazine.com. Alaska's *Official State Guide and Vacation Planner* is available by contacting: Alaska Vacation Planner, Mailing Center, Dept. 501, PO Box 3728, Portland, OR, 972078; phone 907/465-2010. For a calendar of events and state and campground maps, contact Division of Tourism, Dept AP, PO Box 110801, Juneau, AK 99811-0801; phone 907/465-2010.

A number of visitor bureaus and tourist boards are located throughout the state and can provide information on planning stops at points of interest. Their locations are as follows: Anchorage, Delta Junction, Fairbanks, Haines, Homer, Juneau, Kenai, Ketchikan, Kodiak, Matanuska-Susitna Valleys,

Nome, Palmer, Petersburg, Sitka, Skagway, Talkeetna, Tok, and Valdez.

# Anchor Point

**Population** 1,845
**Area Code** 907

Anchor Point is located in the southwestern corner of the Kenai Peninsula. The main claim to fame of this tiny community is that it is the westernmost point on the US highway system, but its spectacular setting is what really makes it so appealing. The town is nestled in the middle of an untamed landscape of rugged, windswept beaches, densely wooded hills, and icy rivers and streams. It's a popular destination for fishermen, who have the option of freshwater fishing in the Anchor River for salmon and steelhead trout or saltwater fishing for halibut and salmon on one of the many charter boats based at the local harbor. The town also has a number of public campgrounds that provide primitive camping facilities along with easy access to the Anchor River and nearby beaches.

## What to See and Do

**Anchor River State Recreation Area.** *Anchor Point. 5 miles N. Phone 907/262-5581. www.dnr.state.ak.us/parks/units/anchoriv.htm.* In the 1770s, this area got its name when Captain James Cook lost an anchor at the mouth of the river. Today, people venture here to catch glimpses of moose, beaver, mink, and bald eagles, along with the beluga whales, harbor seals, and sea otters that hang around near the shore of Cook Inlet. You also can see three volcanoes across the inlet: Mount Augustine to the south and Mount Iliamna and Mount Redoubt to the north. Fishing is quite popular here; anglers can hope to catch salmon, Dolly Varden, and steelhead in the summer months. Nine campsites are available (dump stations).

**Camping.** *Anchor Point.* RV and tent campers will find a range of private and public camping areas along Anchor River Road, all within easy walking distance of the Anchor River, Cook Inlet, and most local hiking trails. Prices and amenities vary by location. To get to the river from the Sterling Highway, turn onto Old Sterling Highway at the Visitor Information Center at mile marker 156. Continue downhill and across the Anchor River Bridge, and then turn right onto Anchor River Road.

**Fishing.** *Anchor Point.* Known for excellent silver and king salmon runs, the Anchor River is also a popular spot to catch steelhead and rainbow trout. Anglers heading out to Cook Inlet for halibut, salmon, and rockfish can launch their own boats for a fee at the end of Anchor River Road or can join one of the fishing charters that depart on most days during the summer. Several companies offer charters to anglers, including Alaska Sport Fishing Tours (phone 907/235-2556) and Tall Tales Charters (phone 907/235-6271). Most fishing charter companies in the area are based on Anchor River Road. For more information about fishing and charters in the Anchor Point area, contact the Anchor Point Chamber of Commerce at phone 907/235-2600.

## Limited-Service Hotel

★★ **ANCHOR RIVER INN.** *34350 Old Sterling Hwy, Anchor Point (99556). Phone 907/235-8531; toll-free 800/435-8531; fax 907/235-2296. www.anchorriverinn.com.* From its location on a bluff overlooking the north fork of the Anchor River, the Anchor River Inn offers quiet, rustic lodging for visitors to the southern Kenai Peninsula. Picturesque views, reasonable prices, and close proximity to fishing charters, wildlife viewing, and some of the best steelhead fishing in the world make this motel a perennial favorite with seasoned travelers on the peninsula. Guest rooms in the main building are slightly worn but offer great views, while those in the newer building across the street have no views but better appointments. 20 rooms. Pets accepted. Check-in 2 pm, check-out 11 am. Restaurant, bar. Fitness room. **$**

## Restaurant

★★ **ANCHOR RIVER INN.** *34350 Old Sterling Hwy, Anchor Point (99556). Phone 907/235-8531; toll-free 800/435-8531; fax 907/235-2296. www.anchorriverinn.com.* For 38 years, the Anchor River Inn Restaurant has been providing family dining in a cozy room with bluff-top views of the Anchor River. The menu selection is varied enough to appeal to most tastes, with classic steak and seafood dishes along with lighter fare like hamburgers, soups, and sandwiches. American, seafood menu. Breakfast, lunch, dinner. Closed Dec 25. Bar. Children's menu. Casual attire. **$$**

# Anchorage (D-5)

*See also Girdwood*

**Population** 260,283
**Area Code** 907
**Information** Anchorage Convention & Visitors Bureau, 524 W Fourth Ave, 99501; phone 907/276-4118
**Web Site** www.anchorage.net

With a population of about 260,000, Anchorage is the largest city in Alaska and one of the most ethnically and culturally diverse. In 1915, three years after Alaska became an official US territory, the site of present day Anchorage was selected as a construction base and supply depot for the rail line being built from Seward into the Interior. With the railroad came people attracted by the lure of jobs, adventure, and uncharted wilderness. The city grew steadily the first few decades after its founding and by 1950 had surpassed Juneau as the largest city in the Territory of Alaska. Upon Alaska's admission to the Union in 1959, Anchorages population stood at 83,000.

In March of 1964, a massive earthquake in the Chugach Range nearby caused widespread damage throughout the state and left some parts of Anchorage devastated, particularly the downtown area, the international airport, and the Turnagain Arm neighbor-

## The Last Great Race on Earth

An event unlike any other, the famed Iditarod Trail Sled Dog Race shakes Alaska out of the winter doldrums, attracting thousands of spectators and volunteers to the state, along with approximately 75 mushers and their respective dog teams. The Iditarod bills itself as "the Last Great Race on Earth." That's a bold claim, but it would be difficult to argue that any race demands more of its competitors. Starting in Anchorage and finishing in Nome, the race covers roughly 1,100 miles along the historic Iditarod Trail. The grueling journey tests the conditioning and resolve of the mushers and their dogs as they endure up to 17 days of subzero temperatures and howling winds, traversing an ever-changing terrain of mountain, forest, tundra, and coastline.

At its core, Alaska's Iditarod is a celebration of sled dogs and their key role in the state's history and development. Sled dogs demonstrated their importance most prominently during the winter of 1925, when diphtheria began to afflict the children of Nome. Medicine could not be delivered to help the ill, as winter storms and a frozen Bering Sea made Nome inaccessible by plane and boat, and neither roads nor railways came near the isolated village in northwestern Alaska. Sled dog teams were called upon to quickly transport a lifesaving serum to Nome. Musher Gunnar Kaasen took the reins for the last leg of the trip, pulled by a team of huskies that was led by a young pup named Balto. The sled dog team rushed toward Nome at a furious clip, refusing to be slowed by fierce winds, blinding snow, and temperatures as low as 60 degrees below zero. The dogs and their musher pulled it off, delivering the serum in time to save the lives of many children. A statue honoring Balto can be found in, of all places, New York City's Central Park.

In 1973, the first Anchorage-to-Nome Iditarod was held, the event staged to help preserve the states mushing heritage. Plane travel had, by this time, diminished the need for sled dogs. Dick Walmarth won the 1973 Iditarod, completing the race in just under three weeks—more than twice the pace of todays winning sled teams. Four-time Iditarod winner Martin Buser and his team of Alaskan huskies finished the 2002 race in a record time of 8 days, 22 hours, and 46 minutes. The day after setting the record, Buser, who was born in Switzerland, became a US citizen, taking the oath while standing under the burled-arch finish line in Nome.

The Iditarod is not the ideal spectator sport, with much of the action unfolding in remote wilderness. Nonetheless, crowds gather at the start and finish lines to cheer on the mushers and their dogs. A great way to be a part of the race is to serve as a volunteer, helping with trail communications, caring for the dogs, or transporting supplies. Check out the official Iditarod Web site (www.iditarod.com) for information about volunteer opportunities.

hood. With turmoil came prosperity as thousands of tradesmen arrived soon after to help rebuild, many of whom ultimately chose to settle in Alaska.

Although it's farther north than St. Petersburg, Russia, Anchorage's weather is surprisingly mild, the result of Japanese currents pushing warm, moisture laden air up into the Gulf of Alaska. Winter daytime highs hover around 20 degrees with an average of 69 inches of snow falling each year. Summer daytime highs average 65 degrees with over 19 hours of daylight on the summer solstice. Geographically, the city is bounded by the Chugach Range and the waters of Knik Arm, Turnagain Arm, and Cook Inlet. Downtown Anchorage sits on a bluff overlooking the Inlet and on a clear day, visitors can see the Alaska Range and Mount McKinley on the horizon—a distance of nearly 150 miles.

In summer, the city comes alive with numerous festivals and exhibits, millions of flowers, and a seemingly endless array of outdoor activities as the residents and tourists make the most of long hours of daylight and mild temperatures. The municipal area is criss-crossed by a network of 120 miles of paved trails and another 180 miles of wilderness trails popular with mountain bikers, hikers, and runners. Within the city limits, Delaney Park, Earthquake Park, Resolution Park and Kincaid Park provide scenic venues for outdoor entertainment and relaxation. One of the most popular attractions downtown during the summer is the huge outdoor market held every Saturday in the 3rd Avenue parking lot between C and E streets. The Summer Solstice Festival also attracts a lot of tourists and locals with a blend of arts and crafts exhibits, Alaskan food stalls, and local dancers, singers, musicians, and poets to entertain the crowds. Visitors arriving in town other times of the year can learn about Alaska's native art, culture, and history by visiting the Anchorage Museum of History and Art located in the middle of downtown.

Another of Anchorage's main roles is that of a convenient staging area and embarkation point for wilderness exploration and adventure. As Alaska's main rail, air, and road hub, it serves as the gateway to the Kenai Peninsula to the south and Denali National Park and Fairbanks to the north and provides access to hundreds of remote towns and villages via Anchorage International Airport, Merrill Field, and the floatplane base at Lake Hood.

## Additional Visitor Information

There are two visitor information centers in Anchorage: downtown at Fourth Ave and F St, phone 907/274-3531; and at the airport, South (Domestic) Terminal Baggage Claim Area, phone 907/266-2437, and North (International) Terminal, phone 907/266-2657.

## Public Transportation

**People Mover** Phone 907/343-6543, www.muni.org.

**Airport** **Ted Stevens Anchorage International Airport.** Phone 907/266-2526.

**Airlines** Air Canada, Alaska Airlines, America West, American Airlines, Asiana Airlines, China Air Lines, Continental Airlines, Delta Air Lines, Era Aviation, Frontier Flying Service, Hawaiian Airlines, Japan Air Lines, Korean Air Lines, Northwest Airlines, PenAir, United Airlines

## What to See and Do

**Alaska Aviation Heritage Museum.** *4721 Aircraft Dr, Anchorage (99502). Phone 907/248-5325. www.alaskaairmuseum.com.* Located on the shores of Lake Hood near Ted Stevens Anchorage International Airport, this private museum aims to preserve and document Alaska's rich aviation history. Interpretive exhibits, vintage photographs, scale models, and an extensive collection of aviation memorabilia offer insight into the evolution of flying in Alaska and the importance it had on the development of the state. An on-site hangar houses an extensive collection of preserved and restored aircraft. (Winter: Fri-Sat 10 am-4 pm, Sun noon-4 pm; summer: Wed-Mon 10 am-6 pm) **$**

**Alaska Botanical Garden.** *4500 Campbell Airstrip Rd, Anchorage (99520). Phone 907/770-3692. www.alaskabg.org.* Encompassing 110 acres of land once used by the Athabascan Indianas, the Alaska Botanical Garden contains more than 480 varieties of cultured plants. Visitors learn about flora in Alaska by exploring the themed gardens, which include two perennial gardens, a rock garden, and an herb garden. The Lowenfels Family Nature Trail, once used by military tanks during World War II maneuvers, features most of the trees native to the area, as well as its wildlife. (Mid-May-mid-Sept: daily 9 am-9 pm; mid-Sept-mid-May: daily dawn-dusk)

**Alaska Center for the Performing Arts.** *621 W 6th Ave, Anchorage (99501). Phone 907/263-2900; toll-free 800/478-7328. www.alaskapac.org.* Opened in

1988, the Alaska Center for the Performing Arts features four state-of-the-art performance spaces and is home to eight resident companies, including the Alaska Dance Theatre, the Anchorage Symphony Orchestra, and the Anchorage Opera. Located in the heart of downtown, the center is within easy walking distance of most major hotels and offers performances throughout the year. **DONATION**

**Alaska Native Heritage Center.** *8800 Heritage Center Dr, Anchorage (99506). Phone 907/330-8000; toll-free 800/315-6608. www.alaskanative.net.* Opened in 1999, the Alaska Native Heritage Center provides visitors with the opportunity to learn about the native cultures of Alaska through interpretive displays; outdoor demonstrations of traditional hunting, fishing, and construction techniques; traditional villages exhibits; and live performances of native songs and dances in the 95-seat Welcome House theater. (Mid-May-Sept: daily 9 am-6 pm; Oct-Apr: Sat noon-5 pm) $$$$ in summer, $$ in winter

★ **Alaska Zoo.** *4731 O'Malley Rd, Anchorage (99507). Phone 907/346-1088. www.alaskazoo.org.* With annual attendance at more than 200,000 visitors, the Alaska Zoo is one of the most frequently visited places in the state. It exhibits 38 species of arctic and subarctic wildlife on 25 acres of land. Exotic animals include elephants, Bactrian camels, snow leopards, Amur tigers, Tibetan yaks, and llamas, but most of the animals housed here are native Alaskan species, such as black and brown bears, polar bears, harbor seals, Sitka black-tailed deer, mink, moose, red foxes, and wolverines. (Daily 10 am-5 pm; closed Thanksgiving, Dec 25) **$$**

**Anchorage Coastal Wildlife Refuge at Potter Marsh.** *333 Raspberry Rd, Anchorage (99518). Mile 117.4, Seward Hwy. Phone 907/267-2182. www.state.ak.us/adfg/wildlife/region2/refuge2/acwr.htm.* Known locally as Potter's Marsh, this 540-acre refuge at the southern edge of Anchorage is a popular spot for bird-watching. At various times of the year, the marshlands are home to arctic terns, Canada geese, trumpeter swans, Pacific loons, and a variety of other shorebirds. A 1,500-foot wooden boardwalk built out over the marsh enables visitors to venture far from the parking lot without damaging the wetlands or disturbing the wildlife in the area. **FREE**

**Anchorage Fifth Avenue Mall.** *320 W 5th Ave, Anchorage (99501). Phone 907/258-5535.* Located in the heart of downtown, the Anchorage Fifth Avenue Mall is one of the largest malls in Alaska, containing 110 shops on the first three levels and a food court on the fourth. Anchored by two large department stores, JCPenney and Nordstrom, it also features smaller national chain stores as well as an array of uniquely Alaskan shops. (Mon-Fri 10 am-9 pm, Sat 10 am-8 pm, Sun 11 am-6 pm)

**Anchorage Museum of History and Art.** *121 W 7th Ave, Anchorage (99501). Phone 907/343-6173. www.anchoragemuseum.org.* This large museum in the middle of downtown is divided into two distinct parts. The ground floor features six art galleries displaying "art of the North," including works by celebrated Alaskan artist Sydney Laurence. The upper floor focuses on Alaskan history and is packed with artifacts, displays, and exhibits that depict the lives and cultures of the groups that have shaped Alaska, from the earliest Native communities to modern-day Alaskans. (Mid-May-mid-Sept: daily 9 am-6 pm, Thurs until 9 pm; mid-Sept-mid-May: Wed-Sat 10 am-6 pm, Sun noon-5 pm) **$$**

**Chugach National Forest.** *3301 C St, Anchorage (99503). Phone 907/743-9500. www.fs.fed.us/r10/chugach.* The Chugach National Forest is the second largest forest in the National Forest System. Roughly the same size as Massachusetts and Rhode Island combined, the Chugach (pronounced CHEW-gatch) is the northernmost national forest, only 500 miles south of the Arctic Circle. One-third of the Chugach is composed of rocks and moving ice. The remainder is a diverse and majestic tapestry of land, water, plants, and animals. The mountains, lakes, and rivers of the Kenai Peninsula, the islands and glaciers of Prince William Sound, and the copious wetlands and birds of the Copper River Delta make this national forest a mecca for adventurers.

**Chugach State Park.** *Mile 115 Seward Hwy, Anchorage (99540). Phone 907/345-5014.* Chugach State Park is an accessible wilderness in the backyard of Anchorage. Wildlife viewing and mountain scenery are year-round pleasures, and campers can choose developed campgrounds or secluded backcountry valleys. Nearly 30 trails take you throughout the park to see some of its most enchanting views. Many visitors may want to stop at the Eagle River Nature Center for a guided tour or interpretive program. You may want to explore a few of the park's 50 glaciers on your own. And for extreme adventure, try climbing a mountainside or plunging through river rapids. Whatever the case, the 495,000-acre park offers a wide variety of activities in all seaons.

**Cyrano's Off Center Playhouse.** *413 D St, Anchorage (99501). Phone 907/274-2599. www.cyranos.org.* This small, independent downtown theater is home to the Eccentric Theatre Company, which puts on a wide variety of plays each year, from classic dramas to contemporary comedies. The atmosphere is decidedly informal, the productions first rate. Before and after shows, theatergoers can browse through the shelves of Cyrano's bookstore or enjoy a drink at the small coffee bar.

**Delaney Park Strip.** *300 W 9th Ave, Anchorage (99501).* Stretching from A to P streets, this narrow park between 9th and 10th avenues was at one time Anchorage's airstrip. Nowadays, it's home to numerous sports fields, playgrounds, the Centennial Rose Garden, and memorials to Alaskan veterans and Martin Luther King Jr. **FREE**

**Earthquake Park.** *Northern Lights Blvd, Anchorage. Phone 907/276-4118.* Located at the west end of Northern Lights Boulevard, this large, forested park was established near the site where a housing development slid into Cook Inlet during the 1964 Good Friday earthquake. The main trail from the parking lot leads to a small interpretive exhibit that explains the geological factors that caused the land beneath the subdivision to collapse. The park also serves as an access point to the Tony Knowles Coastal Trail (see). **FREE**

**Eisenhower Alaska Statehood Monument.** *2nd Ave and E St, Anchorage (99501).* Located at the end of E Street, this small monument overlooking the Alaska Railroad depot features a bust of President Eisenhower and a plaque commemorating the Alaska Statehood Act that Eisenhower signed on January 3, 1959, making Alaska the 49th state. (Daily)

**Eklutna Flats and Palmer Hay Flats.** *Anchorage. N of Anchorage at the head of the Knik Arm in Cook Inlet. Phone 907/267-2182.* The Eklutna Flats and Palmer Hay Flats are a tidally influenced wetlands area at the confluence of the Knik and Matanuska rivers. This flat open area provides the broadest view of the Matanuska Valley bordered by the Chugach Mountains, a stone's throw to the east. The ancient Talkeetna Mountains rise in the distance. This area is teeming with waterfowl and other migratory birds in spring and fall. You may even spot a moose during the long winter months. The Palmer Hay Flats State Game Refuge comprises a large portion of this area.

**Kepler-Bradley State Park.** *Glenn Hwy, Anchorage (99501). Phone 907/269-8400.* A fisherman's paradise, this popular state park comprises several trout-and graylining-filled lakes. Kepler-Bradley State Park is within easy driving distance of Anchorage. The lakes are located in crevasses in between morraine ridges formed by glaciers. Trails from the park connect to the Mat/Su borough Crevasse Morraine Trail System.

**Kincaid Park.** *Raspberry Rd, Anchorage (99502).* The site of a former Nike missile silo during the early years of the Cold War, this park encompasses nearly 1,400 acres of land at the end of Raspberry Road at the extreme western edge of Anchorage. More than 40 miles of maintained trails provide recreational opportunities for runners and cross-country skiers throughout the year. It marks one end of the Tony Knowles Coastal Trail. **FREE**

**Lanie Fleischer Chester Creek Trail.** *Anchorage.* This scenic paved trail follows the course of Chester Creek, providing a green belt connecting eastern Anchorage to the Tony Knowles Coastal Trail (see) and creating a natural divide between downtown Anchorage and the midtown area. With one trailhead at Westchester Lagoon (see) near Cook Inlet and the other at Goose Lake by Alaska Pacific University, it's a popular east-west route across town for bikers, runners, walkers, and cross-country skiers. **FREE**

**Matanuska Glacier State Recreation Area.** *Glenn Hwy, Anchorage (99501). Phone 907/269-8400.* This newly redeveloped recreation area showcases the Matanuska Glacier with an up-close view that will be forever etched into travelers' memories.

★ **Portage Glacier and Begich, Boggs Visitor Center.** *Portage (99587). Phone 907/783-2326. www.fs.fed.us/r10/chugach/chugach_pages/bbvc.html.* Located 50 miles south of Anchorage, Portage Glacier is one of Alaska's most visited tourist attractions. Although the glacier is no longer visible from the shores of Portage Lake, visitors to the area can still marvel at the massive blue icebergs floating in the water and enjoy the area's spectacular scenery. The US Forest Service's Begich, Boggs Visitor Center is one of the best in the state, with daily interpretive walks, interactive glacier and local history exhibits, and an award-winning film called *Voices from the Ice.* Visitors wanting to see the glacier firsthand can board the M/V *Ptarmigan,* a sightseeing boat run by Gray Line Tours (phone 907/277-5581 or toll-free 800/544-2206, www.graylinealaska. com), located on the shore of the lake just past the visitor center. The one-hour cruise ($$$$) takes visitors to the base of the glacier and includes a US Forest Service narration describing the glacier and its impact on the geography of the area. (Visitor center: Memorial Day-Labor Day, daily 9 am-6 pm; rest of year, Sat-Sun 10 am-5 pm)

**Resolution Park.** *300 L St, Anchorage (99501).* Located at 3rd and L streets, this small neighborhood park is named in honor of Captain Cook's ship *Resolution,* which anchored nearby in 1778. With it's imposing statue of Cook, summertime flower gardens, and views of Cook Inlet, its a popular spot for photographers and lunching locals. The Tony Knowles Coastal Trail (see) runs through the park. **FREE**

**Ship Creek fishing area.** *Ship Creek Ave, Anchorage. Just E of the Alaska Railroad depot.* Located in the heart of downtown Anchorage, Ship Creek provides a convenient, though often crowded, place for anglers to try their luck. The king salmon run begins in early June and continues through mid-July; the silver salmon run starts in August. Viewing platforms and a small dam across the river provide excellent spots to observe the action. (Daily)

**Tony Knowles Coastal Trail.** *900 W 2nd Ave, Anchorage (99501).* This scenic paved trail is popular with bicyclists, skaters, and walkers throughout the long days of summer and with cross-country skiers in the winter. Following the contour of Cook Inlet for most of its length, it runs for 11 miles from 2nd Avenue downtown to Kincaid Park (see), providing unobstructed views of Cook Inlet, Mount Susitna, and the Chugach Range, as well as opportunities to observe moose, bald eagles, and other wildlife. **FREE**

**Tours.** *Anchorage. Phone toll-free 800/544-2206. www.graylineofalaska.com.* Gray Line of Alaska offers package tours around Alaska (up to 11 days) as well as glacier cruises, bear-viewing tours, sea kayaking, flightseeing, and city and backcountry tours out of Anchorage.

**Turnagain Pass.** *Anchorage.* The drive through Turnagain Pass may be one of the most scenic on the Byway. This is the highest point on the Byways, and wildlife spotting occurs regularly here. Turnagain Pass is located in the south beyond Turnagain Arm. Two large pullouts are easily accessible from the only section of divided highway outside of the Anchorage bowl. Views from the highway here show off the distinctive U-shaped valley created by retreating glaciers. Northbound travelers are treated to spectacular views of Turnagain Arm and Twentymile glaciers as they head down from this 900-foot pass to sea level. This area is especially popular in the winter for skiing and snowmobiling, and in midsummer for its wildflower displays.

**Westchester Lagoon.** *1915 Hillcrest Rd, Anchorage (99517).* Located near the west end of 15th Avenue, this large, tree-lined lagoon tucked between the downtown and midtown high rises offers scenic walking and biking trails in the summer and ice skating and cross-country skiing in the winter. It also provides easy access to the Tony Knowles Coastal Trail (see) and the Lanie Fleisher Chester Creek Trail (see). **FREE**

## Special Events

**Alyeska Blueberry & Mountain Arts Festival.** *Alyeska Resort, 1000 Arlberg Ave, Anchorage (99587). Phone 907/754-1111; toll-free 800/880-3880. www.alyeskaresort.com.* This small-town summer festival, held beside the pond at the Alyeska Resort, features live entertainment, local artwork, a poetry jam, homemade foods, and lots of blueberry-flavored treats. Beginning in 2004, the festival merges with the annual Alyeska Mountain Run so that visitors to the festival can sit back and bask in blueberry heaven while watching ultra-fit race participants charge up and down the slopes of Mount Alyeska. The festival date varies by year—contact the Alyeska Resort for the current schedule. **FREE**

**Downtown Saturday Market.** *3rd Ave and E St, Anchorage (99501).* Begun in 1992, this wildly popular weekly market features more than 300 vendors offering a wide range of goods, from Alaskan art and souvenirs to locally grown fruits and vegetables. In keeping with its small-town atmosphere, the market features musical performances by local artists as well as booths sponsored by community groups. Held on Saturdays from 10 am to 6 pm regardless of the weather, the market offers something for every taste and style. Mid-May-mid-Sept.

**Fur Rendezvous.** *Anchorage. Phone 907/274-1177. www.furrondy.net.* The Anchorage Fur Rendezvous, locally known as the Fur Rondy, was first held in the 1930s with the aim of bringing people together, showing community support, and celebrating the beginning of the end of winter each year. Now running for 18 days from late February to early March, the festival has evolved into a huge midwinter celebration with more than 140 events and activities, including elaborate fancy dress and costume balls, snow-sculpting competitions, a carnival, and live music and theater productions. The festival was expanded in 2004 to serve as a lead-in to Anchorage's most famous winter event: the ceremonial start of the Iditarod Trail Sled Dog race (see), which begins on the corner of 4th and D streets downtown at 10 am on the first Saturday in March. Equally exciting but less well known is the

World Championship Sled Dog Race, a three-day dog sprint event with mushers covering a 25-mile out-and-back course that begins and ends at 4th and D streets downtown. Late Feb-early Mar.

**Iditarod.** *Anchorage. Phone 907/376-5155. www.iditarod.com.* A famous dogsled race covering more than 1,150 miles from Anchorage to Nome. It's been run since 1973 and usually takes 9 to 12 days. Mar.

**Tesoro Iron Dog 2000 Snowmachine Race.** *Tesoro Iron Dog Headquarters, 7100 Old Seward Hwy, Suite C, Anchorage (99501). Race start and finish dates, times, and locations vary by year. Phone 907/563-4414; fax 907/336-5052. www.irondog.org.* This annual 2,000-mile race pits teams of two racers on separate snowmachines against some of the harshest, most isolated terrain in Alaska. With temperatures dipping to 40 below, speeds as high as 93 mph, and limited daylight for much of the journey, its not a race for the faint of heart. The race runs in segments over the course of a week and usually goes from Fairbanks west to Nome and then southeast to Wasilla, reversing direction in alternating years. Highlights of the competition include a 500-mile full-throttle dash down the frozen Yukon River, a pressure-ridge and snowdrift-plagued traverse across the ice pack on Norton Sound, and a forested climb through deep snow up and over the Alaska Range. Of the 25 teams that started out in 2004, only 12 finished the race, with the first team crossing the line in a cumulative time of 39 hours, 3 minutes. Mid-Feb.

## Limited-Service Hotels

**★ ANCHORAGE GRAND HOTEL.** *505 W 2nd Ave, Anchorage (99501). Phone 907/929-8888; toll-free 888/800-0640; fax 907/929-8899. www.anchoragegrandhotel.com.* Built in 1950, this newly renovated all-suite hotel is a pleasing blend of "old" Anchorage architecture and modern amenities. Located downtown, it's in the midst of Anchorage's restaurant and tourist center, and it's only a short walk downhill to the Alaska Rail Depot. All guest rooms feature full-sized gourmet kitchens, sleeper sofas, and large, enclosed closets, and many have excellent views of Cook Inlet and the mountain ranges that surround the city. 31 rooms. Complimentary continental breakfast. Check-in 3 pm, check-out noon. **$$**

**★ ASPEN HOTEL.** *108 E 8th Ave, Anchorage (99501). Phone 907/868-1605; toll-free 888/506-7848; fax 907/868-3520. www.aspenhotelsak.com.* On the southeastern edge of the downtown area, the 89-room Aspen Hotel caters to a mixture of Alaskan business professionals, local sports groups, and tourists. Its indoor pool, in-room kitchenettes, family suites with bunk beds, and complimentary deluxe continental breakfast—as well as its location near many downtown attractions—make it an inviting place for both families and bargain hunters. 89 rooms. Complimentary continental breakfast. Check-in 3 pm, check-out 11 am. Fitness room. Indoor pool, whirlpool. **$$**

**★ BEST VALUE INN EXECUTIVE SUITES.** *4360 Spenard Rd, Anchorage (99517). Phone 907/243-6366; toll-free 800/770-6366; fax 907/248-2161. www.executivesuitehotel.com.* The 102-room Executive Suite Hotel is an independent, budget-minded hotel located near Anchorage International Airport, within yards of Lake Hood. With frequent manager's specials and 14 different room layouts, most of them suites, it's the kind of place where travelers can always find a bargain. 102 rooms. Pets accepted. Complimentary continental breakfast. Check-in 3 pm, check-out noon. Airport transportation available. **$**

**★ ★ BEST WESTERN GOLDEN LION HOTEL.** *1000 E 36th Ave, Anchorage (99508). Phone 907/561-1522; toll-free 877/935-5466; fax 907/743-4814. www.bestwesterngoldenlion.com.* The most remarkable thing about this clean, comfortable, and affordable hotel is it's "African hunting lodge" décor. Stuffed and mounted African animals dominate the lobby and main staircase, and the meeting rooms are called "Kenya" and "Safari. " Other noteworthy features include a small but well-designed weight room, an oval sauna, and an in-house hair salon. Its location at the intersection of 36th Avenue and the Seward Highway make it a convenient option for travelers looking for a place to stay before or after a trip to the Kenai Peninsula. 83 rooms. Check-in 2 pm, check-out noon. Restaurant. Fitness room. **$$**

**★ CLARION SUITES HOTEL.** *325 W 8th Ave, Anchorage (99501). Phone 907/274-1000; toll-free 888/389-6575; fax 907/274-3016. www.choicehotels.com.* This 111-room hotel is located within a block of Anchorage's main downtown shopping site, the 5th Avenue Mall. The Anchorage Museum of History and Art is less than a block away, as is the Delaney Park Strip, Anchorage's original airfield, now converted into grassy areas, a rose garden, tennis courts, and ball fields. 111 rooms, all suites. Complimentary continental breakfast. Check-in 3 pm, check-out noon. Fitness room. Indoor pool, whirlpool. **$$**

**★ ★ COAST INTERNATIONAL INN.** *3333 W International Airport Rd, Anchorage (99502). Phone 907/243-2233; fax 907/248-3796. www.coasthotels.com.* One of the most attractive things about this 141-room hotel is that its close to the airport without being noisy and only yards from Lake Spenard and the network of walking trails that encircle it. Most guest rooms in this upscale, business-casual hotel have spectacular mountain and lake views, and all of them are comfortable, quiet, and spacious. Corporate travelers, who make up a large part of the client base, frequently stay here because of the quality of the furnishings, the wide range of business amenities offered, and the friendly staff. 141 rooms. Check-in noon, check-out noon. Restaurant. Fitness room. **$$**

**★ COMFORT INN.** *111 W Ship Creek Ave, Anchorage (99501). Phone 907/277-6887; toll-free 800/424-6423; fax 907/274-9830. www.choicehotels.com.* The 100-room Comfort Inn is located alongside Ship Creek near the site where Anchorage's first settlers lived. Although it's a fairly standard outpost of this well-known chain, this family-friendly hotel's spacious lobby is designed with Alaskan touches, including an imposing rock fireplace, an enormous moose antler light fixture, and salmon-themed artwork. Visitors can view salmon spawning in the creek behind the hotel or head uphill into downtown Anchorage for shopping, touring, and dining. With the Alaska Railroad depot a block away, the hotel is an ideal (although somewhat noisy) spot for those arriving from or heading to popular rail destinations like Denali National Park and Seward. Pets accepted. Complimentary continental breakfast. Check-in 4 pm, check-out noon. Fitness room. Indoor pool, whirlpool. **$$**

**★ ★ COURTYARD BY MARRIOTT.** *4901 Spenard Rd, Anchorage (99517). Phone 907/245-0322; toll-free 800/932-2198; fax 907/248-1886. www.courtyard.com.* A five-minute drive from the airport and a ten-minute drive from downtown, this 154-room hotel is within a block of the shores of Lake Spenard and within easy walking distance of a number of restaurants. The Courtyard's main selling point is its on-site recreation facilities, which include a spacious pool area, an indoor sauna, and a well-laid-out exercise room. The small but well-outfitted business center appeals to business travelers. 154 rooms. Check-in 3 pm, check-out noon. Restaurant. Fitness room. Indoor pool, whirlpool. Business center. **$$**

**★ DAYS INN.** *321 E Fifth Ave, Anchorage (99501). Phone 907/276-7226; toll-free 800/329-7466; fax 907/265-5164. www.daysinn.com.* Located on the main east-west road leading to the downtown area, on the eastern edge of downtown, this basic 131-room hotel is a short walk to the Anchorage Museum of History and Art, the Egan Convention and Civic Center, and the 5th Avenue Mall. 131 rooms. Pets accepted. Check-in 3 pm, check-out 11 am. Restaurant. **$$**

**★ ★ ★ DIMOND CENTER HOTEL.** *700 E Dimond Blvd, Anchorage (99515). Phone 907/770-5000; toll-free 866/770-5002; fax 907/770-5001. www.dimondcenterhotel.com.* From the outside, this midtown hotel looks more like an office building than anything else. On entering, though, it's a refreshing surprise: it's filled with custom-made hardwood furniture, native Alaskan artwork from the Kachemak Bay region, and upscale amenities in all areas. The guest rooms, which the hotel bills as being "the most comfortable rooms in the city," are filled with goose-down comforters, original Alaskan artwork, marble counters, deep bathtubs, and custom-made cherry furniture with walnut inlays, all presented in a soothing palette of greens, blues, and earth tones. Because it's located behind the Dimond Mall, it's surrounded by a wide variety of shops, restaurants, and entertainment venues. 109 rooms. Complimentary continental breakfast. Check-in 3 pm, check-out 11 am. Bar. Children's activity center. Fitness room. **$$**

**★ HAMPTON INN.** *4301 Credit Union Dr, Anchorage (99503). Phone 907/550-7000; toll-free 800/426-7866; fax 907/561-7330. www.hamptoninn.com.* This midtown hotel, just 3 miles from the airport, is surrounded by a wide variety of restaurants, from fast food to fine dining. For a chain hotel, it tries hard to be homey and personable, with an Alaska-themed lobby with small fireplace and numerous prints by famed Alaska artist Byron Birdsall. Upgrades to the hotel's amenities are currently underway. 101 rooms. Complimentary continental breakfast. Check-in 3 pm, check-out noon. Fitness room. Indoor pool, whirlpool. Airport transportation available. **$$**

**★ HAWTHORN SUITES.** *1110 W 8th Ave, Anchorage (99501). Phone 907/222-5005; toll-free 888/469-6575; fax 907/222-5215. www.hawthorn.com.* Across the street from Delaney Park Strip—originally an airfield and now converted into ball fields, a rose garden, tennis courts, and grassy areas—the Hawthorn Suites is in a quieter area than most downtown hotels but is still within easy walking distance of all major downtown attractions. Guest rooms have microwaves and refrigerators, making this a convenient choice for families on a budget. 111 rooms, all suites. Complimentary full breakfast. Check-in 3 pm, check-out noon. High-speed Internet access. Fitness room. Indoor pool, whirlpool. **$$**

**★ ★ HILTON GARDEN INN ANCHORAGE.** *100 W Tudor Rd, Anchorage (99503). Phone 907/729-7000; fax 907/729-8000.* Just 3 miles from Anchorage International Airport and within two blocks of midtown Anchorage's dining, shopping, and entertainment venues, the Hilton Garden Inn appeals mainly to business travelers, who appreciate the upgraded amenities, spacious rooms, and on-site exercise facilities. The hotel also has a sunny, Alaskan-themed lobby where guests can sit by the fire, watch television, or just relax and read the paper. Another major selling point is the hotel's complimentary shuttle service to the airport, local shopping areas, and downtown. 125 rooms. Check-in 3 pm, check-out noon. High-speed Internet access. Restaurant. Fitness room. Indoor pool, whirlpool. Airport transportation available. **$$**

**★ ★ THE HISTORIC ANCHORAGE HOTEL.** *330 E St, Anchorage (99501). Phone 907/272-4553; toll-free 800/544-0988; fax 907/277-4483. www.historicanchoragehotel.com.* Located in the heart of downtown, this charming and elegant hotel manages to blend the architectural elegance of the 1930s with the demands of the modern traveler. As Anchorages oldest hotel (it's listed on the National Register of Historic Places), its guest rooms are graced with Queen Anne-style furnishings as well as modern amenities such as cable television, microwave ovens, and high-speed Internet access. Summertime rates are very reasonable by Anchorage standards. 26 rooms. Complimentary continental breakfast. Check-in 3 pm, check-out noon. High-speed Internet access. Restaurant, bar. **$$**

**★ HOLIDAY INN EXPRESS.** *4411 Spenard Rd, Anchorage (99517). Phone 907/248-8848; toll-free 800/465-4329; fax 907/248-8847. www.hiexpress.com.* Five minutes from the airport and ten minutes from downtown, this 128-room hotel is surrounded by a variety of restaurants. A well-designed business center and large in-room desks make it a popular stop for corporate travelers, as well as for families who appreciate the suite accommodations, onsite pool, and complimentary breakfast and nightly cookies and milk. 128 rooms. Pets accepted. Complimentary continental breakfast. Check-in 3 pm, check-out noon. Fitness room. Indoor pool, whirlpool. **$$**

**★ ★ HOWARD JOHNSON ANCHORAGE.** *239 W 4th Ave, Anchorage (99501). Phone 907/793-5500; fax 907/258-4733.* Located on the northern edge of downtown, this family-friendly hotel is close to the Anchorage visitor center and the Alaska Railroad depot. Some rooms have excellent views of Cook Inlet and the surrounding mountains. The indoor pool offers plenty of space for families, regardless of the weather. 251 rooms, 3 story. Check-in 2 pm, check-out noon. Restaurant. Fitness room. Indoor pool. **$$**

**★ ★ INLET TOWER HOTEL & SUITES.** *1200 L St, Anchorage (99501). Phone 907/276-0110; toll-free 800/544-0786; fax 907/258-4914. www.inlettower.com.* A complete renovation in 2003 has recaptured the elegance of this hotel's original 1950s architecture. Renowned New York-based designer Harry Schnaper has created warm and luxurious rooms, but it's the extraordinary views of Cook Inlet, the Chugach Mountains, and the downtown skyline that make this hotel special. The hotel is located in a residential area, but a free 24-hour shuttle to the downtown area offsets any inconvenience. 180 rooms, 14 story. Check-in 4 pm, check-out noon. High-speed Internet access. Restaurant. Airport transportation available. **$$**

**★ LAKESHORE MOTOR INN.** *3009 Lakeshore Dr, Anchorage (99517). Phone 907/248-3485; toll-free 800/770-3000; fax 907/248-1544. www.lakeshoremotorinn.com.* Despite its unassuming appearance, this is not a typical motel. The airy and comfortable lobby pays tongue-in-cheek homage to the fishing and hunting clientele that frequently stays here, and the spacious, crisply clean guest rooms are filled with sturdy wooden furniture, soft fabrics, and local artwork. The motel is only 75 yards from Lake Spenard, the largest floatplane base in the world, so it's ideal for people preparing for or returning from bush-hunting or fishing trips. Better than the usual budget motel, this inn provides a relaxing, refreshing, and

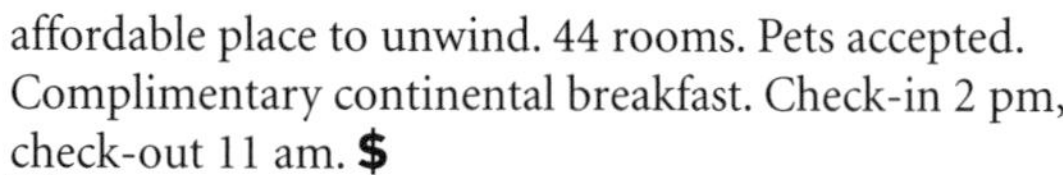


affordable place to unwind. 44 rooms. Pets accepted. Complimentary continental breakfast. Check-in 2 pm, check-out 11 am. **$**

★ **LONG HOUSE ALASKAN HOTEL.** *4335 Wisconsin St, Anchorage (99517). Phone 907/243-2133; toll-free 888/243-2133; fax 907/243-6060. www.longhousehotel.com.* The Long House Alaskan Hotel is set on a quiet street across the road from Lake Hood and within walking distance of many local restaurants. Because of its location, the hotel is a popular stopover for people flying by floatplane to remote hunting and fishing lodges in the Alaskan wilds. The exterior design was inspired by the long houses created by Native Americans as social, cultural, and spiritual gathering places, with honey-colored log siding. 54 rooms. Complimentary continental breakfast. Check-in 4 pm, check-out noon. **$$**

★ **MICROTEL INN & SUITES.** *5205 Northwood Dr, Anchorage (99517). Phone 907/245-5002; toll-free 888/771-7171; fax 907/245-5030. www.microtelinn.com/anchorageak.* About a mile from the airport and ten minutes from downtown, this budget-friendly 79-room motel is also convenient to some of the main traffic arteries for getting into and out of Anchorage quickly from the south. It's not much to look at from the outside, but the interior is much more appealing, with a small but comfortable lobby, breakfast nook, and large, sunny guest rooms with padded window seats and surprisingly good views. The hotel offers free 24-hour shuttle service to the airport, and guests also appreciate the 1 pm check-out time. 79 rooms. Pets accepted. Complimentary continental breakfast. Check-in 4 pm, check-out 1 pm. Whirlpool. Airport transportation available. **$**

★ **PARKWOOD INN.** *4455 Juneau St, Anchorage (99503). Phone 907/563-3590; toll-free 800/478-3590; fax 907/563-5560. www.parkwoodinn.net.* This family-friendly motel isn't the plushest in town, but each of the 50 apartment-style rooms has a full-size stocked kitchen, wide balcony, pull-out sofa, and small dining area. Unlike most lodgings in Anchorage, it's busiest in winter, when low rates attract out-of-towners who come to shop, visit family, take care of medical needs, and escape the hardships of the bush winters. The Parkwood is located close to the city's largest movie theater, the main hospital, Anchorage University, and a large number of restaurants and shops. 50 rooms. Pets accepted. Check-in 2 pm, check-out 11 am. **$**

★ ★ **RAMADA INN.** *115 E 3rd Ave, Anchorage (99501). Phone 907/272-7561; toll-free 800/272-6232; fax 907/272-3879. www.ramada.com.* Opened in the summer of 2003, the Ramada Inn offers clean, quiet, and comfortable rooms decorated with a whimsical Alaskan motif that guests first encounter in the small but tastefully decorated lobby. Most south-facing rooms have spacious, private balconies, while those facing north have sweeping views of Cook Inlet, Sleeping Lady (Mount Susitna), and the Alaska Range. The hotel is also close to the Alaska Railroad depot, making it a convenient choice for those with early-morning departures. In summer, the city's open-air market (held on Saturdays) is nearby. 90 rooms. Check-in 3 pm, check-out 11 am. Restaurant, bar. Fitness room. **$$**

★ **SPRINGHILL SUITES.** *3401 A St, Anchorage (99503). Phone 907/562-3247; toll-free 877/729-0197; fax 907/562-3250. www.springhillsuites.com.* Located about 4 miles from downtown, in the middle of the city's main shopping and dining area, the SpringHill Suites is down the road from Providence Hospital, close to the University of Alaska, and next door to the State of Alaska offices and Anchorage's largest cineplex. The convenient location makes it popular with tourists during the summer and with government groups, college visitors, and school sports teams the rest of the year. Guest suites are spacious and in excellent condition. 102 rooms. Complimentary continental breakfast. Check-in 3 pm, check-out noon. Fitness room. Indoor pool, whirlpool. **$$**

★ **SUPER 8 MOTEL.** *3501 Minnesota Dr, Anchorage (99503). Phone 907/276-8884; toll-free 800/800-8000; fax 907/279-8194. www.super8.com.* About 2 miles from the airport and 3 miles from downtown, the Super 8 puts guests within a mile of all of midtown Anchorage's main attractions: shopping malls, the large multiplex cinema, and a wide array of restaurants. Prices can be high for a motel with few amenities, especially in summer, but rooms are clean, quiet, and in good condition. 85 rooms. Pets accepted; fee. Complimentary continental breakfast. Check-in 2 pm, check-out noon. **$**

★ ★ **THE VOYAGER HOTEL.** *501 K St, Anchorage (99501). Phone 907/277-9501; toll-free 800/247-9070; fax 907/274-0333. www.voyagerhotel.com.* For 25 years, this small, independent hotel has been focusing on customized service delivered by a friendly and dedicated staff. Furious attention is paid to details here, from the placement of quality china and Alaskan coffee in the galley kitchens to the use of fine carpets and extra-soft pillows in the guest rooms. The result is a hotel that draws people in and keeps them coming back year after year. The Voyager is within easy walking distance of most of the area's major attractions and is very close to the Tony Knowles Coastal Trail, which offers spectacular views of Alaskan wildlife and scenery. 40 rooms. Closed week of Dec 25. Complimentary continental breakfast. Check-out 11 am. Restaurant. **$$**

**★ ★ WESTMARK ANCHORAGE HOTEL.** *720 W 5th Ave, Anchorage (99501). Phone 907/276-7676; toll-free 800/544-0970; fax 907/276-3615. www.westmarkhotels.com.* This hotel is an ideal place to stay for those wanting to be right in the midst of all the terrific dining, shopping, live theater, and other diversions downtown Anchorage has to offer. The hotel itself is clean, comfortable, and professionally run, and, as an added bonus, all rooms have their own large private balconies. 198 rooms. Check-in 3 pm, check-out noon. Restaurant, bar. **$$**

## Full-Service Hotels

**★ ★ ★ ANCHORAGE MARRIOTT DOWNTOWN.** *820 W 7th Ave, Anchorage (99501). Phone 907/279-8000; toll-free 800/228-9290; fax 907/279-8005. www.marriott.com.* The first thing that strikes visitors about the Anchorage Marriott Downtown is how bright and cheery it is inside. Every guest room has oversized picture windows that flood the rooms with natural light while providing excellent views of either Cook Inlet or the Chugach Mountains. With an upscale restaurant on-site, a stylish shopping arcade, a sleek indoor pool and fitness center, and a small but well-equipped business center, the hotel is able to provide a high level of comfort and convenience to all of its guests. Its proximity to the Delaney Park Strip and the Tony Knowles Coastal Trail also make it a great location for guests looking for a bit of outdoor recreation. 392 rooms. Check-in 3 pm, check-out noon. Restaurant, bar. Fitness room. Indoor pool, whirlpool. **$$$**

**★ ★ ★ HILTON.** *500 W Third Ave, Anchorage (99501). Phone 907/272-7411; toll-free 800/455-8667; fax 907/265-7044. www.hilton.com.* Located in the heart of downtown, the towers of the Hilton hotel offer sweeping views of the Anchorage area and beyond. On exceptionally clear days, in fact, guests with north-facing rooms can see as far as Mount McKinley, well over 100 miles away. The main draw of the hotel, though, is its ability to bring a sense of grandiose style and glamour to the edge of the Alaskan frontier. From its spacious, tastefully appointed lobby to its intimate, elegant penthouse restaurant, the Hilton is like a wealthy New York aunt on a visit to the country: she's a little out of place but consistently draws a crowd. 600 rooms. Pets accepted. Check-in 3 pm, check-out noon. Two restaurants. Fitness room. Indoor pool, whirlpool. **$$$**

**★ ★ ★ THE HOTEL CAPTAIN COOK.** *4th Ave And K St, Anchorage (99501). Phone 907/276-6000; fax 907/343-2298.*The Hotel Captain Cook is located in the middle of downtown Anchorage. As one of Alaska's premier independent hotels, it prides itself on providing the ultimate in service, comfort, and style to all of its guests. All rooms feature twice-daily housekeeping service, nightly turndown service, and top-quality furnishings, including down comforters, plush towels, and 250-threadcount sheets. Other highlights include three full-service restaurants, a selection of chic boutique shops and art galleries, an onsite athletic club, and a wealth of original artworks and artifacts on display throughout the public areas. 547 rooms. Check-in 3 pm, check-out noon. Three restaurants, bar. Fitness room, fitness classes available. Indoor pool, whirlpool. **$$**

**★ ★ ★ MILLENNIUM ALASKAN HOTEL.** *4800 Spenard Rd, Anchorage (99517). Phone 907/243-2300; toll-free 800/544-0553; fax 907/243-8815. www.millenniumhotels.com.* The spectacular lobby of this 248-room lakefront hotel sets the tone for the whole property, as it's filled with dark woods, slate tiles, leather furniture, and a massive rock fireplace. The guest rooms are also luxurious, immaculate, and spacious, and those facing the lake offer picturesque views and wonderful summer sunsets. The hotel has its own floatplane dock for sportfishing and flightseeing trips. For those looking for upscale accommodations, excellent service, and a scenic location in Anchorage, few properties can rival what this hotel has to offer. 248 rooms. Pets accepted. Check-in 3 pm, check-out noon. Restaurant. Fitness room. Whirlpool. **$$$**

**★ ★ ★ SHERATON ANCHORAGE HOTEL.** *401 E 6th Ave, Anchorage (99501). Phone 907/276-8700;*

*toll-free 800/477-8700; fax 907/276-7561. www.sheratonanchoragehotel.com.* This hotel is located in downtown Anchorage, only a short walk from the Anchorage Museum of History and Art, the 5th Avenue Mall, and the Egan Convention and Civic Center. Most of the large, comfortable guest rooms have terrific views of the mountain ranges and tidal flats that surround the city, and with a friendly, professional staff, a 24-hour on-site gym, and a sophisticated bar and lounge, guests need not leave the hotel to enjoy their stay in Anchorage. Because the Sheraton caters to business professionals, however, it is not as kid-friendly as most other large downtown hotels. 375 rooms, 16 story. Pets accepted. Complimentary continental breakfast. Check-in 3 pm, check-out noon. Restaurant, bar. Fitness room. Whirlpool. **$$$**

## Full-Service Resorts

**★ ★ ★ ALYESKA PRINCE RESORT.** *1000 Arlberg Ave, Anchorage (99587). Phone 907/754-1111; toll-free 800/880-3880; fax 907/754-2200. www.alyeskaresort.com.* The Alyeska Resort is located in the town of Girdwood, about 45 minutes south of Anchorage on the Seward Highway, surrounded by the Chugach Mountains and the waters of Turnagain Arm. It's comprised of a ski area, a golf course (in Anchorage), and the Alyeska Prince Hotel, an appealing blend of Swiss chateau and modern architecture. Everything about this property is first-rate: deluxe guest rooms; world-class skiing, snowboarding, and heli-skiing in winter; extensive hiking and mountain biking in summer; fine-dining restaurants; state-of-the-art fitness facilities; and all-around spectacular views of hanging glaciers, soaring mountains, and miles and miles of pristine wilderness. 307 rooms. Check-in 4 pm, check-out noon. Three restaurants, bar. Fitness room (fee). Indoor pool, whirlpool. Golf, 18 holes. Ski in/ski out. **$$**

## Specialty Lodgings

**A LOON'S NEST BED & BREAKFAST.** *1455 Hillcrest Dr, Anchorage (99503). Phone 907/279-9884; toll-free 800/786-9884. www.aloonsnest.com.* This Frank Lloyd Wright-designed house is poised on a bluff overlooking Westchester Lagoon and features Shaker-style furniture, whirlpool tubs, and wheelchair accessibility. 2 rooms, 2 story. **$**

**ALASKAN LEOPARD BED & BREAKFAST.** *16136 Sandpiper Dr, Anchorage (99501). Phone 907/868-1594; toll-free 877/277-7118. www.alaskanleopard.com.* Hillside chalet with spectacular views of the Anchorage Bowl, Cook Inlet, the Kenai Peninsula, and the volcanoes of the Alaska Range. Known for extraordinary breakfasts. 4 rooms, 2 story. **$**

**FIFTEEN CHANDELEERS B & B.** *14020 Sabine St, Anchorage (99511). Phone 907/345-3032.* This European-style Georgian mansion is set in a botanical garden. Breakfast is served in a formal dining room with fine china and stemware. 5 rooms, 3 story. **$$**

**MAHOGANY MANOR BED & BREAKFAST INN.** *204 E 15th Ave, Anchorage (99501). Phone 907/278-1111; toll-free 888/777-0346. www.mahoganymanor.com.* A luxury-oriented bed-and-breakfast in a secluded environment. All rooms feature private baths, entrances, high-speed Internet connections, and DVD players. 6 rooms, 2 story. **$$$**

**THE OSCAR GILL HISTORIC BED & BREAKFAST.** *1344 W 10th Ave, Anchorage (99501). Phone 907/279-1344. www.oscargill.com.* This 1913 home is located in Delaney Park, bordering the Cook Inlet, and offers views of Denali and Sleeping Lady. Cited as one of Alaska's best lodgings. 3 rooms, 2 story. **$**

**SUSTINA SUNSETS BED & BREAKFAST.** *9901 Conifer St, Anchorage (99507). Phone 907/346-1067.* Features views of Mt. McKinley with breakfast served in-room or on one of the decks. 3 rooms, 3 story. **$**

## Restaurants

**★ THE BAKE SHOP.** *Alyeska Boardwalk, Girdwood (99587). Phone 907/783-2831; fax 907/783-3192. www.thebakeshop.com.* The Bake Shop at Alyeska is a very casual restaurant and bakery serving fresh baked breads, standard breakfast fare, sandwiches, and pizzas. Designed with skiers and outdoor enthusiasts in mind, its counter service and self-seating allows customers to pop in, grab a bite to eat, and get back outdoors without fuss or delay. Deli menu, pizza. Breakfast, lunch, dinner. Casual attire. Outdoor seating. **$**

**★ ★ ★ CAMPOBELLO BISTRO.** *601 W 36th Ave, Anchorage (99501). Phone 907/563-2040.* This midtown bistro features sophisticated Mediterranean cuisine and an impressive wine list and is decorated with modern art. Mediterranean menu. Lunch, dinner. **$$$**

**★ ★ ★ CLUB PARIS.** *417 W 5th Ave, Anchorage (99501). Phone 907/277-6332. www.clubparis*

*restaurant.com.* The grand belle of Anchorage's downtown restaurant scene, Club Paris is considered by many to be "the" steakhouse in Anchorage. Opened in 1957, this local landmark restaurant has weathered earthquakes, blizzards, and urban renewal and still manages to be as charming and as idiosyncratic as always. Designed on the inside to look like part French bistro, part Alaskan saloon, it's a must for those looking for something out of the ordinary. Seafood, steak menu. Lunch, dinner. Closed Thanksgiving, Dec 25. Bar. Casual attire. **$$$**

★ ★ ★ **CORSAIR RESTAURANT.** *944 W 5th Ave, Anchorage (99501). Phone 907/278-4502; fax 907/274-0333. www.corsairrestaurant.com.* Featuring ultra-private wraparound booths, discreet soft lighting, and a well-trained and knowledgeable staff, Corsair is an ideal destination for those looking for a sophisticated dining experience in the heart of Anchorage. The gourmet menu features continental food with an emphasis on French haute cuisine as well as Alaskan seafood dishes prepared with fresh local ingredients by a well-trained, highly professional staff. Winner of the Wine Spectator Best of Award of Excellence and considered one of the top three wine cellars in Alaska, Corsair is above all a wine connoisseur's paradise, with over 700 vintages in its 10,000 bottle cellar. French, seafood menu. Dinner. Closed Sun; holidays. Bar. Casual attire. **$$$**

★ ★ ★ **CROW'S NEST RESTAURANT.** *5th Ave and K St, Anchorage (99501). Phone 907/343-2217.* Featuring one of the best views in Anchorage, this restaurant is best known for its five-course prix fixe menu and an impressive wine list. American menu. Dinner. Closed Sun-Mon. **$$$**

★ **DOLCE EDIBLES CAFE AND BAKERY.** *640 W 36th Ave, Anchorage (99503). Phone 907/770-6680; fax 907/770-6683.* Dolce Edibles is a wonderful find, filled with the tantalizing aroma of fresh-baked pastries, hot bread, and strong coffee. The small seating area's Mediterranean color palette, unobstructed views of the bakers at work, and sturdy wooden chairs and tables create the sense of being a guest in someones kitchen rather than a customer at a café. American menu. Breakfast, lunch. Closed Sun; holidays. Children's menu. Casual attire. **$**

★ ★ **DOWNTOWN DELI & CAFE.** *525 W 4th Ave, Anchorage (99501). Phone 907/276-7116; fax 907/278-7314.* Downtown Deli & Café has been feeding locals and tourists nonstop since 1979. There's lots of booth and table seating inside the comfortable dining area as well as sidewalk seating during the warmer months. The food is traditional American with a Northwest flavor, including such local favorites as sourdough pancakes, reindeer stew, and Alaskan halibut. American menu. Breakfast, lunch. Closed Thanksgiving, Dec 25. Casual attire. Outdoor seating. **$**

★ ★ ★ **FLYING MACHINE RESTAURANT.** *4800 Spenard Rd, Anchorage (99517). Phone 907/266-2249; fax 907/243-8815. www.millenniumhotels.com.* Located a stone's throw from Lake Spenard and offering exceptional dining with sweeping lake and mountain views, this Millennium Alaskan Hotel (see) restaurant manages to be elegant and warm without being overly formal or pricey. The most appealing aspect of the place is its outdoor patio, which during the summer is filled with diners who soak up sunshine while enjoying the top-quality seafood and steaks the restaurant is known for. Even in winter it's an appealing spot, with snow piling up against the bay windows and a cheery fire burning in the rock fireplace. American, seafood menu. Breakfast, lunch, dinner. Bar. Children's menu. Casual attire. Outdoor seating. **$$$**

★ ★ **GLACIER BREWHOUSE.** *737 W 5th Ave, Anchorage (99501). Phone 907/274-2739; fax 907/277-1033. www.glacierbrewhouse.com.* This casually elegant downtown restaurant, the place "where Alaskans meet Alaskans," features a warm and inviting dining area filled with polished woods, slate tile floors, soft lighting, and a huge rock fireplace. The menu contains a wide range of entrées and appetizers, but the rotisserie-grilled meats and fresh Alaskan seafood are what the restaurant is best known for. American menu. Lunch, dinner. Closed July 4, Thanksgiving, Dec 25. Bar. Casual attire. Reservations recommended. **$$**

★ ★ **GWENNIE'S OLD ALASKA RESTAURANT.** *4333 Spenard Rd, Anchorage (99517). Phone 907/243-2090.* Another of Anchorage's perennial breakfast and brunch favorites, Gwennie's takes pride in its strong ties to Anchorage's history, as evidenced by walls lined with framed newspaper clippings and photos depicting Anchorage's wild and sometimes checkered past. This is a real family restaurant, serving wholesome Alaskan food to generations of tourists and locals. American menu. Breakfast, lunch, dinner. Closed Thanksgiving, Dec 25. Bar. Casual attire. **$$**

★ ★ **HOOPER BAY CAFE.** *500 W 3rd Ave, Anchorage (99501). Phone 907/272-7411; fax 907/265-7175.* For travelers looking for prime people-watching venues in Anchorage, the Hooper Bay Café inside the Hilton hotel (see) is the place to go. With only a

waist-high wall separating the café from the spacious Hilton lobby, customers are able to keep an eye on all the action while enjoying quality American, Northwestern, and international dishes from a surprisingly adventurous menu. American menu. Breakfast, lunch, dinner. Children's menu. Casual attire. **$$**

★ ★ **HOW HOW CHINESE RESTAURANT.** *207 Muldoon Rd, Anchorage (99504). Phone 907/337-2116; fax 907/338-6569.* Since the early 1970s, this family-owned restaurant has been serving top quality Chinese food to a devoted local clientele as well as legions of weary travelers staying nearby. With an interior filled with carved animals, hanging lanterns, and graceful architectural features, it provides diners with a terrific visual and culinary experience. American, Chinese menu. Lunch, dinner. Closed Thanksgiving, Dec 25. Bar. Children's menu. Casual attire. Outdoor seating. **$$**

★ ★ **JEN'S.** *701 W 36th Ave, Anchorage (99501). Phone 907/561-5367. www.jensrestaurant.com.* Jen's is a chef-owned, fine dining restaurant exquisitely decorated with Alaskan art. Menu changes daily. French menu. Lunch, dinner. Closed Sun. **$$$**

★ ★ ★ **KATSURA TEPPANYAKI.** *1000 Arlberg Ave, Girdwood (99587). Phone 907/754-2237. www.alyeskaresort.com.* This on-site restaurant at the Alyeska Resort in Girdwood serves "world-class Japanese cuisine with flair" and features a u-shaped seating arrangement whereby guests can watch the master chef prepare their food in front of them. With reservations limited to only 18 diners per seating and a menu of four set courses to choose from, the emphasis here is on creating a unique and memorable dining experience in an intimate, upscale environment. Japanese menu. Dinner. Closed Tues-Wed. Bar. Casual attire. **$$$**

★ ★ ★ **KUMAGORO.** *533 W 4th Ave, Anchorage (99501). Phone 907/272-9905.* This is the only restaurant in Alaska to feature a traditional Japanese breakfast and Shabu Shabu dinners. Japanese menu. Breakfast, lunch, dinner. **$$**

★ ★ **LION'S DEN.** *1000 E 36th Ave, Anchorage (99508). Phone 907/743-4814; fax 907/248-1117. www.bestwesterngoldenlion.com.* This midtown restaurant is located in the Best Western Golden Lion Hotel (see). Featuring a bright, airy dining area and a wide selection of American and seafood entrées, it attracts large numbers of locals as well as hotel guests. Twinkle-toed diners are invited to join in free dance lessons held six nights a week in the adjacent lounge. American menu. Breakfast, lunch, dinner. Closed Jan 1, Dec 25. Bar. Casual attire. **$$**

★ ★ ★ **MARX BROTHERS' CAFE.** *627 W 3rd Ave, Anchorage (99501). Phone 907/278-2133.* A local favorite, this café was built in 1916 and features progressive American cuisine with an award-winning wine list. American menu. Dinner. Closed Sun. **$$$**

★ ★ **PEPPER MILL.** *4101 Credit Union Dr, Anchorage (99503). Phone 907/561-0800; fax 907/563-6382. www.seagalleyalaska.com.* This elegant yet casual steakhouse is one of the most popular in the midtown area, serving top-of-the-line steaks in a private, comfortable setting. It's definitely a unique place to dine, with hundreds of pepper mills on display throughout the dining area, including one so large, it takes four people to operate. Steak menu. Dinner. Closed Thanksgiving, Dec 25. Bar. Children's menu. Casual attire. **$$$**

★ ★ **PIPERS RESTAURANT & LOUNGE.** *3333 W International Airport Rd, Anchorage (99502). Phone 907/249-4444.* The small, slightly upscale dining room at the Coast International Inn (see) features elegant light fixtures, beautiful architectural highlights, and comfortable booth seating that allows for privacy while dining. During summer, the restaurant's biggest attraction is its outdoor patio, which offers diners the chance to enjoy wonderful lake and mountain views while dining under the midnight sun. American menu. Breakfast, lunch, dinner. Closed Jan 1, Thanksgiving, Dec 25. Bar. Children's menu. Casual attire. Outdoor seating. **$$**

★ ★ **THE POND CAFE.** *1000 Arlberg Ave, Girdwood (99587). Phone 907/754-2236. www.alyeskaresort.com.* The highlight of this family-oriented café at the Alyeska Prince Resort (see) is its sunny, spacious dining room that provides terrific views of the hotel's small pond and the Chugach Mountains that encircle the resort. During the long days of summer, diners can opt to relax and unwind on the covered patio that overlooks the pond. American menu. Breakfast, lunch, dinner. Bar. Children's menu. Casual attire. Outdoor seating. **$$**

★ ★ **PTARMIGAN BAR & GRILL.** *401 E 6th Ave, Anchorage (99501). Phone 907/276-8700; fax 907/276-7561. www.sheratonanchorage.com/dining.htm.* This casual, friendly restaurant is located on the ground floor of the Sheraton Anchorage Hotel (see) and specializes in Alaskan cuisine—salmon chowder, reindeer sausage, buffalo meatloaf, and baked halibut. The subtle Alaskan décor and vibrant color scheme in the dining area create a casual, slightly upscale environment that is at once cheerful and inviting. American menu. Breakfast, lunch, dinner. Bar. Casual attire. **$$**

**★ ★ RISTORANTE ORSO.** *737 W 5th Ave, Anchorage (99501). Phone 907/222-3232; fax 907/792-3740. www.orsoalaska.com.* Few, if any, restaurants in Anchorage can rival Ristorante Orso for unique atmosphere and bold continental flair. Designed to resemble the interior of a Tuscan villa, this down-town restaurant is divided into a series of small alcoves and private rooms that enable diners to enjoy fine dining in an intimate setting. Soft lights, warm Mediterranean colors, and beautiful architectural features combine with the gourmet menu to make a visit here a visual and culinary treat. Mediterranean menu. Lunch, dinner. Closed July 4, Thanksgiving, Dec 25. Bar. Casual attire. **$$$**

**★ ★ ★ SACK'S CAFE & RESTAURANT.** *328 G St, Anchorage (99501). Phone 907/274-4022. www.sackscafe.com.* This is an award-winning restaurant specializing in eclectic New American cuisine. American menu. Lunch, dinner. **$$**

**★ ★ SEA GALLEY.** *4101 Credit Union Dr, Anchorage (99503). Phone 907/563-3520; fax 907/563-6382. www.seagalleyalaska.com.* Quality fresh Alaskan seafood is the main draw at this long-time fixture on the midtown restaurant scene, with fresh halibut, Alaska king crab, and fresh oysters flying out the door. A large enclosed atrium permits sunny indoor dining throughout the year, and numerous alcoves make an ideal dining destination for groups, families, and those looking for a bit of privacy. Seafood menu. Lunch, dinner. Closed Thanksgiving, Dec 25. Bar. Children's menu. Casual attire. **$$**

**★ ★ ★ SEVEN GLACIERS.** *1000 Arlberg Ave, Girdwood (99587). Phone 907/754-2237. www.alyeskaresort.com.* Located 2,300 feet above the Girdwood valley floor, the ultra-chic Seven Glaciers restaurant is only accessible by gondola from the Alyeska Prince Resort (see). From this mountainside perch, it provides guests with breathtaking views to the north of seven hanging glaciers on a nearby mountain and to the south, the waters of Turnagain Arm. Winner of the *Wine Spectator* Award of Excellence, the restaurant features award-winning Alaskan cuisine in an exceptionally warm and intimate environment and has a well-deserved reputation for flawless service. Northwestern menu. Dinner. Closed mid-Apr-mid-May and Oct-mid-Nov. Bar. Children's menu. Business casual attire. **$$$**

**★ ★ SIMON & SEAFORT'S SALOON & GRILL.** *420 L St, Anchorage (99501). Phone 907/274-3502.* One of Anchorage's most popular restaurants, Simon & Seafort's Saloon & Grill is located a short walk from the Hotel Captain Hook (see) and offers views of the Cook Inlet from large picture windows. American menu. Lunch, dinner. **$$**

**★ ★ SNOW CITY CAFE.** *1034 W 4th Ave, Anchorage (99501). Phone 907/272-2489; fax 907/272-6338. www.snowcitycafe.com.* Voted Anchorage's best brunch in a citywide poll in 2003, Snow City Café serves up hearty meals and fresh-baked pastries to the office workers, tourists, and locals who drop in throughout the day. With strong ties to the local community, it is host to an ever-changing lineup of art exhibits, local community events, and live music. American menu. Breakfast, lunch. Closed Jan 1, Thanksgiving, Dec 25. Casual attire. Outdoor seating. **$**

**★ ★ SNOW GOOSE RESTAURANT & SLEEPING LADY BREWING COMPANY.** *717 W 3rd Ave, Anchorage (99501). Phone 907/277-7727; fax 907/277-0606. www.alaskabeers.com.* The Snow Goose Restaurant is one of only a few moderately priced restaurants in Anchorage that offers scenic outdoor dining to its summertime clientele. During colder months, oversized picture windows enable customers to enjoy the spectacular mountain and inlet views from the warmth of the restaurant and lounge. Art lovers should plan on extra time to enjoy the colorful hand-made Alaskan quilts and stained glass panels that decorate the walls of the restaurant. American menu. Lunch, dinner, late-night. Closed Jan1, Thanksgiving, Dec 25. Bar. Children's menu. Casual attire. Outdoor seating. **$$**

**★ ★ STUART ANDERSON'S CATTLE COMPANY.** *300 W Tudor Rd, Anchorage (99503). Phone 907/562-2844; fax 907/562-2632. www.stuartandersons.com.* Since opening in Anchorage in 1978, Stuart Anderson's Cattle Company has built a solid reputation for serving up hearty steak and seafood dishes. Weather-beaten boards, enormous wooden rafters, and cowboy memorabilia create a rustic Western feel for the restaurant, but it's the hearty food that draws people back time and again. Steak menu. Lunch, dinner. Closed Dec 25. Bar. Casual attire. **$$**

**★ THAI HOUSE.** *830 E 36th Ave, Anchorage (99503). Phone 907/563-8616; fax 907/562-9490.*

Named best Thai food in a local poll a number of years running, Thai House restaurant has loads of charm, with a gracious and attentive waitstaff and an interior filled with an eclectic array of Thai art, intricate wood carvings, and colorful sarongs. Housed in a former Dairy Queen, its quirky, casual, and inviting. Thai menu. Lunch, dinner. Closed Sun; holidays. Casual attire. **$**

**★★★ TOP OF THE WORLD.** *500 W 3rd Ave, Anchorage (99501). Phone 907/265-7111; fax 907/265-7175. www.hilton.com.* When it comes to fine dining in Anchorage, Top of the World restaurant's combination of elegance, atmosphere, and location is hard to match. Situated on the 15th floor of the Hilton hotel (see), the restaurant offers a carefully crafted gourmet menu along with impeccable service. The real highlight of the restaurant, though, is its stunning panoramic views, which on a clear day extend as far as Mount McKinley. Guests looking for lighter fare can take a seat in the adjoining lounge, which offers rooftop seating during the summer—a chic and unique place to relax and enjoy the midnight sun. Seafood menu. Dinner. Closed Sun-Tues; Dec 25. Bar. Children's menu. Casual attire. **$$$**

**★ UNCLE JOE'S PIZZERIA.** *428 G St, Anchorage (99501). Phone 907/279-3799. www.unclejoespizzeria.com.* Voted "Best Pepperoni Pizza" by University of Alaska Anchorage students in a 2003 poll, Uncle Joe's Pizzeria offers its customers a wide selection of pizzas, calzones, subs, and gyros "made to order, one at a time with pride. " With five locations in and around Anchorage, it's a convenient, casual, and inexpensive place to grab a bite to eat. Pizza. Lunch, dinner. Closed Thanksgiving, Dec 25. Casual attire. **$**

**★ WAYNE'S ORIGINAL TEXAS BAR-B-QUE.** *3400 C St, Anchorage (99503). Phone 907/569-9911; fax 907/569-5582. www.waynesbbq.us.* This ultra-casual family friendly joint focuses on one thing and one thing only: Texas-style barbecue. There's no attempt here to compete with the legions of upscale steakhouses in Anchorage: customers order at a counter and eat and drink from plastic and paper dinnerware. With low prices, a great selection of barbecue favorites, and enormous portions, it's a great place for hungry hombres. American menu. Lunch, dinner. Closed Jan 1, Thanksgiving, Dec 25. Children's menu. Casual attire. **$**

**★★ YUKON YACHT CLUB.** *115 E 3rd Ave, Anchorage (99501). Phone 907/334-8408. www.yukonyachtclub.com.* Proudly billing itself as the northernmost yacht club in North America, the Yukon Yacht Club is open to all with its casual atmosphere, enormous beer selection, live music, and amusing menu. Adventurous customers might consider tackling the 49-ounce Alaskan cut steak, also available in the more "dainty" 22-ounce Texas size. American menu. Breakfast, lunch, dinner. Bar. Children's menu. Casual attire. Outdoor seating. **$$**

# Aniakchak National Monument and Preserve

**Web Site** www.nps.gov/ania

The Aniakchak Caldera, a volcanic crater measuring almost 6 miles in diameter, is a spectacular sight and a truly awesome example of nature's power. Created over the last 3,400 years by a series of volcanic eruptions—the most recent occurring in May 1931—the caldera possesses outstanding examples of volcanic features, with numerous explosion pits, lava flows, and cinder cones. The largest cone, Vent Mountain, rises 1,400 feet above the caldera floor. The walls of the caldera vary in height, generally ranging between 2,000 and 4,400 feet. Surprise Lake glistens within the caldera and serves as the source of the Aniakchak River, which offers an unparalleled whitewater rafting experience. The river cuts a 1,500-foot opening (known as "The Gates") in the caldera wall, and then briskly flows east, winding around the mountains of the Aleutian Range, before spilling out into Aniakchak Bay and the Pacific Ocean. Other popular activities in and around the caldera include camping, fishing, hiking, and wildlife viewing. With its remote location along the Alaska Peninsula, the Aniakchak National Monument and Preserve can be accessed only via floatplane.

# Barrow (A-4)

**Population** 4,581
**Area Code** 907

Barrow, the northernmost city in the United States, is home to a large number of Eskimos, who call the city Ukpeagvik, or "place where owls are hunted." From mid-May to mid-August, the sun never sets—and it never rises above the horizon between mid-December and late January. It's a great place to catch the famous northern lights in winter, and it's also well known as a birding site, with Eider ducks and snowy owls among the 250 species that visit each year. Humorist Will Rogers was killed in Barrow in a plane crash in 1935; two monuments here remember Rogers and the famous pilot of the plane, Wiley Post. No roads connect Barrow to other Alaska cities, but you can catch a (pricey) flight out of Anchorage or Fairbanks. Lodging is available at the King Eider Inn, which was built in 1998 to accommodate the hardy souls who venture here.

## Public Transportation

**Airport** Wiley Post-Will Rogers Memorial Airport (PABR).

## What to See and Do

**Inupiat Heritage Center.** *Barrow (99723). Phone 907/852-5494. www.nps.gov/inup.* The Inupiat Heritage Center recognizes Alaska Natives who participated in commercial whaling during the late 19th and early 20th centuries. Remotely situated along the Arctic Ocean, the center is an affiliated area of the New Bedford Whaling National Historical Park in Massachusetts. More than 2,000 whaling voyages sailed from New Bedford to the frigid waters near Barrow. Alaska Natives, particularly the Inupiat Eskimo people, contributed greatly to the whaling efforts by hunting for food for the whalers, crewing whaling boats, and sheltering crews that had been shipwrecked off the coast. The Heritage Center features exhibits and artifact collections, as well as a library and gift shop. With its location above the Arctic Circle, Barrow is best reached via a commercial flight from Fairbanks or Anchorage. (Mon-Fri 8:30 am-5 pm)

# Bering Land Bridge National Preserve

**Web Site** www.nps.gov/bela

Roughly 13,000 years ago, the continents of Asia and North America were connected by a land bridge thousands of miles wide. Archaeologists believe that the land bridge provided humans the initial means of accessing and populating the Americas. Today, most of this stretch of land, known as the Bering Land Bridge, is submerged beneath the Bering and Chukchi seas. The Bering Land Bridge National Preserve occupies 2. 7 million acres along the Arctic Circle in northwestern Alaska's Seward Peninsula. One of the most isolated areas in the national park system, the preserve offers visitors the opportunity to explore native villages and learn about traditional subsistence lifestyles. Wildlife viewing is popular within the preserve, which is home to grizzly and polar bears, reindeer, wolves, whales, seals, and more than 170 species of birds. Other popular activities include cross-country skiing, fishing, and dog sleddingthe northern terminus of the famous Iditarod Trail can be found just south of the preserve. Winter temperatures here can sink as low at 55 degrees Fahrenheit. Not surprisingly, then, the Serpentine Hot Springs—with water temperatures between 140 and 170 degrees—have become a favorite stop for visitors to the preserve.Phone 907/443-2522

# Cape Krusenstern National Monument

**Web Site** www.nps.gov/cakr

Cape Krusenstern National Monument sprawls out over 660,000 treeless acres along the Chukchi Sea in northwest Alaska. Isolated above the Arctic Circle, the monument possesses a tundra landscape marked by 114 beach ridges, existing as a record of the seas ever-changing coastline. The earliest ridges can be found farther inland. Archaeological excavations at these early beach ridges indicate human presence along the coastline 9,000 years ago. Natives still reside in the area, and, within the monument, they are allowed to hunt marine mammals—whales, walruses, and seals. Polar and grizzly bears patrol the limestone hills of the coastline, as do caribou, moose, and wolves. Each fall brings large numbers of migratory birds to the lagoons at Cape Krusenstern. For visitors to the monument, the most popular recreational activities include camping, hiking, and kayaking. The nearest town, Kotzebue, sits 10 miles to the southeast. During the summer month—swhich are wet, windy, and cool—Cape Krusenstern is accessible by chartered boat or seaplane. Only the hardiest outdoor enthusiasts should consider venturing here during the bitterly cold winter, when a dogsled represents the most effective means of reaching the monument.

# Cordova (D-6)

**Population** 2,454
**Area Code** 907
**Web Site** www.cordovaalaska.com

Accessible only by boat or plane, Cordova sits on the eastern edge of Prince William Sound, the nearest settlement to the vast Copper River Delta, one of the largest and most important migratory bird habitats in North America. Originally developed as the southern terminus of the Copper River & Northwestern Railroad, which transported copper from the Kennecott Mine 200 miles to the north, Cordova flourished from 1911 until the mine shut down in 1938. Eventually, the railroad track was torn up and the bed used as a makeshift roadway until the 1964 Good Friday earthquake destroyed the northernmost span of the Million Dollar Bridge across the Copper River, effectively cutting off Cordova's only land-based link to the outside world. The geographic isolation of the town has turned out to be one of its biggest assets, as it remains largely unaffected by the summer tourists who use it as a home base while they hunt, fish, hike, kayak, and explore the vast wilderness that surrounds the town.

## What to See and Do

**Copper River Highway and Million Dollar Bridge.** *Cordova.* The Copper River Highway begins in Cordova and stretches for 49 miles north follow ing the contours of the Copper River. For most of its length, the road follows the railbed of the old Copper River & Northwestern Railway, which ceased operation in 1938. One of Alaska's most scenic and least traveled roads, it passes through a spectacular landscape of rugged mountains, mammoth glaciers, and icy blue ponds before reaching the Childs Glacier Recreation Area, a popular picnic, hiking, and sightseeing area. Less than a quarter of a mile up the road is the Million Dollar Bridge. Completed in 1910 at a cost of just over a million dollars, its location, length, and design made it an engineering marvel of its time. During the 1964 Good Friday earthquake, the northernmost span collapsed into the Copper River, halting further development of the Copper River Highway and creating one of Cordova's most photographed attractions. A temporary ramp from the third span to the shore was built in 1973, allowing four-wheel-drive vehicles with a high body clearance access to the remaining portions of the road north of the bridge. After a 40-year wait, work to raise and repair the span was begun in early 2004 and is expected to be completed by summer 2005. There are no official plans to rebuild and reopen the highway beyond the bridge, and at present the extremely rough road comes to an abrupt end 10 miles north, at the Allen River. Travelers planning to drive any part of the Copper River Highway are strongly advised to check road and weather conditions before starting out. Much of the highway is unpaved and crosses terrain that can pose significant challenges to unwary drivers.

**Mount Eyak Ski Area.** *Cordova. Phone 907/424-7766.* Downhill skiing, snowboarding, heli-skiing. Thirty trails; longest run 750 feet. Rentals.

**Museum.** *First St, Cordova (99574). Phone 907/424-6665.* Exhibits of native artifacts, early explorers, mining, and the railroad. (Mon-Sat 10 am-6 pm, Sun 2-4 pm)

**Points North Heli Adventures.** *Cordova (99574). Phone toll-free 877/787-6784. www.alaskaheliski.com.* Operating out of the Orca Adventure Lodge (see), this tour company helicopters brave skiers and snowboarders into the Chugach Mountains, dropping them directly onto the slopes for amazing runs in exceptional powder. Most skiers average 20,000 to 25,000 vertical feet in a day, consisting of five to eight runs. At more than $500 an hour, the adventure doesn't come cheap, but it's sure to be an experience you won't soon forget. **$$$$**

## Special Events

**Copper River Delta Shorebird Festival.** *Cordova.* This festival celebrates the annual spring migration of hundreds of thousands of shorebirds through the Copper River Delta. Bird-watchers and wildlife aficionados can take part in educational workshops, attend talks given by noted naturalists, take bird-watching trips out to the delta, and join a dinner and wildlife cruise on Prince William Sound. Early May.

**Copper River Wild! Salmon Festival.** *Cordova. Phone 907/424-7260.* This festival is Cordovas newest tourist draw, celebrating the annual run of salmon up the Copper River. The festival features an assortment of outdoor activities, including nature hikes, community barbecues, and fundraising dinners. One of the main events is the King Salmon Marathon Run, which begins 27 miles up the Copper River Highway and ends in the middle of town. In 2004, the festival merged with the Salmon Jam Music Festival, adding live local music to the slate of public entertainment options. Early June.

**Iceworm Festival.** *Cordova.* Despite its small size, Cordova hosts three large-scale festivals each year, beginning with the Iceworm Festival, held during the first full weekend in February. For more than four decades, this community-wide party has served as a way to lighten spirits and bring people together during the middle of winter. The festival features activities ranging from auctions, arts and crafts exhibits, and baking contests to survival suit races, a Miss Iceworm pageant, and a torch-lit parade. Early Feb.

## Limited-Service Hotel

**★ PRINCE WILLIAM MOTEL.** *501 Second St, Cordova (99574). Phone 907/424-3201; toll-free 888/796-6835; fax 907/424-2260.* Built on the side of a steep hill overlooking Orca Inlet and Hawkins Island, this small, locally owned motel is conveniently located in the heart of downtown Cordova, a five-minute walk to the harbor. The guest rooms are large and half of them have kitchenettes, so its particularly popular with families, budget travelers, and long-term visitors. Unfortunately, none of the rooms take advantage of the motel's setting; they lack the stunning views that many other Alaska lodgings boast. 16 rooms. Pets accepted. Check-in 2 pm, check-out noon. **$**

## Specialty Lodgings

**THE CORDOVA LIGHTHOUSE INN.** *212 Nicholoff Way, Cordova (99574). Phone 907/424-7080; toll-free 888/424-7080; fax 907/424-7081. www.cordovalighthouseinn.com.* The Cordova Lighthouse Inn is a tiny, ultra-cozy inn on the water's edge in Cordova, about three blocks from downtown. Although they lack telephones, each guest room is adorned with framed tintype photos on the dressers, home-style bedspreads and pillows, and an eclectic collection of furniture. Rooms at the front overlook Cordovas small boat harbor, while those at the back have views of Odiak Slough and Mount Eccles. 4 rooms. Check-in 2 pm, check-out 11 am. Restaurant. **$**

**ORCA ADVENTURE LODGE.** *2500 Orca Rd, Cordova (99574). Phone toll-free 866/424-6722. www.orcaadventurelodge.com.* If you're planning a visit to Cordova, it's likely that you'll find yourself at the Orca Adventure Lodge, even if you don't choose to stay here. Many "adventures" depart from the lodge, including river rafting, kayaking, and fly fishing trips. Situated 2 miles north of town on the shores of Prince William Sound, the 1880s cannery town has been refashioned into a rustic lodging with ocean views. All meals are provided in the cookhouse next door. 37 rooms. Wireless Internet access. Airport transportation available. **$**

## Restaurants

**★★★ AMBROSIA RESTAURANT.** *410 Main St, Cordova (99574). Phone 907/424-7175.* Seafood menu. Lunch, dinner. Bar. Business casual attire. Reservations recommended. **$$$**

**★ THE CORDOVA LIGHTHOUSE INN.** *212 Nicholoff Way, Cordova (99574). Phone 907/424-7080; fax 907/424-7081. www.cordovalighthouseinn.com.* Located across the street from the boat harbor, this snug little restaurant and bakery is filled with the delicious smell of coffee and muffins in the morning, pizzas at night, and fresh-baked bread throughout the day. The range of desserts and pastries they offer makes any thought of a diet impossible. American menu. Breakfast, lunch. Closed holidays; also Sun-Mon in winter. Casual attire. Outdoor seating. **$**

# Denali National Park and Preserve

*See also Talkeetna*

**Web Site** www.nps.gov/dena

Like Alaska and Mount McKinley, Denali is big—really big. It ranks among the largest national parks, covering over 6 million acres of pristine wilderness, a broad expanse of land roughly the same size as Massachusetts. Situated within the 600-mile-long Alaska Range, the park's sharp-edged mountains were carved by sprawling glaciers, many of which are still at work—the park contains more than 20 glaciers that are longer than 5 miles, including one, Kahiltna, that stretches 43 miles. Denali also possesses abundant wildlife, and visitors shouldn't be surprised to spot moose, caribou, Dall sheep, and grizzly bears, as well as smaller mammals such as marmots and snowshoe hares.

Hiking and camping are among the most popular activities at Denali. Although the park has few trails, one worth exploring is the Mount Healy Overlook Trail, a

2. 5-mile trek that leads to a stellar view of the fast-flowing Nenana River and majestic peaks of the Alaska Range. The Nenana River offers a stellar whitewater rafting experience that's not for the faint of heart, with stretches of the river categorized as Class IV rapids. Bicycling is another favored activity here, particularly on the 90-mile-long Park Road. Bicycles may be transported on the Park Road shuttle bus, allowing for a one-way bike ride to the center of Denali followed by a one-way bus ride back to the visitor center. For those seeking to truly test their mettle, Mount McKinley stands as one of the most difficult climbs in the world. While not a technically difficult climb, bitterly cold temperatures, fierce winds, and 16,000 feet of snowline make for a daunting expedition. The park is open year-round, and a surprising number of visitors arrive in the winter months to go cross-country skiing or dogsledding.

Deep within Alaska's interior, Mount McKinley boldly emerges from a subarctic desert terrain, the mountain's broad shoulders rising inexorably skyward, culminating at a peak of 20,320 feet—770 feet higher than any other mountain in North America. The massive McKinley is, without question, the star attraction at Denali National Park & Preserve, helping the park to draw nearly 300,000 visitors a year.

Native Alaskans have lived at Denali for many centuries. In fact, Mount McKinley (named for President William McKinley) was originally named Denali, which among the indigenous Athabascan people means "Great One. " With the stroke of a pen, President Woodrow Wilson established Mount McKinley National Park in 1917. Congress changed the park's name to Denali National Park & Preserve 63 years later.

Denali is accessible by car. The park's headquarters sit on Highway 3, 125 miles south of Fairbanks and 240 miles north of Anchorage. Denali's mountaineering headquarters are in Talkeetna, about 100 miles north of Anchorage. The highly regarded Alaska Railroad runs the Denali Star line between Anchorage and Fairbanks, with stops in Talkeetna and Denali. (Daily; hours vary by season)

## What to See and Do

**Tours.** *Denali. Phone toll-free 800/544-2206. www.graylineofalaska.com.* Gray Line of Alaska offers package tours around Alaska (up to 11 days) as well as flightseeing, heli-hiking, rafting, horseback, and backcountry wilderness tours of Denali.

## Limited-Service Hotels

**★ ★ DENALI BLUFFS HOTEL.** *George Parks Hwy, mile 238.3, Denali National Park and Preserve (99755). Phone 907/683-7000; toll-free 866/683-8500; fax 907/683-7500. www.denalialaska.com/bluffs.* This 112-room hotel is actually a series of low-rise buildings located on a bluff overlooking some of the most scenic wilderness in Alaska. All rooms are tidy and appealing, but its the views through the windows that really make staying here a memorable experience. The hotel runs a free shuttle service to Denali National Park, only a mile away, and to the little town nearby. 112 rooms. Closed Oct-Apr. Check-in 3 pm, check-out 11 am. Wireless Internet access. Restaurant, bar. **$$**

**★ ★ DENALI CROW'S NEST LOG CABINS.** *George Parks Hwy, mile 238.3, Denali National Park and Preserve (99755). Phone 907/683-2723. www.denalicrowsnest.com.* Perched on the side of Sugarloaf Mountain 1 mile north of the Denali Park entrance, these one-room log cabins offer magnificent views and cozy, basic accommodations. With neither telephones nor televisions in the rooms, the cabins provide guests with an opportunity to break from routine and enjoy life through nature. 39 rooms. Closed early Sept-mid-May. Check-in 2 pm, check-out 11 am. Restaurant, bar. Whirlpool. **$**

**★ DENALI PARK HOTEL.** *George Parks Hwy, mile 1.5, Denali National Park and Preserve (99743). Phone 907/276-7234; toll-free 866/683-1800; fax 907/683-1801. www.denaliparkhotel.com.* This unassuming complex of long, low buildings offers comparatively inexpensive, comfortable accommodations in a peaceful, rustic setting. Guests check in at a lobby set in a historic Alaska railroad car and then head to their rooms, all of which offer unobstructed views of the Alaska Range and Mount McKinley. Food, souvenirs, and gas are available in the nearby town of Healy. 42 rooms. Closed mid-Sept-mid-May, Pets accepted; fee. Check-in 2 pm, check-out 11 am. **$**

**★ ★ DENALI PRINCESS WILDERNESS LODGE.** *George Parks Hwy, mile 238.5, Denali National Park and Preserve (99755). Phone 907/683-2282; toll-free 800/426-0500; fax 907/683-2545. www.princesslodges.com.* As with all Princess lodges in Alaska, the Denali Princess Wilderness Lodge is an architectural gem set in a stunning Alaskan landscape. From the dramatic two-story rock and wood beam main building, completed in 2004, to the rustic, elegant log buildings that house the guest rooms, the lodge enables its guests to enjoy a taste of Alaskan wilderness without sacrificing comfort or style. The lodge features a number of restaurants, from the casual Lynx Creek Pizza to the unique Music of Denali Dinner Theatre. When not touring, eating, or shopping, guests tend to flock to the lodge's large outdoor deck overlooking the picturesque Nenana River. 440 rooms. Closed mid-Sept-mid-May. Check-in 3:30 pm, check-out 11 am. Three restaurants, two bars. Fitness room. Whirlpool. **$$**

★ ★ **GRANDE DENALI LODGE.** *George Parks Hwy, mile 238.2, Denali National Park and Preserve (99755). Phone 907/683-8500; toll-free 866/683-8500; fax 907/683-8599. www.denalialaska.com.* From its perch at the top of a mountain near the entrance to Denali National Park, this architecturally magnificent lodge dominates the local skyline, literally towering above all other properties in the area. As a full-service, upscale lodge, it features an elegant restaurant, an in-house multi-media theater, and a wide variety of free and fee-based outdoor activities ranging from guided nature walks and mountain bike rentals to tundra wilderness tours and heli-hiking excursions. Most public areas and guest rooms have stunning views of the Denali area, making this one of the most scenic places to stay in the area. 160 rooms. Closed mid-Sept-mid-May. Check-in 3 pm, check-out 10 am. Restaurant, bar. **$$**

★ ★ **MCKINLEY CHALET RESORT.** *George Parks Hwy, mile 239, Denali National Park and Preserve (99755). Phone 907/683-8200; toll-free 800/276-7234; fax 907/683-8211. www.denaliparkresort.com.* Offering upscale rooms and suites, this newly renovated property is located on a hill overlooking the Nenana River and the forested valleys of the Denali wilderness. Guests stay in lodges located near the main building, which houses the resort's restaurants, gift shop, dinner theater, fireside lounge, and interpretive displays. The resort offers guests guided nature walks and twice-daily informational talks given by naturalists familiar with the wildlife and geology of Denali National Park. The centerpiece of the stunning lobby is a large three-dimensional topographical map of the Denali area, which serves as a useful aid in understanding just how big and untamed the Park really is. 345 rooms. Closed mid-Sept-mid-May. Check-in 2 pm, check-out 11 am. Two restaurants, bar. **$$**

★ ★ **MCKINLEY VILLAGE LODGE.** *Mile Post 231, Denali National Park and Preserve (99755). Phone 907/683-8900; toll-free 800/276-7234; fax 907/258-3668.* Located on the Nenana River 8 miles south of the entrance to Denali National Park, this lodge-style hotel offers family-friendly accommodation in a spectacular setting. Rooms here are filled with comfortable wood furniture, soft, soothing colors, and accent pieces featuring local wildlife, reflecting the attractiveness and beauty of the wilderness outside. Guests of the lodge can spend the day panning for gold, riding the Nenana in a whitewater raft, or hiking local trails through the spruce forests that surround the property. On-site dining facilities, outdoor sundecks, and a courtesy shuttle into the park add to the allure of the property. 150 rooms. Closed mid-Sept-late May. Check-in 2 pm, check-out 11 am. Restaurant, bar. **$**

★ ★ **MT. MCKINLEY PRINCESS WILDERNESS LODGE.** *George Parks Hwy, mile 133, Denali National Park and Preserve (99683). Phone 907/733-2900; toll-free 800/426-0500; fax 907/733-2922.* This self-described "true wilderness retreat" is located on the Chulitna River inside Denali State Park. Its 334 guest rooms are housed in seventeen separate buildings on the property, ensuring a quiet, relaxing stay for all guests. The main building houses restaurants, a tour desk, an exercise room, and the Great Room, a magnificent social space with floor-to-ceiling windows offering views of Mt. McKinley, a massive stone fireplace, and plenty of cozy chairs for reading and relaxing. The grounds of the lodge feature a network of hiking trails, a spacious outdoor deck perfect for photographers and sun worshippers, and two hilltop whirlpools designed to help guests unwind after a busy day exploring the area. 334 rooms. Closed mid-Sept-mid-May. Check-in 3 pm, check-out 11 am. Restaurant, bar. Children's activity center. Fitness room. Whirlpool. **$$**

★ ★ **TALKEETNA ALASKAN LODGE.** *Talkeeta Spur Rd, mile 12.5, Talkeetna (99676). Phone 907/733-9500; toll-free 888/959-9590; fax 907/733-9545. www.talkeetnalodge.com.* Run by an Alaskan Native corporation, this hilltop lodge on the outskirts of Talkeetna offers unobstructed panoramic views of Denali and the Alaska Range as well as a bird's-eye view of the Susitna River Valley. The lobby features a four-story vaulted ceiling, a massive river rock fireplace, enormous wooden support pillars, and walls of windows that bathe the room in light and provide guests with front-row seats to the breathtaking scenery outside. Guest rooms are exceptionally comfortable and reflect the same attention to quality and detail seen in

the public areas of the lodge. The on-site restaurant offers casual upscale dining and has been named a winner of the Wine Spectator Award of Excellence. 200 rooms. Closed early Oct-mid-Apr. Check-in 3 pm, check-out 11 am. Two restaurants, bar. **$$$**

**★ WESTMARK DENALI SOURDOUGH CABINS.** *George Parks Hwy, mile 238.8, Denali National Park and Preserve (99755). Phone 907/683-2773; toll-free 800/544-0970; fax 907/683-2357. www.denalisourdoughcabins.com.* These tiny rustic cabins, surrounded by a heavily wooded forest, soar ing mountain peaks, and plenty of wildlife, provide guests with the chance to enjoy Alaska's great outdoors without having to rough it. Each cabin features beautiful cedar paneled walls, a private bathroom and a cozy front porch where guests can sit and take in the sights and sounds of the Denali wilderness. 45 rooms. Closed mid-Sept-late May. Check-in 2 pm, check-out 11 am. **$**

## Specialty Lodgings

**SUSITNA RIVER LODGINGS.** *13.5 Talkeetna Spur Rd, Talkeetna (99676). Phone 907/733-1505; toll-free 866/733-1505; fax 907/733-5051.* This collection of four cabins and a main lodge is a wilderness oasis set beside the Susitna River on the outskirts of Talkeetna. All rooms are suites with kitchenettes, full baths, and separate living and dining areas. The cabins also feature porches with scenic views and easy access to the communal barbecue and picnic area. 8 rooms, all suites. Check-in 3 pm, check-out noon. **$$**

**TALKEETNA ROADHOUSE.** *Main St and C St, Talkeetna (99676). Phone 907/733-1351; fax 907/733-1353. www.talkeetnaroadhouse.com.* This historic, family run hotel has been a Talkeetna landmark since 1944 and is a popular stopover for climbers and independent travelers looking for clean, comfortable, budget-friendly accommodations. Guest rooms are small and spartan and guests share a common bathroom, but the highly social, welcoming atmosphere of the hotel and attached restaurant more than compensates for the lack of modern amenities. 8 rooms. Check-in 2 pm, check-out noon. High-speed Internet access, wireless Internet access. Restaurant. Business center. **$**

## Restaurants

**★ ★ ALPENGLOW RESTAURANT.** *George Parks Hwy, mile 238.2, Denali National Park and Preserve (99755). Phone 907/683-8720; toll-free 866/683-8500; fax 907/683-8599. www.denalialaska.com.* This spacious, lodge-style restaurant at the Grande Denali Lodge (see) features a menu of Alaskan and traditional American dishes prepared with the freshest ingredients available. A two-story wall of windows dominates the main room, offering guests the chance to marvel at the stunning, rugged wilderness surrounding the lodge as they enjoy some of the best casual fine dining in the area. American menu. Breakfast, lunch, dinner. Closed mid-Sept-mid-May. Bar. Children's menu. Casual attire. Reservations recommended. **$$$**

**★ CREEKSIDE CAFE.** *George Parks Hwy, mile 224, Denali National Park and Preserve (99755). Phone 907/683-2277; fax 907/683-1558.* This moderately priced diner-style restaurant is located beside Carlo Creek at McKinley Creekside Cabins. With a casual, rustic décor and good home cooking, its a popular spot for locals as well as tourists, especially on weekdays when patrons are treated to live acoustic music. One of the cafés best-known attractions is its annual chili cook-off, a highly competitive but good-natured event held each summer. American menu. Breakfast, lunch, dinner. Closed mid-Sept-mid-May, children's menu. Casual attire. Outdoor seating. **$$**

**★ ★ ★ FORAKER RESTAURANT.** *Talkeetna Spur Rd, mile 12.5, Talkeetna (99676). Phone 907/733-9509; toll-free 888/959-9590; fax 907/733-9545. www.talkeetnalodge.com.* Earthy elegance and rustic charm characterize this upscale dining spot named after 17,400-foot Mount Foraker, visible in the distance beside Mount McKinley. Featuring an award-winning wine selection, fresh Alaskan seafood, and panoramic views of the Alaska Range, the restaurant offers diners a memorable fine dining experience in the heart of the wilderness. As part of the Native-owned Talkeetna Alaskan Lodge (see), the restaurant has skillfully incorporated original Native Alaskan artwork into the décor of the dining area, adding artistic drama to the natural beauty of the room. American menu. Dinner. Closed Sept-Apr. Bar. Casual attire. Reservations recommended. Outdoor seating. **$$$**

**★ MOUNTAIN HIGH PIZZA PIE.** *Main St, Talkeetna (99676). Phone 907/733-1234; fax 907/733-7437.* With purple walls and funky hand-painted accents, this pizza joint in the heart of historic Talkeetna is the kind of place people go when they want quality food but don't want the formality of a sit-down meal. There's no pretentiousness here, nor high prices, and every calzone, pizza, and Italian flatbread sandwich is hand-made to order. Italian menu. Lunch, dinner, late-night. Children's menu. Casual attire. Outdoor seating. **$**

**★ ★ ★ NENANA VIEW GRILLE.** *George Parks Hwy, mile 238.9, Denali National Park and Preserve (). Phone 907/683-8200; toll-free 800/276-7234.* Located at the McKinley Chalet Resort (see) with sweeping views of the Nenana River from both the bar and grill, this restaurant offers some of the best fine dining in the Denali area. Featuring an open kitchen floor plan and a large stone pizza oven, the dining area is filled with beautiful wooden furniture and striking artwork and accent pieces that give the room a sense of rustic elegance. The menu is a mix of haute cuisine, popular Alaskan dishes, and lighter fare and is complemented by an extensive wine selection. American menu. Breakfast, lunch, dinner, late-night. Closed mid-Sept-mid-May. Bar. Children's menu. Casual attire. Reservations recommended. Outdoor seating. **$$$**

**★ ★ THE OVERLOOK BAR AT THE CROW'S NEST.** *George Parks Hwy, mile 238.5, Denali National Park and Preserve (99755). Phone 907/683-2723.* Boasting "the largest beer selection in all of Alaska," this lively bar and grill at the Denali Crow's Nest Log Cabins (see) has become an area institution in the two decades since its founding. Serving burgers, chili, and other kinds of pub grub in its scenic dining area, it is as popular with locals as it is with tourists. American menu. Lunch, dinner. Bar. Casual attire. Outdoor seating. **$**

**★ PANORAMA PIZZA PUB.** *George Parks Hwy, mile 224, Denali National Park and Preserve (99755). Phone 907/683-2523; toll-free 888/322-2523; fax 907/683-2523. www.denaliparkresorts.com.* Serving piping hot pizzas, hefty burgers, over-sized sandwiches, and fresh-baked pastries prepared from scratch, this little restaurant and pub is an ideal place for a quick, inexpensive meal in the Denali area. Located on Carlo Creek south of the Denali Park entrance, it offers cheerful, friendly service in a beautiful wooded setting. Pizza. Breakfast, lunch, dinner. Children's menu. Casual attire. Outdoor seating. **$**

**★ ★ THE PERCH.** *George Parks Hwy, mile 224, Denali National Park and Preserve. Phone 907/683-2523; toll-free 888/322-2523; fax 907/683-2523. www.denaliperchresort.com.* Part of the Denali Perch Resort, this hilltop restaurant specializes in fine-dining cuisine with an emphasis on popular Alaskan seafood and steak dishes. Multiple bay windows offer dramatic, unobstructed views of the wilderness outside, while the restaurant's rustic architecture and open kitchen provide visual interest inside. Everything here is made from scratch, from the loaves of bread served with meals to the soups, salad dressings, and desserts prepared fresh on site each day. The restaurant also has a full bar featuring Alaskan beers and an extensive wine list. American menu. Dinner. Bar. Children's menu. Casual attire. Outdoor seating. **$$**

# Eagle River

This small town 20 minutes north of downtown Anchorage serves as a bedroom community for the city and as a friendly, relaxing, and inexpensive home base for travelers wanting to explore the Anchorage area. The town serves as the one of the main gateways to Chugach State Park, which at nearly half a million acres ranks as the third largest state park in the United States and contains part of the Iditarod National Historic Trail. Twelve miles up Eagle River Road is the Eagle River Nature Center, offering self-guided hiking trails and hands-on interpretive exhibits. Regardless of the season, visitors to Eagle River can find outdoor recreational activities to suit their ages and fitness levels: hiking, biking, fishing, canoeing, rafting, camping, and rock climbing during the summer; ice climbing, dog mushing, downhill skiing, ice skating, and skijoring during the winter. There are also numerous scenic parks and lakes within a short drive of the downtown area that provide excellent family-friendly locales to relax and enjoy the long days of summer.

## What to See and Do

**Eagle River Nature Center.** *32750 Eagle River Rd, Eagle River (99577). Phone 907/694-2108. www.ernc.org.* The Eagle River Nature Center serves as a gateway to the 500,000-acre Chugach State Park. Indoor and outdoor programs offered by the center teach visitors about the kinds of flora, fauna, and geographic features they might encounter inside the park in order to foster greater appreciation of and respect for one of Alaska's most accessible wilderness areas. The center's Web site provides detailed descriptions of program dates, times, and topics. (June-Aug: Sun-Thurs 10 am-5 pm, Fri-Sat 10 am-7 pm; Oct-Apr: Fri-Sun 10 am-5 pm; May, Sept: Tues-Sun 10 am-5 pm) **FREE**

## Special Event

**Bear Paw Festival.** *Eagle River. Various sites. Phone 907/694-4702. www.cer.org/03bearpw.htm.* First held in 1985, the Bear Paw Festival was created to celebrate the beauty and diversity of the Eagle River and Chugiak area. Visitors to the festival can wander from the Renaissance Village, past the highly popular teddy bear picnic, and end up with prime seats at the Slippery Salmon Olympics. Pet-loving tourists might consider joining the Dog & Owner Look-alike Contest, while faded athletes might gravitate toward an event officially called the "300 Yard* Fun Run (*Because after 300 yards it isn't fun anymore!)." Carnival rides and a grand parade top the list of things to do at this unique small-town event. Contact the Chugiak-Eagle River Chamber of Commerce for detailed information about event dates, times, and locations. **FREE**

## Limited-Service Hotels

**★ EAGLE RIVER MOTEL.** *11111 Old Eagle River Rd, Eagle River (99577). Phone 907/694-5000; toll-free 866/256-6835; fax 907/694-1713. www.eaglerivermotel.com.* Summertime prices at this 14-room motel are about half of what you'd pay in Anchorage, about 15 minutes away, and you get the added bonus of quiet, clean, and comfortable accommodations. Set on the south end of town, the Eagle River Motel is located next to a number of shops and restaurants and is within sight of the highway off-ramp, although it's far enough back from the road to be quiet. It's a family-friendly atmosphere where energetic kids and family pets are very welcome, DVDs can be rented for a nominal fee at the front desk, and guests have access to the motel's laundry facilities. Some rooms have views of the Chugach Mountains rising dramatically a few miles from town. 14 rooms. Pets accepted. Complimentary continental breakfast. Check-in 1 pm, check-out 11 am. **$**

**★ MICROTEL INN & SUITES.** *13049 Old Glenn Hwy, Eagle River (99577). Phone 907/622-6000; toll-free 800/771-7171; fax 907/622-6001. www.eaglerivermicrotel.com.* Located on the main street running through Eagle River, the newer Microtel is very close to the highway on-ramp, enabling guests to leave the motel and be in downtown Anchorage in less than 15 minutes. No restaurant or shop in town is more than a three-minute drive away. The cozy lobby has an appealing river rock fireplace, perfect for lounging on plush couches. With reasonable rates in summer, this is a great choice for families, groups, and travelers looking for reliable accommodations close to Anchorage. 60 rooms. Pets accepted. Complimentary continental breakfast. Check-in 3 pm, check-out noon. **$**

## Restaurant

**★ ★ WATERFALLS RESTAURANT.** *12801 Old Glenn Hwy, Suite #7, Eagle River (99577). Phone 907/622-6160; fax 907/622-6162.* Serving breakfast, lunch, and dinner seven days a week, the owners of this quiet, comfortable little restaurant on Eagle River's main road serve up a great selection of American and international dishes. Open from early morning to late at night, it's a worthwhile stop for the hungry traveler. American menu. Breakfast, lunch, dinner. Closed holidays. Children's menu. Casual attire. **$$**

# Fairbanks (C-5)

**Population** 30,224
**Area Code** 907
**Information** Convention and Visitors Bureau, 550 First Ave, 99701; phone toll-free 800/327-5774
**Web Site** www.explorefairbanks.com

The Fairbanks North Star Borough is about the same size as New Jersey but contains fewer than 90,000 people, a third of whom live in Fairbanks. Centrally located only 120 miles north of Denali National Park and 200 miles south of the Arctic Circle, Fairbanks remains today the largest and most important commercial, social, and tourist center in the Interior.

The origins of modern day Fairbanks can be traced to a series of mishaps that occurred to a would-be goldfield merchant named E. T. Barnette. In 1901, in an attempt to capitalize on the need for supplies at the Tanacross goldfields far up the Tanana River, Barnette loaded a sternwheeler with supplies and set out. After the boat ran aground in the Tanana's shallow waters, Barnette decided to try to reach the area via the nearby Chena River, which proved equally unsuccessful. In defeat, he unloaded the boat on the banks of the Chena and set up a small trading post on the spot, very close to where Italian prospector Felix Pedro struck gold the following year. In the ensuing gold rush, Barnette's business prospered and a town eventually grew up around it. Even today, Fairbanks is still very much a river city, with parks and walkways scattered along the Chena River and tour boats

## Summer Solstice Festival.

Fairbanks comes alive during the week leading up to the summer solstice on June 21. The **Midnight Sun 10K Run** is held the third Saturday in June. Beginning at the Patty Center on the University of Alaska Fairbanks campus, the course winds through residential and riverside neighborhoods before finishing at Pioneer Park. Despite, or because of, its 10 pm start time, the run draws thousands of runners and walkers each year, and the atmosphere is distinctly festive.

Another highlight of the summer solstice events is the **Midnight Sun Baseball Game** held at Growden Memorial Park (at the corner of 2nd Ave and Wilbur St) each June 21. Fairbankss hometown boys, the Alaska Goldpanners, hit the field at 10:30 pm for this one-of-a-kind event. Games are held without artificial lights and are stopped only for the singing of the Alaska Flag song during the half-inning break that falls closest to midnight. Detailed information about the team's history and the Midnight Sun Baseball Game can be found at www.goldpanners.com.

The **Midnight Sun Festival** in downtown Fairbanks is held on the day of the solstice and features crafts, food, shopping, a street fair, and live entertainment. Many downtown stores stay open until midnight to accommodate the huge crowds that turn out for this event each year.

and rental kayaks plying the waters. One of the most popular attractions in the downtown area is a historic sternwheeler that takes passengers for scenic rides on the river during the summer.

One of Fairbanks's main distinctions is that it is subject to some of the widest temperature variations of any city on earth. Summertime temperatures occasionally hit the 90 degree mark, while winter temperatures have dipped as low as -62. Despite this, tourists still visit Fairbanks during winter, primarily because the long hours of darkness and cold night air provides excellent opportunities to view the aurora borealis, Alaska's northern lights. During the summer, the aurora is not visible as the area basks under nearly constant daylight.

## What to See and Do

**Alaska Highway.** *Fairbanks. Phone 907/452-1105.* This 1,522-mile-long road from Dawson Creek, British Columbia, to Fairbanks, Alaska was constructed shortly after the attack on Pearl Harbor, when a need for an inland route to Alaska was vital. Highlights along the way include Muncho Lake, Liard Hot springs, Kluane Lake, and the Trans-Alaska Pipeline Crossing.

**Creamer's Field Migratory Waterfowl Refuge.** *1300 College Rd, Fairbanks (99708). Phone 907/452-5162. www.creamersfield.org.* This 1,800-acre site on the northern edge of Fairbanks serves as an important stopover point for thousands of Canada geese, pintails, golden plovers, and other birds on their spring and fall migrations. Although spring is the best time to see large numbers and varieties of birds at the refuge, sandhill cranes, shovelers, and mallards remain in the area all summer. Visitors walking any of the three trails on the property might happen upon more than just birds: moose, snowshoe hares, squirrels, voles, and red foxes are frequently spotted in the area. Admission to the refuge is free, as are nature walks departing from the Farmhouse Visitor Center. (Refuge always open. Farmhouse Visitor Center: summer: daily 10 am-4 pm; winter: Sat noon-4 pm. Free guided nature walks in summer: Tues and Thurs 7 pm, Wed and Sat 9 am. ) **FREE**

**Dalton Highway.** *Fairbanks.* Eighty-six miles north of Fairbanks, the Dalton Highway begins after branching off from the Elliott Highway. Also known by its original name, the North Slope Haul Road, the Dalton is 414 miles long, most of it hard-packed gravel, and traverses some of the most remote and rugged terrain of any highway in Alaska. The highway crosses the Yukon River at mile marker 55. 6, just over 129 miles from Fairbanks, and it is at this point that many tourists choose to take a break before turning around and heading back down the road. For the truly adventurous with plenty of free time, adequate provisions, and a properly equipped vehicle, the road continues for another 359 miles, passing between the Kanuti National Wildlife Refuge to the west and the Yukon Flats National Wildlife Refuge to the east before passing Gates of the Arctic National Park and Preserve on the climb up and over the Brooks Range. The road

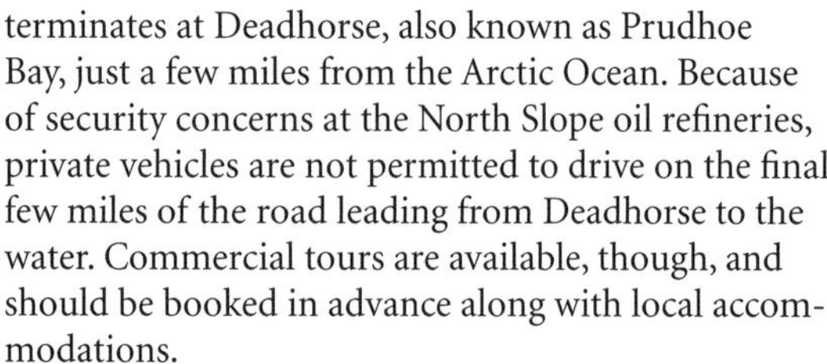

terminates at Deadhorse, also known as Prudhoe Bay, just a few miles from the Arctic Ocean. Because of security concerns at the North Slope oil refineries, private vehicles are not permitted to drive on the final few miles of the road leading from Deadhorse to the water. Commercial tours are available, though, and should be booked in advance along with local accommodations.

**El Dorado Gold Mine.** *Elliott Hwy, mile marker 1.3, Fairbanks (99709). 9 miles N. Phone 907/479-6673; toll-free 866/479-6673. www.eldoradogoldmine.com.* Run by the same family that operates the Riverboat Discovery (see), the El Dorado Gold Mine provides visitors with a chance to watch a real Alaskan gold mine in operation. The two-hour tour begins with a narrated ride on the Tanana Valley Railroad, a narrow-gauge line which travels through some of Fairbanks's original gold fields. Upon arrival at El Dorado mine, guests are given a guided tour of the facility and are taught how to pan for gold. Reservations are strongly recommended. Shuttle service is available; contact the company for details. (Mid-May-mid-Sept: 9:45 am and 3 pm, except Sat, when there is only a 3 pm departure) **$$$$**

**Pioneer Park.** *Airport Way and Peger Rd, Fairbanks (99707). Phone 907/459-1087. www.co.fairbanks.ak.us/parks&rec/pioneerpark.* Formerly known as Alaskaland, this 44-acre park set along the Chena River in the middle of Fairbanks is filled with hundreds of artifacts and mementos of the areas' pioneer past. The 230-foot-long sternwheeler *Nenana*, former belle of the Yukon River route, was transported to the park in 1966 and was faithfully restored to its original glory in 1992. The ship's hold now contains a large diorama depicting life on the Yukon and Tanana rivers during the era of the riverboats. Other highlights of the park include Gold Rush Town, a collection of 35 of Fairbanks's historic buildings transported to the park and restored to serve as a link to the town's past. Adult can also spend time exploring the Pioneer Air Museum and the Alaska Centennial Center for the Arts, while younger visitors can play miniature golf, rent bicycles, explore Mining Valley, or take a ride on the narrow-gauge Crooked Creek & Whiskey Island Railroad. (Park: year-round, admission free. Gold Rush Town and museums: Memorial Day through Labor Day, daily 11 am-9 pm; fees. )

**Riverboat *Discovery*.** *1975 Discovery Dr, Fairbanks (99709). Phone 907/479-6673; toll-free 866/479-6673. www.alaskaone.com/discovery.* Run by an Alaskan family with more than a century of Alaskan riverboating experience, this classic sternwheeler carries tourists on a 3 1/2-hour narrated cruise on the Chena and Tanana rivers. Highlights of the trip include stops at the riverside home of Susan Butcher, four-time winner of the Iditarod Trail Sled Dog race, and at the Old Chena Indian Village, where visitors can experience Alaskan Native culture firsthand and watch a sled dog demonstration. Reservations are required. (Mid-May-mid-Sept: Sun-Fri 8:45 am and 2 pm, Sat 2 pm only) **$$$$**

**Tours.** *Fairbanks. Phone toll-free 800/544-2206. www.graylineofalaska.com.* Gray Line of Alaska offers package tours around Alaska (up to 11 days) as well as sternwheeler, gold-panning, flightseeing, and other tours around Fairbanks.

**University of Alaska Museum of the North.** *907 Yukon Dr, Fairbanks (99775). Phone 907/474-7505. www.uaf.edu/museum.* Located on the campus of the University of Alaska Fairbanks, the Museum of the North houses more than 1. 3 million artifacts relating to Alaska's history and culture. The museum is divided into five galleries, each representing one of Alaska's ecological regions: Southwest, Southcentral, Southeast, Interior, and Western & Artic Coast. Exhibits in the galleries range from a mummified Ice Age bison, affectionately known as Blue Babe, to intricately woven Aleut baskets and Eskimo ivory carvings. During the summer, visitors can stroll among sculptures in the garden outside or sit and watch construction of the newest museum galleries, scheduled for completion by summer 2005. (Mid-May-mid-Sept: daily 9 am-7 pm; mid-Sept-mid-May: Mon-Fri 9 am-5 pm, Sat-Sun noon-5 pm) **$**

## Special Events

**Aurora Borealis (Northern Lights).** *Fairbanks.* One of Alaska's most spectacular and cheapest shows, the best time to see the spectacular streaks of green and red light that make up the Aurora Borealis is from about 10 pm until 2 am on nights with a new moon, although the display is frequently visible at other times. The Web site of the Geophysical Institute at the University of Anchorage (www.gi.alaska.edu) provides daily forecasts for aurora activity, as well as easy-to-understand explanations of the causes of the lights. Visitors should keep in mind that this phenomena is visible in Fairbanks only from late August until mid-April; summer visitors won't see it at all, as the sky never gets dark enough for the lights to be visible.

**World Eskimo-Indian Olympics.** *Big Dipper Ice Arena, 1920 Lathrop St, Fairbanks (99701). Phone 907/452-6646. www.weio.org.* Since 1961, this annual four-day gathering of Native Alaskans has celebrated the skills, traditions, artistry, and spirit of Alaska's six major tribes. Each event in the olympics is based on a traditional Eskimo or Indian hunting, fishing, or survival activity and is designed to measure the competitors' athletic prowess and mental toughness. Strength and endurance of pain are tested in the Knuckle Hop, Ear Weight, and Arm Pull competitions, for example, while athleticism and agility are measured in the One-Hand Reach, Kneel Jump, and Blanket Toss events. The olympics also focuses on the artistry and beauty of Native cultures with arts and crafts booths, performances of traditional dances, and a Miss WEIO pageant. Multiday passes are available. Begins on the third Wednesday in July. **$$**

**World Ice Art Championships.** *Philips Field Rd, Fairbanks (99708). Near Peger Rd. Phone 907/451-8250; fax 907/456-1951. www.icealaska.com.* At the beginning of March each year, ice sculptors from around the world descend on Fairbanks to compete for the title of World Ice Art Champion. The 11-day event consists of three separate contests: single block sculpting, multi-block sculpting, and the Fairbanks Open, a less competitive event open to amateurs. While the competition is underway, visitors are permitted to wander around the Ice Park watching the artists at work. At the conclusion of the contest, the sculptures are outfitted with electric lights and the finished works remain on display until the last Sunday in March. Season passes and group discounts are available. **$$**

## Limited-Service Hotels

**★ ASPEN HOTEL FAIRBANKS.** *4580 Old Airport Rd, Fairbanks (99701). Phone 907/457-2288; toll-free 888/595-2151; fax 907/457-2297. www.aspenhotelsak.com.* Located close to Fairbanks International Airport and the Parks Highway, this clean, comfortable hotel features a wide range of complimentary amenities that appeal to business professionals and families alike. Guests of the hotel enjoy the use of an indoor pool, small exercise room, business center, and coin-operated laundry facility and are treated to a deluxe continental breakfast every morning. 97 rooms. Complimentary continental breakfast. Check-in 3 pm, check-out 11 am. High-speed Internet access. Indoor pool. Airport transportation available. Business center. **$**

**★ ★ BRIDGEWATER HOTEL.** *723 1st Ave, Fairbanks (99701). Phone 907/452-6661; toll-free 800/528-4916; fax 907/452-6126. www.fountainheadhotels.com.* This attractive boutique hotel sits on the banks of the Chena River in downtown Fairbanks, only a short walk to the Visitor Center, Alaskan Railroad depot, and Pioneer Park. Light and bright interiors and the use of soft pastels and floral fabrics give it a warm, folksy charm that sets it apart from larger, standardized hotels. 94 rooms. Closed mid-Sept-mid-May. Check-in 2 pm, check-out 11 am. Restaurant. Airport transportation available. **$**

**★ ★ THE CAPTAIN BARTLETT INN.** *1411 Airport Way, Fairbanks (99701). Phone 907/452-1888; toll-free 800/544-7528; fax 907/452-7674. www.captainbartlettinn.com.* Set in the middle of the main shopping and entertainment area of Fairbanks, this large hotel was built to resemble an Alaskan wilderness lodge. From the totem poles at the entrance to the stuffed musk ox and brown bear in the lobby, the hotel provides its guests with a strong sense of Alaska's history, culture, and grandeur. 197 rooms. Pets accepted; fee. Check-in 3 pm, check-out 11 am. Restaurant, bar. Airport transportation available. **$**

**★ ★ CHENA HOT SPRINGS RESORT.** *565 Chena Hot Springs Rd, Fairbanks (99712). Phone 907/451-8104; toll-free 800/478-4681; fax 907/451-8151. www.chenahotsprings.com.* One of the Interior's most popular and most easily accessed destinations for wilderness adventure and quiet relaxation, this 440-acre resort an hour's drive northeast of Fairbanks is surrounded by the 250,000-acre Chena River State Recreation Area. With a large selection of cozy rooms to choose from and Alaskan wilderness in all directions, the resort appeals to every budget and every type of adventurer. Originally constructed to allow guests to take advantage of the steaming mineral springs in the area, the resort is now at its busiest during the winter when its remoteness results in fantastic opportunities to see, and sometimes hear, the Aurora Borealis dancing across the cold dark sky. 90 rooms. Pets accepted; fee. Check-in 3 pm, check-out 11 am. Restaurant, bar. Indoor pool, whirlpool. **$$**

**★ COMFORT INN CHENA RIVER.** *1908 Chena Landings Loop, Fairbanks (99701). Phone 907/479-8080; toll-free 800/228-5150; fax 907/479-8063. www.choicehotels.com.* The Fairbanks Comfort Inn hotel stands out from most other hotels in the chain because of its fantastic setting by the Chena River near stands of trees frequented by moose and other wildlife. Located near Pioneer Park and only a short drive from downtown, this sparkling, contemporary hotel has an appealing, backcountry feel that belies its central Fairbanks location. 74 rooms. Pets accepted, some restrictions; fee. Complimentary continental breakfast. Check-in 4 pm, check-out 1 pm. High-speed Internet access. Indoor pool, whirlpool. Business center. **$**

★ **FAIRBANKS HOTEL.** *517 3rd Ave, Fairbanks. Phone 907/456-6441; toll-free 888/329-4685; fax 907/456-1792. www.fbxhotl.com.* Travelers looking for budget accommodation in Fairbanks should check out this small independent hotel, the oldest in Fairbanks. With an eye-catching art deco exterior and small but comfortable rooms, it offers guests basic accommodations, good service, and affordable prices. About one-third of the rooms have private baths; all have wireless Internet access. 36 rooms. Check-in 4 pm, check-out 11 am. Wireless Internet access. Airport transportation available. **$**

★ ★ **PIKES WATERFRONT LODGE.** *1850 Hoselton Rd, Fairbanks (99703). Phone 907/456-4500; toll-free 877/774-2400; fax 907/456-4515. www.pikeslodge.com.* Nestled beside the banks of the Chena River across from the airport, this lodge is a relatively new addition to Fairbanks's accommodation scene. Combining striking architectural features with high-quality Alaskan-themed artwork and furnishings, it creates a sense of rustic elegance in an attractive setting. All rooms are spacious and comfortable; some come with features like fireplaces, whirlpools, balconies, and river views. 208 rooms. Pets accepted; fee. Check-in 3 pm, check-out 11 am. Restaurant, bar. Fitness room. Business center. **$$**

★ ★ **REGENCY FAIRBANKS HOTEL.** *95 10th Ave, Fairbanks (99701). Phone 907/452-3200; fax 907/452-6505. www.regencyfairbankshotel.com.* Situated on the western edge of downtown, this medium-sized hotel contains a variety of different room types, from standard rooms to deluxe suites to rooms with their own whirlpool tubs. All guest rooms, regardless of size, feature full kitchens and designated work areas and guests are encouraged to call the 24-hour bell desk whenever they need assistance or have a special request. 129 rooms. Pets accepted; fee. Check-in 3 pm, check-out 11 am. High-speed Internet access. Restaurant, bar. Fitness room. Business center. **$$**

★ ★ **RIVER'S EDGE RESORT.** *4200 Boat St, Fairbanks (99709). Phone 800/770-3343; toll-free 800/770-3343; fax 907/474-3665. www.riversedge.net.* 94 rooms. Closed mid-Sept-early May. Check-in 3 pm, check-out 11 am. Restaurant, bar. **$$**

★ ★ **SOPHIE STATION HOTEL.** *1717 University Ave, Fairbanks (99709). Phone 907/479-3650; toll-free 800/528-4916; fax 907/479-7951. www.fountainheadhotels.com.* Offering spacious and comfortable lodging close to the airport and Fairbanks's main shopping areas, this hotel caters to business and leisure travelers not content to settle for average accommodations. All rooms in this hotel are suites with private balconies, full kitchens, and upscale furnishings including artwork by well-known Alaskan artists. The hotel has it's own restaurant, Zach's (see), which is open for breakfast, lunch, and dinner. Other popular amenities include high-speed Internet stations, a free shuttle service to the airport, and discount passes to a well-equipped local gym. 148 rooms, all suites. Check-in 2 pm, check-out 11 am. Restaurant, bar. Airport transportation available. **$$**

★ ★ **SPRINGHILL SUITES BY MARRIOTT FAIRBANKS.** *575 1st Ave, Fairbanks (99701). Phone 907/451-6552; fax 907/451-6553.* With downtown Fairbanks literally at its doorstep, this all-suite hotel, part of the Marriott chain, offers guests a clean, comfortable place to stay at reasonable rates. Surrounded by shops, restaurants, and numerous riverside walks and attractions, the hotel appeals to just about every taste, from families who appreciate its convenient location, on-site pool, and free continental breakfast to business travelers who are drawn to it for its business center, spacious rooms, and professional staff. 140 rooms, all suites. Complimentary continental breakfast. Check-in 3pm, check-out noon. High-speed Internet access. Restaurant, bar. Fitness room. Indoor pool, whirlpool. Airport transportation available. Business center. **$$**

★ ★ **WEDGEWOOD RESORT.** *212 Wedgewood Dr, Fairbanks (99701). Phone 907/452-1442; toll-free 800/528-4916; fax 907/451-8184. www.fountainheadhotels.com.* Despite being only a mile from downtown, this attractive, campus-style hotel resort on the north side of Fairbanks has a real wilderness feel to it. Guests have the choice of staying in suites or standard rooms, all of which are outfitted with quality furnishings and tasteful accents. The resort is home to the Alaska Bird Observatory and provides easy access to the walking trails and visitor displays found at Creamer's Field Migratory Bird Refuge next door. 157 rooms. Closed mid-Sept-mid-May. Check-in 4 pm, check-out 11 am. Restaurant, bar. Business center. **$$**

★ ★ **WESTMARK FAIRBANKS HOTEL.** *813 Noble St, Fairbanks (99701). Phone 907/456-7722; toll-free 800/544-0970; fax 907/451-7478. www.westmarkhotels.com.* With the recent completion of an eight-story tower addition, this full-service hotel nearly tripled its capacity and now offers guests some of the newest, most spacious rooms in town. As a key property of the Holland America Line Company, the hotel is held to strict standards relating to the levels of quality, comfort, and service it provides. The result is an upscale hotel staffed by friendly, knowledgeable professionals. Its location near most downtown attractions makes it an appealing place to stay for independent travelers and families. 400 rooms. Pets accepted. Check-in noon, check-out noon. High-speed Internet access. Two restaurants, bar. Fitness room. Airport transportation available. **$$**

## Full-Service Hotel

★ ★ ★ **FAIRBANKS PRINCESS RIVERSIDE LODGE.** *4477 Pikes Landing Rd, Fairbanks (99709). Phone 907/455-4477; toll-free 800/426-0500; fax 907/455-4476. www.princesslodges.com.* Set along the banks of the Chena River, this large, semi-secluded hotel is one of the most upscale in Fairbanks. The exterior of the property is painted a striking blue and features a huge open deck overlooking the river, perfect for mid-afternoon lazing and wildlife viewing. The interior, in contrast, is much more lodge-like, with intimate dining and lounge areas, log and stone architectural features, and soft, plush furniture. Open year-round, the hotel is a popular spot for cruise ship passengers during the summer months and northern lights watchers in the winter. 325 rooms. Check-in 3:30 pm, check-out 11 am. Restaurant, bar. Fitness room. Airport transportation available. Business center. **$$**

## Restaurants

★ **BAKERY RESTAURANT.** *69 College Rd, Fairbanks (99701). Phone 907/456-8600; fax 907/456-8602.* This family- and budget-friendly diner-style restaurant just north of downtown serves standard home-style meals all day long. The real draw, though, are the fresh-baked pies, cakes, and other baked goods on display right inside the front door, tempting guests as soon as they walk in. Breakfast is served all day. American menu. Breakfast, lunch, dinner. Children's menu. Casual attire. **$**

★ ★ **BOBBY'S.** *126 N Turner St, Fairbanks (99701). Phone 907/456-3222; fax 907/457-4972.* This cozy, family-owned restaurant near the river in downtown Fairbanks offers a range of traditional Greek and American entrées, including the house specialty, Greek-style rack of lamb. The service is friendly and attentive and the atmosphere decidedly low-key, with attractive leather banquettes and walls covered with pictures of Greece. American, Greek menu. Dinner. Closed holidays. Bar. Casual attire. Reservations recommended. **$$**

★ ★ **CHENA HOT SPRINGS RESORT RESTAURANT.** *565 Chena Hot Springs Rd, Fairbanks (99712). Phone 907/451-8104.* Located at Chena Hot Springs Resort (see), an hour northeast of Fairbanks, this log cabin-style restaurant is the perfect place to enjoy a leisurely meal after a day spent exploring the surrounding wilderness or soaking in the resort's hot springs. The menu features regional Alaskan favorites along with standard American fare, and the décor is rustic Alaska, making for a unique, highly enjoyable dining experience. American menu. Breakfast, lunch, dinner. Bar. Children's menu. Casual attire. Reservations recommended. Outdoor seating. **$$**

★ ★ **CHENA'S AT THE RIVER'S EDGE.** *4200 Boat St, Fairbanks (99709). Phone 907/474-3601; fax 907/474-8023. www.riversedge.net.* This quaint restaurant at River's Edge Resort (see) offers guests a fascinating glimpse into Fairbanks's pioneer past, with artifacts and furnishings dating from the early 20th century. During summer, the outdoor deck beside the river is a popular place to sit and enjoy the savory Alaskan entrées and extensive dessert menu that have made the restaurant a local favorite for years. American menu. Breakfast, lunch, dinner. Closed mid-Sept-early May. Bar. Children's menu. Casual attire. Reservations recommended. Outdoor seating. **$$**

★ **DILLINGER'S RESTAURANT.** *720 Old Steese Hwy, Fairbanks (99701). Phone 907/456-1830; fax 907/456-1544.* With red leather booths, polished chrome fixtures, and spotlessly clean tables, this family-friendly diner just north of the downtown area is a

real local hangout. The menu is typical '50s diner fare, from hamburgers and sandwiches to soft drinks and fries. Outdoor seating is available during the summer. American menu. Breakfast, lunch, dinner. Children's menu. Casual attire. **$**

**★ GAMBARDELLA'S.** *706 2nd Ave, Fairbanks (99701). Phone 907/456-3417; fax 907/456-3420. www.gambardellas.com.* The interior of this well-known downtown restaurant has been designed to resemble a small town in the Italian countryside, complete with a trompe l'oeil street scene, wrought iron window railings, faux stone walls and foliage, and a full-sized vegetable cart. House specialties include homemade Italian bread, "The Mother of All Lasagnas," and a very addictive tiramisu. Italian menu. Lunch, dinner. Children's menu. Casual attire. Reservations recommended. Outdoor seating. **$$**

**★ GERALDO'S RESTAURANT.** *701 College Rd, Fairbanks (99701). Phone 907/452-2299; fax 907/452-7634.* From the sound of Dean Martin crooning on the sound system to the large original oil painting of Don "The Godfather" Corleone, this restaurant embraces its Italian roots with a passion. Featuring award-winning hand-tossed pizzas, huge servings of traditional Italian entrées, and a special "Bambino's Menu," it's a warm, inviting, place to go for a big meal. Italian menu. Lunch, dinner. Children's menu. Casual attire. Reservations recommended. Outdoor seating. **$$**

**★ GOLDEN SHANG HAI.** *1900 Airport Way, Fairbanks (99701). Phone 907/451-1100; fax 907/425-2530.* Serving a wide variety of Mandarin and Szechuan dishes in an ornate dining room filled with Chinese decorative touches, this midtown restaurant is known for its good food and good values. The 60-item buffet, which includes just about every Chinese dish imaginable as well as a selection of Japanese sushi plates, is particularly popular with diners. Chinese menu. Lunch, dinner. Casual attire. **$**

**★ IVORY JACK'S.** *2591 Goldstream Rd, Fairbanks (99709). Phone 907/455-6665; fax 907/455-4254.* Located about 20 minutes from Fairbanks in Gold Stream Valley, this long-time local hangout is part sports bar, part Wild West saloon. Patrons can choose from a long list of burgers, sandwiches, appetizers, and pizzas or can order from the fine dining menu, which features an assortment of New York strip steaks, fresh Alaskan seafood, and barbecued ribs. Bands play in the saloon on Friday nights; Tuesdays and Saturdays are "open mic" amateur nights. American menu. Breakfast, lunch, dinner. Bar. Children's menu. Casual attire. **$$**

**★ ★ LEMON GRASS THAI CUISINE.** *388 Old Chena Pump Rd, Fairbanks (99709). Phone 907/456-2200.* This appealing little restaurant on the extreme western edge of Fairbanks is a family-owned operation that focuses on serving authentic Thai dishes in a relaxed setting. All meals are prepared entirely from scratch and are served in a Thai-themed dining room filled with hand-carved wooden accent pieces, Thai drums, and ornate works of art. Thai menu. Lunch, dinner. Closed Sun. Children's menu. Casual attire. Reservations recommended. Valet parking. **$**

**★ ★ PUMP HOUSE RESTAURANT.** *796 Chena Pump Rd, Fairbanks (99709). Phone 907/479-8452; fax 907/479-8432. www.pumphouse.com.* This restaurant is a must for visitors interested in eating well and learning about the history of the area. Housed in a former pump house once used to help in mine dredging operations, the restaurant is filled with antiques and artifacts of those long ago days. Proud home to the "Farthest North Oyster Bar in the World," the restaurant serves Alaskan cuisine along with less common regional dishes like reindeer steaks and wild musk ox ground sirloin. Throughout the summer, the outdoor riverside patio is a great place to watch the majestic riverboat Discovery paddle its way up the river. American menu. Lunch, dinner. Bar. Children's menu. Casual attire. Reservations recommended. Outdoor seating. **$$**

**★ SAM'S SOURDOUGH CAFE.** *3702 Cameron St, Fairbanks (99709). Phone 907/479-0523.* Often referred to as "Sourdough Sam's" by the hordes of locals that head there each day, this cheerful diner-style restaurant is located right beside the University of Alaska Fairbanks. As a hometown favorite, it's almost always noisy and chaotic, but in an appealing, small-town, friendly way. Patrons can order lunch and dinner items, but the main draw is unquestionably the breakfast menu, available all day. American menu. Breakfast, lunch, dinner. Casual attire. Outdoor seating. **$**

**★ ★ SEÑOR FLANNIGAN'S STEAK PIT.** *354 Old Steese Hwy, Fairbanks (99701). Phone 907/451-6100.* This oddly named restaurant serves an eclectic mix of American and Mexican dishes in a faux alfresco dining room complete with plastic foliage and twinkling "star" lights overhead. Adding to the unique décor is a stunning series of illuminated stained glass panels above the long cantina bar depicting pueblo scenes. With reasonable prices, a large menu, and a game room, it's an enjoyable, family-friendly place to dine. American, Mexican menu. Lunch, dinner, late-night. Bar. Children's menu. Casual attire. Reservations recommended. **$$**

**★ SOAPY SMITH'S.** *541 2nd Ave, Fairbanks (99701). Phone 907/451-8380; fax 907/451-8383.* Named after the most notorious criminal in Alaskan Gold Rush history, this downtown restaurant serves reasonably priced standard American cuisine with local influences and is a must for gold rush and pioneer history buffs. Authentic memorabilia, photographs, and newspaper articles about life in Alaska at the turn of the last century crowd the walls, and the proprietor loves to regale diners with tales of Soapy Smiths colorful life. American menu. Lunch, dinner. Closed Sun; holidays. Casual attire. **$$**

**★ ★ TURTLE CLUB.** *2098 Old Steese Hwy N, Fox (99712). Phone 907/457-3883; fax 907/457-4789.* This spacious, low-key restaurant 11 miles north of Fairbanks has earned a solid reputation for great food thanks to a menu featuring fresh Alaskan seafood and choice cuts of prime rib. Adding to the appeal of the place is a large outdoor seating area and an enormous collection of turtle figurines, the inspiration behind the restaurant's name. The on-site bar offers a separate menu and a low-lit, intimate dining area for those looking for privacy. American menu. Dinner. Closed Jan 1, Dec 25; also Tues-Thurs week of Thanksgiving. Bar. Casual attire. Reservations recommended. Outdoor seating. **$$**

**★ ★ TWO RIVERS LODGE.** *4968 Chena Hot Springs Rd, Fairbanks (99712). Phone 907/488-6815. www.tworiverslodge.com.* Located northeast of Fairbanks on Chena Hot Springs Road, this log-cabin style restaurant is set in a pine forest on the shores of a small lake. Open every day during the summer, it really comes alive from Thursday through Sunday when the outdoor Tuscan Garden section is open. Offering a wide range of Mediterranean dishes featuring fresh local produce, imported meats and cheeses, and herbs grown on the property, the Garden serves "healthy and satisfying" cuisine in a beautiful wilderness setting. American menu. Dinner. Bar. Children's menu. Casual attire. Reservations recommended. Outdoor seating. **$$**

**★ ★ VALLATA.** *2190 Goldstream Rd, Fairbanks (99709). Phone 907/455-7773.* Located in Gold Stream Valley, 20 minutes from downtown Fairbanks, this upscale family-run restaurant specializes in fine Italian and American cuisine made fresh to order. Friday and Saturday nights, guests are treated to live piano music as they enjoy sweeping views of the surrounding wilderness from the comfort of the elegant, intimate dining room. Italian, American menu. Dinner. Closed Mon. Bar. Children's menu. Casual attire. Reservations recommended. **$$**

**★ ★ WILD IRIS CAFE.** *900 Noble St, Fairbanks (99701). Phone 907/455-4747; fax 907/455-4895.* This small café at the Golden Nugget Hotel offers an appealing range of home-style American entrées in a casual, unpretentious setting. The dining room décor features lots of iris prints and spring colors, while the saloon has a more earthy feel to it, courtesy of an enormous circular stone fireplace, soft lighting, and polished wooden furniture. Both rooms share the same menu and are open long hours during the summer. American menu. Breakfast, lunch, dinner. Bar. Casual attire. **$$**

**★ ★ ZACH'S RESTAURANT.** *1717 University Ave S, Fairbanks (99709). Phone 907/479-3650.* This chic restaurant at the Sophie Station Hotel (see) offers fine continental cuisine served with style in a relaxed, intimate setting. New dishes are constantly being added to the menu, but perennial favorites include the Alaskan halibut fillet and the grilled lamb chops. Dessert favorites include a cheesecake burrito described on the menu as being "shamefully good." During the summer, sheltered outdoor dining is available. American menu. Breakfast, lunch, dinner, brunch. Bar. Children's menu. Casual attire. Reservations recommended. Outdoor seating. **$$**

# Gates of the Arctic and National Park and Preserve

**Web Site** www.nps.gov/gaar

Sprawling and remote, Gates of the Arctic National Park & Preserve offers solitude and exceptional natural beauty, along with endless opportunities for wilderness adventure. Only the strongest and best-trained outdoor enthusiasts should consider venturing into the park's 8. 5 million acres of untamed wilderness. Situated above the Arctic Circle, within the rugged peaks and glaciated valleys of northern Alaska's Brooks Range, Gates of the Arctic possesses no roads or established trails. Before trekking off into the park, recreational travelers are required to complete a backcountry orientation program at either the Bettles

Ranger Station, Coldfoot Visitor Center, or Anaktuvuk Pass Ranger Station.

For the trained and hardy, superior wilderness recreation awaits, including river running, dog mushing, and mountaineering. The park is home to Dall sheep, caribou, wolves, moose, grizzlies, black bears, and more than 100 species of birds. Vegetation ranges from boreal forest to alpine tundra. Gates of the Arctic boasts six congressionally designated Wild Rivers and two National Natural Landmarks, as well as a biosphere reserve. The park is best accessed via an air taxi from Fairbanks to either Anaktuvuk Pass or Bettles. Alternately, visitors can take the Dalton Highway from Fairbanks 250 miles north to the Coldfoot Visitor Center, which is open Memorial Day-Labor Day.

# Girdwood

*See also Anchorage*

**Area Code** 907

Forty miles south of Anchorage, nestled among the Turnagain Arm and spectacular Mount Alyeska, Girdwood has evolved from a gold-mining town into Alaska's only year-round resort community. Driving from Anchorage, travelers may see Dall sheep, moose, bald eagles, or Beluga whales in the Turnagain Arm. Girdwood features many bed-and-breakfasts, restaurants, shops, and boutiques and offers many opportunities for outdoor adventure, including kayaking, rafting, hiking, and fishing.

## What to See and Do

**Alaska Wildlife Conservation Center.** *Seward Hwy, mile 79, Portage Glacier (99587). On the W side of the highway, just north of the Portage Glacier exit. Phone 907/783-2025; fax 907/783-2370. www.alaskawildlife.org.* This 140-acre wildlife park 43 miles south of Anchorage, formerly known as Big Game Alaska, was established as a nonprofit refuge for orphaned, injured, and ailing Alaskan wildlife. Now home to hundreds of animals from grizzlies, bison, and moose to smaller creatures like beavers, foxes, and porcupines, the center aims to provide care and rehabilitative therapy to the animals while educating the public about them. Visitors can view the animals up close in outdoor enclosures designed to replicate the natural habitats in which the animals would normally be found. (Apr-mid-May: daily 10 am to 6 pm; mid-May-mid-Sept: daily 8 am-8 pm; mid-Sept-Mar: daily 10 am-5 pm) **$**

**Anton Anderson Memorial Tunnel.** *Whittier/Portage Glacier Access Rd, Girdwood. 6.5 miles from junction Seward Hwy, 18 miles S. Phone 907/566-2244; toll-free 877/611-2586. www.dot.state.ak.us/creg/whittiertunnel/index.htm.* Opened in 2000, this 2. 5-mile tunnel connecting the Portage Glacier area with the town of Whittier is the only one in the world that accommodates alternate passage of vehicles and trains over the same surface. Cars drive on a concrete roadway that has rail lines embedded in it, allowing drivers smooth passage through the narrow, one-lane tunnel. Once all cars are clear of the tunnel on one end, vehicular traffic is allowed into the tunnel heading in the opposite direction. The passage of trains through the tunnel is handled in the same way, with vehicles being held up on both ends while the rail cars are in the tunnel. Although the tunnel serves the practical purpose of linking the sleepy tourist town of Whittier to the Seward Highway, it has become a tourist attraction in its own right owing to its unique construction and designation as North America's longest highway tunnel. Schedule information is available by phone and over the radio at AM 530 (Whittier) and AM 1610 (Portage). Hours vary widely by day and date: check the tunnel Web site or call ahead for times and weather updates. Vehicle toll varies depending on length and type of vehicle; Class A vehicles pay $12 round-trip.

**Crow Creek Mine.** *Crow Creek Rd, Girdwood (99587). Phone 907/278-8060. www.crowcreekgoldmine.com.* Visiting this former gold mining camp 40 miles south of Anchorage is like stepping back in time to the Gold Rush era. Built in 1898, the camp has changed very little in the past hundred years, with small shacks made of rough-hewn timber and logs, unpaved trails, and wagon wheels and mining implements scattered about. Visitors to the camp can view the original bunkhouse, mess hall, blacksmith shop, meat cache, ice house, and barn or, for a small fee, can try their hand at gold panning in Crow Creek. Overnight camping is available on-site, and access is provided to the extensive trail system inside the surrounding Chugach National Forest. (Mid-May-mid-Sept: daily 9 am-6 pm) **$**

## Special Event

**Girdwood Forest Fair.** *Girdwood Fairgrounds, Alyeska Hwy, Mile 2.2, Girdwood. Phone 907/566-3039. www.girdwoodforestfair.com.* Since its inception in 1976, this small-town nature festival has grown into a wildly popular showcase for Alaskan bands and now ranks as the largest free music festival in Alaska. More than 30 groups perform on two stages over the course of the weekend, playing everything from bluegrass and country to pop and rock. As a way to preserve the event's "country fair" ambience, organizers insist that vendors sell only handcrafted goods, thereby eliminating the standard array of mass-produced T-shirts and trinkets sold at most festivals. A chief benefit of this focus on artistry and originality is that it gives fair attendees a chance to meet the artists behind the handicrafts, garments, and works of art they intend to buy. First weekend in July. **FREE**

## Restaurants

★ **ALPINE BAKERY.** *1 Alyeska Hwy, Girdwood (99587). Phone 907/783-2550.* American and European style baked goods and light dinner. American menu. Breakfast, lunch, dinner. **$**

★ **THE DOUBLE MUSKIE INN.** *1 Crow Creek Rd, Girdwood (99587). Phone 907/783-2822.* Renowned local restaurant serving Cajun preparations of local ingredients. Cajun menu. Lunch, dinner. Closed Sun. **$$**

# Glacier Bay National Park and Preserve

**Web Site** www.nps.gov/glba

Glacier Bay National Park & Preserve awes visitors with spectacular scenery that is quintessential Alaska, a varied but universally beautiful and pristine landscape of tidewater glaciers, sheltered coves, deep fjords, freshwater lakes, and snow-capped mountain peaks. The explorer George Vancouver led an expedition here in 1794, bringing a survey crew commanded by Lt. Joseph Whidbey, who charted the narrow passage of the Icy Strait. Whidbey's chart showed Glacier Bay to be a small indentation abutting "solid compact mountains of ice." When legendary naturalist John Muir visited the area in 1879, the bay had grown considerably larger, with the glacier retreating more than 30 miles inland. The glacier's retreat has continued ever since, creating a living laboratory for the study of glaciers and the recolonization of newly exposed land. Recolonizing species on the ground include coyotes, wolves, moose, and brown bears, while humpback and killer whales, Stellar sea lions, and otters have moved into the bay. Glacier Bay was set aside as a national monument in 1925, becoming a national park and preserve in 1980. It was recognized as a UN Biosphere Reserve in 1986.

Like many of Alaska's national parks, accessibility can prove challenging. No roads lead to Glacier Bay, so most visitors arrive by boat. Tour boat, cruise ship, and charter boat services are available, and pleasure boats are welcome, although a free permit is required. Many boat tours begin and end in the small town of Gustavus, which sits 75 miles south of Glacier Bay. Air taxis shuttle passengers between Gustavus and Juneau, roughly 50 miles to the east. Glacier Bay has a maritime climate, with cool summers and mild winters—winter lows at sea level rarely dip below 25 degrees Fahrenheit.

# Haines (E-8)

**Population** 1,811
**Area Code** 907

Haines is a town rich in history and natural beauty. Located near the northern end of the Inside Passage, it's surrounded on all sides by soaring mountains, deepwater inlets, and miles and miles of rugged forests and massive glaciers. In 1898, the Klondike Gold Rush flooded the town with prospectors heading up the nearby Dalton Trail on their way north. Soon after the rush ended, the US Army decided to build its first permanent army post in Alaska on the outskirts of town. In 1972, the fort was listed on the National Register of Historic Places and in 1978 it was designated a National Historic Landmark. To this day, it remains a fascinating visual link to Haines's storied past. Visitors interested in learning more about the area can visit the Sheldon Museum, home to a fascinating mix of pioneer and Gold Rush memorabilia as well as an extensive collection of Chilkat Tlingit art and artifacts.

One of the highlights of Haines's event calendar is its annual Alaska Bald Eagle Festival. Held during the middle of November, the festival celebrates the thousands of bald eagles that congregate in the area to feed on late spawning salmon in the Chilkat River. Photographers and birdwatchers can enjoy the spectacle from any number of highway pullouts adjacent to the 48,000 acre Alaska Chilkat Bald Eagle Preserve northwest of town.

## What to See and Do

**American Bald Eagle Foundation Interpretive Center.** *2nd St and Haines Hwy, Haines (99827). Phone 907/766-3094. www.baldeagles.org.* With a focus on protecting and preserving bald eagles and their habitat, this non-profit foundation aims to achieve its goals by teaching people about bald eagles and the environmental factors necessary for them to flourish in places like Alaska. Located only 20 miles from the Chilkat Bald Eagle Preserve, where upwards of 3,000 eagles congregate each winter, the interpretive center has incorporated more than 180 specimens of fish and wildlife from the preserve into a massive indoor diorama that depicts the interaction of each species in the local ecosystem. The center also contains a screening room where visitors can watch a video showing scenes from the annual migration of eagles to the area, something that most people would otherwise never have a chance to witness.

**Sheldon Museum & Cultural Center.** *First Ave and Main St, Haines (99827). Phone 907/766-2366. www.sheldonmuseum.org.* Established in 1924, the Sheldon Museum houses a wide variety of historical and artistic artifacts relating to the different cultures that reside in the Chilkat Valley. Through on-site displays and exhibits of rare and elaborate Native handicrafts, visitors are able to learn about the Tlingit culture that predominated in the area before the arrival of white settlers. Evidence of Haines's formative days is also presented, with displays of artifacts from the first permanent white settlement in the valley, a Presbyterian mission established in 1879 on the site the museum now occupies. The museum also focuses on the role Haines played in the Klondike Gold Rush, with exhibits and memorabilia that tell the story of the miners who set off on the nearby Dalton Trail leading into the interior and the gold fields of the Klondike. Most summer afternoons, visitors have the chance to observe master Native craftsmen fashioning totem poles in the front yard of the museum. (Summer: Mon-Fri 11 am-6 pm; Sat-Sun 2-6 pm; winter: Mon-Fri 1-4 pm) **$**

## Special Events

**Bald Eagle Preserve and Annual Festival.** *113 Haines Hwy, Haines (99827). Phone 907/766-3094. baldeagles.org/festival.html.* In October, the world's largest number of bald eagles gather in Haines to take advantage of the late salmon run. This amazing gathering of eagles is the basis of this annual festival that is held in the eagles' honor. (Oct)

**Southeast Alaska State Fair.** *Southeast Alaska Fairgrounds,Haines Hwy, Haines (99827). Phone 907/766-2476; fax 907/766-2478. www.seakfair.org. This old-fashioned regional fair is held over five days* at the Southeast Alaska Fairgrounds on the northern edge of town. Friendly, lively, and full of small-town appeal, it features contests to determine everything from the most lovable dog to the best zucchini; volleyball, slow-pitch softball, horseshoes, and basketball tournaments; men's and women's logging competitions; a wide variety of exhibits and demonstrations; live music; and a Grand Parade. Visitors to the fair can also walk around Dalton City, a Gold Rush film set constructed for the Disney movie *White Fang.* Mid-Aug. **$$**

## Limited-Service Hotels

**★ CAPTAIN'S CHOICE INC. MOTEL.** *108 Second Ave N, Haines (99827). Phone 907/766-3111; toll-free 800/478-2345; fax 907/766-3332. www.capchoice.com.* Built on a steeply sloping lot, this family-run motel has terrific views of Lynn Canal and Portage Cove as well as the Fort Seward area of Haines. The small guest rooms are in excellent shape and filled with solid wood furniture, plank walls, and whimsical nautical accents. Reasonable prices, a great location, and warm, friendly service make it an excellent bargain. 40 rooms, 2 story. Pets accepted. Check-in 2 pm, check-out 11 am. **$**

**★ ★ HOTEL HALSINGLAND.** *13 Fort Seward Dr, Haines (99827). Phone 907/766-2000; toll-free 800/359-5627; fax 907/766-2445.* 60 rooms. Closed in winter. Check-in noon, check-out noon. Restaurant, bar. **$**

## Specialty Lodging

**FORT SEWARD LODGE.** *39 Mud Bay Rd, Haines (99827). Phone toll-free 800/478-7772; fax 907/766-2006. www.ftsewardlodge.com.* 10 rooms. Closed Oct-Apr. Check-in 3 pm, check-out noon. **$**

## Restaurants

**★ THE BAMBOO ROOM.** *2nd Ave and Main St, Haines (99827). Phone 907/766-2800.* Seafood menu. Breakfast, lunch, dinner. Bar. Children's menu. Casual attire. Reservations recommended. Outdoor seating. **$$**

**★ ★ FORT SEWARD RESTAURANT.** *39 Mud Bay Rd, Haines (99827). Phone 907/766-2009; toll-free 800/478-7772; fax 907/766-2006. www.ftsewardlodge.com.* Seafood menu. Breakfast, lunch, dinner, brunch.

Closed in winter. Bar. Children's menu. Casual attire. Reservations recommended. **$$**

**★ ★ THE LIGHTHOUSE RESTAURANT.** *2 Front St, Haines (99827). Phone 907/766-2442.* The Lighthouse Restaurant is really a treat: great views and fresh, wholesome steak and seafood dishes without the high prices that often accompany the two. Panoramic views of Lynn Canal and the Chilkoot Range add to the rustic, local charm of the dining room and make for memorable and relaxing dining. Seafood, steak menu. Breakfast, lunch, dinner. Closed Thanksgiving, Dec 25. Bar. Casual attire. **$$**

**★ ★ WILD STRAWBERRY.** *138 Second Ave, Haines (99827). Phone 907/766-3608.* Alaskan seafood menu. Lunch, dinner. Closed in winter. Bar. Casual attire. Outdoor seating. **$$**

# Homer (E-5)

**Population** 3,946
**Area Code** 907

Homer bills itself as the "Halibut Capital of the World" and is known for having some of the best fishing on the Kenai Peninsula. Set on a hillside overlooking Kachemak Bay and Cook Inlet, it plays host to an enormous number of visitors each year, including hundreds who spend the whole summer camped out on the Homer Spit, a 5-mile-long sliver of land that juts out into the waters of the bay, providing unrestricted access to great halibut and salmon fishing. Homer offers a wide range of other diversions for those uninterested in hooks, bait, and flies. In May, the Kachemak Bay Shorebird Festival takes place, celebrating the tens of thousands of shorebirds that stop over on the local mudflats during their annual migration north. Throughout the summer, boats are available to shuttle passengers across the bay to the small fishing villages and artist communities that dot the rugged coastline. For more athletic types, a network of hiking and biking trails throughout the area provides spectacular views of the mountains, waters, and wildlife that make up this region.

## What to See and Do

**Alaska Islands and Ocean Visitor Center.** *95 Sterling Hwy, Homer (99603). Phone 907/235-6961. www.islandsandocean.org.* Opened in December 2003, the Alaska Islands and Ocean Visitor Center is an educational and research facility that offers visitors an opportunity to learn about the Alaska Maritime National Wildlife Refuge and the Kachemak Bay Research Reserve through interactive exhibits, guided tours, and video presentations. One of the primary goals of the center is to enhance people's awareness of the beauty, fragility, and diversity of the remote 4. 9-million-acre refuge, which stretches from the Arctic Ocean all the way to Alaska's southeast panhandle. Another of the center's goals is to make visitors aware of the biologically diverse estuarine and saltwater habitats that exist right outside the windows of the center in the Kachemak Bay region. The center's attractions extend beyond its own walls, too, with trails leading from the back door to nearby Bishop's Beach and Beluga Slough, where guided and self-guided walks bring visitors face to face with the ecosystems the center is dedicated to preserving and protecting. (Memorial Day-Labor Day, daily 9 am-6 pm) **FREE**

**Homer Spit.** *Homer.* Although Homer is nestled in the foothills overlooking Kachemak Bay, the Homer Spit is really the lifeblood of the town during summer. Extending nearly 5 miles into the bay, the Spit is home to an eclectic mix of businesses and attractions, ranging from natural wetlands that teem with wildlife from spring through fall to a large, sheltered boat harbor that buzzes with activity throughout the summer. The Spit's most popular draws, though, are undoubtedly the Fishing Hole and the Salty Dawg Saloon. The former is a man-made lagoon created and stocked by the Alaska Department of Fish & Game. Its small size, large fish population, and relaxed atmosphere make it a prime location for families and novice anglers looking to hook a king or silver salmon without paying to go out on a charter boat. The Salty Dawg Saloon nearby also has a relaxed atmosphere but appeals to a very different crowd. With wood chips on the floors and walls and low-hung ceilings covered with thousands of autographed dollar bills, T-shirts, boat floats, and fishing mementos, this dimly lit, crowded log-cabin saloon has long been a place for hardworking seafarers to blow off steam at the end of the day. Although tourists now make up a sizeable part of its clientele, it still retains a certain rough-and-tumble edginess that is at once intimidating and appealing. Children are not permitted inside.

**Pratt Museum.** *3779 Bartlett St, Homer (99603). Phone 907/235-8635. www.prattmuseum.org.* One of the most attractive things about the Pratt Museum in Homer is that it's not just a historical museum or an art museum or an anthropological museum: it's all of these and more. The interior of this downtown museum houses native and contemporary culture exhibits, natural history artifacts, a gallery of contemporary regional art, and a small room filled with live marine plants and wildlife. Outside, the museum grounds are given over to a fascinating mix of botanical gardens, interpretive forest trails teeming with birds and other wildlife, and historical structures and artifacts from Homer's pioneer days. (Mid-May-mid-Sept: daily 10 am-6 pm; mid-Sept-mid-May: Tues-Sun noon-5 pm; closed Jan) **$$**

**Seldovia day trip.** *Seldovia.* This tiny community across the bay from Homer was at one time the cultural, social, and economic heart of the lower Kenai peninsula. After the Sterling Highway connected Homer to the outside world, Seldovia faded into the background before being rediscovered as a popular tourist destination. The town is small, even by Alaskan standards, making it easy to walk around and explore its spectacular natural setting. Nestled on the shores of Kachemak Bay with the Kenai Mountains towering above it, the town is picture-postcard beautiful. Visitors can spend the day viewing local artists at work, walking the old boardwalk section of town,—hiking along a forest and meadow trail to Outside Beach, or standing on the old town bridge watching anglers struggling to land monster silver and chum salmon. During the summer, numerous charter companies based on the Homer Spit run shuttle boats to the town, making it a readily accessible, highly memorable day trip.

## Special Event

**Kachemak Bay Shorebird Festival.** *Homer (99603). Phone 907/235-7740; fax 907/235-8766. www.homeralaska.org/shorebird.htm.* First held in 1993, this festival was designed as a way to shake off winter's grip and celebrate the annual migration of hundreds of thousands of shorebirds through the Kachemak Bay region. Since then, it has evolved into a four-day event that seeks to track bird migrations, monitor the health of bird populations, and educate the public about the shorebirds and the need for habitat conservation. Throughout the festival, attendees can attend guest lectures and workshops, travel to shorebird viewing stations, take guided bird walks, and join boat tours to remote migration sites. The festival also keeps non-birders entertained by offering kids' activities, an arts and crafts fair, live music, and a wooden boat festival. Events and activities are individually priced and are held at various sites in and around town. Mid-May.

## Limited-Service Hotels

**★ ★ BELUGA LAKE LODGE.** *204 Ocean Dr Loop, Homer (99603). Phone 907/235-5995.* Beluga Lake Lodge is located halfway between downtown Homer and the start of the Homer Spit, providing easy access to all of Homer's main attractions. With unobstructed views of Beluga Slough and Beluga Lake, the lodge's large decks offer nature enthusiasts a unique vantage point from which to view the birds and other wildlife that inhabit the area. Every month, the restaurant hosts Cajun bluegrass bands, earning the Beluga a reputation for good live music as well. 32 rooms. Pets accepted. Check-in 3 pm, check-out 11 am. Restaurant. **$**

**★ ★ BEST WESTERN BIDARKA INN.** *575 Sterling Hwy, Homer (99603). Phone 907/235-8148; toll-free 866/685-5000; fax 907/235-8140. www.bestwestern.com.* Conveniently located at the entrance to Homer, the Bidarka Inn offers rooms with partial views of Kachemak Bay and the Kenai mountains, an impressive new fitness center, conference facilities, and an on-site restaurant and bar. As the only chain lodging facility in Homer, this motel appeals to travelers looking for a familiar, reliable level of comfort and convenience. 74 rooms. Complimentary continental breakfast. Check-in 2 pm, check-out noon. Two restaurants. Fitness room. **$**

**★ ★ LAND'S END RESORT.** *4786 Homer Spit Rd, Homer (99603). Phone 907/235-0400; toll-free 800/478-0400; fax 907/235-0400. www.lands-end-resort.com.* Lands End Resort, at the end of the 4. 5-mile-long Homer Spit, has been providing guests with breathtaking views of the snowcapped Kenai Mountains and the deep blue waters of Kachemak Bay since it opened in 1958. It has grown quite a bit since then, but it remains a popular destination for Alaskans and outsiders alike by continuing to offer guests "beauty, wildlife, serenity, and friendly service." Don't be fooled by the "Resort" part of the name; with no lush beaches, landscaped gardens, or group activities on offer, Land's End is more like an upmarket hotel than a typical resort. 80 rooms, 2 story. Complimentary continental breakfast. Check-in 4 pm, check-out noon. Restaurant. Fitness room, spa. Indoor pool, whirlpool. **$$**

**★ WINDJAMMER SUITES.** *320 W Pioneer Ave, Homer (99603). Phone 907/235-9761; toll-free 888/730-2770; fax 907/235-9764.* Windjammer Suites is located on Pioneer Avenue in downtown Homer, very close to the junction with the Sterling Highway. Most of the guest suites are enormous, with large living rooms and full-sized kitchens. Upstairs suites have spacious balconies with sweeping views of the Kachemak Bay region, making them some of the best bargains in Homer. Note that the ground-floor suites are being converted into regular hotel rooms, with the separate bedroom area available to guests for an additional fee. 13 rooms, all suites. Pets accepted. Check-in 2 pm, check-out 11 am. **$**

## Specialty Lodgings

**ALASKA WATERFRONT HOMER INN & SPA.** *895 Ocean Dr, Homer (99603). Phone 907/235-2501; toll-free 800/294-7823. www.alaskawaterfront.com.* Custom seaside suites on beautiful Kachemak Bay featuring a secluded sand beach, hot tub, king-size beds, spectacular ocean and glacier views, and an array of specialty spa treatments. 5 rooms, 2 story. **$$**

**ARCTIC SUN LODGING.** *61995 Mission Rd, Homer (99603). Phone 907/235-2283; toll-free 888/479-6259. alaskaarcticsun.com.* This inn features clean, comfortable rooms with private baths and views of Kachemak Bay and the Kenai Mountains. 6 rooms, 2 story. **$**

**DRIFTWOOD INN.** *135 W Bunnell Ave, Homer (99603). Phone 907/235-8019; toll-free 800/478-8019. www.thedriftwoodinn.com.* A mom-and-pop operation in the truest sense, the Driftwood Inn is a collection of funky rooms filled with homey, personal touches. With a small breakfast nook and cozy den on the ground floor, the inn has a communal feel that seems to encourage guests to stop and chat with one another. The inn is just uphill from the beach in a quiet area of town, within yards of a great bookstore and a popular bakery, making it ideal for those looking to relax and unwind. The rates are inexpensive, too, making it a great bargain for independent travelers looking for something unique. 20 rooms. Pets accepted. Check-in 3 pm, check-out noon. **$**

**VICTORIAN HEIGHTS BED & BREAKFAST.** *61495 Race Ct, Homer (99603). Phone 907/235-6357.* Located in the hills overlooking Kachemak Bay, the Kenai Mountain Range, and several glaciers. All rooms have private baths, comfortable furnishings, and are decorated simply and elegantly. 4 rooms, 2 story. **$**

## Restaurants

**★ ★ BELUGA BAY LODGE RESTAURANT.** *204 Ocean Drive Loop, Homer (99603). Phone 907/235-5995.* The Beluga Lake Lodge Restaurant is located adjacent to Beluga Lake, about halfway between downtown Homer and the start of the Homer Spit. It is a popular music venue year round, but really comes alive during the monthly Cajun Bluegrass jam nights, some of which draw crowds from as far away as Anchorage. Seafood, steak menu. Dinner. Closed mid-Sept-early May. Bar. Children's menu. Casual attire. Outdoor seating. **$$**

**★ ★ CHART ROOM.** *4786 Homer Spit Rd, Homer (99603). Phone 907/235-0400; toll-free 800/478-0400; fax 907/235-0420. www.endofthespit.com.* The Chart Room restaurant at Land's End Resort (see) features traditional steak and seafood dishes prepared with a fresh Alaskan flavor, including long-time favorites halibut & chips and crab & artichoke dip. The best reason to go, though, is to take in the breathtaking views of the snow-capped Kenai Mountains towering over the waters of Kachemak Bay. During the long days of summer, the outdoor patio facing the water is a popular spot to enjoy fine food while taking in the sights, sounds, and scents of the ocean. Seafood, steak menu. Breakfast, lunch, dinner. Bar. Children's menu. Casual attire. Outdoor seating. **$$$**

**★ COAL BAY SANDWICH COMPANY.** *361 Sterling Hwy, Homer (99603). Phone 907/235-3200.* With the motto "Nobody Leaves Hungry," the Coal Bay Sandwich Company is a real find. It's inexpensive, has a wide variety of hearty and healthy sandwiches, and offers fresh clam chowder and chili along with what the menu claims are the best shakes in town. Its convenient location on the main highway through Homer makes it a popular spot for fishermen and daytrippers looking to grab some food before venturing out for the day. American, deli menu. Lunch, dinner. Closed Sun; Jan 1, Thanksgiving, Dec 25. Casual attire. Outdoor seating. **$**

**★ ★ DON JOSE'S.** *127 W Pioneer Ave, Homer (99603). Phone 907/235-7963; fax 907/235-7964.* Since opening its doors in 1982, Don Jose's has become such a favorite in Homer it has expanded to include restaurants in Kenai and Anchorage. Although known primarily as "the place" to get good Mexican food in a relaxed, comfortable setting, it offers Italian food, too, along with traditional American entrées like cheeseburgers and sandwiches. American, Mexican menu. Lunch, dinner. Bar. Children's menu. Casual attire. **$$**

★ ★ **DUNCAN HOUSE.** *125 W Pioneer Ave, Homer (99603). Phone 907/235-5344.* From the eclectic mix of plates, glasses, and mugs that appear on each table to the antiques and Alaskan memorabilia that fill the walls, Duncan House restaurant exudes an authentic down-home charm that makes you want to linger for hours. The menu features large portions of standard American dishes, making it a family-friendly destination for hungry locals and tourists. American menu. Breakfast, lunch. Closed Tues. Children's menu. Casual attire. **$**

★ ★ **FAT OLIVES.** *276 Ohlson Ln, Homer (99603). Phone 907/235-8488.* Fat Olives is a wonderful blend of urban chic and Alaskan informality. The restaurant is filled with warm Mediterranean colors, polished granite table tops, live plants, and a stylish wooden bar back. And yet, the floors are concrete, the walls cinderblock, and the atmosphere ultra-relaxed. The focal point of the restaurant is its wood-fired oven, used to cook everything except the specialty 28" pizzas, which are so large they have to be baked in a traditional pizza oven. Mediterranean menu. Lunch, dinner. Closed Jan 1, Thanksgiving, Dec 25; Feb. Bar. Casual attire. Outdoor seating. **$$**

★ ★ ★ **THE HOMESTEAD.** *East End Rd, mile 8.2, Homer (99603). Phone 907/235-8723; fax 907/235-3448.* For the past 11 years, the Homestead Restaurant has been providing a dining experience characterized by owner Lisa Nolan as "white tablecloths without the button-up attitude." It's an elegant place without being "formal," a word that Nolan wrinkles up her nose at. The walls are lined with contemporary Alaskan art, the views are breathtaking, and the service and selection are exceptional. Add to the mix a 1,200-bottle wine cellar filled with premium wines from around the world, and the result is one of Homer's most popular, upscale dining spots. Seafood, steak menu. Dinner. Closed Oct-Mar. Bar. Children's menu. Casual attire. **$$$**

★ ★ **THE ROOKERY.** *Phone 907/235-7770; toll-free 800/426-6212. www.ottercoveresort.com.* Located at Otter Cove in Eldred Passage with extensive views of the abundant natural wildlife. Tour and charter boats available. Seafood menu. Lunch, dinner. Closed mid-Sept-late May. Bar. Casual attire. Reservations recommended. Outdoor seating. **$$**

★ **TWO SISTERS BAKERY & CAFÉ.** *106 W Bunnell St, Homer (99603). Phone 907/235-2280. www.twosistersbakery.net.* Two Sisters Bakery & Café is located in the small historic district of Homer in a building with wide, wraparound porches where summertime guests can eat, drink, and relax while taking in the views of Kachemak Bay. In winter, the warm Mediterranean colors inside brighten the bakery while art by local artists livens up the walls. The bakery offers a mouthwatering array of pastries and breads baked on site and uses locally grown ingredients whenever possible. American, deli menu, bakery. Breakfast, lunch. Closed Jan 1, Thanksgiving, Dec 25. Casual attire. Outdoor seating. **$**

# Juneau (E-8)

**Population** 30,711
**Area Code** 907
**Information** Juneau Convention & Visitors Bureau, One Sealalaska Plaza, Suite 305, Juneau, 99801; phone 907/586-1737 or toll-free 800/587-2201
**Web Site** www.juneau.org

Squeezed onto a narrow slip of land between the waters of Gastineau Channel and the base of 3,576-foot-tall Mount Juneau, Alaska's capital city, is literally and figuratively overshadowed by the vast wilderness that surrounds it. Located in the middle of the Tongass National Forest two-thirds of the way up the Inside Passage, Juneau is a former gold rush town that has managed to strike it rich with tourists. Because no roads connect Juneau to the outside world, all visitors must arrive by air or sea. This is an enormous benefit for the city, as it is most striking when viewed against a backdrop of massive glaciers, dense forests, towering peaks, and meandering waterways: a sliver of civilization in the wild. In 2002, more than three-quarters of a million visitors came to this remote region of Alaska, most arriving by cruise ship.

The city was originally called Harrisburg, in recognition of Richard Harris, one of the first prospectors to stake a claim in the area. The town's name was later changed to Rockwell for a short time, before being changed in 1881 to Juneau—in honor of Joe Juneau, Harris's partner and cofounder of the settlement. In 1906, the government was moved from Sitka to Juneau, and it has remained the state capital ever since despite its geographic isolation from the rest of the state. Although Juneau's population is about 31,000, making it the third-largest city in Alaska, it has managed to retain a small-town feel, due in large

## Exploring Juneau's History

The area around Juneau's cruise ship docks is filled with historical statues, memorials, and plaques that commemorate significant historical, social, and cultural events in the city's past.

At the extreme southern end of the cruise ship dock area stands the **Fisherman's Memorial,** dedicated to the memory of local commercial fishermen and women who have died while working in the fishing industry. It is also the site of the annual blessing of the fleet in early May.

The **Archie Van Winkle Memorial** is located nearby in front of the Mount Roberts Tramway terminal. This white granite memorial bears a plaque detailing the gallantry and bravery that led this US Marine Corp Colonel to become Alaska's first Medal of Honor recipient.

Farther north along the waterfront is the **USS *Juneau* Memorial,** dedicated to the memory of the 690 sailors, including the five Sullivan brothers, killed when the USS Juneau was torpedoed and sunk during the Battle of Guadalcanal in World War II.

Just beyond the parking garage and public library to the north is Marine Park, which features two far less solemn memorials. The first is the bronze **Patsy Ann statue** commissioned by the Gastineau Humane Society and dedicated in 1992. It honors Patsy Ann, a deaf English bull terrier living in Juneau in the 1930s that was always one of the first at the docks to meet arriving ships. Patsy Ann's uncanny ability to sense the approach of vessels before they came into view made her such a celebrity that the mayor at the time named her "Official Greeter of Juneau, Alaska."

Also in Marine Park, but closer to Marine Way, is the **Hard Rock Miner sculpture** by Juneau artist Ed Way. Created in 1980, the bronze work depicts hard rock miners at work underground, a powerful reminder of the hard-working men and women who transformed Juneau from an isolated gold mining town into one of Alaska's most important cities.

part to the preservation of the historic district around Front and Franklin streets and the casual, friendly attitude of its residents. It may be the capital, but it's still Alaska. With an average of 222 days of rain each year, it's not surprising that the city is brimming with bookstores, coffeehouses, restaurants, and bars.

## What to See and Do

**AJ Mine/Gastineau Mill Mine Tours.** *500 Sheep Creek Mine Rd, Juneau (99801). Phone 907/463-5017.* The Alaska Juneau Mine, better known as the AJ Mine, began operation in 1916 and within years became the largest gold mine of its type in the world. At its peak, it was also the most important economic force in Juneau, employing 600 workers and helping the town to grow and prosper. Economic factors caused the mine to close in 1944, but not before it had produced more than $75 million in gold. Nowadays, visitors can take a four-hour tour of the mine and the nearby Gastineau Mill that was used to crush the rock extracted from the mine. Tours, conducted daily beginning in May and continuing to the end of September, include an underground walk, a hard rock mining demonstration, and a chance to pan for gold at the mill site. **$$$$**

**Alaska State Capitol.** *4th Ave and Main St, Juneau (99801).* Built between 1929 and 1931, the Alaska State Capitol building was known as the Territorial Federal Building for 28 years until Alaska achieved statehood in 1959. The exterior of the building is somewhat nondescript, featuring Alaskan marble and limestone and a replica of the Liberty Bell beside the 4th Avenue entrance. The interior of the Capitol houses the offices of the governor, lieutenant governor, and state legislature as well as legislative chambers and other state government offices. Throughout the year, visitors can take self-guided tours during regular business hours. During the summer, guided tours are offered on weekdays, with tours beginning every 30 minutes between 8 am and 5 pm.

**Alaska State Museum.** *395 Whittier St, Juneau (99801). Phone 907/465-2901. www.museums.state.ak.us.* Permanent collections and traveling exhibits highlight Alaska's native peoples, its natural history, the Alaska-Yukon gold rushes, and the American period of Alaska's history. Artwork and artifacts include photographs, murals, kayak models, a life-sized eagle tree, and tiny thimble baskets. A children's room features a one-third scale model of the stern of the ship

*Discovery,* used by Captain George Vancouver during his famous explorations of Alaska, as well as dress-up clothes and historic exhibits. (Mid-May-mid-Sept: daily 8:30 am-5:30 pm; mid-Sept-mid-May: Tues-Sat 10 am-4 pm; closed holidays) **$**

**Governor's House.** *716 Calhoun St, Juneau (99801).* Located on the corner of two residential streets, the Governor's House is every bit as unassuming as the State Capitol a short walk away. Built in 1910 in colonial style, it's an attractive, stately building that blends in well with the other attractive homes on the street, giving it an aura of approachability one would not expect to find in a governor's mansion. Public tours of the home are not available, but the governor does host an annual holiday open house for the general public in early December.

**Juneau-Douglas City Museum.** *4th Ave and Main St, Juneau (99801). Phone 907/586-3572. www.juneau.org/parksrec/museum.* Located across the street from the State Capitol, the Juneau-Douglas City Museum was founded to preserve and display materials relating to the cultural and historical development of the Juneau-Douglas area. The small galleries are packed with artifacts and memorabilia of the groups and events that have influenced the development of the Juneau and Douglas region, from ancient Tlingit tribes to turn-of-the-century mining corporations to modern-day tour companies. The museum also features special exhibits throughout the year, details of which are available on the museums Web site. (Mid-May-Sept: Mon-Fri 9 am-5 pm, Sat-Sun 10 am-5 pm; Oct-mid-May: Tues-Sat noon-4 pm) **$**

**The Last Chance Mining Museum.** *1001 Basin Rd, Juneau (99801). Phone 907/586-5338.* Listed on the National Register of Historic Places and Alaska Gold Rush Properties, this museum is housed in a historic compressor building associated with the former Alaska Juneau Gold Mining Company, which operated in Juneau from 1912 until 1944. The museum explores the history of the region's mining industry with exhibits of industrial artifacts associated with hard rock gold mining. (Daily 9:30 am-12:30 pm, 3:30-6:30 pm) **$**

**Mendenhall Glacier.** *Glacier Spur Rd, Juneau (99801). Phone 907/789-0097. www.fs.fed.us/r10/tongass/districts/mendenhall.* Mendenhall Glacier is located about 12 miles from downtown Juneau at the northern end of the Mendenhall Valley. The glacier originates in the Juneau Icefield and stretches for 13 miles before terminating at the northern end of Mendenhall Lake, the waters of which conceal roughly half of the glacier's 200-foot-thick toe. The visitor center offers excellent views of the glacier as well as interpretive exhibits and displays that explain the movement of glaciers and the way they transform landscapes. Five trails originate in and around the center, providing scenic walks for people of all ages and abilities during the summer months. (Summer, daily 8 am-6:30 pm) **$**

**Mount Roberts Tramway.** *490 S Franklin St, Juneau (99801). Phone 907/463-3412; toll-free 888/461-8726. www.alaska.net/~junotram.* The Mount Roberts Tramway runs from the cruise ship dock in downtown Juneau up the side of Mount Roberts to an elevation of about 1,800 feet, providing passengers with magnificent views of Juneau, Douglas Island, and the Gastineau Channel. On arrival at the summit, visitors can walk some of Mount Roberts's most popular alpine trails, enjoy a relaxing meal and great views at the summit restaurant, watch a short documentary on Native culture in the Chilkat Theater, browse through the gift shops, or just sit and enjoy the panoramic views of wilderness Alaska. (May-Sept, daily 9 am-9 pm) **$$$$**

**Tours.** *Juneau. Phone toll-free 800/544-2206. www.graylineofalaska.com.* Gray Line of Alaska offers package tours around Alaska (up to 11 days) as well as a 2 3/4-hour sightseeing tour of historic Juneau and Mendenhall Glacier.

## Limited-Service Hotels

**★ ASPEN HOTEL.** *1800 Shell Simmons Dr, Juneau (99801). Phone 907/790-6435; toll-free 866/483-7848; fax 907/790-6621. www.aspenhotelsak.com.* Like other Aspen hotels, this one is extremely clean and comfortable and staffed by a friendly, professional crew. With affordable rates, a 24-hour business center, and fully equipped meeting rooms, it's a popular spot for business professionals. Families appreciate its deluxe continental breakfast, indoor pool, and family suites featuring a bedroom with bunk beds and a video game console. The hotel is also close to Juneau's two shopping centers, the Nugget Mall and the Mendenhall Mall. 94 rooms. Complimentary continental breakfast. Check-in 3 pm, check-out 11 am. Fitness room. Indoor pool, whirlpool. **$$**

**★ BEST WESTERN COUNTRY LANE INN.** *9300 Glacier Hwy, Juneau (99801). Phone 907/789-5005; toll-free 800/780-7234; fax 907/789-2818. www.bestwestern.com.* Located a half-mile from Juneau International Airport and only a short drive to two local shopping malls and Mendenhall Glacier, this 55-room hotel is popular with visitors looking to do a bit of shopping and sightseeing while in town. Guest accommodations are spacious, clean, and quiet and the staff friendly and knowledgeable, making it a good choice for travelers. 55 rooms. Pets accepted. Complimentary continental breakfast. Check-in 2 pm, check-out noon. **$**

**★ ★ BREAKWATER INN.** *1711 Glacier Ave, Juneau (99801). Phone 907/586-6303; toll-free 800/544-2250; fax 907/463-4820. www.breakwaterinn.com.* The 49-room Breakwater Inn sits across the street from Aurora Harbor about a mile from downtown. Its accommodations—referred to as cabins—are clean and tidy and reflect the nautical theme found in the public areas. The most popular rooms have balconies facing the harbor. and about a third of the rooms have kitchenettes. Another draw is The Breakwater Restaurant (see), which serves steak and seafood and is highly regarded for its menu, views, and atmosphere. 49 rooms. Pets accepted. Check-in 3 pm, check-out noon. Restaurant. **$**

**★ ★ FRONTIER SUITES AIRPORT HOTEL.** *9400 Glacier Hwy, Juneau (99801). Phone 907/790-6600; toll-free 800/544-2250; fax 907/790-6612. www.frontiersuites.com.* Whether staying in a suite or a standard room, guests will be pleased with the prices and the amenities: unique Alaskan artwork, DSL access, full kitchens, big dining tables, and large, comfortable chairs and sofas. The Frontier Suites is about half a mile from the airport, within walking distance of a number of moderately priced restaurants, and a ten-minute drive from Mendenhall Glacier, one of Juneau's top tourist draws. 104 rooms. Pets accepted. Check-in 3 pm, check-out noon. High-speed Internet access. Restaurant. Fitness room. **$**

**★ ★ PROSPECTOR HOTEL.** *375 Whittier St, Juneau (99801). Phone 907/586-3737; fax 907/586-1204.* Thanks to extensive upgrades a few years ago, this 62-room hotel is in remarkable shape. Located across the busy Glacier Highway from Gastineau Channel, the Prospector is only a short walk from downtown but is far enough from the tourist track to avoid being overrun with daytrippers during the summer season. Comfortable, high-quality furnishings are standard here, as is thoughtful and attentive service. Rates are slightly higher than at nearby lodgings, but the views from the ocean-facing rooms make up for it. 62 rooms. Pets accepted. Check-in 3 pm, check-out noon. Restaurant. **$$**

**★ ★ WESTMARK BARANOF HOTEL.** *127 N Franklin St, Juneau (99801). Phone 907/586-2660; toll-free 800/764-0017; fax 907/586-8315. www.westmark-hotels.com.* The Westmark Baranof is one of the oldest hotels in Juneau and one of the most famous in Alaska. Built in 1939, this beautiful Art Deco building recently underwent a $3. 5 million renovation to return its lobby, lounge, restaurant, and guest rooms to their original splendor. For more than six decades, politicians, lobbyists, and pundits have called the downtown hotel their home away from home while the legislature is in session, giving it an aura of refinement, dignity, and gravitas unlike any other in Alaska. The hotel is well suited to business travelers, with plentiful meeting space, a fantastic restaurant, an elegant lounge and formal lobby, and high-speed Internet access available for a fee. 196 rooms. Pets accepted. Check-in 3 pm, check-out 11 am. High-speed Internet access. Two restaurants. **$$**

## Full-Service Hotel

**★ ★ ★ GOLDBELT HOTEL.** *51 Egan Dr, Juneau (99801). Phone 907/586-6900; toll-free 888/478-6909; fax 907/463-3567. www.goldbelthotel.com.* Next door to the Centennial Convention and Visitors' Center, this 105-room hotel is one of the largest in town and has some of the best waterfront views around. A native-owned property, it boasts one of the most extensive collections of Tlingit art found anywhere in Alaska: shields, masks, necklaces, jewelry, baskets, bowls, and many other rare and beautiful items are on display throughout the public areas. The guest rooms are large and feature upscale amenities and a level of comfort and style that is unsurpassed in Juneau. Travelers should book well in advance, as the hotel is generally busy nine months of the year, with cruise ship passengers and business travelers during the summer and politicians and their aides when the legislature is in session. 105 rooms. Pets accepted. Check-in 3 pm, check-out noon. Restaurant. **$$**

## Specialty Lodgings

**ALASKA WOLF HOUSE BED & BREAKFAST.** *1900 Wickersham Ave, Juneau (99802). Phone 907/586-*

*2422; toll-free 888/586-9053.* Built on the mountainside in a 4,000-square-foot western red cedar log home with open beams, natural skylights, and large windows. A large gourmet breakfast is provided every morning. 5 rooms, 2 story. **$**

**THE HIGHLANDS BED & BREAKFAST.** *421 Judy Ln, Juneau (99801). Phone toll-free 877/463-5404. www.juneauhighlands.com.* Located in historic downtown Juneau, this bed-and-breakfast features modern amenities, private entrances and baths. 4 rooms, 2 story. **$**

## Restaurants

**★ BACAR'S.** *230 Seward St, Juneau (99801). Phone 907/463-4202.* Consistently voted Juneau's best breakfast restaurant in a local poll, BaCars derives its name from Barry and Carline Shaw, the longtime owners. Located in the middle of downtown Juneau, the place consistently draws crowds coming to enjoy the fresh breads and "fine specialty home cooking" that has made the restaurant a local favorite for years. American menu. Breakfast, lunch. Closed Jan 1, Thanksgiving, Dec 25. Casual attire. **$**

**★ ★ THE BREAKWATER RESTAURANT & LOUNGE.** *1711 Glacier Ave, Juneau (99801). Phone 907/586-6303; toll-free 800/544-2250; fax 907/463-4820. www.madsens.com/breakwater.* In 2003, Elite Dining named this restaurant one of Juneau's top neighborhood favorites "in recognition of excellence in dining." In addition, *Capital City Weekly* magazine has repeatedly awarded it first place for best seafood, best steaks, best quality, and best dining. Offering Black Angus beef, fresh Alaskan seafood, and one of the largest wine selections in Juneau, this intimate, inviting restaurant is a real treat. Seafood, steak menu. Breakfast, lunch, dinner. Bar. Casual attire. **$$$**

**★ ★ DRAGON INN CHINESE CUISINE.** *213 Front St, Juneau (99801). Phone 907/586-4888; fax 907/586-8074. www.bestchinesefood.com.* Located on one of Juneau's most vibrant streets, this popular local Chinese restaurant is normally packed with an eclectic mix of young couples, large families, day-tripping tourists, and business professionals. The interior sports a subtle Chinese theme, but the main draw is the extensive menu and the restaurant's reputation for relaxed, casual dining. Chinese menu. Lunch, dinner. Closed Sun; Thanksgiving, Dec 25. Casual attire. **$$**

**★ ★ EL SOMBRERO.** *157 S Franklin St, Juneau (99801). Phone 907/586-6770; fax 907/586-6772.* Winner of numerous local awards for best Mexican food, this busy, vibrant restaurant offers a wide selection of traditional Mexican dishes and caters to a widely disparate clientele: from tradesmen and lunch-daters to business professionals and cruise ship tourists. Open long hours throughout the year, it's a great place to go for casual dining in a relaxed, inviting atmosphere. Mexican menu. Lunch, dinner. Closed Jan 1, Thanksgiving, Dec 25; also Sun in winter. Casual attire. **$$**

**★ ★ ★ THE GOLD ROOM.** *127 N Franklin St, Juneau (99801). Phone 907/463-6222; fax 907/586-8315. www.westmarkhotels.com.* This historic restaurant at the Westmark Baranof Hotel (see) is without a doubt one of the most architecturally and artistically attractive restaurants in Alaska. From the exquisite Art Deco skylight rediscovered after a devastating fire in the 1980s to the huge wall mural by Alaskan artist Sydney Lawrence, the restaurant is filled with historical, artistic, and architectural accents that give it an ultra-sophisticated, elegant air. The restaurant's menu is top-rate, too, in keeping with the clientele they servea who's who of Alaska's political, social, and business circles. American menu. Dinner. Closed Thanksgiving, Dec 25. Bar. Children's menu. Casual attire. **$$$**

**★ ★ HANGAR ON THE WHARF.** *#2 Marine Way, #106, Juneau (99801). Phone 907/586-5018. www.hangaronthewharf.com.* Juneau's only waterfront restaurant features southeast Alaska's largest selection of microbrew beers in a converted aircraft hangar. American menu. Lunch, dinner. **$**

**★ JOVANY'S.** *9121 Glacier Hwy, Juneau (99801). Phone 907/789-2339; fax 907/790-3234. www.jovanys.com.* This mom-and-pop family restaurant near the airport in the Mendenhall Valley area of Juneau has been in business for many years and serves an eclectic mix of American, Asian, and European dishes. Friendly service, reasonable prices, and consistently superior food make it a long-time local and tourist favorite. Italian menu. Lunch, dinner. Closed Jan 1, Thanksgiving, Dec 25. Casual attire. **$$**

**★ ★ MICASA.** *9200 Glacier Hwy, Juneau (99801). Phone 907/789-3636.* Frequent winner of local awards for best Mexican food and best brunch in town, MiCasa Mexican restaurant has been serving the Mendenhall Valley area of Juneau since the late 1970s. Architecturally, it has a subtle southwestern feel to it with an appealing blend of earth tones, painted arches, and decorative tiles reminiscent of those found in Mexican haciendas. Mexican menu. Breakfast, lunch, dinner. Bar. Children's menu. Casual attire. **$$**

**★ PARADISE CAFÉ.** *245 Marine Way, Juneau (99801). Phone 907/586-2253.* Set up in a French bistro style, Paradise Café serves a constantly changing variety of breakfast and lunch dishes and fresh pastries, all prepared on site from scratch. On sunny, warm days, the small outdoor patio at the front is an excellent place to sit and watch the harbor and the local action. American menu. Breakfast, lunch. Closed Dec 25; also three weeks late Dec. Casual attire. Outdoor seating. **$**

**★ PASTA GARDEN.** *9400 Glacier Hwy, Juneau (99801). Phone 907/790-8877; toll-free 800/544-2250. www.madsens.com/riverrockrestr.* There's no garden at the Pasta Garden restaurant, but there is a log-cabin seating area in the middle of the otherwise standard dining room. Despite this unusual architectural feature, the extensive menu, packed with an eclectic mix of Italian, Mexican, Asian, and Alaskan seafood dishes and moderate prices, is a real crowd pleaser. International menu. Breakfast, lunch, dinner. Closed Thanksgiving, Dec 25. Children's menu. Casual attire. **$$**

**★ PIZZERIA ROMA.** *2 Marine Way, Suite 104, Juneau (99801). Phone 907/463-5020.* This small pizzeria is located in the Fisherman's Wharf building at the foot of Main Street in downtown Juneau. Well-known in the area for offering consistently excellent pizza, its great location and solid reputation ensure that it's frequently packed with locals and tourists alike. Pizza. Lunch, dinner. Closed Thanksgiving, Dec 25. Casual attire. **$**

**★ ★ T. K. MAGUIRE'S.** *375 Whittier St, Juneau (99801). Phone 907/586-3711; fax 907/586-1204. www.prospectorhotel.com/restaurant.htm.* Windows in this casually upscale steak and seafood restaurant provide excellent views of Gastineau Channel and Douglas Island. Featuring an understated Irish pub theme, its outdoor deck is a great place to dine on warm, sunny days while taking in the sights and sounds of the waterfront. International menu. Breakfast, lunch, dinner. Closed Jan 1, Memorial Day, Dec 25. Bar. Children's menu. Casual attire. Outdoor seating. **$$**

**★ ★ THANE ORE HOUSE.** *4400 Thane Rd, Juneau (99801). Phone 907/586-3442.* Rustic setting with regional Alaskan specialties and unique seating. Song and dance floor show in adjacent theater. American menu. Lunch, dinner. **$**

# Katmai National Park & Preserve

**Web Site** www.nps.gov/katm

Put simply, Katmai is bear country. Katmai National Park and Preserve has one of the world's highest concentrations of brown bears, with more than 2,000 of the giant furry mammals clambering within this remote wilderness along the Alaska Peninsula. The bears are drawn to the area's lakes and rivers, which teem with sockeye salmon. During the months of July and September, it is not uncommon to see dozens of bears gathered at Brooks Falls, feeding on salmon that have migrated up the Naknek River. While the salmon attract bears, the bears in turn attract tourists, thousands of whom make the trip to Katmai via air taxi or boat (no roads lead to the park) to witness North America's largest land predator in its natural habitat. A viewing platform at Brooks Camp enables visitors to safely observe and photograph the brown bears, some of which weigh over 900 pounds. Beyond bears, Katmai is home to numerous other wildlife, including moose, red foxes, weasels, wolves, and porcupines. At the parks southern edge along the Shelikof Strait, hair seals, sea lions, and sea otters inhabit the rugged shoreline, while beluga, killer, and gray whales patrol the waters just off the coast.

Katmai is also famous for its volcanoes, with 14 active volcanoes located in the park. In 1912, the largest volcanic eruption of the 20th century occurred here when the Novarupta Volcano blew its top, launching a plume of smoke and ash 20 miles skyward. The cataclysmic eruption—ten times more powerful than the eruption of Mount St. Helens—created a 40-square-mile ash flow within the Valley of Ten Thousand Smokes, so named by botanist Robert Griggs during a 1916 expedition for *National Geographic.* Today, the area still resembles a lifeless moonscape, possessing a gray landscape devoid of grasses, trees, and shrubs. Aside from wildlife viewing, popular activities at Katmai include hiking, sea kayaking, and sport fishing. The park offers a world-class fishing experience, with the Alagnak and Naknek rivers populated by Pacific salmon, rainbow trout, grayling, and northern pike. Visitors to Katmai should be prepared for cold and wet conditions. The weather is often inhospitable, even during the summer months.

## What to See and Do

**Alagnak Wild River.** *King Salmon (99661). Phone 907/246-3305.* The Alagnak Wild River twists and turns across 67 miles of pristine wilderness in the Aleutian Range of southwestern Alaska. The braided river begins at Kukaklek Lake in the Katmai National Preserve and then flows west, widening along the way, before spilling out into Bristol Bay. In 1980, the Alagnak was included in the national Wild and Scenic Rivers System. Whitewater rafters are drawn to the river's Class IIII rapids and ever-changing landscape, ranging from boreal forest to wet sedge tundra. The Alagnak's western stretch, shallow and marked by numerous sandbars, has become a favored destination for fly fishing. The cool waters of the Alagnak teem with rainbow trout and all five species of Pacific salmon, including the prodigious king salmon, the largest of which can exceed 70 pounds. The Alagnak's designation as a Wild River helps protect the areas abundant wildlife, most notably a large population of brown bears that feed on the salmon. Other wildlife found along the river include bald eagles, caribou, moose, osprey, and wolverines. The Alagank Wild River is accessible only by boat or seaplane. If you make the trip, be sure to bring heavy-duty rain gear and warm wool clothing.

# Kenai (D-5)

**Population** 6,942
**Area Code** 907
**Information** Kenai Convention & Visitors Bureau, 11471 Kenai Spur Hwy, 99611; phone 907/283-1991
**Web Site** www.visitkenai.com

As the oldest settlement on the Alaskan mainland, Kenai has been witness to some of the most significant events in Alaska's history. Originally the home of the Dena'ina Athabascan Indians, the area became a Russian fur trading post in 1791 and remained so for the next 80 years until Alaska was purchased by the US government in 1869. Old Town Kenai, two blocks southeast of the Kenai Visitor Center, contains many artifacts from this period and includes a self-guided walking tour that explores the different cultural and economic influences that have shaped the lives of the Russian, Indian, and American residents of the town over the past two hundred years. In 1947, the Sterling Highway was completed, opening Kenai and the entire Peninsula up to the world and prompting the development of what has become one of the major industries in the area: tourism. Ten years after the Highway was built, oil was discovered at Swanson River northeast of town, opening up a new chapter in the town's history. Despite two centuries of dramatic social, economic, and political change, the Kenai area remains an undeniably appealing place to visit. Set on the edge of Cook Inlet near the mouth of the Kenai River, the town is surrounded on all sides by untamed wilderness, from the muddy shores and frigid waters of the inlet to the pristine lakes, streams, hills, and forests that make up the Kenai National Wildlife Refuge.

With panoramic views across Cook Inlet to three of Alaska's most active volcanoes, Mt. Redoubt, Mt. Spurr, and Mt. Iliamna, few places can match Kenais ability to put on a show, most recently a series of eruptions of Mt. Redoubt in 1990 and similar eruptions of Mt. Spurr in 1992. Visitors not fortunate enough to witness one of these events can always plan on being in town for the annual Kenai River Festival, held in the Green Strip Park the second weekend in June. The festival celebrates the Kenai River and offers an appealing blend of arts and crafts, environmental exhibits, traditional dance and music, and Alaskan food.

## What to See and Do

**Clam Gulch State Recreation Area.** *Soldotna. 11 miles SE on Kenai Spur Hwy. Phone 907/262-5581. www.dnr.state.ak.us/parks/units/clamglch.htm.* This area is famous for the hundreds of thousands of razor clams harvested annually from the sandy beaches adjacent to the State Recreation Area. Visitors may dig clams during any low tide, although an Alaska sportfishing license is required. If you decide to dig, be careful; they are named "razor clams" for good reason! Clam Gulch is located on steep bluffs overlooking Cook Inlet, with sweeping views of the Aleutian Mountains and their three tallest peaks: Mount Iliamna, Mount Redoubt, and Mount Spurr. The park offers tent camping and picnic areas. **$**

**Historic Old Town Kenai.** *Kenai Visitors & Cultural Center, 11471 Kenai Spur Hwy, Kenai (99611). Phone 907/283-1991. www.visitkenai.com.* In an effort to maintain a link with its rich cultural heritage, the city of Kenai has preserved some of its oldest, most historic buildings. Located within sight of the visitor center, the Old Town district consists of everything from grand churches to humble log cabins, each of which helps tell the story of the town's growth and development. Fort Kenay, which is actually a replica of the original, provides visitors with insight into Kenai's tenuous existence during its earliest years, while the Russian Orthodox Church on Mission Avenue serves as an architectural and historic reminder of the importance of religion and Russian culture in the town's development. The homesteader cabins located on Overland Street serve a specific purpose, too, offering a view into the changing living conditions of Kenai's citizens as the town changed and slowly became more established. Elsewhere in Old Town, the Kenai Bible Church, Civic League Building, and American Legion post help bridge the gap between the small, turn-of-the-century town called Kenai and the modern Alaskan city it has become. Walking maps of the Historic Old Town district are available at the Visitors & Cultural Center on the Kenai Spur Highway. (Mid-May-mid-Sept: Mon-Fri 9 am-7 pm, Sat 10 am-6 pm, Sun 11 am-6 pm; mid-Sept-mid-May: Mon-Fri 9 am-7 pm) **FREE**

## Special Event

**Kenai River Festival.** *Kenai Green Strip, Main St, Kenai (99611). Phone 907/260-5449. www.kenaiwatershed.org/kenairiverfestival.html.* This community-wide event celebrates the Kenai River and seeks to raise people's awareness of the need to protect the river's watershed area. The festival features a colorful parade led by a 29-foot salmon, live local music, a 5K foot race, vendor booths featuring local foods and handicrafts by Alaskan artists, and a long list of free activities for children, including face painting and puppet shows. Environmental and conservation groups like the Bird Treatment and Learning Center, the US Forest Service, the Alaska Department of Fish & Game, and the Kenai River Sportfishing Association also are on hand to provide information about the care and conservation of the wildlife and natural resources that make the area such a scenic treasure. Second weekend in June. **FREE**

## Limited-Service Hotel

**★ ★ UPTOWN MOTEL.** *47 Spur View Dr, Kenai (99611). Phone 907/283-3660; toll-free 800/777-3650; fax 907/283-5833. www.uptownmotel.com.* This downtown Kenai motel is more upscale than most motels. The lobby contains a small, ornate staircase and matching reception desk made of beautiful dark, polished woods; the hallways have equally attractive wainscoting; and the guest rooms are accentuated by crown molding and window valances. In all, this level of luxury is entirely unexpected in a motel. The Uptown's proximity to the downtown area and the Kenai River make it a popular place for tourists and outdoor enthusiasts. 49 rooms. Pets accepted. Check-in 2 pm, check-out noon. Restaurant. **$**

## Restaurants

**★ ★ CHARLOTTE'S RESTAURANT.** *115 S Willow St, Kenai (99611). Phone 907/283-2777; fax 907/262-0661.* According to owner Charlotte Legg, Charlotte's serves "contemporary homestyle cooking; comfort food with a flair." It does this by taking foods that people like and making them better: adding extra ingredients or substituting new ingredients to create unexpected, pleasing twists on standard dishes. All of the breads and soups are prepared from scratch and the salads and sandwiches feature vegetables grown on site. California deli menu. Breakfast, lunch. Closed holidays; also first two weeks in Jan. Children's menu. Casual attire. Outdoor seating. **$**

**★ ★ LOUIE'S STEAK & SEAFOOD.** *47 Spur View Dr, Kenai (99661). Phone 907/283-3660; toll-free 800/777-3650; fax 907/283-5833. www.uptownmotel.com.* Louie's is decorated in an '"Alaskan Trophy Room" style, with stuffed native animals, splayed pelts, and mounted fish arranged throughout the room, creating an effect that is far more amusing than shocking. With a long tradition of serving top-quality steak and seafood in a casual fine dining atmosphere, it consistently draws in large crowds of locals and tourists. Seafood, steak menu. Breakfast, lunch, dinner. Closed Dec 25. Bar. Children's menu. Casual attire. **$$$**

**★ ★ MYKEL'S RESTAURANT & LOUNGE.** *35041 Kenai Spur Hwy, Soldotna (99669). Phone 907/262-4305; fax 907/262-4353. www.mykels.com.* Mykel's bills itself as the finest dining on the Kenai Peninsula and features fresh Alaskan seafood and "choice meats" as part of its imaginative menu. In all, it's the kind of place one would go to celebrate a special occasion or to have a long, leisurely meal with a friend. American menu. Lunch, dinner. Closed Jan 1, Thanksgiving, Dec 25. Bar. Children's menu. Casual attire. **$$$**

**★ ★ OLD TOWN VILLAGE RESTAURANT.** *1001 Mission Ave, Kenai (99611). Phone 907/283-4515.* Seafood, steak menu. Breakfast, lunch, dinner. Closed in winter. Bar. Children's menu. Casual attire. Reservations recommended. **$$**

# Kenai Fjords National Park (D-5)

**Web Site** www.nps.gov/kefj

The Seward Highway, a National Scenic Byway, connects Anchorage and the town of Seward in south-central Alaska. The 127-mile trip to Seward twists around steep ridges, reflective lakes, and alpine valleys, leading to a confluence of mountain, ice, and sea at Kenai Fjords National Park. The park's inner landscape is dominated by glaciers and ice caps, the most prominent being the 300-square-mile Harding Icefield, the largest ice cap in the United States. The glaciers stretch all the way to the coastline at the park's southern edge. Here, the narrow inlets of Aialik Bay lead out into the cold, choppy waters of the Gulf of Alaska.

Aside from relaxing amid serene surroundings, the most popular activities at Kenai (pronounced "keen eye") Fjords include fishing, hiking, kayaking, and wildlife viewing. The park is home to mountain goats, moose, puffins, sea otters, and sea lions, while humpback whales can be seen surfacing just off the coast. Many commercial guides offer wildlife viewing tours that begin in Seward.

The park has four public-use cabins, three of which (Aialik, Holgate, and Northarm) are situated along the coast. The fourth cabin (Willow) is available only during the winter months, and accessing it requires a 7-mile journey with the help of cross-country skis, snowshoes, a snowmachine, or a dogsled. Visitors can reserve cabins by calling the National Park Service (phone 907/224-3175).

By Alaska standards, the park is easily accessible, with Seward serviced by both the Alaska Railroad and the Alaska Marine Highway. Commercial flights are available as well, and charter boats and cruise ships offer additional alternatives for reaching the majestic scenery and abundant wildlife of Kenai Fjords National Park.

## What to See and Do

**Exit Glacier.** *Glacier Rd (Herman Leirer Rd), mile 8.6, Seward (99664).* Originating in the massive Harding Icefield that dominates the landscape on the eastern side of the Kenai Peninsula, Exit Glacier flows for 3 miles before coming to an end in a scenic river valley just north of Seward. Visitors can walk from the nature center to the foot of the glacier via the Outwash Plain Trail or branch off onto the relatively easy Overlook Loop Trail, which brings visitors to a small plateau very close to the jagged blue glacier ice. Park Service rangers lead one-hour interpretive tours from the Nature Center to the glacier along these trails twice a day during the summer, at 11 am and 3 pm. Visitors looking for a much more rigorous experience can take the 8-mile round-trip Harding Icefield Trial, which follows the glacier uphill to its source high up in the mountains. Rangers lead tours along this trail at 9 am on Saturdays in July and August. Because the trail climbs to 3,500 feet during the 4-mile ascent, this excursion is recommended only for extremely fit hikers. (Nature Center: summer, daily 9 am-7:30 pm)**$**

# Ketchikan (F-9)

**Population** 7,922
**Area Code** 907
**Information** Ketchikan Visitors Bureau, 131 Front St, 99901; phone 907/225-6166 or toll-free 800/770-3300
**Web Site** www.visit-ketchikan.com

Ketchikan is a town of about 8,500 people, but hosts nearly three-quarters of a million visitors during the summer. It's the first Alaskan stop for most cruise ships touring the Inside Passage and proudly declares itself to be "Alaska's First City." Set in the heart of the Tongass National Forest, the town has one of the highest rainfall totals in the state, with 162 inches of rain falling in an average year. It is also the closest community to Misty Fjords National Monument, a 2.3 million acre wilderness of massive glaciers, deep saltwater fjords, pristine forests, and abundant wildlife. Closer to town, the protected waters of the Inside Passage attract massive runs of salmon each year, leading to Ketchikan's claim to be the "Salmon Capital of the World." The most famous section of the old town area is Creek Street, a former red light district that now houses an appealing blend of restaurants, art galleries, and small shops built on pilings over Ketchikan Creek. Its a pedestrian-only zone and a great place to wander around, do a bit of shopping, and grab a bite to eat. The Ketchikan area is also rich in native culture. Totem Bight State Park, 8 miles north of town, contains a historic collection of totem poles set along a scenic trail on the shores of the Tongass Narrows. Saxman Totem Park, located 2 miles south of town, contains historic totem poles as well as workshops where visitors can watch native carvers fashion totem poles, canoes, and other artwork using the same techniques employed by their ancestors. The Totem Heritage Center in town offers classes in traditional art forms and preserves totems from abandoned villages, and the Southeast Alaska Discovery Center in the middle of downtown has a wide range of exhibits, including a selection of contemporary poles, samples of native basketry, and a model of a traditional fish camp.

## What to See and Do

**Deer MountainTribal Hatchery & Eagle Center.** *1158 Salmon Rd, Ketchikan (99901). On the banks of Ketchikan Creek, 1/4 mile upstream from Creek St. Phone 907/225-6760; toll-free 800/252-5158.* This creekside facility, run by the Ketchikan Indian Community, provides an up-close view of the workings of a modern fish hatchery. Throughout the summer, visitors are able to watch the upstream migration of silver and king salmon, the harvesting of salmon roe, and the feeding of the tiny salmon fry that will one day be released into waterways across Alaska. Also on-site is the Eagle Center, home to injured eagles that can't be returned to the wild. With its walk-through design, the enclosure offers visitors exceptionally close views of one of Alaska's most majestic creatures. (Mid-May-mid-Sept: daily 8 am-4:30 pm; mid-Sept-mid-May: by appointment only) **$$**

**Historic Creek Street and Dolly's House Museum.** *24 Creek St, Ketchikan (99901). Phone 907/225-2279.* One of Ketchikan's most popular tourist destinations is Historic Creek Street, a former red-light district built on pilings over the rushing waters of Ketchikan Creek. Visitors can stroll the narrow, pedestrian-only wooden boardwalks and take time to admire the beauty and architectural grace of the district's turn-of-the-century buildings, most of which have long since been converted into restaurants, art galleries, gift shops, and private residences. Visitors looking for a glimpse into Creek Street's bawdy past should visit the Dolly's House Museum at #24 Creek St. This building was one of Ketchikan's most infamous brothels during the town's early days and was owned and operated by Madam Dolly Arthur. Nowadays, it serves as a tangible link to the past, with fixtures and furnishings seemingly unchanged from the time when Dolly ran the show. (Summer, daily 8 am-5 pm; closed Oct-Apr) **$**

**Misty Fiords National Monument.** *3031 Tongass Ave, Ketchikan (99901). Phone 907/225-7535. www.fs.fed.us/r10/tongass.* This area at the southern border of the Tongass National Forest, accessible only by floatplane and boat, derives its name from the almost constant precipitation that occurs in the region; the area receives almost 14 feet of precipitation annually, giving rise to its many lakes, streams, and waterfalls. Behm Canal stretches more than 100 miles through the heart of the area, flowing past active glaciers and towering sea cliffs. Despite the rainy climate, kayaking and camping are popular with adventurers here.

**Saxman Native Village.** *S Tongass Hwy, mile 2.5, Ketchikan (99901). Phone 907/225-4846. www.capefoxtours.com.* Saxman Native Village, located a short drive south of downtown Ketchikan, offers visitors a chance to immerse themselves in the rich cultural and artistic heritage of the Tlingit tribe of southeast Alaska. The village features a park filled with 28 totems recovered from surrounding villages and restored by members of the Civilian Conservation Corps during the early part of the 20th century. Also on-site is the Beaver Clan House, a replica of a traditional winter house once used by the Tlingits. While in the house, visitors can learn about the history and language of the Tlingits and observe a Native dance demonstration. The highlight of the trip is the Saxman Carving Center, where visitors have the opportunity to observe master totem carvers and their apprentices at work, preserving their cultural heritage while creating objects of great beauty. Although there is no cost to visit the park, there is a fee for guided tours and demonstrations run by the park. Contact Cape Fox Tours for prices and tour availability.

**Southeast Alaska Discovery Center.** *50 Main St, Ketchikan (99901). Phone 907/228-6220; fax 907/228-6234. www.fs.fed.us/r10/tongass/districts/discovery center.* As one of four Public Lands Information Center's in Alaska, this centers mission is to provide information about the cultures, people, ecosystems, and history of Alaska's southeast. Throughout the day, the onsite theater shows *Mystical Southeast Alaska*, a short multimedia presentation that provides a general introduction to the region. In the center's exhibit halls, life-size ecosystem displays, historic artifacts, and scenic and wildlife photographs give visitors a more detailed view of the region's beauty and diversity. The center also features a staffed trip-planning room filled with information and pictures about each of Alaska's six geographic regions. (May-Sept: daily 8 am-5 pm; Oct-Apr: Tues-Sat 10 am-4:30 pm) **$**

**Totem Bight State Historical Park.** *Ranger Station,9883 N Tongass Hwy, Ketchikan (99901). Phone 907/247-8574. www.dnr.state.ak.us/parks/units/totembgh.htm.* In 1938, the US Forest Service began salvaging and reconstructing magnificent examples of Tlingit, Haida, and Tsimshian symbolic carvings. Decaying totem poles were copied in freshly cut cedar logs using traditional tools and techniques; even the paints used were made of natural materials like clam shells and salmon eggs. Today, this state park houses the largest collection of totem poles in the world. **$**

## Limited-Service Hotels

**★ ★ BEST WESTERN LANDING HOTEL.** *3434 Tongass Ave, Ketchikan (99901). Phone 907/225-5166; toll-free 800/428-8304; fax 907/225-6900. www.bestwestern.com.* This clean, comfortable, friendly hotel has the added advantage of being close to the main shopping, transportation, and tourist destinations in Ketchikan. It's directly across the street from the Alaska Marine ferry dock and two blocks from the city's small airport. With two restaurants, a small fitness center, and a free shuttle service anywhere within the city limits, it's a popular place for tourists looking to avoid the congestion and expense of downtown lodging and dining. 76 rooms. Pets accepted. Check-in 3 pm, check-out noon. Two restaurants. Fitness room. **$**

**★ ★ GILMORE HOTEL.** *326 Front St, Ketchikan (99901). Phone 907/225-9423; toll-free 800/225-9423; fax 907/225-7442. www.gilmorehotel.com.* Built in 1927, the Gilmore Hotel is one of the oldest, best-known hotels in Ketchikan. Located across the street from the cruise ship dock and in the heart of the historic downtown district, it was recently remodeled to bring it up to code while retaining as much of the building's original beauty and charm as possible. The result is a hotel that offers an eclectic mix of modern amenities like cable television and soda machines alongside such traditional features as cast-iron radiators and wooden window frames. Guest rooms are small and can be noisy, as the lounge downstairs is the place to party in Ketchikan. 42 rooms. Pets accepted. Complimentary continental breakfast. Check-in 1 pm, check-out noon. Restaurant. **$**

**★ ★ NARROWS INN.** *4871 N Tongass Hwy, Ketchikan (99901). Phone 907/247-2600; toll-free 888/686-2600; fax 907/247-2602. www.narrowsinn.com.* The Narrows Inn is the only year-round hotel on the water in Ketchikan. It's also one of the most scenic, with many of its 47 small rooms featuring private decks overlooking the water. With its own restaurant, lounge, boat dock, and waterfront grounds, the inn provides ample opportunities for guests to relax and unwind without having to drive anywhere, yet it's still relatively close to downtown, the airport, and the city's main shopping areas. 47 rooms. Complimentary continental breakfast. Check-in 4 pm, check-out noon. Restaurant. **$**

**★ SUPER 8.** *2151 Sea Level Dr, Ketchikan (99901). Phone 907/225-9088; toll-free 800/800-8000; fax 907/225-1072. www.super8.com.* Located on the water's edge in the same vast parking lot as the main shopping mall, the 82-room Super 8 is one of the best deals in Ketchikan. Rates are lower than at other lodgings in town, and some rooms have great views of Tongass Narrows and the cruise ships and floatplanes that pass in front of the motel. Rooms lack some common amenities, like coffee makers and ironing boards, but for a basic economy accommodation, it fits the bill just fine. 82 rooms. Pets accepted. Complimentary continental breakfast. Check-in 2 pm, check-out noon. **$**

**★ ★ WESTCOAST CAPE FOX LODGE.** *800 Venetia Way, Ketchikan (99901). Phone 907/225-8001; fax 907/225-8286.* The views from this architecturally stunning clifftop hotel are spectacular, with south-facing guest rooms overlooking downtown Ketchikan and the Tongass Narrows and north-facing ones looking out on the dramatic mountain range that rises up on the edge of town. The interior is magnificent, too, featuring a grand lobby framed by massive wooden posts and beams, a fireside lounge filled with live plants, museum-quality native artwork displays, and a sweeping central staircase accentuated by a huge totem carving by renowned local artist Nathan Jackson. Guests looking to shop, dine, and sightsee can ride the hotel's funicular from the lobby down the bluff and step off onto Creek Street, the main tourist area downtown. 72 rooms. Pets accepted. Check-in 3 pm, check-out 11 am. Restaurant. **$$**

## Restaurants

**★ ★ ANNABELLE'S FAMOUS KEG AND CHOWDER HOUSE.** *326 Front St, Ketchikan (99901). Phone 907/225-6009.* Annabelle's is located in an elegant 1927 dining room complete with mahogany panels, Scottish wool carpets, and beautiful sconce lighting. The attached lounge is impressive, too, with historic murals of old-time Creek Street, pressed tin ceilings, a colorful stained glass ceiling, and a handcrafted wooden bar. Located on the ground floor of the Gilmore Hotel (see), it's well worth a visit for its architectural, artistic, and historic appeal. American, seafood menu. Lunch, dinner. Closed Thanksgiving, Dec 25; also Sun in winter. Bar. Casual attire. **$$**

★ **DIAZ CAFE.** *335 Stedman St, Ketchikan (99901). Phone 907/225-2257.* American menu. Breakfast, lunch. Closed in winter. Casual attire. **$**

★ **DOCKSIDE DINER.** *1287 Tongass Ave, Ketchikan (99901). Phone 907/247-7787; fax 907/247-7737.* This diner is one of those places tourists are always looking for: a "real" Alaskan restaurant. With a menu offering a wide range of American "homestyle food for family dining" at reasonable prices, it's a place locals like to hang out in to catch up with one another and hear the latest news. American menu. Breakfast, lunch, dinner. Children's menu. Casual attire. Outdoor seating. **$$**

★ ★ ★ **HEEN KAHIDI.** *800 Venetia Way, Ketchikan (99901). Phone 907/225-8001; toll-free 866/225-8001; fax 907/225-8286. www.westcoasthotels.com.* Heen Kahidi, which translates as "House by the River," is perched on the side of a bluff overlooking downtown Ketchikan and the waters of the Tongass Narrows. The dining area has the feel of an après ski lodge, with massive wooden roof beams, a river rock fireplace, subtle lighting, and soft colors that enhance the stylish ambience of the place. Towering literally and figuratively above all of its competitors, this restaurant offers an appealing array of succulent seafood, chicken, and pasta dishes prepared by Chef Tim, the creative mastermind behind the restaurant's success. American, seafood menu. Breakfast, lunch, dinner. Closed Thanksgiving, Dec 25. Bar. Casual attire. **$$**

★ **JEREMIAH'S.** *3434 Tongass Ave, Ketchikan (99901). Phone 907/225-6530; fax 907/225-5526.* Jeremiah was a bullfrog and the inspiration for this restaurant's name as well as its signature drink, the Midori-based "Bullfrog." Designed with style and sophistication in mind, the bistro-style dining area features comfortable booths, a sleek curved wooden bar, soft lighting, and a small outdoor patio overlooking the ferry terminal. Pizza. Lunch, dinner. Closed Dec 25. Bar. Children's menu. Casual attire. Outdoor seating. **$$**

★ **THE LANDING RESTAURANT.** *3434 Tongass Ave, Ketchikan (99901). Phone 907/225-5166; toll-free 800/428-8304; fax 907/225-6900.* This restaurant functions as a popular hangout for people who live at the northern end of Ketchikan. The décor is retro '50s with big, padded booths, stark white floors and walls, glass-block partitions between tables, and plenty of counter seating. Waitresses and customers call each other by name, giving the place a real neighborly, hometown feel. American menu. Breakfast, lunch, dinner. Closed Dec 25. Bar. Children's menu. Casual attire. **$$**

★ ★ **THE NARROWS RESTAURANT.** *4871 N Tongass Hwy, Ketchikan (99901). Phone 907/247-5900; fax 907/247-2602. www.narrowsinn.com.* One of the best reasons to visit this restaurant is to take in the exceptional views it offers of the floatplanes, boats, and wildlife that share the waters of Tongass Narrows. The menu is another big selling point, featuring standard American dishes as well as house specialties such as stuffed halibut, Coffman Cove oysters, and Alaskan king crab. American, seafood menu. Breakfast, lunch, dinner. Closed Dec 25. Bar. Children's menu. Casual attire. Reservations recommended. **$$**

★ ★ **NEW YORK CAFE.** *207 Stedman St, Ketchikan (99901). Phone 907/225-0246; toll-free 866/225-0246; fax 907/225-1803. www.thenewyorkhotel.com.* American menu. Breakfast, lunch, dinner. Closed in winter. Bar. Children's menu. Casual attire. Reservations recommended. Outdoor seating. **$$**

★ ★ **OCEAN VIEW RESTAURANTE.** *1831 Tongass Ave, Ketchikan (99901). Phone 907/225-7566; fax 907/247-7566.* The décor of this popular local restaurant can best be described as "upscale Mexican villa," with polished wood chairs, petite tea candles, a colorful Mexican bar, and walls and ceilings painted in vibrant oranges, yellows, and reds. Although the emphasis is on Mexican food, the restaurant also serves a wide range of Italian, Greek, and American dishes. Italian, Mexican menu. Breakfast, lunch, dinner. Closed Jan 1, July 4, Dec 25. Bar. Children's menu. Casual attire. Reservations recommended. **$$**

★ **THE PIZZA MILL.** *808 Water St, Ketchikan (99901). Phone 907/225-6646; fax 907/247-8080.* This family-run restaurant proudly bills itself as Ketchikan's original pizza place, having been established in the early 1970s. It offers subs, Mexican food, burgers, and spaghetti, but is most proud of its "pizza with an attitude:" thirty-five different pizza choices, including eleven "Yuppie Pies" with names like Dead Head, Fish Hippie, and Generation X. Pizza. Lunch, dinner, late-night. Casual attire. **$**

**★ RED ANCHOR CAFE & DELI.** *1935 Tongass Ave, #A, Ketchikan (99901). Phone 907/247-5287.* American deli menu. Breakfast, lunch. Closed Sun. Casual attire. **$**

**★ ★ SALMON FALLS RESTAURANT.** *16707 N Tongass Hwy, Ketchikan (99901). Phone 907/225-2752; toll-free 800/247-9059; fax 907/225-2710.* Seafood menu. Breakfast, lunch, dinner. Closed in winter. Bar. Casual attire. Outdoor seating. **$$**

**★ THAI HOUSE.** *127 Stedman St, Ketchikan (99901). Phone 907/225-8424; fax 907/247-8424.* With window seating on two floors and a small outdoor deck built over the waters of Ketchikan Creek, this bustling restaurant offers guests terrific views of Ketchikan's popular Creek Street as well as savory Thai and Chinese dishes. The atmosphere inside is relaxed and informal, making it a great place to unwind after a long day working or sightseeing. Chinese menu, Thai menu. Lunch, dinner. Closed Thanksgiving, Dec 25. Casual attire. Outdoor seating. **$$**

# Kobuk Valley National Park

**Web Site** www.nps.gov/kova

An unexpected sight awaits visitors who venture above the Arctic Circle to Kobuk Valley National Park: sand dunes rising as high as 150 feet. The landscape is not a mirage, and, no, this is not Arizona; the sands were created by the grinding of glaciers during the last ice age and deposited here by shifting sands and water. Squeezed between the Baird Mountains to the north and the Warring Mountains to the south, the Kobuk Valley is perhaps best explored by paddling along the calm, wide waters of the Kobuk River. The ideal time to visit the park is late summer, when more than 300,000 western arctic caribou—the largest caribou herd in North America—cross the river during their migration south. The caribou, known as "the nomads of the north," move constantly across the alpine tundra in search of food to support their body weight, which for a bull ranges from 150 to 300 pounds. Getting to Kobuk Valley is challenging, typically requiring two flights: a commercial flight to either Kotzebue or Nome, followed by an air-taxi ride to the park. There are no roads in or around the park. The Kotzebue Public Lands Information Center offers educational and interpretive programs throughout the year. (Daily; closed holidays)

# Kodiak (E-5)

**Population** 6,334
**Area Code** 907
**Information** Kodiak Island Convention & Visitors Bureau, phone 907/486-4782 or toll-free 800/789-4782
**Web Site** www.kodiak.org

Located on Chiniak Bay at the northeastern tip of Kodiak Island, the town of Kodiak is home to more than 770 commercial fishing vessels that ply the waters of the Gulf of Alaska and the Bering Sea in search of king crab, salmon, halibut, cod, shrimp, and many other varieties of seafood. Although the Alutiit people have called the island their home for nearly 8,000 years, it wasn't until the arrival of Alexander Baranov in 1792 that a permanent settlement was established next to the sheltered natural harbor he christened St. Paul. In creating a fur trading outpost on the site, he also founded what was to become the first capital of Russian America. By 1804, just twelve years after the Russian's arrival, the sea otters had been hunted to near extinction, so Baranov moved the company's operations far to the west where he founded a new settlement known today as Sitka. With the demise of the fur trade and the 1867 purchase of Alaska by the United States, the local economy shifted to commercial salmon fishing, which has remained a mainstay of the local economy ever since. Two hundred years after the departure of Baranov and his workers, Kodiak still maintains ties to its Russian heritage, most notably in the Holy Resurrection Russian Orthodox Church, with its blue onion-dome spire and Russian cross; in the Baranov Museum nearby, which was built by Baranov's men as an otter pelt warehouse; and in numerous street, place, and business names throughout the town.

Kodiak today offers visitors far more than just fresh Alaskan seafood, liquid sunshine, and spectacular views. An estimated 3,000 Kodiak brown bears live on the island along with large numbers of deer, foxes, mountain goats, bald eagles, and shore birds and the waters near shore are home to orcas, humpback whales, sea otters, and Stellar seal lions. Visitors need only walk the shores, hike the trails, drive the roads, or paddle the rivers and bays to immerse themselves in the natural wonders that make Kodiak such an extraordinary destination in Alaska.

## What to See and Do

**Baranov Museum.** *101 Marine Way, Kodiak (99615). Phone 907/486-5920; fax 907/486-3166. www.baranov.us.* Housed in the oldest wooden building in Alaska, this historical museum was built by the Russian-American Company as an otter pelt warehouse during Kodiak's heyday as a Russian fur trading post. Nowadays, it's home to a collection of photographs, exhibits, artworks, and artifacts tracing Kodiaks history from the time the Alutiit Indian culture thrived in the area, through the Russian fur trading frenzy, and into Alaska's territorial era and early statehood years. (Summer: Mon-Sat 10 am-4 pm, Sun noon-4 pm; winter: Tues-Sat 10 am-3 pm; special openings on request) **$**

**Fort Abercrombie State Historic Park.** *Kodiak District Office, 1400 Abercrombie Dr, Kodiak (99615). Phone 907/486-6339. www.dnr.state.ak.us/parks/units/kodiak/ftaber.htm.* This scenic oceanside park on 186 acres north of downtown Kodiak was the site of a defensive military installation during World War II and still contains visual reminders of its wartime function. Nowadays, the site plays a completely different role: that of scenic park, crisscrossed by a ribbon of trails passing through lush meadows, trout-filled lakes, and seaside cliffs with excellent whale-watching vantage points. Only 3 1/2 miles from downtown and connected to it by a paved bike trail, it's a popular spot for outdoor enthusiasts and those looking to spend a couple of hours relaxing in a wild, beautiful environment. Hiking and camping are available on-site, as is a visitor center run by the Alaska Department of Natural Resources. **FREE**

**Kodiak Island.** *Kodiak. Phone 907/486-4782; toll-free 800/789-4782. www.kodiak.org.* Unlike the frozen wilderness that's usually associated with Alaska, Kodiak Island is known as the state's Emerald Isle because of its green snow-tipped mountains and tree-lined fjords. Located off the southern coast of Alaska, it is one of the largest commercial fishing ports in the nation and is famous for its Kodiak brown bears. Outdoor activities here include fishing, kayaking, hiking, biking, and wildlife viewing.

**Kodiak Island National Wildlife Refuge Visitor Center.** *1390 Buskin River Rd, Kodiak (99615). Phone 907/487-2600. kodiak.fws.gov.* Located beside the Buskin River a half-mile from Kodiak Airport, this visitor center is designed to educate people about the animals, plants, and ecosystems that make up the 1. 9-million-acre Kodiak National Wildlife Refuge. Encompassing two-thirds of Kodiak Island and a few neighboring islands, the refuge is a haven for red foxes, river otters, weasels, Sitka deer, mountain goats, and 250 species of birds, including an estimated 600 pairs of bald eagles. The most famous inhabitants, though, are the approximately 3,000 Kodiak brown bears that roam the island. The largest of the brown bears, they average 10 feet tall and weigh as much as 1,600 pounds. The refuge is accessible only by boat or floatplane, so the visitor center also serves as an invaluable resource for travelers planning trips into the area. (Memorial Day-Labor Day: Mon-Fri 8 am-7 pm, Sat-Sun noon-4 pm; rest of year: Mon-Fri 8 am-4:30 pm)

## Special Events

**Bear Country Music Festival.** *State Fair and Rodeo Grounds, W Rezanof Dr, Kodiak (99615). Phone 907/486-4829.* This annual musical event features two days of live performances of folk, country, bluegrass, soft rock, and native Alaskan music by bands from all around the state. The festival draws thousands of visitors each year and features performances on three stages, one of which is indoors to hedge against Kodiak's unpredictable weather. Camping is available nearby, and shuttle service is provided between downtown and the festival site. Mid-July. **$$**

**Kodiak State Fair & Rodeo.** *Kodiak State Fair & Rodeo Grounds, W Rezanof Dr, Kodiak (99615). Phone 907/486-6380.* This local version of the larger state fair held in Palmer retains much of the old-fashioned, hometown charm of a traditional county fair. Rodeo events like calf roping, barrel racing, and bull and bronc riding offer guaranteed excitement for adults and teens, while pony rides, a petting zoo, pie eating, seed spitting, and bubble gum blowing competitions keep the younger crowd entertained. Live local music and vendor booths selling everything from local artwork to kettle corn round out the fairs attractions. Labor Day weekend. **$$**

## Limited-Service Hotels

**★★ BEST WESTERN KODIAK INN.** *236 Rezanof Dr W, Kodiak (99615). Phone 907/486-5712; toll-free 888/563-4254; fax 907/486-3430. www.kodiakinn.com.* Built on the side of a hill on the edge of downtown Kodiak, the Best Western Kodiak Inn is considered one of the top two places to stay in town. It has terrific views of Kodiak's two harbors and the orcas, seals, and other wildlife that inhabit the bay. Guests enjoy clean, comfortable, and spacious rooms and access to an outdoor cabana with a whirlpool in it. Book early if you want a harbor-view room, as these rooms tend to sell out more quickly. 80 rooms. Pets accepted. Complimentary continental breakfast. Check-in 2 pm, check-out noon. Restaurant, bar. Whirlpool. **$**

★★ **COMFORT INN.** *1395 Airport Way, Kodiak (99615). Phone 907/487-2700; toll-free 800/544-2202; fax 907/487-4447.* The Buskin River Inn is an ideal place to stay for those looking for quiet, comfortable accommodations in an idyllic setting, surrounded by excellent fishing, hiking, and sightseeing spots. It's located 6 miles from downtown Kodiak, alongside the Buskin River. Although the river isn't visible from any room in the hotel, west-facing rooms have terrific views of nearby Mount Barometer and other peaks. Wildlife enthusiasts will be in their element here: the area around the hotel is a haven for bald eagles, white-tailed deer, foxes, and other small animals. The hotel's restaurant, the Eagle's Nest (see), is a local favorite. 50 rooms. Pets accepted. Check-in 2 pm, check-out noon. Restaurant, bar. **$**

★★ **SHELIKOF LODGE.** *211 Thorsheim Ave, Kodiak (99615). Phone 907/486-4141; fax 907/486-4116. www.ptialaska.net/~kyle.* A longtime favorite in downtown Kodiak, the Shelikof Lodge is a popular destination for travelers who use it as a home base while they hunt, fish, and explore Kodiak Island during the summer and fall. Its central location, knowledgeable staff, and friendly service make it a good place to go to be in the middle of the action. 38 rooms. Pets accepted. Check-in upon availability, check-out noon. Restaurant, bar. Airport transportation available. **$**

## Restaurants

★★ **2ND FLOOR.** *116 W Resanof Dr, Kodiak (99615). Phone 907/486-8555; fax 907/486-8559.* In keeping with its Japanese theme, the interior of this popular restaurant is subtly decorated, with waist-high screens and large plants creating intimate nooks throughout the dining room. Paper lanterns hanging from the ceiling and colorful Japanese prints on the wall create an appealing, casually elegant ambience. Japanese menu. Lunch, dinner. Closed holidays. Children's menu. Casual attire. **$$**

★★ **THE CHART ROOM.** *236 Resanof Dr W, Kodiak (99615). Phone 907/486-5712; fax 907/486-3430. www.kodiakinn.com.* Located on the second floor of the Best Western Kodiak Inn, the Chart Room offers captivating views of Kodiak's waterfront and the mountains and bays that surround the town. The restaurant provides casual fine dining in a relaxing, slightly upscale environment. Particularly noteworthy are the pre- and post-tsunami photos of Kodiak that line the entryway. American menu. Breakfast, lunch, dinner. Closed Dec 25. Bar. Children's menu. Casual attire. **$$$**

★★ **EAGLE'S NEST RESTAURANT.** *1395 Airport Way, Kodiak (99615). Phone 907/487-2700; toll-free 800/544-2202; fax 907/487-4447.* Eagle's Nest Restaurant is the on-site restaurant at the Buskin River Inn (see). With large picture windows looking out onto a dark green forest and jagged mountains rising above the tree tops, it's a casual, though elegant setting for dining and celebrating. During warmer weather, a large outdoor deck provides an opportunity to dine alfresco with excellent views amid a peaceful setting. American menu. Breakfast, lunch, dinner. Closed Thanksgiving, Dec 25. Bar. Children's menu. Casual attire. Outdoor seating. **$$$**

★★ **EL CHICANO MEXICAN RESTAURANT & CANTINA.** *103 Center Ave, Kodiak (99615). Phone 907/486-6116. www.elchicano.com.* El Chicano is the place to go in Kodiak for quality Mexican food in a family-friendly atmosphere in the heart of downtown. With a street-side outdoor patio, extensive menu, and a huge lounge offering live music, karaoke, and weekend DJs, the restaurant is a major player in the local social scene. Mexican menu. Lunch, dinner. Bar. Children's menu. Casual attire. Outdoor seating. **$$**

★★ **EUGENE'S RESTAURANT.** *1815 Selief Ln, Kodiak (99615). Phone 907/486-2625; fax 907/486-8589.* This popular Chinese restaurant in downtown Kodiak offers a vast menu selection and ultra-friendly service. There's nothing skimpy or delicate here; owner James Chong is a real meat lover and serves no steaks less than 14 ounces. The only complaint they hear at Eugene's is that the portions are so large, customers can't finish them. Chinese menu. Lunch, dinner. Closed Mon; Thanksgiving, Dec 25, children's menu. Casual attire. **$$**

★ **HENRY'S GREAT ALASKAN RESTAURANT.** *512 Marine Way, Kodiak (99615). Phone 907/486-8844.* American menu. Lunch, dinner. Bar. Children's menu. Casual attire. Reservations recommended. Outdoor seating. **$**

**★ PEKING SIZZLER BURGER RESTAURANT.** *116 W Rezanof Dr, Kodiak (99615). Phone 907/486-3300; fax 907/486-8559.* This newly renovated, oddly named restaurant has been serving an eclectic mix of Chinese food, hamburgers, fish and chips, and shakes to Kodiak locals and tourists since the early 1980s. The extensive menu, inexpensive prices, and convenient downtown location make it a family- and budget-friendly place to grab a bite while on the go. American menu, Chinese menu. Lunch, dinner. Closed holidays. Casual attire. **$$**

**★ SHELIKOF LODGE RESTAURANT.** *211 Thorsheim Ave, Kodiak (99615). Phone 907/486-4300; fax 907/486-4116. www.ptialaska.net/~kyle.* Billing itself as one of the cheapest restaurants in town, the Shelikof Lodge Restaurant offers a variety of daily specials, fresh soups, and other hearty American and seafood dishes. Although tucked away inside the Shelikof Lodge (see), it's not just hotel guests who eat here—the place is frequently crowded with locals who appreciate the good food and friendly, reliable service. American, Italian menu. Breakfast, lunch, dinner. Closed Thanksgiving, Dec 25. Bar. Children's menu. Casual attire. **$**

# Lake Clark National Park and Preserve

**Web Site** www.nps.gov/lacl

Lake Clark National Park & Preserve encompasses 4 million acres of pristine wilderness, extending from Cook Inlet, across the craggy peaks of the Chigmit Mountans, farther west to the tundra-covered hills of Interior Alaska. Two active volcanoes can be found in the park: Mount Redoubt and Mount Iliamna. The park's namesake, Lake Clark, stretches for 40 miles. Teeming with red salmon, grayling, Dolly Varden, and northern pike, Lake Clark offers tremendous fishing opportunities, as do the parks many other lakes and rivers—three of which have been designated National Wild and Scenic Rivers. Fishing season runs from May until October, although a few of the lakes may not fully thaw until June. Hiking is another popular activity, but it requires considerable backcountry experience and know-how. The park contains no trails, and even the most physically fit hikers will be challenged—and slowed—by streams that must be forded and dense vegetation, particularly near the coast. For those willing to take on the challenge, spectacular rewards await: awe-inspiring scenery, incomparable solitude, and frequent wildlife sightings. Dall sheep, moose, and black and brown bears call the park home, as do more than 125 species of birds. Beluga whales, harbor seals, and sea lions can be seen in Chinitna Bay and Tuxedni Bay. No roads lead to the park, but floatplanes regularly shuttle visitors to the waters of Lake Clark from Anchorage, about 150 miles to the northeast.

# Moose Pass

**Settled** 1909
**Population** 206
**Area Code** 907
**Information** Moose Pass Chamber of Commerce & Visitors Bureau, PO Box 147, 99631
**Web Site** www.moosepass.net

This tiny hamlet of 200 people on the southern shores of Trail Lake in the middle of the Kenai Peninsula is renown for its scenic beauty and its laid back, rustic charm. Throughout the summer, floatplanes skim in over the mountains and land on the lake, dropping off hikers, hunters, and fishermen who come to take advantage of the town's easy access to wild Alaska. From mid-May to mid-September, the Alaska Railroad winds down the eastern side of the lake, stopping in Moose Pass each day on its journey to and from Seward, 29 miles to the south. In winter, when heavy winter snows close the rail line, the town remains accessible via the Seward Highway, which passes by the edge of town, connecting Anchorage with Seward. Located less than 20 miles from Cooper Landing and the spectacular fishing of the Kenai River, Moose Pass is a popular spot for travelers looking for beauty and tranquility in the heart of one of Alaska's most popular regions.

## Special Event

**Summer Solstice Festival.** *Main St, Moose Pass (99631). www.moosepass.net/solstice.html.* Despite having a population of only 200 people, Moose Pass throws a lively festival to celebrate the summer solstice each year. Held on the weekend of or immediately preceding June 21, this two-day event features live music from local bands, arts and crafts booths, a community barbecue, and a huge bake sale of cakes, cookies, pies, and brownies baked by local residents. Sponsored by the local Sportsman's Club, the festival proceeds are used to support community projects and organizations, making it truly an Alaskan hometown event.

## Limited-Service Hotel

★ ★ **TRAIL LAKE LODGE.** *Seward Hwy, mile 29.5, Moose Pass (99631). Phone 907/288-3101; toll-free 888/395-3624; fax 907/288-3106. www.traillakelodge.com.* The Trail Lake Lodge is actually two buildings: a motel with small, clean rooms and basic amenities and a main building with six newer, more spacious rooms (with telephones) and a restaurant. Located 30 minutes from Seward and 20 minutes from world-class river fishing, it's in a convenient, peaceful, and spectacular setting, ideal for river and lake anglers and daytrippers who don't want to be stuck in a "large" city like Seward. During the winter, it's popular with snowmachiners who like to explore the trails around Moose Pass. In the long days of summer, guests enjoy scenery from the lodge's long, wide veranda. 35 rooms. Check-in 2 pm, check-out 10 am. Restaurant, bar. **$**

## Restaurants

★ ★ **SUMMIT LAKE LODGE.** *Seward Hwy, mile 45.5, Moose Pass. Phone 907/244-2031. www.summitlakelodge.com.* American menu. Breakfast, lunch, dinner. Closed in winter. Bar. Children's menu. Casual attire. Reservations recommended. **$**

★ ★ **TRAIL LAKE LODGE RESTAURANT.** *Seward Hwy, mile 29.5, Moose Pass (99631). Phone 907/288-3101; toll-free 888/395-3624; fax 907/288-3106. www.traillakelodge.com.* This small restaurant is one of those warm, inviting, homey places that are so enjoyable to visit while on a road trip. It offers hearty meals at reasonable prices as well as some unexpected treats like jambalaya, quiche Lorraine, and the house specialty and local favorite, quesadillas, listed on the menu as being "World Famous (in Moose Pass)." International menu. Breakfast, lunch, dinner. Closed Oct; also Tues-Thurs in Nov-Apr. Bar. Children's menu. Casual attire. **$$**

# Noatak National Preserve

Far above the Arctic Circle in northwest Alaska, Noatak National Preserve offers an extraordinary float-trip experience for canoeists and kayakers. The Noatak River, designated a National Wild and Scenic River, flows for 350 miles, passing through dense coniferous forests and wide-open tundra as it cuts a path through the rugged peaks of the Brooks Range to Kotzebue Sound, just east of the Bering Strait. Wildlife-watching and photography are other popular activities within the preserve, which is home to musk oxen, grizzly bears, and caribou. There are no trails or roads within the park. Winters are extremely harsh here—only the hardiest of dog mushers should consider a visit during the winter months. Summer days are long and temperatures comparatively mild—July highs often eclipse 60 degrees. Alaska Airlines serves the town of Kotzebue, which is a short air-taxi ride from the preserve.

# Palmer (D-5)

**Population** 4,533
**Area Code** 907
**Information** Greater Palmer Chamber of Commerce, PO Box 45, 99645; phone 907/745-2880
**Web Site** www.palmerchamber.org

Tucked into a fertile valley between the rugged Talkeetna Range to the north and the towering Chugach Range to the south, Palmer was originally established as a trading post on the Matanuska River by George Palmer around 1890. It remained a sleepy little town until 1935 when it was chosen as the site of a New Deal agricultural experiment called the Matanuska Valley Colony. Two hundred farm families from the American Midwest arrived in the area that year and were given 40-acre tracts of land in the hopes of establishing a permanent agricultural colony that would help in the development of Alaska. Although the colony ultimately proved unsuccessful, descendents of the original colonists continue to live in the area today and many of the original buildings they constructed are listed on the National Register of Historic Places. Nowadays, Palmer is home to the Alaska State Fair, a 12-day event that begins in late August and runs through Labor Day. The Palmer area also offers a broad array of activities year round, ranging from fishing, hiking, and berry picking during the summer to ice-fishing, cross-country skiing, and dog sled racing during the winter.

## What to See and Do

**Colony House Museum.** *316 E Elmwood Ave, Palmer (99645). Phone 907/745-1935.* Housed in a farmhouse constructed as part of the Matanuska Colony during the 1930s, this small historical museum brings to life the story of the Depression-era agricultural experiment that led to the development of modern Palmer.

Run by the Palmer Historical Society, the museum offers free guided tours, some led by descendents of the original colonists. (May-Aug: Tues-Sat 10 am-4 pm; closed in winter) **DONATION**

**Independence Mine State Historical Park.** *Hatcher Pass Rd, mile 18 (Fishhook Willow Rd), Palmer. 19.5 miles NW of Palmer; 22 miles E of Wasilla. The road connects with the Parks Hwy near the town of Willow for tourists heading N to Denali National Park. Phone 907/745-2827. www.dnr.state.ak.us/parks.* The site of gold mining operations from 1906 to 1951, this 271-acre park is set in a scenic, tundra landscape of steep rock mountains, treeless plains, and icy streams. Thirteen of the mine's original structures dating from the 1930s and 40s have been preserved at the site, giving visitors a glimpse into living and working conditions at the mine during its heyday. With a network of year-round trails and relatively easy access from nearby towns, the Hatcher Pass area surrounding the mine is a popular destination for hikers, mountain bikers, casual gold panners, and berry pickers during the summer months and sledders, snowboarders, and cross-country skiers during the winter. Guided tours are offered at 1 pm and 3 pm every day during the summer, with an additional tour at 4:30 pm on weekends. (Visitor center, early June-early Sept, daily 10 am-7 pm)

**Musk Ox Farm.** *Glenn Hwy, mile 50.1, Palmer (99645). Phone 907/745-4151; fax 907/746-4831. www.muskoxfarm.org.* For more than four decades, this one-of-a-kind nonprofit farm has been raising domesticated musk oxen in the Matanuska Valley. Visitors to the farm can tour the grounds, taking photographs and learning about the history of these shaggy holdovers from the last ice age. The farm is more than just a tourist attraction, though; it's an important player in a thriving cottage industry. Each spring, the musk oxen's soft underwool, called qiviut, is combed out and shipped to native communities in Alaska's far north, where it's fashioned into traditional wool garments, which are then sold in stores throughout the state. Providing eight times the warmth of regular sheep's wool, clothes made from qiviut have long been a highly valued commodity in Alaska. Guided tours are given every half-hour until 5:30 pm. (Mothers Day-late Sept, daily 10 am-6 pm)

## Special Event

**Alaska State Fair.** *Alaska State Showgrounds, 2075 Glenn Hwy, Palmer (99645). Phone 907/745-4827; toll-free 800/850-3247. www.alaskastatefair.org.* This annual state fair is one of the highlights of Alaska's summer season, with 12 days of live entertainment, carnival rides, rodeo events, and exhibitors displaying everything from handcrafted jewelry and local artwork to homemade quilts, cakes, pies, jams, and jellies. One of the most popular highlights of the fair is the agricultural weigh-off, where locally grown cabbages frequently top 100 pounds and carrots have been known to tip the scales at more than 70 pounds. Located less than 45 miles from downtown Anchorage, the fair makes for an easy day trip for visitors to the Anchorage area. Late Aug-early Sept. **$$**

## Limited-Service Hotels

**★ ★ COLONY INN.** *325 E Elmwood, Palmer (99645). Phone 907/745-3330; fax 907/746-3330.*
This quaint little inn, with only 12 rooms, was built in 1935 as a teacher's dormitory for the Matanuska Colony. Easily accessible from the Glenn Highway, it's located in the middle of downtown Palmer, next to the visitor information center and within sight of most of Palmer's main shops. The lobby features a stately fireplace, period smoking chairs, and tasteful antique furniture and memorabilia, while the former dorm rooms have been transformed into ultra-cozy guest rooms filled with furniture harkening back to the 1930s. For those looking for something elegantly different, it's well worth a visit. Guests register and pick up keys at the Valley Hotel nearby. 12 rooms. Check-in upon availability, check-out 11 am. Restaurant. **$**

**★ ★ GOLD MINER'S HOTEL.** *918 S Colony Way, Palmer (99645). Phone 907/745-6160; toll-free 800/725-2752; fax 907/745-6173. www.goldminershotel.com.* This 28-room hotel began as the town's theater and has been extensively remodeled on numerous occasions since then, which accounts for the unusual floor plan. Overlooking the park area of town, it offers enormous rooms, a convenient midtown location, and inexpensive rates as well as magnificent views of Pioneer Peak, Sleeping Lady, and the towering Chugach Range. Seven of the rooms have access to the large rooftop deck, which brings many guests back to the Gold Miner's Hotel year after year. Pets accepted. Check-in 2 pm, check-out noon. Restaurant. **$**

**★ ★ VALLEY HOTEL.** *606 S Alaska St, Palmer (99645). Phone 907/745-3330; fax 907/746-3330.* One of the most striking new features of this 1948 hotel is the extensive woodwork featured throughout; guest room headboards, bedside tables, window valances, and hallway moldings and partitions have all been carefully handcrafted by one of the current owners. The result is striking, adding warmth, artistry, and a personal touch to each of the cozy rooms. The downtown hotel is within walking distance of the visitor center and most of the town's restaurants and shops. A 24-hour restaurant—a rarity in Alaska—adds convenience. 43 rooms. Check-out 11 am. Restaurant. **$**

## Restaurants

**★ ★ GOLD MINER'S STEAKHOUSE & RESTAURANT.** *918 S Colony Way, Palmer (99645). Phone 907/745-6160; toll-free 800/725-2752; fax 907/745-6173. www.goldminershotel.com.* Combining local history and Alaskan artistry, the owners of this downtown restaurant have incorporated mining memorabilia and a gigantic nature mural into their spacious, rustic dining area. With a relaxed staff, all-day breakfast, and daily all-you-can-eat specials, it's an enticing place to stop for a meal. American menu. Breakfast, lunch, dinner. Closed Thanksgiving, Dec 25. Bar. Children's menu. Casual attire. **$$**

**★ ★ INN CAFÉ.** *325 E Elmwood, Palmer (99645). Phone 907/746-6118.* Located in one of Palmer's oldest buildings, Inn Café offers casual dining in a visually and historically appealing setting, with hardwood floors and walls, an understated but elegant lobby, and beautiful six-pane windows that let in plenty of light and provide stunning views of the Chugach and Talkeetna mountain ranges that surround. American menu. Lunch, dinner. Closed Mon; Jan 1, Thanksgiving, Dec 25. Casual attire. **$$**

**★ ★ OPEN CAFE.** *606 S Alaska St, Palmer (99645). Phone 907/745-3330; fax 907/746-3330.* This restaurant is notable for two reasons: its open 24 hours a day, every day of the year and it offers fresh baked pastries and more than 25 kinds of pie prepared on site by a local pastry chef. With an open-seating plan, lots of windows, and an extensive menu, it's bright, sunny, and family-friendly. American menu. Breakfast, lunch, dinner, late-night. Bar. Children's menu. Casual attire. **$$**

# Petersburg (E-8)

**Founded** 1910
**Population** 3,224
**Area Code** 907
**Web Site** www.petersburg.org

Petersburg is both geographically and culturally far removed from the rest of the towns and villages that dot the Inside Passage. In a region with centuries-old ties to Russian and native cultures, this remote fishing port at the northern tip of Mitkof Island proudly celebrates its rich Norwegian heritage. Founded at the end of the 19th century by Norwegian businessman Peter Buschmann, Petersburg soon attracted other Norwegian immigrants who felt at home amid the snowy mountains and deep fjords of the area. Set in the heart of the Tongass National Forest, Mitkof Island features a landscape dominated not by shady forests and craggy peaks but by muskeg bogs, dense brush, and rolling hills. The best time to visit is around May 17, when the town holds its annual "Little Norway Festival" to coincide with Norway's Constitution Day. Visitors can enjoy traditional Norwegian music, dancing, and food, view the works of local artists, and even get their pictures taken with "real" Vikings and Valkyries.

## What to See and Do

**Clausen Memorial Museum.** *203 Fram St, Petersburg (99833). Phone 907/772-3598. www.clausenmuseum.alaska.net.* This small city-run museum in the center of town focuses on the historical development of Petersburg and Mitkof Island, on which the town is located. Exhibits and artifacts relating to Tlingit culture introduce visitors to the earliest society that lived in the region, while fishing gear and nautical memorabilia bring to life the history of the Norwegian fishermen who settled in the region during the latter part of the 19th century. Logging tools and artifacts also are on display, providing insight into another industry that helped fuel Petersburgs economy during the 20th century. (May-mid-Sept: Mon-Sat 10:30 am-4:30 pm; winter hours vary)

**Petroglyph Beach State Historic Park.** *Wrangell (99929). Phone 907/874-2381. www.wrangell.com/visitors/attractions/history/petroglyph.* Petroglypho—or rock carvings—were artistic works by Native Americans, and Petroglyph Beach offers some of the best examples that still survive today.

**Sing Lee Alley.** *Sing Lee Alley, Petersburg.* Running parallel to the waters of Middle and South harbors and on a boardwalk over Hammer Slough, this narrow street is one of Petersburg's oldest and most historic. Originally the social and commercial center of the town, the street is no longer a major thoroughfare but does pass by a number of Petersburg landmarks. The Sons of Norway Hall, located at 23 S. Sing Lee Alley was built in 1912 by local Norwegian immigrants and has played a key role in the preservation of the town's unique Norwegian heritage. Next to the Hall is the Bojer Wikan Fishermen's Memorial Park, built on pilings above Hammer Slough. Featuring an oversized statue of a fisherman and a simple memorial gazebo, its a powerful, but understated tribute to the local men and women who have lost their lives while working in the fishing industry. Hammer Slough is itself an important local landmark, as it provides a picturesque backdrop for tourist's photographs of the historic district.

### Special Event

**Little Norway Festival.** *Petersburg. Phone 907/772-3646. www.petersburg.org/visitor/festivals.html.* This community-wide event celebrates Norwegian Constitution Day and Petersburg's Norwegian heritage. Events include live performances of Norwegian music, songs, and dances; a Scandinavian pageant; downtown arts and crafts booths; and the annual Fish-O-Rama Seafood Feast. The festival's colorful parade is a highlight of the weekend, with the Viking ship *Valhalla* "sailing" through downtown to the strains of traditional Norwegian songs. Third full weekend in May.

### Limited-Service Hotels

**★ ★ SCANDIA HOUSE.** *110 N Nordic Dr, Petersburg (99833). Phone 907/772-4281; toll-free 800/722-5006; fax 907/772-4301. www.scandiahousehotel.com.* This hotel offers spacious, bright, and affordable accommodations, some of which have terrific views of the water and the mountains around Petersburg. It also provides guests with a large, comfortable lobby with a wide range of traveler's amenities, including wireless Internet access, on-site car and boat rentals, a fish and game freezer, a hairstyling salon, and a coffee shop. 33 rooms. Pets accepted. Complimentary continental breakfast. Check-in 2 pm, check-out 11 am. Restaurant. Airport transportation available. **$**

**★ TIDES INN.** *307 N 1st St, Petersburg (99833). Phone 907/772-4288; toll-free 800/665-8433; fax 907/772-4286. www.tidesinnalaska.com.* Located in the heart of downtown, this 47-room motel is convenient to all local attractions and provides its guests with an on site car rental desk and free e-mail access in the lobby. Some rooms have terrific water and mountain views, and all are clean, quiet, and reasonably priced, making the Tides Inn a relaxing and affordable home away from home for guests. 47 rooms. Complimentary continental breakfast. Check-in 1 pm, check-out 11 am. Airport transportation available. **$**

### Restaurant

**★ ROONEY'S NORTHERN LIGHTS RESTAURANT.** *203 Sing Lee Alley, Petersburg (99833). Phone 907/772-2900; fax 907/772-2901.* Located on pilings above Hammer Slough overlooking Middle Harbor, this restaurant offers a fairly extensive menu and a line of desserts that are so popular, locals have been known to call ahead and reserve them. Regardless of the weather, the views are terrific, giving guests a chance to watch the local fishermen and tides flow in and out of the harbor. International menu. Breakfast, lunch, dinner. Closed Thanksgiving, Dec 24-25. Children's menu. Casual attire. Outdoor seating. **$$**

## Seldovia

**Population** 286
**Area Code** 907

### Restaurants

**★ ★ THE MAD FISH.** *221 Main St, Seldovia (99663). Phone 907/234-7676. www.madfishalaska.com.* Seafood, steak menu. Lunch, dinner. Closed Mon; also winter. Bar. Children's menu. Casual attire. Reservations recommended. Outdoor seating. **$$**

## Seward (D-5)

**Population** 2,830
**Area Code** 907
**Information** Chamber of Commerce, PO Box 749, 99664; phone 907/224-8051
**Web Site** www.sewardak.org

This town of 3,000 people on the shores of Resurrection Bay is named after William H. Seward, the US Secretary of State who was responsible for negotiating the purchase of Alaska from Russia in 1867. The town sits on the eastern side of the Kenai Peninsula, 127 miles from Anchorage via the Seward Highway. Founded in 1903 as an ocean terminus for the Alaska Railroad, the town's economy originally relied almost exclusively on the fishing and railroad industries. With the opening of the Seward and Sterling Highways on the Kenai Peninsula after World War II, Seward's economy gradually shifted, making tourism and fishing the leading industries today. Throughout the summer, the town vibrates with life as thousands of visitors arrive each day by road, sea, and rail to explore the area. From the bustling small boat harbor, visitors can join halibut and salmon fishing charters, take tour boats to view the abundant wildlife and magnificent tidewater glaciers of Kenai Fjords National Park, or rent kayaks and paddle the shores of Resurrection Bay. After a day on the water, visitors leaving the harbor can either head directly downtown via 4th Avenue or opt to walk part of the Iditarod National Historic Trail that parallels the shoreline all the way to one of Seward's newest and most impressive attractions, the Alaska SeaLife Center. Opened in 1998, its a combination marine research station, wildlife rehabilitation center, and hands-on interpretive venue. The highlight of the summer is the town's 4th of July celebration, the largest in Alaska. A multi-day event, it's capped off by the Mount Marathon run, a grueling 3 mile out-and-back course in which runners run through the downtown area, claw their way to the top of 3,022-foot-high Mount Marathon, and then turn around and come pounding back down the scree-filled hillside, ending up in the center of town to the cheers of thousands of spectators lining the streets. For athletes and spectators alike, it's a breathtaking event.

## What to See and Do

**Alaska Sealife Center.** *301 Railway Ave, Seward (99664). Phone 907/224-6300; toll-free 800/224-2525. www.alaskasealife.org.* The Alaska SeaLife Center offers an unrivaled up-close-and-personal experience with Gulf of Alaska marine wildlife. Witness 1,500-pound Stellar sea lions gliding past underwater viewing windows, puffins diving in a carefully crafted naturalistic habitat, and harbor seals hauled out on rocky beaches. Alaskan king crab, sea stars, and Pacific octopus also await you, as well as a variety of intertidal creatures and deep-sea fishes. (Daily; closed Thanksgiving, Dec 25) **$$$**

**Benny Benson Memorial Park.** *Seward Hwy, mile 1.4, Seward (99664).* This newly renovated roadside park is dedicated to Benny Benson, Seward's most famous citizen. In 1927, 13-year-old Benson, an orphan living at Seward's Jesse Lee Home, entered and won a competition sponsored by the Alaska Department of the American Legion to design Alaska's territorial flag. In his contest application, Benson described what the flag symbolized: "The blue field is for the Alaska sky and the forget-me-not, an Alaska flower. The North Star is for the future state of Alaska, the most northerly of the union. The dipper is for the Great Bear symbolizing strength." The park is located beside the lagoon at the entrance to town, across the street from the small boat harbor.

**Seward Museum.** *336 Third Ave, Seward (99664). Phone 907/224-3902.* Operated by the Resurrection Bay Historical Society, the Seward Museum aims to tell the story of Seward's history, from its founding as a railway terminus at the beginning of the 20th century to its role as a strategic port during World War II to its current incarnation as one of the most popular destinations on the Kenai Peninsula. Highlights of the museum include the earthquake exhibits detailing the local devastation caused by the Good Friday Earthquake that rocked Alaska in 1964 and the Iditarod room, which details Seward's role in the development of the Iditarod trail and honors hometown hero Mitch Seavey, winner of the 2004 Iditarod Trail Sled Dog Race. (May-Sept: daily 9 am-5 pm; Oct-Apr, days and hours varycall for information) **$**

**Two Lakes Park.** *2nd Ave and C St, Seward (99664).* This forested park at the foot of Mount Marathon does not appear on any visitor center maps or tourist brochures, making it one of Seward's best-kept secrets. The two "lakes" are actually small, glassy ponds surrounded by groves of cottonwood and spruce trees, connected to one another by an easy mile-long loop trail. During summer, visitors can dip their feet in the lakes, watch for salmon in the creeks, and gorge themselves on the blueberries and salmonberries that grow wild throughout the park. Barbecue grills, picnic tables, and a covered pavilion are located beside First Lake, only a few yards from the main park entrance tucked behind the AVTEC building at 2nd Avenue and C Street.

## Special Events

**Fourth of July Festival and Mount Marathon Race.** *Seward. Phone 907/224-8051.* Considered by many to be the best Independence Day festival in Alaska. Thousands of people flood into town for parades, food booths, music, and craft fairs. The festival is capped off by the Mount Marathon Race, one of the oldest and toughest footraces in America (a 3.25-mile run from just above sea level to the top of Mount Marathon—3,020 feet—and crashing back down again). Early July.

**Polar Bear Jump-Off Festival.** *Seward. Citywide. Phone 907/224-5688.* Costumed jumpers take the plunge into icy Resurrection Bay in an effort to raise money for the American Cancer Society. Parade, ice bowling, oyster slurping, dogsled race, salmon toss, basketball tournament, and more. Third weekend in Jan.

## Limited-Service Hotels

**★ ★ BREEZE INN MOTEL.** *1306 Seward Hwy, Seward (99664). Phone 907/224-5237; toll-free 888/224-5237; fax 907/224-7024. www.breezeinn.com.* Located at Seward's small-boat harbor near the train depot, this 86-room hotel's convenient location and wide range of accommodation types and prices—from small, clean, and comfortable economy rooms to spacious suites with Jacuzzis and great views—make it a popular place for tourists arriving by train or cruise ship and for those going on fishing charters and sightseeing cruises. It has its own gift shops, restaurant, lounge, and espresso shop. 86 rooms. Pets accepted. Check-in 3 pm, check-out 11 am. Restaurant, bar. **$**

**★ HARBORVIEW INN.** *804 Third Ave, Seward (99664). Phone 907/224-3217; toll-free 888/324-3218; fax 907/224-3218. www.sewardhotel.com.* This 37-room motel is in an excellent location for people going on day trips out of Seward's small-boat harbor as well as landlubbers staying in town to go sightseeing and shopping. Guest rooms are relaxing and inviting, with sturdy wooden furniture, colorful bedding and window treatments, and a subtle Alaskan outdoors motif that really adds to the appeal of the place. 37 rooms. Closed Thanksgiving weekend; also late Dec-early Jan. Check-in 3 pm, check-out 11 am. **$**

**★ ★ HOTEL EDGEWATER AND CONFERENCE CENTER.** *202 Fifth Ave, Seward (99664). Phone 907/224-2700; toll-free 888/793-6800; fax 907/224-2701. www.hoteledgewater.com.* Built in 1999, this waterfront hotel—the largest and most popular in downtown Seward—is filled with comfortably appointed rooms, some with fantastic views of Resurrection Bay and the southern Chugach Mountains. Architecturally modern from the outside, the hotel's incorporation of simple wood railings, earth tones, and a dramatic three-story central atrium into the interior design evokes romantic images of the frontier hotels of the Wild West. Free shuttle service is available to the Seward small-boat harbor, where glacier cruises and fishing charters depart throughout the day during the summer. 76 rooms. Complimentary continental breakfast. Check-in 2 pm, check-out 11 am. Whirlpool. **$$**

**★ HOTEL SEWARD.** *221 5th Ave, Seward (99664). Phone 907/224-2378; toll-free 800/478-4050; fax 907/224-3114. www.hotelsewardalaska.com.* This downtown hotel is physically connected to the much older New Seward Hotel but charges different rates and offers more upscale and appealing accommodations. Bonus features of staying here include in-room VCRs with complimentary videos available at the front desk and a concierge in the lobby who will make tour and restaurant reservations for guests. 38 rooms. Check-in 3 pm, check-out noon. **$$**

**★ MARINA MOTEL.** *Seward Hwy, mile 1, Seward (99664). Phone 907/224-5518; fax 907/224-5553. www.sewardmotel.com.* This 18-room motel isn't the flashiest place in town, but its clean, tidy, sunny accommodations reflect the pride the owners take in maintaining and updating the property. Located at Mile 1 of the Seward Highway, it's the closest lodging to the railroad depot and a short walk to the small boat harbor, making it an excellent bargain in a good location. 18 rooms. Check-in 2 pm, check-out 11 am. **$**

**★ THE VAN GILDER HOTEL.** *308 Adams St, Seward (99664). Phone 907/224-3079; toll-free 800/204-6835; fax 907/224-3689. www.vangilderhotel.com.* Built in 1916, this charming 24-room hotel was placed on the National Register of Historical Places in 1980 and is gradually being restored to its former glory. Whenever guests are not in their cozy, tastefully decorated rooms, they are free to relax in the ornate lobby filled with antiques, stained-lass windows, and a magnificent wooden bar from England. Although many of the rooms are small and lack the array of amenities found in more contemporary hotels, the Van Gilder is a popular stopover for independent travelers looking for a unique and memorable lodging. 24 rooms. Check-in 4 pm, check-out noon. **$**

## Restaurants

**★ ★ BREEZE INN RESTAURANT.** *1306 Seward Hwy, Seward (99664). Phone 907/224-5237; toll-free 888/224-5237; fax 907/224-7024. www.breezeinn.com.* This harborside restaurant is a popular casual dining spot for tourists during the summer and locals throughout the year. Offering standard American and seafood dishes, one of the most popular menu selections is "halibut chunks" made from halibut caught in local waters. In keeping with the restaurant's hometown flair, the walls are lined with photographs and paintings done by local artists. American menu. Breakfast, lunch, dinner. Bar. Children's menu. Casual attire. **$$**

**★ CHRISTO'S PALACE.** *133 Fourth Ave, Seward (99664). Phone 907/224-5255.* This chic downtown restaurant serves an eclectic mix of American and international foods in a dining room filled with dark polished woods, soft lights, exposed beams, and dark carpets. The highlight of the dining area, though, is the enormous 150-year-old polished wood back bar that gives the room a sleek and stylish ambience. American menu. Lunch, dinner. Closed Thanksgiving, Dec 25. Bar. Children's menu. Casual attire. **$$**

**★ ★ HARBOR DINNER CLUB.** *220 5th Ave, Seward (99664). Phone 907/224-3012.* This family-run restaurant has been in business since 1958, serving steaks and fresh local seafood such as Alaskan halibut and Kachemak Bay steamer clams to generations of locals and a long line of daytripping tourists. Its casual atmosphere and large outdoor patio make it a popular destination for those seeking good food in a friendly setting. Seafood, steak menu. Lunch, dinner. Closed holidays. Bar. Children's menu. Casual attire. Outdoor seating. **$$$**

**★ RAY'S WATERFRONT.** *1316 4th Ave, Seward (99664). Phone 907/224-5606.* Seafood menu. Lunch, dinner. Closed in winter. Bar. Casual attire. Outdoor seating. **$**

**★ RESURRECTION ROADHOUSE.** *Herman Leirer Rd, mile 66, Seward (99664). Phone 907/224-7116. www.sewardwindsong.com.* Seafood, steak menu. Lunch, dinner. Closed in winter. Bar. Business casual attire. Outdoor seating. **$$**

# Sitka (E-8)

**Population** 8,835
**Area Code** 907
**Information** Sitka Convention and Visitors Bureau, PO Box 1226, 99835; phone 907/747-5940
**Web Site** www.sitka.org

One of the oldest Western settlements in Alaska, Sitka was established at the beginning of the 19th century as a fur trading outpost and fort by the Russian American Company under the leadership of Alexander Baranov. Originally called New Archangel, it served as the capital of Russian Alaska until 1867, when a waning fur trade and domestic economic upheaval led the Russian government to sell its stake in the New World. The transfer of ownership of Alaska from Russian to the United States took place on Castle Hill and a series of plaques on the site now provide visitors with a detailed account of that event. Modern Sitka retains strong ties to its past, as evidenced by the Russian architecture of Saint Michael's Cathedral in the middle of downtown—a replica of the original that burned to the ground in 1966, the restored Russian Bishop's house across from Crescent harbor, and Russian Cemetery at the end of Observatory Street. Evidence of the older, Tlingit civilization in the area can be found on the east end of town at the Sheldon Jackson Museum, which contains a stunning display of native arts and crafts. Further down the road is Sitka National Historic Park, which features a collection of 15 totem poles set along a meandering forest trail. Pamphlets available in the park's visitor center provide detailed explanations of each of the totems, so it's best to stop off there first. The center also houses an extensive native history museum, a collection of delicate wood carvings that could not survive outdoors in Sitka's rainy climate, and a woodworking shop where native Alaskan crafts are fashioned and art classes taught.

## What to See and Do

**Castle Hill.** *Sitka. Located in downtown Sitka, next to O'Connell Bridge. Parking lot and pathway are located beside the bridge. An additional pathway begins on the Lincoln Street side of the hill.* Officially known as Baranov Castle Hill State Historic Site, this small hill in the middle of Sitka marks the site where Russia formally transferred ownership of Alaska to the United States in October 1867. Easily accessible via wheelchair ramps and stairs, the summit plaza contains numerous interpretive displays recounting the history of Sitka and the role the Castle Hill area played in so many of the town's major developments. The site also offers exceptional views of downtown Sitka and the waterfront area.

**Old Sitka State Historical Site.** *Halibut Point Rd, mile 7.5, Sitka (99835). www.dnr.state.ak.us/parks/units/sitka.htm.* Located 7 miles north of downtown, this national historic landmark is the site of the original 1799 Russian-American Company settlement in the area. After the Russian fort was destroyed during fighting with the local Tlingit tribe in 1803, the Russians responded by attacking and capturing the nearby Tlingit settlement of Shee-Atika. The Russians then built a new settlement on the site, naming it New Archangel. When the United States purchased Alaska from the Russians in 1867, the town's name was changed to Sitka, a European version of the area's Tlingit name. The Old Sitka site contains numerous outdoor interpretive displays that tell the history of the native and Russian settlements that once thrived in the area. Visitors with time to spare can walk the sites trail network, which includes the Forest & Muskegs Trail, the Estuary Life Trail, and the slightly longer Mosquito Cove Loop Trail. Overnight visitors can stay at Starrigavan Campground, a US Forest Service facility on the northern edge of the historic site.

**Sheldon Jackson Museum.** *104 College Dr, Sitka (99835). Phone 907/747-8981. museums.state.ak.us.* This small, oddly shaped museum on the Sheldon Jackson College campus near downtown Sitka houses what is generally regarded as one of the best collections of Native arts and crafts in the state. It is also Alaska's oldest museum, founded in 1887 by Reverend Sheldon Jackson, who sought to create a museum in Alaska that would preserve and exhibit the cultural and artistic history of Native Alaskan cultures. Highlights of the collection include Eskimo masks, Tlingit and Haida headdresses, and a full-sized Aleut baidarka, a specialized form of sea kayak. (Mid-May-mid-Sept: daily 9 am-5 pm; mid-Sept-mid-May: Tues-Sat 10 am to 4 pm) **$**

**Sitka National Historical Park.** *103 Monastery St, Sitka (99835). Phone 907/747-0110. www.nps.gov/sitk.* Sitka National Historical Park is one of Alaska's smallest but most popular national parks, with nearly 300,000 annual visitors making the trip to the 113-acre park. Located in a temperate rain forest at the mouth of the Indian River on Baranof Island, the park marks the site of the 1804 Battle of Sitka, a fight that pitted the native Tlingit Indians against the Russians. Led by Alexander Baranof, the Russians won the battle, but only after the natives exhausted their supply of gunpowder. The outlines of Tlingit Fort can be seen at the park. Another popular attraction is the Russian Bishop's House, constructed in 1843, a time when the Tsar ruled Alaska. The log structure survives as one of four remaining examples of Russian-period architecture in North America. The park also features a remarkable collection of original and replica totem poles from villages throughout southeastern Alaska. Bold in color and design, the totem poles are exhibited along a scenic coastal trail. The park's visitor center offers interpretive talks, exhibits, and slide programs. Alaska's oldest federally designated park, Sitka National Historical Park is a short drive from downtown Sitka. The Alaska Marine Highway serves Sitka, and the town is a ten-hour ferry ride from Juneau to the north. **$**

**St. Michael's Cathedral.** *Lincoln St, Sitka (99835). Phone 907/747-8120. www.sitka.org/attractions.html.* A local landmark since its construction in 1848, this beautiful Russian Orthodox cathedral is actually a replica of the original, which burned to the ground in 1966. Featuring classic Russian Orthodox architectural elements like a large onion dome and three-bar crosses, the cathedral houses an exquisite collection of historic icons and religious artifacts dating back to the days when Russian culture dominated the region. Because the cathedral is still in use, visitors are permitted to wander around inside only during posted hours, when religious services are not being conducted. Hours vary depending on cruise ship schedules and time of year and are posted on the cathedral door. **DONATION**

**Tongass National Forest.** *204 Siginaka Way, Sitka (99835). Phone 907/747-6671. www.fs.fed/us/r10/tongass.* Tongass National Forest, the largest national forest in the United States, is the definition of "wilderness"; in fact, one-third of the Tongass (5. 7 million acres) is managed as wilderness so that Alaska retains its undeveloped character. Hardy visitors can expect to see eagles, bears, deer, and a variety of other animals, birds, and fish in this vast national forest. Hunting, fishing, cabins (fee).

## Special Event

**Sitka Summer Music Festival.** *Sitka. Harrigan Centennial Hall. Phone 907/747-6774. www.sitkamusicfestival.org.* Although many towns in Alaska host summer music festivals, Sitka is the only place that features classical music. First held in 1972 as an informal reunion event for musicians from around the world, the festival begins on the first Friday in June and ends on the fourth Friday in June, with concerts held on Tuesday and Friday evenings and on one Saturday evening. In an effort to appeal to all ages, the festival also features a string of free lunchtime concerts and a community-wide concert and ice cream social. Special charity fundraising events are also part of the festivities, with a pair of concerts aboard a tour boat drawing some of the biggest crowds. **$$$$**

## Limited-Service Hotels

**★★ SITKA HOTEL.** *118 Lincoln St, Sitka (99835). Phone 907/747-3288; fax 907/747-8499. www.sitkahotel.com.* Built in 1939 and listed on the National Register of Historic Places, this 63-room hotel's Victorian architecture has recently been beautifully restored and preserved, resulting in an atmosphere of graceful elegance and old-time charm. The pressed-tin ceilings, real and reproduction Victorian furniture, and period architecture of the lobby and hallways are reminiscent of a time when vacation travel was a slower, more genteel pursuit. The hotel sits on the main commercial road through Sitka's small downtown area, close to the main tourist attractions and within easy walking distance of Sitka's three harbors. 63 rooms. Check-in 2 pm, check-out 11 am. Restaurant. **$**

**★ ★ WESTMARK SITKA.** *330 Seward St, Sitka (99835). Phone 907/747-6241; toll-free 800/544-0970; fax 907/747-5486. www.westmarkhotels.com.* From the sleek, native-themed lobby and elegant on-site restaurant on the ground floor to the crisp, comfortable rooms on the upper floors, the focus at this hotel is on providing guests with much more than just a place to sleep. Given this emphasis, it's not surprising to find that the hotel recommends making summertime reservations up to a year in advance. Occupying a prominent position on Seward Street in the middle of downtown, the Westmark Sitka, owned by the Carnival Cruise Line corporation, is the largest hotel in town. 101 rooms. Check-in 3 pm, check-out 11 am. Restaurant, bar. **$$**

**★ WESTMARK TOTEM SQUARE INN.** *201 Katlian, Sitka (99835). Phone 907/747-6302; toll-free 800/544-0970; fax 907/747-6307.* 59 rooms. Closed Oct-Apr. Check-in 3 pm, check-out noon. **$**

## Restaurants

**★ BAYVIEW RESTAURANT.** *407 Lincoln St, Sitka (99835). Phone 907/747-5440.* This charming little restaurant is located on the second floor of a small shopping arcade across the street from Crescent Harbor in downtown Sitka. Popular with tourists and locals alike, guests can choose from a broad menu of traditional American and seafood dishes while enjoying spectacular views of the waters and islands of Sitka Sound. American menu. Breakfast, lunch, dinner. Children's menu. Casual attire. **$$**

**★ ★ RAVEN DINING ROOM & KADATAAN LOUNGE.** *330 Seward St, Sitka (99835). Phone 907/747-6241; fax 907/747-5486. www.westmarkhotels.com.* This upscale restaurant has a menu diverse enough to suit most tastes but specializes in fresh local seafood, including the perennial favorite, Halibut Olympia. The layout and décor of the restaurant are very appealing, with large windows providing excellent views of Crescent Harbor and upscale furniture and appointments adding a sense of sleek elegance to the room. Seafood menu. Breakfast, lunch, dinner. Closed Dec 25. Bar. Casual attire. **$$$**

**★ ★ VICTORIA'S.** *118 Lincoln St, Sitka (99835). Phone 907/747-3288; fax 907/747-8499. www.sitkahotel.com/food.htm.* The front windows of this small, quaint restaurant located in the Sitka Hotel look out on the Pioneer Building and Totem Square, both popular destinations for daytrippers. Filled with lace curtains, pressed tin ceilings, antique pictures, and bathed in sunlight, it's the kind of place one can imagine going for breakfast and staying through lunch. American, seafood menu. Breakfast, lunch, dinner. Bar. Casual attire. **$$**

# Skagway (D-8)

**Population** 862
**Area Code** 907
**Information** Skagway Convention & Visitors Bureau, PO Box 1029, 99840; phone 907/983-2854
**Web Site** www.skagway.org

Skagway is located at the northernmost point of the Inside Passage near the Canadian border and derives its name from the Tlingit word "skaqua"—windy place. It was a hunting and fishing camp for local Indian tribes for centuries until the discovery of gold 600 miles north at Bonanza Creek in 1896. By 1898, the town had grown to nearly 10,000 people and had become an important staging area for gold prospectors preparing to make the arduous trek through White Pass north of town to seek their fortunes in the Klondike. The nearby settlement of Dyea offered a different route, through Chilkoot Pass, but both routes merged at Bennett Lake just inside the Canadian border and formed a single route, now referred to as the Trail of '98. Skagway's fortunes declined with the end of the gold rush, but its downtown area still retains its late 1890s charm, with wooden sidewalks, false-fronted wooden buildings, and the restored turn-of-the-century White Pass & Yukon Railroad passenger depot and steam engine. Much of downtown Skagway is now part of Klondike Gold Rush National Historic Park and well-prepared adventurers can once again hike the 33-mile Chilkoot Trail, beginning at the long-abandoned Dyea townsite.

## What to See and Do

**Arctic Brotherhood Hall.** *Broadway St, Skagway (99840). Between 2nd and 3rd aves. Phone 907/983-2854; toll-free 888/762-1898. www.skagway.org.* Easily the most recognizable structure in Skagway, if not all of Alaska, this two-story wooden building dating to 1899 features an exterior covered with more than 10,000 pieces of driftwood. Built by the Fraternal Order of the Arctic Brotherhood, the building served as a social, cultural, and charitable center for its members during Skagway's heyday as a boomtown. In its current incarnation, it is home to the Skagway Visitor Center and an excellent place to begin a sightseeing tour of the area. (Mid-May-mid-Sept: Sun-Friday 8 am-6 pm, Sat 9 am-6 pm; mid-Sept-mid-May: call for hours)

**Klondike Gold Rush National Historical Park.** *Second Ave and Broadway St, Skagway (99840). Phone 907/983-2921. www.nps.gov/klgo.* It may be hard to believe, but in 1897, Skagway, a one-building town situated along a narrow inlet in southeastern Alaska, suddenly became the most prosperous city in the Pacific Northwest. In the summer of that year, news spread around the world of a gold strike in the Klondike region of the Yukon Territory. Almost overnight, thousands of stampeders descended on the newly created town of Skagway. The town served as a base during the Klondike Gold Rush, a place to gather supplies and prepare for the arduous 500-mile trek to the gold fields in Canada, where those entering the country were required to be equipped with a year's worth of food. The trip began with a steep climb over Chilkoot Pass, following an aboriginal trail created by Alaska natives many years before the gold rush.

Today, the 33-mile-long Chilkoot Trail is administered by the park, and it makes for a challenging but rewarding three- to five-day hike. Most stampeders abandoned Skagway, along with dreams of instant riches, in 1898. The town now has a year-round population of only 800, although the historical park receives around 750,000 annual visits. From the gold-rush era, approximately 100 buildings remain, 15 of which have been restored by the National Park Service. Nestled within the Taiya Inlet and surrounded by snow-capped mountains, the park offers guided tours of the Skagway Historic District, along with exhibits, ranger presentations, and films. Many visitors arrive in Skagway by boat, as the town is served by the Alaska Marine Highway. **FREE**

**Skagway Museum.** *City Hall/McCabe Building, 700 Spring St, Skagway (99804). Phone 907/983-2420. www.skagwaymuseum.org.* Located inside Skagway's historic City Hall, the Skagway Museum is filled with artifacts, photographs, and personal accounts that tell of life in Skagway before and after the Klondike Gold Rush of 1898. A Tlingit canoe and a Bering Sea kayak are just some of the exhibits that paint a picture of the Tlingit culture that once thrived in the area. Displays of gold rush relics, tools, and supplies tell another tale, that of the tens of thousands of gold prospectors who flooded into the region at the end of the 19th century to seek their fortunes in the Klondike. The museum is a few blocks north of most of Skagway's other attractions but is one of the most comprehensive and engaging museums in town. (May-Sept: Mon-Fri 9 am-5 pm, Sat-Sun 1-4 pm; Oct-Apr: hours varycall for times) **$**

**Tours.** *Skagway. Phone toll-free 800/544-2206. www.graylineofalaska.com.* Gray Line of Alaska offers package tours around Alaska (up to 11 days) as well as a historic tour of the city and a combination flightseeing/dogsledding tour.

**White Pass and Yukon Route of the Scenic Railway of the World.** *White Pass & Yukon Route Depot,Second Ave and Spring St, Skagway (99840). Phone 907/983-2217; toll-free 800/343-7373. www.whitepassrailroad.com.* Built in only 20 months during the Klondike Gold Rush, the White Pass & Yukon Route connecting Skagway with Whitehorse, Yukon Territory remains one of the most spectacular railways in the world and has been designated an International Historic Civil Engineering Landmark. Modern travelers on this rail line can choose from four different excursions, depending on how much time they have. The White Pass Summit Excursion is a three-hour, 40-mile round-trip that climbs 2,865 feet from Skagway to the summit at White Pass. Covering many of the railway's most scenic sections, this tour is the least expensive from Skagway and the most popular. The Lake Bennett Excursion takes 8 1/2 hours and travels an additional 20 miles on the line to Canada's Lake Bennett, where the Chilkoot Trail comes to an end. The railway also offers a Chilkoot Trail Hikers Service for people interested in hiking up the 33-mile historic Chilkoot Trail and then hopping aboard the train as it heads back to Skagway. Another option is the combination bus and train service that transports travelers from Skagway to Whitehorse. Prices and departure times vary, and reservations are required for all excursions. **$$$$**

## Special Event

**Buckwheat Ski Classic.** *Skagway. Phone 907/983-2544.* Amateurs and professionals alike compete in this cross-country ski race along White Pass Mountain. Late Mar.

## Limited-Service Hotels

**★ SGT. PRESTON'S LODGE.** *370 Sixth Ave, Skagway (99840). Phone 907/983-2521; fax 907/983-3500.* Set in the middle of downtown Skagway, this motel has 30 rooms ranging from tiny and very cheap to large and reasonably priced. There's a central courtyard with a BBQ grill, picnic table, and ice machine for warm-weather gatherings and a snug lobby with big couches and residential-style armchairs for wintertime socializing and an Internet-connected computer for staying in touch with folks back home. 30 rooms. Pets accepted. Check-in 2 pm, check-out 11 am. **$**

**★ ★ WESTMARK SKAGWAY.** *3rd and Spring sts, Skagway (99840). Phone toll-free 800/544-0970. www.westmarkhotels.com.* 151 rooms. Closed Oct-Apr. Check-in 3 pm, check-out noon. Restaurant, two bars. **$**

## Restaurants

**★ ★ BONANZA BAR & GRILL.** *3rd Ave and Broadway St, Skagway (99840). Phone 907/983-6214.* American menu. Lunch, dinner. Closed Nov-Apr. Bar. Children's menu. Casual attire. Outdoor seating. **$**

**★ HAVEN CAFÉ.** *9th Ave and State St, Skagway (99840). Phone 907/983-3553; fax 907/983-3554.* This funky little place focuses on "espresso and light fare," but in a town as small as Skagway, it's a heavy hitter. Owner Susan Jabal has created a very hip, fresh cafe with a real bistro atmosphere. Serving all meals during the summer, its real focus is on its ever-changing, eclectic selection of panini sandwiches, green salads, and fresh-baked pastries. Deli menu. Breakfast, lunch, dinner. Closed Jan 1, Thanksgiving, Dec 25. Casual attire. Outdoor seating. **$**

# Soldotna (D-5)

**Population** 3,759
**Web Site** www.soldotnachamber.com

Soldotna exists due to the confluence of two events in 1947: the granting of homesteading rights on the Kenai Peninsula to veterans of World War II and the selection of the Soldotna area as the site for a highway bridge across the Kenai River. When the Sterling Highway was completed soon after, Soldotna was suddenly connected to the Alaskan road system and rapidly became a major stopping point for travelers and outdoor enthusiasts on the Kenai Peninsula. Nowadays, Soldotna's enormous popularity stems mainly from its greatest natural asset, the Kenai River, from whose waters the current world record king salmon, weighing in at 97.2 lbs, was pulled in 1985. Other highlights of Soldotna are its two campgrounds, nine parks, and network of trails and walks that provide visitors with plenty of opportunities to enjoy the natural beauty of the area. During the summer, it's possible to go hiking, canoeing, biking, wildlife viewing, and berry picking without straying far from town. During winter, snow machining and cross-country skiing keep locals and off-season visitors active.

## What to See and Do

**Kenai National Wildlife Refuge.** *Refuge Visitor Center, 2139 Ski Hill Rd, Soldotna (99669). Phone 907/262-7021. kenai.fws.gov.* Originally created as the 1. 7 million-acre Kenai National Moose Range in 1941, this refuge now totals nearly 2 million acres, covering much of the western half of the Kenai Peninsula. Containing every type of Alaskan habitat and supporting an enormous amount of wildlife including moose, bears, caribou, eagles, and lynxes, the refuge is visited by more than half a million travelers each year, many of whom come to try their luck fishing in the nine rivers that run through it. The Kenai National Wildlife Refuge Visitor Center in Soldotna is open year-round and contains exhibits about local wildlife, information about recreational activities available in the area, and a range of displays explaining the geological and ecological make-up of the refuge. Visitors to the center also can view a short film about the wildlife found within the refuge. (Summer: Mon-Fri 8 am-4:30 pm, Sat-Sun 9 am-6 pm; winter: Mon-Fri 8 am-4:30 pm; Sat-Sun 10 am-5 pm) **FREE**

## Limited-Service Hotels

**★ ASPEN HOTEL SOLDOTNA.** *326 Binkley Cir, Soldotna (99669). Phone 907/260-7736; toll-free 888/308-7848; fax 907/260-7786. www.aspenhotel-sak.com.* The Kenai River flows at the back of this midtown property, providing fishermen and outdoor enthusiasts with easy access to one of Soldotna's greatest assets. Tourist- and family-friendly features such as an indoor pool, deluxe continental breakfast, in-room kitchens, and free Internet access make it an especially appealing place to stay when visiting the Kenai Peninsula. 63 rooms. Complimentary continental breakfast. Check-in 3 pm, check-out 11 am. Fitness room. Indoor pool, whirlpool. **$**

★ ★ **BEST WESTERN KING SALMON MOTEL.** *35546A Kenai Spur Hwy, Soldotna (99669). Phone 907/262-5857; toll-free 888/262-5857; fax 907/262-9441. www.bestwestern.com.* The main appeal of this modest brand-name motel is its convenient location. It's in the heart of the Kenai Peninsula and close to the world-class fishing of the Kenai River, so it tends to attract a steady stream of tourists, fishermen, and outdoor enthusiasts in the summer and an eclectic mix of off-season travelers and hunters in the winter. A variety of good restaurants can be found within sight of the front door. 49 rooms. Check-in 3 pm, check-out noon. Restaurant. **$$**

★ **KENAI RIVER LODGE.** *393 Riverside Dr, Soldotna (99669). Phone 907/262-4292; fax 907/262-7332. www.kenairiverlodge.com.* This family-run motel on the Kenai River has been drawing a devoted repeat clientele since it opened in 1969. In an area where "combat fishing" is often the norm, the motel's ability to offer its guests exclusive access to nearly 100 yards of riverbank is a huge draw, as is the owners' in-depth knowledge of the river and how to fish it. Other benefits include BBQ pits and picnic areas, fish-cleaning facilities, boat moorage, and river views from all guest rooms. Prices are very reasonable, so the Kenai River Lodge tends to be popular with bargain hunters. 25 rooms. Complimentary continental breakfast. Check-in 3 pm, check-out noon. **$**

★ ★ **SOLDOTNA INN.** *35041 Kenai Spur Hwy, Soldotna. Phone 907/262-9169; toll-free 866/262-9169; fax 907/262-1099. www.thesoldotnainn.com.* Located near a major junction of the Sterling Highway and the Kenai Highway spur road, this combination hotel and motel has 18 rooms and ten deluxe suites available for rent by the day, week, or month. All of the rooms are in very good condition and are being steadily upgraded by the new owners. Its excellent downtown location near world-class fishing and outdoor recreation sites and its reasonable rates make the Soldotna Inn an excellent home base for active tourists. 28 rooms. Pets accepted. Complimentary continental breakfast. Check-in 3 pm, check-out 11 am. Restaurant. Fitness room. **$**

# Talkeetna (D-5)

*Also see Denali National Park and Preserve*

**Population** 772
**Area Code** 907
**Information** Talkeetna Denali Visitor Center, PO Box 688, 99676; phone 907/733-2499 or toll-free 800/660-2688
**Web Site** www.alaskan.com/talkeetnadenali

## What to See and Do

**Tours.** *Talkeetna. Phone toll-free 800/544-2206. www.graylineofalaska.com.* Gray Line of Alaska offers package tours around Alaska (up to 11 days) as well as flightseeing tours, a jet boat safari, and guided fishing tours.

## Special Event

**Moose Dropping Festival.** *Talkeetna. Phone 907/733-2487.* This festival ranks high in terms of small-town charm: food and craft booths, slow-pitch softball tournaments, a mini parade, a footrace, pancake breakfasts, and the Mountain Mother Contests, where local women compete for the title of Mountain Mother (crossing a "stream" with a baby doll on their backs, shooting an arrow, casting a fishing pole, cutting firewood, etc.). Mid-July.

# Unalaska (F-2)

**Settled** 1758
**Population** 4,283
**Area Code** 907
**Web Site** www.ci.unalaska.ak.us

## What to See and Do

**Aleutian World War II National Historic Area.** *Visitor Center, 2716 Airport Beach Rd, Unalaska (99685). Phone 907/581-1276. www.nps.gov/aleu.* Situated 800 miles west of Anchorage on Amaknak Island, the Aleutian World War II National Historic Area serves to educate present and future generations about the critical role the Aleutian Islands played in the defense of North America during the Second World War. The Historic Area spreads out over 134 acres, encompassing the ruins of the US Army base Fort Schwatka, which stood 1,000 feet above the Bering Sea. During the summer of 1942, the United States and Japan engaged in fierce fighting in the Aleutians, with Japan seizing occupation of the islands of Agattu, Attu, and Kiska. The US grew increasingly concerned that these islands would be used as a staging area for attacks on the North American mainland. US forces focused their efforts on reclaiming the islands, doing so in May 1943—although both sides suffered significant casualties. The Historic Area also exists to honor the island natives, the Aleut or Unangan people, many of whom were killed or placed in internment camps during the war.

# Valdez (D-6)

**Population** 4,036
**Area Code** 907
**Information** Valdez Convention and Visitors Bureau, 200 Fairbanks St, PO Box 1603, 99686; phone 907/835-4636 or toll-free 800/770-5954
**Web Site** www.valdezalaska.org

Valdez was founded in the spring of 1898 by a group of hucksters who printed advertisements touting the speedy, established "All-American Route" from Prince William Sound to the Klondike gold fields. Thousands of prospectors discovered upon arriving that the route they had heard about was little more than a rough-hewn trail up and over a glacier. Despite its ignominious beginnings, Valdez remains today the "Gateway to the Interior," providing a vital link between the Interior and the rest of the world. As North America's northernmost ice-free port, it also serves as the terminus for the Alaska Pipeline. With an average of 325 inches of snow per year, the town boasts some of the best snowcat, helicopter, and extreme skiing in the world as well as world-class ice climbing in nearby Keystone Canyon. In recent years, an extensive network of hiking trails has been developed to provide better access to the wild beauty of the area.

## What to See and Do

**Historic and scenic hiking trails.** *Valdez. Various locations. Phone 907/835-4636. www.valdezalaska.org/maps/maps.html.* With mountains and rugged wilderness surrounding it on all sides, Valdez is graced with some of the best hiking trails in Alaska, some of which follow historic gold prospector routes through the mountains. Of the seven main trails in or near town, the easiest is the Dock Point Trail, a scenic 3/4-mile round-trip beginning at the east end of the dock harbor and looping around a narrow peninsula jutting out into Valdez Bay. Hikers looking for more of a challenge can try the historic lower section of the Keystone Canyon Pack Trail, running for 2. 6 miles from the Old Richardson Highway Loop at mile 12. 5 to Bridal Veil Falls. Rated easy to moderate, this 1899 trail was abandoned for nearly a century before being hand-cleared and reopened to foot traffic in the late 1990s. This trail provides excellent views of the canyon and the waterfalls, river, and forests inside it. Another easy to moderate hike nearby is the Goat Trail & Wagon Road, which replaced the northern part of the Keystone Canyon Pack Trail. This 4. 8-mile hike takes travelers from Bridal Veil Falls north to mile 18 on the Richardson Highway and offers spectacular views of Snowslide Gulch, Bear Creek, and the Lowe River. Other trails in the Valdez area are equally scenic, though not as historic. One runs up Mineral Creek, another along Shoup Bay, and a third through Solomon Gulch. The Valdez Convention & Visitors Bureau (200 Fairbanks St, 99686) offers free maps and detailed information about each of the trails in the area.

**Tours.** *Valdez. Phone toll-free 800/544-2206 www.graylineofalaska.com.* Gray Line of Alaska offers package tours around Alaska (up to 11 days) as well as flightseeing tours, a jetboat safari, and guided fishing tours.

**Valdez Museum and Annex.** *217 Egan Dr, Valdez (99686). Phone 907/835-2764. www.alaska.net/~vldzmuse/index.html.* The Valdez Museum is located in the center of downtown Valdez and features displays and exhibits that tell the story of Valdez and the Prince William Sound area. The museum annex is located in a warehouse at the southern end of Hazelet Avenue, by the ferry dock and Ruth Pond Park. Walking through the museum and its annex, visitors can trace the history of the town, from its origins as a trailhead supply depot during the Klondike Gold Rush of 1897-1898 through its destruction and relocation after the 1964 Good Friday Earthquake to its rejuvenation after being chosen as the southern terminus of the Alaska pipeline. Other exhibits focus on the 1989 *Exxon Valdez* oil spill that occurred in Prince William Sound and detail both the massive cleanup effort that was made and the steps that have been taken locally and nationally to learn from the accident. Visitors to the museum should save time to visit the museum annex located a short walk southeast of the museum. The annex contains an exquisitely detailed 1:20 scale model of Old Town Valdez as it looked just prior to the 1964 earthquake, including more than 400 buildings and covering more than 20 city blocks. Archival news footage and written accounts of the earthquake and its aftermath are also on public display in the annex. (Museum: summer: Mon-Sat 9 am-6 pm, Sun 8 am-5 pm; winter: Mon-Fri 1-5 pm; Sat noon-4 pm. Annex: summer, daily 9 am-4 pm. ) **$**

## Special Events

**Gold Rush Days.** *Valdez. Phone 907/835-4636. www.valdezalaska.org.* Held for five days at the start of

August, Valdez's Gold Rush Days festival celebrates the town's rich Gold Rush history. Highlights of the festival include the coronation of the king and queen of Gold Rush Days, a fashion show put on by local residents, roaming costumed can-can dancers, and a free community halibut and salmon fish fry held oudoors in one of the town's parks.

**Last Frontier Theater Conference.** *Valdez. Prince William Sound Community College. Phone 907/834-1614; toll-free 800/478-8800; fax 907/834-1627. http://137.229.240.35/gen/newtc/01tc.htm.* Co-hosted each year by Prince William Sound Community College and Edward Albee, Pulitzer Prize-winning playwright—best known for his work *Whos Afraid of Virginia Woolf?*—this lively, highly social event begins in mid-June and runs for nine days. During its run, panel discussions and small-group seminars feature well-known actors, directors, and playwrights talking about their craft and giving advice to conference attendees, some of whose plays are later read and critiqued. Evenings feature live performances of works by featured guests with professional and amateur actors filling the roles. Past invitees have included playwrights Arthur Miller, Tony Kushner, and Terrence McNally and television and actors Angela Bassett, Laura Linney, and Chris Noth. Individual and multi-event tickets are available. Mid-June.

## Limited-Service Hotels

**★ ASPEN HOTEL.** *100 Meals Ave, Valdez (99686). Phone 907/835-4445; toll-free 800/478-4445; fax 907/835-2437. www.aspenhotelsak.com.* This comfortable downtown hotel appeals on different levels to the eclectic mix of people who stay here. Business professionals appreciate the small, private business center and in-room DSL and wireless Internet access. Families and groups enjoy the large family suites and the host of freebies the hotel offers: an on-site pool and hot tub, a small fitness center, e-mail access, and deluxe continental breakfast. 102 rooms. Complimentary continental breakfast. Check-in 3 pm, check-out 11 am. High-speed Internet access, wireless Internet access. Fitness room. Indoor pool, whirlpool. **$$**

**★ ★ BEST WESTERN VALDEZ HARBOR INN.** *100 Fidalgo Dr, Valdez (99686). Phone 907/835-3434; fax 907/835-2308.* This newly renovated waterfront hotel (the only hotel in Valdez that's right on the water) is located at the Valdez boat harbor with unobstructed views of Prince William Sound and the Chugach Mountains. Although it's a popular hotel for people heading out on glacier cruises and fishing charters, its slow-paced, rustic charm makes thoughts of napping and relaxing equally appealing. 88 rooms. Pets accepted. Check-in 2 pm, check-out noon. Restaurant. Fitness room. **$**

**★ ★ TOTEM INN HOTEL.** *144 E Egan Dr, Valdez (99686). Phone 907/835-4443; toll-free 888/808-4431; fax 907/834-4430. www.toteminn.com.* Built in 1973, this well-known family-owned hotel is actually a collection of buildings, the oldest of which houses a restaurant, a reception area, and the motel-like original rooms. All accomoodations on the property, which marks the start of downtown Valdez, are clean, comfortable, and in excellent shape; those in the newer buildings are more upscale. The inn's restaurant is the place to go for weekend brunch, attracting a steady stream of longtime local customers. 70 rooms. Pets accepted. Check-in 2 pm, check-out 11 am. Restaurant. **$**

## Specialty Lodgings

**BROOKSIDE INN BED & BREAKFAST.** *1465 Richardson Hwy, Valdez (99686). Phone 907/835-9130. www.brooksideinnbb.com.* Built in 1898, this inn is located three minutes away from downtown Valdez and Prince William Sound. 6 rooms, 2 story. **$**

**L & L'S BED & BREAKFAST.** *533 W Hanagita St, Valdez (99686). Phone 907/835-4447. www.lnlalaska.com.* Located minutes from downtown Valdez, the Alaska Marine Ferry Terminal, nature trails, and a visitors center, this bed-and-breakfast offers drop-off and pickup from airport and ferry. 5 rooms, 3 story. **$**

## Restaurants

**★ ★ ALASKA'S BISTRO.** *100 Fidalgo Dr, Valdez (99686). Phone 907/835-5688; fax 907/835-4240. www.valdezharborinn.com.* This harborside restaurant is a great location to watch fishing charters return with their catches at the end of the day. A local favorite for fine dining, it features "nouveau Mediterranean" cuisine in a casually upscale dining room. Of the many items on the menu, the crab-stuffed halibut, paella, and homemade cheesecake are far and away the most popular. Mediterranean menu. Breakfast, lunch, dinner. Bar. Casual attire. **$$**

★★★ **THE ROSE CACHE.** *321 Egan St, Valdez (99686). Phone 907/835-8383.* Relaxed and elegant dining with local ingredients. American menu. Dinner. Closed Mon. Reservations recommended. **$$**

★★ **TOTEM INN RESTAURANT.** *144 E Egan Dr, Valdez (99686). Phone 907/835-4443; fax 907/834-4426. www.toteminn.com.* For decades now, this friendly family restaurant has been serving hearty American dishes along with fresh Alaskan seafood, homemade soups, and fresh-baked biscuits and gravy to hungry tourists and locals. Adding to the appeal of the place is the wood and stone dining room filled with historic photos of Valdez as well as a spectacular array of stuffed Alaskan wildlife.
American menu. Breakfast, lunch, dinner. Closed Dec 25. Bar. Children's menu. Casual attire. **$$**

# Wasilla (D-5)

**Population** 5,469
**Area Code** 907
**Information** Greater Wasilla Chamber of Commerce, 415 E Railroad Ave, 99654; phone 907/376-1299
**Web Site** www.wasillachamber.org

Like many small towns in Alaska, Wasilla owes its existence to the Alaska Railroad. In 1917, the rail line being constructed between Anchorage and Fairbanks reached Wasilla. Practically overnight, the tiny community that had been little more than a wayside stop on the Carle Wagon Road became a vital commercial and industrial center for the surrounding area. With the completion of the Parks Highway from Anchorage to Fairbanks in 1971, the area once again began an era of rapid growth and change as it suddenly became possible to live amid the scenic beauty and tranquility of the Wasilla area and work in Anchorage, 43 miles away. These days, visitors can learn more about the characters, events, and decisions that shaped the region at the Dorothy Page Museum and Historical Townsite, located in downtown Wasilla. Other noteworthy local attractions are the Iditarod Trail Sled Dog Race Headquarters and the Knik Museum and Dog Mushers Hall of Fame, both of which spotlight the history and evolution of dog sledding through interpretive exhibits and historical artifacts.

## What to See and Do

**Iditarod Trail Sled Dog Race Headquarters.** *Knik Goose Bay Rd, mile 2.2, Wasilla (99687). From the Parks Hwy, head S on Knik Goose Bay Rd for 2.2 miles. Phone 907/376-5155. www.iditarod.com.* This rustic log cabin headquarters and visitor center just south of the Parks Highway contains interpretive displays and historical artifacts relating to the Iditarod dogsled race. Visitors can view videos of past races, wander through the museum, and take dogsled rides during summer months (fee). Unlike many attractions in Alaska, the headquarters stays open all year and really begins to get crowded in the weeks leading up to the race, which officially starts in Wasilla the day after its ceremonial—and much publicized—start in Anchorage. Hours change during the weeks surrounding the Iditarod Trail Sled Dog race, so call for details. (Mid-May-mid-Sept: daily 8 am-7 pm; mid-Sept-mid-May: Mon-Fri 8 am-5 pm) **FREE**

**Knik Museum & Sled Dog Mushers' Hall of Fame.** *Knik Rd, mile 13.9, Wasilla (99654). Phone 907/376-2005.* This small historical museum is housed in Knik Hall, one of only two buildings remaining in Knik, once a bustling port used by miners heading up the Iditarod Trail to Alaska's western goldfields. Although the town has faded into history, the museum's collection of old photographs, period furniture, and unique artifacts still attracts visitors interested in gold rush and local history. The main draw of the museum, though, is undoubtedly the Sled Dog Mushers' Hall of Fame located on the second floor. The Hall contains portraits and detailed descriptions of the Iditarod's top mushers dating to the first years of the race. In recognition of the vital role that individual dogs can play in determining the success of a musher, the museum honors famous sled dogs, too. A nearby memorial garden is dedicated to Joe Redington, known as the Father of the Iditarod for his work in the early 1970s to establish the race and make it an annual event. Hours are subject to change depending on staffing and public interest, so call ahead. (June-Aug: Fri-Sun 2-6 pm, other days by appointment; rest of year: by appointment) **DONATION**

## Special Event

**Tesoro Iron Dog 2000 Snowmachine Race.** *Tesoro Iron Dog Headquarters, 7100 Old Seward Hwy, Suite C, Anchorage (99501). Race start and finish dates, times, and locations vary by year. Phone 907/563-4414; fax 907/336-5052. www.irondog.org.* This annual 2,000-mile race pits teams of two racers on separate snowmachines against some of the harshest, most isolated terrain in Alaska. With temperatures dipping to 40 below, speeds as high as 93 mph, and limited daylight for much of the journey, it's not a race for the faint of heart. The race runs in segments over the course of a week and usually goes from Fairbanks west to Nome and then southeast to Wasilla, reversing direction in alternating years. Highlights of the competition include a 500-mile full-throttle dash down the frozen Yukon River, a pressure-ridge and snowdrift-plagued traverse across the ice pack on Norton Sound, and a forested climb through deep snow up and over the Alaska Range. Of the 25 teams that started out in 2004, only 12 finished the race, with the first team crossing the line in a cumulative time of 39 hours, 3 minutes. Mid-Feb.

## Limited-Service Hotels

**★ ALASKAN VIEW MOTEL.** *2650 E Parks Hwy, Wasilla (99654). Phone 907/376-6787; fax 907/376-6726. www.alaskanviewmotel.com.* The primary selling point of this inexpensive, cozy motel is the spectacular, panoramic view it offers of Cook Inlet and the Chugach Range towering above the landscape in the distance. The motel is also only a short distance from Wasilla's main shopping areas and most of the towns restaurants and shops. 24 rooms. Pets accepted. Check-in 4 pm, check-out 11 am. **$**

**★ ★ BEST WESTERN LAKE LUCILLE INN.** *1300 W Lake Lucille Dr, Wasilla (99654). Phone 907/373-1776; toll-free 800/897-1776; fax 907/376-6199. www.bestwesternlakelucilleinn.com.* Set on the shores of Lake Lucille, every lakeside room has a private balcony with breathtaking views of the wooded lake and the snowcapped Chugach mountain range soaring into the sky some 15 miles away. Offering comfortable, tranquil accommodations in a lodge-like setting, this hotel would be a great place to stop while in transit to or from the Denali area. 54 rooms. Pets accepted. Complimentary continental breakfast. Check-in 3 pm, check-out noon. Restaurant, bar. Fitness room. Whirlpool. **$**

**★ ★ GRAND VIEW INN & SUITES.** *2900 Parks Hwy, Wasilla (99654). Phone 907/357-7666; toll-free 866/710-7666; fax 907/357-6776.* Located at the crest of a hill on the southern edge of Wasilla, this hotel offers magnificent, unobstructed views of nearby Cook Inlet, the Chugach Mountains, and Knik Glacier. The spacious, comfortable lobby and immaculate rooms provide guests with plenty of room to relax and unwind, but its the views that make this a terrific place to stop. 79 rooms. Pets accepted. Complimentary continental breakfast. Check-in 3 pm, check-out noon. Restaurant. Fitness room. Indoor pool, whirlpool. **$**

## Restaurant

**★ ★ SHORELINE RESTAURANT.** *1300 W Lake Lucille Dr, Wasilla (99654). Phone 907/373-1776; fax 907/376-6199. www.bestwestern.com/lakelucilleinn.* The interior of this popular restaurant is both muted and classy, but the focus here is undeniably on whats outside: strikingly beautiful views of wooded Lake Lucille and the snowy Chugach Range rising behind it. During the long days of summer, the outdoor patio enables guests to dine alfresco while still enjoying the white tablecloth service they would get inside. American menu. Lunch, dinner. Closed Dec 25. Bar. Children's menu. Casual attire. Outdoor seating. **$$**

# Wrangell-St. Elias National Park and Preserve

**Web Site** www.nps.gov/wrst

While its name may neither sound familiar nor roll easily off the tongue, Wrangell-St. Elias National Park & Preserve is definitely worth a visit, as it boasts North America's greatest collection of mountain peaks above 16,000 feet, highlighted by 18,008-foot-high Mount St. Elias, the second highest peak in the United States. Wrangell-St. Elias is the nation's largest national park, with over 13 million acres of rugged wilderness, a landscape of towering mountains, sweeping valleys, massive glaciers, and powerful rivers. Wrangell-St. Elias is one of four contiguous parks situated along the US-Canada border, the other three being Glacier Bay National Park & Preserve (Alaska), Kluane National Park Reserve (Yukon Territory), and the Alsek-Tatshenshini Provincial Park (British Columbia). Together, these four parks comprise the world's largest internationally protected area. Wrangell-St. Elias's headquarters can be found in Copper Center, a four-hour drive from Anchorage on the Alaska Highway. Two gravel roads provide access into the park. Nabesna Road (42 miles long) offers spectacular scenery, whil McCarthy Road (60 miles long) leads to exceptional hiking, fishing, and camping. The National Park Service recommends drivers

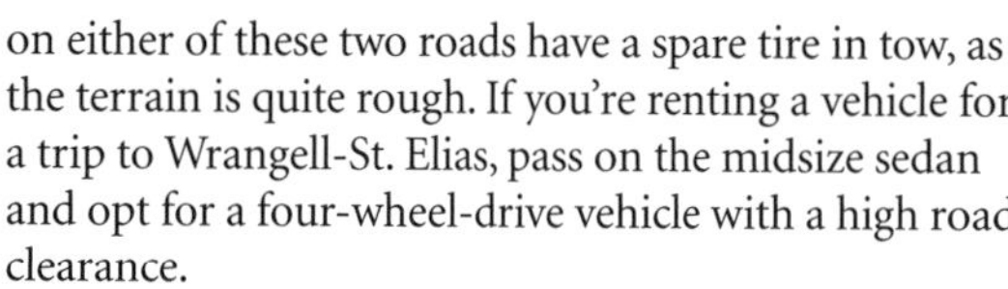

on either of these two roads have a spare tire in tow, as the terrain is quite rough. If you're renting a vehicle for a trip to Wrangell-St. Elias, pass on the midsize sedan and opt for a four-wheel-drive vehicle with a high road clearance.

# Yukon-Charley Rivers National Preserve

**Web Site** www.nps.gov/yuch

Yukon-Charley Rivers National Preserve is notable for its abundant wildlife. Bordering Canada in east-central Alaska, the preserve has North America's highest nesting density of peregrine falcons. Summer brings a wide variety of other bird species to the area, some traveling from as far away as South America. Grizzlies and black bears roam the hills here, as do herds of caribou and packs of wolves. The preserve protects the entire 1. 1 million-acre watershed of the Charley River, as well as 115 miles of the 1,800-mile-long Yukon River. Rafting, kayaking, and canoeing are popular on both rivers, particularly on the Charley, which has been designated a National Wild River. Yukon-Charley Rivers has seven public-use cabins, all available on a first-come, first-served basis. A visitor center in the town of Eagle features exhibits on the preserves history and ecology. Situated at the northern terminus of Highway 5, Eagle is accessible by car, about a days drive from Anchorage.

# Idaho

When the Idaho Territory was created (it included much of Montana and Wyoming as well), President Abraham Lincoln had difficulty finding a governor who was willing to come to this wild and rugged land. Some appointees, including Gilman Marston and Alexander H. Conner, never appeared.

They had good reason to be timorous—the area was formidable and still is. For there is not just one Idaho; there are at least a half-dozen: a land of virgin rain forests (more than one-third of the state is wooded); a high desert covering an area bigger than Rhode Island and Delaware combined; gently sloping farmland, where soft Pacific winds carry the pungency of growing alfalfa; an alpine region of icy, isolated peaks and densely forested valleys hiding more lakes and streams than have been named, counted, or even discovered; an atomic energy testing station as modern as tomorrow, only a few miles from the Craters of the Moon, where lava once poured forth and congealed in fantastic formations; and the roadless, nearly uninhabited, 2.3-million-acre Frank Church-River of No Return Wilderness, where grizzly bear, moose, and bighorn sheep still run wild.

**Population:** 1,293,593
**Area:** 83,557 square miles
**Elevation:** 710-12,662 feet
**Peak:** Borah Peak (Custer County)
**Entered Union:** July 3, 1890 (43rd state)
**Capital:** Boise
**Motto:** Let it be perpetual
**Nickname:** Gem State
**Flower:** Syringa
**Bird:** Mountain Bluebird
**Tree:** White Pine
**Fair:** Eastern, September in Blackfoot; Western, August in Boise
**Time Zone:** Mountain and Pacific
**Web Site:** www.visitid.org
**Fun Facts:**

- The world's longest floating boardwalk surrounds the marina at the Coeur d'Alene Resort in Coeur d'Alene, Idaho. Built in 1986, it is 12 feet wide and 3,300 feet long.
- Idaho's statehouse in Boise is geothermally heated by underground hot springs.
- Rivers flow across 3,100 miles of Idaho, more than any other state.
- Idaho's Hells Canyon is the deepest river gorge (7,913 feet) in North America.
- Ernest Hemingway finished *For Whom the Bell Tolls* while living in Sun Valley, and he is buried in Ketchum.

Stretching southward from Canada for nearly 500 miles and varying dramatically in terrain, altitude, and climate, Idaho has the deepest canyon in North America (Hell's Canyon, 7,913 feet), the largest stand of white pine in the world (in Idaho Panhandle National Forests), the finest big game area in the country (Chamberlain Basin and Selway), the largest wilderness area in the United States (the Frank Church-River of No Return Wilderness), and the largest contiguous irrigated area in the United States (created by American Falls and several lesser dams). Idaho's largest county, named after the state itself, would hold the entire state of Massachusetts; its second-largest county, Owyhee, would hold New Jersey.

In addition to superlative scenery, fishing, and hunting, visitors find such diversions as buried bandit treasure, lost gold mines, hair-raising boat trips down the turbulent Salmon River (the "River

## Calendar Highlights

### February

**Lionel Hampton Jazz Festival** *(Moscow). University of Idaho. Phone 208/885-6765.* Four-day festival hosted by Lionel Hampton featuring all-star headliners and student performers.

**Pacific Northwest Sled Dog Championship Races At Priest Lake Airport.** *Phone Chamber of Commerce, 208/263-2161.* Approximately 100 teams from the US and Canada compete in various races from 1/2 mile to 35 miles.

### April

**Cowboy Poet Festival** *(St. Anthony). Phone South Fremont Chamber of Commerce, 208/624-4870.* Entertainment, clogging demonstrations.

### June

**Boise River Festival** *(Boise). Phone 208/338-8887.* Nighttime parade, contests, entertainment, and fireworks.

**National Oldtime Fiddlers' Contest** *(Weiser). Phone 800/437-1280.* One of the oldest such contests in the country, attracting some of the nation's finest fiddlers. Also parade, barbecue, and arts and crafts.

**Western Days** *(Twin Falls). Phone 208/733-3974.* Three-day event features a shoot-out, barbecue contests, dances, and a parade.

### July

**smART Festival St. Marie's City Park.** *Phone 208/245-3417.* Paintings and crafts by local and regional artists. Food, entertainment, and swimming.

**Snake River Stampede** *(Nampa). Phone 208/466-4641.* Among the nation's top professional rodeos. All seats reserved.

### August

**The Festival at Sandpoint.** *(Sandpoint) Phone 208/265-4554.* Since 1982, thousands have gathered in this arts town to enjoy music performed by internationally acclaimed musicians representing just about every genre imaginable. Past artists include the likes of B.B. King, Shawn Colvin, Tony Bennett, Wynton Marsalis, and Johnny Cash.

**Shoshone-Bannock Indian Festival** *(Blackfoot). Fort Hall Indian Reservation. Phone 208/238-3700.* Tribes from many western states and Canada gather for this festival. Dancing, parades, rodeo, Native American queen contest, buffalo feast, and other events.

**Western Idaho Fair** *(Boise). Phone 208/376-3247.* Largest fair in the state. Four entertainment stages, grandstand for nationally known musicians. Livestock, rodeo, agricultural pavilion, antique tractors, indoor and outdoor commercial exhibits, and midway rides.

### September

**Eastern Idaho State Fair** *(Blackfoot). Phone 208/785-2480.* 70-acre fairground. Livestock, machinery exhibits, four-, six-, and eight-horse hitch competition, racing (pari-mutuel betting), rodeo, tractor pull, demolition derby, parade, and nightly outdoor musical shows.

of No Return"), and ghost mining towns. For those who prefer less strenuous activities, Sun Valley and Coeur d'Alene have luxurious accommodations.

Millions of years ago herds of mammoth, mastodon, camels, and a species of enormous musk ox roamed the Idaho area. When Lewis and Clark entered the region in 1805, they found fur-bearing animals in such great numbers that they got in each other's way. The promise of riches in furs brought trappers, who fought the animals, the Native Americans, the country, and each other with equal gusto. They were aided and abetted by the great fur companies, including the legendary Hudson's Bay Company. The first gold strike in the Clearwater country in 1860, followed by rich strikes in the Salmon River and Florence areas, the Boise Basin, and Coeur d'Alene (still an important mining area in the state) brought hordes of miners who were perfectly willing to continue the no-holds-barred way of life initiated by fur trappers. Soon afterward the shots of warring sheepmen and cattlemen mingled with those of miners.

Mining, once Idaho's most productive and colorful industry, has yielded its economic reign, but the state still produces large amounts of silver, zinc, pumice, antimony, and lead. It holds great reserves (268,000 acres) of phosphate rock. Copper, thorium, limestone, asbestos, graphite, talc, tungsten, cobalt, nickel, cinnabar, bentonite, and a wealth of other important minerals are found here. Gems, some of the finest quality, include agate, jasper, garnets, opals, onyx, sapphires, and rubies.

Today, Idaho's single largest industry is farming. On more than 3.5 million irrigated acres, the state produces an abundance of potatoes, beets, hay, vegetables, fruit, and livestock. The upper reaches of the Snake River Valley, once a wasteland of sagebrush and greasewood, are now among the West's most fertile farmlands. Manufacturing and processing of farm products, timber, and minerals is an important part of the state's economic base. Tourism is also important to the economy.

## When to Go/Climate

Summer and fall are usually pleasant times to visit Idaho, although it can snow at almost any time of year here. The state's varied topography makes for a wide range of weather conditions. Winter temperatures are cold but not so cold as to make outdoor activities uncomfortable.

### AVERAGE HIGH/LOW TEMPERATURES (°F)

**Boise**

| | | |
|---|---|---|
| **Jan** 36/22 | **May** 71/44 | **Sep** 77/48 |
| **Feb** 44/28 | **Jun** 81/58 | **Oct** 65/39 |
| **Mar** 53/32 | **Jul** 90/58 | **Nov** 49/31 |
| **Apr** 61/37 | **Aug** 88/57 | **Dec** 38/23 |

**Pocatello**

| | | |
|---|---|---|
| **Jan** 32/14 | **May** 68/40 | **Sep** 75/43 |
| **Feb** 38/20 | **Jun** 78/53 | **Oct** 63/34 |
| **Mar** 47/26 | **Jul** 88/53 | **Nov** 45/26 |
| **Apr** 58/32 | **Aug** 86/51 | **Dec** 34/16 |

## Parks and Recreation

Water-related activities, hiking, riding, various other sports, picnicking, visitor centers, and camping are available in most of Idaho's state parks. Camping: $16/site per night with all hookups; $12/site per night with water; $10/site per night for primitive site. Extra vehicle $7/night. FIfteen-day maximum stay at most parks. Reservations available only at Bear Lake, Farragut, Hells Gate, Ponderosa and Priest Lake parks ($8 fee). Motorized vehicle entrance fee (included in camping fee), $3/day or $35 annual pass; no entrance fee for persons walking, riding a bicycle, or horseback riding. All camping parks in the Idaho system feature at least one site designed for use by the disabled. Most visitor centers and restrooms also accommodate the disabled. For further information, contact the Idaho Dept of Parks & Recreation, PO Box 83720, Boise 83720-0065; phone 208/334-4199 or toll-free 800/847-4843.

### FISHING AND HUNTING

Nowhere in Idaho is the outdoor enthusiast more than an hour's drive from a clearwater fly-fishing stream. From 2,000 lakes, 90 reservoirs, and 16,000 miles of rivers and streams, anglers take several million fish each year. Kokanee, trout (steelhead, rainbow, Kamloops, cutthroat, brown, brook, Dolly Varden, and Mackinaw), bass, perch, channel catfish, and sunfish are the most common varieties, with trout the most widespread and certainly among the scrappiest. Big game includes whitetail and mule deer, elk, antelope, bighorn sheep, mountain goat, and black bear. There are 12 kinds of upland game birds, plus ducks, Canada geese, and doves in season. Nonresident fishing license: season $53; one-day $10; each additional day $4/day; three-day salmon/steelhead $31.50. Nonresident hunting license: game $110; turkey tag $40; deer tag $240; elk tag $340; other tag fees required for some game. There are nonresident quotas for deer and elk; apply mid-Dec. State permit validation is required for hunting waterfowl and some upland bird species, $6.50; archery and muzzleloader permits, $16.50. Prices may vary; for full information contact the Idaho Dept of Fish and Game, 600 S Walnut St, Box 25, Boise 83707; phone 208/334-3700 or toll-free 800/635-7820.

## ICE-AGE LAKES AND DEEP RIVER CANYONS

This tour starts at a gold rush town at the heart of the Rockies, passes an ice-age glacial lake, and drops down through farm country to the desert canyons of the Snake River.

Stately Wallace sits in the shadows of a steep Rocky Mountain valley that contains some of the richest silver and lead veins in the world. There has been This This tour starts at a gold rush town at the heart of the Rockies, passes an ice-age glacial lake, and drops down through farm country to the desert canyons of the Snake River. Stately Wallace sits in the shadows of a steep Rocky Mountain valley that contains some of the richest silver and lead veins in the world. There has been extensive industrial mining here since the 1880s, and the town of Wallace possesses one of the best-preserved Victorian town centers in Idaho. The entire town is listed on the National Historic Register. Visit the Wallace District Mining Museum, which tells the story of the region's silver boom. Then walk to the Northern Pacific Depot Railroad Museum, located in the town's lovely old depot.

A number of silver mines still operate in the Wallace area. If you're interested in what goes on underground in a silver mine, take a tour of the Sierra Silver Mine. From downtown Wallace, old trolleys drive you to the mine, where underground tours demonstrate the techniques and equipment of hard-rock mining.

Continue west on I-90 to Cataldo. The Mission of the Sacred Heart, now a state park, is Idaho's oldest building. Built by Catholic "Blackrobe" Jesuits in 1848, this simple church, constructed of mortised and tenoned beams, sits above a bluff on the Coeur d'Alene River. For decades this was the spiritual and educational center of northern Idaho. The state park now includes a visitor center with interpretive information, picnic area, and a self-guiding nature trail.

Continue west on I-90, climbing up over the Fourth of July Pass before dropping down onto Lake Coeur d'Alene, a large glacier-dug lake flanked by green forested mountains. The town of Coeur dAlene sits at the west end of the lake and is the center of a large resort community. The heart of Coeur d'Alene is City Park and Beach at the edge of downtown. During summer a crush of people enjoy the sun and water here, indulging in such pastimes as swimming, sailing, jet-skiing, and windsurfing. From the marina in front of the Coeur dAlene Resort, lake cruises depart to explore the lake. The streets behind the beachfront preserve period storefronts with good casual restaurants and shops.

From Coeur d'Alene, turn south on Highway 95 and pass through the Coeur dAlene Indian Reservation. The landscape transforms from pine and fir forests to rolling farmland. Amid the wheat fields are more curious crops: this is the center of lentil production in the United States. Moscow is home to the University of Idaho. The compact downtown area has a pleasant alternative feel, with bookstores, coffee shops, food co-ops, and brew pubs.

From Moscow south on Highway 95, the farmland begins to fall away and the road begins to wind down the Snake River Canyon. During the early settlement days, the canyon wall north of Lewiston was an impediment to transport and commerce with farms in the Moscow area. Finally in 1914, with improved engineering and technology, a road was devised that snaked down Lewiston Hill, slowly dropping 2,000 feet in 9 1/2 miles, with 64 switchbacks, to reach the valley floor. Nowadays, a freeway zips up and down the hill, but the old road is preserved as the Old Spiral Highway. Take this side road for more leisurely and scenic views onto Lewiston and the confluence of the Snake and Clearwater rivers.

Lewiston is the departure point for jet boat trips up the Hells Canyon of the Snake River, the deepest river canyon in North America. The tours depart from Hells Gate Park, south of the city on Snake River Avenue. **(Approximately 164 miles).**

## THE WILDS OF IDAHO

This route begins in the Snake River Canyon and follows a series of dramatic river valleys into the very heart of the Rockies, finally climbing up to crest the Continental Divide. Lewiston sits at the junction of the Snake and Clearwater rivers, which meet beneath 1,000-foot desert cliffs. (Lewiston is the starting point for jet boat trips to popular Hells Canyon, the gorge formed by the Snake River.) Highway 30 follows the

Clearwater River east, where the valley quickly turns forested and green. This portion of the route passes through the Nez Perce National Historic Park, where several sites of mythic and historic interest to the Nez Perce people are highlighted and interpreted. As the route continues east, the valley becomes more narrow and dramatic, with small, venerable fishing resorts clinging to the rocky river bank. East from Kooskia, Highway 12 wedges into the canyon of the Lochsa River, a mountain terrain so formidable (and scenically dramatic) that completion of this section of the highway was not possible until 1962, when modern engineering and construction processes became available. This near-wilderness area is popular with experienced whitewater rafters, who are often seen on the coursing river. Near the pass into Montana, easy hiking trails lead to undeveloped, natural hot springs. **(Approximately 172 miles)**

## Driving Information

Safety belts are mandatory for all persons in the front seat of a vehicle. Children under 4 years must be in an approved safety seat anywhere in the vehicle. For further information, phone 208/334-8100.

### INTERSTATE HIGHWAY SYSTEM

The following alphabetical listing of Idaho towns in this book shows that these cities are within 10 miles of the indicated interstate highways. Check a highway map for the nearest exit.

| Highway Number | Cities/Towns within 10 miles |
|---|---|
| Interstate 15 | Blackfoot Idaho Falls, Lava Hot, Springs, Pocatello. |
| Interstate 84 | Boise, Burley, Caldwell, Jerome, Mountain Home, Nampa, Twin Falls. |
| Interstate 86 | American Falls, Pocatello. |
| Interstate 90 | Coeur d' Alene, Kellogg, Wallace. |

## Additional Visitor Information

Idaho Travel Council, PO Box 83720, 700 W State St, Boise 83720-0093, publishes a number of attractive and helpful pamphlets, among them an Idaho Travel Guide. Phone 208/334-2470 or 800/714-3246.

Visitor centers in Idaho are located in or near the Oregon/Idaho, Washington/Idaho, and Utah/Idaho borders, as well as throughout the state. Visitors who stop by will find information and brochures helpful in planning stops at points of interest.

# American Falls (F-4)

*See also Pocatello*

**Population** 3,757
**Elevation** 4,404 ft
**Area Code** 208
**Zip** 83211
**Information** Chamber of Commerce, 239 Idaho St, PO Box 207; phone 208/226-7214
**Web Site** www.americanfallschamber.org

After a party of American Fur Company trappers was caught in the current of the Snake River and swept over the falls here, the fur company gave its name to both the community and the falls. American Falls boasts an important hydroelectric plant and is the capital of a vast dry-farming wheat belt; agricultural reclamation projects stretch westward for 170 miles.

## What to See and Do

**American Falls Dam.** *239 Idaho St, American Falls (83211). I-86 exit 40, follow signs on ID 39 Bypass. Phone 208/226-7214.* Impounds 25-mile-long lake; Willow Bay Recreation Area has swimming (beaches), fishing, boating (ramp; fee); picnicking, camping (hookups; fee).

**Indian Springs.** *3249 Indian Springs Rd, American Falls (83211). 4 miles S on Hwy 37.* Hot mineralized springs, pools, and baths; camping. (May-Labor Day, daily)**$$**

**Massacre Rocks State Park.** *3592 Park Ln, American Falls (83211). 12 miles SW on I-86 at exit 28. Phone 208/548-2672.* Covers 995 acres. Along the Old Oregon Trail, emigrants carved their names on Register Rock. Nearby, at Massacre Rocks, is the spot where a wagon train was ambushed in 1862. River, juniper-sagebrush area; extensive bird life. Waterskiing, fishing, boating (ramps); hiking, bird-watching,

picnicking. 52 tent and trailer sites (dump station). Interpretive programs; info center. (Daily) **$**

**Trenner Memorial Park.** *Near Idaho Power Company plant, SW of dam.* Honors an engineer who played a key role in the development of the area; includes a miniature power station, fountain, and lava terrace. **FREE**

## Special Event

**Massacre Rocks Rendezvous.** *Massacre Rocks State Park, 3592 Park Ln, American Falls (83211). Phone 208/548-2672.* Reenactment of Wild West past with black powder shoots and knife-throwing contest. First weekend in June.

# Arco (E-3)

**Settled** 1879
**Population** 1,016
**Elevation** 5,318 ft
**Area Code** 208
**Zip** 83213

Arco, the seat of Butte County, was the first town to be lighted by power derived from atomic energy. Wildcat Peak casts its shadow on this pleasant little community located in a bend of the Big Lost River. Visitors pause here while exploring the Craters of the Moon National Monument, 20 miles southwest.

## What to See and Do

**Experimental Breeder Reactor Number 1 (EBR-1).** *Hwy 20/26, Arco (83213). 18 miles SE via Hwy 20/26. Phone 208/526-0050.* The first nuclear reactor developed to generate electricity (Dec 20, 1951). Visitor center exhibits include the original reactor and three other nuclear reactors, equipment, and control room, as well as displays on the production of electricity. Self-guided or one-hour tours (Memorial Day weekend-Labor Day: daily; rest of year: by appointment). Contact INEL Tours, PO Box 1625, Idaho Falls 83415-3695. **FREE**

# Ashton (E-5)

*See also Driggs, Rexburg, Saint Anthony*

**Population** 1,114
**Elevation** 5,260 ft
**Area Code** 208
**Zip** 83420
**Information** Chamber of Commerce, City Hall, 64 N 10th St, PO Box 689; phone 208/652-3987
**Web Site** www.ashtonidaho.com

Ashton's economy is centered on the flow of products from the rich agricultural area that extends to Blackfoot. Equally important to the town, which has a view of the Twin Teton Peaks in Wyoming, is the influx of vacationers bound for the Targhee National Forest, Warm River recreation areas, and Bear Gulch winter sports area. A Ranger District office of the forest is located here.

## What to See and Do

**Harriman State Park.** *3489 Hwy 20, Ashton (83420). 19 miles N on Hwy 20/191, S of Island Park. Phone 208/558-7368.* Located in the heart of a 16,000-acre wildlife refuge; home of the rare trumpeter swan. Nature is the main attraction here with Golden and Silver lakes, wildflowers, lodgepole pines, and thriving wildlife. The world-famous fly-fishing stream, Henry's Fork of the Snake River, winds through the park. Historic Railroad Ranch. Hiking, horseback riding, cross-country skiing. (Daily) **$**

**Henry's Lake State Park.** *3489 Hwy 20, Ashton (83420). 37 miles N on Hwy 20, then 1 mile W; N of Island Park, on the S shore of famous fishing area, Henry's Lake. Phone 208/558-7368.* This 586-acre park offers waterskiing, boating (ramp); hiking, picnicking, 50 campsites (26 with hookups, 24 without hookups; dump station). (Mid-May-Oct, daily) **$**

★ **Targhee National Forest.** *1405 Highway Park Dr, Idaho Falls (83402). Phone 208/524-7500.* Approximately 1.8 million acres include two wilderness areas: Jedediah Smith (W slope of the Tetons, adjacent to Grand Teton National Park) and Winegar Hole (grizzly bear habitat, bordering Yellowstone National Park); no motorized vehicles allowed in wilderness areas. Fishing (including trout fishing on Henry's Fork of the Snake River and Henry's Lake Reservoir); big game hunting, camping (fee), picnicking, winter sports; Grand Targhee Resort (see DRIGGS) ski area. Float trips on the Snake River; boating, sailing, waterskiing, and canoeing on the Palisades Reservoir; outfitters and guides for the Jedediah Smith Wilderness. Closed Sat-Sun. In the forest are

**Big Springs.** *33 miles N on Hwy 20/191 to Mack's Inn, then 5 miles E on paved road.* Source of the north fork of the Snake River, which gushes from a subterranean cavern at a constant 52°F; it quickly becomes 150 feet wide. Schools of salmon and rainbow trout can be seen from the bridge. The stream was designated the first National Recreation Water Trail. Moose, deer, sandhill cranes, trumpeter swans, and bald eagles can be seen along the banks.

**Lower Mesa Falls.** *14 miles NE on Hwy 47.* N Fork drops another 65 feet here; scenic overlook; camping.

**Upper Mesa Falls.** *18 miles NE on Hwy 47 on Forest Service land.* North Fork of Snake River takes a 114-foot plunge here; scenic overlook.

# Bellevue (E-3)

*See also Shoshone, Sun Valley Area*

**Population** 1,275
**Elevation** 5,190 ft
Area Code 208
**Zip** 83313

## What to See and Do

**Sawtooth National Forest.** *2647 Kimberly Rd E, Twin Falls (83301). Phone 208/737-3200.* Elevations from 4,500-12,100 feet. Swimming, water sports, fishing, boating; nature trails, downhill and cross-country skiing, snowmobiling, picnicking, saddle and pack trips, hunting, camping. Fee at certain designated campgrounds. **FREE**

# Blackfoot (E-4)

*See also Idaho Falls, Pocatello*

**Founded** 1878
**Population** 9,646
**Elevation** 4,504 ft
**Area Code** 208
**Zip** 83221
**Information** Chamber of Commerce, Riverside Plaza, #1, PO Box 801; phone 208/785-0510
**Web Site** www.blackfootidaho.net

Blackfoot is situated in southeastern Idaho, halfway between Idaho Falls and Pocatello. The community bills itself as the "Potato Capital of the World", a boast supported by the downtown presence of the Idaho Potato Expo, a museum celebrating the state's most famous export. Blackfoot was originally called Grove City, an homage to the town's abundance of trees. Its present name is derived from the Blackfoot River, which flows through town. The Fort Hall Indian Reservation sprawls across 544,000 acres to the south. Authentic Shoshone and Bannock arts and crafts are available at nearby stores, a favorite being the Clothes Horse, a marketplace located on the reservation.

## What to See and Do

**Airport Park.** *Parkway Dr, 1/2 miles N via I-15 exit 93.* Racetrack; picnicking, playground, golf, BMX track.

**Bingham County Historical Museum.** *190 N Shilling Ave, Blackfoot (83221). Phone 208/785-8065.* Restored 1905 homestead of Brown family containing gun collection, Native American artifacts, early 20th-century furnishings and kitchen utensils. (Mar-Nov, Wed-Fri; closed holidays) **DONATION**

**Jensen Grove Park.** *Airport Rd, on Snake River.* Boating, waterskiing, paddleboat rentals, varied water activities, disc golf, skateboard park, hockey.

## Special Events

**Blackfoot Pride Days.** *Blackfoot (83221). Phone 208/785-0510.* Late June.

**Eastern Idaho State Fair.** *Blackfoot. 70-acre fairground, N of town. Phone 208/785-2480.* Livestock, machinery exhibits, four-, six-, and eight-horse hitch competition, racing (pari-mutuel betting), rodeo, tractor pull, demolition derby, parade, nightly outdoor musical shows. Sept.

**Shoshone-Bannock Indian Festival.** *, Blackfoot. Fort Hall Indian Reservation, S on I-15, Simplot Rd exit 80, then 2 miles W.* Tribes from many western states and Canada gather for this festival. Dancing, parades, rodeo, Native American queen contest, buffalo feast, and other events. Early Aug.

# Boise (E-2)

*See also Caldwell, Idaho City, Mountain Home, Nampa*

**Settled** 1862
**Population** 125,738
**Elevation** 2,726 ft
**Area Code** 208
**Information** Convention and Visitors Bureau, 312 S 9th St, Suite 100, 83701; phone 208/344-7777 or toll-free 800/635-5240
**Web Site** www.boise.org

Capital and largest city in Idaho, Boise (BOY-see) is also the business, financial, professional, and transportation center of the state. It is home to Boise State University (1932) and the National Interagency Fire Center, the nation's logistical support center for wildland fire suppression. Early French trappers labeled this still tree-rich area as les bois (the woods). Established during gold rush days, Boise was overshadowed by nearby Idaho City until designated the territorial capital in 1864. Abundant hydroelectric power stimulated manufacturing, with electronics, steel fabrication, and mobile homes the leading industries. Several major companies have their headquarters here. Lumber, fruit, sugar beets, and livestock are other mainstays of the economy; the state's main dairy region lies to the west of Boise. Natural hot water from the underground springs (with temperatures up to 170°F) heats some of the homes in the eastern portion of the city. A Ranger District office and the headquarters of the Boise National Forest are located here.

Extending alongside the Boise River is the Greenbelt, a trail used for jogging, skating, biking, and walking. When complete, the 22-mile trail will connect Eagle Island State Park on the west side of the city with Lucky Peak State Park on the east side of the city.

## Public Trasnsportation

**Buses.** ValleyRide, phone 208/846-8547, www.valleyride.org.

**Airport.** Boise Airport. Information phone 208/838-3110

**Airlines.** Alaska Airlines, America West Airlines, Big Sky Airlines, Delta Air Lines, Frontier Airlines, Horizon Air, Northwest Airlines, Salmon Air, SkyWest Airlines, Southwest Airlines, United Airlines

### Boise Fun Fact

- Idaho's statehouse in Boise is geothermally heated by underground hot springs.

## What to See and Do

**Basque Museum and Cultural Center.** *611 Grove St, Boise (83702). Phone 208/343-2671.*(1864) The only museum in North America dedicated solely to Basque heritage; historical displays, paintings by Basque artists, changing exhibits, restored boarding house used by Basque immigrants in 1900s. (Tues-Sat, limited hours) **$$**

**Bogus Basin Ski Resort.** *2405 Bogus Basin Rd, Boise (83702). 16 miles N on Bogus Basin Rd. Phone 208/342-2100; toll-free 800/367-4397.www.bogusbasin.com.* Four double chairlifts, two high-speed quad, paddle tow; patrol, school, rentals; two lodges, restaurants, bar; day care. Longest run 1 1/2 miles; vertical drop 1,800 feet. Night skiing. Cross-country trails. (Nov-Apr, daily) **$$$$**

**Boise National Forest.** *1387 S Vinnell Way, Boise (83709). Phone 208/373-4007.* This 2,646,341-acre forest includes the headwaters of the Boise and Payette rivers, two scenic byways, abandoned mines and ghost towns, and access to the Sawtooth Wilderness and the Frank Church River of No Return Wilderness. Trout fishing, swimming, rafting; hunting, skiing, snowmobiling, mountain biking, motorized trail biking, hiking, picnicking, camping. Visitor Center.

**Bronco Stadium.** *1400 Bronco Ln, Boise (83725). Phone 208/426-4737.* Although it is not one of the largest or most hallowed arenas in college football, Boise State University's Bronco Stadium has one thing that few other places (if any at all) have: blue turf. The trademark blue Astroturf makes this stadium unique not only to the Western Athletic Conference, but to stadiums in general. Fans can see teams from places like the University of Hawaii on the mainland in Boise in one of the most unique places to watch a sporting event of any kind.

**Discovery Center of Idaho.** *131 Myrtle St, Boise (83702). Phone 208/343-9895.www.scidaho.org.* Hands-on exhibits explore various principles of science; large bubblemaker, catenary arch, magnetic sand. (Tues-Sun; closed holidays) **$$**

**Eagle Island State Park.** *2691 Mace Rd, Eagle (83616). 8 miles W via Hwy 20/26 to Linder Rd. Phone 208/939-0696.* This 546-acre park was once a prison farm. Situated between the north and south channels of the Boise River, the park has cottonwoods, willows, and a variety of native flowers, as well as an abundance of wildlife including the great blue heron, eagle, hawk, beaver, muskrat, fox, and weasel. Facilities include a 15-acre man-made lake (no fishing), swimming beach, water slide (fee); picnicking, concession. No pets. No glass beverage bottles. (Memorial Day-Labor Day, daily) **$$**

## Exploring Downtown Boise

Boise is a high-spirited city that manages to meld the vestiges of the cowboy Old West with the sophistication of the urban Pacific Northwest. The downtown core is relatively small, which makes it fun to explore on foot. There's plenty of street life and activity, and much of the late-19th-century architecture—born of a gold rush—is still intact.

Begin at the state capitol building, at Capitol Boulevard and Jefferson Street. This vast structure is constructed of local sandstone and faced on the interior with four kinds of marble and mahogany paneling. On the first floor, wander across the rotunda and gaze upward at the interior of the 200-foot dome, ringed with 43 stars (Idaho was the 43rd state in the Union). The legislative chambers are on the third floor. The Idaho capitol is the only geothermally heated statehouse in the country: water from hot springs five blocks away is pumped into the building's radiators.

From the capitol, proceed down Capitol Boulevard to Main Street. From this corner east on Main Street to about 3rd Street is a district of fine old homes—many renovated into shops and restaurants—that recalls Boise's early-20th-century opulence. Referred to as Old Boise, this street is home to the Egyptian Theatre (at Main and Capital Boulevard), an architecturally exuberant early vaudeville theater and movie palace in full King Tut drag.

One block farther west, at Grove and 8th Street, is The Grove, Boise's unofficial city center. The grove is a brick-lined plaza with a large fountain, public art, and a pedestrian area. Summer concerts are held here, and it's the place to gather for skateboarders, cyclists, and lunchtime office workers.

Continue down Grove to 6th Street to the Basque Museum and Cultural Center (611 Grove St). Idaho contains one of the largest Basque settlements outside of Europe, and this interesting museum tells the story of their culture and settlement in southwest Idaho. Next door, and part of the museum, is the Cyrus Jacobs-Uberuaga House, built as a boarding house for Basque immigrants in 1864.

Continue up Capitol Boulevard to Julia Davis Park, a large park along the Boise River that contains many of the city's important museums and cultural institutions. Follow the posted sign trails to the Idaho Historical Museum (610 N Julia Davis Dr), which gives an excellent overview of the states rich historic heritage. Especially good are the exhibits devoted to Idaho native Indian history and to Oregon Trail pioneers. Immediately next door is Pioneer Village, a re-created town with vintage buildings dating from the late 19th century. Also in the park is the Boise Art Museum (670 Julia Davis Dr), with a permanent collection that focuses on American Realism.

At the center of Julia Davis Park is Zoo Boise. In addition to the traditional exotic zoo animal favorites from Africa, the zoo is home to a collection of large Rocky Mountain mammals like moose, mountain lions, elk, and bighorn sheep. Zoo Boise has the largest display of birds of prey in the Northwest. Return to the downtown area along 5th Street.

**Idaho Botanical Gardens.** *2355 N Penitentiary Rd, Boise (83712). Phone 208/343-8649.* Twelve theme and display gardens include meditation, cactus, rose, water, and butterfly/hummingbird gardens; 3/4-mile nature trail, plaza. (Daily) **$$**

★ **Julia Davis Park.** *1104 Royal Blvd, Boise (83706). Between Capitol Blvd and Broadway on the Boise River. Phone 208/384-4240.* Rose garden, tennis courts, picnicking, (shelters), playground. Boat rentals, Gene Harris bandshell. On grounds are

**Boise Art Museum.** *670 S Julia Davis Dr, Boise (83702). Phone 208/345-8330.* Northwest, Asian, and American art featured in changing and permanent exhibits. (Tues-Sun; closed holidays) **$$**

**Boise Tour Train.** *9824 Gurdon Ct, Boise (83704). Phone 208/342-4796.* Narrated, one-hour tour of the city and historical areas aboard motorized 1890s-style tour train. Departure point in Julia Davis Park. (Memorial Day-Labor Day: daily; early May-Memorial Day and after Labor Day-Oct: weekends) **$$$**

**Idaho Black History Museum.** *508 N Julia Davis Dr, Boise (83702). Phone 208/443-0017.* Changing exhibits highlight the history and culture of African Americans, with special emphasis on Idaho African Americans. Lectures, films, workshops, storytelling, and musical performances. (Summer: Tues-Sun 10 am-4 pm; winter: Wed-Sat 10 am-4 pm)

**Idaho Historical Museum.** *610 N Julia Davis Dr, Boise (83702). Phone 208/334-2120.* History of Idaho and Pacific Northwest. Ten historical interiors; Native American exhibits; fur trade, mining, ranching, forestry displays. (Daily) **$**

**Zoo Boise.** *355 N Julia Davis Dr, Boise (83702). Phone 208/384-4260.* Home to 285 animals; large birds of prey area; otter exhibit, primates, variety of cats, petting zoo. Education center; gift shop. (Daily; closed Jan 1, Thanksgiving, Dec 25) **$$**

**Lucky Peak State Park.** *10 miles SE on Hwy 21. Phone 208/334-2679.* A 237-acre park comprised of three units: Spring Shores Marina (boating, day use), Sandy Point (swimming beach below dam), and Discovery unit (picnicking, three group shelters, river) **$$**

**M-K Nature Center.** *600 S Walnut St, Boise (83712). Phone 208/334-2225.* River observatory allows visitors to view activities of fish life; aquatic and riparian ecology displays; also visitor center with hands-on computerized exhibits; nature trails. (Tues-Sun) **$$**

**Old Idaho Penitentiary.** *2445 Old Penitentiary Rd, Boise (83712).2 1/2 miles E via Warm Springs Ave (Hwy 21). Phone 208/368-6080.* (1870) Self-guided tour through the cells, compounds, and other areas of the prison. Guided tours by appointment (Memorial Day-Labor Day). Displays about famous inmates, lawmen, and penal methods. Slide show on history. Under 13 only with adult. (Daily; closed holidays) **$$**

**St. Michael's Episcopal Cathedral.** *518 N 8th St, Boise (83702). Phone 208/342-5601.www.stmichaelscathedral.org. (1900)* The Tiffany window in the south transept is a fine example of this type of stained glass. (Mon-Fri, call for schedule)

**State Capitol.** *8th and Jefferson sts, Boise. Phone 208/334-5174* (1905-1922) Neoclassical design, faced with Boise sandstone; mounted statue of George Washington in lobby on second floor. Murals on fourth floor symbolically tell state's past, present, and future. Changing exhibits. Self-guided tours (Mon-Sat). Guided tours (Mon-Fri, by appointment) **FREE**

**Table Rock.** *4 miles E at end of Shaw Mountain Rd.* Provides panoramic view of entire valley, 1,100 feet below. Road may be closed in winter.

**World Center for Birds of Prey.** *5668 W Flying Hawk Ln, Boise (83709). I-84, exit 50 to S Cole Rd, then 6 miles S. Phone 208/362-8687.* Originally created to prevent extinction of peregrine falcon; scope has been expanded to include national and international conservation of birds of prey and their environments. Visitors can see breeding chamber of California condors and other raptors at interpretive center; gift shop. (Daily; closed Jan 1, Thanksiving, Dec 25) **$$**

## Special Events

**Boise River Festival.** *7032 S Eisenman Rd, Boise (83716). Phone 208/338-8887.* Night parade, contests, entertainment, fireworks. Last full weekend in June.

**Idaho Shakespeare Festival.** *Amphitheater and Reserve, 5657 Warm Springs Ave, Boise (83716). Phone 208/429-9908. www.idahoshakespeare.org.* Enjoy an outdoor summer performance of one of Shakespeares famous tragedies or comedies. The 600-seat amphitheater is situated in a nature preserve in the scenic Boise foothills. June-Sept. **$$$$**

**Western Idaho Fair.** *Les Bois Park,5610 Glenwood St, Boise (83714) Phone 208/376-3247.* The largest fair in the state. Aug.

## Limited-Service Hotels

**★ ★ DOUBLETREE HOTEL.** *2900 Chinden Blvd, Boise (83714). Phone 208/343-1871; toll-free 800/222-8733; fax 208/344-1079. www.doubletree.com.* Right on the banks of the Boise River, this hotel is only 1 mile from the city center, near golf, white water rafting, and the Bogus Basin Ski Area. 304 rooms, 2 story. Pets accepted, some restrictions; fee. Check-in 3 pm, check-out noon. Restaurant, bar. Fitness room. Outdoor pool, children's pool, whirlpool. Airport transportation available. **$**

**★ ★ DOUBLETREE HOTEL.** *475 Parkcenter Blvd, Boise (83706). Phone 208/345-2002; toll-free 800/222-8733; fax 208/345-8354. www.boiseclub.doubletree.com.* Near the Boise River and just minutes from the airport, this property offers guest rooms with large workstations and data ports. Shopping and dining options of downtown Boise can be found nearby. 158 rooms, 6 story. Check-in 3 pm, check-out noon.

Restaurant, bar. Fitness room. Outdoor pool. Airport transportation available. Business center. **$**

★ ★ **HOLIDAY INN.** *3300 Vista Ave, Boise (83705). Phone 208/343-4900; toll-free 800/465-4329; fax 208/343-9635. www.holiday-inn.com.* 265 rooms, 2 story. Pets accepted; fee. Check-out noon. Restaurant, bar. Fitness room. Indoor pool, children's pool. Airport transportation available. **$**

★ ★ **OWYHEE PLAZA HOTEL.** *1109 Main St, Boise (83702). Phone 208/343-4611; toll-free 800/233-4611; fax 208/336-3860. www.owyheeplaza.com.* This historic property in the Owyhee Mountains offers an outdoor pool, two restaurants, and a complimentary airport shuttle, making the beauty of Idaho accessible. 100 rooms, 3 story. Pets accepted, some restrictions; fee. Check-in 3 pm, check-out noon. Two restaurants, bar. Outdoor pool. Airport transportation available. **$**

★ ★ **RED LION.** *1800 Fairview Ave, Boise (83702). Phone 208/344-7691; toll-free 800/733-5466; fax 208/336-3652. www.redlion.com.* 182 rooms, 7 story. Check-out noon. Restaurant, bar. Fitness room. Outdoor pool. Airport transportation available. **$**

★ **SAFARI INN.** *1070 Grove St, Boise (83702). Phone 208/344-6556; fax 208/344-7240. www.safariinndowntown.com.* 103 rooms, 3 story. Complimentary con-tinental breakfast. Check-out 1 pm. Fitness room. Outdoor pool, whirlpool. Airport transportation available. **$**

★ **SHILO INN.** *3031 Main St, Boise (83702). Phone 208/344-3521; toll-free 800/222-2244; fax 208/384-1217. www.shiloinns.com.* 112 rooms, 3 story. Pets accepted, some restrictions; fee. Complimentary continental breakfast. Check-in 3 pm, check-out noon. Fitness room. Indoor pool, whirlpool. Airport transportation available. **$**

★ ★ **STATEHOUSE INN.** *981 Grove St, Boise (83702). Phone 208/342-4622; toll-free 800/243-4622; fax 208/344-5751. www.statehouse-inn.com.* 112 rooms, 6 story. Complimentary full breakfast. Check-in 1 pm, check-out 1 pm. Restaurant, bar. Fitness room. Whirlpool. Airport transportation available. **$**

## Full-Service Hotel

★ ★ ★ **GROVE HOTEL.** *245 S Capitol Blvd, Boise (83702). Phone 208/333-8000; toll-free 800/549-9099; fax 208/333-8800. www.grovehotelboise.com.* Steps from the Boise Convention Center, this hotel situates guests in the heart of the downtown area. Rooms are comfortably appointed with modern furnishings. With over 17,000 square feet of flexible meeting space, The Grove Hotel has much to offer business travelers. The hotel is attached to the 5,000-seat Bank of America Centre, which hosts a variety of sporting and entertainment events. Fine dining is available at Emilios, which offers a menu of New American cuisine. Julia Davis Park and the Boise River are a short stroll away.254 rooms. Check-in 3 pm, check-out 11 am. High-speed Internet access, wireless Internet access. Two restaurants, bar. Fitness room (fee). Indoor pool, whirlpool. Airport transportation available. Business center. **$**

## Specialty Lodging

**IDAHO HERITAGE INN.** *109 W Idaho St, Boise (83702). Phone 208/342-8066; toll-free 800/342-8445; fax 208/342-3325. www.idheritageinn.com.* 6 rooms, 3 story. Complimentary full breakfast. Check-in 3 pm, check-out 11 am. Built in 1904. **$**

## Restaurants

★ **BARDENAY RESTAURANT DISTILLERY.** *610 Grove St, Boise (83702). Phone 208/426-0538. www.bardenay.com.* American menu. Lunch, dinner, late-night. Bar. Children's menu. Casual attire. Outdoor seating. **$$**

★ ★ **GERNIKA BASQUE PUB.** *202 S Capitol Blvd, Boise (93702). Phone 208/344-2175.* Mediterranean menu. Lunch, dinner, late-night. Closed Sun. Casual attire. Outdoor seating. **$$**

★ **RICK'S CAFE AMERICAN AT THE FLICKS.** *202 S Capitol Blvd, Boise (93702). Phone 208/344-2175.* Mediterranean menu. Lunch, dinner, late-night. Closed Sun. Casual attire. Outdoor seating. **$$**

# Bonners Ferry (A-2)

*See also Sandpoint*

**Settled** 1864
**Population** 2,193
**Elevation** 1,777 ft
**Area Code** 208
**Zip** 83805
**Information** Visitors Center, PO Box X; phone 208/267-5922
**Web Site** www.bonnersferrychamber.com

E. L. Bonner offered ferry service from this point on the Kootenai River, near the northern tip of the state, and gave this community its name. Today, Bonner's Ferry services the agricultural and lumbering districts of Boundary County, of which it is the county seat. From here the broad, flat, and fertile Kootenai Valley stretches north to British Columbia. This scenic area features many lakes and streams; fishing, hunting, and hiking are popular pastimes. A Ranger District office of the Idaho Panhandle National Forest-Kaniksu is located here.

## What to See and Do

**Kootenai National Wildlife Refuge.** *Riverside Rd, Bonners Ferry (83805). 5 miles W on Riverside Rd. Phone 208/267-3888.* This 2,774-acre refuge was created as a resting area for waterfowl during migration. Its wide variety of habitat supports many species of birds and mammals, including bald eagles. Auto tour (4 1/2 miles). Hunting, fishing. **FREE**

**Moyie Falls.** *Bonners Ferry. 9 miles E on Hwy 2, then N at Moyie Springs on small road; watch for sign for overlook just E of first bridge over Moyie River.* Park and look down into 400-foot canyon at spectacular series of plunges. Greater flow during the spring runoff.

## Special Event

**Kootenai River Days.** *Main St, Bonners Ferry (83805). Phone 208/267-3888.www.bonnersferrychamber.com/pages/KootenaiRiverDays.* This annual festival features fun activities for the entire family: a community barbecue, a teen dance and karaoke, and a children's movie. You might also choose to peruse the food stands, browse the arts and crafts fair, and enter the softball or golf tournaments. Early Aug.

## Limited-Service Hotels

**★ KOOTENAI VALLEY MOTEL.** *6409 S Main St, Bonners Ferry (83805). Phone 208/267-7567; fax 208/267-2600. www.kootenaivalleymotel.com.* 22 rooms, 1 story. Pets accepted, some restrictions; fee. Check-in 1 pm, check-out 11 am. Whirlpool. **$**

**★ TOWN & COUNTRY MOTEL.** *Hwy 95 S, Bonners Ferry (83805). Phone 208/267-7915.*12 rooms. Pets accepted; fee. Complimentary continental breakfast. Check-in noon, check-out 11 am. Whirlpool. **$**

## Restaurant

**★ PANHANDLE RESTAURANT.** *7168 Main St, Bonners Ferry (83805). Phone 208/267-2623.* American menu. Breakfast, lunch, dinner. Children's menu. Casual attire. **$**

# Buhl (F-2)

*See also Twin Falls*

**Population** 3,516
**Elevation** 3,793 ft
**Area Code** 208
**Zip** 83316
**Information** Chamber of Commerce, 716 Hwy 30 E; phone 208/543-6682
**Web Site** buhlidaho.us

Named for Frank Buhl, an early empire builder, this community processes the outpouring of farm goods produced in the farmlands of "Magic Valley." A Ranger District office of Nevada's Humboldt National Forest is located here.

## What to See and Do

**Balanced Rock.** *12 miles SW on local roads.* This 40-foot rock tower, resembling the mushroom cloud of an atomic bomb, rests on an 18-by-36-inch base; picnic area nearby.

## Special Events

**Farmers Market.** *Buhl (83316). Phone 208/733-3974.* Last week in June-Sept.

**Sagebrush Days.** *Buhl. Phone 208/543-6682.* Sidewalk sales, arts in the park, fireworks, parade. Early July.

**Twin Falls County Fair and Magic Valley Stampede.** *215 Fair Ave, Filer (83328). 6 miles E. Phone 208/326-4396.* Carnival, 4-H exhibits, flower, art, and antique shows; RCA rodeo. First weekend in Sept.

# Burley (F-3)

*See also Twin Falls*

**Population** 8,702
**Elevation** 4,165 ft
**Area Code** 208
**Zip** 83318
**Information** Mini-Cassia Chamber of Commerce, 324 Scott Ave, Rupert, 83350;

Burley was created by a 210,000-acre irrigation project that turned a near-desert area into a thriving agricultural center ideal for alfalfa, grain, sugar beet, and potatoes. The town is a center for potato processing and has one of the largest sugar beet processing plants in the world. A Ranger District office of the Sawtooth National Forest is located here.

## What to See and Do

**Boating.** *Burley.* Thirty miles of the Snake River, with constant water levels, provide great boating opportunities throughout the summer.

**Cassia County Historical Museum.** *E Main St and Hiland Ave, Burley (83318). Phone 208/678-7172.* Railroad cars, pioneer cabins, wagon collection, other pioneer relics. (Apr-mid-Nov, Tues-Sat; closed July 4) **DONATION**

**City of Rocks National Reserve.** *3010 Elba Almo Rd, Almo (83312). 22 miles S on Hwy 27 to Oakley, then 16 miles S and follow signs; or 32 miles S on Hwy 77 to Almo, then 2 miles W and follow signs. Phone 208/824-5519.* A pioneer stopping place, this 25-square-mile area of granite spires and sculptured rock formations resembles a city carved from stone; granite walls are inscribed with messages and names of westward-bound settlers, and remnants of the California Trail are still visible. Well known for technical rock climbing. Hiking, picnicking, primitive camping.

**Sawtooth National Forest.** *2647 Kimberly Rd, Twin Falls (83301). 9 miles E on Hwy 30 to Declo, then 15 miles S on Hwy 77; other areas E and W. Phone 208/737-3200.* Fishing, camping, hiking, horseback riding, snowmobiling, cross-country and downhill skiing, scenic views. Includes Howell Canyon, Lake Cleveland and four other glacial lakes. Fee for certain designated campgrounds. In forest is

> **Pomerelle Ski Area.** *Albion. 25 miles SE on Hwy 77, off I-84 Exit 216. Phone 208/673-5599.* Double, triple chairlifts, rope tow; patrol, school, rentals; cafeteria. Longest run 2.2 miles; vertical drop 1,000 feet. Night skiing (Jan-mid-Mar, Tues-Sat). (Mid-Nov-Mar: daily; Apr: weekends) **$$$$**

## Special Events

**Cassia County Fair and Rodeo.** *Burley. County Fairgrounds, E end of E 10th and E 12th sts. Phone 208/678-9150.* Racing, pari-mutuel betting. Third week in Aug.

**Idaho Powerboat Regatta.** *Burley Marina. Phone 208/436-4793.* Boat racers from throughout the western United States compete in this American Power Boat Association's national championship series event. Last weekend in June.

## Limited-Service Hotel

**★ ★ BEST WESTERN BURLEY INN & CONVENTION CENTER.** *800 N Overland Ave, Burley (83318). Phone 208/678-3501; toll-free 800/599-1849; fax 208/678-9532. www.bestwestern.com.* 126 rooms, 2 story. Pets accepted, some restrictions. Check-out noon. Restaurant, bar. Outdoor pool, children's pool. **$**

# Caldwell (E-1)

*See also Boise, Nampa; also see Ontario, OR*

**Founded** 1883
**Population** 18,400
**Elevation** 2,369 ft
**Area Code** 208
**Zip** 83605
**Information** Chamber of Commerce, 704 Blaine St, PO Box 819, 83606; phone 208/459-7493
**Web Site** www.cityofcaldwell.com

Caldwell, seat of Canyon County, is situated in the triangle formed by the confluence of the Snake and Boise rivers. Founded by the Idaho and Oregon Land Improvement Company, the town was named for the company's president, C. A. Caldwell. Livestock, diversified agriculture, and vegetable-processing plants are mainstays of the economy.

## What to See and Do

**Albertson College of Idaho.** *2112 Cleveland Blvd, Caldwell (83605). At 20th St. Phone 208/459-5500.* (1891) (800 students) Oldest four-year college in the state. Private liberal arts college. Evans Mineral Collection, the Orma J. Smith Natural Science Museum, and a planetarium are in Boone Science Hall; Blatchley Hall houses the Rosenthal Gallery of Art (Sept-May, inquire for hours).

**Ste. Chapelle Winery and Vineyards.** *7.5 miles S via Hwy 55, Caldwell (83605). Phone 208/459-7222.* Vineyards spread over slopes of the beautiful Snake River Valley. Reception area; tasting room; 24-foot cathedral windows offer spectacular view of valley and distant Owyhee Mountains. 30-minute tours. (Daily) **FREE**

**Succor Creek Canyon.** *Caldwell. 33 miles W on Hwy 19, just across Oregon line.* Two-mile stretch of spectacular canyon scenery and interesting earth formations. An abundance of prehistoric fossils has been found here.

**Warhawk Air Museum.** *Caldwell Industrial Airport, 4917 Aviation Way, Caldwell (83605). Phone 208/465-6446.* Displays World War II aviation artifacts. (Tues-Sun; call for schedule) **$$**

## Special Events

**Canyon County Fair & Festival.** *Equine & Event Center, 111 S 22nd Ave, Caldwell (83605). Phone 208/455-8500. www.canyoncountyfair.org.* The Canyon County Fair hosts a carnival, music and comedy acts, and livestock exhibits. It also features several special events like a tractor driving contest, Barn Yard Game Show, and the Ag Challenge. Late July-early Aug. **$**

**Night Rodeo.** *CNR Arena,2301 Blaine St, Caldwell (83605). Phone 208/459-2060. www.caldwellnightrodeo.com.* Caldwell's Night Rodeo features several PRCA and WPRA events, but the week also includes activities like the Buckaroo Breakfast and performances by the Horsemanship Drill Team. Second or third week in Aug. **$$$**

## Limited-Service Hotels

**★ LA QUINTA INN.** *901 Specht Ave, Caldwell (83605). Phone 208/454-2222; fax 208/454-9334.* 65 rooms, 3 story. Pets accepted, some restrictions. Complimentary continental breakfast. Check-in 2 pm. Check-out noon. Fitness room. Indoor pool, whirlpool. **$**

**★ SUNDOWNER MOTEL.** *1002 Arthur, Caldwell (83605). Phone 208/459-1585; toll-free 800/588-5268; fax 208/467-5268. www.sundownerinc.com.* 66 rooms, 2 story. Pets accepted; fee. Complimentary continental breakfast. Check-in 2 pm. Check-out 11 am. **$**

# Challis (D-3)

*See also Boise, Nampa, Ontario*

**Founded** 1876
**Population** 1,073
**Elevation** 5,288 ft
**Area Code** 208
**Zip** 83226
**Web Site** www.challisidaho.com

Cloud-capped mountains, rocky gorges, and the Salmon River make this village one of the most picturesque in the Salmon River "Grand Canyon" area. Challis is the seat of Custer County and the headquarters for Challis National Forest. Two Ranger District offices of the forest are located here.

## What to See and Do

**Challis National Forest.** *HC63, Hwy 93 S and Hwy 75, Challis (83226). Phone 208/879-2285.* More than 2 1/2 million acres of forestland surrounds Challis on all sides, crossed by Hwy 93 and Hwy 75. Hot springs, ghost towns, nature viewing via trails; portion of the Frank Church River of No Return Wilderness; trout fishing; camping, picnicking, hunting. Guides, outfitters available in Challis and vicinity. Idaho's highest point is here Mount Borah (12,665 feet). For further info contact the Recreation Staff Officer, Forest Supervisor Bldg, HC 63, Box 1671. Flowing through the forest is the

> **Middle Fork of the Salmon Wild and Scenic River.** *Hwy 93 S, Challis (83226). Phone 208/879-4101.* One of the premier whitewater rafting rivers in the United States. Permits are required to float this river (apply Oct-Jan, permits issued June-Sept by lottery; fee). For permit information, contact the Middle Fork Ranger, PO Box 750.

**Grand Canyon in miniature.** *Challis. 13 miles S and SE on Hwy 93.* Walls cut 2,000 feet down on either side. Best seen at dusk.

## Limited-Service Hotels

**★ NORTHGATE INN.** *Hwy 93, Challis (83226). Phone 208/879-2490; fax 208/879-5767.* 60 rooms, 3 story. Pets accepted, some restrictions; fee. Check-in 3 pm. Check-out 11 am. **$**

**★ ★ VILLAGE INN.** *Hwy 93, Challis (83226). Phone 208/879-2239; fax 208/879-2813.* 54 rooms, 2 story. Pets accepted, some restrictions; fee. Check-in 2 pm, check-out 11 am. Restaurant. Whirlpool. **$**

# Coeur d'Alene (B-1)

*See also Kellogg, St. Marie's, Wallace; also see Spokane, WA*

**Settled** 1878
**Population** 24,563
**Elevation** 2,152 ft
**Area Code** 208
**Zip** 83814
**Information** Coeur d'Alene Area Chamber of Commerce, PO Box 850, 83816; phone 208/664-3194
**Web Site** www.coeurdalene.org

Nestled amid lakes and rivers, Coeur d'Alene (cor-da-LANE) is a tourist and lumbering community, but particularly a gateway to a lush vacation area in the Idaho Panhandle. Irrigation has opened vast sections of nearby countryside for agricultural development; grass seed production is of major importance. The city is the headquarters for the three Idaho Panhandle National Forests, and there are three Ranger District offices here.

### Coeur d'Alene Fun Fact

- The world's longest floating boardwalk surrounds the marina at the Coeur d'Alene Resort in Coeur d'Alene, Idaho. Built in 1986, it is 12 feet wide and 3,300 feet long.

## What to See and Do

**Coeur d'Alene Greyhound Park.** *5100 W Riverbend Rd, Post Falls (83854). 11 miles W via I-90, at Idaho/Washington state line. Phone 208/773-0545.* Pari-mutuel betting; clubhouse, restaurant, concessions. (Daily) **FREE**

**Farragut State Park.** *13400 E Ranger Rd, Athol (83801). 20 miles N on Hwy 95, then 4 miles E on Hwy 54. Phone 208/683-2425.* Comprised of 4,000 acres on south end of Lake Pend Oreille; some open landscape, heavy woods. Swimming, bathhouse, fishing, boating (ramps); hiking and bicycle route, cross-country skiing, sledding, and snowshoeing in winter. Model airplane field. Picnicking. Tent and trailer sites (hookups Apr-mid-Oct, dump station; reservations recommended). Campfire programs; interpretive displays and talks; information center. (Daily) **$**

**Idaho Panhandle National Forests–Coeur d'Alene.** *3815 Schreiber Way, Coeur d'Alene (83815). Other national forests that lie in the panhandle are Kaniksu and St. Joe. Phone 208/765-7223. www.fs.fed.us/ipnf.* Boating, fishing; camping (fee), cabins, picnicking, hiking, cross-country skiing, snowmobiling trails. Visitors are welcome at the Coeur d'Alene Tree Nursery, 1 mile NW on Ramsey Rd.

**Lake Coeur d'Alene.** *1201 W Ironwood Dr, Coeur d'Alene (83814).* Partially adjacent to the Idaho Panhandle National Forest. This lake, 26 miles long with a 109-mile shoreline, is considered one of the loveliest in the country and is popular for boating, fishing, and swimming. Municipal beach, picnic grounds at point where lake and town meet. At S end of lake is

**Lake Coeur d'Alene Cruises, Inc.** *1115 S Second St, Coeur d'Alene (83814). Phone 208/765-4000.* Makes a 6-hour trip up Lake Coeur d'Alene into the St. Joe River (Mid-June-early Sept: Wed and Sun; late Sept-Oct: Sun only). Also 90-minute lake cruises (Mid-May-mid-Oct, daily). Dinner cruises (June-mid-Sept, Sun-Thurs). Sun brunch cruises (Mid-June-Sept). **$$$$**

**St. Joe River.** *Chatcolet.* One of the rivers that feed Lake Coeur d'Alene. Trout and lovely scenery abound. Stretch between Lake Chatcolet and Round Lake is said to be the world's highest navigable river.

**Museum of North Idaho.** *115 Northwest Blvd, Coeur d'Alene (83814). Adjacent to City Park, near the waterfront. Phone 208/664-3448.www.museumni.org.* Exhibits at this museum feature steamboating, the timber industry, and Native American history. There is also a big game trophy collection. (Apr-Oct, Tues-Sat 11 am-5 pm) **$** Admission includes entrance to

**Fort Sherman Museum.** *115 Northwest Blvd, Coeur d'Alene (83814). On the North Idaho College campus. Phone 208/664-3448.* Housed in the old powder house of Fort Coeur d'Alene (circa 1880). Exhibits include a log cabin once used by US Forest Service firefighters, as well as logging, mining, and pioneer implements. (May-Sept, Tues-Sat 1-4:45 pm)

**Scenic drives.** *Coeur d'Alene. In any direction from city.* Some of the most spectacular drives are S on Hwy 97, along E shore of Lake Coeur d'Alene; E on Hwy 10, through Fourth of July Canyon; and N, along Hwy 95.

**Silverwood Theme Park.** *26225 N Hwy 95, Athol (83801). 15 miles N on I-95. Phone 208/683-3400.* Turn-of-the-century park and village with Victorian buildings includes restaurants, saloon, general store, theater featuring old newsreels and classic movies, aircraft museum, air shows, and entertainment; adjacent to amusement park with rides and attractions. (Memorial Day weekend-Labor Day, daily) **$$$$**

## Special Events

**Art on the Green.** *Hubbard St and Rosenberry Dr, Coeur d'Alene (83814). Phone 208/667-9346. www.artonthegreen.org.* Art on the Green is an annual marketplace for more than 130 artists who sell their glass, metal, and clay pieces to the more than 50,000 people who attend the festival each year. The event also hosts hands-on craft instruction for both children and adults. First weekend in Aug.

**North Idaho Fair.** *Kootenai County Fairgrounds,4060 N Government Way, Coeur d'Alene (83815). Phone 208/765-4969. www.northidahofair.com.* Five days of nonstop fun including a carnival, two entertainment stages, three PRCA rodeo performances, 4-H exhibits, and countless food selections. Late Aug. **$$**

## Limited-Service Hotels

**★ AMERITEL INN.** *333 Ironwood Ave, Coeur d'Alene (83814). Phone 208/665-9000; toll-free 800/600-6001; fax 208/665-9900. www.ameritelinns.com.* 114 rooms, 4 story. Complimentary continental breakfast. Check-in 3 pm, check-out 11 am. High-speed Internet access. Fitness room. Indoor pool, whirlpool.**$**

**★ ★ BEST WESTERN COEUR D'ALENE INN.** *506 W Appleway Ave, Coeur d'Alene (83814). Phone 208/765-3200; toll-free 800/251-7829; fax 208/664-1962. www.cdainn.com.* 122 rooms, 2 story. Pets accepted; fee. Check-out noon. Restaurant, bar. Fitness room, spa. Indoor pool, outdoor pool. Airport transportation available. **$**

**★ DAYS INN.** *2200 Northwest Blvd, Coeur d'Alene (83814). Phone 208/667-8668; fax 208/765-0933. www.daysinn.com.* 62 rooms, 2 story. Pets accepted; fee. Complimentary continental breakfast. Check-in 3 pm. Check-out noon. Fitness room. Whirlpool. **$**

**★ ★ RED LION TEMPLINS HOTEL ON THE RIVER.** *414 E 1st Ave, Post Falls (83854). Phone 208/773-1611; toll-free 800/733-5466; fax 208/773-4192. www.redlion.com.* 167 rooms, 3 story. Pets accepted, some restrictions; fee. Check-in 2 pm, check-out noon. Restaurant, bar. Fitness room. Indoor pool, whirlpool. Tennis. Airport transportation available. **$**

**★ RIVERBEND INN.** *4105 W Riverbend Ave, Post Falls (83854). Phone 208/773-3583; toll-free 800/243-7666; fax 208/773-1306. www.riverbend-inn.com.* 71 rooms, 2 story. Complimentary continental breakfast. Check-in 3 pm. Check-out noon. Outdoor pool, whirlpool. **$**

**★ SHILO INN.** *702 W Appleway Ave, Coeur d'Alene (83814). Phone 208/664-2300; toll-free 800/222-2244; fax 208/667-2863. www.shiloinns.com.* 139 rooms, 4 story. Pets accepted; fee. Complimentary continental breakfast. Check-in 4 pm, check-out noon. Fitness room. Indoor pool, whirlpool. **$**

## Full-Service Resort

**★ ★ ★ THE COEUR D'ALENE RESORT.** *115 S 2nd St, Coeur d'Alene (83814). Phone 208/765-4000; fax 208/664-7276.* Northern Idaho's Coeur d'Alene Resort is a superb destination for active travelers. This lakeside resort enjoys a parklike setting filled with a multitude of outdoor activities. From boat cruises, water-skiing, and marina access to downhill skiing, championship golf, and nearby shopping, this resort has something to satisfy every guest. This spot is particularly notable for its golf, both for its premier golf academy and its amazing floating green, accessible by a small boat. A European-style spa primps and pampers, while five lounges and bars entertain. Sophisticated Northwestern regional cuisine is highlighted at Beverly's restaurant (see), and Tito Macaroni's enjoys a lively Italian spirit.336 rooms,

18 story. Pets accepted; fee. Check-in 4 pm, check-out noon. Three restaurants, bar. Children's activity center. Fitness room, spa. Beach. Indoor pool, outdoor pool, children's pool, whirlpool. Golf, 18 holes. Tennis. Airport transportation available. Business center. **$**

## Specialty Lodging

**THE ROOSEVELT.** *105 E Wallace Ave, Coeur d'Alene (83814). Phone 208/765-5200; toll-free 800/290-3358; fax 208/664-4142. www.therooseveltinn.com.* Take one look at this inns charming red brick exterior and you won't be at all surprised to learn that it originally served as a schoolhouse. Built in 1905 and listed on the National Register of Historic Places, the four-story building was converted into a cozy bed-and-breakfast in 1994. The innnamed in honor of Theodore Roos-eveltfeatures 15 antique-furnished rooms. A complimentary gourmet breakfast awaits guests each morning.15 rooms, 4 story. Pets accepted, some restrictions; fee. Children over 6 years only. Complimentary full breakfast. Check-in 3 pm, check-out noon. Fitness room. Whirlpool. Airport transportation available. **$**

## Restaurants

**★ ★ ★ BEVERLY'S.** *115 S 2nd St, Coeur d'Alene (83816). Phone 208/765-4000; toll-free 800/688-5253; fax 208/664-7276. www.cdaresort.com.* This 7th-floor restaurant is the signature dining room at the Coeur d'Alene Resort (see). Enjoy great lake views, a fine wine cellar, and Northwest-inspired cuisine that includes the popular firecracker prawns with angel hair pasta. International menu. Breakfast, lunch, dinner, late-night, brunch. Bar. Children's menu. Casual attire. Valet parking. **$$$**

**★ IRON HORSE.** *407 Sherman Ave, Coeur d'Alene (83814). Phone 208/667-7314.* American menu. Breakfast, lunch, dinner, brunch. Bar. Children's menu. Casual attire. Valet parking. Outdoor seating. **$$**

# Craters of the Moon National Monument (E-3)

*See also Kellogg, St. Marie's, Wallace, Spokane*

*18 miles W of Arco on Hwy 20*

**Web Site** www.nps.gov/crmo

So named because it resembles the surface of the moon as seen through a telescope, this 83-square-mile monument has spectacular lava flows, cinder cones, and other volcanic creations. Geologists believe a weak spot in the earth's crust permitted outbursts of lava at least eight times during the last 15,000 years. These eruptions produced the lava flows, the 25 cinder cones, spatter cones, lava tubes, natural bridges, and tree molds within the monument. Geological and historical exhibits are on display at the visitor center (daily 8 am-4:30 pm, until 6 pm in summer; closed winter holidays). Autos may follow the 7-mile loop drive, which is closed by snow in winter. Interpretive programs of nature walks, campfire talks (mid-June-Labor Day). Campsites (no hookups, showers, or dump station) are found near the entrance (mid-May-Oct; fee). Golden Eagle, Golden Age, and Golden Access passports are accepted (see MAKING THE MOST OF YOUR TRIP), and pets on leash are allowed. Per vehicle **$**

# Driggs (E-5)

*See also Ashton, Rexburg, Saint Anthony*

**Population** 846
**Elevation** 6,116 ft
**Area Code** 208
**Zip** 83422

This mountain town sits in eastern Idaho, a short drive from the Wyoming state line and Grand Teton National Park. The Teton Basin Ranger Station of the Targhee National Forest is located here.

## What to See and Do

**Grand Targhee Ski and Summer Resort.** 1200 E Ski Hill Rd, Alta, WY (83422). 12 miles E on county road. Phone 307/353-2300; toll-free 800/827-4433. Three chairlifts, surface lift; patrol, school, rentals; three lodges, three restaurants, cafeteria, bar; nursery; whirlpools, heated outdoor pool. Longest run 2.7 miles; vertical drop 2,200 feet. (Mid-Nov-early Apr, daily). Second mountain for powder skiing only. Crosscountry trails; snowboard half-pipe. Summer activities include fishing, rafting; horseback riding, biking, hiking, golf, tennis, music festivals (July-Aug); chairlift rides (June-Aug, daily). Half-day rates. **$$$$**

## Limited-Service Hotels

**★ BEST WESTERN TETON WEST.** *476 N Main St, Driggs (83422). Phone 208/354-2363; toll-free 800/780-7234; fax 208/354-2962. www.bestwestern.com.* 40 rooms, 2 story. Pets accepted; fee. Complimentary continental breakfast. Check-in 3 pm, check-out noon. Indoor pool, whirlpool. **$**

**★ ★ GRAND TARGHEE SKI AND SUMMER RESORT.** *1200 E Ski Hill Rd, Alta, WY (83422). Phone 307/353-2300; toll-free 800/827-4433; fax 307/353-8619. www.grandtarghee.com.* Located at the main gateway to Grand Teton and Yellowstone national parks, this self-contained resort with panoramic views of three states offers a variety of outdoor activities. Skiing (both downhill and cross-country) is the main draw here, but summer brings opportunities to ride horses, mountain bike, hike, play Frisbee, golf on a designated 18-hole course, and more. Adventurers can challenge themselves on the climbing wall or on the ropes course and zip line, while scenic chairlift rides cater to those who prefer simply to enjoy the beautiful vistas. On-site shopping and dining options include the Targhee Steakhouse, the Trap Bar & Grill, and a general store that sells snacks and sundries.120 rooms, 4 story. Closed mid-Apr-May and mid-Sept-mid-Nov. Check-in 4 pm, check-out 11 am. Three restaurants, bar. Children's activity center. Fitness room, fitness classes available. Outdoor pool, whirlpool. Tennis. Ski in/ski out. Airport transportation available. Business center. **$**

## Specialty Lodging

**TETON RIDGE RANCH.** *200 Valley View Rd, Tetonia (83452). Phone 208/456-2650; fax 208/456-2218. www.tetonridge.com.* More of a lodge or guest house than a dude ranch, this casually elegant property offers well appointed guest rooms, incredible views of the Grand Tetons, and gourmet dining on 4,000 private acres. Horseback riding and fishing are available.5 rooms. Closed Nov-mid-Dec, Apr-May. Pets accepted. Children over 12 years only. Complimentary full breakfast. Check-in 1 pm, check-out 11 am. Airport transportation available. **$$$$**

# Grangeville (C-2)

*See also Ashton, Rexburg, Saint Anthony*

**Founded** 1876
**Population** 3,226
**Elevation** 3,390 ft
**Area Code** 208
**Zip** 83530
**Information** Chamber of Commerce, Hwy 95 and Pine St, PO Box 212; phone 208/983-0460
**Web Site** www.grangevilleidaho.com

Grangeville is a light industrial and agricultural community. It was a focal point in the Nez Perce Indian War and a gold rush town in the 1890s, when rich ore was found in the Florence Basin and the Elk City areas. The seat of Idaho County, it is also the gateway to several wilderness areas. The headquarters and two Ranger District offices of the Nez Perce National Forest are located here.

## What to See and Do

**Hells Canyon National Recreation Area.** *Grangeville. Access approximately 16 miles S on Hwy 95 to White Bird, then W on County Rd 493 to Pittsburg Landing; access also from Riggins, from Hwy 95 take Rd 241 (Race Creek) N of Riggins; paved access via Hwy 71 from Cambridge (see WEISER). Phone 541/426-4978. www.fs.fed.us/hellscanyon.* Created by the Snake River, at the Idaho/Oregon border, Hell's Canyon is the deepest gorge in North America—1/2 miles from He Devil Mountain (elevation 9,393 feet) to the Snake River at Granite Creek (elevation 1,408 feet). Overlooks at Heaven's Gate, W of Riggins, and in Oregon (see JOSEPH, OR). The recreation area includes parts of the Nez Perce and Payette National Forests in Idaho and the Wallowa-Whitman National Forest in Oregon. Activities include float trips, jet boat tours; auto tours, backpacking, and horseback riding; boat trips into canyon from Lewiston, Grangeville, and Riggins, also via Pittsburg Landing or the Hells Canyon Dam. Developed campgrounds in Oregon and Idaho; much of the area is undeveloped, some is designated wilderness. Be sure to inquire about road conditions before planning a trip; some roads are rough and open for a limited season. For further information, contact Hells Canyon National Recreation Area, 88401 Hwy 82, Enterprise, OR 97828, phone 541/426-4978; or 2535 Riverside Dr, Box 699, Clarkston, WA 99403, phone 509/758-0616. For river information and float reservations, phone 509/758-1957.

★ **Nez Perce National Forest.** *Main St and E Hwy 13, Grangeville (83530). S on Hwy 95. Phone 208/983-1950.* More than 2.2 million acres with excellent fishing; camping, cabins (fee at some campgrounds), picnicking, cross-country skiing, and snowmobiling. The Salmon (the River of No Return), Selway, South Fork Clearwater, and Snake rivers, all classified as wild and scenic, flow through or are adjacent to the forest. Pack and float trips are available; contact the Idaho Outfitters and Guides Association, PO Box 95, Boise 83701; Phone 208/342-1438. High elevations are open only in summer and fall; low elevations are open Mar-Nov. For further info contact Office of Information, Hwy 2, Box 475.

**Snowhaven.** *Grangeville. 7 miles SE via Fish Creek Rd. Phone 208/983-3866.* T-bar, rope tow; patrol, school, rentals; cafeteria. Vertical drop 400 feet. Night skiing; half-day rates. (Dec-early Mar, Fri-Sun) **$$$$**

**White Bird Hill.** *Rte 95, Grangeville (83530). 5 miles S on Hwy 95. Phone 208/983-0460.* Site of the famous Whitebird Battle of the Nez Perce Indian Wars. View of Camas Prairie, canyons, mountains, and Seven Devils Peaks. Self-guided tour brochures available from Chamber of Commerce.

## Special Events

**Border Days.** *Hwy 95, Grangeville (83530). Phone 208/983-0460.* Three-day rodeo and parades, dances. Art-in-the-park; food. July 4 weekend.

**Oktubberfest.** *Hwy 95, Grangeville (83530). Phone 208/983-0460.* Three-day event features tub races on Main St, arts and crafts, street dance, entertainment. Last weekend in Sept.

# Idaho City (E-2)

*See also Boise*

**Settled** 1862
**Population** 322
**Elevation** 3,906 ft
**Area Code** 208
**Zip** 83631
**Information** Chamber of Commerce, PO Box 70; phone 208/392-4148
**Web Site** www.idahocitychamber.com

Flecks of gold persist in the gravel beneath most of Idaho City, and the community is steeped in gold rush lore. From the 18-square-mile Boise Basin, said to have produced more gold than all of Alaska, Idaho City's fame once spread far and wide. Idaho City also is home to the state's first Pioneer Lodge (established in 1864) and the birthplace of the Grand Lodge of Idaho (established in 1867).

## What to See and Do

**Boise Basin Museum.** *Commercial Montgomery, Idaho City (83631). Montgomery and Wall sts. Phone 208/392-4550.* (1867) Restored building houses artifacts of gold rush era. Walking tours of Idaho City available (fee). (Memorial Day-Labor Day: daily; May and Sept: weekends only; rest of year: by appointment) **$**

**Boise National Forest.** *1750 Front St, Idaho City (87302).* Fishing, hunting, swimming; camping, skiing, and snowmobiling. A Ranger District office of the forest is located here.

**Boot Hill.** *Idaho City. Phone 208/392-4148.* Restored 40-acre cemetery, last resting place of many gunfight victims.

**Gold Hill.** *Idaho City. 1 mile N on Main St. Phone 208/392-4148.* Rich Boise Basin placer ground.

# Idaho Falls (E-2)

*See also Blackfoot, Pocatello, Rexburg, Saint Anthony*

**Population** 43,929
**Elevation** 4,710 ft
**Area Code** 208
**Information** Chamber of Commerce, 505 Lindsay Blvd, PO Box 50498, 83405; phone 208/523-1010 or toll-free 800/634-3246
**Web Site** www.visitidahofalls.com

An industrial, transportation, and trading center in the upper Snake River Valley, Idaho Falls is a center of potato production and headquarters for the Idaho Operations Office of the Department of Energy. The Idaho National Engineering Laboratory is located on the Lost River Plains, 30 miles west on Highway 20. Potato processing is important; the stockyards here are the state's largest; and one of the nation's leading safety research centers for nuclear reactors is located here. A Ranger District office of Targhee National Forest (see ASHTON) can be found in Idaho Falls.

## What to See and Do

**Bonneville Museum.** *200 N Eastern Ave, Idaho Falls (83402). Phone 208/522-1400.* Displays of early county, state, and city history; natural history; Native American artifacts; early settler and mountain-man relics; replica of early (circa 1890) Idaho Falls (Eagle Rock); 30-minute video on county history and other subjects of local interest. Art exhibits featuring works of area artists; special and traveling exhibits. (Mon-Fri; also Sat afternoons; closed Jan 1, Thanksgiving, Dec 25) **$**

**Heise Hot Springs.** *5116 E Heise Rd, Ririe (83443). 23 miles E on Hwy 26. Phone 208/538-7312.* Mineral water pool, freshwater pools, water slide, fishing; golf, camping. Fee for activities. (Mid-May-Sept)

**Idaho Falls.** *On river downtown, Idaho Falls (83409). Phone 208/523-1010.* Falls run for 1,500 feet along the Snake River. Picnic tables nearby.

**The Lavas.** *Shelley. 10 miles S via Hwy 91 to Shelley, then 4 miles W on local road. Phone 208/523-1010.* Lava-created caves, fissures, and rock flows, fringed by dwarf trees. Native American relics are also plentiful.

**Tautphaus Park.** *2725 Carnival Way, Idaho Falls (83405). Rollandet Ave or South Blvd. Phone 208/528-5552.*Zoo (fee); amusement rides (Memorial Day weekend-Labor Day weekend, fee); picnic and barbecue areas; lighted tennis courts and softball diamonds; horseshoe pits; ice skating, hockey (seasonal). Park (Daily; closed Jan 1, Thanksgiving, Dec 25). **FREE**

## Special Event

**War Bonnet Roundup.** *Sandy Downs Park Rodeo Grounds,6855 S 15 E, Idaho Falls (83404). Phone 208/523-1010.www.idahofallschamber.com.* Rodeo. Four nights in early Aug.

## Limited-Service Hotels

**★ AMERITEL INN IDAHO FALLS.** *645 Lindsay Blvd, Idaho Falls (83402). Phone 208/523-1400; toll-free 800/600-6001; fax 208/523-0004. www.ameritelinns.com.* 126 rooms, 4 story. Complimentary full breakfast. Check-in 3 pm, check-out noon. Fitness room. Indoor pool, whirlpool. Airport transportation available. **$**

**★ ★ RED LION HOTEL ON THE FALLS.** *475 River Pkwy, Idaho Falls (83402). Phone 208/523-8000; toll-free 800/733-5466; fax 208/529-9610. www.redlion.com.* 138 rooms. Pets accepted. Check-in 3 pm, check-out noon. High-speed Internet access, wireless Internet access. Restaurant, bar. Fitness room. Outdoor pool, whirlpool. **$**

**★ SHILO INN.** *780 Lindsay Blvd, Idaho Falls (83402). Phone 208/523-0088; toll-free 800/222-2244; fax 208/522-7420. www.shiloinns.com.* 162 rooms, 4 story. Pets accepted, some restrictions. Complimentary full breakfast. Check-in 2 pm, check-out noon. Restaurant, bar. Fitness room. Indoor pool, whirlpool. Airport transportation available. **$**

## Restaurant

**★ JAKERS.** *851 Lindsay Blvd, Idaho Falls (83402). Phone 208/524-5240; fax 208/524-1937. www.jakers.com.* American menu. Lunch, dinner. Bar. Children's menu. Casual attire. **$$**

# Jerome (F-3)

*See also Shoshone, Twin Falls*

**Population** 6,529
**Elevation** 3,781 ft
**Area Code** 208
**Zip** 83338
**Information** Chamber of Commerce, 1731 S Lincoln, Suite A; phone 208/324-2711
**Web Site** www.visitjerome.com

## What to See and Do

**Jerome County Historical Museum.** *220 N Lincoln, Jerome (83338). Phone 208/324-5641.* Located in historic Pioneer Hall building. Changing displays. Guided tours. (May-Sept: Mon-Sat; rest of year: Tues-Sat) **FREE**

**Malad Gorge State Park.** *1074 E 2350 S, Hagerman (83332). Phone 208/837-4505.*More than 650 acres with the 2 1/2-mile-long, 250-feet-deep Malad Gorge. A footbridge spans a waterfall at Devil's Washbowl. Interpretive trails, picnicking. (Schedule varies)

## Special Events

**Chariot Races.** *Jerome County Fairgrounds,200 N Fir St, Jerome (83338). Phone 208/324-2711.* Weekends, Dec-Feb.

**Horse racing.** *Jerome County Fairgrounds,200 N Fir St, Jerome (83338). Phone 208/324-2711.* Pari-mutuel racing. Two weekends in mid-June.

**Jerome County Fair & Rodeo.** *Jerome County Fairgrounds, 200 N Fir St, Jerome (83338). Phone 208/324-2711.* Concert, rodeo, carnival, parade. First week in Aug.

## Limited-Service Hotel

**★ BEST WESTERN SAWTOOTH INN & SUITES.** *2653 S Lincoln Ave, Jerome (83338). Phone 208/324-9200; toll-free 800/780-7234; fax 208/324-9292. www.bestwestern.com.* 57 rooms, 2 story. Pets accepted; fee. Complimentary continental breakfast. Check-out noon. Fitness room. Indoor pool, whirlpool. **$**

# Kellogg (B-2)

*See also Coeur d'Alene, Wallace*

**Population** 2,591
**Elevation** 2,308 ft
**Area Code** 208
**Zip** 83837
**Information** Greater Kellogg Area Chamber of Commerce, 608 Bunker Ave; phone 208/784-0821
**Web Site** www.kellogg-idaho.com

In this rich mining region are the country's largest silver and lead mines. One of the state's most violent miners' strikes took place here in 1899. Today, the former mining town is being transformed into a ski resort.

## What to See and Do

**Old Mission State Park.** *Cataldo (83810). 10 miles W off I-90, exit 38. Phone 208/682-3814. www.idahoparks.org.* (1850) A 100-acre park. Tours of the Coeur d'Alene Mission of the Sacred Heart, a restored Native American mission, which is the oldest existing building in the state. Information center, interpretive programs, history trail. (Daily 9 am-5 pm)

**Silver Mountain Ski Area.** *610 Bunker Ave, Kellogg (83837). 1/2 mile SW, off I-90 exit 49. Phone 208/783-1111; toll-free 800/204-6428. www.silvermt.com.* Double, quad, three triple chairlifts, surface lift; patrol, school, rentals; lodges, restaurants, cafeteria, bar, nursery. Fifty trails, longest run 2 1/2 miles; vertical drop 2,200 feet. (Mid-Nov-Apr, Wed-Sun) **$$$$**

**Sunshine Mine Disaster Memorial.** *Frontage Rd, Hwy 90 exit 54, Kellogg (83837). 3 miles E on I-90, exit 54, Big Creek. Phone 208/784-0821.* Double-life-size statue constructed of steel is memorial to all miners; created by Kenn Lonn, a native of Kellogg. The helmet's light burns perpetually and the miner holds a typical jackleg drill.

## Special Event

**Christmas Dickens Festival.** *608 Bunker Ave, Kellogg (83837). Phone 208/784-0821.* Entire town dressed in period costume. Plays, skits, puppet shows, parade. Second weekend in Dec.

## Limited-Service Hotel

**★ SUPER 8.** *601 Bunker Ave, Kellogg (83837). Phone 208/783-1234; fax 208/784-0461.www.baymontinn-kellogg.com.* 61 rooms, 2 story. Pets accepted, some restrictions; fee. Complimentary continental breakfast. Check-in 3 pm, check-out 11 am. Indoor pool, whirlpool. Ski in/ski out. **$**

# Ketchum (E-3)

*See also Sun Valley Area*

**Founded** 1880
**Population** 3,003
**Elevation** 5,845 ft
**Area Code** 208
**Zip** 83340
**Information** Sun Valley/Ketchum Chamber & Visitors Bureau; phone toll-free 800/634-3347
**Web Site** www.visitsunvalley.com

While Ketchum may not receive as much attention as its sister city, Sun Valley, it's not for a lack of charm and natural beauty. Main Street is a pleasant stretch of shops, restaurants, and art galleries. The town sits just to the south of the Sawtooth National Recreation Area, a four-season playground for outdoor enthusiasts. Trapper and guide David Ketchum, the towns namesake, settled here in 1879. Writer Ernest Hemingway spent his final years in Ketchum and is buried in the town cemetery.

## Limited-Service Hotels

**★ ★ BEST WESTERN KENTWOOD LODGE.** *180 S Main St, Ketchum (83340). Phone 208/726-4114; toll-free 800/805-1001; fax 208/726-2417. www.bestwestern.com.* 57 rooms, 3 story. Check-in 3 pm, check-out 11 am. Restaurant. Fitness room. Indoor pool, whirlpool. **$$**

**★ TAMARACK LODGE.** *291 Walnut Ave N, Ketchum (83340). Phone 208/726-3344; toll-free 800/521-5379; fax 208/726-3347. www.tamaracksunvalley.com.* 26 rooms, 3 story. Check-in 3 pm, check-out noon. Indoor pool, whirlpool. **$**

## Full-Service Inn

**★ ★ ★ KNOB HILL INN.** *960 N Main St, Ketchum (83340). Phone 208/726-8010; toll-free 800/526-8010; fax 208/726-2712. www.knobhillinn.com.* This charming country-style inn draws skiers who flock to Sun Valley for its top-notch slopes, as well as summer vacationers who come here take advantage of the area's golf courses, hiking trails, and river rafting. Each guest room has a balcony, enabling guests to revel in the mountain views. You'll also find a dressing room and a separate tub and shower. The inn prides itself on serving healthy breakfasts using no artificial ingredients; coffee, tea, wine, and pastries are available at the Knob Hill Cafe in the afternoons.26 rooms, 4 story. Check-in 3 pm, check-out noon. Fitness room. Indoor pool, whirlpool. **$$**

## Restaurant

**★ ★ ★ CHANDLER'S RESTAURANT.** *200 S Main St, Ketchum (83340). Phone 208/726-1776; fax 208/725-5665.www.chandlersrestaurant.com.*This 1940s home has antique furnishings and open beamed ceilings. American menu. Dinner. Bar. Children's menu. Casual attire. Reservations recommended. Outdoor seating. **$$$**

# Lava Hot Springs (F-4)

*See also Pocatello*

**Population** 420
**Elevation** 5,060 ft
**Area Code** 208
**Zip** 83246
**Web Site** www.lavahotsprings.org

Hot water pouring out of the mountains and bubbling up in springs, believed to be the most highly mineralized water in the world, makes Lava Hot Springs a busy year-round resort. Fishing, swimming; hunting, camping, and golf are available in the surrounding area.

## What to See and Do

**Lava Hot Springs.** *430 E Main, Lava Hot Springs (83246). 1/2 mile E on Hwy 30 N. Phone 208/776-5221. www.lavahotsprings.org.* Outdoor mineral pools, fed by 30 different springs, range from 104°-112°F. Olympic-size swimming pool with diving tower (Memorial Day-Labor Day). (Daily; closed Thanksgiving, Dec 25) **$$**

**South Bannock County Historical Center.** *110 Main St, Lava Hot Springs (83246). Phone 208/776-5254.* Museum artifacts, photographs, transcripts, and memorabilia trace history of town from the era of Native American and fur trappers to its development as a resort area. Slide show and guided walking tour (by appointment). (Daily) **DONATION**

# Lewiston (C-1)

*See also Moscow, Clarkston*

**Founded** 1861
**Population** 28,082
**Elevation** 739 ft
**Area Code** 208
**Zip** 83501
**Information** Chamber of Commerce, 111 Main St, Suite 120; phone 208/743-3531 or toll-free 800/473-3543
**Web Site** www.lewistonchamber.org

The Clearwater River, starting in the Bitterroot Mountains and plunging through the vast Clearwater National Forest, joins the Snake River at Lewiston. The two rivers and the mountains that surround the town give it one of the most picturesque settings in the state. A thriving tourist trade supplements Lewiston's grain, lumber, and livestock industries.

## What to See and Do

**Auto tours.** *Lewiston.* The Lewis and Clark Highway (Hwy 12) parallels the famous Lewis and Clark Trail east to Montana. Interpretive signs along the way explain the human and natural history of the canyon. A Forest Service Information Station is at Lolo Pass on the Idaho/Montana border. The Chamber of Commerce has maps for other tours.

**Castle Museum.** *202 State St, Juliaetta (83535). 23 miles N on Hwy 3; 1 block off main hwy. Phone 208/276-3081.* Three-story, handmade cement block house built in 1906 and patterned after Scottish castle; embossed metal ceilings, antiques. (By appointment) **DONATION**

**Clearwater National Forest.** *12730 Hwy 12, Orofino (83544). Phone 208/476-4541.* About 1,850,000 acres with trout fishing; hunting, skiing and snowmobiling trails, camping (fee for some developed campsites), cabins, picnicking, lookout towers (fee). Pack trips. Higher elevations accessible July-Sept; lower elevations accessible Mar-Oct or Nov. Lolo Pass Visitor Center and Lochsa Historical Ranger Station on Highway 12 (Mid-May-mid-Sept; daily).

**Hells Canyon excursions.** *Lewiston.* Jet boat trips and fishing charters into Hells Canyon National Recreation Area (see GRANGEVILLE). For information, contact the Chamber of Commerce.

**Hells Gate State Park.** *Lewiston. 4 miles S on Snake River Ave. 960 acres on Snake River, 40 miles N of Hells Canyon National Recreation Area. Phone 208/799-5015.* Swimming, fishing, boating (marina, concession, ramp); hiking and paved bicycle trails, horseback riding area, picnicking, playground, tent and trailer campsites (hookups, dump station; 15-day maximum). Info center, interpretive programs, exhibits; excursion boats. Park (Mar-Nov).

**Luna House Museum.** *0306 3rd St, Lewiston (83501). 3rd and C sts. Phone 208/743-2535.*On site of first hotel in town (1861). Exhibits on Nez Perce and pioneers; displays on town and county history. (Tues-Sat; closed holidays) **FREE**

**Nez Perce National Historical Park.** *Hwy 95 S, Spalding (83541). Headquarters has visitor center and museum, 39063 Hwy 95, Lapwai, ID 83540. Phone 208/843-2261.* The park is composed of 38 separate sites scattered throughout Washington, Oregon, Montana, and Idaho. All of the sites relate to the culture and history of the Nez Perce; some relate to the westward expansion of the nation into homelands. **FREE**

## Special Events

**Lewiston Roundup.** *Lewiston Round-Up grounds,7000 Tammany Creek Rd, Lewiston (83501). Phone 208/746-6324. www.lewistonroundup.org.* The Lewiston Round-up has a longstanding tradition of excellence and entertainment. It is a top 50 PRCA rodeo, and several world champions have participated in the event since it began in 1935. Weekend after Labor Day.

**Nez Perce County Fair.** *Fairgrounds,1229 Burrell Ave, Lewiston (83501). Phone 208/743-3302. www.npcfair.org.* The fair includes several 4-H exhibits, live entertainment, pony rides, and a cowboy church service with cowboy poetry as well as Western and Gospel music. Four days in late Sept. **$$**

## Limited-Service Hotels

**★ GUESTHOUSE INN & SUITES.** *1325 Main St, Lewiston (83501). Phone 208/746-3311; toll-free 800/214-8378; fax 208/746-7955. www.guesthouseintl.com.* 75 rooms, 4 story. Pets accepted. Check-in 3 pm, check-out noon. Fitness room. Outdoor pool. **$**

**★ ★ INN AMERICA.** *702 21st St, Lewiston (83501). Phone 208/746-4600; toll-free 800/469-4667; fax 208/746-7756. www.lewiston.innamerica.com.* 61 rooms, 3 story. Check-in 2 pm, check-out 1 pm. Restaurant. Outdoor pool. **$**

**★ ★ RED LION HOTEL LEWISTON.** *621 21st St, Lewiston (83501). Phone 208/799-1000; toll-free 800/733-5466; fax 208/748-1155. www.redlion.com.* 183 rooms, 4 story. Pets accepted, some restrictions. Check-in 3 pm, check-out noon. Restaurant, bar. Indoor pool, outdoor pool, whirlpool. Airport transportation available. **$**

**★ ★ SACAJAWEA SELECT INN.** *1824 Main St, Lewiston (83501). Phone 208/746-1393; toll-free 800/333-1393; fax 208/743-3620. www.selectinn.com.* 90 rooms, 2 story. Pets accepted, some restrictions; fee. Complimentary continental breakfast. Check-in 1 pm, check-out noon. Restaurant, bar. Fitness room. Outdoor pool, whirlpool. Airport transportation available. **$**

# McCall (D-2)

*See also Moscow, Clarkston*

**Population** 2,005
**Elevation** 5,030 ft
**Area Code** 208
**Zip** 83638
**Information** Chamber of Commerce, PO Box D; phone 208/634-7631 or toll-free 800/260-5130
**Web Site** www.mccall.id.us

At the southern tip of Payette Lake, McCall is a resort center for one of the state's chief recreational areas. Fishing, swimming, boating, and waterskiing are available on Payette Lake. McCall is also the headquarters for Payette National Forest, and three Ranger District offices of the forest are located here.

## What to See and Do

**Brundage Mountain Ski Area.** *McCall. 8 miles NW via Hwy 55, unnumbered road. Phone 208/634-4151; toll-free 888/255-7669. www.brundage.com.* Two triple chairlifts, Quadlift, Pomalift, platter tow; patrol, school, rentals; bar, cafeteria; nursery. (Mid-Nov-mid-Apr, daily) **$$$$**

**Cascade Dam Reservoir.** *Cascade. 25 miles S on Hwy 55. Phone 208/382-4258. www.parksandrecreation.idaho.gov.* Situated alongside the West Mountains, this 30,000-acre body of water offers exceptional fishing and boating opportunities. Notable fish species include smallmouth bass, rainbow trout, yellow perch, and coho salmon. Open year-round, ice fishermen dot the frozen reservoir in the winter.

**Pack trips into Idaho primitive areas.** *McCall. Phone 208/634-7631.* Check with the Chamber of Commerce for a list of outfitters.

**Payette National Forest.** *800 W Lakeside, McCall (83638). Phone 208/634-0700.* More than 2.3 million acres surrounded by the Snake and Salmon rivers, the River of No Return Wilderness, Hell's Canyon National Recreation Area, and the Boise National Forest. Trout and salmon fishing in 300 lakes and 3,000 miles of streams, boating; 2,100 miles of hiking trails, hunting, camping, and picnic areas; winter sports.

**Ponderosa State Park.** *Miles Standish Rd, McCall. 2 miles NE, on Payette Lake. Phone 208/634-2164.* Approximately 1,280 acres. Large stand of ponderosa pines. Swimming, waterskiing, fishing, boating (ramps); hiking; cross-country skiing, picnicking, camping (except winter; reservations accepted Memorial Day-Labor Day); tent and trailer sites (hookups; 15-day maximum; dump station). Park (Daily). Contact Park Manager, PO Box A.

**River rafting.** *Salmon River Outfitters,1734 W Roseberry Rd, Donnelly (83615). ; toll-free 800/346-6204. www.salmonriveroutfitters.com.* Offers five and six-day guided raft trips along the Salmon River. **$$$$**

## Special Events

**McCall Folk Music Festival.** *McCall (83638). University of Idaho Field Campus Ponderosa State Park. Phone 208/634-7631.* Fiddle music; Western, swing, Irish, folk, blues, and jazz; square dancing. Third weekend in July.

**Winter Carnival.** *McCall. Phone 208/634-7631.* Parades, fireworks; ice sculptures, snowmobile and ski races, snowman-building contest, carriage and sleigh rides, ball. Ten days in early Feb.

## Limited-Service Hotel

**★ BEST WESTERN MCCALL.** *415 N 3rd St, McCall (83638). Phone 208/634-6300; toll-free 800/780-7234; fax 208/634-2967.www.bestwestern.com.* 79 rooms, 2 story. Pets accepted, some restrictions. Check-in 2 pm, check-out 11 am. Fitness room. Indoor pool, whirlpool. **$**

## Specialty Lodging

**HOTEL MCCALL.** *1101 N 3rd St, McCall (83638). Phone 208/634-8105; toll-free 866/800-1183; fax 208/634-8755.* 32 rooms, 3 story. Complimentary full breakfast. Check-in 2 pm, check-out 11 am. **$**

## Restaurant

**★ ★ MILL STEAKS & SPIRITS.** *324 N 3rd St, McCall (83638). Phone 208/634-7683. www.themillmccallidaho.com.* Photo collection of history of the Northwest. Steak menu. Dinner. Closed Thanksgiving, Dec 25. Bar. Children's menu. Casual attire. Reservations recommended. **$$**

# Meridian (E-1)

## Restaurant

**★ ★ EPI'S A BASQUE RESTAURANT.** *1115 1st St, Meridian (83642). hone 208/884-0142.* Spanish menu. Dinner. Closed Sun-Mon. Bar. Casual attire. Reservations recommended. Outdoor seating. **$$**

# Montpelier (F-5)

**Founded** 1864
**Population** 2,656
**Elevation** 5,964 ft
**Area Code** 208
**Zip** 83254
**Information** Bear Lake Convention & Visitors Bureau, PO Box 26, Fish Haven 83287; phone 208/945-2072 or toll-free 800/448-2327

Located in the highlands of Bear Lake Valley, Montpelier is surrounded by lakes, rivers, creeks, and grazing ranges. The average yearly temperature is 45°F. First called Clover Creek, then Belmont, it was finally designated by the Mormon leader, Brigham Young, as Montpelier, after the capital of Vermont. There are Mormon tabernacles throughout this area. Phosphate is mined extensively nearby. A Ranger District office of the Caribou National Forest is located here.

## What to See and Do

**Bear Lake.** *Montpelier. 20 miles S on Hwy 89.* Covering 71,000 acres, this 20-mile-long, 200-foot-deep body of water lies across the Idaho/Utah border. Fishing for Mackinaw, cutthroat, whitefish, and the rare Bonneville cisco. On the north shore is

> **Bear Lake State Park.** *81 S Main, Montpelier (83261). Phone 208/945-2790.* Provides swimming beach, waterskiing, fishing, boating (ramp); picnicking, park (Mid-May-mid-Sept), camping on east shore (dump station, hookups).

**Bloomington Lake.** *Bloomington. 12 miles S on Hwy 89, then W on local road, W of Bloomington.* Spring-fed lake of unknown depth. Camping, fishing.

**Caribou National Forest.** *322 N 4th St, Montpelier (83254). Phone 208/847-0375.* Fishing; camping (fee at certain designated campsites), hunting, picnicking, winter sports. Within the forest is

> **Minnetonka Cave.** *322 N 4th St, Montpelier (83254). 10 miles W of St. Charles off Hwy 89. Phone 208/847-0375.* Cave is 1/2 mile long and has nine rooms; 40°F. Guided tours (Mid-June-Labor Day, daily). **$$**

## Special Event

**Bear Lake County Fair.** *Montpelier. Bear Lake County Fairgrounds. Phone 208/945-2072. www.bearlake.org/calendar.* At the fair, you can choose from a variety of activities like watching the rodeo, visiting the carnival, browsing the artisans' booths, and attending the demolition derby. Third weekend in Aug.

## Limited-Service Hotel

**★ ★ BEST WESTERN CLOVER CREEK INN.** *243 N 4th St, Montpelier (83254). Phone 208/847-1782; toll-free 800/528-1234; fax 208/847-3519. www.bestwestern.com.* 65 rooms, 2 story. Pets accepted, some restrictions; fee. Complimentary continental breakfast. Check-in 2 pm, check-out 11 am. Restaurant. Fitness room. Whirlpool. **$**

# Moscow (B-1)

*See also Lewiston*

**Population** 18,519
**Elevation** 2,583 ft
**Area Code** 208
**Zip** 83843
**Information** Chamber of Commerce, PO Box 8936; phone 208/882-1800 or toll-free 800/380-1801
**Web Site** www.moscowchamber.com

This northern Idaho town is nestled between Moscow Mountain and the scenic rolling hills of the Palouse. A quaint college town, Moscow is home to the University of Idaho, and Washington State University is only a 15-minute drive west, just across the state line in Pullman. Moscow bills itself as the "Heart of the Arts", an appropriate moniker given the town's well-attended arts festivals, renowned summer theater program, and vibrant live music scene. The nearby Palouse hills possess rich soils, producing high yields of dry peas and lentils. The USA Dry Pea and Lentil Council is headquartered in Moscow.

## What to See and Do

**Appaloosa Museum and Heritage Center.** *2720 W Pulman Rd, Moscow (83843). Moscow-Pullman Hwy. Phone 208/882-5578. www.appaloosamuseum.org.* Exhibit of paintings and artifacts relating to the appaloosa horse; early cowboy equipment; saddle collection; Nez Perce clothing, tools. Also houses national headquarters of the Appaloosa Horse Club, Inc. (June-Aug: Mon-Sat; rest of year: Mon-Fri; closed holidays) **FREE**

**Latah County Historical Society.** *110 S Adams St, Moscow (83843). Mc Connell Mansion (1886). Phone 208/882-1004.* Historic rooms, exhibits, and artifacts depicting local history. Local history and genealogy library, children's activities. Museum (Tues-Sat, limited hours; closed holidays); library, 327 E 2nd St (Tues-Fri). **DONATION**

**University of Idaho.** *415 W 6th St, Moscow (83843). W off Hwy 95. Phone 208/885-6424. www.uidaho.edu.*(1889) (11,000 students) Graduate and undergraduate programs. On campus is a major collection of big game specimens from the estate of well-known hunter Jack O'Connor; art gallery and performing arts center; mining, forestry, and wildlife exhibits in the mining and forestry bldgs; 18,000-seat, covered Kibbie-ASUI Activities Center with award-winning barrel-arch dome. Tours (daily).

## Special Events

**Idaho Repertory Theater.** *E.W. Hartung Theater, University of Idaho,6th St and Stadium Dr, Moscow (83843). Phone 208/885-7986.* Shakespeare, musicals, dramas, comedies. June-early Aug.

**Latah County Fair.** *Fairgrounds,1021 Harold St, Moscow (83843). E of town. Phone 208/883-5722.www.latah-countyfair.com.* Home economics, horticultural, and livestock 4-H exhibits; nightly entertainment; and carnival rides are just some of the fun features of the Latah County Fair. Second week in Sept, after Labor Day.

**Lionel Hampton Jazz Festival.** *University of Idaho, Perimeter Dr and Rayburn St, Moscow (83843). Phone 208/885-6765.* Four-day festival hosted by Lionel Hampton featuring all-star headliners and student performers. Late Feb.

**Rendezvous in the Park.** *East City Park,1021 Harold St, Moscow (83843). Phone 208/882-1178.* Arts and crafts festival, juried art shows, silent movies, concerts under the stars. Two weekends in July.

## Limited-Service Hotels

**★ ★ BEST WESTERN UNIVERSITY INN.** *1516 Pullman Rd, Moscow (83843). Phone 208/882-0550; toll-free 800/325-8765; fax 208/883-3056. www.bestwestern.com.* 173 rooms, 2 story. Pets accepted; fee. Check-in 4 pm, check-out noon. Restaurant, bar. Fitness room. Indoor pool, children's pool, whirlpool. Airport transportation available. **$**

**★ ★ MARK IV MOTOR INN.** *414 N Main St, Moscow (83843). Phone 208/882-7557; fax 208/883-0684.*86 rooms, 2 story. Pets accepted; fee. Check-in 3 pm, check-out noon. Restaurant, bar. Indoor pool, whirlpool. Airport transportation available. **$**

**★ SUPER 8.** *175 Peterson Dr, Moscow (83843). Phone 208/883-1503; toll-free 800/800-8000; fax 208/883-4769.www.super8.com.*60 rooms, 3 story. Check-in 2 pm, check-out 11 am. **$**

# Mountain Home (E-2)

*See also Boise*

**Population** 7,913
**Elevation** 3,143 ft
**Area Code** 208
**Zip** 83647
**Information** Desert Mountain Visitor Center, 2900 American Legion Blvd, PO Box 3; phone 208/587-4464
**Web Site** www.mountain-home.org/chamber

A transportation center in the Boise-Owyhee Valley of southwest Idaho, Mountain Home affords a fine starting point for side trips. Within a few hours' drive are forested ranges of the Boise National Forest, sand dunes, ghost towns, reservoirs, and canyons; a Ranger District office of the forest (see BOISE) is located here.

## What to See and Do

**Bruneau Canyon.** *Hwy 51, Mountain Home (83647). 20 miles S on Hwy 51 to Bruneau, then SE on Hot Springs Road. Phone 208/366-7919. www.idahoparks.org.* A 61-mile gorge, 800 feet deep but narrow enough in places to toss a rock across. Bruneau Dunes State Park (4,800 acres) has small lakes, sand dunes, and the highest single-structured dune in North America (470 feet). Fishing for bass and bluegill, boating (ramps; no motors); nature trails, picnicking, tent and trailer sites

(15-day maximum; hookups, dump station). Information center, public observatory, interpretive programs (by appointment).

**Elmore County Historical Foundation Museum.** *180 S 3rd St E, Mountain Home (83647). Phone 208/587-6847.* Contains historical info about Mountain Home and Elmore County. (Mar-Dec, Fri-Sat afternoons). **DONATION**

**Fishing, swimming, boating, camping.** *Mountain Home.* Strike Reservoir, 23 miles S on Hwy 51; or Anderson Ranch Reservoir, 22 miles NE on Hwy 20.

**Soldier Mountain Ski Area.** *Fairfield. NE on Hwy 20 to Fairfield, then 10 miles N on Soldier Creek Rd. Phone 208/764-2526. www.soldiermountain.com.* Two double chairlifts, rope tow; patrol, school, rentals; snowmaking; cafeteria, concession. Longest run 2 miles; vertical drop 1,400 feet. Half-day rates. (Mid-Nov-Apr: Thurs-Sun and holidays; Christmas and Easter weeks: daily) **$$$$**

**Three Island Crossing State Park.** *W Madison St, Mountain Home (83623). 35 miles SE in Glenns Ferry, I-84 at Glenns Ferry exit. Phone 208/366-2394. www.idahoparks.org.* On 513 acres. The site was once a river crossing on the Oregon Trail. Camping (reservations recommended; fee). Interpretive center; gift shop.

## Limited-Service Hotel

**★ BEST WESTERN FOOTHILLS MOTOR INN.** *1080 Hwy 20, Mountain Home (83647). Phone 208/587-8477; toll-free 800/604-8477; fax 208/587-5774. www.bestwestern.com/foothillsmotorinn.* 76 rooms, 2 story. Pets accepted; fee. Complimentary continental breakfast. Check-in 3 pm, check-out noon. Outdoor pool, whirlpool. **$**

# Nampa (E-1)

*See also Boise, Caldwell*

**Founded** 1885
**Population** 28,365
**Elevation** 2,490 ft
**Area Code** 208
**Information** Chamber of Commerce, 1305 3rd St S, PO Box A, 83653; phone 208/466-4641
**Web Site** www.nampa.com

Nampa, the most populous city in Canyon County, is located in southwestern Idaho's agriculturally rich Treasure Valley. Crops such as sweet corn, onions, mint, and potatoes thrive in the area's sun-soaked, high desert climate. Nampa is a short drive west of Boise on I-84, a few miles north of the Snake River Birds of Prey National Conservation Area, home to North Americas largest concentration of nesting raptors.

## What to See and Do

**Canyon County Historical Society Museum.** *1200 Front St, Nampa (83651). Phone 208/467-7611.* Historical artifacts and memorabilia inside a 1903 train depot once used as offices of the Union Pacific Railroad. (Tues-Sat, limited hours) **DONATION**

**Deer Flat National Wildlife Refuge.** *13751 Upper Embankment, Nampa (83686). 5 miles SW off I-84. Phone 208/467-9278.* Thousands of migratory waterfowl pause at this 10,500-acre refuge while on their journey (Oct-Dec). Wildlife observation. Fishing, hunting in season. Visitor center (Mon-Fri; closed holidays). **FREE** Within the refuge is

> **Lake Lowell.** *13751 Upper Embankment Rd, Nampa. Phone 208/467-9278.* Approximately 8,800 acres. Boating, sailing, water-skiing; picnicking (mid-Apr-Sept, daily).

**Lakeview Park.** *Garrity Blvd and 16th Ave, Nampa (83686). Phone 208/465-2215.* A 90-acre park with gardens, sports facilities, tennis, picnic areas. Pool (June-Labor Day; fee). Antique fire engine, locomotive, steam roller, jet fighter plane on display. Amphitheater. Park (Daily). **FREE**

## Special Event

**Snake River Stampede.** *109 12th Ave S, Nampa (83651). Phone 208/466-8497.* Among nation's top professional rodeos. All seats reserved. For tickets contact PO Box 231, 83653. Tues-Sat, third week in July.

## Limited-Service Hotels

**★ HAMPTON INN AT IDAHO CENTER.** *5750 E Franklin Rd, Nampa (83687). Phone 208/442-0036; toll-free 800/426-7866; fax 208/442-0037. www.hamptoninn.com.* 101 rooms. Pets accepted; fee. Complimentary continental breakfast. Check-in 3 pm, check-out noon. High-speed Internet access. Fitness room. Indoor pool, whirlpool. Airport transportation available. Business center. **$**

★ **SHILO INN.** *617 Nampa Blvd, Nampa (83687). Phone 208/466-8993; toll-free 800/222-2244; fax 208/465-5929. www.shiloinns.com.* 84 rooms, 3 story. Pets accepted; fee. Complimentary continental breakfast. Check-in 3 pm, check-out noon. Indoor pool, whirlpool. **$**

# Pocatello (F-4)

*See also American Falls, Blackfoot, Idaho Falls, Lava Hot Springs*

**Founded** 1882
**Population** 46,080
**Elevation** 4,464 ft
**Area Code** 208
**Information** Greater Pocatello Chamber of Commerce, 343 W Center St, PO Box 626, 83204; phone 208/233-1525
**Web Site** www.pocatelloidaho.com

At the heart of the intermontane transportation system is Pocatello. Once the site of a reservation, the city was named for the Native American leader who granted the railroad rights of way and building privileges. A Ranger District office and the headquarters of the Caribou National Forest are located here.

## What to See and Do

**Caribou National Forest.** *1405 Hollipark Dr, Pocatello (83201). S, W, and E of city. Phone 208/523-3278.* Scenic drives, pack trips, camping (fee in some designated developed campgrounds), picnic grounds, hunting, fishing, downhill and cross-country skiing, snowmobiling. For further info contact the Forest Supervisor, 670 Broadway Ave, Idaho Falls, 83401. In the forest is

> **Pebble Creek Ski Area.** *3340 E Green Canyon Rd, Inkom (83245). 10 miles SE on I-15 to Inkom, then 5 miles E on Green Canyon Rd. Phone 208/775-4452.* Two triple, one double chairlifts; beginner-to-expert trails; patrol, school, rentals; restaurant, bar. Longest run 1 1/2 miles; vertical drop 2,200 feet. Night skiing. Half-day rates. (Second week in Dec-early Apr; daily) **$$$$**

**Idaho State University.** *921 S 8th Ave, Pocatello (83201). Phone 208/236-3620.*(1901) (13,500 students) Undergraduate and graduate programs. Art gallery in Fine Arts Building has changing exhibits (academic year, daily; summer by appointment, phone 208/236-3532); art gallery in Student Union Building (daily); both galleries free. On campus is 12,000-seat Holt Arena, indoor football stadium and sports arena. Tours. Also here is

> **Idaho Museum of Natural History.** *066 S 5th Ave, Pocatello (83201). Phone 208/282-3168.* Exhibits on Idaho fossils, especially large mammals of the Ice Age; Native American basketry and beadwork; "Discovery Room" for educational activities; museum shop. (Mon-Sat; closed holidays) **$$**

**Rocky Mountain River Tours.** *314 Stevens Ave, Pocatello (83707). Middlefork Salmon River Canyon. Phone 208/345-2400.* Six-day wilderness rafting tours; equipment provided.

**Ross Park.** *911 N 7th Ave, Pocatello (83201). S 2nd Ave. Phone 208/234-6232.* Zoo; swimming pool (June-Aug), water slide; playground, picnic area with shelter, band shell. Fee for some activities. Park (Daily). On upper level are

> **Bannock County Historical Museum.** *3000 Alvord Loop, Pocatello (83204). Phone 208/233-0434.* Relics of the early days of Pocatello and Bannock County; Bannock and Shoshone display. (Memorial Day-Labor Day: daily; rest of year: Tues-Sat, limited hours; closed holidays, also mid-Dec-mid-Jan) **$**

> **Old Fort Hall Replica.** *Pocatello.* Reproduction of 1834 Hudson's Bay Trading Post; period displays. (June-mid-Sept: daily; Apr-May: Tues-Sat) **$**

## Special Events

**Bannock County Fair and Rodeo.** *10588 Fairgrounds Rd, Pocatello (83201). Phone 208/237-1340.* North: Bannock County Fairgrounds. South: Downey Fairgrounds. Carnival, rodeo, exhibits, food booths, livestock and horse shows. Mid-Aug.

**Shoshone-Bannock Indian Festival.** *Festival and Rodeo Grounds, 10588 Fairgrounds Rd, Pocatello (83201). Phone 208/237-1340. www.sho-ban.com/festival.htm.* Experience centuries-old traditions nightly at the tribal dancing, singing, and drumming performances in the arbor. Other activities include an all-Indian rodeo, an arts and crafts fair, a juried art show, and a softball tournament. Second weekend in Aug.

**Summer Band Concert Series.** *2901 S 2nd Ave, Pocatello. Guy Gates Memorial Band Shell, in lower level of Ross Park. Phone 208/234-6232.* Sun, July-Aug.

## Limited-Service Hotels

★ ★ **HOLIDAY INN.** *1399 Bench Rd, Pocatello (83201). Phone 208/237-1400; toll-free 800/200-8944; fax 208/238-0225. www.holiday-inn.com.* 205 rooms, 2 story. Pets accepted, some restrictions. Complimentary continental breakfast. Check-in 3 pm, check-out noon. Restaurant, bar. Fitness room. Indoor pool, whirlpool. Airport transportation available. **$**

★ ★ **RED LION.** *1555 Pocatello Creek Rd, Pocatello (83201). Phone 208/233-2200; toll-free 800/325-4000; fax 208/234-4524. www.redlion.com.* 150 rooms, 2 story. Pets accepted, some restrictions. Check-out noon. Restaurant, bar. Fitness room. Indoor pool, children's pool, whirlpool. Airport transportation available. Business center. **$**

# Priest Lake Area (A-1)

*See also Sandpoint*

*25 miles N of Priest River via Hwy 57.*

Among the few remaining unspoiled playgrounds of the Pacific Northwest are lovely and spectacular Priest Lake and the Idaho Panhandle National Forest. North of the confluence of the Pend Oreille and Priest rivers, giant lake trout, big game, towering mountains, waterfalls, lakes, and tall trees make this area one of the most attractive in the country. Mountain ranges and Pacific breezes keep the climate moderate. This entire water and forest domain was explored by a Jesuit priest, Father Peter John DeSmet, also known as "great black robe" and the "first apostle of the Northwest." Priest Lake and Priest River were both named in his honor. A Ranger District office of the Idaho Panhandle National Forests-Kaniksu is located at Priest Lake.

## What to See and Do

**Idaho Panhandle National Forests–Kaniksu.** *Nordman Hwy, Priest River. Surrounds Priest Lake and Lake Pend Oreille; other areas NE. Phone 208/443-2512.* Rich with huge trees, wildflowers, fishing streams. Boating, swimming, fishing in Pend Oreille and Priest lakes; big game hunting, cross-country skiing, snowmobiling trails, picnicking, 12 forest-run campgrounds on the west side of Priest Lake; other state-run campgrounds in the area. For more information, contact the Priest Lake Ranger District, 32203 Hwy 57, Priest River 83856.

**Priest Lake.** *32203 Hwy 57, Priest River (83856). 22 miles N of town of Priest River via Hwy 57, then approximately 6 miles E on East Shore Rd; or approximately 6 miles farther on Hwy 57, then 1 mile E on Outlet Bay Rd.* Lower Priest, the main lake, is 18 1/2 miles long and about 4 miles wide and has a 63-mile shoreline. Upper Priest (inaccessible by road; best reached by boat) is 3 1/4 miles long and 1 mile wide and has an 8-mile shoreline. The area is popular for picnics, overnight cruises, and campouts. There are three state-run campgrounds on the east side: Dickensheet, Indian Creek, and Lionhead; the US Forest Service operates other campgrounds in the area, on the west side. Nearby is the Roosevelt Grove of ancient cedars with 800-year-old trees standing as tall as 150 feet. Granite Falls is within the grove. Priest Lake is famous for its giant lake trout (Mackinaw trout) and cutthroat trout. The main lake contains six islands ideal for picnicking and camping (ten-day maximum). Recreation around the lake includes swimming, boating (ramp), ice fishing, cross-country skiing, snowmobiling, ice skating, and sledding. On the east side of the lake is

> **Priest Lake State Park.** *423 Indian Creek Bay, Priest Lake Area (83821). Phone 208/443-6710.* This park comprises three state-run campgrounds: the **Dickensheet** unit is 1 mile off Highway 57, on the Coolin Rd (46 acres; 11 campsites); the **Indian Creek** unit is 11 miles N of Coolin, on Eastshore Rd (park headquarters; 295 acres; 93 campsites, two camper cabins, store, boating facilities, RV hookups, trails); and the **Lionhead** unit is 23 miles N of Coolin, on Eastshore Rd (415 acres; 47 tent sites, group camp, boating facilities, trails). Reservations are available for Indian Creek campsites; reservations are required for the group camp at Lionhead.

**Priest River.** *Priest Lake. Winds for 44 miles S of the lake through wild, forested country.* Old logging roads parallel much of it. Only at the north and south stretches is it easily reached from Highway 57. Long whitewater stretches provide adventure for canoe experts; riffles, big holes, smooth-flowing sections make it a tantalizing trout stream (fishing: June-Oct).

## Special Events

**Pacific Northwest Sled Dog Championship Races.** *Priest Lake. On Hwy 57 at Priest Lake Airport, W shore.* Last weekend in Jan.

**Spring Festival.** *Priest Lake. Phone 208/443-3191.* Auction, parade. Memorial Day weekend.

### Full-Service Resorts

★ ★ **ELKINS ON PRIEST LAKE.** *404 Elkins Rd, Nordman (83848). Phone 208/443-2432; fax 208/443-2527. www.elkinsresort.com.* 31 rooms. Closed Mar-Apr. Pets accepted, some restrictions; fee. Check-in 4 pm, check-out 11 am. Restaurant, bar. **$**

★ ★ **HILLS RESORT.** *4777 W Lakeshore Rd, Priest Lake (83856). Phone 208/443-2551; fax 208/443-2363. www.hillsresort.com.* 77 rooms, 2 story. Pets accepted; fee. Check-in 4:30 pm, check-out 10:30 am. Restaurant, bar. Tennis. **$**

# Rexburg (E-4)

*See also Ashton, Driggs, Idaho Falls, Saint Anthony*

**Founded** 1883
**Population** 14,302
**Elevation** 4,865 ft
**Area Code** 208
**Zip** 83440
**Information** Chamber of Commerce Tourist & Information Center, 420 W 4th St; phone 208/356-5700
**Web Site** www.rexcc.com

Rexburg enjoys its position as a farm and trading center. Founded on instructions of the Mormon Church, the community was named for Thomas Ricks; common usage changed it to Rexburg.

### What to See and Do

**Beaver Dick.** *Rexburg. 7 miles W on Hwy 33.* A 12-acre preserve on west bank of the north Fork of Snake River. Fishing, boating, ramp; picnic facilities, primitive camping. (Mar-Dec)

**Idaho Centennial Carousel.** *Porter Park,12 N Center St, Rexburg (83440). Phone 208/359-3020.*Restored Spillman Engineering carousel. (June-Labor Day, daily) **$**

**Teton Flood Museum.** *51 N Center, Rexburg (83440). Phone 208/359-3063.* Artifacts, photographs, and films document the 1976 flood caused by the collapse of the Teton Dam, which left 11 persons dead and $1 billion in damage. Also various historical displays. (May-Aug: Mon-Sat; rest of year: Mon-Fri, limited hours; closed holidays except July 4) **$**

**Twin Bridges.** *Rexburg. 13 miles SE on Archer-Lyman Rd. Phone 208/356-3102.*A 30-acre preserve on the north bank of the south Fork of Snake River. Fishing, boating, ramp; picnic facilities, camping. (Apr-Nov)

**Yellowstone Bear World.** *6010 S 4300 W, Rexburg (83440). 5 miles S on Hwy 20. Phone 208/359-9688.* Drive-through preserve near Yellowstone National Park features bears, wolves, other wildlife; "Cub Yard" shows bear cubs at play; "Duck Deck" waterfowl observation/feeding deck. (May-Oct, daily) **$$$**

### Special Event

**Idaho International Folk Dance Festival.** *Rexburg. Phone 208/356-5700.* Dance teams from around the world, events. Last week in July-first weekend in Aug.

### Limited-Service Hotels

★ ★ **BEST WESTERN COTTONTREE INN.** *450 W 4th St S, Rexburg (83440). Phone 208/356-4646; toll-free 800/662-6886; fax 208/356-7461. www.bestwestern.com.* 98 rooms, 2 story. Pets accepted, some restrictions. Check-in 2 pm, check-out noon. Restaurant. Indoor pool, whirlpool.**$**

★ **COMFORT INN.** *885 W Main St, Rexburg (83440). Phone 208/359-1311; toll-free 800/228-5150; fax 208/359-1387. www.choicehotels.com.* 52 rooms, 2 story. Pets accepted. Complimentary continental breakfast. Check-in 3 pm, check-out 11 am. Fitness room. Indoor pool, whirlpool. **$**

### Restaurant

★ **FRONTIER PIES RESTAURANT.** *460 W 4th St, Rexburg (83440). Phone 208/356-3600; fax 208/356-3673.*American menu. Breakfast, lunch, dinner. Children's menu. Casual attire. **$**

# Saint Anthony (E-4)

*See also Ashton, Driggs, Idaho Falls, Rexburg*

**Population** 3,010
**Elevation** 4,972 ft
**Area Code** 208
**Zip** 83445
**Information** Chamber of Commerce, City Hall, 114 N Bridge St; phone 208/624-4870

Seat of Fremont County, headquarters for the Targhee National Forest and a center of the seed potato industry, Saint Anthony is named for Anthony Falls, Minnesota. Tourists make it a base for exploring Idaho's tiny (30 miles long, 1 mile wide) "sahara desert," the Saint Anthony Sand Dunes.

## What to See and Do

**Fort Henry Trading Post Site.** *St. Anthony. 7 miles W along Henry's Fork of Snake River.* (1810) First fort on what early voyageurs called the "accursed mad river."

**St. Anthony Sand Dunes.** *St. Anthony. 12 miles W. Phone 208/624-3494.* More than 10,000 acres of ever-shifting white quartz sand dunes. The area is popular among dune buggy, ATV, and horseback riders. During the winter months, kids and kids at heart—arrive to sled and tube down the snow-covered dunes.

## Special Events

**Fremont County Fair.** *St. Anthony. Fairgrounds. Phone 208/624-4870.* Features demolition derby. Aug.

**Fremont County Pioneer Days.** *St. Anthony. Phone 208/624-4870.* Rodeo, parade, carnival. Late July.

**Summerfest.** *Main St, St. Anthony (83445). Phone 208/624-4870. www.ci.saint-anthony.id.us.* This annual street festival features an open air market. Aug.

# St. Marie's (B-1)

*See also Coeur d'Alene*

**Population** 2,442
**Elevation** 2,216 ft
**Area Code** 208
**Zip** 83861
**Information** Chamber of Commerce, 906 Main St, PO Box 162; phone 208/245-3563

St. Marie's (St. Mary's) is a center for lumbering and the production of plywood, a crossroads for lake, rail, and road transportation, and the jumping-off place for exploring the shadowy St. Joe River country. A Ranger District office of the Idaho Panhandle National Forests-St. Joe is located in St. Marie's.

## What to See and Do

**Benewah, Round, and Chatcolet lakes.** *St. Marie's. Along the St. Joe River.* Famous as one of the state's best bass fishing and duck hunting areas. The three lakes became one with the construction of the Post Falls Dam. Also here is

> **Heyburn State Park.** *1291 Chatcolet Rd, Plummer (83851). 7 miles W on Hwy 5. Phone 208/686-1308.* More than 7,800 acres. Swimming beach, fishing, boating (ramps, fee), ice skating, ice fishing; hiking and bridle trails, mountain biking, self-guided nature walks, picnicking, concession, tent and trailer campsites (15-day maximum; hookups), dump station. Campfire and interpretive programs. Dinner and interpretive cruises. Park (Daily).

**Idaho Panhandle National Forests-St. Joe.** *St. Marie's. Access from Hwy 95 and I-90; other areas E on local roads. Phone 208/245-2531.* Hunting, fishing, hiking, camping, cabins, picnicking, summer and winter sports areas, cross-country skiing, snowmobiling trails; digging for garnets; scenic drives. For more information, contact the Avery Ranger District, HC Box 1, Avery 83802, phone 208/245-4517; or the Supervisor, 3815 Schreiber Way, Coeur d'Alene 83815, phone 208/765-7223.

**St. Joe Baldy Mountain.** *St. Marie's. 8 miles E on St. Joe River Rd (Forest Hwy 50).* Lookout at top has view of Washington and Montana.

**St. Joe River.** *St. Marie's Just E on Hwy 5.* Called "the river through the lakes," one of the world's highest navigable rivers. Connects St. Marie's with Lake Coeur d'Alene.

## Special Events

**Paul Bunyan Days.** *St. Marie's. Phone 208/245-3563.* Includes parade, fireworks, logging events, water show, carnival. Labor Day weekend.

**smART Festival.** *St. Marie's City Park,827 Main Ave, St. Marie's (83861). Phone 208/245-3417.* Paintings and crafts by local and regional artists. Food, entertainment, swimming. Third weekend in July

# Salmon (D-3)

**Settled** 1866
**Population** 2,941
**Elevation** 4,004 ft
**Area Code** 208
**Zip** 83467
**Information** Salmon Valley Chamber of Commerce, 200 Main St, Suite 1; phone 208/756-2100 or toll-free 800/727-2540
**Web Site** www.salmonidaho.com

This town, at the junction of the Salmon and Lemhi rivers, serves as a doorway to the Salmon River country. It has towering mountains, lush farmland, timberland, and rich mines. The Salmon River runs through the town on its way to the Columbia River and the Pacific Ocean. Fishing and boating are available along the Salmon and Lemhi rivers and in more than 250 lakes. The headquarters and two Ranger District offices of the Salmon National Forest are located here.

## What to See and Do

**River rafting, backpack, fishing, and pack trips.** Salmon. Trips along the Lemhi, Salmon, Middle Fork, and other rivers can be arranged. Contact the Chamber of Commerce for a list of outfitters in the area.

**Salmon National Forest.** *50 Hwy 93 S, Salmon (83467). N, E, and W of town along Hwy 93. Phone 208/756-2215.* Approximately 1.8 million acres. Boat trips, fishing; hunting, picnicking, camping. Includes portion of the Frank Church–River of No Return Wilderness.

## Special Events

**High School Rodeo.** *Salmon (83467). Phone 208/756-2100.* First weekend in June.

**Lemhi County Fair & Rodeo.** *Salmon (83467).* Third week in Aug.

**Salmon River Days.** *Salmon. Phone 208/756-2100.* July 4.

## Limited-Service Hotel

**★ STAGECOACH INN MOTEL.** *201 Hwy 93 N, N Salmon (83467). Phone 208/756-4251; fax 208/756-3456.* 100 rooms, 3 story. Complimentary continental breakfast. Check-in 3 pm, check-out 11 am. Beach access. Outdoor pool. Airport transportation available. **$**

## Restaurant

**★ SALMON RIVER COFFEE SHOP.** *608 Main St, Salmon (83467). Phone 208/756-3521.* American menu. Breakfast, lunch, dinner. Children's menu. Casual attire. **$**

# Sandpoint (A-1)

*See also Bonners Ferry, Priest Lake Area; see also Spokane, WA*

**Population** 5,203
**Elevation** 2,085 ft
**Area Code** 208
**Zip** 83864
**Information** Chamber of Commerce, 900 N 5th, PO Box 928; phone 208/263-2161 or toll-free 800/800-2106
**Web Site** www.sandpointchamber.com

At the point where the Pend Oreille River empties into Lake Pend Oreille (pon-da-RAY, from a Native American tribe given to wearing pendant ear ornaments), Sandpoint straddles two major railroads and three US highways. All of these bring a stream of tourists into town. In the surrounding area are dozens of smaller lakes and streams. A Ranger District office of the Idaho Panhandle National Forests-Coeur d'Alene is located here.

## What to See and Do

**Bonner County Historical Society Museum.** *611 S Ella St, Sandpoint (83864). In Lakeview Park, at Ontario and Ella sts. Phone 208/263-2344. www.bonnercountyhistory.org.* Exhibits depict the history of Bonner County. There is also a research library with a newspaper collection dating from 1899. (Tues-Sat 10 am-4 pm; closed holidays) **$**

**Coldwater Creek on the Cedar Street Bridge.** *334 N 1st Ave, Sandpoint (83864). Phone 208/263-2265.* Shopping mall built on a bridge over Sand Creek. Inspired by the Ponte Vecchio in Florence, Italy, the Coldwater Creek shops provide panoramic views of Lake Pend Oreille and nearby mountains. (Daily)

**Lake Pend Oreille.** *Sandpoint.* The largest lake in Idaho, and one of the largest natural lakes wholly within the United States, Lake Pend Oreille is more than 43 miles long and 6 miles wide, with more than 111 miles of shoreline. Anglers catch approximately 14 varieties of game fish, including the famous Kamloops, the largest rainbow trout in world (they average 16 to 26 pounds). Boating, swimming, water-skiing; camping, picnicking.

**Round Lake State Park.** *Sagle. 10 miles S on Hwy 95, then 2 miles W. Phone 208/263-3489.* Approximately 140 acres of coniferous woods. Swimming, skin diving, fishing, ice fishing, ice-skating, boating (ramp, no motors); hiking, cross-country skiing, sledding, tobogganing, snowshoeing in winter, picnicking. Camping (15-day maximum; no hookups), dump station. Campfire programs. Park (Daily).

**Sandpoint Public Beach.** *Sandpoint. Foot of Bridge St, E edge of town.* Nearly 20 acres. Bathhouse, swimming, waterskiing, boat docks, ramps; picnic tables, fireplaces, volleyball and tennis courts; concession (seasonal). Park (Daily). **FREE**

**Schweitzer Mountain Resort.** *10000 Schweitzer Mountain Rd, Sandpoint (83864). 11 miles NW off Hwy 2 and Hwy 95, in Selkirk Mts of Idaho Panhandle National Forests; toll-free 800/831-8810.* Five chairlifts, high-speed quad; school, rentals; lodging, restaurants, bars, cafeteria; nursery. Longest run 2.7 miles; vertical drop 2,400 feet. (Nov-Apr, daily) Summer chairlift rides (fee).

## Special Events

**Festival at Sandpoint.** *Sandpoint. Phone 208/265-4554.* Since 1982, thousands have gathered in this arts town to enjoy music performed by internationally acclaimed musicians representing just about every genre imaginable. Past artists have included the likes of B.B. King, Shawn Colvin, Tony Bennett, Wynton Marsalis, and Johnny Cash. Aug.

**Winter Carnival.** *Sandpoint. Phone 208/263-2161.* Two weekends of festivities include snow sculpture, snowshoe softball, and other games, races, torchlight parade. Mid-Jan.

## Limited-Service Hotels

**★ ★ BEST WESTERN EDGEWATER RESORT.** *56 Bridge St, Sandpoint (83864). Phone 208/263-3194; toll-free 800/635-2534; fax 208/263-3194. www.sandpointhotels.com/edgewater.* 55 rooms, 3 story. Pets accepted; fee. Complimentary full breakfast. Check-in 3 pm, check-out noon. Restaurant, bar. Indoor pool, whirlpool. **$**

**★ ★ LA QUINTA INN.** *415 Cedar St, Sandpoint (83864). Phone 208/263-9581; toll-free 800/282-0660; fax 208/263-3395. www.laquinta.com.* 70 rooms, 3 story. Check-out 1 pm. Restaurant, bar. Fitness room. Outdoor pool, whirlpool. **$**

**★ ★ THE SELKIRK LODGE, A RED LION HOTEL.** *10000 Schweitzer Mountain Rd, Sandpoint (83864). Phone 208/265-0257; toll-free 800/831-8810; fax 208/263-7961. www.schweitzer.com.* 78 rooms. Check-in 4 pm, check-out 11 am. High-speed Internet access, wireless Internet access. Restaurant, bar. Children's activity center. Fitness room. Outdoor pool, whirlpool. Ski in/ski out. Business center. **$**

**★ ★ WHITE PINE LODGE AT SCHWEITZER MOUNTAIN.** *10000 Schweitzer Mountain Lodge, Sandpoint (83864). Phone 208/265-0257; toll-free 800/831-8810; fax 208/263-0775. www.schweitzer.com.* 43 rooms. Check-in 4 pm, check-out 11 am. High-speed Internet access, wireless Internet access. Children's activity center. Fitness room. Whirlpool. Ski in/ski out. **$$**

## Specialty Lodging

**THE COIT HOUSE BED & BREAKFAST.** *502 N Fourth Ave, Sandpoint (83864). Phone 208/265-4035; toll-free 866/265-2648; fax 208/265-5558. www.coithouse.com.* This charming B&B is located in downtown Sandpoint, steps away from shopping, restaurants, and the City Beach at Lake Pend Oreille. Antiques and handmade crafts can be found throughout this restored 1907 Victorian manor. Each of the four bedrooms has a private bath. The upstairs master suite charms guests with a beautiful sleigh bed and clawfoot tub. A mural of an English garden graces the wall alongside the staircase. A cheery sun room is the perfect place to relax before or after a day of outdoor fun in this year-round vacation community. 5 rooms. Pets accepted, some restrictions; fee. Children over 10 years only. Complimentary full breakfast. Check-in 4 pm, check-out 11 am. High-speed Internet access, wireless Internet access. $

## Restaurants

**★ ★ BANGKOK CUISINE.** *202 N 2nd Ave, Sandpoint (83864). Phone 208/265-4149.* Thai menu. Lunch, dinner. Closed Sun. Casual attire. **$$**

**★ ★ FLOATING RESTAURANT.** *Hwy 200 E, Hope (83836). Phone 208/264-5311.* Enjoy panoramic views of Lake Pend Oreille, while dining on the restaurant's floating deck or in the indoor dining room. Seafood menu. Dinner, Sun brunch. Closedd Mon-Tues; also Nov-Mar. Bar. Children's menu. Outdoor seating. **$$**

★ **HYDRA.** *115 Lake St, Sandpoint (83864). Phone 208/263-7123. www.thehydrarestaurant.com.* Steak menu. Lunch, dinner. Bar. Children's menu. Casual attire. Outdoor seating. **$$**

★ ★ **IVANO'S RISTORANTE.** *102 S First Ave, Sandpoint (83864). Phone 208/263-0211; fax 208/255-4225. www.ivanos.com.* Cathedral ceiling in main dining room. Italian menu. Lunch, dinner. Bar. Children's menu. Casual attire. Reservations recommended. Outdoor seating. Cathedral ceiling in main dining room. **$$**

★**JALAPENO'S.** *314 N 2nd Ave, Sandpoint (83864). Phone 208/263-2995.* Mexican menu. Lunch, dinner. Bar. Children's menu. Casual attire. Outdoor seating. **$$**

# Shoshone (E-3)

*See also Bellevue, Jerome, Twin Falls*

**Founded** 1882
**Population** 1,249
**Elevation** 3,970 ft
**Area Code** 208
**Zip** 83352
**Information** City Hall, 207 S Rail St W, Box 208; phone 208/886-2030 Located in the Magic Valley region of south-central Idaho, Shoshone serves as the seat of Lincoln County. The town is surrounded by ranches and farms, and the area retains an aura of the untamed old West. Popular recreational activities include boating, fishing, and big-game hunting. Shoshone marks the beginning of the Sawtooth Scenic Route, a stretch of State Highway 75 leading northward to the resort community of Sun Valley (see).

## What to See and Do

**Mary L. Gooding Memorial Park.** *300 N Rail St, Shoshone (83324). Phone 208/886-2030.* Playground, pool (May-Aug, daily), picnic area along Little Wood River. (Daily)

★ **Shoshone Indian Ice Caves.** *1561 N Hwy 75, Shoshone (83352). 17 miles N on Hwy 75. Phone 208/886-2058.* The caves function as a natural refrigerator, with temperatures ranging from 18° to 33°F. The cave is three blocks long, 30 feet wide, and 40 feet high, and local legend has it that long ago a princess named Idahow was buried under the ice. To this day, visitors report hearing strange voices and footsteps that seem to come from nowhere. On the grounds are a statue of Shoshone Chief Washakie and a museum of Native American artifacts, as well as minerals and gems (free). The caves are a good place to take children. 45-minute guided tours (May-Sept, daily). **$$$**

## Special Events

**Arts in the Park.** *Shoshone.* Arts and crafts fair. Second weekend in July.

**Lincoln County Fair.** *Shoshone. Phone 208/886-2030.* Third week in July.

**Manty Shaw Fiddlers' Jamboree.** *Shoshone. Phone 208/886-2030.* Second weekend in July.

# Stanley (D-2)

*See also Bellevue, Jerome, Twin Falls*

**Population** 71
**Elevation** 6,260 ft
**Area Code** 208
**Zip** 83278
**Information** Chamber of Commerce, PO Box 8; phone 208/774-3411
**Web Site** www.stanleycc.org

Situated on the Salmon River (the famous "river of no return"), Stanley is located at the center of the Sawtooth Wilderness, Sawtooth Valley, and scenic Stanley Basin. A Ranger District office of the Sawtooth National Forest is located here.

## What to See and Do

**Salmon River.** *Stanley. Phone 208/879-4101.*Rafting, kayaking, fishing; camping.

**River expeditions.** *Hwy 21, Stanley. Phone 208/774-3411.* Many outfitters offer wilderness float trips on the Middle Fork of the Salmon River. Along the river are Native American pictographs, caves, abandoned gold mines, and abundant wildlife. Activities include boating, fishing, hiking, natural hot water springs, and photography. For a list of outfitters contact the Chamber of Commerce or the Idaho Company Outfitters and Guides Association.

**Sawtooth National Recreation Area.** *Ketchum. In Sawtooth National Forest. Phone 208/727-5000.* Fishing, boating, waterskiing; hiking, biking, camping (fee). Many lakes are here, including Stanley, Redfish, and Alturas. Contact Area Ranger, HC 64, Box 8291, Ketchum 83340. In recreation area are

**Redfish Lake Visitor Center.** *Ketchum. 5 miles S on Hwy 75, then 2 miles SW. Phone 208/774-3376.* Historical, geological, naturalist displays and dioramas. Self-guided trails. Campfire programs, guided tours. (Memorial Day-Labor Day, daily) **FREE**

**Sawtooth Wilderness.** *Ketchum. 8 miles N. Phone 208/727-5000.* Many lakes; wilderness hiking, backpacking, and mountain climbing.

**Sawtooth Valley and Stanley Basin.** *Stanley. Phone 208/774-3411.* Fishing; cross-country skiing, snowmobiling, mountain biking, backpacking, hunting. Dude ranches featuring pack trips; big game guides. Contact Chamber of Commerce.

## Special Events

**Sawtooth Mountain Mamas Arts and Crafts Fair.** *Stanley (83278). Phone 208/774-3411; toll-free 800/878-7950. www.stanleycc.org.* The Mountain Mamas are a group of women who coordinate activities that raise money for local causes. This fair is their largest event, and it is also one of the best arts and crafts fairs in the state. Third weekend in July.

**Sawtooth Quilt Festival.** *Stanley (83278). Community Building. Phone 208/774-3411; toll-free 800/878-7950. www.stanleycc.org.* Third weekend in Sept.

## Limited-Service Hotel

**★ ★ MOUNTAIN VILLAGE LODGE.** *Hwy 75 and 21, Stanley (83278). Phone 208/774-3661; fax 208/774-3761. www.mountainvillage.com.* 54 rooms, 2 story. Pets accepted; fee. Check-in 3 pm, check-out 11 am. Restaurant, bar. Airport transportation available. **$**

## Specialty Lodging

**IDAHO ROCKY MOUNTAIN RANCH.** *HC 64, Box 9934, Stanley (83278). Phone 208/774-3544; fax 208/774-3477. www.idahorocky.com.* 21 rooms. Complimentary full breakfast. Check-in 3 pm, check-out 11 am. Restaurant. Outdoor pool. **$**

# Sun Valley Area

*See also Bellevue, Ketchum*

**Elevation** 5,920 ft
**Area Code** 208
**Information** Sun Valley/Ketchum Chamber of Commerce, PO Box 2420, Sun Valley 83353; phone 208/726-3423 or toll-free 800/634-3347

In a sun-drenched, bowl-shaped valley, this is one of the most famous resorts in the world. Developed by the Union Pacific Railroad, this area was established after an extensive survey of the West. Sheltered by surrounding ranges, it attracts both winter and summer visitors and offers nearly every imaginable recreational opportunity. Powder snow lasts until late spring, allowing long skiing seasons, and there is hunting, mountain biking, and superb fly fishing. Two Ranger District offices of the Sawtooth National Forest are located in Ketchum.

## What to See and Do

**Sawtooth National Recreation Area.** *Sun Valley. NW via Hwy 75, in Sawtooth National Forest. Phone 208/727-5000. www.fs.fed.us/r4/sawtooth.* Fishing, boating, water-skiing; hiking, camping (fee). Many lakes are here, including Stanley, Redfish, and Alturas. For more information, contact the Area Ranger, HC 64, Box 8291, Ketchum 83340. In the recreation area on Highway 75 is

**Headquarters Visitor Information Center.** *Hwy 75 and Chocolate Gulch, Sun Valley Area. Phone 208/727-5013.* Orientation exhibits, maps, brochures, interpretive material. Evening programs (summer). Center (daily; schedule may vary). **FREE**

**Sun Valley Resort.** *1 Sun Valley Rd, Sun Valley (83353). Phone 208/622-4111.* Sports director, supervised recreation for children; three outdoor pools (two glass-enclosed), lifeguard; sauna, massage, bowling, indoor and outdoor ice skating, movies, dancing; Sun Valley Center for the Arts and Humanities. For more information, contact Sun Valley Resort.

**Summer.** *Sun Valley.* Three outdoor pools, fishing, boating, whitewater river rafting trips; tennis (school), 18-hole Robert Trent Jones golf course (pro), Olympic ice show, skeet and trap shooting, lawn games, horseback riding (school), mountain biking, hiking, pack trips, hay rides. Auto trips may be arranged to Redfish Lake near Stanley.

**Winter.** *Sun Valley.* Seventeen ski lifts to slopes for every level of skier; ski school, rentals. Longest run 3 miles; vertical drop 3,400 feet. Ice skating, sleigh rides, and groomed cross-country trails. (Thanksgiving-Apr, daily)

## Special Event

**Wagon Days.** *Sun Valley. Phone 208/726-3423.* A celebration of the area's mining history; large, nonmotorized parade, band concerts, entertainment, arts and crafts fair, dramas. Labor Day weekend.

## Full-Service Resort

**★ ★ ★ SUN VALLEY LODGE.** *1 Sun Valley Rd, Sun Valley (83353). Phone 208/622-2001; toll-free 800/786-8259; fax 208/622-2015. www.sunvalley.com.* Everyone from Ernest Hemingway to Clark Gable came to Sun Valley to rusticate in luxury, and the Sun Valley Lodge has been this resort towns shining star since 1936. The guest rooms and suites are decorated in a French country style with oak furnishings and cozy fabrics, and modern amenities make guests feel at home. A heated pool, fitness center, day spa and salon, bowling alley, and game room are among the many features at this property, while Sun Valleys legendary skiing and fishing lure visitors away from the sophisticated confines of the hotel. The Duchin Lounges hot buttered rum hits the spot after a day on

### Wandering the Sun-Drenched Sun Valley Area

Begin a tour of the resort towns of Ketchum and Sun Valley at the Ketchum-Sun Valley Heritage and Ski Museum, in Ketchum's Forest Service Park at 1st Street and Washington Avenue. The museum tells the story of the indigenous Tukudeka tribe, the early mining settlement, and the building of Sun River Resort. There is also information about past and present residents like Ernest Hemingway, Olympic athletes, and the Hollywood glitterati who come here to ski. Walk north along Washington Ave, passing coffee shops and gift boutiques, to the Sun Valley Center for the Arts and Humanities (191 5th St E), the hub of the valley's art world. The center presents exhibits, lectures, and films and is a great place to find out whats going on in Ketchum.

Walk one block east to Main Street. For a city of its size, downtown Ketchum has an enormous number of art galleries, restaurants, and high-end boutiques. It would be easy to spend a day wandering the small town center, looking at art, trying on sheepskin coats, and stopping for lattes. While you wander, be sure to stop at the Chapter One Bookstore (160 Main St), which offers a good selection of regional titles. Charles Stuhlberg Furniture (571 East Ave N) is filled with the faux-rustic New West furniture and accessories popular with the areas upscale residents. For art galleries, go to the corner of Sun Valley Road and Walnut Avenue. The Walnut Avenue Mall (620 Sun Valley Rd) is a boutique development with four independent galleries. Directly across the street is the Colonnade Mill (601 Sun Valley Rd) with four more top-notch galleries.

Continue east on Sun Valley Road, picking up the walking and biking trail north of the road. Follow the trail 1 mile east through forest to the Sun Valley Resort, a massive complex with an imposing central lodge, condominium developments, home tracts, and golf courses. The lodge was built in 1936 by Averill Harriman, chairman of the Union Pacific Railroad, and was modeled after European ski resorts in Switzerland and Austria. Harriman hired an Austrian count to tour the western United States in search of a suitable locale; the count chose the little mining town of Ketchum for the resort.

Wander the interior of the vast lodge, looking at the photos of the celebrities who have skied here. In its heyday, Sun Valley hosted the likes of Lucille Ball, the Kennedys, Gary Cooper, and dozens of other stars of film and politics. Just west of the lodge, easily glimpsed through the windows that look out onto the Bald Mountain ski area, is an outdoor skating rink. Kept frozen even in summer, the rink is usually a-spin with novice ice skaters. On Saturday evenings, professional ice skaters take to the ice to perform.

For a longer hike, return to Sun Valley Road and walking trail and continue east up Trail Creek, past golf courses and meadows. In a mile, the valley narrows. Here, in a grove of cottonwoods overlooking the river, is the Hemingway Memorial, a simple stone bust that commemorates the author, who died in Ketchum in 1961. Etched in the stone are the words Hemingway wrote upon the death of a friend: "Best of all he loved the fall. The leaves yellow on the cottonwoods. Leaves floating on the trout streams. And above the hills the high blue windless skies... now he will be a part of them forever."

the slopes; Gretchens (see) pleases with casual fare; and the Lounge Dining Room is a stand-out with its epicurean delights. 148 rooms, 4 story. Check-in 4 pm, check-out 11 am. Two restaurants, bar. Children's activity center. Fitness room. Outdoor pool, children's pool. Golf, 18 holes. Tennis. Ski in/ski out. Airport transportation available. **$$**

## Restaurants

★ ★ ★ **GRETCHEN'S.** *Sun Valley Rd, Sun Valley (83353). Phone 208/622-2144; fax 208/622-2030. www.sunvalley.com.* After a day on the slopes, guests can relax and unwind at this beautifully decorated restaurant located in the Sun Valley Lodge (see), which has a cozy, country-French atmosphere. Gretchen's serves a variety of specialty salads, pastas, seafood, and poultry. Continental menu. Breakfast, lunch, dinner. Bar. Children's menu. Casual attire. Reservations recommended. Valet parking. Outdoor seating. **$$**

★ ★ **ZOU 75.** *416 N Main, Hailey (83313). Phone 208/788-3310.* Japanese menu. Dinner. Closed Mon. Bar. Children's menu. Business casual attire. Reservations recommended. Valet parking. Outdoor seating. **$$$**

# Twin Falls (F-3)

*See also Buhl, Burley, Jerome, Shoshone*

**Founded** 1904
**Population** 27,591
**Elevation** 3,745 ft
**Area Code** 208
**Zip** 83301
**Information** Chamber of Commerce, 858 Blue Lakes Blvd N; phone 208/733-3974 or toll-free 800/255-8946
**Web Site** www.twinfallschamber.com

After rising "like magic" on the tide of irrigation that reached this valley early in the century, Twin Falls has become the major city of south central Idaho's "Magic Valley" region. Seat of agriculturally rich Twin Falls County, it is also a tourist center, boasting that visitors in the area can enjoy almost every known sport. The headquarters and a Ranger District office of the Sawtooth National Forest are located here.

## What to See and Do

**Fishing.** *Twin Falls.* In the Snake River and numerous other rivers and lakes. Sturgeon of up to 100 pounds may be caught, but by law cannot be removed from the water. The Twin Falls Chamber of Commerce can provide detailed information.

**Herrett Center.** *315 Falls Ave, Twin Falls (83301). On College of Southern Idaho campus. Phone 208/733-9554.* Exhibits on archaeology of North, Central, and South America; gallery of contemporary art; Faulkner Planetarium. (Tues-Sat; closed holidays)

**Perrine Memorial Bridge.** *Twin Falls. 1 1/2 miles N on Hwy 93. Phone 208/733-3974.* Bridge, 486 feet high and 1,500 feet long, crosses the Snake River canyon.

**Sawtooth Twin Falls Ranger District.** *2647 Kimberly Rd, Twin Falls (83301). 9 miles E on Hwy 30 to Hansen, then 28 miles S on local roads, in Sawtooth National Forest. Phone 208/737-3200.* Fishing; camping (fee at some designated campgrounds), picnicking, hiking trails, snowmobile trails, downhill and cross-country skiing.

★ **Shoshone Falls.** *Twin Falls. 5 miles NE, on Snake River.* "Niagara of the West" drops 212 feet (52 feet more than Niagara Falls). During irrigation season, the flow is limited; it is best during spring and fall. Access to the falls is available through

> **Shoshone Falls Park.** *136 Maxwell Ave, Twin Falls (83301). S bank of river. Phone 208/736-2265.* Picnic tables, stoves, fireplace, trails, waterskiing. (Mar-Nov, daily) **$$**

**Twin Falls.** *Twin Falls. 5 1/2 miles NE.* These 132-foot falls are accessible via

**Twin Falls Park.** *3593 Twin Falls Grade, Twin Falls (83301). S bank of river. Phone 208/423-4223.* Boating (dock, ramp), fishing, waterskiing; picnic area. (Daily)

## Special Events

**Twin Falls County Fair and Magic Valley Stampede.** *County Fairgrounds, 215 Fair Ave, Filer (83328). 6 miles W via Hwy 30. Phone 208/326-4396; toll-free 888/865-4398. www.tfcfair.com.* Events at the fair include a PRCA rodeo, destruction derby, and extreme motorcross races. One week starting the Wed before Labor Day.

**Western Days.** *Twin Falls. Phone toll-free 800/255-8946.* Three-day event featuring shoot-out, barbecue contests, dances, parade. Dates may vary, call for schedule; usually the weekend following Memorial Day.

## Limited-Service Hotels

★ **AMERITEL INN TWIN FALLS.** *1377 Blue Lakes Blvd N, Twin Falls (83301). Phone 208/736-8000; toll-free 800/600-6001; fax 208/734-7777. www.ameritelinns.com.* 118 rooms, 3 story. Complimentary continental breakfast. Check-out 11 am. Fitness room. Indoor pool, whirlpool. Airport transportation available. **$**

★★ **RED LION HOTEL CANYON SPRINGS.** *1357 Blue Lakes Blvd N, Twin Falls (83301). Phone 208/734-5000; toll-free 800/733-5466; fax 208/734-3813. www.redlion.com.* 112 rooms, 2 story. Check-out 1 pm. Restaurant, bar. Fitness room. Outdoor pool. Airport transportation available. **$**

★ **SHILO INN.** *1586 Blue Lakes Blvd N, Twin Falls (83301). Phone 208/733-7545; toll-free 800/222-2244; fax 208/736-2019. www.shiloinns.com.* 128 rooms, 4 story. Pets accepted; fee. Complimentary continental breakfast. Check-out noon. Fitness room. Indoor pool, whirlpool. **$**

## Restaurant

★ **JAKER'S.** *1598 Blue Lakes Blvd, Twin Falls (83301). Phone 208/733-8400; fax 208/736-8652. www.jakers.com.* American menu. Lunch, dinner. Bar. Children's menu. Casual attire. Outdoor seating. **$$**

# Wallace (B-2)

*See also Coeur d'Alene, Kellogg*

**Founded** 1884
**Population** 1,010
**Elevation** 2,744 ft
**Area Code** 208
**Zip** 83873
**Information** Chamber of Commerce, 10 River St, PO Box 1167; phone 208/753-7151
**Web Site** www.wallaceidahochamber.com

Gold was discovered in streams near here in 1882; lead, zinc, silver, and copper deposits were found in 1884. A Ranger District office of the Idaho Panhandle National Forests-Coeur d'Alene is located in nearby Silverton.

## What to See and Do

**Auto tour.** *Wallace.* A 15-mile drive through spectacular scenery in Idaho Panhandle National Forests–Coeur d'Alene and St. Joe. Local roads follow Nine Mile Creek, Dobson Pass, and Two Mile Creek to Osburn. This trip may be extended by traveling north and east out of Dobson Pass along Beaver and Trail creeks to Murray, then west to Prichard; then follow Coeur d'Alene River west and south to Kingston; return to Wallace on Highway 10, I-90.

**Lookout Pass Ski Area.** *73888 Lookout Pass Rd, Mullan. 12 miles E on I-90, in Idaho Panhandle National Forests. Phone 208/744-1301. www.skilookout.com.* Chairlift, rope tow; patrol, school, rentals; cafeteria; bar. Longest run 1 mile; vertical drop 850 feet. Half-day rate. Cross-country skiing is also available. Snowmobiling. (Mid-Nov-mid-Apr, Thurs-Sun) **$$$$**

**Northern Pacific Depot Railroad Museum.** *219 6th St, Wallace (83873). Phone 208/752-0111.* (1901) Houses artifacts, photographs, and memorabilia that portray railroad history of the Coeur d'Alene Mining District; display of railroad depot (circa 1910). (May-Oct, hours vary) **$**

**Oasis Bordello Museum.** *605 Cedar St, Wallace (83873). Phone 208/753-0801.* Former bordello (circa 1895); moonshine still. (May-Oct, daily) **$$**

**Sierra Silver Mine Tour.** *420 5th St, Wallace (83873). Phone 208/752-5151.*Offers 1 1/4-hour guided tour through actual silver mine. Demonstrations of mining methods, techniques, and operation of modern-day equipment. Departs every 30 minutes. (May-mid-Oct, daily) **$$$**

**Wallace District Mining Museum.** *509 Bank St, Wallace (83873). Phone 208/556-1592.* Material on the history of mining, 20-minute video, old mining machinery. Information on mine tours and old mining towns in the area. (May-Sept: daily; rest of year: Mon-Sat) **$**

## Limited-Service Hotel

★★ **BEST WESTERN WALLACE INN.** *100 Front St, Wallace (83873). Phone 208/752-1252; toll-free 800/643-2386; fax 208/753-0981. www.bestwestern.com.* 63 rooms, 2 story. Pets accepted; fee. Check-out noon. Restaurant, bar. Fitness room. Indoor pool, whirlpool. **$**

# Weiser (D-1)

*See also Ontario, OR*

**Founded** 1888
**Population** 4,571
**Elevation** 2,117 ft
**Area Code** 208
**Zip** 83672
**Information** Chamber of Commerce, 8 E Idaho St; phone (208) 414-0452 or toll-free 800/437-1280
**Web Site** www.weiserchamber.com

Located at the confluence of the Weiser and Snake rivers, the town of Weiser (WEE-zer) is both a center for tourism for Hells Canyon National Recreation Area to the north and a center for trade and transportation for the vast orchards, onion, wheat, and sugar beet fields of the fertile Weiser Valley to the east. Lumbering, mining, the manufacture of mobile homes, and the raising of cattle also contribute to the town's economy. A Ranger District office of the Payette National Forest is located in Weiser.

## What to See and Do

**Fiddlers' Hall of Fame.** *10 E Idaho St, Weiser (83672). Phone 208/549-0452.* Mementos of past fiddle contests, pictures of champion fiddlers, state winners; collection of old-time fiddles; state scrapbook on view. (Mon-Fri; also weekend during Fiddlers' Contest; closed holidays)

**Hells Canyon National Recreation Area.** *Weiser. Stretching N for 100 miles; access approximately 55 miles NW via Hwy 95 to Cambridge, then via Hwy 71.* Spanning the Idaho/Oregon border, this canyon, the deepest in North America, was created by the Snake River, which rushes nearly 8,000 feet below Seven Devils rim on the Idaho side. Three dams built by the Idaho Power Company have opened up areas that were once inaccessible and created man-made lakes that provide boating, fishing, and water-skiing. Whitewater rafting and jet boat tours are available below the dams, on the Snake River. Also here are

> **Brownlee Dam.** *Weiser.* The southernmost dam of the three, at end of Hwy 71. This 395-foot rockfill dam creates Brownlee Lake, 57 1/2 miles long, reaching to 10 miles north of Weiser. Woodhead Park, a short distance south, and McCormick Park, a short distance north, provide picnicking, boat ramps; tent and trailer sites, showers. **$$$**

> **Hells Canyon Dam.** *Weiser. 23 miles N of Oxbow Dam.* This structure (330 feet high) creates a water recreation area. The improved Deep Creek trail, Idaho side, provides angler and other recreational access to the Snake River below Hells Canyon Dam.

> **Oxbow Dam.** *Weiser. 12 1/2 miles N of Brownlee Dam.* This 205-foot-high barrier makes a 12 1/2-mile-long reservoir. Copperfield Park, just below the dam on the Oregon side, has trailer and tent spaces, showers, and day-use picnicking; 9 miles north of dam on the Idaho side is Hell's Canyon Park, offering boat ramp; tent and trailer sites, showers, picnicking. **$$$**

**Snake River Heritage Center.** *Hooker Hall,2295 Paddock Ave, Weiser (83672). Phone 208/549-0205.* Artifacts and memorabilia portray the history of Snake River Valley. (By appointment only) **$**

**Trips into Hells Canyon.** *Weiser.* Several companies offer river rafting, jet boat, and pack trips into and around Hells Canyon National Recreation Area. For information on additional outfitters, contact the Chamber of Commerce.

> **Hells Canyon Adventures.** *Weiser. Phone 503/785-3352; toll-free 800/422-3568.* Jet boat and whitewater rafting trips down the Snake River. For more information, contact PO Box 159, Oxbow, OR 97840.

> **Hughes River Expeditions.** *95 First St, Cambridge (83610). 26 miles N on Hwy 95. Phone 208/257-3477.* Outfitters for whitewater and fishing trips on backcountry rivers of Idaho and eastern Oregon, including three-, four-, and five-day trips on the Snake River through Hell's Canyon. Advance reservations required. (May-Oct, several dates) **$$$$**

## Special Event

**National Oldtime Fiddlers' Contest.** *Weiser. Phone toll-free 800/437-1280.* One of the oldest such contests in the country, attracting some of the nation's finest fiddlers. Also parade, barbecue, arts and crafts. Mon-Sat, third full week in June.

# Oregon

This is the end of the famous Oregon Trail, over which came scores of pioneers in covered wagons. The state abounds in the romance of the country's westward expansion. Meriwether Lewis and William Clark, sent by President Thomas Jefferson to explore the vast area bought in the Louisiana Purchase, ended their explorations here. This was also the scene of John Jacob Astor's fortune-making fur trade and that of Hudson's Bay Company, which hoped to keep the area for England, as well as gold rushes and the traffic of stately clippers of the China trade.

**Population:** 3,421,399

**Area:** 97,073 square miles

**Elevation:** 0-11,235 feet

**Peak:** Mount Hood (between Clackamas and Hood River counties)

**Entered Union:** February 14, 1859 (33rd state)

**Capital:** Salem

**Motto:** She Flies with Her Own Wings

**Nickname:** Beaver State

**Flower:** Oregon Grape

**Bird:** Western Meadowlark

**Tree:** Douglas Fir

**Fair:** August-September in Salem

**Time Zone:** Mountain and Pacific

**Web Site:** www.traveloregon.com

**Fun Facts:**

- At 1,932 feet, Crater Lake is the deepest lake in the United States.
- Oregon has more ghost towns than any other state.

English Captain James Cook saw the coast in 1778. Others had seen it before him and others after him, but it remained for Lewis and Clark to discover what a prize Oregon was. On their return to St. Louis in 1806, they spread the word. In 1811, Astor's Pacific Fur Company built its post at Astoria, only to be frightened into selling to the British North West Company during the War of 1812. (In 1818, it again became US territory.) Other fur traders, missionaries, salmon fishermen, and travelers followed them, but the Oregon country was far away and hard to reach. The first true settlers did not make their way there until 1839, four years before a great wagon train blazed the Oregon Trail.

Cattle and sheep were driven up from California and land was cleared for farms. Oregon was settled not by people hungry for gold but by pioneers looking for good land that could support them. The Native Americans resented the early settlers and fought them until 1880. The Oregon Territory, established in 1848, received a flood of immigrants; they continued to arrive after statehood was proclaimed under President James Buchanan 11 years later.

The rich forests grew rapidly in the moist climate west of the mountains called the Cascades, and lumber was an early product of this frontier. The streams were full of fish, the woods offered nuts and berries, and the lush, green scenery lifted hearts and hopes at the end of the weary journey. The rivers—Columbia, Willamette, Rogue, and many others—offered transportation to the sea. Steamboats plied the Willamette and Columbia as early as 1850. The first full ship's cargo of wheat went from Portland to Liverpool in 1868, and when the railroad reached Portland in 1883, the world began receiving the fish, grain, lumber, and livestock that Oregon was ready to deliver.

Vast rivers provide more than transportation. Dammed, they are the source of abundant electric power and water to irrigate farms east of the Cascades. Timber is still important; a quarter of

## Calendar Highlights

### MAY

**Boatnik Festival** *(Grants Pass). Riverside Park. Phone toll-free 800/547-5927.* Parade, concessions, carnival rides, boat races, and entertainment. A 25-mile whitewater hydroboat race from Riverside Park to Hellgate Canyon and back. Square dance festival at Josephine County Fairgrounds.

### JUNE

**Bach Festival** *(Eugene). Phone toll-free 800/457-1486; www.bachfest.uoregon.edu.* Numerous concerts by regional and international artists; master classes; family activities.

**Portland Rose Festival** *(Portland). Phone 503/227-2681; www.rosefestival.org.* Held for more than 90 years, this festival includes the Grand Floral Parade (reservations required for indoor parade seats) and two other parades; band competition; rose show; championship auto racing; hotair balloons; air show; carnival; Navy ships.

**Return of the Sternwheeler Days** *(Hood River). Phone 541/374-8619.* Celebration of the sternwheeler Columbia Gorge's return to home port for the summer. Wine and cheese tasting, crafts, food.

**Sandcastle Contest** *(Cannon Beach). Phone 503/436-2623.* Nationally known event features sand sculptures on beach.

**Scandinavian Midsummer Festival** *(Astoria). Astoria Warrenton Chamber of Commerce, phone 503/325-6311.* Parade, folk dancing, display booths, arts and crafts demonstrations, Scandinavian food.

### JULY

**Da Vinci Days** *(Corvallis). Phone 541/757-6363.* Festival celebrating the relationship between art, science, and technology.

**Oregon Coast Music Festival** *(Coos Bay). Phone toll-free 877/897-9350.* Variety of musical presentations ranging from jazz and dance to chamber and symphonic music.

**Salem Art Fair & Festival** *(Salem). Bush's Pasture Park. Phone 503/581-2228.* Arts and crafts booths and demonstrations, children's art activities and parade, ethnic folk arts, performing arts, street painting, 5K run, food; tours of historic Bush House.

### AUGUST

**Oregon State Fair** *(Salem). Fairgrounds. Phone 503/378-FAIR.* Horse racing, wine competition and tastings, agricultural exhibits, horse show, livestock, food, carnival, entertainment.

### SEPTEMBER

**Pendleton Round-Up** *(Pendleton). Stadium. Phone toll-free 800/457-6336.* Rodeo and pageantry of the Old West, held annually since 1910. Gathering of Native Americans, PRCA working cowboys, and thousands of visitors.

Oregon is national forest land. Sustained yield practices by the big lumber companies ensure a continuing supply.

One of the most beautiful drives in Oregon extends from Portland (see) to The Dalles (see) along the Columbia River. Here is the spectacular Columbia Gorge, designated a National Scenic Area, where waterfalls, streams, and mountains abound. The area offers many recreational activities such as camping—the Cascade Locks Marina Park lies 4 miles east of the Bonneville Dam (see also HOOD RIVER), skiing (see also MOUNT HOOD NATIONAL FOREST), snowmobiling, windsurfing, and hiking.

Whether your taste is for an ocean beach, a ski slope, a mountain lake, or ranch life with riding and rodeos, the visitor who loves the outdoors or the American West loves Oregon. Each year, millions of tourists enjoy the state's magnificent coastline, blue lakes, mountains, and forests.

## When to Go/Climate

Temperatures along the Pacific coast are mild, while Portland and the Willamette Valley experience more extreme weather conditions. Heavy snow falls in the Cascades, and to the east there's a high desert area that experiences typical desert heat and dry conditions.

### AVERAGE HIGH/LOW TEMPERATURES (°F)

**Burns**

| | | |
|---|---|---|
| **Jan** 34/13 | **May** 66/36 | **Sep** 74/36 |
| **Feb** 40/19 | **Jun** 74/42 | **Oct** 62/28 |
| **Mar** 48/25 | **Jul** 85/47 | **Nov** 45/22 |
| **Apr** 57/29 | **Aug** 83/45 | **Dec** 35/15 |

**Portland**

| | | |
|---|---|---|
| **Jan** 45/34 | **May** 67/47 | **Sep** 75/52 |
| **Feb** 51/36 | **Jun** 74/53 | **Oct** 64/45 |
| **Mar** 56/39 | **Jul** 80/57 | **Nov** 53/40 |
| **Apr** 61/41 | **Aug** 80/57 | **Dec** 46/35 |

## Parks and Recreation

Water-related activities, hiking, riding, various other sports, picnicking, and visitor centers, as well as camping, are available in many of Oregon's state parks. Many camping facilities in these parks stay open year-round, while others remain open as long as the weather permits, usually March through October. All campgrounds are open from mid-April to late October. Campers are limited to ten days in any 14-day period from May 15 to September 14, and 14 days out of 18 the rest of the year. Discount rates are available at most campgrounds from October to April. Fees per night are as follows: primitive campsites $4-$6; tent sites $10-$13; electrical sites $12-$17; full hookup sites $12-$18; extra vehicle $5-$7. Firewood is available. Campsites may be reserved at 25 state parks throughout the year with a $6 fee plus the first night's camping rate. A day-use fee of $3 is charged for each motor vehicle entering 24 state parks. For more information, contact the Oregon Parks and Recreation Department, 725 Summer St, Suite C, Salem 97301; phone 503/378-6305 or toll-free 800/551-6949; www.oregon-stateparks.org. For campsite reservations, phone toll-free 800/452-5687.

### FISHING AND HUNTING

Oregon has 15,000 miles of streams, hundreds of lakes, and surf and deep-sea fishing. Fishing is good for Chinook and coho salmon, steelhead, rainbow and cutthroat trout, striped bass, perch, crappie, bluegill, catfish, and many other varieties. Hunters will find mule and black-tailed deer, elk, ring-necked pheasant, Hungarian and chukar partridge, quail, blue and ruffed grouse, band-tailed pigeons, mourning doves, waterfowl, jackrabbits, coyotes, foxes, and bears.

Nonresident fishing license, annual $61.50; seven-day license $43.75; combined angling harvest tag, $21.50; one-day license, $12. Nonresident hunting license, annual $76.50. Special tags are required in addition to a license for big game. All licenses include an agent-writing fee.

For synopses of the latest angling and big-game regulations, contact Oregon Department of Fish and Wildlife, PO Box 59, Portland 97207; phone 503/872-5268; www.dfw.state.or.us.

## Driving Information

Safety belts are mandatory for all persons anywhere in a vehicle. Children under age 4 (or 40 pounds in weight) must use approved safety seats anywhere in a vehicle. For more information, phone 503/986-4190 or toll-free 800/922-2022 (in Oregon).

### INTERSTATE HIGHWAY SYSTEM

The following alphabetical listing of Oregon towns in this book shows that these cities are within 10 miles of the indicated interstate highways. Check a highway map for the nearest exit.

| Highway Number | Cities/Towns within 10 Miles |
|---|---|
| Interstate 5 | Albany, Ashland, Beaverton, Corvallis, Cottage Grove, Eugene, Grants Pass, Jacksonville, Medford, Oregon City, Portland, Roseburg, Salem. |
| Interstate 84 | Baker City, Beaverton, Biggs, Hermiston, Hood River, La Grande, Ontario, Oregon City, Pendleton, Portland, The Dalles, Umatilla. |

## Additional Visitor Information

The Oregon Tourism Commission, 775 Summer St NE, Salem 97301 (phone toll-free 800/547-7842; www.traveloregon.com) will provide visitors with an Oregon travel guide and other informative brochures upon request.

There are nine staffed state welcome centers in Oregon (April-October): Astoria (downtown); Brookings (OR-CA border, S on Hwy 101); Lakeview (downtown); Siskiyou (OR-CA border, S on I-5); Ontario (OR-ID border, E on I-84); Seaside (at the Chamber of Commerce on Hwy 101); Umatilla (on Brownell Blvd); Jantzen Beach-Portland (I-5, exit 308); and Klamath Falls (OR-CA border, S on Hwy 97).

# Albany

*See also Corvallis, Salem, Sweet Home*

**Founded** 1848
**Population** 29,462
**Elevation** 212 ft
**Area Code** 541
**Zip** 97321
**Information** Visitors Convention & Association, 300 SW 2nd Ave, PO Box 965; phone 541/928-0911 or toll-free 800/526-2256
**Web Site** www.albanyvisitors.com

The gateway to Oregon's covered bridge country, Albany was founded by Walter and Thomas Monteith and named for their former home, Albany, New York. The city boasts the state's largest collection of Victorian homes. The seat of Linn County, Albany is nestled in the heart of the Willamette Valley along the I-5 corridor of the Cascades. The Calapooia River joins the Willamette here.

## What to See and Do

**Flinn's Heritage Tours.** *222 First Ave W, Albany (97321). Phone 541/928-5008; toll-free 800/636-5008.* Twenty different narrated tours take visitors through historic areas in the Mid Willamette Valley. Tours range from 45 minutes to 6 hours and feature the covered bridges of Linn County, Albany's three historic districts, ghost towns, a 100-year-old apple orchard, and historic homes. (Daily; closed Dec 25) **$$$$**

## Special Events

**Historic Interior Homes Tours.** *300 2nd Ave SW, Albany (97321). Phone 541/928-0911; toll-free 800/526-2256.* Summer and late Dec.

**Veteran's Day Parade.** *626 Harrison St, Albany (97321). Phone 541/258-2873.* One of the nation's largest. Mid-Nov.

## Limited-Service Hotel

**★ LA QUINTA INN.** *251 Airport Rd SE, Albany (97321). Phone 541/928-0921; fax 541/928-8055. www.lq.com.* 62 rooms, 2 story. Pets accepted, some restrictions. Complimentary continental breakfast. Check-out 1 pm. Fitness room. Indoor pool, whirlpool. **$**

# Ashland (E-2)

*See also Jacksonville, Medford*

**Founded** 1852
**Population** 16,234
**Elevation** 1,951 ft
**Area Code** 541
**Zip** 97520
**Information** Chamber of Commerce, 110 E Main St, PO Box 1360; phone 541/482-3486
**Web Site** www.ashlandchamber.com

When the pioneers climbed over the Siskiyou Mountains and saw the green expanse of the Rogue River Valley ahead of them, many decided to go no further and settled here. Later, when mineral springs were found, their Lithia water was piped in; it now gushes from fountains on this city's plaza. Tourism, education, and small industry support the town. Southern Oregon University College (1926) makes Ashland a regional education center. The Rogue River National Forest is on three sides; a Ranger District office is located here.

## What to See and Do

**Lithia Park.** *E Main St and Winburn Way, Ashland (97520). Adjacent to City Plaza. Phone 541/488-5340.* Has 100 acres of woodlands and ponds. Nature trails, tennis, picnicking, sand volleyball. Rose and Japanese gardens. Concerts. (Daily) **FREE**

**Mount Ashland Ski Area.** *Ashland. 8 miles S on I-5, then 9 miles W on access road. Phone 541/482-2897. www.*

## THE COLUMBIA RIVER HIGHWAY AND BEYOND

The magnificent canyon of the Columbia River slices through the spine of the Cascade Range just east of Portland. The Columbia, over a mile wide, winds through a 3,000-foot-deep gorge flanked by volcanic peaks and austere bands of basalt. The gorge contains one of the greatest concentrations of waterfalls in North America–chutes of water tumble from its edge to fall hundreds of feet to the river.

Begin in Portland, driving east on I-84. As the walls of the river canyon rise in the distance, take exit 22 and climb up the forested valley to join Highway 30, the Historic Columbia River Highway, atop the gorge wall. Modeled on European mountain roads, the Columbia River Highway was built in the 1910s as a scenic automobile route through the Gorge–quite an engineering feat at that time.

Famous as the western entry to the Gorge, Crown Point is a viewpoint and interpretive center atop a craggy 800-foot-high point of basalt. To the east, as far as the eye can see, the Columbia River unfurls between green cliffs. The famed Columbia Gorge waterfalls start almost immediately. Latourell Falls is the first major falls, a chute of water dropping 249 feet into a misty pool. To see churning Bridal Veil Falls requires a mile round-trip walk through deep forest and odd rock formations. Hike up the trail at Wahkeena Falls to see why it is named after an Indian term meaning "the most beautiful."

Half a mile east of Oneonta Gorge is Horsetail Falls, which drops out of a notch in the rock to fall 176 feet. While the waterfall is easily seen from the turnout along Highway 30, hikers should consider the 3-mile Horsetail-Oneonta Loop Trail, an easy hike that takes in another waterfall and the narrow Oneonta chasm.

From there, continue east on Highway 30, rejoining I-84 at Dodson. Built in 1937 at the height of the Depression, Bonneville Dam was one of the largest of the New Deal projects and was the first major hydropower dam on the Columbia. The visitor center, at exit 40, has a good collection of Native American artifacts, as well as exhibits about the building of the dam. From the lower floors of the visitor center, you can watch through underwater windows as fish negotiate the dam's fish ladders. Walk to the Bonneville Fish Hatchery, where salmon and sturgeon are reared to restock the Columbia River. Nearby, the Columbia River Sternwheeler offers cruises through the Columbia River Gorge departing from Cascade Locks Marine Park.

Continue on I-84 to Hood River, an old orchard town on the Columbia River that has found new life as a world capital of windsurfing. From Hood River, turn south on Highway 35. As you climb out of the Gorge, Mount Hood–Oregon's highest peak at 11,240 feetfills the skyline, a slim white incisor towering above a valley filled with apple, pear, and cherry orchards. As the orchards thin, Highway 35 winds up around the base of Mount Hood, through fir forests and along rushing streams. At Government Camp, turn north into Timberline Lodge and climb 6 steep miles to 6,000 feet. Here, at the foot of soaring Mount Hood, sits one of the unquestioned masterpieces of WPA-funded Depression-era public works, Timberline Lodge (phone 503/272-3311). The interior of this 43,700-square-foot lodge is spectacular: the central stone fireplace rises 92 feet through three open stories of lobby. The third floor bar and café is a wonderful place to take in the inspiring handiwork that created this architectural gem.

The ski lifts at Timberline operate almost all year, so strap on skis or a snowboard and head to the lifts. Hiking trails lead out from the lodge in almost all directions. For food, check out the Blue Ox Pub, tucked away in a cavernlike corner, or splurge at the wood-beamed Cascade Dining Room.

Return to Highway 30, and continue west to the Portland suburbs. **(Approximately 75 miles)**

## DRIVING OREGON'S CENTRAL COAST

Oregon's central coast has some of the state's most dramatic scenery, with volcanic mountains dropping into the pounding Pacific surf. Along this route, you'll encounter many enchanting small towns, as well as an excellent aquarium and a sand dune recreation area.

Begin in Newport, Oregon's second-largest commercial port. Dominated by the high-arching Yaquina Bay Bridge, old downtown Newport is still a very lively seafront, complete with seafood markets, the smells of a working port, and the bark of seals. Bay Boulevard is lined with fish-processing plants on one side, chandlers, fish restaurants, art galleries, and brew pubs on the other. A number of ship owners offer boat excursions around Yaquina Bay and trips out into the Pacific to view whales.

Besides Newport's mile-long beaches, the city's biggest draw is the Oregon Coast Aquarium. Exhibits are grouped by ecosystem with interactive displays to explain the dynamics of the various forms of life found there. Outside, trails lead around natural-looking enclosures for seals, sea lions, and sea otters; the seabird aviary includes puffins and murres.

Drive south along Highway 101 to Seal Rock State Park, where a massive hump of rock protects a beach and tide pools, making this a good place for young children to explore the coast. Waldport is a quiet town on the mouth of the Alsea River with an unusual museum of transport. Travel along Oregon's rugged coast was not always simple, as The Alsea Bay Bridge Historical Interpretive Center makes evident. The facility traces the history of transportation routes along the coast, beginning with trails used by Native Americans and moving on to the sea, rail, and road routes now in use. From Waldport south to Yachats (pronounced Ya-HOTS) are more wide sandy beaches, easily accessed at state park access points.

Some of Oregon's most spectacular shoreline begins at Yachats and continues south about 20 miles. This entire area was once a series of volcanic intrusions, which resisted the pummeling of the Pacific long enough to rise as oceanside peaks and promontories. Tiny beaches lined by cliffs seem almost serendipitous; acres of tide pools appear and disappear according to the fancy of the tides and are home to starfish, sea anemones, and sea lions. Picturesque lighthouses rise above the surf.

Cape Perpetua, 2 miles south of Yachats, was first sited and named by England's Captain James Cook in 1778. This volcanic remnant is one of the highest points on the Oregon coast. Views from the cape are incredible, taking in coastal promontories from Cape Foulweather to Cape Arago. Deep fractures in the old volcano allow waves to erode narrow channels into the headland, creating the compelling Devils Churn. Waves race up a deep trench between basalt ledges, then shoot up the 30-foot inlet only to explode against the narrow sides of the channel. From the base of the Devils Churn trail, turn south to explore acres of tide pools.

To continue, follow Highway 101 south. Stop at Devils Elbow State Park and the Heceata Head Lighthouse, complete with an 1893 lighthouse keeper's house. From here, the road tunnels through mountains and edges along cliffs to reach Sea Lion Caves, an enormous natural sea grotto filled with smelly, shrieking sea lions. A 208-foot elevator drops down a small natural shaft that opens onto the larger grotto. From this observation point 50 feet above the surging waves, watch Steller's sea lions clambering onto rocks, jockeying for position at the top of ledges, and letting loose with mighty roars.

From the Sea Lion Caves, Highway 101 drops down from the volcanic peaks to a broad sandy plain fronted by extensive beaches preserved in state parks. Florence is an old fishing port that boomed in the 1890s. Detour from the unlovely Highway 101 strip to Old Town Florence, the historic port area on the Siuslaw River. The towns small fishing fleet ties at the base of restored Victorian storefronts, now filled with restaurants, coffee shops, and galleries.

From Florence southward to Reedsport is the Oregon Dunes National Recreation Area. These massive dunes front the Pacific Ocean but undulate east as much as 3 miles to meet coastal forests, with a succession of curious ecosystems and formations between. A number of hiking trails, bridle paths, and boating and swimming areas have been established throughout this unique place, and the entire region is noted for its abundant wildlife, especially birds.

Reedsport, once an important fishing and log milling town, is home to the Umpqua Lighthouse State Park. The still-operating lighthouse was built in 1894 and is open for tours. Directly opposite the lighthouse is a whale-watching platform, with displays that explain various whale species and their habits. **(Approximately 75 miles)** *mtashland.com.* Area has two triple, two double chairlifts; patrol, school, rentals; cafeteria, bar. Longest run 1 mile; vertical drop 1,150 feet. (Thanksgiving-Apr)

## Special Events

**Oregon Cabaret Theatre.** *241 Hargadine St, Ashland (97520). 1st and Hargadine sts. Phone 541/488-2902.* Musicals, revues, and comedies in dinner club setting. Schedule varies. Feb-Dec.

**Oregon Shakespeare Festival.** *15 S Pioneer St, Ashland (97520). Phone 541/482-4331.* You wouldn't expect to find world-class theater productions in a quiet town of 20,000 people, but that's exactly what you get with the Oregon Shakespeare Festival (OSF). From its humble beginnings with a 1935 staging of *Twelfth Night,* this repertory theater has evolved in size and scope, earning a reputation for consistently excellent productions and making Ashland a must-stop destination for drama lovers. *Time* magazine recognized OSF in 2003, heralding the company as one of the five best regional theaters in the United States. The name is something of a misnomer, as Shakespeare's plays, though featured prominently, are not the only offerings here. Running from February to early November, the 2003 season featured four Shakespeare productions, including *A Midsummer Night's Dream* and *Romeo and Juliet,* while seven works from other playwrights also were staged, ranging from the Ibsen classic *Hedda Gabler* to August Wilson's modern masterpiece, *The Piano Lesson.* OSF actually consists of three separate theaters: the intimate New Theatre, the versatile Angus Bowmer Theatre, and the open-air Elizabethan Stage, which is fashioned after the Bard's legendary Globe Theatre. Feb-early Nov.

## Limited-Service Hotels

**★ ★ ASHLAND SPRINGS HOTEL.** *212 E Main St, Ashland (97520). Phone 541/488-1700; toll-free 888/795-4545; fax 541/488-0240. www.ashlandspringshotel.com.* With a stately exterior that employs gothic and Beaux Arts architectural elements, the nine-story Ashland Springs Hotel towers impressively over the intersection at Main and 1st streets. The elegant hotel serves as the perfect home base for exploring the Rogue River Valley. Listed on the National Register of Historic Places, the hotel has been a southern Oregon landmark since opening its doors as the Lithia Hotel in 1925. After years of ups and downs, the hotel was closed and abandoned in 1997, only to be exhaustively renovated a few years later and reopened as the Ashland Springs Hotel. The hotel now includes modern amenities, but it retains many original details, including six chandeliers in the ballroom and the original stained glass that bears the LH crest. 70 rooms. Complimentary continental breakfast. Check-in 3 pm, check-out 11 am. High-speed Internet access. Restaurant, bar. **$**

**★ BEST WESTERN BARD'S INN.** *132 N Main St, Ashland (97520). Phone 541/482-0049; toll-free 800/528-1234; fax 541/488-3259. www.bestwestern.com.* Near Shakespeare Festival theater. 91 rooms, 3 story. Pets accepted; fee. Complimentary continental breakfast. Check-in 3 pm, check-out 11 am. Outdoor pool, whirlpool. **$**

**★ STRATFORD INN.** *555 Siskiyou Blvd, Ashland (97520). Phone 541/488-2151; toll-free 800/547-4741; fax 541/482-0479. www.stratordinnashland.com.* 55 rooms, 3 story. Complimentary continental breakfast. Check-out 11 am. Indoor pool, whirlpool. **$**

**★ ★ WINDMILL INN AND SUITES OF ASHLAND.** *2525 Ashland St, Ashland (97520). Phone 541/482-8310; toll-free 800/547-4747; fax 541/488-1783. www.windmillinns.com.* Easily accessible from Interstate 5, this downtown hotel features a hair salon, lending library, and bikes available for guests to enjoy.230 rooms, 3 story. Pets accepted. Complimentary continental breakfast. Check-out 11 am. Restaurant, bar. Fitness room. Outdoor pool, whirlpool. Tennis. Airport transportation available. **$**

## Full-Service Inns

**★ ★ ★ MT. ASHLAND INN.** *550 Mt. Ashland Rd, Ashland (97520). Phone 541/482-8707; toll-free 800/830-8707. www.mtashlandinn.com.* With slopes and cliffs on one side and the mountain ranges on the other, guests are guaranteed a breathtaking view no matter where they look. Whatever the season, guests will enjoy such activities as hiking, skiing, rafting, sledding, and fishing. A truly exciting getaway. 5 rooms, 4 story. Children over 10 years only. Complimentary full breakfast. Check-in 3-5 pm, check-out 11 am. **$$**

**★ ★ ★ THE WINCHESTER INN & RESTAURANT.** *35 S Second St, Ashland (97520). Phone 541/488-1113; toll-free 800/972-4991; fax 541/488-4604. www.winchesterinn.com.* Located just one block from downtown Ashland, this restored Victorian house once served as the area's first hospital. 18

rooms, 3 story. Complimentary full breakfast. Check-in 3 pm, check-out 11 am. Restaurant. **$$**

## Specialty Lodgings

**CHANTICLEER INN.** *120 Gresham St, Ashland (97520). Phone 541/482-1919; toll-free 800/898-1950; fax 541/488-4810. www.ashlandbnb.com.* This inn is convenient to many area attractions such as the Shakespeare Festival, Cascade volcanoes, and the Oregon Caves. Antiques, fine art, and a beautifully manicured garden welcome guests for a romantic getaway. 6 rooms, 3 story. Complimentary full breakfast. Check-in 3-6 pm, check-out 11 am. Wireless Internet access. **$$**

**COUNTRY WILLOWS BED & BREAKFAST INN.** *1313 Clay St, Ashland (97520). Phone 541/488-1590; toll-free 800/945-5697; fax 541/488-1611. www.countrywillowsinn.com.* This restored 1890s farmhouse is surrounded by 5 acres of farmland in the Siskiyou and Cascade Mountain Ranges. Breakfast is served every morning at your own private table. 9 rooms, 2 story. Children over 12 years only. Complimentary full breakfast. Check-in 3-5 pm, check-out 11 am. High-speed Internet access. Outdoor pool, whirlpool. **$$**

**OAK HILL BED & BREAKFAST.** *2190 Siskiyou Blvd, Ashland (97520). Phone toll-free 888/482-1554; fax 541/482-1378. www.oakhillbb.com.*6 rooms, 2 story. Children over 12 years only. Complimentary full breakfast. Check-in 3-6 pm, check-out 11 am. **$**

**ROMEO INN BED & BREAKFAST.** *295 Idaho St, Ashland (97520). Phone 541/488-0884; toll-free 800/915-8899; fax 541/488-0817. www.romeoinn.com.* Established in 1982, this property has all the amenities to help guests relax and enjoy their time away from the hustle and bustle of life. Whether your idea of relaxing is swinging in the hammock amid the garden, unwinding in the jacuzzi, or swimming in the pool, this bed-and-breakfast has it all. 6 rooms, 2 story. Children over 12 years only. Complimentary full breakfast. Check-in 3-6 pm, check-out 11 am. Outdoor pool, whirlpool. **$**

## Restaurants

**★ ASHLAND BAKERY & CAFE.** *38 E Main St, Ashland (97520). Phone 541/482-2117.* American menu. Breakfast, lunch, dinner. Closed Tues in winter. Children's menu. Casual attire. **$**

**★★ CHATEAULIN.** *50 E Main St, Ashland (97520). Phone 541/482-2264. www.chateaulin.com.* French menu. Dinner. Closed Mon-Tues in winter. Bar. Business casual attire. Reservations recommended. **$$$**

**★★ LELA'S BAKERY.** *258 A St, #3, Ashland (97520). Phone 541/482-1702. www.lelascafe.com.* Italian menu. Lunch, dinner. Closed Sun-Mon. Business casual attire. Reservations recommended. **$$**

**★ MACARONI'S.** *58 E Main St, Ashland (97520). Phone 541/488-3359.* Italian menu. Lunch, dinner. Bar. Casual attire. Outdoor seating. **$$**

**★★ WINCHESTER COUNTRY INN.** *35 S Second St, Ashland (97520). Phone 541/488-1113; toll-free 800/972-4991; fax 541/488-4604. www.winchesterinn.com.* International menu. Dinner, brunch. Closed Jan; also Sun-Mon in Feb-Mar. Bar. Business casual attire. Reservations recommended. Outdoor seating. Built in 1886. **$$**

# Astoria (A-1)

*See also Cannon Beach, Fort Clatsop National Memorial, Seaside*

**Settled** 1811
**Population** 10,069
**Elevation** 18 ft
**Area Code** 503
**Zip** 97103
**Information** Astoria-Warrenton Chamber of Commerce, 111 W Marine Dr, PO Box 176; phone 503/325-6311 or toll-free 800/875-6807
**Web Site** www.oldoregon.com

John Jacob Astor's partners sailed around Cape Horn and picked this point of land 10 miles from the Pacific, overlooking the mouth of the Columbia River, for a fur-trading post. The post eventually lost its importance, but the location and natural resources attracted immigrants, and the town continued to grow. A 4-mile-long bridge crosses the mouth of the Columbia here.

## What to See and Do

**Astoria Column.** *Astoria. Follow scenic drive signs to Coxcomb Hill. Phone 503/325-7275.* (1926) A 125-foot tower commemorates first settlement; observation deck at top. Gift shop. (Daily) Information booth (Memorial Day-Labor Day, daily). **FREE**

**Columbia River Maritime Museum.** *1792 Marine Dr, Astoria (97103). Phone 503/325-2323. www.crmm.org.* Rare maritime artifacts and memorabilia of the Columbia River, its tributaries, and the Northwest coast. *Columbia,* Lightship 604 at moorage in Maritime Park. Fishing industry, discovery and exploration, steamship, shipwreck, navigation, and steamboat exhibits. Coast Guard and Navy exhibits. (Daily 9:30 am-5 pm; closed Thanksgiving, Dec 25) **$$**

**Flavel House.** *441 8th St, Astoria (97103). Phone 503/325-2203. www.oldoregon.com/pages/flavel.htm.* (1883-1887) Built by Captain George Flavel, pilot and shipping man; an outstanding example of Queen Anne architecture. The restored Victorian home houses antique furnishings and fine art, along with a collection of 19th- and 20th-century toys. Carriage house, museum store, orientation film. (Daily 10 am-5 pm; closed holidays) **$$**

★ **Fort Clatsop National Memorial.** *Astoria. 6 miles SW on Hwy 101A. www.nps.gov/focl/.* (see).

**Fort Stevens State Park.** *Astoria. 5 miles W on Hwy 101, then 5 miles N on Ridge Rd. Phone 503/861-1671.* A 3,763-acre park adjacent to old Civil War fort. Wreck of the *Peter Iredale* (1906) is on the ocean shore. Fort Stevens is the only military post in the lower 48 states to be fired upon by foreign forces since 1812. On June 21, 1942, a Japanese submarine fired several shells from its 5-inch gun; only one hit land while the others fell short. Visitor center and self-guided tour at the Old Fort Stevens Military Complex. Ocean beach, lake swimming, fishing, clamming on beach, boating (dock, ramp); bicycling, picnicking at Coffenbury Lake. Improved tent and trailer sites (daily; standard fees, dump station).

## Special Events

**Astoria Regatta.** *1609 E Habor Dr, Astoria (97146). Phone 503/325-2353.* Parade, arts festival, public dinner, barbecue, boating competition. Mid-Aug.

**Astoria-Warrenton Crab and Seafood Festival.** *1090 1st Ave, Hammond (97121). Phone 503/325-6311.* Hammond Mooring Basin on Columbia River. Crab feast, Oregon wines, food and craft booths. Carnival, water taxi, crabbing and fishing boats. Last weekend in Apr.

**Great Columbia Crossing Bridge Run.** *Port of Astoria, 1 Portway, Astoria (97103). Phone 503/325-6311.* One of the most unusual and scenic runs; 8 mile course begins at Chinook, WA, and ends at Astoria port docks. Mid-Oct.

**Scandinavian Midsummer Festival.** *Astoria. Phone 503/325-4600.* Parade, folk dancing, display booths, arts and crafts demonstrations, Scandinavian food. Mid-June.

## Limited-Service Hotels

★ **BEST WESTERN LINCOLN INN.** *555 Hamburg Ave, Astoria (97103). Phone 503/325-2205; toll-free 800/621-0641; fax 503/325-5550. www.bestwestern.com.* 76 rooms, 4 story. Pets accepted; fee. Complimentary continental breakfast. Check-in 3 pm, check-out 11 am. High-speed Internet access. Indoor pool, whirlpool. **$**

★★ **RED LION.** *400 Industry St, Astoria (97103). Phone 503/325-7373; fax 503/325-8727. www.redlion.com.* 124 rooms, 2 story. Pets accepted; fee. Check-out noon. Restaurant, bar. Airport transportation available. Overlooks harbor; on Columbia River. **$**

★★ **SHILO INN.** *1609 E Harbor Dr, Warrenton (97146). Phone 503/861-2181; toll-free 800/222-2244; fax 503/861-2980. www.shiloinns.com.* 63 rooms, 4 story. Pets accepted, some restrictions; fee. Check-out noon. Restaurant, bar. Fitness room. Indoor pool, whirlpool. Airport transportation available. **$**

## Specialty Lodging

**ROSEBRIAR HOTEL.** *636 14th St, Astoria (97103). Phone 503/325-7427; toll-free 800/487-0224; fax 503/325-6937. www.rosebriar.net.* Built in 1902 as a residence; was also used as a convent. 10 rooms, 2 story. Complimentary full breakfast. Check-in 3 pm, check-out 11 am.

## Restaurants

★★ **SHIP INN.** *1 2nd St, Astoria (97103). Phone 503/325-0033.* Seafood menu. Lunch, dinner. Closed holidays. Bar. **$$**

★★ **SILVER SALMON GRILLE.** *1105 Commercial St, Astoria (97103). Phone 503/338-6640. www.silversalmongrille.com.* Located on the beautiful Oregon coast in a 1924 commercial building with a renovated interior and featuring an abundance of regional specialties. American, seafood menu. Lunch, dinner. **$$**

★★ **T. PAUL'S URBAN CAFE.** *1119 Commercial St, Astoria (97103). Phone 503/338-5133. www.*

## Sleepy Astoria

The oldest American settlement in the Pacific Northwest, Astoria was founded as a fur-trading fort in 1811. Thereafter, thanks to its fortuitous location at the mouth of the mighty Columbia River, the town became a prosperous shipping and fishing port. During the 1880s, sea captains and other captains of industry built magnificent homes overlooking the Columbia River. Astoria contains some of the most lovingly restored and precipitously poised Victorian homes outside of San Francisco.

Begin a walking tour of Astoria at the Columbia River Maritime Museum (1792 Marine Dr), a modern 25,000-square-foot facility that tells the story of the city's two centuries of seafaring history. The galleries explore Astoria's maritime past with exhibits on the salmon-packing industry, local lighthouses, the evolution of boat design, and delicate ivory scrimshaw work. There is also a creepy display on harpoons.

From the museum, follow Highway 30/Marine Drive to the west, and turn south on 16th Street. Housed in the former City Hall building, the Astoria Heritage Museum (1618 Exchange St) contains a commemoration of Astoria's fishing past, as well as an exhibit dedicated to the various ethnic communities that came together to form the city; take note of the Tong shrine. Another room is dedicated to the Clatsop Indians and the early days of exploration.

A block to the west, at 15th and Exchange streets, is the site of old Fort Astoria, founded in 1811 by the Pacific Fur Company. While nothing remains of the original structure, volunteers have rebuilt the blockhouse and stockade to original drawings.

Astoria's landmark Victorian mansions line the steep hills behind downtown. Climb up 16th Street to Grand Avenue. One block east is the Foard House (690 17th St), an elaborate Queen Anne mansion that is now a wildly painted bed-and-breakfast. Walk back west, past more restored mansions and below the St. Mary's Catholic Church (1465 Grand Ave), built in 1902.

Drop down to Franklin Street and continue walking westward past street after street of mammoth Victorian homes. At 137 Franklin Avenue is the oldest surviving house in Astoria, built in 1853. Other notable homes, now bed-and-breakfasts, include the Columbia River Inn (1681 Franklin St) and the Rosebriar Hotel (636 14th St), formerly a convent.

At 8th Street, turn north and walk downhill to Duane Street. Captain George Flavel, one of Astoria's leading citizens during the 1870s and 1880s, built a highly ornamented mansion, Flavel House (441 8th St), with great views over the harbor (especially from the three-story corner tower) to keep an eye on his ships. The house is now a museum that has been restored throughout and repainted with its original colors; the grounds have been returned to Victorian-era landscaping. Tours are offered daily.

From the Flavel House, drop down to Commercial Street, and walk west through sleepy downtown Astoria to again reach the Maritime Museum.

*tpaulsurbancafe.com.* Located on the north coast in the heart of Astoria, this restaurant features eclectic, local cuisine; regional wines; and microbrew beer. American menu. Lunch, dinner. Closed Sun. **$**

# Baker City (C-5)

*See also La Grande*

**Population** 9,140
**Elevation** 3,443 ft
**Area Code** 541
**Zip** 97814
**Information** Baker County Visitor & Convention Bureau, 490 Campbell St; phone 541/523-3356 or toll-free 800/523-1235
**Web Site** www.visitbaker.com

The Baker City Historic District includes more than 100 commercial and residential buildings, many built from stone quarried in town at the same place where gold was found. A 15-block area, from the Powder River to 4th Street and from Estes to Campbell streets, has many structures built between 1890 and 1910 that are being restored. Baker City, on the "old Oregon trail," is also the home of the Armstrong Gold Nugget found by George Armstrong on June 19, 1913. It weighs more than 80 ounces. A Ranger District office and the office of the supervisor of the Wallowa-Whitman National Forest are located here.

## What to See and Do

**Eastern Oregon Museum.** *610 3rd St, Baker City (97814). 9 miles NW on old Hwy 30. Phone 541/856-3233.* A large collection of relics and implements used in the development of the West; turn-of-the-century logging and mining tools; period rooms; doll collection; children's antique furniture. On the grounds is an 1884 railroad depot. (Mid-Apr-Labor Day, daily) **$**

**National Historic Oregon Trail Interpretive Center.** *Hwy 86, Baker City (97814). 5 miles E on Hwy 86, at summit of Flagstaff Hill. Phone 541/523-1843; toll-free 800/523-1235.* Exhibits, living history presentations, multimedia displays. (Daily; closed Jan 1, Dec 25) **$$$**

**Oregon Trail Regional Museum.** *2490 Grove St, Baker City (97814). Phone 541/523-9308; toll-free 800/523-1235.* Houses one of the most outstanding collections of rocks, minerals, and semiprecious stones in the West. Also, an elaborate sea-life display; wildlife display; period clothing and artifacts of early Baker County. (Late Mar-Oct, daily) **$**

**Sumpter Valley Railway.** *Baker City. 30 miles SW on Hwy 7. Phone 541/894-2268; toll-free 800/523-1235. www.svry.com.* A restored gear-driven Heisler steam locomotive and two observation cars travel 7 miles on a narrow-gauge track through a wildlife game habitat area where beavers, muskrats, geese, waterfowl, herons, and other animals can be seen. The train also passes through the Sumpter mining district, the location of the Sumpter Dredge, which brought up more than $10 million in gold between 1913 and 1954 from as far down as 20 feet. (Memorial Day-Sept, weekends and holidays) **$$**

**Unity Lake State Park.** *Hwy 26, Mount Vernon. 45 miles SW on Hwy 245, near junction Hwy 26. Phone 541/932-4453.* A 39-acre park with swimming, fishing, boat ramp on Unity Lake; picnicking, tent and improved-site camping.

**Wallowa-Whitman National Forest.** *47794 Oregon Hwy 244, Baker City (97850). Sections W, NE, and S. Phone 541/523-6391.* More than 2 million acres with 14,000-acre North Fork John Day Wilderness; 7,000-acre Monument Rock Wilderness; 358,461-acre Eagle Cap Wilderness; 215,500-acre Hells Canyon Wilderness. Snowcapped peaks, Minam River; alpine meadows, rare wildflowers; national scenic byway, scenic drive Hells Canyon Overlook, which overlooks deepest canyon in North America—Hells Canyon National Recreation Area; Buckhorn Lookout; Anthony Lake and Phillips Lake. Stream and lake trout fishing; elk, deer, and bear hunting; float and jet boat trips; saddle and pack trips. Picnic area. Camping. For further information contact Supervisor, PO Box 907. In the forest is

**Anthony Lakes Ski Area.** *47500 Anthony Lake Hwy, North Powder (97867). 35 miles NW, off I-84. Phone 541/856-3277.* Triple chairlift, Pomalift; patrol, school, rentals; nursery; day lodge, cafeteria, concession area, bar. Longest run 1 1/2 miles; vertical drop 900 feet. Cross-country trails. (Mid-Nov-mid-Apr, Thurs-Sun) Fishing, hiking, cabin rentals, store (summer). **$$$$**

## Special Event

**Miner's Jubilee.** *490 Campbell St, Baker City (97814). Phone 541/523-5855.* Third weekend in July.

## Limited-Service Hotels

**★ ★ BEST WESTERN SUNRIDGE INN.** *1 Sunridge Ln, Baker City (97814). Phone 541/523-6444; toll-free 800/233-2368; fax 541/523-6446. www.bestwestern.com.* 154 rooms, 2 story. Pets accepted; fee. Check-in 3 pm, check-out noon. High-speed Internet access. Restaurant, bar. Outdoor pool, whirlpool. **$**

**★ ★ GEISER GRAND HOTEL.** *1996 Main St, Baker City (97814). Phone 541/523-1889; toll-free 888/434-7374; fax 541/523-1800. www.geisergrand.com.* 30 rooms. Pets accepted; fee. Check-in 3 pm, check-out noon. High-speed Internet access, wireless Internet access. Restaurant, bar. **$**

## Restaurant

**★ ★ GEISER GRILL.** *1966 Main St, Baker City (97814). Phone 866/826-3850.* Located in the Geiser Grand Hotel with the largest stained glass ceiling in the West. American menu. Breakfast, lunch, dinner. **$$**

# Bandon (D-1)

*See also Coos Bay, North Bend, Port Orford*

**Population** 2,215
**Elevation** 67 ft
**Area Code** 541

**Zip** 97411
**Information** Chamber of Commerce, 300 2nd St, PO Box 1515; phone 503/347-9616
**Web Site** www.bandon.com

A fine beach, known for its picturesque beauty, legendary rocks, and a harbor at the mouth of the Coquille River attracts many travelers to Bandon. From November through March, the town is known for its short-lived storms followed by sunshine; it even has a group called the Storm Watchers. Popular seashore activities include beachcombing, hiking, fishing from the south jetty, and crabbing from the docks. Summer and early autumn bring the salmon run in the Coquille River. Rockhounds search for agate, jasper, and petrified wood.

## What to See and Do

**Bandon Museum.** *300 2nd St, Bandon (97411). Hwy 101 and Filmore Ave. Phone 541/347-2164.* Exhibits on maritime activities of early Bandon and Coquille River; coastal shipwrecks, Coast Guard operations; extensive collection of Native American artifacts; old photos. (Schedule varies) **$**

**Bullards Beach State Park.** *52470 Hwy 101, Bandon (97411). 2 miles N on Hwy 101. Phone 541/347-3501.* A 1,266-acre park with 4 miles of ocean beach. Fishing; boating (dock, ramp with access to Coquille River). Picnicking. Improved trailer campsites (dump station). Coquille River Lighthouse (1896); interpretive plaques (May-Oct, daily). **FREE**

**Face Rock State Park.** *Bandon (97411). 4 miles S on Hwy 101, then 1 mile W on Bradley Lake Rd. Phone 541/347-3501.* An 879-acre park on coastal dune area with access to beach; fishing. Picnicking. **FREE**

**West Coast Game Park.** *Hwy 101, Bandon (97411). 7 miles S on Hwy 101. Phone 541/347-3106. www.gameparksafari.com.* A 21-acre park with more than 450 exotic animals and birds. Visitors meet and walk with free-roaming wildlife. Animal keepers demonstrate the personalities of many large predators residing at the park. (Mar-Nov: daily; rest of year: weekends and holidays) **$$$**

## Special Events

**Cranberry Festival.** *Bandon. Phone 541/347-9616.* Parade, barbecue, square dances, harvest ball, sports events. Sept.

**Wine & Food Festival.** *300 2nd, Bandon (97121). Phone 541/347-9616.* Featuring handmade crafts as well as a variety of Oregon wineries, regional foods, and music. Memorial Day weekend.

## Limited-Service Hotels

**★ ★ BEST WESTERN INN AT FACE ROCK RESORT.** *3225 Beach Loop Rd, Bandon (97411). Phone 541/347-9441; toll-free 800/638-3092; fax 541/347-2532. www.facerock.net.* 74 rooms. Pets accepted, some restrictions; fee. Check-in 4 pm, check-out 11 am. Restaurant. Children's activity center. Fitness room. Beach. Indoor pool, whirlpool. Golf, 9 holes. Business center. **$$**

**★ ★ SUNSET OCEANFRONT LODGING.** *1865 Beach Loop Dr, Bandon (97411). Phone 541/347-2453; toll-free 800/842-2407; fax 541/347-3636. www.sunset-motel.com.* Located on Bandon's scenic Beach Loop Drive just south of the mouth of the Coquille River, this hotel offers exceptional views of the Pacific and its rugged coastline. The large family-owned property is made up of a motel-like structure as well as cabins, houses, and studios, many of which have kitchen facilities. With easy access to a private beach, all outdoor activities here are oriented toward the ocean. 71 rooms, 2 story. Pets accepted; fee. Check-in 4 pm, check-out 11 am. Restaurant, bar. Indoor pool, whirlpool. **$**

## Full-Service Resort

**★ ★ ★ LODGE AT BANDON DUNES.** *57744 Round Lake Dr, Bandon (97411). Phone 541/347-4380; toll-free 888/345-6008; fax 541/347-8161. www.bandon-dunes.com.* The Lodge at Bandon Dunes sits alongside the windswept coast of the Pacific Ocean. The property offers luxurious accommodations for the Bandon Dunes Golf Resort, home to two of the Northwest's premiere 18-hole courses. All guest rooms feature scenic views, and some have fireplaces and private balconies. Just off the lobby, The Gallery Restaurant serves three meals a day, specializing in fresh Pacific Northwest seafood. 153 rooms. Check-in 4 pm, check-out 11 am. High-speed Internet access. Two restaurants, two bars. Fitness room. Beach. Whirlpool. Golf, 36 holes. Airport transportation available. Business center. **$$**

## Restaurants

**★ ★ BANDON BOATWORKS.** *275 Lincoln Ave SW, Bandon (97411). Phone 541/347-2111.* Seafood menu. Lunch, dinner. Closed Dec 25. Children's menu. Casual attire. Valet parking. **$$**

**★ ★ LORD BENNETT'S.** *1695 Beach Loop Dr, Bandon (97411). Phone 541/347-3663; fax 541/347-9032. www.lordbennetts.com.* Come relish this restaurant's spectacular Pacific Ocean view and fresh, straightforward preparations of pasta, beef, pork, veal, chicken, and seafood. The atmosphere is refined but casual with a slightly nautical feel, and the adjacent lounge offers great cocktails and live entertainment. Seafood, steak menu. Lunch, dinner, late-night, Sun brunch. Bar. Children's menu. Casual attire. **$$**

**★ ★ WHEELHOUSE.** *125 Chicago Ave, Bandon (97411). Phone 541/347-9331.* Seafood, steak menu. Lunch, dinner. Bar. Children's menu. In restored fish warehouse. Casual attire. **$$**

# Beaverton (B-2)

*See also Forest Grove, Newberg, Oregon City, Portland*

**Population** 53,310
**Elevation** 189 ft
**Area Code** 503
**Zip** 97005
**Information** Beaverton Area Chamber of Commerce, 4800 SW Griffith Dr, Suite 100; phone 503/644-0123
**Web Site** www.beaverton.org

Nestled amid the scenic rolling hills and lush forests of the Tualatin Valley, Beaverton appeals to those who love to explore the great outdoors, with more than 100 public parks, 30 miles of hiking trails, and a 25-mile network of bike paths. In fact, every home in the city is within a half mile of a park. Beaverton is situated midway between the beaches of the Pacific Ocean and the ski slopes at Mount Hood, an enviable location to find oneself, allowing for either destination to be reached in an hour's drive. Oregon's fifth-most-populous city, Beaverton boasts strong public schools and close-knit residential neighborhoods. Economically, the city has been strengthened by the tremendous success of Nike, which is headquartered here. Each July, Beaverton's SummerFest features a parade, live music, freshly prepared food, and an arts and crafts marketplace. The event draws thousands to this friendly community 7 miles west of Portland.

## Limited-Service Hotels

**★ ★ BEST WESTERN GREENWOOD INN & SUITES.** *10700 SW Allen Blvd, Beaverton (97005). Phone 503/643-7444; toll-free 800/289-1300; fax 503/626-4553. www.greenwoodinn.com.* Located minutes from downtown Portland, this modern hotel is known best for its design and service. 250 rooms, 2 story. Pets accepted; fee. Check-out 1 pm. Restaurant, bar. Outdoor pool, whirlpool. Business center. **$**

**★ ★ COURTYARD BY MARRIOTT.** *8500 SW Nimbus Dr, Beaverton (97008). Phone 503/641-3200; toll-free 800/831-0224; fax 503/641-1287. www.courtyard.com.* 149 rooms, 3 story. Check-out noon. Bar. Fitness room. Indoor pool, whirlpool. **$**

**★ FAIRFIELD INN.** *15583 NW Gateway Ct, Beaverton (97006). Phone 503/972-0048; fax 503/972-0049. www.fairfieldinn.com/pdxfh.* 106 rooms, 4 story. Complimentary continental breakfast. Check-out noon. Fitness room. Indoor pool, whirlpool. **$**

## Restaurants

**★ ★ ★ PAVILION TRATTORIA.** *10700 SW Allen Blvd, Beaverton (97005). Phone 503/626-4550. www.paviliontrattoria.citysearch.com.* American menu. Breakfast, lunch, dinner, Sun brunch. Bar. Children's menu. Outdoor seating. **$$**

**★ ★ SAYLER'S OLD COUNTRY KITCHEN.** *4655 SW Griffith Dr, Beaverton (97005). Phone 503/644-1492; fax 503/644-5424.* American menu. Dinner. Closed holidays. Bar. Children's menu. **$$**

# Bend (C-3)

*See also Prineville, Redmond*

**Settled** 1900
**Population** 50,779
**Elevation** 3,628 ft
**Area Code** 541
**Information** Chamber of Commerce, 777 NW Wall St; phone 541/382-3221 or toll-free 800/905-2363
**Web Site** www.bendchamber.org

The early town was named Farewell Bend after a beautiful wooded area on a sweeping curve of the Deschutes River, where pioneer travelers had their last view of the river. The Post Office Department shortened it, but there was good reason for this nostalgic name. As westward-bound settlers approached, they found the first lush, green forests and good water they had seen in Oregon.

Tourists are attracted year-round to the region by its streams, lakes, mountains, great pine forests, ski slopes, and golf courses. There is also much of interest to geologists and rockhounds in this area. Movie and television producers often take advantage of the wild western scenery.

Two Ranger District offices of the Deschutes National Forest are located here.

## What to See and Do

**Deschutes National Forest.** *1645 Hwy 20 E, Bend (97701). Phone 541/383-5300. www.fs.fed.us/r6/central-oregon/index.shtml.* The Deschutes National Forest encompasses 1.6 million acres of ruggedly scenic wilderness, a broad and diverse expanse of land marked by snow-capped mountains, craggy volcanic formations, old-growth forests, and deep rivers knifing through high-desert canyons. Established as a national forest in 1908, Deschutes has become one of the Pacific Northwest's most popular year-round tourist destinations, attracting over 8 million visitors annually. The winter months bring hordes of skiers and snowmobilers. Oregon's largest ski resort can be found alongside the 9,065-foot-high Mt. Bachelor. Hikers arrive after the spring thaw, eager to take advantage of the areas 1,388 miles of trails—including 60 miles of the **Pacific Crest National Scenic Trail.** Cars carrying strapped-down canoes and kayaks are a common sight, with paddlers headed to the Deschutes River, which has been designated both a National Scenic River and a National Recreational River. Anglers are drawn to the forest's 157 trout-filled lakes and reservoirs. Situated on the eastern side of the Cascade Mountains, the Deschutes National Forest gets significantly more sunshine than the rainier western side, but drier conditions also create a greater risk for forest fires. In the summer of 2003, the Booth and Bear Butte fires burned nearly 91,000 acres over the course of 39 days. The rapidly growing town of Bend lies just to the east of Deschutes, offering visitors a return to civilization after an exhausting day of outdoor adventure.

★ **Driving Tour in Deschutes National Forest.** *1645 Hwy 20 E, Bend (97701). Phone 541/383-5300.* An 89-mile paved loop (Century Dr, Cascade Lakes Hwy) provides a clear view of Three Sisters peaks, passes many mountain lakes and streams. Go west on Franklin Ave past Drake Park, follow the signs. Continue south past Mt. Bachelor, Elk Lake, Lava Lakes, and Cultus Lake. After passing Crane Prairie Reservoir, turn left (east) on Forest Rd 42 to Highway 97, then left (north) for return to Bend. Also in the forest are Newberry National Volcanic Monument, the Lava Cast Forest and Lava Butte Geological Area, Mt. Bachelor Ski Area, Crane Prairie Osprey Management Area, as well as Mt. Jefferson, Diamond Peak, Three Sisters, and Mt. Washington wildernesses. Fishing, hiking, camping, picnicking, and rafting are popular. The forest includes 1.6 million acres with headquarters in Bend. Ten miles south of Bend, at the base of Lava Butte, is Lava Lands Visitor Center, operated by the US Forest Service, with dioramas and exhibits on history and geology of volcanic area. For further information contact Supervisor, 1645 Hwy 20 E, 97701.

**High Desert Museum.** *59800 S Hwy 97, Bend (97702). 6 miles S on Hwy 97. Phone 541/382-4754. www.highdesertmuseum.org.* A regional museum with indoor/outdoor exhibits featuring live animals and cultural history of Intermountain Northwest aridlands; hands-on activities; ongoing presentations. The galleries house wildlife, Western art, and Native American artifacts; landscape photography; and walk-through dioramas depicting the opening of the American West. The desertarium showcases seldom-seen bats, burrowing owls, amphibians, and reptiles. (Daily 9 am-5 pm; closed Jan 1, Thanksgiving, Dec 25) **$$**

**LaPine.** *15800 State Recreation Rd, Bend (97739). 22 miles S on Hwy 97, then 4 miles W. Phone 541/388-6055.* A 2,333-acre park on Deschutes River in Ponderosa pine forest. Scenic views. Swimming, bathhouse, fishing, boating; picnicking, improved trailer campsites (dump station).

**Lava Butte and Lava River Cave.** *58201 Hwy 97 S, Bend (97707). 11 miles S on Hwy 97. Phone 541/593-2421.* Lava Butte is an extinct cinder cone. Paved road to top provides view of Cascades; interpretive trails through pine forest and lava flow. One mile south, Lava River Cave offers a lava tube 1.2 miles long (fee); ramps and stairs ease walking. Visitor center has audiovisual shows (May-Sept, daily). **$$**

**Mount Bachelor Ski Area.** *Bend (97702). 22 miles SW on Century Dr. Phone 541/382-2442; toll-free 800/829-2442. www.mtbachelor.com.* Panoramic, scenic view of forests, lakes, and Cascade Range. Facilities at base of 6,000 feet; 6,000 acres. Ten chairlifts; patrol, school, rentals; cafeterias, concession areas, bars, lodges; day care. Longest run 1 1/2 miles; vertical drop 3,365 feet. (Mid-Nov-May, daily) 56 miles of cross-country trails. **$$$$**

**Newberry National Volcanic Monument.** *1645 Hwy 20 E, Bend (97701). 24 miles S on Hwy 97, then 14 miles E on Forest Rd 21, in Deschutes National Forest. Phone 541/383-5300. www.fs.fed.us/r6/centraloregon/newberrynvm/index.shtml.* This monument, an active volcano, has a wide range of volcanic features and deposits similar to Mount Etna; obsidian flow, pumice deposits. On same road are East and Paulina lakes, both of which have excellent fishing as well as boat landings; hiking, picnicking (stoves, fireplaces), resorts, tent and trailer sites. You can get a view of the entire area from Paulina Peak, at nearly 8,000 feet. **$$**

**Pilot Butte.** *2880 NE 27th St, Bend (97701). 1 mile E on Hwy 20. Phone 541/388-6055.* A 101-acre park noted for a lone cinder cone rising 511 feet above the city. Summit affords an excellent view of the Cascade Range. No water, no camping.

**Pine Mount Observatory.** *Bend. 26 miles SE near Millican, via Hwy 20, then 9 miles S. Phone 541/382-8331.* University of Oregon astronomical research facility. Visitors may view stars, planets, and galaxies through telescopes. (Memorial Day-Sept, Fri and Sat) **$$**

**Tumalo.** *Bend. 5 1/2 miles NW off Hwy 20. Phone 541/382-3586.* A 320-acre park situated along the banks of the Deschutes River; swimming nearby, fishing; hiking, picnicking, tent and trailer campsites; solar-heated showers.

**Tumalo Falls.** *Skyliner Rd and Tumalo Falls, Bend (97701). W via Franklin Ave and Galveston Ave, 12 miles beyond city limits, then 2 miles via unsurfaced forest road. Phone 541/383-5300.* A 97-foot waterfall deep in pine forest devastated by 1979 fire.

**Whitewater rafting.** *Sun Country Tours, 531 SW 13th St, Bend (97702). Phone 541/382-6277. www.suncountrytours.com.* Choose from 2-hour or all-day trips. Also canoeing and special programs. (May-Sept) **$$$$**

## Limited-Service Hotels

**★ ★ MOUNT BACHELOR VILLAGE RESORT.** *19717 Mount Bachelor Dr, Bend (97701). Phone 541/389-5900; toll-free 800/452-9846; fax 541/388-7401. www.mountbachelorvillage.com.* Woodland setting along Deschutes River. 130 rooms, 2 story. Check-out noon. Restaurant. Outdoor pool, children's pool. Tennis. Business center. **$$**

**★ ★ RED LION.** *1415 NE 3rd St, Bend (97701). Phone 541/382-7011; toll-free 800/733-5466; fax 541/382-7934. www.redlion.com.* 75 rooms, 2 story. Pets accepted. Check-out noon. Restaurant. Outdoor pool, whirlpool. **$**

**★ ★ THE RIVERHOUSE.** *3075 N Hwy 97, Bend (97701). Phone 541/389-3111; toll-free 800/547-3928; fax 541/389-0870. www.riverhouse.com.* This resort is located on the Deschutes River and features such amenities as refrigerators and microwaves, an indoor/outdoor pool, and golfing and skiing packages. 220 rooms, 2 story. Pets accepted. Check-out noon. Restaurant. Indoor pool, outdoor pool. Golf. **$**

**★ ★ SHILO INN.** *3105 NE O. B. Riley Rd, Bend (97701). Phone 541/389-9600; toll-free 800/222-2244; fax 541/382-4310. www.shiloinns.com.* On Deschutes River. 151 rooms, 2 story. Pets accepted, some restrictions; fee. Check-out noon. Restaurant, bar. Fitness room. Indoor pool, outdoor pool, whirlpool. Airport transportation available. **$**

## Full-Service Resorts

**★ ★ ★ INN OF THE SEVENTH MOUNTAIN.** *18575 SW Century Dr, Bend (97702). Phone 541/382-8711; toll-free 800/452-6810; fax 541/382-3517. www.7thmtn.com.* With breathtaking views both in summer and winter, this beautiful oasis is set in Deschutes National Forest. Activities such as whitewater rafting, horseback riding, golfing, and canoeing make it Oregon's premier resort destination. 300 rooms, 3 story. Check-out noon. Restaurant, bar. Children's activity center. Two outdoor pools, children's pool, whirlpool. Tennis. **$**

**★ ★ ★ SUNRIVER RESORT.** *1 Center Dr, Sunriver (97707). Phone 541/593-1000; toll-free 800/801-8765; fax 541/593-4167. www.sunriver-resort.com.* Central Oregon's Sunriver Resort is one of the state's best vacation destinations. This full-service, all-season resort on the sunny side of the scenic Cascade Mountain Range offers visitors a complete getaway with an endless supply of recreational opportunities, including sparkling pools, three 18-hole golf courses, a state-of-the-art fitness center, and an elegant spa. Recreational opportunities run the gamut from canoe and kayak trips to 30 miles of biking trails to a challenge ropes course, while the Sunriver Nature Center and Observatory offers stargazing, a botanical garden, and nature trails. Whether you plan to stay for just a few days or enjoy a longer visit, the accommodations range from deluxe rooms in the River Lodges and rooms and suites in the Lodge Village to private home and condominium rentals. Several restaurants entice diners with distinctive Northwestern cuisine or classic pub-food favorites, and regional beers and wines are a special highlight. 441 rooms, 2 story. Check-in 4 pm, check-out 11 am. Three restaurants, bar. Children's activity center. Fitness room, fitness classes available, spa. Three outdoor pools, children's pool, whirlpool. Golf, 54 holes. Tennis. Airport transportation available. Business center. **$**

## Specialty Lodgings

**DIAMOND STONE GUEST LODGE.** *16693 Sprague Loop, LaPine (97739). Phone 541/536-6263; toll-free 800/600-6263. www.diamondstone.com.* This lodge sits adjacent to Quail Run Golf Course, at the gateway to Newberry National Volcanic Monument, with the Cascade Mountains as a backdrop. Surrounded by open meadows and pines, there are plenty of trails for hiking and exploring. 3 rooms, 2 story. **$**

**ROCK SPRINGS GUEST RANCH.** *64201 Tyler Rd, Bend (97701). Phone 541/382-1957; toll-free 800/225-3833; fax 541/382-7774. www.rocksprings.com.* 26 rooms. Check-in 4:30 pm, check-out 11 am. Restaurant. Children's activity center. Fitness room. Outdoor pool, whirlpool. Tennis. Airport transportation available. **$$**

## Restaurants

**★ ★ COWBOY DINNER TREE.** *Hager Mountain Rd, Silver Lake (97638). Phone 541/576-2426. www.cowboydinnertree.homestead.com.* A very traditional Old West restaurant with a very limited menu and hours, but worth a visit for the great food and atmosphere. Located in a turn-of-the-century ranch. American menu. Dinner. Closed Mon-Tues, Thurs. No credit cards accepted. **$$**

**★ ★ ★ ERNESTO'S ITALIAN RESTAURANT.** *1203 NE 3rd St, Bend (97701). Phone 541/389-7274; fax 541/389-1686. www.ernestositalian.com.* This former church is now a family restaurant featuring basic Italian fare. Service is courteous and helpful, but the food may be a little heavy at times. Italian menu. Dinner. Bar. Children's menu. **$$**

**★ ★ ★ MEADOWS.** *1 Center Dr, Sunriver, (97707). Phone 541/593-1000. www.sunriver-resort.com.* American menu. Dinner. Bar. **$$**

**★ ★ PINE TAVERN.** *967 NW Brooks St, Bend (97701). Phone 541/382-5581. www.pinetavern.com.* 100-foot pine tree in dining room. Seafood, steak menu. Lunch, dinner. Bar. Children's menu. Outdoor seating. **$$**

**★ ROSZAK'S FISH HOUSE.** *1230 NE 3rd St, Bend (97701). Phone 541/382-3173.* Seafood, steak menu. Lunch, dinner. Closed Memorial Day, Labor Day. Bar. Children's menu. **$$**

**★ WESTSIDE BAKERY & CAFE.** *1005 NW Galveston Ave, Bend (97701). Phone 541/382-3426.* American menu. Breakfast, lunch. Closed Thanksgiving, Dec 25. Children's menu. **$**

# Biggs (B-3)

*See also The Dalles*

**Population** 30
**Elevation** 173 ft
**Area Code** 541
**Zip** 97065

## What to See and Do

**John Day Locks and Dam.** *Biggs. 5 miles E off I-84 N.* A $487-million unit in the US Army Corps of Engineers Columbia River Basin project. Visitors may view turbine generators from powerhouse observation room; fish-viewing stations. Self-guided tours (daily; guided tours by appointment; closed holidays). **FREE** The dam creates

**Lake Umatilla.** A 100-mile reservoir. The eastern part of the lake is a national wildlife management area for the preservation of game waterfowl and fish.

# Bridal Veil (B-2)

## Restaurant

**★ ★ MULTNOMAH FALLS LODGE.** *50000 Historic Columbia River Hwy, Bridal Veil (97010). Phone 503/695-2376. www.multnomahfallslodge.com.* Elegant dining room with scenic views. American menu. Breakfast, lunch, dinner. **$**

# Brookings (E-1)

*See also Coos Bay, Gold Beach*

**Population** 4,400
**Elevation** 130 ft
**Area Code** 541
**Zip** 97415
**Information** Brookings-Harbor Chamber of Commerce and Information Center, 16330 Lower Harbor Rd, PO Box 940; phone 541/469-3181 or toll-free 800/535-9469
**Web Site** www.brookingsor.com

Beachcombers, whale-watchers, and fishermen find this coastal city a haven for their activities. A commercial and sportfishing center, Brookings lies in an area that produces a high percentage of the nation's Easter lily bulbs. A Ranger District office of the Siskiyou National Forest is located here.

## What to See and Do

**Azalea Park.** *Hwy 101 and N Bank Chetco River Rd, Brookings (97415). Just E off Hwy 101. Phone 541/469-2021.* A 36-acre city park with five varieties of large native azaleas, some blooming twice a year. Observation point. Hiking. Picnicking.

**Harris Beach.** *1655 Hwy 101 N, Brookings (97415). 2 miles N on Hwy 101. Phone 541/469-2021.* A 171-acre park with scenic rock cliffs along ocean. Ocean beach, fishing; hiking trails, observation point, picnicking, improved tent and trailer campsites (dump station).

**Loeb.** *1601 Hwy 101 N, Brookings (97415). 10 miles NE off Hwy 101. Phone 541/469-2021.* A 320-acre park on the Chetco River with an area of beautiful old myrtle trees; also redwoods. Swimming, fishing; picnicking, improved camping.

**Samuel H. Boardman.** *4655 Hwy 101 N, Brookings (97415). 4 miles N on Hwy 101. Phone 541/469-2021.* A 1,473-acre park with observation points along 11 miles of spectacular coastline. Fishing, clamming; hiking, picnicking.

## Special Event

**Azalea Festival.** *Azalea Park, Brookings. Phone 541/469-2021.* Parade, seafood, art exhibits, street fair, crafts fair, music. Memorial Day weekend.

## Limited-Service Hotel

**★ ★ BEST WESTERN BROOKINGS INN.** *1143 Chetco Ave, Brookings (97415). Phone 541/469-2173; toll-free 800/822-9087; fax 541/469-2996. www.bestwestern.com.* 68 rooms. Check-in 3 pm, check-out noon. Restaurant, bar. Indoor pool, whirlpool. Business center. **$**

# Burns (D-5)

**Population** 2,913
**Elevation** 4,170 ft
**Area Code** 541
**Zip** 97720
**Information** Harney County Chamber of Commerce, 18 W D St; phone 541/573-2636
**Web Site** www.harneycounty.com

This remote trading center and county seat serves a livestock-raising and forage production area bigger than many eastern states. Ranger District offices of the Malheur National Forest and Ochoco National Forest are located here.

## What to See and Do

**Harney County Historical Museum.** *18 West D St, Burns (97720). Phone 541/573-5618.* Displays include arrowheads, quilts, wildlife, artifacts, furniture, clothing, cut glass, old-fashioned kitchen, Pete French's safe and spurs. The Hayes Room contains a bedroom and dining room furnished in antiques. Also old wagons, tools, and machinery. (Apr-Oct, Mon-Sat; closed July 4) **$$**

**Malheur National Wildlife Refuge.** *36391 Sodhouse Ln, Princeton (97721). 32 miles S on Hwy 205. Phone 541/493-2612. pacific.fws.gov/malheur.* Established in 1908 by Theodore Roosevelt, the 185,000-acre refuge was set aside primarily as a nesting area for migratory birds. It is also an important fall and spring gathering point for waterfowl migrating between the northern breeding grounds and the California wintering grounds. More than 320 species of birds and 58 species of mammals have been recorded on the refuge. The headquarters has a museum. (Daily dawn-dusk) **FREE**

## Special Events

**Harney County Fair, Rodeo and Race Meet.** *Burns. Phone 541/573-6166.* Includes rodeo and pari-mutuel racing. Tues-Sun after Labor Day.

**John Scharff Migratory Bird Festival.** *76 E Washington St, Burns (97720). Phone 541/573-2636.* Includes bird-watching and historical tours, films, arts and crafts. First weekend in Apr.

**Steens Mountain Rim Run.** *Frenchglen. Approximately 48 miles S on Hwy 205. Phone 541/573-2636.* Features a 6-mile run at high elevation, pit barbecue, all-night street dance, team-roping, horse cutting. First Sat in Aug.

## Limited-Service Hotel

**★ DAYS INN.** *577 W Monroe St, Burns (97720). Phone 541/573-2047; toll-free 800/303-2047; fax 541/573-3828. www.daysinn.com.* 52 rooms, 2 story. Pets accepted, some restrictions; fee. Complimentary continental breakfast. Check-in 2 pm, check-out 11 am. Outdoor pool. **$**

# Cannon Beach (A-1)

*See also Astoria, Rockaway Beach, Seaside*

**Population** 1,588
**Elevation** 25 ft
**Area Code** 503
**Zip** 97110
**Information** Cannon Beach Chamber of Commerce Visitor Information Center, 207 N Spruce, PO Box 64; phone 503/436-2623
**Web Site** www.cannonbeach.org

The cannon and capstan from the survey schooner USS *Shark,* which washed ashore near here in 1846, are now on a small monument 4 miles south of this resort town. Swimming (with a lifeguard on duty in summer), surfing, and surf fishing can be enjoyed here, and the 7-mile stretch of wide beach is wonderful for walking. Among the large rocks offshore is the 235-foot Haystack Rock, the third-largest monolith in the world. Migrating gray whales often can be spotted heading south from mid-December to early February and then heading back north in early to mid-spring.

## What to See and Do

**Ecola State Park.** *Ecola Rd, Cannon Beach. 2 miles N off Hwy 101. Phone 503/861-1671.* End of the trail for Lewis and Clark expedition. A 1,303-acre park with 6 miles of ocean frontage; sea lion and bird rookeries on rocks and offshore islands; Tillamook Lighthouse. Beaches, fishing; hiking (on the Oregon Coast Trail), picnicking at Ecola Point. Whale-watching at observation point.

**Oswald West State Park.** *9500 Sandpiper Ln, Nehalem (97131). 10 miles S on Hwy 101. Phone 503/368-5943. www.oregonstateparks.org/park_195.php.* A 2,474-acre park with outstanding coastal headland, towering cliffs, low dunes, and rain forest with massive spruce and cedar trees. The road winds 700 feet above sea level and 1,000 feet below the peak of Neahkahnie Mountain. Surfing (at nearby Short Sands Beach), fishing; hiking trails (on the Oregon Coast Trail), picnicking, primitive campgrounds accessible only by a 1/4-mile foot trail. **FREE**

## Special Event

**Sandcastle Contest.** *Cannon Beach. Phone 503/436-2623.* Nationally known event features sand sculptures on beach. Early June.

## Limited-Service Hotels

**★ HALLMARK RESORT.** *1400 S Hemlock St, Cannon Beach (97110). Phone 503/436-1566; toll-free 800/345-5676; fax 503/436-0324. www.hallmarkinns.com.* Located in Cannon Beach, this property overlooks Haystack Rock.137 rooms, 3 story. Pets accepted, some restrictions; fee. Check-in 4 pm, check-out noon. Fitness room. On beach. Indoor pool, children's pool, whirlpool. **$**

**★ ★ SURFSAND RESORT.** *Oceanfront, Cannon Beach (97110). Phone 503/436-2274; toll-free 800/547-6100; fax 503/436-9116. www.surfsand.com.* On ocean, beach. 82 rooms, 2 story. Pets accepted, some restrictions; fee. Check-out noon. Restaurant, bar. Indoor pool, whirlpool. **$$**

**★ TOLOVANA INN.** *3400 S Hemlock, Cannon Beach (97145). Phone 503/436-2211; toll-free 800/333-8890; fax 503/436-0134. www.tolovanainn.com.* 175 rooms, 3 story. Pets accepted, some restrictions; fee. Check-out noon. Indoor pool, whirlpool. **$**

## Restaurant

**★ ★ DOOGER'S.** *1371 S Hemlock, Cannon Beach (97110). Phone 503/436-2225.* Seafood, steak menu. Breakfast, lunch, dinner. Closed Thanksgiving Dec 25. Bar. Children's menu. **$$$**

# Cave Junction (E-1)

*See also Grants Pass, Oregon Caves National Monument*

**Population** 1,126
**Elevation** 1,295 ft
**Area Code** 541
**Zip** 97523
**Information** Illinois Valley Chamber of Commerce, 201 Caves Hwy, PO Box 312; phone 541/592-3326
**Web Site** www.cavejunction.com

This small rural community in the picturesque Illinois Valley is the gateway to the Oregon Caves National Monument. Surrounding forest lands offer opportunities for fishing, hiking, and backpacking. A Ranger District office of the Siskiyou National Forest is located here.

## What to See and Do

**Kerbyville Museum.** *24195 Redwood Hwy, Kerby (97531). 2 miles N on Hwy 199. Phone 541/592-5252.* Home (circa 1870) furnished in the period; outdoor display of farm, logging, and mining tools; Native American artifacts; rock display; log schoolhouse, blacksmith shop, general store. Picnic tables. (Mar-Dec, daily) **$$**

## Special Event

**Wild Blackberry Festival.** *Cave Junction. Phone 541/592-3326.* Blackberry foods, cooking, games, crafts and music. Mid-Aug.

## Limited-Service Hotel

**★ ★ OREGON CAVES LODGE.** *20000 Caves Hwy, Cave Junction (97523). Phone 541/592-5020; fax 541/592-3800.* 22 rooms, 3 story. Closed Nov-Apr. Check-out 11 am. Restaurant. Business center. **$**

# Coos Bay (D-1)

*See also Bandon, Brookings, North Bend, Reedsport*

**Founded** 1854
**Population** 15,374
**Elevation** 11 ft
**Area Code** 541
**Zip** 97420
**Information** Bay Area Chamber of Commerce, 50 E Central, PO Box 210; phone 541/269-0215 or toll-free 800/824-8486
**Web Site** www.oregonsbayareachamber.com

This charming port town borders a bay that shares its name. The bay itself is the largest natural harbor between San Francisco and Seattle, and since the earliest pioneer days it has served as a key means of commercial passage to and from the sea. Coos Bay is the state's second busiest maritime center, supported by such industries as forestry, shipbuilding, and fishing. Outdoor enthusiasts appreciate the areas mild climate (the temperature rarely falls below 45 degrees F) and the terrific recreational opportunities available at three local state parks: Cape Arago, Shore Acres, and Sunset Bay. Anglers flock to the shores of the nearby Coos River, which is considered one of best places in Oregon to catch salmon and steelhead.

## What to See and Do

**Cape Arago.** *Cape Arago Hwy, Coos Bay. 14 miles SW off Hwy 101 on Cape Arago Hwy. Phone 541/888-8867. www.oregonstateparks.org.* This 134-acre promontory juts 1/2 mile into the ocean. Two beaches, fishing; hiking (on Oregon Coast Trail), picnicking. Observation point (whale and seal watching).

**Charleston Marina Complex.** *63534 Kingfisher Dr, Charleston (97420). 9 miles SW. Phone 541/888-2548. www.charlestonmarina.com.* Charter boats; launching and moorage facilities (fee); car and boat trailer parking (free); dry boat storage, travel park; motel; marine fuel dock; tackle shops; restaurants. Office (Mon-Fri).

**Oregon Connection/House of Myrtlewood.** *1125 S 1st St, Coos Bay (97420). Just off Hwy 101 in S Coos Bay. Phone 541/267-7804.* Manufacturing of myrtlewood gift items. Tours. (Daily; closed holidays) **FREE**

**Shore Acres.** *89814 Cape Arago Hwy, Coos Bay (97420). 13 miles SW off Hwy 101 on Cape Arago Hwy. Phone 541/888-3732. www.shoreacres.net.* Former grand estate of Coos Bay lumberman, noted for its unusual botanical and Japanese gardens and spectacular ocean views (743 acres). Ocean beach; hiking (on the Oregon Coast Trail), picnicking. Standard fees.

**South Slough National Estuarine Research Reserve.** *61907 Seven Devils Rd, Charleston (97420). 4 miles S on Seven Devils Rd. Phone 541/888-5558. www.southsloughestuary.org.* A 4,400-acre area reserved for the study of estuarine ecosystems and life. Previous studies here include oyster culture techniques and water pollution. Special programs, lectures, and exhibits at Interpretive Center. Trails and waterways (Daily); guided trail walks and canoe tours (June-Aug; fee). Interpretive Center (June-Aug: daily; rest of year: Mon-Fri). **FREE**

**Sunset Bay.** *Cape Arago Hwy, Coos Bay. 12 miles SW off Hwy 101 on Cape Arago Hwy. Phone 541/888-4902. www.oregonstateparks.org.* A 395-acre park with swimming beach on sheltered bay, fishing; hiking, picnicking, tent and trailer sites. Observation point. Standard fees.

## Special Events

**Bay Area Fun Festival.** *Coos Bay. Phone 541/267-3341; toll-free 800/738-4849.* The festival features activities for all ages including a quilt show, duck derby, sock hop, vendor booths, and car shows. Third weekend in Sept.

**Blackberry Arts Festival.** *Coos Bay. Phone 541/269-0215.* Features arts, crafts, jewelry, photography, paintings, and prints. Fourth weekend in Aug.

**Oregon Coast Music Festival.** *Coos Bay. Phone toll-free 877/897-9350.* Variety of musical presentations ranging from jazz and dance to chamber and symphonic music. Also free outdoor picnic concerts. Last two full weeks in July.

## Limited-Service Hotel

**★ ★ RED LION HOTEL.** *1313 N Bayshore Dr, Coos Bay (97420). Phone 541/267-4141; toll-free 800/733-5466; fax 541/267-2884. www.redlion.com.* Located at the north end of downtown Coos Bay on busy Highway 101, this motel-style facility offers nicely renovated guest rooms. Most have refrigerators and microwaves. For entertainment, there's an on-site putting green, and the lounge hosts stand-up comedy shows on weekend nights. 143 rooms, 2 story. Pets accepted. Check-in 3 pm, check-out noon. Restaurant, bar. Fitness room. Outdoor pool, whirlpool. Airport transportation available. **$**

## Restaurant

**★ ★ PORTSIDE.** *8001 Kingfisher Rd, Charleston (97420). Phone 541/888-5544. www.portsidebythebay.com.* Seafood menu. Lunch, dinner. Bar. Children's menu. Outdoor seating. **$$**

# Corvallis (C-2)

*See also Albany, Eugene, Salem*

**Settled** 1845
**Population** 44,757
**Elevation** 225 ft
**Area Code** 541
**Information** Convention & Visitors Bureau, 553 NW Harrison, 97330; phone 541/757-1544 or toll-free 800/334-8118
**Web Site** www.visitcorvallis.com

Located in the heart of Oregon's fertile Willamette Valley and built on the banks of the Willamette River, Corvallis is a center for education, culture, and commerce. It is the home of Oregon State University, the state's oldest institution of higher education. The Siuslaw National Forest headquarters is here.

## What to See and Do

**Avery Park.** *1310 SW Avery Pk Dr, Corvallis (97331). S 15th St and Hwy 20. Phone 541/757-6918.* A 75-acre park on the Marys River. Bicycle, cross-country, and jogging trails. Picnicking, playground, ballfield. Rose and rhododendron gardens, community gardens; 1922 Mikado locomotive. Playground (accessible to the disabled). (Daily) **FREE**

**Benton County Historical Museum.** *1101 Main St, Philomath (97370). 6 miles W. Phone 541/929-6230. www.bentoncountymuseum.org.* Located in the former Philomath College building. Features displays on history of the county; art gallery. Reference library (by appointment). (Tues-Sat) **FREE**

**Oregon State University.** *Corvallis (97331). Phone 541/737-2416. www.oregonstate.edu.* (1868) (14,500 students) On its 400-acre campus are Memorial Union Concourse Gallery (daily). **FREE**

**Siuslaw National Forest.** *4077 Research Way, Corvallis (97333). W via Hwy 34. Phone 541/750-7000.* Includes 50 miles of ocean frontage with more than 30 campgrounds; public beaches, sand dunes and overlooks; visitor center and nature trails in the Cape Perpetua Scenic Area. Mary's Peak, highest peak in the Coast Range, has a road to picnic grounds and campground near the summit. Swimming; ocean, lake, and stream fishing; hunting for deer, bear, elk, and migratory birds; clam digging; boating. Hiking. Picnicking. Camping (fee in most areas); dune buggies (in designated areas). Forest contains 630,000 acres including the Oregon Dunes National Recreation Area.

**Tyee Wine Cellars.** *26335 Greenberry Rd, Corvallis (97333). 7 miles S via Hwy 99 W, 3 miles W on Greenberry Rd. Phone 541/753-8754.* Located on 460-acre Century farm. Offers tastings, tours, interpretive hikes, picnicking. (July-Aug: Fri-Mon; Apr-June and Oct-Dec: weekends; also by appointment) **FREE**

## Special Events

**Benton County Fair and Rodeo.** *110 SW 53rd St, Corvallis (97333). Phone 541/757-1521. www.bentoncountyfair.com.* The festival features activities for all ages including a quilt show, pony show, and livestock show. Late July-early Aug.

**Da Vinci Days.** *760 SW Madison Ave, Corvallis (97333). Phone 541/757-6363.* Festival celebrating the relationship between art, science, and technology. Third weekend in July.

**Fall Festival.** *Corvallis. Phone 541/752-9655. www.corvallisfallfestival.com.* Features over 150 Arts and Crafts booths including original designs in a variety of art such as: textiles, wearable art, hand-crafted ceramics, decorative and functional wood, jewelry, leather, photography, paintings, drawings, prints, and metal work. Last weekend in Sept.

**Oregon Folklife Festival.** *Corvallis. Phone 541/754-3601.* Traditional and contemporary folk music; crafts. Late June.

## Limited-Service Hotel

**★ BEST WESTERN GRAND MANOR INN.** *925 NW Garfield Ave, Corvallis (97330). Phone 541/758-8571; toll-free 800/626-1900; fax 541/758-0834. www.bestwestern.com.* 55 rooms, 3 story. Complimentary continental breakfast. Check-out 11 am. Fitness room. Outdoor pool. **$**

## Specialty Lodging

**HARRISON HOUSE B&B.** *2310 NW Harrison Blvd, Corvallis (97330). Phone 800/233-6248; toll-free 800/233-6248; fax 541/754-7679. www.corvallis-lodging.com.* Located within walking distance to Oregon State University, this bed-and-breakfast is convenient to such area activities as kayaking, rafting, and hiking. 4 rooms, 2 story. Complimentary full breakfast. Check-in 4 pm, check-out 11 am. **$**

## Restaurants

**★ ★ GABLES.** *1121 NW 9th St, Corvallis (97330). Phone 541/752-3364; toll-free 800/815-0167; fax 541/757-0351.* Seafood menu. Dinner. Bar. Children's menu. **$$**

**★ ★ MICHAEL'S LANDING.** *603 NW Second St, Corvallis (97330). Phone 541/754-6141. www.michaelslanding.com.* Old train depot overlooking river, built 1909. American menu. Lunch, dinner. Closed Dec 25. Bar. Children's menu. **$$**

# Cottage Grove (D-2)

*See also Eugene*

**Population** 7,402
**Elevation** 641 ft
**Area Code** 541
**Zip** 97424
**Information** Cottage Grove Area Chamber of Commerce, 700 E Gibbs, PO Box 587; phone 541/942-2411
**Web Site** www.cgchamber.com

Cottage Grove is the lumber, retail, and distribution center for south Lane County. A Ranger District office of the Umpqua National Forest is located here.

## What to See and Do

**Chateau Lorane Winery.** *27415 Siuslaw River Rd, Lorane (97451). 12 miles W on Cottage Grove-Lorane Rd to Siuslaw River Rd. Phone 541/942-8028.* A 30-acre vineyard is located on this 200-acre wooded estate. Features a lakeside tasting room in which to enjoy great variety of traditional, rare and handmade wines. (June-Oct: daily; Mar-May and Nov-Dec: weekends and holidays; also by appointment). **FREE**

**Cottage Grove Lake.** *75819 Short Ridge Hill Rd, Cottage Grove (97424). S via I-5, Cottage Grove Lake exit 170, turn left, then 5 miles S on London Rd. Phone 541/942-8657.* A 3-mile-long lake. Lakeside (west shore) and Wilson Creek (east shore) parks have swimming, boat launch, and picnicking. Shortridge Park (east shore) has swimming, waterskiing, fishing, and picnicking. Primitive and improved camping (showers, dump station) at Pine Meadows on east shore (mid-May-mid-Sept, 14-day limit; no reservations; fee). **$$$**

**Cottage Grove Museum.** *147 H St, Cottage Grove (97424). Birch Ave and H St. Phone 541/942-3963.*

Displays of pioneer homelife and Native American artifacts housed in a former Roman Catholic Church (1897), octagonal, with stained-glass windows made in Italy. Adjacent to annex houses model of ore stamp mill showing how gold was extracted from the ore; working model of a green chain; antique tools. (Mid-June-Labor Day: Wed-Sun afternoons; rest of year: weekends) **FREE**

**Covered Bridges.** *710 Row River Rd, Cottage Grove (97424). Phone 541/942-2411.* Five old-time covered bridges within 10-mile radius of town. Inquire at Chamber of Commerce.

**Dorena Lake.** *34979 Shoreview Dr, Cottage Grove (97424). 5 miles E on Row River Rd. Phone 541/942-1418.* A 5-mile-long lake. Schwarz Park (camping fee), on Row River below the dam, has fishing, picnicking, and camping (dump station). Lane County maintains Baker Bay Park, on the south shore, and offers swimming, waterskiing, fishing, boating (launch, marina, rentals); picnicking, concession, camping (fee). Harms Park, on the north shore, offers boat launching and picnicking. For further information, inquire at the Cottage Grove project office. **$$$**

## Special Event

**Bohemia Mining Days Celebration.** *Cottage Grove. Phone 541/942-5064.* Commemorates area's gold-mining days; parades; flower, art shows; rodeo, entertainment. Third week in July.

## Limited-Service Hotel

**★ ★ VILLAGE GREEN RESORT.** *725 Row River Rd, Cottage Grove (97424). Phone 541/942-2491; toll-free 800/343-7666; fax 541/942-2386. www.villagegreenresortandgardens.com.* 96 rooms. Pets accepted. Check-out 11 am. Restaurant, bar. Outdoor pool, whirlpool. Tennis. **$**

## Restaurant

**★ COTTAGE.** *2915 Row River Rd, Cottage Grove (97424). Phone 541/942-3091.* American menu. Lunch, dinner. Closed Sun; week of Thanksgiving. Bar. Children's menu. **$$**

# Crater Lake National Park (D-3)

**Web Site** *www.nps.gov/crla*

*57 miles N of Klamath Falls on Hwys 97, 62.*

One of Crater Lake's former names, Lake Majesty, probably comes closest to describing the feeling visitors get from the deep blue waters in the caldera of dormant Mount Mazama. More than 7,700 years ago, following climactic eruptions, this volcano collapsed and formed a deep basin. Rain and snow accumulated in the empty caldera, forming the deepest lake in the United States (1,932 feet). Surrounded by 25 miles of jagged rim rock, the 21-square-mile lake is broken only by Wizard and Phantom Ship islands. Entering by road from any direction brings you to the 33-mile Rim Drive (July-mid-Oct or the first snow), leading to all observation points, park headquarters, and a visitor center at Rim Village (June-Sept, daily). The Sinnott Memorial Overlook with a broad terrace permits a beautiful view of the area. On summer evenings, rangers give campfire talks at Mazama Campground (late June-Sept, phone 541/594-2211). The Steel Center located at Park Headquarters (open daily) has exhibits about the natural history of the park and shows a movie daily.

The park can be explored on foot or by car following spurs and trails extending from Rim Drive. Going clockwise from Rim Village to the west, The Watchman Peak is reached by a trail almost 1 mile long that takes hikers 1,800 feet above the lake with a full view in all directions; Mount Shasta in California, 105 miles away, is visible on clear days. The road to the north entrance passes through the Pumice Desert, once a flood of frothy debris from the erupting volcano.

On the northeast side, Cleetwood Trail descends 1 mile to the shore and a boat landing, where 2-hour launch trips depart hourly each day in summer (fee). From the boats, Wizard Island, a small volcano, and Phantom Ship, a craggy mass of lava, can be seen up close.

Six miles farther on Rim Drive, going clockwise, is the start of a 2 1/2-mile hiking trail, 1,230 feet to Mount Scott, soaring 8,926 feet, the highest point in the park. Just to the west of the beginning of this trail is a 1-mile drive to the top of Cloudcap, 8,070 feet high and 1,600 feet above the lake. Four miles beyond this point, a road leads 7 miles from Rim Drive to The Pinnacles, pumice spires rising like stone needles from the canyon of Wheeler Creek.

Back at Rim Village, two trails lead in opposite directions. Counterclockwise, a 1 1/2-mile trek mounts the top of Garfield Peak. The other trail goes to Discovery Point, where in 1853 a young prospector, John Hillman, became the first settler to see the lake.

In winter, the south and west entrance roads are kept clear in spite of the annual 45-foot snowfall; the north entrance road and Rim Drive are closed from mid-Oct-June, depending on snow conditions. A cafeteria is open daily at Rim Village for refreshments and souvenirs.

Depending on snow, the campground (fee) is open from late June-mid-October. Mazama, at the junction of the south and west entrance drives, has a camp store, fireplaces, showers, laundry facilities, toilets, water, and tables; no reservations. There are six picnic areas on Rim Drive. The wildlife includes black bears—keep your distance and never feed them. There are also deer, golden-mantled ground squirrels, marmots, and coyotes. Do not feed any wildlife in park.

The park was established in 1902 and covers 286 square miles. For park information, contact Superintendent, Crater Lake National Park, PO Box 7, Crater Lake 97604; phone 541/594-2211, ext 402. Golden Eagle Passports are accepted (see MAKING THE MOST OF YOUR TRIP).

***Note:*** Conservation measures may dictate the closing of certain roads and recreational facilities. In winter, inquire locally before attempting to enter the park. **$$$**

## Full-Service Resort

**★ ★ ★ CRATER LAKE LODGE.** *565 Rim Village Dr, Crater Lake (97604). Phone 541/594-2255; fax 541/594-2342. www.crater-lake.com.* This grand lodge has been welcoming guests to its lakeside location since 1915. The lodge captures the essence of Pacific Northwest beauty and rusticity. Guests can relax with a good book in front of the Great Hall's massive stone fireplace. The Dining Room restaurant prepares dishes using Oregon-grown ingredients. It's also the perfect place to enjoy a cup of coffee as you watch the sun rise over Crater Lake, the morning light reflecting on the placid blue surface of the second deepest lake in the Western Hemisphere. Guest rooms are without TVs and phones, but, at a destination as blissful as this, you won't miss them. 71 rooms, 4 story. Closed mid-Oct-mid-May. Check-out 11 am. Restaurant. **$**

# The Dalles (B-3)

*See also Biggs, Hood River, Mount Hood National Forest*

**Founded** 1851
**Population** 10,200
**Elevation** 98 ft
**Area Code** 541
**Zip** 97058
**Information** Chamber of Commerce, 404 W 2nd St; phone 541/296-2231 or toll-free 800/255-3385
**Web Site** www.thedalleschamber.com

At one time The Dalles was the end of the wagon haul on the Oregon Trail. Here the pioneers loaded their goods on boats and made the rest of their journey westward on the Columbia River. The falls and rapids that once made the river above The Dalles unnavigable are now submerged under water backed up by the Columbia River dams. The Dalles Dam is part of a system of dams extending barge traffic inland as far as Lewiston, Idaho, and Pasco, Washington. The port has berthing space for all types of shallow draft vessels. The chief source of income in the area is agriculture. The Dalles is noted for its cherry orchards and wheat fields located in the many canyons along the river.

## What to See and Do

**Columbia Gorge Discovery Center.** *5000 Discovery Dr, The Dalles (97058). 3 miles NW at Crate's Point. Phone 541/296-8600.* Over 26,000-square-feet building is official interpretive center for the Columbia River Gorge National Scenic Area. Hands-on and electronic exhibits detail the volcanic upheavals and raging floods that created the Gorge, describe the history and importance of the river, and look to the Gorge's future. Also Early Explorers, Steamboats and Trains, Industry and Stewardship exhibits. Guided tours, seminars, classes, and workshops (some fees). Library and collections (by appointment). Café. (Daily; closed Jan 1, Thanksgiving, Dec 25) **$$$** Admission includes

**Oregon Trail Living History Park.** Includes 80,000 square feet of outdoor exhibits and gardens. Costumed interpreters demonstrate life of Oregon Trail emigrants, members of Lewis and Clark ex-

pedition, and Native Americans. Footpaths wind through park; offers stunning views of river from high bluff. (Schedule and phone same as Center)

**Wasco County Historical Museum.** Reveals colorful history of over 10,000 years of county's occupation and importance of Columbia River on area history. Artifacts and exhibits feature Native Americans, missionaries, early pioneers and explorers; history of area railroad industry, farming, and shipping. Interactive displays include a late-19th-century town, railroad depot and barn. (Schedule and phone same as Center)

**Dalles Dam and Reservoir.** *The Dalles. 3 miles E of town off I-84 and 1 mile E of The Dalles Hwy Bridge, which crosses the Columbia just below the dam (use I-84 exit 87 in summer, exit 88 off-season). Phone 541/296-1181.* Two-mile train tour with views of historic navigation canal, visitor center, petroglyphs, and fish ladder facilities (Memorial Day-Labor Day: daily; Apr-May and Oct-Mar: Wed-Sun). **FREE** On south shore, 8 1/2 miles east of dam is

**Celilo Park.** *The Dalles. Adjacent to ancient fishing grounds, now submerged under waters backed up by The Dalles Dam.* Swimming, sailboarding, fishing, boating (ramp); picnicking, playground. Comfort station. Recreational areas with similar facilities also are on north and south shores.

**Fort Dalles Museum.** *500 W 15th St, The Dalles (97058). At Garrison St. Phone 541/296-4547.* Only remaining building of the 1856 outpost is the Surgeon's Quarters. Rare collection of pioneer equipment; stagecoaches, covered wagons. (Mar-Oct: daily; rest of year, Wed-Sun: closed holidays, also first two weeks in Jan)

**Mayer State Park.** *The Dalles. 10 miles W, off I-84, exit 77. www.oregonstateparks.org/park_161.php.* A 613-acre park comprised of an undeveloped area with an overlook on Rowena Heights and a developed area on the shores of the Columbia River, with a swimming beach, dressing rooms, and boat ramp. Windsurfing, fishing. Wildflowers bloom in March/April. Picnicking. **$**

**Mount Hood National Forest.** *The Dalles. W of city.* (see).

**Sorosis Park.** *The Dalles.* This 15-acre park overlooks the city from the highest point on Scenic Drive, with view of the Columbia River, Mt. Adams, and Mt. Hood. Located on part of the bottom of ancient Lake Condon. The bones of three types of camels, the ancient horse, and mastodons were found near here. Jogging trail; tennis courts. Picnic area. Rose Garden.

**Riverfront Park.** *Off I-84, exit 85.*Swimming beach, windsurfing, fishing, boating (launch), jet boat excursions; picnicking.

## Special Events

**Fort Dalles Rodeo.** *The Dalles. Phone 541/296-2231.* CASI sanctioned. Thurs-Sun, third week in July.

**Northwest Cherry Festival.** *The Dalles. Phone 541/296-5481.* Some of the activities are quilt show, car show, and parade. Fourth weekend in Apr.

## Limited-Service Hotel

**★ ★ COUSINS COUNTRY INN.** *2114 W 6th St, The Dalles (97058). Phone 541/298-5161; toll-free 800/848-9378; fax 541/298-6411. www.cousinscountry-inn.com.* 85 rooms, 2 story. Pets accepted; fee. Check-out 11 am. Restaurant. Outdoor pool, whirlpool. **$**

## Restaurants

**★ COUSIN'S.** *2115 W 6th St, The Dalles (97058). Phone 541/298-2771. www.cousins-restaurant.com.* American menu. Breakfast, lunch, dinner. Closed Dec 25. Bar. Children's menu. **$$**

**★ WILDFLOWER CAFE.** *904 2nd Ave, Mosier (97040). Phone 541/478-0111.* Excellent pancakes; live music on weekends. American menu. Breakfast, lunch, dinner. **$**

**★ WINDSEEKER.** *1535 Barge Way Rd, The Dalles (97058). Phone 541/298-7171.* Small supper club style restaurant featuring contemporary American and Pan Asian cuisine. American menu. Breakfast, lunch, dinner. **$**

# Depoe Bay (B-1)

*See also Lincoln City, Newport*

**Population** 870
**Elevation** 58 ft
**Area Code** 541
**Zip** 97341
**Information** Chamber of Commerce, PO Box 21; phone 541/765-2889
**Web Site** www.depoebaychamber.org

The world's smallest natural navigable harbor, with six acres, Depoe Bay is a base for the US Coast Guard and a good spot for deep-sea fishing. The shoreline is rugged at this point. Seals and sea lions inhabit the area, and whales are so often seen that Depoe Bay claims to be the "whale watching capital of the Oregon coast." In the center of town are the "spouting horns," natural rock formations throwing geyserlike sprays high in the air. There are nine state parks within a few miles of this resort community.

## What to See and Do

**Depoe Bay Park.** *Hwy 101 and Shell Ave, Depoe Bay (97341). N on Hwy 101. Phone 541/765-2361.* Covers three acres. Ocean observation building with view of bay, spouting horn, and fishing fleets. Small picnic area.

**Fogarty Creek State Park.** *Depoe Bay. 2 miles N on Hwy 101. Phone 541/265-9278.* A 142-acre park with beach area and creek, swimming (dressing rooms), fishing; hiking, picnicking. **$$**

## Special Events

**Classic Wooden Boat Show and Crab Feed.** *Depoe Bay. Phone 541/765-2889.* Boat exhibitors display handcrafted boats of original and classed designs. Boat exhibitors explain boat-building techniques, boat renovation history, and hull and power plant design. Also available are crab dinners at the Community Hall. Last weekend Apr.

**Fleet of Flowers Ceremony.** *Depoe Bay. Phone 541/765-2889.* After services on shore, flowers are cast on the water to honor those who lost their lives at sea. Memorial Day.

**Salmon Bake.** *Depoe Bay Park, Depoe Bay. Phone 541/765-2889.* Salmon prepared in the Native American manner. Third Sat in Sept.

## Limited-Service Hotels

**★★ INN AT OTTER CREST.** *301 Otter Crest Loop Rd, Otter Rock (97369). Phone 541/765-2111; toll-free 800/452-2101; fax 541/765-2047. www.innatottercrest.com.* 120 rooms. Check-out noon. Restaurant, bar. Fitness room. Outdoor pool, whirlpool. Tennis. **$**

**★★ SURFRIDER RESORT.** *3115 NW Hwy 101, Depoe Bay (97341). Phone 541/764-2311; toll-free 800/662-2378; fax 541/764-4634. www.surfriderresort.com.* 52 rooms, 2 story. Check-out 11 am. Restaurant, bar. Indoor pool, whirlpool. Airport transportation available. **$**

## Specialty Lodging

**CHANNEL HOUSE.** *35 Ellington St, Depoe Bay (97341). Phone 541/765-2140; toll-free 800/447-2140; fax 541/765-2191. www.channelhouse.com.* 14 rooms, 3 story. Children over 16 years only. Complimentary full breakfast. Check-in 4 pm, check-out 11 am. Modern oceanfront building overlooking Depoe Bay. **$$**

# Eugene (C-2)

*See also Corvallis, Cottage Grove, McKenzie Bridge*

**Settled** 1846
**Population** 112,669
**Elevation** 419 ft
**Area Code** 541
**Information** Lane County Convention & Visitors Association, 754 Olive, PO Box 10286, 97440; phone 541/484-5307 or toll-free 800/547-5445
**Web Site** www.visitlanecounty.org

Eugene sits on the west bank of the Willamette (Wil-AM-et) River, facing its sister city Springfield on the east bank. The Cascade Range rises to the east, mountains of the Coast Range to the west. Bicycling, hiking, and jogging are especially popular here, with a variety of trails to choose from. Forests of Douglas fir support a lumber industry that accounts for 40 percent of the city's manufacturing. Eugene-Springfield is at the head of a series of dams built for flood control of the Willamette River Basin. Willamette National Forest headquarters is located here.

## What to See and Do

**Armitage County Park.** *90064 Coburg Rd, Eugene (97408). 6 miles N off I-5 on Coburg Rd. Phone 541/682-2000. www.ecomm.lanecounty.org.* A 57-acre park on partially wooded area on the south bank of the McKenzie River. Fishing, boating (ramp); hiking, picnicking.

**Camp Putt Adventure Golf Park.** *4006 Franklin Blvd, Eugene (97403). Phone 541/741-9828.* An 18-hole course with challenging holes like "Pond O' Peril," "Thunder Falls," and "Earthquake." Lakeside patio with ice cream bar. (Late Mar-mid-Nov, daily) **$$**

**Fall Creek Dam and Lake.** *40386 W Boundary Rd, Lowell (97452). 20 miles SE on Hwy 58 to Lowell, then follow signs to Big Fall Creek Rd. Phone 541/937-2131.* Winberry Creek Park has swimming beach, fishing, boating (ramp); picnicking. (May-Sept) Some fees. North Shore Ramp has fishing, boat launching facilities; picnicking. (Daily with low-level ramp) Cascara Campground has swimming, fishing, boating (ramp); camping (May-Sept). Some fees.

**Hendricks Park Rhododendron Garden.** *Summit and Skyline drs, Eugene (97401). Phone 541/682-5324. www.eugene-or.gov.* A 20-acre, internationally known garden features more than 6,000 aromatic plants, including rare species and hybrid rhododendrons from the local area and around the world (peak bloom mid-Apr-mid-May). Walking paths, hiking trails, picnic area. (Daily) **FREE**

**Hult Center.** *1 Eugene Ctr, Eugene (97401). 7th Ave and Willamette St. Phone 541/682-5000.* Performing arts center offering more than 300 events each year ranging from Broadway shows and concerts to ballet.

**Lane County Historical Museum.** *740 W 13th Ave, Eugene (97402). Phone 541/682-4242. www.lchmuseum.org.* Changing exhibits depict history of county from mid-19th century to 1930s; includes artifacts of pioneer and Victorian periods; textiles; local history research library. (Wed-Fri 10 am-4 pm, Sat-Sun noon-4 pm) **$**

**Lookout Point and Dexter Dams and Lakes.** *40386 W Boundary Rd, Lowell (97452). 20 miles SE on Hwy 58. Phone 541/937-2131.* The 14-mile-long Lookout Point Lake has Black Canyon Campground (May-Oct; fee) with trailer parking. Fishing; picnicking. Hampton Boat Ramp with launching facilities and four camp sites (all year; fee) with trailer parking, picnicking; fishing, closed to launching during low water (usually Oct-Apr). **Lowell Park** on 3-mile-long Dexter Lake has swimming, waterskiing, boating (moorage, ramp), sailboating; picnicking. **Dexter Park** has waterskiing, fishing, boating (ramp), sailboating; picnicking. The Powerhouse at Lookout Point Dam is open to the public (by appointment).

**Owen Municipal Rose Garden.** *North Jefferson at the river, Eugene. N end of Jefferson St, along the Willamette River. Phone 541/682-5025.* A 5-acre park with more than 300 new and rare varieties of roses, as well as wild species (best blooms late June-early July); a recognized test garden for experimental roses. Also here is a collection of antiques and miniatures. Picnic area. (Daily) **FREE**

**South Breitenbush Gorge National Recreation Trail.** *Eugene. From Detroit Ranger Station, travel E on Hwy 22 for approximately 1 mile, turn left onto Breitenbush Rd 46, travel about 14 miles, turn right on Forest Rd 4685. Access 1 is 1/2 mile up Rd 4685. Access 2 is 2 miles on Rd 4685 at Roaring Creek, and access 3 is 1/4 mile past access 2. Phone 541/225-6301.* Meandering through giant trees in an old-growth grove, this popular trail follows the Wild & Scenic-eligible South Breitenbush River. A small Forest Service-operated campground is near the trailhead.

**Spencer Butte Park.** *Ridgeline and Willamette St, Eugene. 2 miles S of city limits on Willamette St. Phone 541/682-4800.* Park has 305 acres of wilderness, with Spencer Butte Summit, at 2,052 feet, dominating the scene. Hiking trails. Panoramic views of Eugene, Cascade Mountains. (Daily) **FREE** Starting at edge of park is

**South Hills Ridgeline Trail.** *52nd St and Spencers Butte Park, Eugene (97405). Begins at 52nd St and Willamette St. Phone 503/325-7275.* A 5-mile trail extending from Blanton Road east to Dillard Road; a spur leads to top of Butte. The trail offers magnificent views of the Cascade Mountains, Coburg Hills, and Mount Baldy; the wildflowers along the trail reach their peak bloom in late Apr.

**University of Oregon.** *1205 University of Oregon, Eugene (97403). Bounded by Franklin Blvd and Agate St, Alder and 18th sts. Phone 541/346-3014. www.uoregon.edu.* (1876) (19,000 students) The 250-acre campus includes more than 2,000 varieties of trees. Points of interest include the Museum of Natural History, Robinson Theatre, Beall Concert Hall, Hayward Field, and the Erb Memorial Union. Campus tours depart from Information and Tour Services, Oregon Hall (Mon-Sat). Also on campus are

**Jordan Schnitzer Museum of Art.** *1430 Johnson Ln, Eugene (97403). Phone 541/346-3027.* Diverse collections include large selection of Asian art representing cultures of China, Japan, Korea, Cambodia, and American and British works of Asian influence; official court robes of the *Ch'ing* dynasty (China, 1644-1911); Russian icon paintings from the 17th-19th centuries; Persian miniatures and ceramics; photography; works by contemporary artists and craftsmen from the Pacific Northwest, including those of Morris Graves. Special exhibits. Gift shop. (Wed-Sun afternoons; closed holidays) **FREE**

**Knight Library.** *University of Oregon Library, 1299 University of Oregon, Eugene (97403). Phone 541/346-3054.* With more than 2 million volumes, this is the largest library in Oregon. Main lobby features changing exhibits of rare books, manuscripts; Oregon Collection on second floor. Fine arts pieces, wrought iron gates and carved panels. (Daily)

**Whitewater rafting.** *Eugene. Phone toll-free 800/547-5445.* Numerous companies offer trips on the McKenzie, Deschutes, and Willamette rivers. Trips range from two hours to five days. Contact Convention and Visitors Association for details.

**Willamette National Forest.** *211 E 7th Av, Eugene (97401). E via Hwy 20, Hwy 126. Phone 541/225-6300.* More than 1 1/2 million acres. Home to more than 300 species of wildlife; including Cascade Mountain Range summit; Pacific Crest National Scenic Trail with views of snowcapped Mt. Jefferson, Mt. Washington, Three Fingered Jack, Three Sisters, Diamond Peak; Koosah and Sahalie Falls on the Upper McKenzie River; Clear Lake; the lava beds at summit of McKenzie Pass; Waldo Lake near summit of Willamette Pass. Fishing; hunting, hiking, skiing, snowmobiling, camping (fee at some sites).

**Willamette Pass Ski Area.** *Cascade Summit. S via I-5, E on Hwy 58. Phone 541/345-7669. www.willamette-pass.com.* Double, three triple chairlifts; patrol, school, rentals (ski and snowboard). Lodge, restaurant, lounge. Longest run 2.1 miles; vertical drop 1,583 feet. Also 20 kilometers of groomed nordic trails. Night skiing (late Dec-late Feb, Fri-Sat). (Late-Nov-mid-Apr) **$$$$**

**Willamette Science and Technology Center.** *2300 Leo Harris Pkwy, Eugene (97401). Phone 541/682-7888.* Participatory science center encourages hands-on learning; features exhibits illustrating physical, biological, and earth sciences and related technologies. Planetarium shows. (Wed-Sun) **$$**

## Special Events

**Bach Festival.** *Eugene. Phone toll-free 800/457-1486.* Numerous concerts by regional and international artists; master classes; family activities. Mid-June-early July.

**Lane County Fair.** *796 W 13th Ave, Eugene (97402). Phone 541/682-4292.* Features local talents in art, baking, photography, and livestock; also included is a Midway and entertainment. Mid-Aug.

## Limited-Service Hotels

**★ PHOENIX INN SUITES EUGENE.** *850 Franklin Blvd, Eugene (97403). Phone 541/344-0001; toll-free 800/344-0131; fax 541/686-1288. www.phoenixinnsuites.com.* 97 rooms, 4 story. Complimentary continental breakfast. Check-out noon. Fitness room. Indoor pool, whirlpool. **$**

**★ ★ RED LION.** *205 Coburg Rd, Eugene (97401). Phone 541/342-5201; toll-free 800/733-5466; fax 541/485-2314. www.redlion.com.* 137 rooms, 2 story. Pets accepted. Check-out noon. Restaurant, bar. Fitness room. Outdoor pool, whirlpool. Airport transportation available. **$**

## Full-Service Hotels

**★ ★ ★ HILTON EUGENE AND CONFERENCE CENTER.** *66 E 6th Ave, Eugene (97401). Phone 541/342-2000; toll-free 800/445-8667; fax 541/342-6661. www.hiltoneugene.com.* In the heart of downtown Eugene, the Hilton is adjacent to the Hult Center for the Performing Arts (see), which holds Broadway shows, concerts, and other performances throughout the year. It's within walking distance of shops and restaurants. At the hotel, the Big River Grille serves Pacific Northwest cuisine, and the lobby bar offers local microbrews. 272 rooms, 12 story. Pets accepted, some restrictions; fee. Check-in 3 pm, check-out noon. High-speed Internet access. Restaurant, bar. Fitness room. Indoor pool, whirlpool. Airport transportation available. Business center. **$$**

**★ ★ ★ WESTCOAST VALLEY RIVER INN.** *1000 Valley River Way, Eugene (97401). Phone 541/743-1000; toll-free 800/543-8266; fax 541/687-0289. www.valleyriverinn.com.* This hotel is conveniently located downtown and minutes from the airport, shopping, the University of Oregon, and the convention center. Some rooms have views of the Willamette River.257 rooms, 3 story. Pets accepted, some restrictions. Check-out 11 am. Restaurant, bar. Fitness room. Outdoor pool, children's pool, whirlpool. Airport transportation available. **$$**

## Specialty Lodging

**THE CAMPBELL HOUSE, A CITY INN.** *252 Pearl St, Eugene (97401). Phone 541/343-1119; toll-free*

*800/264-2519; fax 541/343-2258. www.campbellhouse.com.* Comfort and elegance await you at this intimate bed-and-breakfast, which offers views of the city from a hill. Each room is tastefully and uniquely furnished. 19 rooms, 3 story. Complimentary full breakfast. Check-in 4 pm, check-out noon. **$$**

## Restaurants

**★★ AMBROSIA.** *174 E Broadway, Eugene (97401). Phone 541/342-4141. www.ambrosiarestaurant.com.* Italian menu. Lunch, dinner. Closed holidays. Bar. Outdoor seating. **$$**

**★★★ CHANTERELLE.** *207 E 5th Ave, Eugene (97401). Phone 541/484-4065.* European cuisine set in an intimate, relaxed atmosphere. Chef Ralf Schmidt creatively uses fresh, local ingredients to create such flawless dishes as lamb Provencale, tournedo of beef "Chanterelle," and sautéed prawns Maison. International menu. Dinner. Closed Sun-Mon; holidays. **$$**

**★ EXCELSIOR INN.** *754 E 13th, Eugene (97401). Phone 541/342-6963. www.excelsiorinn.com.* Italian menu. Breakfast, lunch, dinner, Sun brunch. Bar. Children's menu. Outdoor seating. **$$**

**★★ NORTH BANK.** *22 Club Rd, Eugene (97401). Phone 541/343-5622. www.mcmenamins.com.* Seafood, steak menu. Lunch, dinner. Closed Dec 25. Bar. **$$**

**★★ OREGON ELECTRIC STATION.** *27 E 5th Ave, Eugene (97401). Phone 541/485-4444; fax 541/484-6149. www.oesrestaurant.com.* Former train station (1912); memorabilia. Outdoor seating. American menu. Lunch, dinner. Closed July 4, Dec 25. Bar. Children's menu. **$$**

**★★★ SWEETWATERS.** *1000 Valley River Way, Eugene (97401). Phone 541/687-0123. www.valleyriverinn.com.* With a beautiful view of the Willamette River, this casually elegant restaurant delights guests with ample portions of Northwest cuisine and Mediterranean-inspired dishes. Fresh seafood, game meats, exotic fruits, and seasonal, local ingredients make up the majority of the menu. Breakfast, lunch, dinner, Sun brunch. Bar. Children's menu. Outdoor seating. **$$**

**★★ ZENON CAFE.** *898 Pearl St, Eugene (97401). Phone 541/343-3005.* American menu. Breakfast, lunch, dinner, Sun brunch. Closed Thanksgiving, Dec 25. Outdoor seating. **$$**

# Florence (C-1)

*See also Reedsport, Yachats*

**Settled** 1876
**Population** 5,162
**Elevation** 23 ft
**Area Code** 541
**Zip** 97439
**Information** Florence Area Chamber of Commerce, Hwy 101 and 2nd St, PO Box 26000; phone 541/997-3128
**Web Site** www.el.com/to/florence

At the northern edge of the National Dunes Recreation Area, with some of the highest sand dunes in the world, Florence is within reach of 17 lakes for fishing, swimming, and boating. River and ocean fishing, crabbing, and clamming are also popular. Along the Siuslaw River is "Old Town," an historic area with galleries, restaurants, and attractions.

## What to See and Do

**C&M Stables.** *90241 Hwy 101, Florence (97439). 8 miles N on Hwy 101. Phone 541/997-7540.* Experience spectacular scenery of Oregon coast on horseback. Beach (1 1/2-2 hours), dune trail (1-1 1/2 hours), sunset (2 hours, with or without meal), and coast range (1/2-day or all day) rides. Must be 8 years or older. (Daily; closed Thanksgiving, Dec 25) **$$$$**

**Carl G. Washburne Memorial.** *93111 Hwy 101, Florence (97439). 14 miles N on Hwy 101. Phone 541/547-3416.*This 1,089-acre park is a good area for study of botany. Features a 2-mile-long beach, swimming, fishing, clamming; hiking, picnicking, tent and trailer campsites with access to beach. Elk may be seen in campgrounds and nearby meadows.

**Darlingtonia.** *84505 Hwy 101 S, Florence (97439). 5 miles N on Hwy 101. Phone 541/997-3641.* An 18-acre park with short loop trail through bog area noted for Darlingtonia, a carnivorous, insect-eating plant also known as cobra lily. Picnicking, viewing deck.

**Devils Elbow.** *84505 Hwy 101, Florence (97439). 13 miles N on Hwy 101, below Heceta Head Lighthouse. Phone 541/997-3641.* A 545-acre park. Ocean beach, fishing; hiking, picnicking. Observation point. **$$**

**Heceta Head Lighthouse.** *92072 Hwy 101 S, Yachats (97498). 12 miles N on Hwy 101. Phone 541/547-3696.* (1894) Picturesque beacon set high on rugged cliff.

**Jessie M. Honeyman Memorial.** *84505 Hwy 101, Florence (97439). 3 miles S on Hwy 101. Phone 541/997-3641.* Park has 522 coastal acres with wooded lakes and sand dunes, an abundance of rhododendrons and an excellent beach. Swimming, waterskiing, fishing, boat dock and ramps; hiking, picnicking, improved camping, tent and trailer sites (dump station). (Daily)

**Sand Dunes Frontier.** *83960 Hwy 101, Florence (97439). 3 1/2 miles S on Hwy 101. Phone 541/997-3544. sanddunesfrontier.com.* Excursions aboard 20-passenger dune buggies or drive-yourself Odysseys; miniature golf; flower garden; gift shop, snack bar. (Daily, weather permitting) **$$$$**

**Sea Lion Caves.** *91560 Hwy 101, Florence (97439). 12 miles N on Hwy 101. Phone 541/547-3111. www.sealioncaves.com.* Descend 208 feet under basaltic headland into a 1,500-foot-long cavern that is home to wild sea lions. These mammals (up to 12 feet long) are generally seen on rocky ledges outside the cave in spring and summer and inside the cave in fall and winter. Self-guided tours; a light jacket and comfortable shoes are suggested. (Daily from 9 am; closed Dec 25) **$$**

**Siuslaw Pioneer Museum.** *85294 Hwy 101 S, Florence (97439). 1 mile S. Phone 541/997-7884.* Exhibits preserve the history of the area; impressive display of artifacts and items from early settlers and Native Americans. Library room; extensive genealogy records; hundreds of old photographs. (Jan-Nov, Tues-Sun; closed holidays) **$**

## Special Event

**Rhododendron Festival.** *Florence. Phone 541/997-3128.* Activities include the crowning of the Queen Rhododendra, parades, carnival rides, and entertainment. Third weekend in May.

## Limited-Service Hotels

**★ BEST WESTERN PIER POINT INN.** *85625 Hwy 101, Florence (97439). Phone 541/997-7191; fax 541/997-3828. www.bestwestern.com.* Overlooks Siuslaw River. 55 rooms, 3 story. Complimentary continental breakfast. Check-out 11 am. Whirlpool. **$**

**★ ★ DRIFTWOOD SHORES RESORT & CONFERENCE CENTER.** *88416 1st Ave, Florence (97439). Phone 541/997-8263; fax 541/997-5857. www.driftwoodshores.com.* 128 rooms. Check-in 3 pm, check-out noon. Restaurant, bar. Indoor pool, whirlpool. **$$**

## Restaurant

**★ ★ CLAWSON WINDWARD INN.** *3757 Hwy 101 N, Florence (97439). Phone 541/997-8243; fax 541/997-8243.* American menu. Breakfast, lunch, dinner. Closed Dec 25. Bar. Children's menu. **$$**

# Forest Grove (B-2)

*See also Beaverton, Oregon City, Portland*

**Settled** 1845
**Population** 13,559
**Elevation** 175 ft
**Area Code** 503
**Zip** 97116
**Information** Chamber of Commerce, 2417 Pacific Ave; phone 503/357-3006
**Web Site** www.fgchamber.org

Forest Grove traces its beginning to missionaries who brought religion to what they called the "benighted Indian." The town is believed to have been named for a forest of firs which met a grove of oaks.

## What to See and Do

**Pacific University.** *2043 College Way, Forest Grove (97116). Main entrance on College Way. Phone 503/357-6151. www.pacificu.edu.* (1849) (1,600 students) Founded as Tualatin Academy, it is one of the Northwest's oldest schools. On campus is art gallery and Old College Hall (academic year, Tues, Thurs; also by appointment). Tours of campus.

**Scoggin Valley Park and Hagg Lake.** *50250 SW Scoggins Valley Rd, Gaston (97119). 7 miles SW via Hwy 47, Scoggin Valley Rd exit. Phone 503/359-5732.* Features 11 miles of shoreline. Swimming, windsurfing, fishing, boating (ramps); picnic sites. (Feb-Nov)

## Special Events

**Barbershop Ballad Contest.** *Pacific University, 2331 Main St, Forest Grove (97116). Phone 503/357-3006.* First weekend in Mar.

**Concours d'Elegance.** *Pacific University, 2043 College Way, Forest Grove (97116). Phone 503/357-2300.* Classic and vintage auto display. Third Sun in July.

**Founders Day Corn Roast.** *2417 Pacific Ave, Forest Grove (97116). Phone 503/357-3006.* Late Sept.

**Hawaiian Luau.** *Pacific University, 2043 College Way, Forest Grove (97116). Phone 503/357-6151.* Hawaiian traditions celebrated in food, fashions, and dance. Mid-Apr.

## Limited-Service Hotel

**★ BEST WESTERN UNIVERSITY INN AND SUITES.** *3933 Pacific Ave, Forest Grove (97116). Phone 503/992-8888; toll-free 800/780-7234; fax 503/992-8444. www.bestwestern.com.* 54 rooms. Complimentary continental breakfast. Check-in 3 pm, check-out noon. Fitness room. Indoor pool, whirlpool. **$**

# Fort Clatsop National Memorial (A-1)

*See also Astoria*

**Web Site** *www.nps.gov/focl*

*(6 miles SW of Astoria off Hwy 101A)*

This site marks the western extremity of the territory explored by Meriwether Lewis and William Clark in their expedition of 1804-1806. The fort is a reconstruction of their 1805-1806 winter quarters. The original fort was built here because of its excellent elk hunting grounds, its easy access to ocean salt, its protection from the westerly coastal storms, and the availability of fresh water.

The expedition set out on May 14, 1804, to seek "the most direct and practicable water communication across this continent" under orders from President Thomas Jefferson. The first winter was spent near Bismarck, North Dakota. In April, 1805, the party, then numbering 33, resumed the journey. On November 15, they had their first view of the ocean from a point near McGowan, Washington. The company left Fort Clatsop on March 23, 1806, on their return trip and was back in St. Louis on September 23 of the same year. The Lewis and Clark Expedition was one of the greatest explorations in the history of the United States, and its journals depict one of the most fascinating chapters in the annals of the American frontier. The visitor center has museum exhibits and provides audiovisual programs. The canoe landing has replicas of dugout canoes of that period. Ranger talks and living history demonstrations are presented mid-June-Labor Day. (Daily; closed Dec 25) For further information contact Superintendent, Hwy 3, Box 604 FC, Astoria 97103; phone 503/861-2471. Apr-Sept **$$**, Rest of year **FREE**

# Gold Beach (E-1)

*See also Brookings, Port Orford*

**Population** 1,546
**Elevation** 51 ft
**Area Code** 541
**Zip** 97444
**Information** Chamber of Commerce & Visitors Center, 94080 Shirley Ln; phone 541/247-7526 or toll-free 800/525-2334
**Web Site** www.goldbeach.org

Until floods in 1861 washed the deposits out to sea, placer mining in the beach sands was profitable here; hence the name. There is still some mining farther up the Rogue River. Gold Beach is at the mouth of the Rogue River, on the south shore; Wedderburn is on the north bank. Agate hunting is popular at the mouth of the Rogue River. The river is also well-known for steelhead and salmon fishing. Surf fishing and clamming are possible at many excellent beaches. The Siskiyou National Forest is at the edge of town and a Ranger District office of the forest is located here.

## What to See and Do

**Cape Sebastian State Park.** *Gold Beach. 7 miles S on Hwy 101. Phone 541/469-2021.* Approximately 1,143 acres of open and forested land. Cape Sebastian is a precipitous headland, rising more than 700 feet above the tide with a view of many miles of coastline. One-and-a-half-mile trail to the tip of the cape; beach access. A short roadside through the forest area is marked by wild azaleas, rhododendrons, and blue ceanothus in season. Trails; no restrooms or water.

**Curry County Historical Museum.** *29984 Ellensburg Ave, Gold Beach (97444). Phone 541/247-9396.* Collections and interpretive displays of early life in Curry County. (Feb-Dec, Tues-Sat afternoons) **DONATION**

**Jerry's Rogue River Jet Boat Trips.** *Gold Beach. S end of Rogue River Bridge at port of Gold Beach Boat Basin. Phone 541/247-4571; toll-free 800/451-3645.* A 6-hour (64-mile) round trip into wilderness area; 2-hour lunch or dinner stop at Agness. Also 8-hour (104-

mile) and 6-hour (80-mile) round-trip whitewater excursions. Rogue River Museum and Gift Shop (all year). (May-Oct, daily). **$$$$**

**Mail Boat Whitewater Trips.** *94294 Rouge River Rd, Gold Beach (97444). Mail Boat Dock. Phone 541/247-7033; toll-free 800/458-3511.* A 104-mile round trip by jet boat into wilderness and whitewater of the upper Rogue River. Narrated 7 1/2-hour trip. (Mid-May-mid-Oct, daily) Also 80-mile round trip to the middle Rogue River. Narrated 6 3/4-hour trip departs twice daily. Reservations advised for all trips. (Mid-June-Sept) **$$$$**

**Official Rogue River Mail Boat Hydro-Jet Trips.** *94294 Rogue River Rd, Gold Beach (97444). Mail Boat Dock, 1/4 mile upstream from N end of Rogue River Bridge. Phone 541/247-7033; toll-free 800/458-3511.* A 64-mile round trip by jet boat up the wild and scenic Rogue River; 2-hour lunch stop at Agness. Reservations advised. (May-Oct, daily) **$$$$**

**Prehistoric Gardens.** *36848 Hwy 101, Port Orford (97465). 14 miles N on Hwy 101, located in Oregon's rain forest. Phone 541/332-4463.* Life-size sculptures of dinosaurs and other prehistoric animals that disappeared more than 70 million years ago are set among primitive plants, which have survived. (Daily) **$$$**

## Special Events

**Curry County Fair.** *29392 Ellensburg Ave, Gold Beach (97444).* Last weekend in July.

**Festival of Quilts.** *Gold Beach. Phone 541/247-7526.* Sept.

**Spring Flower, Art, & Clam Chowder Festival.** *Gold Beach. Phone 541/247-6550.* First weekend in May.

**Whale of an Art and Wine Festival.** *Gold Beach. Phone 541/247-7526.* Mid-May.

## Limited-Service Hotel

**★ GOLD BEACH INN.** *29346 Ellensburg Ave, Gold Beach (97444). Phone 541/247-7091; toll-free 888/663-0608; fax 541/247-0225. www.shorecliffinn.com.* On Highway 101, this rather nondescript but well maintained hotel has a beautiful location to recommend it. Most guest rooms overlook the ocean, as does the hotel's balcony. Beachcombing for driftwood is popular here. 40 rooms, 2 story. Pets accepted; fee. Complimentary continental breakfast. Check-in 2 pm, check-out 11 am. Beach. **$**

## Full-Service Inn

**★ ★ ★ TU TU' TUN LODGE.** *96550 N Bank Rogue, Gold Beach (97444). Phone 541/247-6664; toll-free 800/864-6357; fax 541/247-0672. www.tututun.com.* Tu Tu' Tun Lodge corners the market on sophisticated rustication. From its flower-filled gardens to its scenic spot on the banks of the Rogue River, this place seems to ooze serenity. Entered from covered walkways, the guest rooms and suites are true havens from the outside world with wood-burning fireplaces, deep-soaking tubs, overstuffed furnishings, and luxuriously soft bed linens. A peaceful slumber is virtually guaranteed here, where romantics enjoy the blissful quietude. Nature is the inspiration behind this great resort, where large windows bring the outdoors in, and river rock fireplaces and distinctive wood furnishings celebrate nature's bounty. Don't miss a boat ride on the Rogue River, which can be arranged through the lodge. There's also a four-hole pitch-and-putt course and horseshoe courts. Inventive Pacific Northwest cuisine accounts for memorable dining experiences at this unique lodge. 18 rooms. Closed Jan 1, Thanksgiving, Dec 25. Check-in 3 pm, check-out 11 am. Restaurant, bar. Outdoor pool. Airport transportation available. **$$**

# Grants Pass (E-2)

*See also Cave Junction, Jacksonville, Medford, Oregon Caves National Monument*

**Population** 17,488
**Elevation** 948 ft
**Area Code** 541
**Information** Visitor & Convention Bureau, 1995 NW Vine St, PO Box 1787, 97526; phone 541/476-5510 or toll-free 800/547-5927
**Web Site** www.visitgrantspass.org

Grants Pass was named by the rail constructors who were here when news reached them of General Grant's victorious siege of Vicksburg in 1863. On the Rogue River, Grants Pass is the seat of Josephine County. Tourism is the chief source of income; agriculture and electronics are next in importance. Fishing in the Rogue River is a popular activity. A Ranger District office and headquarters of the Siskiyou National Forest is located here.

## What to See and Do

**Grants Pass Museum of Art.** *229 SW G St, Grants Pass (97527). Phone 541/479-3290.* Permanent and changing exhibits of photography, paintings, art objects. (Tues-Sat afternoons; closed holidays) **FREE**

**Rogue River Raft Trips.** *Grants Pass. Phone toll-free 800/547-5927.* One- to five-day whitewater scenic or fishing trips through the wilderness, past abandoned gold-mining sites; overnight lodges or camping en route. Some of these are seasonal; some all year. For details, contact the Visitor and Convention Bureau. Also available is

> **Hellgate Jetboat Excursions.** *966 SW 6th St, Grants Pass (97526). Depart from Riverside Inn. Phone 541/479-7204; toll-free 800/648-4874.* Interpretive jet boat trips down the Rogue River: 2-hour scenic excursion (May-Sept, daily); 4-hour country dinner excursion (Mid-May-Sept); 4-hour champagne brunch excursion (Mid-May-Sept, weekends); 5-hour whitewater trip (May-Sept, daily). **$$$$**

**Siskiyou National Forest.** *Grants Pass. N, S, and W off Hwy 199 or W of I-5. Phone 541/471-6516.* Over 1 million acres. Famous for salmon fishing in lower Rogue River gorge and early-day gold camps. Many species of trees and plants are relics of past ages; a botanist's paradise. An 84-mile stretch of Rogue River between Applegate River and Lobster Creek Bridge is designated a National Wild and Scenic River; nearly half is in the forest. Boat, pack, and saddle trips into rugged backcountry. Picnic sites. Camping. For further information contact Visitor Information Office, PO Box 440, 200 NE Greenfield Rd.

**Valley of the Rogue State Park.** *3792 N River Rd, Grants Pass (97525). 8 miles S on I-5. Phone 541/582-1118.* A 275-acre park with fishing, boat ramp to Rogue River; picnicking, improved tent and trailer sites. (Daily; dump station)

## Special Events

**Amazing May.** *Grants Pass. Phone 541/476-7717.* Eclectic mixture of events heralding the arrival of spring. May.

**Boatnik Festival.** *Grants Pass. Riverside Park. Phone 541/474-2361.* Parade, concessions, carnival rides, boat races; entertainment. A 25-mile whitewater hydroboat race from Riverside Park to Hellgate Canyon and back. Square dance festival at Josephine County Fairgrounds. Memorial Day weekend.

**Heritage Days.** *Grants Pass. Phone 541/476-7717.* Historical and ethnic related events of the pioneers that settled the southern Oregon territory. Sept-mid-Oct.

**Jedediah Smith Mountain Man Rendezvous.** *Grants Pass. Sportsman Park. Phone 541/476-5020.* Muzzle-loader/black powder shoots, costume contests, exhibits. Early Aug.

**Josephine County Fair.** *Fairgrounds, 1451 Fairgrounds Rd, Grants Pass (97527). Redwood Hwy and W Park St. Phone 541/476-3215.* Mid-Aug.

**Pari-mutuel horse racing.** *Fairgrounds, 1451 Fairgrounds Rd, Grants Pass (97527). Phone 541/476-3215.* Late May-early July.

## Limited-Service Hotels

**★ BEST WESTERN INN AT THE ROGUE.** *8959 Rogue River Hwy, Grants Pass (97527). Phone 541/582-2200; toll-free 800/238-0700; fax 541/582-1415. www.bestwestern.com.* Easily accessible from I-5, this hotel is a convenient overnight stopover. It's also a destination unto itself; the nearby Rogue River offers fishing, rafting, and jet boat excursions. Guest rooms have microwaves and small refrigerators, and VCRs are available. 54 rooms, 2 story. Pets accepted; fee. Complimentary continental breakfast. Check-in 2 pm, check-out 11 am. Fitness room. Outdoor pool, whirlpool. **$**

**★ COMFORT INN.** *1889 NE 6th St, Grants Pass (97526). Phone 541/479-8301; toll-free 800/626-1900; fax 541/955-9721. www.choicehotels.com.* 59 rooms, 2 story. Pets accepted; fee. Complimentary continental breakfast. Check-in 2 pm, check-out 11 am. Outdoor pool. **$**

**★ HOLIDAY INN EXPRESS.** *105 NE Agness Ave, Grants Pass (97526). Phone 541/471-6144; toll-free 800/838-7666; fax 541/471-9248. www.hiexpress.com.* 81 rooms, 4 story. Pets accepted, some restrictions; fee. Complimentary continental breakfast. Check-in 3 pm, check-out 11 am. Outdoor pool, whirlpool. Airport transportation available. Business center. **$**

**★ ★ MORRISON'S ROGUE RIVER LODGE.** *8500 Galice Rd, Merlin (97532). Phone 541/476-3825; toll-free 800/826-1963; fax 541/476-4953. www.morrisonslodge.com.* 22 rooms. Closed Dec-Apr. Check-out 11 am. Restaurant. Outdoor pool. Tennis. Business center. **$**

## Specialty Lodgings

**FLERY MANOR.** *2000 Jumpoff Joe Creek Rd, Grants Pass (97526). Phone 541/476-3591; fax 541/471-2303. www.flerymanor.com.* Set on 7 rural acres about 10 miles north of Grants Pass, Flery Manor is an elegant country bed-and-breakfast. The grounds include gardens, three ponds, a small waterfall, and a gazebo. True to the period of the home, the unique guest rooms are furnished with antiques, canopied feather beds with lots of pillows, and clawfoot tubs. Breakfast is a highlight here: three gourmet courses are served on fine china and heirloom linens. 5 rooms, 3 story. Children over 11 years only. Complimentary full breakfast. Check-in 4 pm, check-out 11 am. **$**

**PINE MEADOW INN.** *1000 Crow Rd, Grants Pass (97532). Phone 541/471-6277; toll-free 800/554-0806; fax 541/471-6277. www.pinemeadowinn.com.* Situated on 9 acres of meadow and private forest, this Midwest-style farmhouse is furnished with turn-of-the-century antiques. 4 rooms, 2 story. Closed Nov-Jan. Children over 11 years only. Complimentary full breakfast. Check-in 4 pm, check-out 11 am. Whirlpool. **$**

**WEASKU INN.** *5560 Rogue River Hwy, Grants Pass (97527). Phone 541/471-8000; toll-free 800/493-2758; fax 541/471-7038. www.countryhouseinns.com.* A secluded setting on the Rogue River amid towering pine trees lends this 1924 inn an air of tranquility. Originally a vacation spot for Hollywood stars, including Clark Gable, Bing Cosby, and Carole Lombard, the Weasku is a high-end lodge that offers guests the opporunity to fish for salmon, go river rafting, or simply relax on the expansive lawn. Choose from five rooms in the main lodge, with its rustic great room complete with roaring fire, and the surrounding cabins, which have river rock fireplaces of their own. All accommodations feature pine furnishings, homey quilts, and beamed ceilings with ceiling fans. Guests enjoy an evening wine-and-cheese reception, nightly milk and cookies, and summertime barbecues. 17 rooms, 2 story. Complimentary continental breakfast. Check-in 4 pm, check-out noon. High-speed Internet access. **$$**

# Hermiston (A-4)

*See also Pendleton, Umatilla*

**Population** 10,040
**Elevation** 457 ft
**Area Code** 541
**Zip** 97838
**Information** Greater Hermiston Chamber of Commerce, 415 S US Hwy 395, PO Box 185; phone 541/567-6151 or 541/564-9109
**Web Site** www.el.com/to/hermiston/

Centrally located between the major cities of the Northwest, Hermiston offers an abundant array of recreational opportunities. The Columbia River, second largest river in the country, flows 5 miles to the north and the Umatilla River skirts the city limits; both are popular for fishing. The nearby Blue Mountains offer a variety of summer and winter activities. Agriculture, processing, and production form the economic base of this community, which has become a trading center for this area of the Columbia River Basin.

## Special Event

**Stock Car Racing.** *Race City, USA, Hwy 395, Hermiston. Phone 541/564-8674.* Apr-Oct.

## Limited-Service Hotel

**★ BEST WESTERN HERMISTON INN.** *2255 S Hwy 395, Hermiston (97838). Phone 541/564-0202; toll-free 800/780-7234; fax 541/567-5512. www.bestwestern.com.* 54 rooms. Complimentary continental breakfast. Check-in 2 pm, check-out 11 am. Fitness room. Indoor pool. **$**

# Hood River (B-3)

*See also The Dalles, Mount Hood National Forest*

**Settled** 1854
**Population** 4,632
**Elevation** 155 ft
**Area Code** 541
**Zip** 97031
**Information** Chamber of Commerce Visitor Center, 405 Portway Ave; phone 541/386-2000 or toll-free 800/366-3530
**Web Site** www.hoodriver.org

Hood River, located in the midst of a valley producing apples, pears, and cherries, boasts a scenic view of Oregon's highest peak, Mount Hood; its slopes are accessible in all seasons by road. Highway 35, called the Loop Highway, leads around the mountain and up to the snowline. The Columbia River Gorge provides perfect conditions for windsurfing in the Hood River Port Marina Park.

## What to See and Do

**Bonneville Lock & Dam.** *Cascade Locks (97014). US Army Corp of Engineers Bonneville Lock & Dam Cascade Locks, 23 miles W on I-84. Phone 541/374-8820.* The dam consists of three parts—one spillway and two powerhouses. It has an overall length of 3,463 feet and extends across the Columbia River to Washington. It was a major hydroelectric project of the US Army Corps of Engineers. On the Oregon side is a five-story visitor center with underwater windows into the fish ladders and new navigation lock with viewing facilities. Audiovisual presentations and tours of fish ladders, and the original powerhouse (June-Sept, daily or by appointment; closed Jan 1, Thanksgiving, Dec 25). State salmon hatchery adjacent. Fishing (salmon and sturgeon ponds); picnicking. Powerhouse II and Visitor Orientation Building on Washington side, Highway 14; underwater fish viewing, audiovisual presentations, fish ladder and powerhouse tours (June-Sept, daily or by appointment; closed Jan 1, Thanksgiving, Dec 25); accessible via Bridge of the Gods from I-84. **FREE**

**Columbia Gorge.** *Hood River. Port of Cascade Locks. 10 miles W on I-84, exit 44. Phone 541/374-8427.* Sternwheeler makes daytime excursions, sunset dinner and brunch cruises, harbor tours, and special holiday cruises. Reservations required except for daily excursions (mid-June-Sept).

**Flerchinger Vineyards.** *4200 Post Canyon Dr, Hood River (97031). Phone 541/386-2882.* Tours; tasting room. (Daily) **FREE**

**Hood River County Museum.** *Port Marina Park,300 E Port Marina Dr, Hood River (97031). Phone 541/386-6772.* Items from early settlers to modern residents. An outdoor display includes a sternwheeler paddle wheel, beacon light used by air pilots in the Columbia Gorge, steam engine from the *Mary.* (Apr-Oct, daily) **DONATION**

**Hood River Vineyards.** *4693 Westwood Dr, Hood River (97031). Phone 541/386-3772.* Tours; tasting room. (Mar-Dec, daily) **FREE**

**Lost Lake.** *Hwy 26 and LoLo Pass, ZigZag. 28 miles SW off I-84 on Dee Secondary Hwy and paved Forest Service road in Mount Hood National Forest. Phone 541/386-6366.*bSwimming, fishing, boat rentals; hiking, picnicking, concession, day lodge, camping.

**Mount Hood National Forest.** *S and W of Hood River.* (see).

**Mount Hood Scenic Railroad.** *110 Railroad Ave, Hood River (97031). Phone 541/386-3556; toll-free 800/872-4661. www.mthoodrr.com.* This historic railroad (1906) makes 44-mile round-trip excursions. Dinner, brunch, and murder mystery and comedy excursions are available. Reservations are recommended. (Mar-Dec, schedule varies) **$$$$**

**Panorama Point.** *Hwy 35 S and Eastside Rd, Hood River (97031). 1/2 mile S on Hwy 35 to Eastside Rd. Phone toll-free 800/366-3530.* Observation point for Hood River Valley and Mount Hood.

## Special Events

**Blossom Festival.** *Hood River.* Third weekend in Apr.

**Cross Channel Swim.** *405 Portway Ave, Hood River (97031). Phone toll-free 800/366-3530.* Labor Day.

**Hood River County Fair.** *3020 Wyeast Rd, Hood River (97031). Phone 541/354-2865.* July.

**Hood River Valley Harvest Fest.** *Hood River. Phone toll-free 800/366-3530.* Fresh local fruit, art and crafts, wine tasting, contests. Third weekend in Oct.

**Hood River Valley Sternwheeler Days.** *355 Wanapa St, Hood River (97031). Phone 541/386-2000.* Celebration of the sternwheeler *Columbia Gorge*'s return to home port for the summer. Wine and cheese tasting, crafts, food. July.

## Limited-Service Hotel

**★ ★ BEST WESTERN HOOD RIVER INN.** *1108 E Marina Way, Hood River (97031). Phone 541/386-2200; toll-free 800/828-7873; fax 541/386-8905. www.hoodriverinn.com.* In Columbia River Gorge. 149 rooms, 3 story. Pets accepted, some restrictions; fee. Check-out noon. Restaurant, bar. Outdoor pool. **$**

## Full-Service Hotels

**★ ★ ★ COLUMBIA GORGE HOTEL.** *4000 Westcliff Dr, Hood River (97031). Phone 541/386-5566; toll-free 800/345-1921; fax 541/386-9141. www.columbiagorgehotel.com.* Nestled in the Columbia Gorge National Scenic Area, trees and mountain peaks surround this hotel, which features a waterfall, beautiful scenic gardens, and a Jazz Age atmosphere. 40 rooms, 3 story. Pets accepted, some restrictions; fee. Complimentary full breakfast. Check-out noon. Restaurant, bar. **$$**

★ ★ ★ **HOOD RIVER HOTEL.** *102 Oak St, Hood River (97031). Phone 541/386-1900. www.hoodriverhotel.com.* Charm and elegance await guests at the Hood River Hotel, which is listed on the National Register of Historic Places. Each room is uniquely decorated with antique reproductions and artwork evoking the hotel's history, dating back to its construction as an annex to the Mt. Hood Hotel in 1913. Suites include kitchens. The hotel graces downtown Hood River, a stone's throw from the Columbia River Gorge. Pasquale's Ristorante can be found in the hotel, specializing in Italian and Pacific Northwest cuisines. 41 rooms. Complimentary continental breakfast. Check-in 3 pm, check-out noon. Restaurant, bar. **$$**

## Full-Service Resort

★ ★ ★ **DOLCE SKAMANIA LODGE.** *1131 SW Skamania Lodge Way, Stevenson (98648). Phone 509/427-7700; toll-free 800/376-9116; fax 509/427-2547. www.skamania.com.* At once rugged and sophisticated, the Dolce Skamania Lodge is a perfect mountain getaway. Tucked among the mountain peaks, waterfalls, and canyons of the Columbia River Gorge, just 45 minutes north of Portland, Oregon, this resort enjoys a picture-perfect setting. Comprehensive yet intimate, this hideaway is an ideal spot for large groups or couples escaping the daily grind. From golf and tennis to hiking and biking, this resort offers an endless supply of recreational opportunities. The guest rooms and suites pay tribute to the area's Native American heritage with unique decorative accents, while the clean lines of Pacific Northwestern architecture come shining through here. Three restaurants enchant diners with refined renditions of American classics. 254 rooms, 4 story. Check-in 4 pm, check-out noon. Wireless Internet access. Three restaurants, bar. Fitness room. Indoor pool, whirlpool. Golf, 18 holes. Tennis. Business center. **$**

## Specialty Lodging

**INN OF THE WHITE SALMON.** *172 W Jewett Blvd, White Salmon (98672). Phone 509/493-2335; toll-free 800/972-5226. www.innofthewhitesalmon.com.* European-style inn built in 1937; antique décor, original art. 16 rooms, 2 story. Pets accepted, some restrictions; fee. Complimentary full breakfast. Check-in 3 pm, check-out noon. Outdoor pool. **$**

## Restaurant

★ ★ ★ **COLUMBIA GORGE DINING ROOM.** *4000 Westcliff Dr, Hood River (97031). Phone 541/386-5566; fax 541/386-9141. www.columbiagorgehotel.com.* Located in the historic Columbia Gorge Hotel. Visitors are urged to try the signature "farm" breakfast, a five-course extravaganza. Evening meals focus on Northwest cuisine, especially salmon, lamb, and venison. International menu. Breakfast, lunch, dinner, brunch. Bar. **$$**

# Jacksonville (E-2)

*See also Ashland, Grants Pass, Medford*

**Founded** 1852
**Population** 1,896
**Elevation** 1,569 ft
**Area Code** 541
**Zip** 97530
**Information** Historic Jacksonville Chamber of Commerce, PO Box 33; phone 541/899-8118
**Web Site** www.jacksonvilleoregon.org

Gold was discovered here in 1851 and brought prospectors by the thousands. An active town until the gold strike played out in the 1920s, Jacksonville lost its county seat to the neighboring town of Medford in 1927. Now a national historic landmark, the town is one of the best preserved pioneer communities in the Pacific Northwest. Approximately 80 original buildings can be seen and some visited. A Ranger District office of the Rogue River National Forest is located about 20 miles southwest of town, in Applegate Valley.

## What to See and Do

**Jacksonville Museum.** *206 N 5th St, Jacksonville (97530). Phone 541/773-6536.* In Old County Courthouse (1883), has exhibits of southern Oregon history, pioneer relics, early photographs, Native American artifacts, quilts, natural history. (Wed-Sun; closed Jan 1, Thanksgiving, Dec 25) Children's Museum is in Old County Jail. (1911) **$$** Also maintained by the Southern Oregon Historical Society is

**Beekman House.** *352 E California St, Jacksonville (97530).* (1875) Country Gothic house; former home of a prominent Jacksonville citizen. Living history exhibit. (Memorial Day-Labor Day, Wed-Sun)**$$**

**Oregon Vortex Location of the House of Mystery.** *4303 Sardine Creek L Fork Rd, Gold Hill (97525). Approximately 10 miles NW on county road. Phone 541/855-1543. www.oregonvortex.com.* The Vortex is a spherical field of force half above the ground, half below. Natural, historical, educational, and scientific phenomena are found in former assay office and surrounding grounds. Guided lecture tours (Mar-Oct, daily). **$$**

## Special Event

**Britt Musical Festivals.** *350 1st St, Jacksonville (97530). Phone 541/779-0847; toll-free 800/882-7488.* Hillside estate of pioneer photographer Peter Britt forms a natural amphitheatre. Festivals in classical, jazz, folk, country, dance, and musical theater. Mid-June-Sept.

## Specialty Lodging

**JACKSONVILLE INN.** *175 E California St, Jacksonville (97530). Phone 541/899-1900; toll-free 800/321-9344; fax 541/899-1373. www.jacksonvilleinn.com.* 12 rooms, 2 story. Pets accepted, some restrictions. Complimentary full breakfast. Check-in 4 pm, check-out 11:30 am. High-speed Internet access. Two restaurants, bar. Airport transportation available. Built in 1860s; gold-rush era atmosphere. **$$**

## Restaurants

★★★ **JACKSONVILLE INN.** *175 E California St, Jacksonville (97530). Phone 541/899-1900. www.jacksonvilleinn.com.* Set in a gold rush-era guesthouse, this nationally recognized restaurant serves hearty country fare seasoned with fresh herbs from the inn's garden. American menu. Breakfast, lunch, dinner. Closed Thanksgiving, Dec 24-25. Bar. Outdoor seating. **$$**

★★★ **MCCULLY HOUSE.** *240 E California St, Jacksonville (97530). Phone 541/899-1942. www.mccullyhouseinn.com.* Housed in a historic Gothic Revival mansion—one of the first houses built in town—that is now the McCully House Inn, the dining room features contemporary Pacific Northwest cuisine. Emphasizing only the freshest ingredients, chef Mark Bender provides tempting selections, including pan-seared scallops with cilantro crème fraîche and an extensive wine list. American menu. Dinner. Bar. Outdoor seating. Rose garden. **$$**

# John Day (C-5)

**Population** 1,836
**Elevation** 3,085 ft
**Area Code** 541
**Zip** 97845
**Information** Grant County Chamber of Commerce, 281 W Main; phone 541/575-0547 or toll-free 800/769-5664

John Day, named for a heroic scout in the first Astor expedition, was once a Pony Express stop on trail to The Dalles. Logging and cattle raising are the major industries in the area. Headquarters for the Malheur National Forest is located here; two Ranger District offices of the forest are also located here.

## What to See and Do

**Grant County Historical Museum.** *101 S Canyon City Blvd, Canyon City (97820). 2 miles S on Hwy 395. Phone 541/575-0362.* Mementos of gold-mining days, Joaquin Miller cabin, Greenhorn jail (1910). (Mid-May-Sept, Mon-Sat, also Sun afternoons) **$**

**John Day Fossil Beds National Monument.** *Hwys 19 and 26, John Day (97848). 40 miles W on Hwy 26, then 2 miles N on Hwy 19. Phone 541/987-2333.* The monument consists of three separate units in Wheeler and Grant counties of north central Oregon; no collecting within monument. Wayside exhibits at points of interest in each unit. **FREE** These units include

**Clarno Unit.** *Hwy 218 and Hwy 19, Fossil (97830). 20 miles W of Fossil on Hwy 218. Phone 541/763-2203.* Consists of hills, bluffs, towering rock palisades, and pinnacles. Self-guided Trail of the Fossils features abundant plant fossils visible in the 35-50 million-year-old rock. Picnicking.

**Painted Hills Unit.** *37375 Bear Creek Rd, Mitchell (97750). 9 miles NW of Mitchell, off Hwy 26 on a county road. Phone 541/462-3961.* Displays a colorful, scenic landscape of buff and red layers in the John Day Formation. Self-guided Painted Cove Trail and Leaf Hill Trail. Exhibits; picnicking.

**Sheep Rock Unit.** *Hwys 19 and 26, Kimberly (97848). 7 miles W of Dayville on Hwy 19. Phone 541/987-2333.* Here are outstanding examples of the buff and green layers of the fossil-bearing John Day Formation, Mascall Formation, and Rattlesnake Formation. Visitor center offers picnicking and browsing among fossil displays. Self-guided Island in Time Trail and Story in Stone Trail includes exhibits.

**Kam Wah Chung and Co Museum.** *250 NW Canton, John Day (97845). Adjacent to city park. Phone 541/575-0028.* Originally constructed as a trading post on The Dalles Military Rd (1866-1867). Now houses Chinese medicine herb collection, shrine, kitchen, picture gallery, Doc Hay's bedroom. (May-Oct, Mon-Thurs, Sat-Sun)

**Malheur National Forest.** *431 Patterson Bridge Rd, John Day (97845). N and S on Hwy 395; E and W on Hwy 26. Camping. Phone 541/575-3000.* Nearly 1 1/2 million acres in southwestern part of Blue Mountains include Strawberry Mountain and Monument Rock wilderness areas. Trout fishing in Magone and Yellowjacket Lakes, stream fishing, elk and deer hunting. Hiking. Winter sports. Picnicking. **FREE**

## Special Events

**"62" Day Celebration.** *Canyon City. 1 mile S. Phone 541/575-0329.* Celebrates the discovery of gold in 1862. Medicine wagon and fiddling shows, parade, booths, barbecue, dancing, selection of queen. Second weekend in June.

**Grant County Fair and Rodeo.** *Grant County Fairgrounds, 411 NW Bridge St, John Day (97845). Phone 541/575-1900.* Oregon's oldest continuous county fair. Late Aug.

## Limited-Service Hotel

**★ BEST WESTERN JOHN DAY INN.** *315 W Main St, John Day (97845). Phone 541/575-1700; toll-free 800/780-7234; fax 541/575-1558. www.bestwestern.com.* 39 rooms. Complimentary continental breakfast. Check-in 3 pm, check-out noon. **$**

# Joseph (B-6)

**Population** 1,073
**Elevation** 4,190 ft
**Area Code** 541
**Zip** 97846
**Information** Wallowa County Chamber of Commerce, 115 Tejaka, PO Box 427, Enterprise 97828; phone 541/426-4622 or toll-free 800/585-4121
**Web Site** www.josephoregon.com

Joseph is located in the isolated wilderness of northeast Oregon. Remote from industry, the town attracts vacationers with its beautiful surroundings. There are fishing lakes here and hunting in the surrounding area. At the north end of Wallowa Lake is Old Joseph Monument, a memorial to the Nez Perce chief who resisted the US government. A Ranger District office of the Wallowa-Whitman National Forest is located in nearby Enterprise.

## What to See and Do

**Hells Canyon National Recreation Area.** *612 SW 2nd St, Enterprise (97828). 30 miles NE on County Rd 350 in Wallowa-Whitman National Forest. Phone 541/426-5546. www.fs.fed.us/hellscanyon.* Created by the Snake River at the Idaho/Oregon border, Hells Canyon is the deepest river-carved gorge in North America—1 1/2 miles from Idaho's He Devil Mountain (elevation 9,393 feet) to the Snake River at Granite Creek (elevation 1,408 feet). Overlooks at Hat Point, southeast of Imnaha, and in Idaho (see GRANGEVILLE); both are fire lookouts. The recreation area includes parts of the Wallowa-Whitman National Forest in Oregon and the Nez Perce and Payette national forests in Idaho. Activities include float trips, jet boat tours, boat trips into the canyon from Lewiston, ID (see) or the Hells Canyon Dam (see WEISER, ID), as well as auto tours, backpacking, and horseback riding. There are developed campgrounds in Oregon and Idaho; much of the area is undeveloped, and some is designated wilderness. Be sure to inquire about road conditions before planning a trip; some roads are rough and open for a limited season. For a commercial outfitters guide list and further information, contact Hells Canyon National Recreation Area Office, 88401 OR 82, Enterprise 97828. (See BAKER.)

**Valley Bronze of Oregon.** *307 W Alder St, Joseph (97846). Phone 541/432-7445. www.valleybronze.com.* Company produces finished castings of bronze, fine and sterling silver, and stainless steel. Showroom displays finished pieces. Tours of foundry depart from showroom (by reservation). (May-Nov: daily; rest of year: by appointment) **$$**

**Wallowa Lake State Park.** *72214 Marina Ln, Joseph (97846). 6 miles S on Hwy 82. Phone 541/432-4185.* Park has 201 forested acres in an alpine setting formed by a glacier at the base of the rugged Wallowa Mountains. Swimming, water sport equipment rentals, fishing, boating (dock, motor rentals); picnicking, concession, improved tent and trailer sites (dump station).

Park at edge of Eagle Cap wilderness area; hiking and riding trails begin here. Horse stables nearby.

**Wallowa Lake Tramway.** *Joseph. 6 miles S on Hwy 82. Phone 541/432-5331.* Gondola rises from valley to Mt. Howard summit. Snack bar at summit. (June-Sept: daily; May: weekends, weather permitting) **$$$$**

## Special Event

**Chief Joseph Days.** *102 E 1st St, Rodeo Grounds, Joseph (97846). Phone 541/432-1015.* PRCA rodeo, parades, Native American dances, cowboy breakfasts. Contact Chamber of Commerce. Last full weekend in July.

## Limited-Service Hotel

★ ★ **WALLOWA LAKE LODGE.** *60060 Wallowa Lake Hwy, Joseph (97846). Phone 541/432-9821; fax 503/432-4885. www.wallowalake.com.* 22 rooms, 3 story. Check-in 2 pm, check-out 11 am. Restaurant. **$**

## Restaurant

★ **WILDFLOWER BAKERY.** *600 N Main St, Joseph (97846). Phone 541/432-7225.* Organic baked goods, breakfast items, and sandwiches in a small out of the way building. American menu. Breakfast, lunch. Closed Thurs-Sat. **$**

# Klamath Falls (E-3)

**Settled** 1867
**Population** 17,737
**Elevation** 4,105 ft
**Area Code** 541
**Information** Klamath County Department of Tourism, 205 Riverside Dr, 97601; phone 541/884-0666 or toll-free 800/445-6728
**Web Site** www.klamathcountytourism.com

The closest sizable town to Crater Lake National Park with more than 100 good fishing lakes nearby, Klamath Falls is host to sports-minded people. Upper Klamath Lake, the largest body of fresh water in Oregon, runs north of town for 30 miles. White pelicans, protected by law, nest here each summer, and a large concentration of bald eagles winter in the Klamath Basin. Headquarters and a Ranger District office of the Winema National Forest are located here.

## What to See and Do

**Collier Memorial State Park and Logging Museum.** *46000 Hwy 97 N, Chiloquin (97624). 30 miles N, on both sides of Hwy 97. Phone 541/783-2471.* A 655-acre park located at the confluence of Spring Creek and Williamson River. Open-air historic logging museum with display of tools, machines, and engines; various types of furnished 1800s-era pioneer cabins; gift shop (daily; free). Fishing; hiking, picnicking. Tent and trailer campsites (hookups, dump station).

**Favell Museum of Western Art and Native American Artifacts.** *125 W Main, Klamath Falls (97601). Phone 541/882-9996.* Contemporary Western art; working miniature gun collection; extensive display of Native American artifacts. Also art and print sales galleries. Gift shop. (Tues-Sat) **$$**

**Jackson F. Kimball State Recreation Site.** *46000 Hwy 97, Chiloquin (97624). 40 miles N on Hwy 97, Hwy 62 to Fort Klamath, then 3 miles N on Hwy 232. Phone 541/783-2471. www.oregonstateparks.org/park_229.php.* A 19-acre pine- and fir-timbered area at the headwaters of the Wood River, noted for its transparency and deep blue appearance. Fishing, picnicking, ten primitive campsites (mid-Apr-Oct; no water). **FREE**

**Klamath County Baldwin Hotel Museum.** *31 Main St, Klamath Falls (97601). Phone 541/883-4208.* Restored turn-of-the-century hotel contains many original furnishings. Guided tours (June-Sept, Tues-Sat; closed holidays). **$$**

**Klamath County Museum.** *1451 Main St, Klamath Falls (97601). Phone 541/883-4208.* Local geology, history, wildlife, and Native American displays; research library has books on history, natural history, and anthropology of Pacific Northwest. (Tues-Sat; closed holidays) **$**

**Winema National Forest.** *2819 Dahlia, Klamath Falls (97601). N, E, and W, reached by Hwy 97, Hwy 62 or Hwy 140. Phone 541/883-6714.* This forest (more than 1 million acres) includes former reservation lands of the Klamath Tribe; high country of Sky Lakes; portions of Pacific Crest National Scenic Trail; recreation areas in Lake of the Woods, Recreation Creek, Mountain Lakes Wilderness, and Mt. Theilson Wilderness. Swimming, boating; picnicking, camping (some areas free). **$$$**

## Special Events

**Bald Eagle Conference.** *Klamath Falls. Phone toll-free 800/445-6728.* Mid-Feb.

**Jefferson State Stampede.** *Klamath Falls. Phone 541/883-3796.* Early Aug.

**Klamath County Fair.** *3531 S 6th St, Klamath Falls (97603). Phone 541/883-3796.* Early Aug.

**Klamath Memorial Powow and Rodeo.** *Klamath Falls. Phone toll-free 800/524-9787.* Late May.

## Limited-Service Hotels

**★ BEST WESTERN OLYMPIC INN.** *2627 S 6th St, Klamath Falls (97603). Phone 541/882-9665; toll-free 800/600-9665; fax 541/884-3214. www.klamathfallshotelmotel.com.* 92 rooms, 3 story. Complimentary full breakfast. Check-in 4 pm, check-out 11 am. Outdoor pool, whirlpool. Airport transportation available. Business center. **$**

**★ HOLIDAY INN EXPRESS.** *2500 S 6th St, Klamath Falls (97601). Phone 541/884-9999; toll-free 800/465-4329; fax 541/882-4020. www.hiexpress.com.* 58 rooms, 2 story. Complimentary continental breakfast. Check-in 2 pm, check-out noon. High-speed Internet access. Fitness room. Indoor pool, whirlpool. Business center. **$**

## Full-Service Resort

**★ ★ ★ THE RUNNING Y RANCH RESORT.** *5500 Running Y Rd, Klamath Falls (97601). Phone 541/850-5500; toll-free 888/850-0275; fax 541/850-5593. www.runningy.com.* This 3,600-acre resort is a nature lover's paradise, set amid wooded hills and open meadows at the edge of the Cascade Range. The Running Y Ranch overlooks Klamath Lake, the largest natural lake in the Northwest. The resort's lodge has comfortably appointed rooms with golf course views. Also offered are 2- and 3-bedroom townhouses and chalets, each equipped with a full kitchen, washer and dryer, fireplace, and private deck. Guests can take advantage of the resort's fitness center, pool complex, and Sandhill Spa. The Ranch House Restaurant serves up steak, seafood, and pasta dishes, while the Sugar Pine Café provides lighter fare and snack foods. An on-site Arnold Palmer-designed golf course is among the best public links in the nation. 350 rooms. Check-in 3 pm, check-out noon. Two restaurants, bar. Fitness room. Indoor pool, whirlpool. Airport transportation available. **$**

## Specialty Lodgings

**CRYSTAL WOOD LODGE.** *38625 Westside Dr, Klamath Falls (97601). Phone toll-free 866/381-2322. www.crystalwoodlodge.com.* Located just outside Crater Lake National Park and offering morel mushroom hunting, boating, and fly fishing. 7 rooms, 3 story. **$**

**PROSPECT HOTEL.** *391 Millcreek Dr, Prospect (97536). Phone 541/560-3664; toll-free 800/944-6490. www.prospecthotel.com.* Historic hotel built in the late 1800s was home to many famous figures in American history such as Theodore Roosevelt, Jack London. 24 rooms, 2 story. **$**

## Restaurant

**★ GREY GULL RESTAURANT.** *601 Harbor Isles Blvd, Klamath Falls (97601). Phone 541/882-0663. www.greygullrestaurant.com.* Located next to Klamath Lake at the Harbor Links Golf Course with outdoor seating available. American menu. Lunch, dinner. Outdoor seating. **$$**

# La Grande (B-5)

*See also Baker City, Pendleton*

**Settled** 1861
**Population** 11,766
**Elevation** 2,771 ft
**Area Code** 541
**Zip** 97850
**Information** La Grande/Union County Visitors & Conventions Bureau, 102 Elm; phone 541/963-8588 or toll-free 800/848-9969
**Web Site** www.unioncountychamber.org

Located in the heart of Northeast Oregon amid the Blue and Wallowa mountains, La Grande offers visitors breathtaking scenery and numerous exhilarating activities. Rafting and fishing enthusiasts enjoy the Grande Ronde River; hikers and mountain bikers navigate the Eagle Cap Wilderness and the tracks of the Oregon Trail. A Ranger District office of the Wallowa-Whitman National Forest is located here.

## What to See and Do

**Catherine Creek State Park.** *La Grande. 8 miles SE on Hwy 203. Phone toll-free 800/551-6949. www.oregonstateparks.org/park_17.php.* A 160-acre park in a pine forest along the creek. Fishing, biking, hiking, picnicking. Twenty primitive campsites (mid-Apr-Oct). **FREE**

**Eastern Oregon University.** *1 University Blvd, La Grande (97850). Phone 541/962-3672. www.eou.edu.* (1929) (2,000 students) Campus overlooks the town. Liberal arts college. Rock and mineral collection displayed in science building (Mon-Fri; closed holidays; free). Nightingale Gallery, concerts, theatrical productions, in Loso Hall; changing exhibits.

**Hilgard Junction State Park.** *La Grande. 8 miles W off I-84 N. Phone toll-free 800/551-6949. www.oregonstateparks.org/park_20.php.* A 233-acre park on the old Oregon Trail. Fishing, picnicking, 18 primitive campsites (mid-Apr-Oct). Exhibits at the Oregon Trail Interpretive Center (Memorial Day-Labor Day, daily). **FREE**

**Turns of the Brick.** *105 Fir, Suite 321, La Grande (97850).* Self-guided walking tour of 30 turn-of-the-century buildings and ghost signs. Approximately one-hour tour includes McGlasson's Stationery (1890), Masonic Lodge and JC Penney Company (circa 1900), Fire Station Building (1898) and Helm Building (1891). Unique brickwork and architecture explained in brochure available from La Grande Downtown Development Association. **FREE**

## Special Event

**Union County Fair.** *Union County Fairgrounds, 3604 N 2nd St, La Grande (97850). Phone toll-free 800/848-9969.* Early Aug.

## Specialty Lodging

**STANG MANOR BED & BREAKFAST.** *1612 Walnut St, La Grande (97850). Phone 541/963-2400; toll-free 888/286-9463. www.stangmanor.com.* 4 rooms, 2 story. Children over 10 years only. Complimentary full breakfast. Check-in 3 pm. Check-out 11 am. **$**

## Restaurants

**★ ★ FOLEY STATION.** *1011 Adams, La Grande (97850). Phone 541/963-7473.* Chef-owned restaurant known for eclectic breakfasts. American menu. Breakfast, lunch, dinner. Closed Mon. **$$**

**★ ★ TEN DEPOT STREET.** *10 Depot St, La Grande (97850). Phone 541/963-8766.* Innovative cuisine in a turn of the century brick two-flat with antique furnishings. American menu. Lunch, dinner. Closed Sun. **$$**

# Lakeview (E-4)

**Founded** 1876
**Population** 2,526
**Elevation** 4,798 ft
**Area Code** 541
**Zip** 97630
**Information** Lake County Chamber of Commerce, 126 N E St; phone 541/947-6040
**Web Site** www.lakecountychamber.org

General John C. Fremont and Kit Carson passed through what is now Lake County in 1843. There are antelope and bighorn sheep in the area, many trout streams, and seven lakes nearby. A supervisor's office of the Fremont National Forest is located here; also here is a district office of the Bureau of Land Management and an office of the US Department of Fish and Wildlife.

## What to See and Do

**Drews Reservoir.** *Lakeview. 15 miles W on Dog Lake Rd. Phone 541/947-3334.* Fishing, boating (launch); camping.

**Fort Rock Valley Historical Homestead Museum.** *Fort Rock. Phone 541/576-2468. www.fortrockmuseum.com.* The purpose of this village museum is to preserve some of the homestead era structures by moving them from original locations to the museum site, just west of the town of Fort Rock. The Webster cabin and Dr. Thom's office were the two buildings that were in place for the opening in 1988. Since that time, several homes and a church have been moved to the village, as well as pieces of equipment. As this is an ongoing project; more structures and other pieces will be moved in the future. The moving of the buildings has been accomplished by volunteers from the community, Lake County Road Department, and Midstate Electric Cooperative. Restoration has been done by a few local members. (Open Memorial Day weekend-weekend after Labor Day Fri-Sun 9 am-dusk)

**Fremont National Forest.** *1301 S G St, Lakeview (97630). E and W via Hwy 140, N and S via Hwy 395 and Hwy 31. Phone 541/947-2151.* More than 5 million acres. Includes remnants of ice-age lava flows and the largest and most defined exposed geologic fault in North America, Abert Rim, on east side of Lake Abert. Abert Rim is most spectacular at the east side of Crooked Creek Valley. Many of the lakes are remnants of post-glacial Lake Lahontan. Gearhart Mountain Wilderness is rough and forested with unusual rock formations, streams and Blue Lake. Fishing; hunting, picnicking, camping.

**Geyser and Hot Springs.** *Lakeview. 1 mile N on Hwy 395.* "Old perpetual," said to be largest continuous hot water geyser in the Northwest. Spouts as high as 70 feet occur approximately every 90 seconds. Hot springs nearby.

**Hart Mountain National Antelope Refuge.** *Plush. Phone 541/947-3315. sheldonhartmtn.fws.gov.* The 275,000-acre Hart Mountain National Antelope Refuge was established in 1936 to provide spring, summer, and fall range for remnant antelope herds. These herds usually winter in Catlow Valley, to the east, and on the Sheldon National Wildlife Refuge about 35 miles southeast in Nevada. Since then, the purpose of the refuge has been expanded to include management of all wildlife species characteristic of this high-desert habitat and to preserve natural, native ecosystems for the enjoyment, education, and appreciation of the public.

**Paisley.** *303 Hwy 31, Paisley (97636). 45 miles N on Hwy 31. Phone 541/943-3114.* Unspoiled old Western town.

**Schminck Memorial Museum.** *128 South E St, Lakeview (97630). Phone 541/947-3134.* Pressed-glass goblets, home furnishings, dolls, toys, books, clothing, quilts, guns, saddles, tools, and Native American artifacts. (Feb-Nov, Tues-Sat; also by appointment; closed holidays) **$**

## Special Events

**Festival of Free-Flight.** *Lakeview. Phone toll-free 877/947-6040.* July 4 weekend.

**Irish Days.** *Lakeview. Phone toll-free 877/947-6040.* Mid-Mar.

**Junior Rodeo.** *Lakeview. Phone toll-free 877/947-6040.* Last weekend in June.

**Lake County Fair and Roundup.** *1900 N 4th St, Lakeview (97630). Phone toll-free 877/947-6040.* Labor Day weekend.

## Limited-Service Hotel

**★ BEST WESTERN SKYLINE MOTOR LODGE.** *414 N G St, Lakeview (97630). Phone 541/947-2194; toll-free 800/528-1234; fax 541/947-3100. www.bestwestern.com.* 38 rooms, 2 story. Pets accepted, some restrictions; fee. Complimentary continental breakfast. Check-out 11 am. Indoor pool, whirlpool. **$**

## Specialty Lodging

**HERYFORD HOUSE INN.** *108 S F St, Lakeview (97630). Phone 541/947-2380; toll-free 888/295-3402.* Located in a 1911 brick Queen Anne Victorian mansion in downtown Lakeview.6 rooms, 3 story. **$**

## Restaurant

**★ HOMESTEAD.** *Hwy 31 N, Paisley (97636). Phone 541/943-3187.* Classic American food is served at this restaurant in a historic location. American menu. Breakfast, lunch, dinner. **$**

# Lincoln City (B-1)

*See also Depoe Bay, Newport, Tillamook*

**Population** 5,892
**Elevation** 11-115 ft
**Area Code** 541
**Zip** 97367
**Information** Visitor & Convention Bureau, 801 SW Hwy 101, Suite #1; phone 541/994-8378 or toll-free 800/452-2151
**Web Site** www.oregoncoast.org

Nicknamed the "kite capital of the world," Lincoln City is a popular recreation, art, and shopping area offering many accommodations with ocean view rooms.

## What to See and Do

**Alder House II.** *611 Immonen Rd, Lincoln City (97367). 1/2 mile E off Hwy 101.* Set in a grove of alder trees, this is the oldest glass-blowing studio in Oregon. Watch molten glass drawn from a furnace and shaped into pieces of traditional or modern design. (Mid-Mar-Nov, daily) **FREE**

**Chinook Winds Casino & Convention Center.** *1777 NW 44th St, Lincoln City (97367). Phone 541/996-5825; toll-free 888/244-6665. www.chinookwinds.com.* About 80 miles south of the Washington border on the scenic Oregon coast, Chinook Winds is the largest convention facility between Seattle and San Francisco. With more than 1,200 machines and tables, the modern casino has all the requisite games—slots, blackjack, keno, poker, roulette, craps, and even bingo—with a betting limit of $500. The cavernous showroom sees regular performances by classic rock bands, country artists, and comedians, many of them household names. There are also three restaurants (an upscale room, a buffet, and a deli), a lounge, and childcare services and an arcade for the kids, but no hotel rooms. (There are plenty of the latter in Lincoln City, however.) Best of all, the casino's beachfront location is serene, and there's plenty of public access in the area.

**Devils Lake State Park.** *1452 NE 6th Dr, Lincoln City (97367). S of town, off Hwy 101. Phone 541/994-2002.* A 109-acre park with swimming, fishing, boating (ramp on east side of Devils Lake). Tent and trailer sites (on northwest side of lake).

**Theatre West.** *3536 SE Hwy 101, Lincoln City (97367). Phone 541/994-5663.* Community theater featuring comedy and drama. (Thurs-Sat)

## Limited-Service Hotels

**★ BEST WESTERN LINCOLN SANDS SUITES.** *535 NW Inlet Ave, Lincoln City (97367). Phone 541/994-4227; toll-free 800/445-3234; fax 541/994-2232. www.bestwestern.com.* 33 rooms, 3 story. Complimentary continental breakfast. Check-out 11 am. Fitness room. Beach. Outdoor pool, whirlpool. **$**

**★ ★ CHINOOK WINDS RESORT & CASINO.** *1501 NW 40th Pl, Lincoln City (97367). Phone 541/994-3655; fax 541/994-2199. www.shiloinn.com.* 247 rooms, 4 story. Pets accepted, some restrictions; fee. Check-out noon. Restaurant, bar. Fitness room. Indoor pool, whirlpool. Airport transportation available. Business center. **$**

**★ COHO INN.** *1635 NW Harbor Ave, Lincoln City (97367). Phone 541/994-3684; toll-free 800/848-7006; fax 541/994-6244. www.thecohoinn.com.* 50 rooms, 3 story. Pets accepted, some restrictions; fee. Check-out 11 am. Whirlpool. **$**

**★ ★ INN AT SPANISH HEAD.** *4009 SW Hwy 101, Lincoln City (97367). Phone toll-free 800/452-8127; fax 541/996-4089. www.spanishhead.com.* Built on side of cliff; oceanfront. Colorful sunsets and sandy beaches are the setting for this oceanfront hotel on the Oregon coast. 120 rooms, 10 story. Check-out noon. Restaurant, bar. Fitness room. Outdoor pool, whirlpool. **$$**

## Full-Service Resort

**★ ★ ★ SALISHAN LODGE & GOLF RESORT.** *7760 Hwy 101 N, Gleneden Beach (97388). Phone 541/764-2371; toll-free 800/452-2300; fax 541/764-3663. www.salishan.com.* Carved out of a scenic stretch of Oregon coastline, the Salishan Lodge & Golf Resort is paradise for nature lovers who love their creature comforts. This traditional Pacific Northwest lodge knows how to pamper its guests with fireside massages, fine dining, and a multitude of recreational pursuits, but it is perhaps best loved for its magnificent views of the region's ruggedly beautiful landscape. Private beach access and an 18-hole Scottish-style golf course rank among the property's favorite amenities, which also include an indoor tennis center, fitness center, and two indoor pools. Diners enjoy laid-back sophistication at the resort's eateries, where fresh, flavorful Pacific Northwest cuisine and classic American favorites provide rewarding ways to end the day. 205 rooms, 3 story. Pets accepted; fee. Check-out noon. Restaurant, bar. Fitness room. Indoor pool, whirlpool. Golf, 18 holes. Tennis. **$**

## Specialty Lodging

**THE O'DYSIUS HOTEL.** *120 NW Inlet Ct, Lincoln City (97367). Phone 541/994-4121; toll-free 800/869-8069; fax 541/994-8160.* The O'dysius Hotel appeals to water lovers, with the Pacific Ocean to the immediate west, the D-River (the world's shortest river) bordering to the south, and Devil's Lake a short walk to the east. Each room has a fireplace, whirlpool tub, and custom décor. Select rooms have balconies overlooking a sandy beach and the ocean's pounding surf. Nightly wine tastings are offered in the lobby and parlor. Antique furnishings and lacquer-finished wainscoted walls evoke warmth and sophistication throughout the hotel. 30 rooms. No children allowed. Complimentary continental breakfast. Check-in 4 pm, check-out noon. Whirlpool. **$$**

## Restaurants

**★ ★ ★ BAY HOUSE.** *5911 SW US 101, Lincoln City (97367). Phone 541/996-3222. www.bayhouserestaurant.com.* Located at the south end of the city, this romantic restaurant offers spectacular views of Siletz Bay. American menu. Dinner, brunch. **$$**

**★ ★ THE DINING ROOM AT SALISHAN.** *7760 N Hwy 101, Gleneden Beach (97388). Phone 541/764-*

2371. *www.salishan.com.* American menu. Breakfast, lunch, dinner, Sun brunch. Children's menu. Valet parking. **$$$**

★ **DORY COVE.** *5819 Logan Rd, Lincoln City (97367). Phone 541/994-5180. www.dorycove.com.* Seafood menu. Lunch, dinner. Children's menu. **$$**

# Madras (C-3)

*See also Prineville, Redmond*

**Population** 3,443
**Elevation** 2,242 ft
**Area Code** 541
**Zip** 97741
**Information** Chamber of Commerce, 274 SW 4th St, PO Box 770; phone 541/475-2350 or toll-free 800/967-3564

Although the area was explored as early as 1825, settlement here was difficult because of Native American hostility. Settlement east of the Cascades, considered a wall of separation between the Native Americans and the settlers, was officially forbidden in 1856. In 1858 the order was revoked, and in 1862 the first road was built across the Cascades to provide a passage for traders. Shortly thereafter, settlement began in earnest.

## What to See and Do

**Cove Palisades State Park.** *7300 SW Jordan Rd, Madras (97734). 15 miles SW off Hwy 97. Phone 541/546-3412. www.oregonstateparks.org/park_32.php.* A 4,130-acre park on Lake Billy Chinook behind the Round Butte Dam; scenic canyon of geological interest; spectacular views of the confluence of the Crooked, Deschutes, and Metolius rivers forming Lake Billy Chinook in a steep basaltic canyon. Swimming, fishing, boating (ramp, dock, rentals, marina with restaurant, groceries), houseboat rentals; hiking (nearly 10 miles of trails), picnicking, tent and trailer sites (dump station). **$**

**Jefferson County Museum.** *34 SE D St, Madras (97741). 1 block off Main St. Phone 541/475-3808.* Located in the old courthouse; old-time doctor's equipment; military memorabilia; homestead and farm equipment. (May-Oct, Mon-Fri) **$**

**Rockhounding.** *Richardson's Recreational Ranch, Mile Post 81 on Hwy 87, Madras (97741). 11 miles N on Hwy 97, then right 3 miles to ranch office. Phone 541/475-2680.* All diggings accessible by road; highlight of ranch are famous agate beds, featuring Thunder Eggs and ledge agate material. Rockhound campground area (no hookups). Digging fee.

## Special Event

**Collage of Culture.** *Madras. Friendship Park. Phone 541/475-2350.* Music and balloon festival celebrating cultural diversity. Mid-May.

## Limited-Service Hotel

★ **SONNY'S MOTEL.** *1539 SW Hwy 97, Madras (97741). Phone 541/475-7217; fax 541/475-6547. www.sonnysmotel.net.* 44 rooms, 2 story. Pets accepted; fee. Complimentary continental breakfast. Check-out 11 am. Outdoor pool, whirlpool. **$**

## Full-Service Resort

★ ★ ★ **KAH-NEE-TA LODGE.** *6823 Hwy 8, Warm Springs (97761). Phone 541/553-1112; toll-free 800/554-4786; fax 541/553-1071. www.kah-nee-ta.com.* Overlooking the Warm Springs River, this resort gives each guest a view of the sunrise from each room. There is a casino on site for those who enjoy testing their luck. Authentic Native American dances are featured on Sundays (May-Sept). 139 rooms, 4 story. Pets accepted, some restrictions. Check-in 4:30 pm, check-out 11:30 am. Restaurant, bar. Fitness room. Outdoor pool. Golf. Tennis. Casino. **$**

# McKenzie Bridge (C-2)

*See also Eugene*

**Population** 200
**Elevation** 1,337 ft
**Area Code** 541
**Zip** 97413
**Information** McKenzie River Chamber of Commerce and Information Center, MP 24 McKenzie Hwy East (Hwy 126), PO Box 1117, Leaburg 97489; phone 541/896-3330 or -9011
**Web Site** www.el.com/to/Mckenzierivervalley

McKenzie Bridge and the neighboring town of Blue River are located on the beautiful McKenzie River, with covered bridges, lakes, waterfalls, and wilderness trails of the Cascades nearby. Fishing, float trips, ski-

ing, and backpacking are some of the many activities available. Ranger District offices of the Willamette National Forest (see EUGENE) are located here and in Blue River.

## What to See and Do

**Blue River Dam and Lake.** *51668 Blue River Dr, Vida. 7 miles W on Hwy 126, then N on Forest Rd 15 in Willamette National Forest. Phone 541/822-3317.* Saddle Dam Boating Site offers boat ramp. Mona Campground offers swimming; fishing. Picnicking (fee). Dam is a US Army Corps of Engineers project. Recreation areas administered by the US Forest Service. Camping (mid-May-mid-Sept; fee).

**Carmen-Smith Hydroelectric Development.** *McKenzie Bridge. 14 miles NE on Hwy 126, on Upper McKenzie River. Phone 541/484-2411.* Salmon spawning facility near Trail Bridge Dam; three stocked reservoirs—Trail Bridge, Smith and Carmen (daily). Boat launching (free). Picnicking. Camping at Lake's End, north end of Smith Reservoir, at Ice Cap Creek on Carmen Reservoir and at Trail Bridge (10-day limit). **$$$**

**Cougar Dam and Lake.** *51668 Blue River Dr, Vida. 5 miles W on Hwy 126, then S on Forest Rd 19 (Aufderheide Forest Dr), in Willamette National Forest. Phone 541/822-3317.* A 6-mile-long reservoir. Echo Park is a day-use area with boat ramp (free). Slide Creek campground offers swimming, water-skiing, fishing, and a boat ramp. Picnicking; camping (fee). Delta and French Pete campgrounds offer fishing and picnicking. The campgrounds are maintained and operated by the US Forest Service. The dam is a US Army Corps of Engineers project. For further information, inquire at Blue River Ranger Station. (May-Sept; most areas closed rest of year, inquire)

## Limited-Service Hotels

**★ ALL SEASONS MOTEL.** *130 Breitenbush Rd, Detroit (97342). Phone 503/854-3421.* Situated on 2 1/2 acres of wooded land in the foothills of central Oregon, the location is ideal for hiking, boating, and recreation. 10 rooms, 1 story. **$**

**★ ★ RAINBOW RESORT.** *54466 McKenzie River Dr, Blue River (97413). Phone 541/822-3715; toll-free 800/823-3715.* Located on 90 acres of woods and streams with guides for fishing and rafting available. 15 rooms, 2 story. Restaurant. **$$**

**★ SUTTLE LAKE RESORT & MARINA.** *Hwy 20, Sisters (97759). Phone 541/595-2628.* Historic 1920s cabins and houseboat are available for rental featuring a full-service marina with boat and bike rental. 15 rooms, 1 story. **$**

## Specialty Lodgings

**BELKNAP LODGE & HOT SPRINGS.** *59296 N Belknap Springs Rd, Blue River (97413). Phone 541/822-3512.* Extensive grounds and perennial gardens make this mountain retreat on the banks of the McKenzie River one of the state's most enjoyable. 24 rooms, 2 story. **$$**

**MCKENZIE RIVER INN.** *49164 McKenzie River Hwy, Vida (97488). Phone 541/822-6260. www.mckenzieriverinn.com.* Built in 1929, this inn is one of the oldest bed-and-breakfasts on the river. All special needs are catered to. 6 rooms, 2 story. **$**

**METOLIUS RIVER RESORT.** *25551 SW F.S. Rd, #1419, Camp Sherman (97730). Phone toll-free 800/818-7688. www.metolius-river-resort.com.* Located on one of Oregon's premier fly fishing rivers, this area offers fully furnished cabins with kitchens and private decks. All linens are provided. 12 rooms, 2 story. **$$**

**WAYFARER RESORT.** *46725 Goodpasture Rd, Vida (97488). Phone 541/896-3613; toll-free 800/627-3613. www.wayfarerresort.com.* Located on the banks of the McKenzie River with fully applianced cabins, open-beamed ceilings, spacious decks, and fireplaces. 13 rooms, 2 story. **$$**

## Restaurants

**★ ★ BRONCO BILLY'S RANCH GRILL.** *190 E Cascade, Sisters (97759). Phone 541/549-7427. www.broncobillysranchgrill.com.* Located in the historic Sisters Hotel, this establishment serves up modern interpretations of Old West cooking in a unique period environment. American menu. Dinner. **$**

**★ THE CEDARS RESTAURANT & LOUNGE.** *200 Detroit Ave, Detroit (97432). Phone 503/854-3636.* Serving authentic local cuisine for more than 50 years in beautiful downtown Detroit. American menu. Breakfast, lunch, dinner. **$**

**★ KORNER POST RESTAURANT.** *100 S Detroit Ave, Detroit (97342). Phone 503/854-3735. www.kornerpost.com.* Located in a former post office, this restaurant and gift shop serves classic American cuisine with a kitschy atmosphere. American menu. Breakfast, lunch, dinner. **$**

★ **THE LAKESIDE BISTRO.** *13653 Hawks Beard Rd, Black Butte Ranch (97759). Phone toll-free 800/452-7455. www.blackbutteranch.com.* This country-style Western barbecue restaurant features ingredients from the Northwest. American menu. Lunch, dinner. **$**

★ ★ **THE LODGE RESTAURANT.** *13653 Hawks Beard Rd, Black Butte Ranch (97759). Phone toll-free 800/452-7455. www.blackbutteranch.com.* Located in an elegant setting with incredible views of the surrounding mountains and lake, this restaurant serves modern French cuisine utilizing Northwest products. French menu. Dinner. **$**

★ ★ **LOG CABIN INN.** *56483 McKenzie Hwy, McKenzie Bridge (97413). Phone 541/822-3432; toll-free 800/355-3432; fax 541/822-6173. www.logcabininn.com.* Situated in the deep woods in an 1886 river house, this restaurant features an extensive menu of Northwestern specialties. American menu. Lunch, dinner. Bar. Children's menu. Outdoor seating. **$$**

★ **MARION FORKS RESTAURANT.** *Hwy 22, mile 66, Marion Forks (97350). Phone 503/854-3669.* Offering classic American road food in a family-oriented environment. American menu. Lunch, dinner. **$**

★ **SEASON'S CAFÉ AND WINE SHOP.** *411 E Hood, Sisters (97759). Phone 541/549-8911.* The freshly unique sandwiches and light fare here are complemented by a great by-the-glass wine selection. American menu. Lunch. Closed Mon. **$**

# McMinnville (B-2)

*See also Newberg, Oregon City, Salem*

**Population** 17,894
**Elevation** 160 ft
**Area Code** 503
**Zip** 97128
**Information** Chamber of Commerce, 417 NW Adams; phone 503/472-6196
**Web Site** www.mcminnville.org

McMinnville is in the center of a wine-producing area. Many of the wineries offer tours.

## What to See and Do

**Community Theater.** *210 NE Ford St, McMinnville (97128). At 2nd St. Phone 503/472-2227.* Musical, comedy and drama productions by the Gallery Players of Oregon (Fri-Sun).

**Evergreen Aviation Museum.** *500 NE Capt. Michael King Smith Way, McMinneville (97128). Phone 503/434-4180. www.sprucegoose.com.* Home of Howard Hughes "Spruce Goose" aircraft. **$$**

**Linfield College.** *900 SE Baker St, McMinnville (97128). Phone 503/883-2200. www.linfield.edu.* (1849) (2,100 students) Liberal arts. On the 100-acre campus are Miller Fine Arts Center, Linfield Anthropology Museum and the Linfield Theater. The music department offers concerts. Lectures and events throughout the year.

## Special Events

**Turkey Rama.** *417 NW Adams St, McMinnville (97128). Phone 503/472-6196.* Mid-July.

**Wine & Food Classic.** *McMinnville. Phone 503/472-6196.* Mid-Mar.

**Yamhill County Fair & Rodeo.** *2070 NE LaFayette Ave, McMinnville (97128). Phone 503/434-7524.* Late July-early Aug.

## Limited-Service Hotel

★ **BEST WESTERN VINEYARD INN.** *2035 S Hwy 99 W, Mcminnville (97128). Phone 503/472-4900; toll-free 800/285-6242; fax 503/434-9157. www.bestwestern.com.* 65 rooms. Complimentary continental breakfast. Check-in 4 pm, check-out noon. Fitness room. Indoor pool, whirlpool. **$**

## Specialty Lodgings

**FLYING M RANCH.** *23029 NW Flying M Rd, Yamhill (97148). Phone 503/662-3222; fax 503/662-3202. www.flying-m-ranch.com.* 31 rooms. Pets accepted. Check-in 4 pm, check-out 11 am. Restaurant, bar. **$**

**STEIGER HAUS BED & BREAKFAST.** *360 SE Wilson St, McMinnville (97128). Phone 503/472-0821; fax 503/472-0100. www.steigerhaus.com.* Northern European country-style house; stained-glass windows. 5 rooms, 3 story. Children over 10 years only. Complimentary full breakfast. Check-in 3-6 pm. Check-out 11 am. **$**

**YOUNGBERG HILL VINEYARDS INN.** *10660 SW Youngberg Hill Rd, McMinnville (97128). Phone 503/472-2727; toll-free 888/657-8668; fax 503/472-1313. www.youngberghill.com.* Set on a hillside high above the Willamette Valley, this cozy inn possesses

an idyllic location in Oregon's wine country. The inn overlooks Youngberg Hills award-winning Pinot Noir vineyards. Accommodations are nicely appointed with elegant furnishings. The Martini room has a fireplace and Jacuzzi tub, as well as French doors leading to a private deck. Guests are welcome to relax in the library and lounging salon. Covered decks wrap around the perimeter of the inn, affording breathtaking views of the valley below and mountain peaks on the horizon. 7 rooms. Check-in 4 pm. Whirlpool. **$$**

# Medford (E-2)

*See also Ashland, Grants Pass, Jacksonville*

**Founded** 1885
**Population** 46,951
**Elevation** 1,380 ft
**Area Code** 541
**Information** Visitors and Convention Bureau, 101 E 8th St, 97501; phone 541/779-4847 or toll-free 800/469-6307
**Web Site** www.medfordchamber.com

Medford is a name known throughout the US for pears: Comice, Bartlett, Winter Nellis, Bosc, and d'Anjou. The city, on Bear Creek 10 miles from its confluence with the Rogue River, is surrounded by orchards. Trees make the city parklike; lumbering provides a large share of the industry. Mild winters and warm summers favor outdoor living and also encourage outdoor sports: boating and fishing on the Rogue River, fishing in 153 stocked streams and 17 lakes; camping and hunting in 56 forest camps within an 80-mile radius. The Rogue River National Forest headquarters is here.

## What to See and Do

**Butte Creek Mill.** *402 Royal Ave N, Eagle Point (97524). 10 miles N on Hwy 62. Phone 541/826-3531.* Water-powered gristmill (1872) grinds whole grain products with original millstones. Museum (summer, Sat). Mill (Mon-Sat; closed holidays). **FREE**

**Crater Rock Museum.** *2002 Scenic Ave, Central Point (97502). N on I-5, exit 35, then S on Hwy 99. Phone 541/664-6081.* Gem and mineral collection; Native American artifacts; fossils, geodes and crystals. Gift shop. (Tues, Thurs, and Sat; closed holidays) **DONATION**

**Joseph H. Stewart State Park.** *35251 Hwy 62, Trail (97451). 35 miles NE on Hwy 62. Phone 541/560-3334. www.oregonstateparks.org/park_30.php.* A 910-acre park located on a lake formed by the Lost Creek Dam. Swimming, fishing (trout, bass); boat dock and ramp to the Rogue River. Hiking, bike trails (11 miles). Picnicking. Tent and improved campsites (dump station). **FREE**

★ **Rogue River National Forest.** *333 W 8th St, Medford (97501). S off I-5 and NE on Hwy 62, 140. Phone 541/858-2200.* Forest has 632,045 acres with extensive stands of Douglas fir, ponderosa, and sugar pine. Rogue-Umpqua National Forest Scenic Byway offers a day-long drive through southern Oregon's dramatic panorama of mountains, rivers, and forest; viewpoints. A part of the Pacific Crest National Scenic Trail and portions of three wilderness areas are included in the forest. For fishermen, the upper reaches of the Rogue River, and other streams and lakes yield rainbow, cutthroat, and brook trout. Union Creek Historic District, on Highway 62 near Crater Lake National Park. Forest is in two separate sections, located in the Siskiyou Mountains (W of I-5) and Cascade Range (E of I-5). Swimming; hiking, backpacking, downhill and cross-country skiing, picnic areas, camping. Some fees.

**Southern Oregon Historical Society.** *106 N Central Ave, Medford (97501). Phone 541/773-6536. www.sohs.org.* More than 2,000 items from Southern Oregon Historical Society's cultural history collection. Exhibits, public programs, research library. (Mon-Fri) **FREE**

**TouVelle State Recreation Site.** *Medford. 3 miles NE on I-5, then 6 miles N on Table Rock Rd. Phone 541/582-1118. www.oregonstateparks.org/park_106.php.* A 51-acre park. Fishing on the Rogue River; boat ramp. Swimming, hiking, bird-watching, picnicking. **$**

## Special Events

**Jackson County Fair.** *Medford. Jackson County Fairgrounds. Phone 541/774-8270.* Entertainment, dance, music, 4-H fair. Third weekend in July.

**Pear Blossom Festival.** *Medford. Phone 541/779-4847.* Parade; 10-mile run; band festival. Second weekend in Apr.

## Limited-Service Hotels

★★ **RED LION.** *200 N Riverside Ave, Medford (97501). Phone 541/779-5811; toll-free 800/733-5466; fax 541/779-7961. www.redlion.com.* 185 rooms, 2 story. Pets accepted; fee. Check-in 3 pm, check-out noon. High-speed Internet access. Two restaurants, bar. Fitness room. Outdoor pool. Airport transportation available. Business center. **$**

**★ ★ ROGUE REGENCY INN.** *2300 Biddle Rd, Medford (97504). Phone 541/770-1234; toll-free 800/535-5805; fax 541/770-2466. www.rogueregency.com.* 203 rooms, 4 story. Complimentary continental breakfast. Check-in 3 pm, check-out 11 am. High-speed Internet access. Restaurant, bar. Fitness room. Indoor pool, whirlpool. Airport transportation available. Business center. **$**

**★ WINDMILL INN OF MEDFORD.** *1950 Biddle Rd, Medford (97504). Phone 541/779-0050; toll-free 800/547-4747; fax 541/779-0050. www.windmillinns.com.* 123 rooms, 2 story. Pets accepted. Complimentary continental breakfast. Check-in 3 pm, check-out 11 am. Fitness room. Outdoor pool, whirlpool. Airport transportation available. Business center. **$**

## Restaurant

**★ SATIN SLIPPER.** *6463 Table Rock Rd, Central Point (97502). Phone 541/826-6000.* Home-style cooking in a fun, family-oriented environment. American menu. Breakfast, lunch, dinner. **$**

# Mount Hood National Forest (B-3)

*See also Hood River, The Dalles*

**Web Site** www.mthood.org

Mount Hood (11,235 feet) is the natural focal point of this 1,064,573-acre forest with headquarters in Sandy. Its white-crowned top, the highest point in Oregon, can be seen for miles on a clear day. It is also popular with skiers, who know it has some of the best slopes in the Northwest. There are five winter sports areas. Throughout the year, however, visitors can take advantage of the surrounding forest facilities for camping (1,600 camp and picnic sites), hunting, fishing, swimming, mountain climbing, golfing, horseback riding, hiking and tobogganing. The Columbia Gorge, which cuts through the Cascades here, has many spectacular waterfalls, including Multnomah (620 feet). There are nine routes to the summit, which has fumed and smoked several times since the volcanic peak was discovered. Only experienced climbers should try the ascent and then only with a guide. For further information contact the Mount Hood Information Center, 65000 E Hwy 26, Welches 97067; phone 503/622-7674, 503/622-4822, or toll-free 888/622-4822.

## What to See and Do

**Mount Hood Meadows.** *Government Camp. 11 miles NE of Government Camp on Hwy 35. Phone 503/337-2222. www.skihood.com.* Quad, triple, seven double chairlifts, free rope tow; patrol, school, rentals; restaurant, cafeteria, concession, bar, daycare, two day lodges. Longest run 3 miles; vertical drop 2,777 feet. Also 550 acres of expert canyon skiing. (Nov-May, daily) Groomed, ungroomed cross-country trails; night skiing (Wed-Sun).

**River cruise.** *Cascade Locks. 45 miles E of Portland via I-84. Phone 503/224-3900.* 2-hour narrated cruise of Columbia Gorge aboard the 599-passenger *Columbia Gorge,* an authentic sternwheeler. (Mid-June-Sept, three departures daily; reservations required for dinner cruise) Also here: museum; marina; travel information; picnicking; camping. **$$$$**

**Timberline Lodge.** *Timberline (97028). Timberline Ski Area, 6 miles N of Hwy 26. Phone 503/272-3311. www.timberlinelodge.com.* Four Quads, triple, one double chairlift; patrol, school, rentals; restaurant, cafeteria, concession, bar, lodge. Longest run more than 2 miles; vertical drop 3,580 feet. Chairlift also operates (daily, weather permitting; fee). (Mid-Nov-June, daily) **$$$$**

## Limited-Service Hotels

**★ MOUNT HOOD INN.** *87450 Government Camp Loop, Government Camp (97028). Phone 503/272-3205; toll-free 800/443-7777; fax 503/272-3307. www.mounthoodinn.com.* 56 rooms, 2 story. Pets accepted, some restrictions; fee. Complimentary continental breakfast. Check-out noon. Whirlpool. **$**

**★ ★ TIMBERLINE LODGE.** *Timberline, Timberline Lodge (97028). Phone 503/272-3311; fax 503/272-3710. www.timberlinelodge.com.* 70 rooms, 4 story. Check-in 4 pm, check-out 11 am. Restaurant, bar. Children's activity center. Outdoor pool, whirlpool. Ski in/ski out. **$**

## Staying in a Fire Lookout in the Cascades

The Cascades possess a majestic beauty rivaling that of any other mountain range in the lower 48. To fully appreciate the splendor of the Cascades, you must set off on foot and spend several days navigating your way through dense forests and across open meadows, up and over rocky ridges and alongside deep alpine lakes. Most trekkers choose to sleep in tents, which means bringing along a tarp, rainfly, poles, and stakes, along with the tent itself, all of which must be assembled and disassembled, as well as kept clean and dry. But a tent is not your only option when it comes to shelter. In the Pacific Northwest, the US Forest Service (www.fs.fed.us) rents out dozens of fire lookouts to the public. Lookout amenities are wide-ranging. Some are furnished with just a cot and table, while others have such luxuries as propane-powered heaters, refrigerators, and stoves. With all fire lookouts, a spectacular view comes standard.

If you're ready to leave the tent behind and stay in a fire lookout, here are several worthy of consideration:

Pickett Butte Lookout stands on a ridge near the southern Oregon town of Tiller, a short drive north of Medford and west of Crater Lake. Nestled amid the pines of Umpqua National Forest, the lookout is well equipped with a heater, lantern, stove, and refrigerator, all of which are powered by complimentary propane. The lookout can be rented for up to three consecutive nights from early November through May. The fee is $40 per night. To make a reservation, contact the Tiller Ranger Station at phone 541/825-3100.

Set high above Hidden Lake in Willamette National Forest, Indian Ridge Lookout offers breathtaking views of the Three Sisters mountain peaks. An hour's drive east of Eugene, the lookout is surrounded by pine trees, beargrass, and huckleberries. Amenities are minimal; you'll find two twin beds and a table but no heat, so bring your flannel pajamas. The 16 x 16 structure is available from July through September for $40 a night. Make a reservation by calling the ranger station in McKenzie Bridge at phone 541/822-3381.

East of Portland, Clear Lake Lookout is perched on a 40-foot tower in Mount Hood National Forest. The lookout rents for $30 per night and accommodates four people. This one's a good option for those who love snow, as it's available only from November through May. Nearby, the Timberline Lodge offers year-round skiing on the shoulders of 11,239-foot-high Mount Hood. To reserve the lookout, contact the Barlow Ranger Station at phone 541/467-2291.

Evergreen Mountain Lookout sits atop a mountain ridge at an elevation of 5,587 feet. A two-hour drive east of Seattle in Mount Baker-Snoqualmie National Forest, the structure was used to detect fires from 1935 until the early 1980s, and even served as an Air Warning Station during World War II. After nearly 20 years of neglect, the lookout was renovated in 2001 and made available for public rental. Furnishings include a stove, two lanterns, four mattresses, a table, and folding chairs. The lookout can be rented from early August until mid-November, depending on the weather, at a fee of $40 per night. Contact the Skykomish Ranger Station at phone 360/677-2414 for more information.

While a lookout may offer more protection than a tent, you still need to bring along such essentials as flashlights, bedding, and ample food and water. It also must be noted that reaching a fire lookout typically involves driving on an unpaved Forest Service road to an unattended parking area, followed by a mile-plus hike, and finishing with a climb up a narrow switchback of stairs to the enclosed lookout. Those willing to make the effort are rewarded with a unique and enchanting experience that will make their travels in the Cascades all the more memorable..

## Full-Service Resort

**★★★ THE RESORT AT THE MOUNTAIN.** *68010 E Fairway Ave, Welches (97067). Phone 503/622-3101; toll-free 800/669-7666; fax 503/622-2222. www.theresort.com.* Situated on 300 acres of forest at Salmon River. Scottish amenities reminiscent of Highlands. 160 rooms, 2 story. Check-in 4 pm, check-out noon. Restaurant, bar. Fitness room. Outdoor pool, whirlpool. Golf. Tennis. **$**

# Newberg (B-2)

*See also Beaverton, McMinnville, Oregon City, Portland, Salem, Silverton*

**Founded** 1889
**Population** 13,086
**Elevation** 176 ft
**Area Code** 503
**Zip** 97132
**Information** Chamber of Commerce, 415 E Sheridan; phone 503/538-2014
**Web Site** www.chehalemvalleychamberofcommerce.com

Quakers made their first settlement west of the Rockies here and established Pacific Academy in 1885. Herbert Hoover was in its first graduating class (1888).

## What to See and Do

**Champoeg State Heritage Area.** *7679 Champoeg Rd NE, Saint Paul (97137). 5 miles W off I-5. Phone 503/678-1251.* A 615-acre park on site of early Willamette River settlement, site of settlers' vote in 1843 for a provisional territorial government, swept away by flood of 1861. Fishing, boat dock on Willamette River; hiking, picnicking, improved camping (dump station). Visitor information, interpretive center; monument. French Prairie Loop 40-mile auto or bike tour begins and ends here. (See SPECIAL EVENT) **$$** In the area are

**Newell House Museum.** *8089 Champoeg Rd NE, Newberg (97132). Just W of park entrance. Phone 503/678-5537.* Reconstructed home of Robert Newell, one-time mountain man and friend of the Native Americans. Contains period furnishings, quilts, coverlets and examples of fine handiwork; collection of inaugural gowns worn by wives of Oregon governors; Native American artifacts. Old jail (1850) and typical pioneer one-room schoolhouse. (Feb-Nov, Wed-Sun; closed Thanksgiving) **$**

**Pioneer Mother's Memorial Log Cabin.** *8035 Champoeg Rd NE, Newberg (97137). Located in the park, on the banks of the Willamette River. Phone 503/633-2237.* A replica, much enlarged, of the type of log cabin built by early pioneers. Constructed of peeled hand-hewn logs, with a shake roof, it has a massive stone fireplace in the living room, a sleeping loft and two small bedrooms; many pioneer items include an old Hudson's Bay heating stove, collection of guns and muskets dating from 1777-1853, a fife played at Lincoln's funeral, china and glassware and original furnishings from pioneer homes. (Feb-Nov, Wed-Sun; closed Thanksgiving) **$**

**Visitor Center.** *8239 Champoeg Rd NE, Newberg. Phone 503/678-1251.* Interpretive historical exhibits tell the story of "Champoeg: Birthplace of Oregon"; films; tours. (Daily) **DONATION**

**George Fox University.** *414 N Meridian, Newberg (97132). Phone 503/538-8383.* (1891) (2,600 students) Founded as Friends Pacific Academy; renamed in 1949 for English founder of the Society of Friends. Herbert Hoover was a student here; Hoover Building has displays. Brougher Museum has Quaker and pioneer exhibits. Campus tours.

**Hoover-Minthorn House Museum.** *115 S River St, Newberg (97132). Phone 503/538-6629.* Herbert Hoover lived here with his uncle, Dr. Henry Minthorn. Quaker house built in 1881 contains many original furnishings, photographs, and souvenirs of Hoover's boyhood. (Mar-Nov: Wed-Sun; Dec and Feb: Sat-Sun; closed Jan) **$**

## Special Event

**Vintage Celebration.** *115 N Washington St, Newberg (97132). Phone 503/538-2014.* Classic automobiles and airplanes, arts and crafts, wine tasting. Sat-Sun after Labor Day.

## Limited-Service Hotel

**★ SHILO INN.** *501 Sitka Ave, Newberg (97132). Phone 503/537-0303; toll-free 800/222-2244; fax 503/537-0442. www.shiloinns.com.* 60 rooms, 3 story. Pets accepted, some restrictions; fee. Complimentary continental breakfast. Check-out noon. Fitness room. Outdoor pool, whirlpool. **$**

## Restaurants

**★★ DON GUIDO'S ITALIAN CUISINE.** *73330 E Hwy 26, Rhododendron (97049). Phone 503/622-5141. www.donguidos.com.* Italian menu. Dinner. Closed holidays. Bar. Children's menu. **$$**

**★★★ HIGHLANDS DINING ROOM.** *68010 E Fairway Ave, Welches (97067). Phone 503/622-2214; fax 503/622-2222. www.theresort.com.* International/Fusion menu. Breakfast, lunch, dinner, Sun brunch. Bar. Children's menu. Outdoor seating. **$$**

# Newport (C-1)

*See also Depoe Bay, Lincoln City, Yachats*

**Settled** 1882
**Population** 8,437
**Elevation** 160 ft
**Area Code** 541
**Zip** 97365
**Information** Chamber of Commerce, 555 SW Coast Hwy; phone 541/265-8801 or toll-free 800/262-7844
**Web Site** www.newportchamber.org

This fishing port at the mouth of the Yaquina River has been a resort for more than 100 years. Crabbing is a popular activity here; Dungeness crabs can be caught in the bay year-round.

## What to See and Do

**Beverly Beach.** *198 NE 123rd St, Newport (97365). 7 miles N on Hwy 101. Phone 541/265-9278; toll-free 800/452-5687.* A 130-acre park with beach access; fishing. Hiking. Picnicking. Tent and trailer sites (dump station).

**Devils Punch Bowl.** *Newport. 8 miles N off Hwy 101. Phone 541/265-9278.* An 8-acre park noted for its bowl-shaped rock formation that fills at high tide; ocean-carved caves, marine gardens. Beach. Trails. Picnicking. Observation point.

**Hatfield Marine Science Center of Oregon State University.** *2030 SE Marine Science Dr, Newport (97365). S side of Yaquina Bay, just E of Newport Bridge, off Hwy 101. Phone 541/867-0100.* Conducts research on oceanography, fisheries, water quality, marine science education and marine biology; research vessel *Wecoma;* nature trail; aquarium-museum; films; special programs in summer. Winter and spring grey whale programs. Braille text and other aids for the hearing and visually impaired. (Daily; closed Dec 25) **DONATION**

**Lincoln County Historical Society Museums.** *Phone 541/265-7509. Log Cabin Museum, 545 SW 9th St, Newport (97365).* Artifacts from Siletz Reservation; historical, pioneer and maritime exhibits. (Tues-Sun; closed Jan 1, Thanksgiving, Dec 25) Also **Burrows House Museum,** 579 SW 9th St. Victorian-era household furnishings, clothing; history of Lincoln County. (Same days as log cabin museum) **FREE**

**Marine Discovery Tours.** *345 SW Bay Blvd, Newport (97365). Phone 541/265-6200; toll-free 800/903-2628.* Whale-watching and river cruises. Hands-on activities. (Hours vary seasonally; closed Dec 25) **$$$$**

**Mineral collecting.** *Newport. Phone toll-free 800/262-7844.* Gemstones, marine fossils, other stones are found on beaches to north and south of Newport, particularly at creek mouths.

**Ona Beach.** *Newport. 8 miles S on Hwy 101. Phone 541/867-7451.* A 237-acre day-use park with ocean beach, swimming; fishing, boat ramp on creek. Picnicking.

**Oregon Coast Aquarium.** *2820 SE Ferry Slip Rd, Newport (97365). S side of Yaquina Bay. Phone 541/867-3474.* Houses 15,000 animals representing 500 species in unique habitats. (Daily; closed Dec 25) **$$$**

**Ripley's—Believe It or Not.** *250 SW Bay Blvd, Newport (97365). Phone 541/265-2206.* Exhibits include replicas of a backwards fountain; King Tut's tomb; the *Titanic*; the Fiji mermaid. (Daily; closed Dec 25) **$$$**

**South Beach.** *5580 S Coast Hwy, South Beach (97366). 2 miles S on Hwy 101. Phone 541/867-7451.* Over 400 acres. Botanically interesting area, sandy beach, dunes. Fishing. Hiking. Picnicking. Improved campsites (dump station).

**Undersea Gardens.** *250 SW Bay Blvd, Newport (97365). On Yaquina Bay just off Hwy 101 in the Bay Front district. Phone 541/265-2206.* Visitors descend beneath the sea for underwater show. Watch native sea life through viewing windows; guides narrate as scuba divers perform; features Armstrong, the giant octopus. (Daily; closed Dec 25) **$$$**

**Wax Works.** *250 SW Bay Blvd, Newport (97365). Phone 541/265-2206.* Events of the past and future shown with animation and special effects. (Daily; closed Dec 25) **$$$**

**Yaquina Bay.** *5580 S Coast Hwy, Newport (97365). N end of bridge on Hwy 101. Phone 541/867-7451.* Over 30 acres. Ocean beach, fishing, picnicking. Agate beaches nearby. Old Yaquina Bay Lighthouse (1871) has been restored; exhibits. (Memorial Day-Labor Day: daily; rest of year: weekends) **DONATION**

**Yaquina Head.** *Lighthouse Dr and Hwy 101, Newport (97365). 1/2 mile N on Hwy 101. Phone 541/574-3100.* Lighthouse here is a popular spot for whale-watching and fully accessible tidal pool viewing. Also interpretive center.

## Special Events

**Loyalty Days and Sea Fair Festival.** *555 SW Coast Hwy, Newport (97365). Phone 541/867-3798.* Military ships, parade, sailboat races; entertainment. First weekend in May.

**Seafood and Wine Festival.** *Newport. Phone 541/265-8801.* Last full weekend in Feb.

## Limited-Service Hotels

**★ ★ EMBARCADERO RESORT HOTEL.** *1000 SE Bay Blvd, Newport (97365). Phone 541/265-8521; toll-free 800/547-4779; fax 541/265-7844. www.embarcadero-resort.com.* View of bay. 85 rooms, 3 story. Check-out 11 am. Restaurant, bar. Fitness room. Indoor pool, whirlpool. Airport transportation available. **$**

**★ ★ SHILO INN.** *536 SW Elizabeth St, Newport (97365). Phone 541/265-7701; fax 541/265-5687. www.shiloinns.com.* 179 rooms, 4 story. Pets accepted, some restrictions; fee. Check-out noon. Restaurant, bar. Indoor pool. **$**

**★ WHALER MOTEL.** *155 SW Elizabeth St, Newport (97365). Phone 541/265-9261; toll-free 800/433-9444; fax 541/265-9515. www.whalernewport.com.* 73 rooms, 3 story. Complimentary continental breakfast. Check-out noon. Fitness room. Indoor pool, whirlpool. Airport transportation available. **$**

## Restaurant

**★ WHALE'S TALE.** *452 SW Bay Blvd, Newport (97365). Phone 541/265-8660.* Seafood menu. Breakfast, lunch, dinner, brunch. Closed Wed. Children's menu. **$$**

# North Bend (D-1)

*See also Bandon, Coos Bay, Reedsport*

**Settled** 1853
**Population** 9,614
**Elevation** 23 ft
**Area Code** 541
**Zip** 97459
**Information** Bay Area Chamber of Commerce, 50 Central, PO Box 210, Coos Bay 97420; phone 541/269-0215 or toll-free 800/824-8486. The North Bend Info Center is located at 1380 Sherman Ave, phone 541/756-4613.

This town sits on the "north bend" of Coos Bay, one of the largest and deepest ports in the Northwest. Forestry has long been the town's lifeblood industry, followed by shipbuilding and fishing. Situated at the southern edge of Oregon Dunes National Recreation Area, North Bend is intersected by Hwy 101. The Conde B. McCullough Memorial Bridge stands as the towns most prominent landmark, a 5,300-foot-long expanse of steel constructed during the Depression and bearing the name of its architect.

## What to See and Do

**Coos County Historical Society Museum.** *1220 Sherman Ave, North Bend (97459). In Simpson Park, on Hwy 101, N edge of town. Phone 541/756-6320.* Local history; permanent and changing exhibits. (Tues-Sat) **$**

**Oregon Dunes National Recreation Area.** *855 Hwy 101, Reedsport (97467). Phone 541/271-3611.* Area is 2 miles wide and 40 miles long. One of largest bodies of sand outside of the Sahara. (See REEDSPORT)

**The Real Oregon Gift.** *68752 Hauser Depot Rd, North Bend (97459). 5 miles N on Hwy 101. Phone 541/756-2220.* Manufacturers of myrtlewood products. Tour of factory; gift shop. (Daily) **FREE**

## Limited-Service Hotel

**★ ★ COMFORT INN NORTH BEND.** *1503 Virginia Ave, North Bend (97459). Phone 541/756-3191; fax 541/756-5818.* 96 rooms. Check-in 3 pm, check-out noon. Restaurant, bar. Fitness room. Whirlpool. **$**

## Restaurant

**★ ★ HILLTOP HOUSE.** *166 N Bay Dr, North Bend (97459). Phone 541/756-4160.* International menu. Lunch, dinner. **$$**

# Ontario (C-6)

*See also Caldwell, ID; Weiser, ID*

**Founded** 1883
**Population** 9,392
**Elevation** 2,154 ft
**Area Code** 541
**Zip** 97914
**Information** Visitors & Convention Bureau, 676 SW 5th

Ave; phone 541/889-8012 or toll-free 888/889-8012
**Web Site** www.ontariochamber.com

Ontario, the largest town in Malheur County, is a trading center at the eastern border of Oregon. Irrigation from the Snake River has made possible the cultivation of sugar beets, potatoes, onions, corn, hay, and alfalfa seed, but there is still a vast wilderness of rangeland, lakes and reservoirs, mountains, and canyons. Quartz crystals, jaspers, thundereggs, marine fossils, petrified wood, and obsidian are abundant in the area.

## What to See and Do

**Farewell Bend.** *23751 Old Hwy 30, Huntington (97907). 25 miles NW on I-84. Phone 541/869-2365.* A 72-acre park named by pioneers who left the Snake River at this point in their trek west. Fishing; boat ramp. Picnicking. Primitive and improved camping (dump station).

**Fishing and hunting.** *Ontario. Phone 208/746-6276; toll-free 800/262-8874.* Rainbow trout, crappie, and bass are plentiful. Mallard and Canada geese are found on the Snake River; sage grouse, chukars, antelope, mule deer in the sagebrush areas; pheasant on irrigated land.

**Lake Owyhee.** *Ontario. 33 miles SW off Hwy 201. Phone 541/339-2331.* A 730-acre park with a 52-mile-long lake created by the Owyhee Dam. Fishing; boating (ramp). Picnicking. Improved camping (dump station).

**Ontario.** *Ontario. On I-84 at N end of town. Phone 541/869-2365.* A 35-acre day-use area. Fishing; boat ramp. Picnicking.

**Owyhee Canyon.** *Rome. Phone 208/384-3300.* Fossils and utensils of Native Americans; petroglyphs. Boating. Fishing and hunting. Contact office, 3948 Development Ave, Boise, ID 83705.

## Special Events

**American Musical Jubilee.** *Ontario. Phone toll-free 888/889-8012.* Early June.

**Malheur County Fair.** *795 NW 9th St, Ontario (97914). Phone 541/889-3431.* First week in Aug.

**Obon Festival.** *Ontario. Phone toll-free 888/889-8012.* Japanese dancing, food; art show. Mid-July.

## Limited-Service Hotel

★ **BEST WESTERN INN & SUITES.** *251 Goodfellow St, Ontario (97914). Phone 541/889-2600; toll-free 800/828-0364; fax 541/889-2259. www.bestwestern.com.* 61 rooms, 2 story. Complimentary continental breakfast. Check-in 2 pm, check-out 11 am. High-speed Internet access. Fitness room. Indoor pool, whirlpool. Business center. **$**

# Oregon Caves National Monument (E-2)

*See also Cave Junction, Grants Pass*

*(20 miles E of Cave Junction on Hwy 46)*

This area was discovered in 1874, when hunter Elijah Davidson's dog followed a bear into the cave. After a visit in 1907, frontier poet Joaquin Miller called this "The Marble Halls of Oregon." In 1909, the cave and 480 acres of the Siskiyou Mountains were made a national monument.

The cave has many chambers—Paradise Lost, Joaquin Miller's Chapel, Ghost Room, and others. Guide service is required. The average temperature is 42° F. Evening talks are given by National Park Service naturalists in summer.

On the surface, the area is covered with a beautiful old growth forest with abundant wildlife, birds, wildflowers, and an interesting variety of trees and shrubs. A maintained and marked system of trails provides access to these areas; stay on the trail. Dogs aren't allowed on trails.

Forest Service campgrounds (fee) are located 4 miles and 8 miles NW on Hwy 46 in Siskiyou National Forest (see GRANTS PASS). (Mid-May-Labor Day) Phone 541/592-3400.

Cave tours (daily; closed Thanksgiving, Dec 25). Children must be at least 3' 6" (42 inches) in height and complete a step test to be permitted into the cave. Cave tours are strenuous; recommended only for those in good physical condition. A jacket and walking shoes with nonslip soles should be worn. Lodge, dining room (May-mid-Oct). For further information contact Oregon Caves Co, 19000 Caves Hwy, Cave Junction 97523; phone 541/592-2100. Cave tours

# Oregon City (B-2)

*See also Beaverton, Forest Grove, McMinnville, Newberg, Portland, Salem, Silverton*

**Settled** 1829
**Population** 14,698
**Elevation** 55 ft
**Area Code** 503
**Zip** 97045
**Information** Oregon City Chamber of Commerce and Visitors Center, PO Box 226; phone 503/656-1619 or toll-free 800/424-3002
**Web Site** www.oregoncity.org

Below Willamette Falls, where the river spills over a 42-foot drop, is historic Oregon City. Steamers were built here in the 1850s and locks around the falls opened the upriver to navigation in 1873. Salmon fishing in the Willamette and Clackamas rivers is from early Mar-mid-May. The city is built on terraces and there is an enclosed elevator to an observation platform.

## What to See and Do

**End of the Oregon Trail Interpretive Center.** *1726 Washington St, Oregon City (97045). Phone 503/657-9336.* Exhibits on journey made by early settlers over the Oregon Trail. (Daily; closed holidays) **$$$**

**Holmes Family Home.** *Holmes Ln and Rilance St, Oregon City (97045). Phone 503/656-5146.* (Rose Farm). Oldest standing American home in Oregon City, built in 1847. First Territorial governor gave his first address here in 1849; the upstairs ballroom was the scene of many social events. (Apr-Oct, Sun; closed holidays) **$**

**John Inskeep Environmental Learning Center.** *19600 S Molalla, Oregon City (97045). On N side of Clackamas Community College's campus. Phone 503/657-6958.* Eight acres developed on former industrial site to demonstrate wildlife habitat in an urban setting. Includes extensive birds of prey exhibits, various plant and wildlife displays, and plant nursery. Haggart Astronomical Observatory (Wed, Fri-Sat; fee). **$**

**McLoughlin House National Historic Site.** *713 Center St, Oregon City (97045). Between 7th and 8th sts. Phone 503/656-5146. www.mcloughlinhouse.org.* Georgian frame building built in 1845-1846 by Dr. John McLoughlin, chief factor of the Hudson's Bay Company, who ruled the Columbia River region from 1824-1846. Period furnishings; many are original pieces, most having come around Cape Horn on sailing ships. (Tues-Sun; closed holidays, also Jan) **$$**

**Milo McIver State Park.** *24101 S Entrance Rd, Estacada (97023). 4 miles N on Hwy 213, then 12 miles SE via Hwys 212, 211. Phone 503/630-7150. www.oregonstateparks.org/park_142.php.* On the Clackamas River, this 937-acre park offers a panoramic view of Mount Hood. Fishing; boating (ramp to the river). Hiking, horseback trails. Disc golf course. Interpretive programs. Picnicking. Improved campsites (dump station, electric hook-ups, showers). **$**

**Old Aurora Colony Museum.** *15018 2nd St, Aurora (97002). 15 miles SW via Hwy 99 E. Phone 503/678-5754. www.auroracolonymuseum.com.* Complex of buildings forming historical museum of the Aurora Colony, a German religious communal society, founded by Dr. William Keil (1856-1883). Includes Kraus House (1863), a colony house with original artifacts; Steinbach Cabin (1876); wash house used by colony women for washing, soapmaking and canning; herb garden divided into various uses—teas, cooking, medicinal, fragrances. Exhibits of furniture, musical instruments, quilts, tools. Tours. (May-mid-Oct: Tues-Sun; mid-Oct-Dec and Mar-Apr: Fri-Sun; Jan-Feb: by appointment only) **$$**

**Stevens Crawford Heritage House.** *603 6th St, Oregon City (97045). Phone 503/655-2866.* (Mertie Stevens Residence, 1908). Fifteen fully furnished period rooms. Working kitchen, bedrooms, living room, dining room; doll collection. (Feb-Dec, Wed-Sun) **$$**

**Willamette Falls Locks.** *West Linn. On Willamette River. Phone 503/656-3381.* National Historical site; oldest multilift navagation lock, built 1873. Four locks, canal basin and guard lock operated by US Army Corps of Engineers. Picnic areas. Information Center. (Daily) **FREE**

## Limited-Service Hotel

★★ **RIVERSHORE HOTEL.** *1900 Clackamette Dr, Oregon City (97045). Phone 503/655-7141; toll-free 800/443-7777; fax 503/655-1927. www.rivershorehotel.com.* 120 rooms, 4 story. Pets accepted, some restrictions; fee. Check-out noon. Restaurant, bar. Outdoor pool, whirlpool. **$**

# Pendleton (B-5)

*See also Hermiston, La Grande, Umatilla*

**Founded** 1868
**Population** 15,126
**Elevation** 1,068 ft
**Area Code** 541
**Zip** 97801
**Information** Chamber of Commerce, 501 S Main; phone 541/276-7411 or toll-free 800/547-8911
**Web Site** www.pendletonchamber.com

Located on the old Oregon Trail, Pendleton is a trading center for the extensive cattle, wheat, and green pea production in the area. Seat of Umatilla County, it is famous for its annual Round-up.

## What to See and Do

**Emigrant Springs State Park.** *Pendleton. 26 miles SE off I-84. Phone 541/983-2277.* A 23-acre park near summit of Blue Mountains (nearly 4,000 feet); ponderosa pine forest. Winter sports. Picnicking, lodge. Tent and trailer sites. Oregon Trail display.

**Pendleton Woolen Mills.** *1307 SE Court Pl, Pendleton (97801). Phone 541/276-6911.* Woolen manufacturing; carding, spinning, rewinding and weaving processes. Guided tours (30 minutes; Mon-Fri; closed holidays). **FREE**

**Ukiah-Dale Forest State Park.** *Pendleton. 50 miles S on Hwy 395, 3 miles SW of Ukiah. Phone 541/983-2277; toll-free 800/551-6949. www.oregonstateparks.org/park_22.php.* A 3,000-acre scenic forest canyon extending along Camas Creek and the north fork of the John Day River. Fishing for trout, steelhead, and salmon. Twenty-seven primitive campsites. **FREE**

**Umatilla Indian Reservation.** *51 Umatilla Loop, Pendleton (97801). 5 miles E via Mission Hwy (Hwy 30). Phone 541/276-3873.* Created by the Walla Walla Valley Treaty of 1855. Firsthand view and understanding of a Native American community in transition. Historic significance as well as a lifestyle different from modern-day, American-style development. One of the first Catholic missions in the United States is here. Reservation always open for unguided touring. Indian Lake has good fishing, camping and beautiful scenery. The foothills and lowlands of the Blue Mountains provide excellent upland game and waterfowl hunting. In addition, the Umatilla Tribes have reestablished runs of chinook salmon and steelhead within the Umatilla River. Some fees.

**Umatilla National Forest.** *2517 SW Hailey Ave, Pendleton (97801). NE and S of Pendleton. Reached by I-84, Hwys 395, 11, 204, 82, 244, 207, and 12. Phone 541/276-3811.* More than 1 million acres, partly in Washington. Lewis and Clark passed through this region on the Columbia River in 1805. Includes spectacular views of the Tucannon, Umatilla, Grande Ronde, North Fork John Day, and Wenaha River canyons. Remnants of historic gold mining can be found in the Granite, OR, area in sight of the Greenhorn Mountain Range. North Fork John Day, North Fork Umatilla and the Wenaha-Tucannon wilderness areas may be reached on horseback or on foot. Stream fishing (steelhead, rainbow trout), big-game hunting (elk, deer); boating, river rafting. Hiking. Skiing, snowmobiling. Picnicking. Camping (fee at some campgrounds). In forest are

> **Spout Springs.** *Hwy 204 to Mile Post 22, Pendleton. 21 miles NE on Hwy 11 to Weston, then 20 miles E on Hwy 204 to Tollgate.* **Ski Bluewood.** *45 miles NE to Walla Walla, WA, 29 miles NE on Hwy 12 to Dayton, then 23 miles SE on country road. Phone 541/276-7411.* (see LA GRANDE)

## Special Event

**Pendleton Round-up.** *Pendleton. Stadium. Phone toll-free 800/457-6336.* Rodeo and pageantry of Old West, annually since 1910. Gathering of Native Americans, PRCA working cowboys and thousands of visitors. Mid-Sept.

## Limited-Service Hotel

**★★ RED LION.** *304 SE Nye Ave, Pendleton (97801). Phone 541/276-6111; toll-free 800/733-5466; fax 541/278-2413. www.redlion.com.* 170 rooms, 3 story. Pets accepted. Check-in 3 pm, check-out noon. High-speed Internet access, wireless Internet access. Two restaurants, bar. Fitness room. Outdoor pool, whirlpool. Airport transportation available. **$**

# Port Orford (E-1)

*See also Bandon, Gold Beach*

**Founded** 1851
**Population** 1,025
**Elevation** 56 ft

## Portland's Outstanding Parks

The glory of Portland is its parks. Settled by idealistic New Englanders, Portland had an extensive park system in the 1850s, decades before other West Coast cities were even founded. Begin at Portland State University in the North Park Blocks, a swath of twenty blocks of parkland that cuts right through the heart of the city. The park was established in the 1850s and for generations was the best address for civic structures. Numerous historic churches, plus the Portland Art Museum, the Oregon History Center, the Portland Center for the Performing Arts, and the Schnitzer Concert Hall (home to the Oregon Symphony) flank the park. The park is also home to the largest remaining stand of American elm (killed elsewhere by Dutch elm disease), numerous heroic statues, and a farmers market (on Wednesdays and Saturdays).

Drop down to Pioneer Courthouse Square at 6th and Morrison, often referred to as Portland's living room. This is where many outdoor festivals, concerts, and demonstrations take place. (Dan Quayle got such a raucous reception here that he thenceforward refused to visit Portland, referring to the city as "America's Beirut.") The Square is a great place for people-watching and sunbathing, and there are many food carts and cafés here. In the blocks around Pioneer Courthouse Square are many of Portland's major shopping venues. Adjacent is the Pioneer Courthouse itself, built in 1875.

Follow 5th Avenue south, noting the abundance of public art along the pedestrian friendly bus mall. At 5th Avenue and Main Street is the Portland Building, a noted postmodern structure designed by Michael Graves. The front is surmounted by a massive statue called Portlandia. This is the second-largest hammered copper statue in the world, the largest being the Statue of Liberty.

Head over to the Willamette River waterfront. The park that runs the length of downtown along the river is recent. In the 1970s, the city ripped out a freeway that ran along the river and replaced it with this park, which in summer is loaded with joggers, sun worshipers, and any number of summer festivals. Also along the river are boat tour operators, a large marina with some shops and cafés, and, at the north end, a memorial to Japanese-American internment during World War II. Under the Burnside Bridge, adjacent to Waterfront Park, is the Portland Saturday Market (open both Saturday and Sunday), which is reputed to be the largest open-air crafts market in the nation.

Turn north along 3rd Avenue and walk through Portland's Old Town (most buildings date from the 1880s) to Chinatown. Here, between 2nd and 3rd avenues and Everett and Flanders streets is the Portland Chinese Garden, a traditional Chinese garden that is a joint project of Portland and the city of Suzhou. It is the largest Chinese-style garden outside of China itself.

**Area Code** 541
**Zip** 97465
**Information** Chamber of Commerce, 502 Battle Rock City Park, PO Box 637; phone 541/332-8055
**Web Site** www.portorfordoregon.com

The westernmost incorporated city in the contiguous United States, Port Orford overlooks the Pacific Ocean with spectacular views. This was the first settlement in Coos and Curry counties. Captain George Vancouver sighted this area in 1792 and named it for the Earl of Orford. The cedar trees that grow in the area (sometimes called Lawson cypress and later named for the Earl) are highly favored for boat construction.

## What to See and Do

**Battle Rock Wayside.** *520 Jefferson, Port Orford (97465). S edge of town on Hwy 101. Phone 541/332-4106.* Site of one of the fiercest Native American battles on the Oregon Coast (1851); explanation of battle is inscribed on a marker in the park. Battle Rock offers one of the best seascapes in the state and has an ocean beach, surfing. Hiking trail.

**Cape Blanco State Park.** *91814 Cape Blanco Rd, Port Orford (97465). 9 miles N off Hwy 101. Phone 541/332-6774.* A 1,880-acre park with an ocean beach, observation point, and historic lighthouse (1870). Fishing; river access for boats. Hiking, picnicking. Horse camp, beach access/horse trails. Rustic cabins, improved campsites. **FREE** In the park is the

**Historic Hughes House.** *Hwy 101 and Cape Blanco Rd, Port Orford (97465). Phone 541/332-4106.* Restored Victorian house. (1898) (May-Sept, Thurs-Mon and holidays) **DONATION**

**Fishing.** *300 Dock Rd, Port Orford (97465). Phone 541/332-7121.* Ocean fishing provides salmon, ling cod, perch, snapper, and crabs. Fall fishing in the Elk and Sixes rivers provides catches of chinook salmon and trout. **Garrison Lake,** at the northwest edge of town, is open all year for trout and bass fishing. Also swimming, waterskiing; boat ramp.

**Humbug Mountain State Park.** *Port Orford. 6 miles S on Hwy 101. Phone 541/332-6774. www.oregonstateparks.org/park_56.php.* A 1,842-acre park with a winding trail leading to the summit of Humbug Mountain (elevation 1,756 feet); the peak looks out on virgin forest, trout streams, and a sand beach. Windsurfing, scuba diving. Fishing, hiking, picnicking. Tent and trailer sites (dump station). **FREE**

# Portland (B-2)

*See also Beaverton, Forest Grove, Newberg, Oregon City, Salem*

**Founded** 1851
**Population** 437,319
**Elevation** 77 ft
**Area Code** 503
**Information** Portland Oregon Visitors Association, 2701 SW 6th Ave, 97204; phone 503/222-2223 or toll-free 877/678-5263
**Web Site** www.travelportland.com

**Suburbs** Beaverton, Forest Grove, Hillsboro, Newburg, Oregon City; also Vancouver, WA.

Oregon's largest city sprawls across both banks of the Willamette River, just south of its confluence with the Columbia. The lush and fertile Willamette Valley brings it beauty and riches. Portland's freshwater harbor is visited by more than 1,400 vessels annually from throughout the world. The city enjoys plentiful electric power, captured from river waters, which drives scores of industries with minimal amounts of smoke or smog.

Portland is surrounded by spectacular scenery. The Columbia River Gorge, Mount Hood, waterfalls, forests, ski slopes, fishing streams, and hunting and camping areas are within easy access. It attracts many conventions, for which it is well equipped, with four large auditoriums: the Memorial Coliseum Complex, the Metropolitan Exposition Center, and the Oregon Convention Center. Portland's reputation as "The City of Roses" is justified by its leadership in rose culture, as seen in its International Rose Test Garden and celebrated during the annual Portland Rose Festival, which attracts visitors worldwide. Mount St. Helens, in Washington's Gifford Pinchot National Forest, 50 miles to the northeast, can be seen from numerous vantage points in Portland.

Portland is also an educational center, with Portland State University, the University of Portland (1901), Lewis & Clark College (1867), and Reed College (1911).

## Additional Visitor Information

For further information, contact the Portland Oregon Visitors Association, 26 SW Salmon, 97204, phone 503/222-2223. For a recorded message describing major theater, sports, and music events in Portland for the current month, phone 503/225-5555.

## Public Transportation

**Buses, MAX light rail trains** (Tri-County Metropolitan Transportation District), phone 503/238-7433, www.trimet.org.

**Airport Portland International Airport (PDX).** NE of the city off I-205.

**Information** Phone 503/460-4234, toll-free 877/739-4636

**Lost and Found** Phone 503/460-4277; toll-free 800/547-8411, ext 4272

**Airlines** Air Canada Jazz, Alaska Airlines, America West Airlines, American Airlines, Continental Airlines, Delta Air Lines, Frontier Airlines, Hawaiian Air, Horizon Air, Lufthansa, Mexicana Airlines, Northwest Airlines, Skywest Airlines, Southwest Airlines, Sun Country Airlines, United Airlines

## What to See and Do

**American Advertising Museum.** *211 NW 5th Ave, Portland (97209). Phone 503/226-0000.* This museum is devoted to the history and evolution of advertising and its impact on culture. Boasting the industry's

## Portland's Passion for Microbrews

San Francisco has wine and Seattle has coffee, but in unpretentious and easygoing Portland, the beverage of choice is beer. And if you appreciate fresh, handcrafted beer, you're certain to enjoy your stay here. Portland has been dubbed "America's Microbrew Capital", an appropriate moniker given the city's numerous thriving microbreweries. Portland stakes claim to having more microbreweries and brewpubs per capita than any other city in the nation. Beer drinkers flock daily to brewpubs such as the **Laurelwood Public House** (1728 NE 40th Ave) and **BridgePort BrewPub** (1313 NW Marshall St), where they enjoy a variety of ales crafted in the old-world tradition, often using locally grown barley and hops.

Portland's beer history dates to 1852, when German brewer Henry Saxer moved to the Oregon Territory, opening Liberty Brewery in the village of Portland near First and Davis streets. Saxer's brewery experienced immediate success, and other breweries opened soon after to tap into the local's seemingly insatiable thirst for beer. The city's enthusiasm for beer continued into the 20th century, although it slowed during the Prohibition period. In the mid-1980s, Portland's brew tastes focused on European-style microbrews, a trend driven by a law passed by the Oregon state legislature that enabled brewers to sell beer directly to the public. Suddenly, microbreweries and brewpubs were popping up all over the state. Nobody took better advantage of the new law than Mike and Brian McMenamin, who in 1984 opened the **Hillsdale Brewery and Public House** (www.mcmenamins.com), the state's first brewpub since Prohibition. The McMenamins admit that their first brew, Hillsdale Ale, needed improvement, but after experimenting with different recipes—one doomed effort included Mars Bars—they were able to concoct colorfully named beers (Hammerhead, Terminator) that quickly became popular. The McMenamin brothers parlayed these early successes into a brewmeisting empire, opening more than 50 breweries and brewpubs in the Northwest, as well as seven theater pubs and six hotels.

A fun and safe way to experience the city's many microbrews is to book a trip on the **Portland Brew Bus** (www.brewbus.com). The five-hour tour aboard the Brew Bus takes you to three or four local brewers, where you'll sample 15 to 25 beers, recording your impressions of each on a complimentary sampling scorecard. The bus often stops at **Widmer Brothers Gasthaus Restaurant & Pub** (955 N Russell), founded by siblings Kurt and Rob in 1984. Widmer Brothers Brewing Company has emerged as one of the most successful brewers in the Northwest, thanks largely to the popularity of its Hefeweizen, a strongly aromatic beer that goes unfiltered from the lagering tank to the bottle, creating a golden-hued cloudy appearance.

Another way to enjoy beer in Portland is to attend the **Oregon Brewers Festival (OBF)**. Since 1987, OBF (www.oregonbrewfest.com) has been attracting tens of thousands of beer drinkers to Tom McCall Waterfront Park in downtown Portland, where the annual event is held on the last full weekend in July. Whatever your favored beer style, be it a pale ale, robust porter, or a Bavarian-style lager, you're certain to find a brew—or two or three—that appeals to your tastes.

most comprehensive collection of advertising and business artifacts, the American Advertising Museum features permanent as well as changing exhibits. (Thurs-Sat 11 am-5 pm) **$**

**Benson State Recreation Area.** *Portland. 30 miles E on I-84, exit 30. Phone 503/695-2261. www.oregonstateparks.org/park_147.php.* Thirty miles east of Portland, near Multnomah Falls, the Benson State Recreation Area has a lake that's perfect for fishing, swimming, and boating (non-motorized boats only). Picnicking is also popular here, and the park even has a disc golf course. (Daily) **$**

**Children's Museum 2nd Generation.** *4015 SW Canyon Rd, Portland (97221). Off Hwy 26 opposite the Oregon Zoo. Phone 503/223-6500. www.portlandcm2.org.* CM2 offers plenty of hands-on play spaces, including the Vroom Room, where kids can race in a variety of wheeled objects, and KidCity Market, a children-sized grocery store with miniature carts and aisles of fake food. The museum also features temporary exhibits, a recent example being a replica of the television set of *Mister Roger's Neighborhood.* (Sun 11 am-5 pm; Mon-Thurs, Sat 9 am-5 pm; Fri 9 am-8 pm; closed holidays) **$**

**Council Crest Park.** *SW Council Crest Dr, Portland (97201). S on SW Greenway Ave (follow the blue and white scenic tour signs). Phone 503/823-2223. www.parks.ci.portland.or.us/parks/councilcrest.htm.* Council Crest Park is not just the city's highest park— it's the site of Portlands highest point, topping off at 1,073 feet above sea level. That may not sound all that high, but it's high enough to afford wonderful views of the Tualatin Valley, the Willamette River, Mount St. Helens, and the truly high and mighty Mount Hood. **FREE**

**Crown Point.** *40700 Historic Columbia River Hwy, Corbett (97019). E on I-84, exit 22; on Hwy 30. Phone 503/695-2240. www.oregonstateparks.org/park_150.php.* This 307-acre park possesses a 725-foot-high vantage point alongside the Columbia River Gorge, allowing for spectacular views of the gorge's rock walls, which rise 2,000 feet above the river. The historic Vista House, an octagonal building with a copper dome, can be found here, though it was recently closed indefinitely while restoration work is performed. **FREE**

**Crystal Springs Rhododendron Garden.** *SE 28th Ave, Portland (97202). N of SE Woodstock Blvd. Phone 503/823-2223. www.parks.ci.portland.or.us/parks/crysspringrhodgar.htm.* The pathways at Crystal Springs wind through a woodland setting, passing by some 2,500 rhododendrons, azaleas, and companion plants. A spring-fed lake attracts many species of birds and waterfowl. Admission is free from Labor Day through February. (Daily) **$**

**Dabney State Recreation Area.** *Portland. 19 miles E off I-84 exit 18, at Stark St Bridge on Hwy 30. Phone 503/695-2261. www.oregonstateparks.org/park_151.php.* East of Portland, this 135-acre park is a popular summertime destination, thanks to its idyllic swimming hole and picnic area. The park even offers electric cooking stations to fry up those hamburgers and tofu dogs. Other amenities include a reservable group shelter, walking trails, beach, boat ramp, and disc golf course. Many visitors enjoy fishing for salmon and steelhead in the Sandy River. **$**

**Forest Park.** *NW Skyline and Helens Rd, Portland. Off Hwy 30, NW of Fremont Bridge. Phone 503/823-7529. www.parks.ci.portland.or.us/parks/forestpark.htm.* Park encompasses over 5,000 wooded acres, making it the largest wilderness park within city limits in the US. Visitors can take advantage of 74 miles of hiking, bicycling, and equestrian trails. Wildwood Trail begins at the Vietnam Veterans Living Memorial in Hoyt Arboretum and extends 27 miles, ending deep in the park, beyond Germantown Road. Some 100 bird species and 60 mammal species inhabit the park. (Daily) **FREE**

**Gray Line bus tours.** *4320 N Suttle Rd, Portland (97217). Phone 888/684-3322; toll-free 800/422-7042. www.grayline.com.* Gray Line offers seven tours that originate in Portland, including a three-hour tour of the city and a nine-hour tour that retraces Lewis and Clarks journey along the Columbia River. **$$$$**

**The Grotto.** *8840 N E Skidmore, Portland (97220). NE 85th Ave at Sandy Blvd, on Hwy 30. Phone 503/254-7371. www.thegrotto.org.* The National Sanctuary of Our Sorrowful Mother—commonly called The Grotto—is a 62-acre Catholic shrine and botanical garden. Created in 1924, The Grotto cuts into the side of a 110-foot cliff and is surrounded by beautiful plants and flowers. An elevator takes visitors to the Natural Gallery in the woods, where you'll find more than 100 statues. The landscaped upper level has a meditation chapel overlooking the Columbia River, with Mount St. Helens visible in the distance. (Daily; closed Thanksgiving, Dec 25) **DONATION**

**Guy W. Talbot State Park.** *Columbia River Hwy, Troutdale (97062). E on I-84, exit 27; on Hwy 30. Phone 503/695-2261. www.oregonstateparks.org/park_154.php.* These 371 lush acres served as the estate of Guy Webster Talbot and his family until the property was donated to the state in 1929. The park is regarded as a wonderful picnicking destination, as it's rarely crowded and features beautiful natural surroundings, including 250-foot-high Latourell Falls, the second-highest falls along the Columbia River Gorge. **FREE**

**Howell Territorial Park and the Bybee House.** *13901 NW Howell Park Rd, Portland (97231). 12 miles N via Hwy 30, cross bridge to Sauvie Island, 1 mile W to Howell Territorial Park Rd. Phone 503/797-1850.* The Howell Territorial Park, occupying 93 pastoral acres on Sauvie Island, is home to the Bybee House, an impressive example of Greek Revival architecture. Originally a private home, the Bybee House was purchased in 1961 by Multnomah County and soon after restored to appear as it would have at the time of its construction in 1858. Guided tours of the home are conducted on the half-hour. (Park open daily year-round; Bybee House open weekend afternoons from June-Labor Day) **DONATION**

**Hoyt Arboretum.** *4000 SW Fairview Blvd, Portland (97221). Phone 503/865-8733. www.hoytarboretum.org.* Within its 175 acres, the Hoyt Arboretum boasts more than 900 species of trees and shrubs, including one of the largest collections of conifers in the US. The arboretum sits upon a ridge overlooking the Oregon Zoo. Guided tours are offered April-October on Saturdays and Sundays at 2 pm. The park and visitor center are open daily. **FREE**

**Lewis and Clark College.** *0615 SW Palatine Hill Rd, Portland (97219). 3 miles E of I-5 Terwilliger Exit. Phone 503/768-7000. www.lclark.edu.* The campus at Lewis and Clark College is simply gorgeous, highlighted by the floral display at the Memorial Rose Garden. Established in 1867, the college has an enrollment of about 3,000 students. Two campus buildings, the Manor House and Gatehouse, are listed in the National Register of Historic Places.

**Lewis and Clark State Recreation Area.** *Portland. 16 miles E on I-84, exit 18. Phone 503/695-2261. www.oregonstateparks.org/park_159.php.* Situated near the confluence of the Columbia and Sandy rivers, this park offers picnic tables, a beach, and a boat ramp. Anglers and swimmers are a common sight in the cool waters of the Sandy River. Hiking also is popular here, particularly along a trail that leads to Broughton's Bluff. The park's namesakes camped and explored the area in November 1805. **FREE**

**Lloyd Center.** *2201 Lloyd Center, Portland (97232). Phone 503/282-2511. www.lloydcentermall.com.* Billing itself as the biggest mall in Oregon, the trilevel Lloyd Center features anchor stores such as Nordstrom and Meier & Frank, discount stores like Marshalls, numerous eateries, and an 18-screen movie theater.

**Mount Hood-Columbia Gorge Loop Scenic Drive.** *Portland. Phone toll-free 877/678-5263.* This 163-mile scenic drive along the Columbia River and through Mount Hood National Forest offers splendid views of the river basin, visits to waterfalls, many state parks, and spectacular mountain scenery. Drive east 17 miles on Highway 30, I-84 to Troutdale. At this point, for approximately 24 miles, there are two routes: you may turn right and take the mountainous upper-level scenic route or continue on the main river-level freeway. The two roads rejoin about 10 miles west of Bonneville Dam. Continue east on Highway 30, I-84 for 23 miles to Hood River, turning south on Highway 35 for 47 miles through Mount Hood National Forest to Highway 26. Drive northwest on Highway 26, 56 miles back to Portland. A description of this tour may be found in a free visitors guide from the Portland Visitors Association.

**Mount Tabor Park.** *SE 60th Ave and Salmon St, Portland (97215). Phone 503/823-2223. www.parks.ci.portland.or.us/Parks/MtTabor.htm.* This 195-acre park has something for everyone, with a basketball court, volleyball court, horseshoe pit, playground, picnic shelter, and tennis courts, as well as an off-leash area for dogs. The park contains an extinct volcano, making Portland one of only two US cities to have an extinct volcano within its city limits. (Daily)

**Multnomah Falls.** *I-84 to Multnomah Falls turnoff, Bridal Veil. 32 miles E on I-84. Phone 503/695-2372.* Chief among the 11 waterfalls along 11 miles of this highway; 620-foot drop in two falls, fourth-highest in United States. Hiking. Restaurant. Visitor center.

**Oaks Park.** *7100 SE Oaks Park Way, Portland (97202). SE Oaks Park Way, E end of Sellwood Bridge. Phone 503/233-5777. www.oakspark.com.* Opened in 1905, Oaks Park is one of the oldest continuously operating amusement parks in the US. It features thrill rides, a children's area, a roller rink (Tues-Sun; rentals available), miniature golf, and waterfront picnicking. (Spring and fall: weekends; summer: daily).

**Oregon Convention Center.** *777 NE Martin Luther King Jr. Blvd, Portland (97232). Phone 503/235-7575; toll-free 800/791-2250. www.oregoncc.org.* Located within Portlands city center, the Oregon Convention Center (OCC) hosts conferences, exhibitions, and parties year round within its 255,000-square-foot facility. OCC provides Wi-Fi access throughout the property, a big plus for visitors seeking a high-speed connection to the Internet. The MAX light rail stops at OCCs front door.

**Oregon Historical Society.** *1200 SW Park Ave, Portland (97205). Phone 503/222-1741. www.ohs.org.* The Oregon Historical Society features a broad range of exhibits and collections within its museum and research library. The history of Oregon and the Pacific Northwest is documented through photographs, audio recordings, artifacts, and books. The library houses a book collection exceeding 35,000 titles (Wed-Sat). The museum offers permanent and changing exhibits. (Tues-Sun; closed holidays) **$$**

**Oregon Museum of Science and Industry.** *1945 SE Water Ave, Portland (97214). Phone 503/797-4000. www.omsi.edu.* The museum has six exhibit halls and labs, with an emphasis on putting the fun in such topics as astronomy, electronics, Earth science, biology, and dinosaurs. The museum is also home to a planetarium and OMNIMAX Theater (daily, fee), as well as the USS *Blueback*, the Navy's last non-nuclear, fast attack submarine. (Labor Day-Memorial Day: Tues-Sun; rest of the year: daily; closed Dec 25) **$$**

**Oregon Zoo.** *4001 SW Canyon Rd, Portland (97221). Phone 503/226-1561. www.oregonzoo.org.* Specializing in breeding and protecting rare and endangered species, the Oregon Zoo has about 1,029 living specimens, 54 of which are considered either endangered or threatened. Opened as the Washington Park Zoo in 1887, the Oregon Zoo houses creatures large and small, ranging from elephants and giraffes to millipedes and scorpions. The botanical gardens have more than 1,000 species of exotic plants. The zoo is a five-minute ride from downtown Portland on the MAX light rail. A separate zoo railway links to the popular Washington Park. (Daily; closed Dec 25) **$$**

**Peninsula Park and Community Center.** *700 N Portland Blvd, Portland (97217). N Portland Blvd and Albina Ave. Phone 503/823-2223. www.parks.ci.portland.or.us/parks/peninsulapkrosegar.htm.* Home to Portland's first public rose garden and community center, Peninsula Park has extensive facilities, including softball, football, and soccer fields; a basketball court; an outdoor swimming pool; tennis courts; a horseshoe pit; a playground; and a picnic shelter. An amazing 8,900 plantings grow in the 2-acre rose garden. The parks community center (Mon-Fri; closed most holidays) is impressively fashioned as an Italian villa. (Daily) **FREE**

**PGE Park.** *1844 SW Morrison, Portland (97205). Take I-405 to the Salmon St exit. www.pgepark.com.* PGE Park serves as the home for two professional sports teams, the Portland Beavers and the Portland Timbers, as well as the football team at Portland State University. The Beavers are the AAA affiliate of the San Diego Padres, while the Timbers compete in the USLs A-League, soccer's highest level of play in the US and Canada. PGE Park sits on a plot of land that has been used for athletic events since 1893, a time when it was known as Multnomah Field. Over the years, the versatile facility has hosted a wide range of athletic events, including tennis, cricket, and ski jumping. In 2001, PGE Park underwent a $38.5 million renovation, turning it into one of the most modern and comfortable stadiums of its size. Tickets may be purchased at the PGE Park box office or by calling Ticketmaster at 503/224-4400. **$$$**

**Pittock Mansion.** *3229 NW Pittock Dr, Portland (97210). Phone 503/823-3624. www.pittockmansion.com.* This restored and furnished French Chateau-esque mansion, dating to 1914, is surrounded by 46 forested and landscaped acres. Spectacular views of rivers, the city, and snowcapped mountains, including Mount St. Helens and Mount Hood, are an added bonus. (Summer, daily 11 am-4 pm; noon-4 pm rest of year; closed holidays) **$$**

**Police Historical Museum.** *16th floor of Justice Center, 1111 SW 2nd Ave, Portland (97204). Phone 503/823-0019.* The museum features a collection of police uniforms, badges, photos, confiscated weapons, and other police memorabilia. One of the most popular museum pieces is a police motorbike with sidecar. (Mon-Thurs; closed holidays) **FREE**

★ **Portland Art Museum.** *1219 SW Park Ave, Portland (97205). At Jefferson St. Phone 503/226-2811. www.portlandartmuseum.org.* Founded in 1892, the Portland Art Museum holds a collection of more than 32,000 works of art, including European paintings and sculptures from the Renaissance to the present; 19th- and 20th-century American works; a noted collection of Northwest Coast Native American art; Asian, pre-Columbian, West African, and classical Greek and Roman art; British silver; and creative photography. The museum hosts lectures, films, concerts, and other arts-related special events. (Tues-Sun; closed holidays) **$$$**

**Portland Saturday Market.** *108 W Burnside, Portland (97209). Under the Burnside Bridge. Phone 503/222-6072. www.portlandsaturdaymarket.com.* One of largest, oldest open-air community markets in the US. More than 350 vendor booths feature arts and crafts made by Pacific Northwest artisans and a wide variety of foods, from sushi to curry. Street entertainers, face painters, and the like enliven the atmosphere and keep kids smiling. (Mar-Dec 24, Sat 10 am-5 pm, Sun 11 am-4:30 pm)

**Portland State University.** *724 SW Harrison St, Portland (97201). Visitor information center at SW Broadway and College sts. Phone 503/725-3000. www.pdx.edu.* Located in the woodsy South Park Blocks area, the university enrolls more than 21,000 students in its undergraduate and graduate programs. Art exhibits are often featured in the Smith Memorial Center and Neuberger Hall.

**Portland Trail Blazers (NBA).** *Rose Garden, 1 Center Ct, Portland (97227). Phone 503/797-9600. www.nba.com/blazers.* Portland loves its Trail Blazers, the city's lone major sports franchise. The Blazers, as they're better known, compete in the Pacific Division of the National Basketball Association, playing their home games in the 19,980-seat Rose Garden. Founded in

1970, the Blazers have made it to the NBA Finals on three occasions, taking home the championship in 1977 behind the stellar play of center Bill Walton and forward Maurice Lucas. The Blazers host 41 regular-season games, beginning in late October and finishing in mid-April. **$$$$**

**Powell's City of Books.** *1005 W Burnside, Portland (97209). Phone toll-free 866/201-7601. www.powells.com.* A must-stop for bibliophiles, Powells City of Books stocks more than a million new and used titles within a sprawling 68,000-square-foot facility that occupies an entire city block in downtown Portland. First-time visitors should pick up a complimentary store map to help them navigate through nine color-coded rooms, perusing an inventory that's divided into 122 major subject areas and approximately 3,500 subsections. If you're a collector looking for, say, a signed first edition of *The Hobbit,* be sure to check out the Rare Book Room, which houses autographed first editions and other collectible volumes. (Daily 9 am-11 pm)

**Rooster Rock State Park.** *Portland. E on I-84, milepost 25. Phone 503/695-2261. www.oregonstateparks.org/park_175.php.* A short drive east of Portland, Rooster Rock offers 3 miles of sandy beaches along the Columbia River. The park is a popular destination for windsurfing, boating, fishing, swimming, hiking, and picnicking. One of Oregon's two designated nude beaches is located at the park's eastern edge. The nude beach is secluded, and it cannot be seen from the clothing-required area. **$**

**Rose Quarter.** *One Center Ct, Portland (97227). Phone 503/231-8000. www.rosequarter.com.* The Rose Quarter is Portland's home for big-name live entertainment. Two venues comprise the Rose Quarter: the Memorial Coliseum, which seats a shade under 13,000, and the Rose Garden, a modern arena with a capacity near 20,000. The Rose Garden serves as the home court for the NBAs Trail Blazers. The Portland Winter Hawks, a minor-league hockey team, take to the ice in both venues. Musical acts also perform in both venues, with more popular artists taking to the stage in the Rose Garden.

***Sternwheeler* Columbia Gorge.** *1200 NW Naito Pkwy, Portland (97209). Cruises leave from Marine Park in Cascade Locks, E on I-84, exit 44. Phone 439/003-3928. www.sternwheeler.com.* Climb aboard the Sternwheeler *Columbia Gorge,* an authentic triple-deck paddle wheeler, and enjoy spectacular views as you journey along the Columbia River. A variety of excursions are offered, including champagne brunch cruises and dinner cruises. **$$$$**

★ **Washington Park.** *400 S W Kingston, Portland (97211). Accessible via W Burnside St, SW Park Place, or Canyon Rd. Phone 503/823-2223. www.parks.ci.portland.or.us/Parks/Washington.htm.* Washington Park encompasses 129 scenic acres on a hill overlooking the city. On a clear day, the views are simply spectacular, with Mount Hood towering majestically in the east and Mount St. Helens visible in the northern horizon. The Shakespeare Garden, Lewis and Clark Memorial, and Sacajawea Memorial Statue can be found in the park, as well as the popular International Rose Test Garden and Japanese Garden. Washington Park facilities include softball and soccer fields, lighted tennis courts, covered picnic areas, a playground, and hiking trails. The MAX light rail stops at Washington Park. Also here are

**International Rose Test Garden.** *400 SW Kingston, Portland (97201). Phone 503/823-7529.* In a city rich with natural wonders, perhaps no Portland location can match the beauty found at the International Rose Test Garden. The garden sits on a hillside in Washington Park, with a clear view of snowcapped Mount Hood rising majestically in the distance. The garden was created in 1917 by three prominent nurserymen, established, in part, to serve as a safe haven for hybrid roses grown in war-torn Europe. Today, the garden features more than 8,000 rosebushes, enhancing the city's reputation as the "City of Roses." Near the garden's parking lot, the Rose Garden Store offers an impressive array of rose-related arts and crafts. (Daily 7:30 am-9 pm)

**Japanese Garden.** *611 SW Kingston Ave, Portland (97205). Phone 503/223-1321.* This 5-acre enclave of tranquility is considered one of the most authentic Japanese gardens outside of Japan. Masterly designed by Professor Takuma Tono, the garden opened in 1967 as a place for reflection and serenity within an environment of natural beauty and quietude. The Japanese Garden possesses five formal garden styles: Natural Garden, Sand and Stone Garden, Tea Garden, Strolling Pond Garden, and Flat Garden. The Japanese Garden Gift Store offers an eclectic array of arts and crafts merchandise, most of which comes from Japan. (Daily; closed holidays) **$$**

**Willamette Stone State Heritage Site.** *Skyline Blvd and W Burnside, Portland (97229). 4 miles W. Phone toll-free 877/678-5263. www.oregonstateparks.org/park_246.php.* The land in the US is divided into a grid, and markers such as Willamette Stone are used as starting points from which grid lines are established. Willamette Stone serves as the "zero point" for the Willamette Meridian region, encompassing all of the land west of the Cascade Mountains in Oregon and Washington. A 500-foot trail cuts through dense forest as it leads to the actual marker and a plaque describing its relevance. **FREE**

**World Forestry Center.** *4033 SW Canyon Rd, Portland (97221). Phone 503/228-1367. www.worldforestry.org.* The World Forestry Center is highlighted by the Forest Discovery Center, a museum celebrating the importance and diversity of tree life. Opened in 1971, the museum features educational programs, gallery shows, and exhibits. The museum's most popular exhibit is a 70-foot-high talking tree, a replica Douglas fir that teaches tree biology in five different languages: English, French, Japanese, Spanish, and German. (Daily; closed Dec 25) **$$**

## Special Events

**Chamber Music Northwest.** *522 SW 5th Ave, #725, Portland (97204). Phone 503/294-6400. www.cmnw.org.* Catlin Gabel School and Reed College. Nationally acclaimed summer chamber music festival offers 25 concerts featuring 40-50 artists (Mon, Tues, Thurs-Sat). A catered picnic precedes each concert. Children under 7 only permitted at Family Concert. Mid-June-late July.

**Elephant Garlic Festival.** *Jessie Mayes Community Center, 30955 NW Hillcrest, North Plains (97133). Phone 503/647-2207. www.funstinks.com.* How can you go wrong with a festival whose motto is "Where fun stinks?" Garlic ice cream, garlic beer, and other delicacies dominate this yearly extravaganza that is almost surely devoid of vampires. Elephant garlic has been the theme only since 1998, when it was made the focus after almost ten years of lackluster attendance at "North Plains Days." Since then, the festival has blossomed, and attendance (which is still free) has increased almost every year. Third weekend in Aug.

**Holiday Parade of Christmas Ships.** *Portland. Along Willamette and Columbia rivers.* More than 50 boats cruise the two rivers in a holiday display. Early-mid-Dec.

**Horse racing.** *Portland Meadows, 1001 N Schmeer Rd, Portland (97217). 6 miles N on I-5. Phone 503/285-9144.* Parimutuel betting. Thoroughbred and quarter horse racing. (Fri evenings, Sat and Sun matinee) Under 12 years not permitted at evening races. Late Oct-Apr.

**Mount Hood Jazz Festival.** *Main and Powell sts, Gresham (97030). 15 miles E on I-84.* International, national and local jazz acts presented in outdoor festival. First weekend in Aug.

**Multnomah County Fair.** *Portland. Phone 503/761-7577.* Agricultural and horticultural exhibits; entertainment. Mid-July.

**Portland Center Stage.** *Portland Center for the Performing Arts,1111 SW Broadway, Portland (97205). Phone 503/274-6588.* Series of contemporary and classical plays. Daily except Mon. Call for fees, performance and title schedules. Sept-Apr.

**Portland Marathon.** *1221 SW 4th Ave, Portland (97204). Phone 503/226-1111. www.portlandmarathon.org.* World-class running event featuring international competition. Early Oct.

**Portland Rose Festival.** *5603 SW Hood Ave, Portland (97239). Phone 503/227-2681.* Held for more than 90 years, this festival includes the Grand Floral Parade (reservations required for indoor parade seats) and two other parades; band competition; rose show; championship auto racing; hot-air balloons; air show; carnival; Navy ships. Late May-June.

**Portland Scottish Highland Games.** *Mt. Hood Community College, 26000 SE Stark St, Gresham (97030). 15 miles E. Phone 503/293-8501. www.phca.com.* Mid-July.

**St. Patrick's Irish Festival.** *Portland. Phone 503/227-4057.* One of the largest Irish festivals in the Pacific Northwest. Three days in Mar.

## Limited-Service Hotels

**★ COMFORT SUITES.** *1477 NE 183rd St, Portland (97060). Phone 503/661-2200; toll-free 877/771-7768; fax 503/465-1414. www.comfortsuites.com.* Conveniently located, this Comfort Suites property is just 5 miles from the airport. Directly off Interstate 84, it is close to outlet malls and restaurants. 83 rooms, all suites. Pets accepted, some restrictions; fee. Complimentary continental breakfast. Check-in 4 pm, check-out noon. High-speed Internet access. Fitness room. Outdoor pool. **$**

**★ DAYS INN.** *1414 SW 6th Ave, Portland (97201). Phone 503/221-1611; toll-free 800/544-8313; fax 503/226-0447. www.daysinn.com.* On-site parking is offered at this location near Portland's financial district. Many businesses are nearby, and the waterfront is just a stroll away. The full-service restaurant, Portland Bar & Grill, is open for breakfast, lunch, and dinner and features seasonal theater performances. 173 rooms, 5 story. Pets accepted; fee. Check-in 3 pm, check-out noon. High-speed Internet access. Restaurant, bar. Fitness room. Outdoor pool. **$**

**★ DAYS INN PORTLAND SOUTH.** *9717 SE Sunnyside Rd, Clackamas (97015). Phone 503/654-1699; toll-free 800/241-1699; fax 503/659-2702. www.daysinn.com.* This hotel on the south side of Portland is across the street from the Clackamas Town Center Mall, which includes a movie theater. Several restaurants are within walking distance, and there's a public golf course one block away. 110 rooms, 3 story. Complimentary continental breakfast. Check-in 4 pm, check-out noon. Bar. Outdoor pool, whirlpool. **$**

**★ ★ DOUBLETREE HOTEL.** *1000 NE Multnomah St, Portland (97232). Phone 503/281-6111; toll-free 800/222-8733; fax 503/284-8553. www.doubletree.com.* Although this property is not located downtown, it sits across from the Lloyd Center, with shopping, restaurants, movie theaters, and the infamous ice-skating rink. For convenient downtown transportation, the MAX Light Rail is a 20-minute ride. The lobby features an atrium with a glass elevator through the middle. 476 rooms, 15 story. Check-in 3 pm, check-out noon. High-speed Internet access. Two restaurants, bar. Fitness room. Outdoor pool. Business center. **$$**

**★ FAIRFIELD INN.** *11929 NE Airport Way, Portland (97220). Phone 503/253-1400; toll-free 800/228-2800; fax 503/253-3889. www.fairfieldinn.com.* This airport location is amid many fast food restaurants. The Expo Center, Oregon Convention center, Columbia River Gorge, and Oregon Zoo are all nearby. 106 rooms, 3 story. Complimentary continental breakfast. Check-in 3 pm, check-out noon. Wireless Internet access. Fitness room. Outdoor pool, whirlpool. Airport transportation available. **$**

**★ HOLIDAY INN EXPRESS TROUTDALE.** *1000 NW Graham Rd, Portland (97060). Phone 503/492-2900; toll-free 800/465-4329. www.holiday-inn.com.* An accommodating staff awaits guests at this location near shopping malls and restaurants. Just off exit 16, it is situated in Troutdale, approximately 15 minutes from the airport. 77 rooms. Pets accepted; fee. Complimentary full breakfast. Check-in 4 pm, check-out noon. High-speed Internet access, wireless Internet access. Fitness room. Whirlpool. **$**

**★ ★ HOTEL DELUXE.** *729 SW 15th Ave, Portland (97205). Phone 503/223-6311; fax 503/223-0522.* 136 rooms, 8 story. Pets accepted; fee. Check-out 1 pm. Restaurant, bar. **$**

**★ QUALITY INN & SUITES.** *2323 NE 181st Ave, Portland (97230). Phone 503/492-4000; toll-free 800/527-1133; fax 503/492-3271. www.qualityinn.com.* Approximately 10-12 minutes from the airport, this location is convenient with easy access to Interstate 84. Area attractions include the Columbia River Gorge, Oregon Zoo, and Portland International Raceway. 70 rooms, 3 story. Pets accepted; fee. Complimentary full breakfast. Check-in, check-out noon. High-speed Internet access, wireless Internet access. Fitness room. Indoor pool, whirlpool. Business center. **$**

**★ SHILO INN PORTLAND I-5 SOUTH.** *7300 SW Hazel Fern Rd, Portland (97224). Phone 503/639-2226; toll-free 800/222-2244; fax 503/639-9130. www.shiloinns.com.* This convenient Shilo Inn location is directly accessible to the freeway, approximately 15 minutes to downtown, and close to many restaurants and shops. A microwave and refrigerator are provided in each guest room, and complimentary popcorn and fruit are offered in the lobby. 116 rooms. Pets accepted; fee. Complimentary continental breakfast. Check-in 4 pm, check-out noon. High-speed Internet access. Fitness room. Outdoor pool, whirlpool. **$**

## Full-Service Hotels

**★ ★ ★ 5TH AVENUE SUITES HOTEL.** *506 SW Washington St, Portland (97204). Phone 503/222-0001; toll-free 888/207-2201; fax 503/417-3386. www.5thavenuesuites.com.* This centrally located, full-service historic hotel dating to 1912 was once the Lipman, Wolf & Co. department store. It has been renovated, and its guest rooms feature upholstered headboards, fluffy bedspreads, and Egyptian cotton robes to snuggle up in. The accommodations are decorated in soft colors, with subtle lighting and comfortable furniture adding to the cozy feel. The elegant lobby features soaring ceilings of molded plaster and wood, floor-to-ceiling windows, and a large corner fireplace surrounded by marble and topped with an antique mirror. Dine on Pacific Northwest cuisine at the Red Star Tavern & Roast House (see). 221 rooms, 10 story. Pets accepted; fee. Check-in 3 pm, check-out noon. High-speed Internet access, wireless Internet access. Restaurant, bar. Fitness room. Business center. **$$**

★ ★ **AVALON HOTEL & SPA.** *0455 SW Hamilton Ct, Portland (97239). Phone 503/802-5800; toll-free 888/556-4402; fax 503/802-5820. www.avalonhoteland-spa.com.* Carefree yet sophisticated, Portland's Avalon Hotel & Spa is a unique destination. On the edge of downtown, this boutique hotel offers guests the best of both worlds. Its proximity to the city's attractions lures cosmopolitan travelers, while its location on the Willamette River draws those seeking a tranquil retreat. Blending styles from Asia and the Pacific Northwest, the hotel is a splendid contemporary showpiece. Dark and light woods combine to create a soothing space, while large windows capitalize on the superior setting. The two-story lobby is an inviting place to take in local artwork displays or to rest by the fire. When you enter the guest accommodations, an instant calm washes over you, largely due to the floor-to-ceiling windows that showcase the rivers beautiful surroundings. Standard rooms feature marble baths, plush bathrobes, CD players, cordless phones, and private balconies; suites add fireplaces and double vanities. The Avalon Spa captures the essence of the region while paying tribute to Asian and European traditions. Dedicated to well-being, the spas carefully selected treatment menu utilizes natural ingredients, ancient wisdom, and innovative therapies to completely relax you. The excellent Avalon Fitness Club offers cutting-edge classes like Pilates, kickboxing, and Neuromuscular Integrative Action (NIA) in addition to free weights and cardio equipment, with personal trainers on duty to help customize workous for optimum results. 99 rooms, 6 story. Check-in 3 pm, check-out noon. High-speed Internet access, wireless Internet access. Restaurant, bar. Fitness room, fitness classes available, spa. Whirlpool. Business center. Credit cards accepted. **$$**

★ ★ ★ **BENSON HOTEL.** *309 SW Broadway, Portland (97205). Phone 503/228-2000; toll-free 888/523-6766; fax 503/471-3920. www.bensonhotel.com.* Presidents and celebrities alike have stayed in this landmark downtown hotel, whose owners have spared no expense since it was built in 1912. Feast your eyes on the lobby's paneling and Russian pillars, Austrian crystal chandeliers, and Italian marble staircase. The guest rooms are equally elegant, offering pleasantries like complimentary coffee, tea, and apples. With the hotel's one-to-one ratio of employees to guests, expect top servicefrom wine tastings to afternoon tea to the hotel's jazz club (the first ever to open in Portland). Don't miss the popular London Grill (see) restaurant, which offers an extensive wine collection and live jazz. 287 rooms, 14 story. Pets accepted, some restrictions; fee. Check-in 3 pm, check-out 1 pm. High-speed Internet access, wireless Internet access. Two restaurants, bar. Fitness room. Airport transportation available. Business center. **$$**

★ ★ ★ **CROWNE PLAZA.** *14811 Kruse Oaks Blvd, Lake Oswego (97035). Phone 503/624-8400; toll-free 800/227-6963; fax 503/684-8324. www.crowneplaza.com.* Located just minutes from the downtown area, this hotel is quite convenient to the convention center as well as many of the area universities. 161 rooms, 6 story. Pets accepted; fee. Check-out noon. Restaurant, bar. Fitness room. Indoor pool, outdoor pool, whirlpool. Business center. **$$**

★ ★ ★ **EMBASSY SUITES PORTLAND DOWNTOWN.** *319 SW Pine St, Portland (97204). Phone 503/279-9000; toll-free 800/362-2779; fax 503/497-9051. www.embassyportland.com.* Unlike a typical Embassy Suites, the downtown Portland location is a historic hotel, originally opened in 1912. The restored lobby remains true to its origins, adorned with gold-leafed columns, marble stairways, and crystal chandeliers. The two-room suites have comfortable, traditional-style furnishings, as well as refrigerators and microwaves. Guests dine at Portland Steak and Chophouse, which offers more than 100 fine scotches and whiskies. Also onsite is the Salon Nyla Day Spa. 276 rooms, 8 story, all suites. Complimentary full breakfast. Check-in 4 pm, check-out noon. High-speed Internet access, wireless Internet access. Restaurant, bar. Fitness room. Indoor pool, whirlpool. Business center. Credit cards accepted. **$$**

★ ★ ★ **GOVERNOR HOTEL.** *614 SW 11th Ave, Portland (97205). Phone 503/224-3400; toll-free 800/554-3456; fax 503/241-2122. www.govhotel.com.* The historic building sports a unique Lewis & Clark theme, with Native American flair throughout. The lobby, for example, features a totem pole, wood-burning fireplace, panoramic murals retracing Lewis & Clark's expedition, and turn-of-the-century frescoes.

Some guest rooms have fireplaces, wet bars, and balconies offering panoramic city views. The clubby Jakes Grill (see) serves American food. 100 rooms, 6 story. Check-in 4 pm, check-out noon. High-speed Internet access, wireless Internet access. Restaurant, bar. Fitness room, fitness classes available. Indoor pool, whirlpool. Business center. **$$**

★ ★ ★ **THE HEATHMAN HOTEL.** *1001 SW Broadway, Portland (97205). Phone 503/241-4100; toll-free 800/551-0011; fax 503/790-7110. www.heathman-hotel.com.* Dating to 1927, this grand "Arts Hotel of Portland" features a mix of artwork—from Art Deco mirrors in the Marble Bar to 18th-century French canvases in the historic Tea Court to silkscreens by Andy Warhol in the Heathman Restaurant (see). It's worth a tour for art lovers of any style and period. The guest rooms also have varied pieces of art. Personalized service at the front desk adds a warm and inviting touch. Distinguishing touches include a 400+ film library, afternoon tea, and nightly jazz in the Tea Court. 150 rooms, 10 story. Pets accepted, some restrictions; fee. Check-in 3:30 pm, check-out noon. High-speed Internet access. Restaurant, bar. Fitness room. Business center. **$$**

★ ★ ★ **HILTON PORTLAND & EXECUTIVE TOWER.** *921 SW Sixth Ave, Portland (97217). Phone 503/226-1611; toll-free 800/774-1500; fax 503/220-2565. www.portland.hilton.com.* Located in Portland's entertainment and financial districts, this hotel features fine dining and an athletic club with an indoor pool, tanning beds, sauna, and more. It is near the Performing Arts Center, shopping, and many restaurants. 782 rooms, 23 story. Pets accepted, some restrictions; fee. Check-in 4 pm, check-out noon. High-speed Internet access. Three restaurants, three bars. Children's activity center. Fitness room. Indoor pool, whirlpool. Business center. **$$**

★ ★ **HOLIDAY INN.** *1441 NE 2nd Ave, Portland (97232). Phone 503/233-2401; toll-free 800/465-4329; fax 503/238-7016. www.holiday-inn.com.* This welcoming hotel is located next to the Rose Garden Arena and within walking distance to the Convention Center. The MAX Light Rail is three blocks from the hotel and makes frequent trips to downtown (approximately 10-minute rides). A sport court, directly outside the meeting space, is available to guests. 239 rooms, 10 story. Check-in 3 pm, check-out noon. High-speed Internet access, wireless Internet access. Restaurant, bar. Fitness room. Indoor pool, whirlpool. Airport transportation available. Business center. **$**

★ ★ **HOLIDAY INN GRESHAM.** *2752 NE Hogan Dr, Gresham (97030). Phone 503/907-1777; toll-free 800/465-4329; fax 503/674-5985. www.holiday-inn.com.* This up-to-date property is attractively decorated in greens, yellows, and reds. With a convenient suburban location, it is near a shopping area and approximately 1 mile from Interstate 84. Ski resorts, water sports, and golf are all nearby.168 rooms. Pets accepted, some restrictions. Check-in 4 pm, check-out noon. High-speed Internet access, wireless Internet access. Restaurant, bar. Children's activity center. Fitness room. Indoor pool. Business center. **$**

★ ★ **HOTEL LUCIA.** *400 SW Broadway at Stark, Portland (97205). Phone 503/225-1717; toll-free 800/225-1717; fax 503/225-1919. www.hotellucia.com.* Hotel Lucia, in the downtown area, offers guests a memorable stay. The décor is unique, with rich chocolate brown furniture, black-and-white photographs by David Kennerly, and an interesting collection of artwork and sculptures. 127 rooms, 9 story. Check-in, check-out noon. High-speed Internet access, wireless Internet access. Restaurant, bar. Fitness room. Business center. **$$**

★ ★ ★ **HOTEL VINTAGE PLAZA.** *422 SW Broadway, Portland (97205). Phone 503/228-1212; toll-free 800/263-2305; fax 503/228-3598. www.vintageplaza.com.* What started out as the Imperial Hotel in 1894 is now the elegant Hotel Vintage Plaza, listed on the National Register of Historic Places. The hotel celebrates local winemaking by offering tastings of Oregon vintages in the evenings in the warm and inviting lobby. Guest accommodations feature Tuscan wine country décor, with Italian tapestries, ornately carved wooden mirrors, and bright colors and textures. Special rooms include the Garden Spa rooms, with their own outdoor patios and private spa tubs; and Starlight rooms, with slanted skylights and power shades. Pazzo Ristorante (see) offers fine Italian cuisine and wines. 107 rooms, 10 story. Pets accepted. Check-in 3 pm, check-out noon. Wireless Internet access. Two restaurants, bar. Fitness room. Business center. **$$**

★ ★ ★ **MARRIOTT PORTLAND CITY CENTER.** *520 SW Broadway, Portland (97205). Phone 503/226-6300; toll-free 800/228-9290; fax 503/227-*

*7515. www.marriott.com.* This Marriott location is in the heart of Portland, close to everything you may be looking for in a downtown property. 249 rooms, 20 story. Pets accepted; fee. Check-in 4 pm, check-out noon. High-speed Internet access. Restaurant, bar. Fitness room. Whirlpool. Business center. **$$**

★ ★ ★ **MARRIOTT PORTLAND DOWNTOWN.** *1401 SW Naito Pkwy, Portland (97201). Phone 503/226-7600; toll-free 800/228-9290; fax 503/221-1789. www.marriott.com.* This convenient location is situated within the financial/business district, on the west bank of the Willamette River. The guest rooms are decorated in warm tones of green, gold, and rust, and some rooms overlook a city park, giving way to a view of the river. The modern lobby is equally inviting with its comfortable furniture, marble floors, glass atrium, and soft lighting. 503 rooms, 16 story. Pets accepted, some restrictions. Check-in 4 pm, check-out noon. High-speed Internet access. Two restaurants, two bars. Fitness room. Indoor pool, whirlpool. Business center. **$$**

★ ★ ★ **PARAMOUNT HOTEL.** *808 SW Taylor St, Portland (97205). Phone 503/223-9900; toll-free 800/663-1144; fax 503/223-7900. www.portland-paramount.com.* Fashioned in the neoclassical style, this 15-story boutique hotel is located smack dab in the middle of downtown Portland, within walking distance of Pioneer Square and the Center for the Performing Arts. The hotels marble-tiled lobby creates a favorable first impression, with soaring ceilings, hand-loomed Persian rugs, and original artwork. Rooms are colored in warm tones, the walls adorned by black-and-white photography. Jetted tubs and private balconies are available in some rooms. Just off the hotel lobby, the Dragonfish Asian Café melds flavors and styles from all across East Asia, creating an eclectic Pan-Asian cuisine. 154 rooms. Pets accepted; fee. Check-in 3 pm, check-out noon. High-speed Internet access, wireless Internet access. Restaurant, bar. Fitness room. Business center. **$**

★ ★ **RED LION HOTEL ON THE RIVER - JANTZEN BEACH.** *909 N Hayden Island Dr, Portland (97217). Phone 503/283-4466; toll-free 800/733-5466; fax 503/735-4847. www.redlion.com.* This facility is conveniently located just 15 minutes from the Portland International Airport and easily accessible to Intertate 5. A courtesy van transports guests to the airport. Situated directly on Hayden Island/Jantzen Beach, it is adjacent to the Columbia River and features its own boat dock. This convention/business hotel is also popular for weekend stays due to its beach location. 318 rooms, 4 story. Pets accepted, some restrictions; fee. Check-in 3 pm, check-out noon. High-speed Internet access, wireless Internet access. Two restaurants, bar. Fitness room. Outdoor pool, whirlpool. Airport transportation available. Business center. **$**

★ ★ ★ **RIVERPLACE HOTEL.** *1510 SW Harbor Way, Portland (97201). Phone 503/228-3233; toll-free 800/227-1333; fax 503/295-6161. www.riverplacehotel.com.* Situated on the Willamette River, the RiverPlace Hotel is adjacent to Tom McCall Park and the marina, only a few blocks from downtown. Guests can relax on patio rocking chairs while enjoying the views. Kayaks and bikes are available for rental to tour the esplanade. 84 rooms, 4 story. Pets accepted; fee. Check-in, check-out noon. High-speed Internet access, wireless Internet access. Restaurant, bar. Whirlpool. Business center. **$$**

★ ★ ★ **SHERATON PORTLAND AIRPORT HOTEL.** *8235 NE Airport Way, Portland (97220). Phone 503/281-2500; toll-free 800/325-3525; fax 503/249-7602. www.sheratonpdx.com.* This hotel is conveniently located on the grounds of the airport and offers many services and amenities. 218 rooms, 5 story. Pets accepted; fee. Check-in 3 pm, check-out noon. Wireless Internet access. Restaurant, bar. Fitness room. Indoor pool, whirlpool. Airport transportation available. Business center. **$**

## Specialty Lodgings

**HERON HAUS.** *2545 NW Westover Rd, Portland (97210). Phone 503/274-1846; fax 503/248-4055. www.heronhaus.com.* This restored 1904 Tudor-style house is as charming on the outside as it is inside. The interior is traditional and features a TV room, an enclosed east-view sunroom, and a library. Downstairs, guests can take in the view of a small apple and pear orchard. Located in a historic area, it is approximately ten minutes from the city center. 6 rooms, 3 story. Complimentary continental breakfast. Check-in 4-6 pm, check-out 11 am. High-speed Internet access. **$$**

**MCMENAMINS EDGEFIELD.** *2126 SW Halsey St, Troutdale (97060). Phone 503/669-8610; toll-free 800/669-8610; fax 503/665-4209. www.mcmenamins.*

*com/edge.* 103 rooms, 3 story. Complimentary full breakfast. Check-out 11 am. Restaurant, bar. Golf. Renovated in the style of a European village complete with theater, winery, distillery, and brewery. **$**

**PORTLAND'S WHITE HOUSE BED AND BREAKFAST.** *1914 NE 22nd Ave, Portland (97212). Phone 503/287-7131; toll-free 800/272-7131; fax 503/249-1641. www.portlandswhitehouse.com.* Located in a historic neighborhood within walking distance to shopping, dining, fitness facilities and local attractions, this bed-and-breakfast offers finely furnished rooms, each with a full bath. A white southern colonial mansion with Greek columns and a fountain at the entrance, it bears a striking resemblance to Washington, DC's White House. 9 rooms, 2 story. Complimentary full breakfast. Check-in 4 pm, check-out noon. High-speed Internet access, wireless Internet access. **$$**

## Spa

★ ★ ★ **AVALON SPA.** *0455 SW Hamilton Ct, Portland (97239). Phone 503/802-5900; toll-free 888/556-4402. www.avalonhotelandspa.com.* The Avalon Spa captures the essence of the Pacific Northwest while paying tribute to Asian and European traditions. Dedicated to well-being, the spa's carefully selected treatment menu utilizes natural ingredients, ancient wisdom, and innovative therapies to relax you. Warm and attentive, the exceptional staff enhances the experience. Whether you need help with a fitness machine or require more information to select the right spa treatment, the staff is there to assist you in every possible way. If you would like to run on a treadmill or to join a group exercise class, the state-of-the-art fitness center warrants a visit. The juice bar welcomes you to catch your breath and refuel yourself with a fresh drink. Pamper yourself with an Ayurvedic ritual or a body care therapy. Choose from rose, coastal evergreen, aromatherapy, chamomile, and Turkish aroma for your exfoliation treatment, or take advantage of the detoxifying benefits of a natural spirulina or moor mud body wrap. Relish a renew or a revitalize facial. Traditional European kurs, including Hungarian thermal mineral, thalasso, and Kruter, are available to experience, or surrender to the heated waters of a themed bath. If stress has you tied up in knots, a heated stone, Swedish, sports, or reflexology massage can help melt away your tension. Expectant mothers in their second or third trimesters enjoy customized massages designed for them. The spa also offers salon services, including hair care, manicures, pedicures, waxing, and makeup instruction and applications.

## Restaurants

★ ★ **AL-AMIR LEBANESE RESTAURANT.** *223 SW Stark St, Portland (97204). Phone 503/274-0010. www.alamirrestaurant.com.* This uniquely decorated restaurant is located in a historic building on Stark Street. A beautiful mosaic of a palace arch leads into the dining room, and exposed brick walls and Persian rugs add to the ambience. Authentic Middle Eastern dishes are served by a pleasant, accommodating staff. Lebanese menu. Dinner, late-night. Bar. Children's menu. Casual attire. Reservations recommended. **$$**

★ **ALESSANDRO'S.** *301 SW Morrison, Portland (97204). Phone 503/222-3900; fax 503/224-9613. www.alessandrosrestaurant.com.* The tried and true Italian cuisine at Alessandro's is consistent. A good choice for families and groups, this local favorite offers a cozy atmosphere, with light blond furniture, green tablecloths, red napkins, and light yellow walls. Italian menu. Lunch, dinner. Bar. Children's menu. Casual attire. Reservations recommended. Outdoor seating. **$$**

★ **ALEXIS.** *215 W Burnside, Portland (97209). Phone 503/224-8577; fax 503/224-9354. www.alexisfoods.com.* Guests looking for traditional Greek fare will be tempted by Alexis's menu options, which include moussaka, pastitso, kalamarakia, and turkey souvlaki. The interior of the blue and white-stuccoed building is inviting and decorated with Greek knick knacks. Greek menu. Lunch, dinner. Closed Sun; holidays. Bar. Casual attire. Reservations recommended. **$$**

★ ★ **BUGATTI'S.** *18740 Willamette Dr, West Linn (97068). Phone 503/636-9555.* Italian menu. Dinner. Closed holidays. Children's menu. Outdoor seating. **$$**

★ ★ **BUSH GARDEN.** *900 SW Morrison, Portland (97205). Phone 503/226-7181; fax 503/226-7184. www.bush-garden.com.* This downtown area restaurant serves up Japanese dishes in a traditional Japanese setting. The lively atmosphere at the sushi bar and the DJ/karaoke on Fridays and Saturdays make for a fun night out. Japanese menu. Lunch, dinner. Closed holidays. Bar. Casual attire. Reservations recommended. **$$**

★ ★ ★ **CAPRIAL'S BISTRO.** *7015 SE Milwaukie Ave, Portland (97202). Phone 503/236-6457; fax 503/238-8554. www.caprialandjohnskitchen.com.* Located in the Westmoreland section of Portland, Caprial's Bistro is within ten minutes of downtown. The interior features an open kitchen and many wine bottles on display. The seasonal Northwest menu changes monthly and includes fresh local ingredients. Cooking classes and wine tastings are also offered here. American menu. Lunch, dinner. Closed Sun-Mon. Bar. Casual attire. Reservations recommended. **$$$**

**★ ★ CHART HOUSE RESTAURANT.** *5700 SW Terwilliger Blvd, Portland (97201). Phone 503/246-6963; fax 503/246-8437. www.chart-house.com.* Views of the Willamette River, Mt. Hood, and downtown Portland can be seen while driving to this restaurant situated high in the Willamette hills. Vibrant paintings adorn the walls, and the views from the large windows are spectacular. Seafood, steak menu. Lunch, dinner. Bar. Children's menu. Casual attire. Reservations recommended. Valet parking. **$$$**

**★ CORBETT FISH HOUSE.** *5901 SW Corbett Ave, Portland (97239). Phone 503/246-4434. www.corbettfishhouse.com.* All the food and dressings are gluten free (except the bread used in sandwiches) at Corbett Fish House. A local favorite, it is just outside downtown Portland. The yellow perch, halibut, and walleye are among the house favorites. Seafood menu. Lunch, dinner. Bar. Children's menu. Casual attire. Outdoor seating. **$$**

**★ DAN & LOUIS OYSTER BAR.** *208 SW Ankeny St, Portland (97204). Phone 503/227-5906. www.danandlouis.com.* You'll feel as if you were in a small New England fishing town when you step into Dan & Louis Oyster Bar. Large ship wheels and black-and-white photographs are among the old-time nautical décor at this local favorite. Seafood menu. Lunch, dinner. Closed holidays. Bar. Children's menu. Casual attire. **$$**

**★ ESPARZA'S TEX MEX CAFE.** *2725 SE Ankeny St, Portland (97214). Phone 503/234-7909; fax 503/232-3589.* Just across East Burnside—the main drag that divides North and South Portland—sits this restaurant offering Tex-Mex favorites. The décor is kitschy, with marionettes and animal skulls on the ceiling and walls. Southwestern menu. Lunch, dinner, brunch. Closed Sun. Bar. Children's menu. Casual attire. Outdoor seating. **$$**

**★ ★ FERNANDO'S HIDEAWAY.** *824 SW First Ave, Portland (97204). Phone 503/248-4709; fax 503/248-0798. www.fernandosportland.com.* Guests can choose from more than 47 tapas choices and an impressive sherry selection at this historic waterfront location along the Willamette River. Classical Spanish guitar and flamenco music add to the Spanish ambience. Salsa lessons are offered Thursday through Saturday. Spanish menu. Lunch, dinner, late-night. Bar. Children's menu. Casual attire. Reservations recommended. Outdoor seating. **$$**

**★ ★ ★ GENOA.** *2832 SE Belmont St, Portland (97214). Phone 503/238-1464; fax 503/238-9786. www.genoarestaurant.com.* Housed in a windowless, unassuming storefront that offers outsiders no clue as to the wonders just beyond the front door, Genoa is a hidden gem where glorious Italian feasts are served nightly. However, if you require predictability and control in your life, this restaurant may not be the place for you. There is no printed menu at Genoa. Your gracious waiter will offer you a choice of three entrées, but all other decisions rest with the chef. The menu is seven courses, prix fixe, and includes antipasto, soup, pasta, fish or salad, your chosen entrée, dessert, and then fruit. (A trip to the gym should be scheduled for the following day.) With this much food to consume, dinner at Genoa is a lengthy, leisurely, and lovely affair. The service is hospitable and knowledgeable, and nothing is rushed (a terrific concept), giving you time to savor the food and your company. Italian menu. Dinner. Bar. Casual attire. Reservations recommended. **$$$**

**★ GROLLA RESTAURANT & WINE BAR.** *2930 NE Killingsworth, Portland (97211). Phone 503/493-9521.* Mediterranean menu. Dinner. Closed Sun, Mon. Bar. Outdoor seating. **$$**

**★ ★ ★ HEATHMAN.** *1001 SW Broadway, Portland (97205). Phone 503/241-4100; fax 503/790-7110. www.heathmanhotel.com.* Executive chef Philippe Boulot offers classic French cooking, with an emphasis on Normandy, in a three-level dining room with a kitchen on one side and views of Broadway Street on the other. A prix fixe menu is offered for hurried theatergoers. American, French menu. Breakfast, lunch, dinner, late-night. Bar. Children's menu. Casual attire. Reservations recommended. Valet parking. Outdoor seating. **$$$**

**★ ★ ★ HIGGINS RESTAURANT & BAR.** *1239 SW Broadway, Portland (97205). Phone 503/222-9070; fax 503/222-1244.* Elegantly designed like a French bistro, this trilevel restaurant has taken special efforts to create an inviting atmosphere. Passionate about using local, organic ingredients, the chef creates a menu that leaves palates pleased. American menu. Lunch, dinner, late-night. Closed holidays. Bar. Children's menu. Casual attire. Reservations recommended. **$$$**

**★ ★ HUBER'S CAFE.** *411 SW 3rd Ave, Portland (97204). Phone 503/228-5686; fax 503/227-3922. www.hubers.com.* This eatery was originally a saloon established in 1879; it became a restaurant during Prohibition. The décor includes an arched stained-glass skylight, mahogany paneling, and a terrazzo floor. American, seafood menu. Breakfast, lunch, dinner, late-night. Bar. Children's menu. Casual attire. Reservations recommended. Outdoor seating. **$$**

**★ ★ JAKE'S FAMOUS CRAWFISH.** *401 SW 12th Ave, Portland (97205). Phone 503/226-1419; fax 503/220-1856. www.jakesfamouscrawfish.com.* At more than 110 years old, this downtown landmark restaurant doesn't hide its age; dark woods, turn-of-the-century décor, and scenes of old-time Portland give it a classic feel. An upbeat mood pervades the place, especially in the lively bar area, which is a local favorite. Jake's serves fresh regional seafood dishes as well as several varieties of the crawfish that made it famous. If you're feeling especially adventurous (not to mention hungry), try the 1-pound crawfish platter. Seafood menu. Breakfast, lunch, dinner, late-night. Closed Dec 25. Bar. Children's menu. Casual attire. Valet parking. Outdoor seating. **$$**

**★ ★ ★ JAKE'S GRILL.** *611 SW 10th St, Portland (97205). Phone 503/220-1850; fax 503/226-8365. www.mccormickandschmicks.com.* This timeless restaurant is a local favorite in downtown Portland. Decorated with dark woods, red leather chairs, tables topped with white tablecloths, and unique chandeliers, it exudes an old-fashioned steakhouse atmosphere. American menu. Breakfast, lunch, dinner, late-night, brunch. Bar. Children's menu. Casual attire. Reservations recommended. Valet parking. Outdoor seating. **$$$**

**★ ★ MANDARIN COVE.** *111 SW Columbia, Portland (97201). Phone 503/222-0006; fax 503/274-9800.* Located in the financial section of Portland, Mandarin Cove serves up some amazing Chinese cuisine. Don't miss the affordable lunch specials. Mandarin, Chinese menu. Lunch, dinner. Bar. Casual attire. **$$**

**★ ★ MARRAKESH MOROCCAN RESTAURANT.** *1201 NW 21st Ave, Portland (97209). Phone 503/248-9442; fax 503/294-7191. www.marrakesh.city.com.* A traditional Moroccan feast awaits guests at this colorful eatery. Adding to the ambience, belly dancers perform on Wednesday through Saturday evenings. For those interested in a cocktailwine, beer, and champagne are the only alcoholic beverages served. Moroccan menu. Dinner. Children's menu. Casual attire. **$$**

**★ ★ MURATA.** *200 SW Market St, Portland (97201). Phone 503/227-0080.* Murata is a traditional Japanese restaurant located in Portland's financial district. Authentic dishes are served here, and guests can dine at the sushi bar. Japanese menu. Lunch, dinner. Closed Sun. Casual attire. Reservations recommended. Valet parking. **$$**

**★ ★ NOHO'S HAWAIIAN CAFE.** *2525 SE Clinton, Portland (97202). Phone 503/233-5301; fax 503/239-0990. www.nohos.com.* The chef/owner of Noho's grew up in Hawaii and brought traditional Hawaiian recipes to Portland. Authentic cuisine is served in a fun atmosphere. Hawaiian menu. Lunch, dinner. Casual attire. Outdoor seating. **$$**

**★ ★ ★ PALEY'S PLACE.** *1204 NW 21st Ave, Portland (97209). Phone 503/243-2403; fax 503/223-8041. www.paleysplace.citysearch.com.* The bistro fare here features imaginative and beautifully presented entrées, using only the freshest local ingredients. Homemade chocolates arrive with the bill. Wine Wednesdays include wine tastings and a menu to match. French bistro menu. Dinner. Bar. Casual attire. Reservations recommended. Outdoor seating. **$$$**

**★ ★ PAPA HAYDN.** *5829 SE Milwaukie, Portland (97202). Phone 503/232-9440; fax 503/236-5815. www.papahaydn.com.* This warm and inviting restaurant has a Viennese feel, decorated with fabric touches and antiques. First a pastry/coffee house, it has expanded its menu to include a full lunch, dinner, and Sunday brunch menu. Papa Haydn's is a local favorite for dessert. American menu. Lunch, dinner, late-night, brunch. Bar. Children's menu. Casual attire. Outdoor seating. **$$**

**★ ★ ★ PAZZO RISTORANTE.** *627 SW Washington, Portland (97205). Phone 503/228-1515; fax 503/228-5935. www.kimptongroup.com.* A cozy, friendly atmosphere is the setting for an authentically northern Italian restaurant that is a favorite among the locals. The open kitchen gives guests a preview of what's to come: handmade pastas and hearty dishes such as leg of lamb with goat cheese. Italian menu. Breakfast, lunch, dinner, brunch. Bar. Children's menu. Casual attire. Reservations recommended. Valet parking. Outdoor seating. **$$**

**★ ★ PERRY'S ON FREMONT.** *2401 NE Fremont, Portland (97212). Phone 503/287-3655; fax 503/287-6216.* American menu. Dinner. Closed Sun. Bar. Children's menu. Casual attire. Valet parking. Outdoor seating. **$$**

**★ ★ ★ PLAINFIELD.** *852 SW 21st Ave, Portland (97205). Phone 503/223-2995; fax 503/292-9893. www.plainfields.com.* Plainfields Mayur (in Sanskrit, mayur means peacock) is located downtown in a historic Victorian house near the Civic Stadium. The waitstaff, donned in white shirts with black ties and cummerbunds, serves up East Indian food, including vegan and vegetarian entrées. An extensive wine list is also offered. Indian menu. Dinner. Bar. Children's menu. Casual attire. Reservations recommended. Outdoor seating. Credit cards accepted. **$$**

**★ POOR RICHARDS.** *3907 NE Broadway, Portland (97232). Phone 503/288-5285; fax 503/493-1449. www.poorrichardstwofer.com.* Fun and informal, Poor Richards has been serving up steakhouse favorites since 1959. It is a popular stop for the "two-fer" meals, where two value meals are offered at one price. Situated on the corner of 39th and Broadway, it is on the east side of Portland (east of the Willamette River). Steak menu. Lunch, dinner. Bar. Children's menu. Casual attire. Reservations recommended. Outdoor seating. **$$**

**★ ★ ★ RED STAR TAVERN & ROAST HOUSE.** *503 SW Alder St, Portland (97204). Phone 503/222-0005; fax 503/417-3334. www.redstartavern.com.* With views overlooking downtown Portland, this tavern turns out Northwestern fare that centers on spit-roasted meats, fresh seafood (especially shellfish) and great flatbread appetizers. Diners can watch their food being prepared in the semi-exposed kitchen. American menu. Breakfast, lunch, dinner, late-night, brunch. Bar. Children's menu. Casual attire. Reservations recommended. Valet parking. Outdoor seating. **$$**

**★ ★ RHEINLANDER.** *5035 NE Sandy Blvd, Portland (97213). Phone 503/288-5503. www.gutenfoods.com.* German menu. Lunch, dinner. Closed July 4, Dec 24-25. Bar. Children's menu. **$$**

**★ ★ ★ RINGSIDE.** *2165 W Burnside St, Portland (97210). Phone 503/223-1513; fax 503/223-6908. www.ringsidesteakhouse.com.* Established in the 1940s, Ringside is a classic steakhouse located on top of Nob Hill, just a few minutes from the center of downtown. Pictures of famous patrons and various awards decorate the walls. The dining area is low lit and intimate. Seafood, steak menu. Dinner, late-night. Bar. Casual attire. Reservations recommended. Valet parking. **$$$**

**★ ★ RINGSIDE EAST AT GLENDOVEER.** *14021 NE Glisan, Portland (97230). Phone 503/255-0750. www.ringsidesteakhouse.com.* This family-owned and -operated steakhouse is within 15 minutes of downtown Portland. A variety of seafood and steak options are offered, including prime pepper New York steak and fried oysters Romano. Seafood, steak menu. Lunch, dinner. Bar. Children's Menu. Casual attire. Reservations recommended. **$$**

**★ ★ SALTY'S ON THE COLUMBIA RIVER.** *3839 NE Marine Dr, Portland (97211). Phone 503/288-4444; fax 503/288-3426. www.saltys.com.* Situated 15 minutes from the airport and northeast of downtown, Salty's offers waterfront dining on the Columbia River. The views are appealing and the nautical touches add to the ambience. Seafood menu. Lunch, dinner, Sun brunch. Bar. Children's menu. Casual attire. Reservations recommended. Outdoor seating. **$$$**

**★ SANTORINI.** *11525 SW Barnes Rd, Portland (97201). Phone 503/646-6889.* Italian, Greek menu. Lunch, dinner. Bar. Children's menu. Outdoor seating. **$**

**★ ★ SAUCEBOX.** *214 SW Broadway, Portland (97205). Phone 503/241-3393. www.saucebox.com.* A favorite among the locals, Saucebox offers authentic Pan-Asian cuisine in a modern, hip atmosphere. The Javenese salmon is a specialty here, and specialty cocktails are what made this hot spot popular. Pan-Asian menu. Dinner. Closed Sun-Mon. Bar. Casual attire. Reservations recommended. Outdoor seating. **$$**

**★ SAYLER'S OLD COUNTRY KITCHEN.** *10519 SE Stark, Portland (97216). Phone 503/252-4171.* A good spot for families and groups, Saylers Old Kitchen offers diners a good value in a comfortable setting. The motto here is A Huge Honkin Steak with No Frills. This suburban location is accessible to the freeway. American, steak menu. Dinner. Closed holidays. Bar. Children's menu. Casual attire. **$$**

**★ ★ TYPHOON!** *2310 NW Everett St, Portland (97210). Phone 503/243-7557; fax 503/243-7144.* Thai menu. Lunch, dinner. Closed holidays. Outdoor seating. **$$**

**★ ★ WIDMER GASTHAUS.** *955 N Russell St, Portland (97227). Phone 503/281-3333. www.widmer.com.* German menu. Lunch, dinner. Closed Jan 1, Thanksgiving, Dec 25. Bar. Outdoor seating. **$$**

**★ ★ ★ WILDWOOD RESTAURANT AND BAR.** *1221 NW 21st Ave, Portland (97209). Phone 503/248-9663; fax 503/222-5153. www.wildwoodrestaurant.com.* This acclaimed Oregon restaurant serves the freshest seafood and seasonal Northwest ingredients in elegant combinations that highlight the indigenous flavors. A wood-burning oven turns out crisp pizzas and adds warmth to the dining room's comforting natural tones. American menu. Lunch, dinner, Sun brunch.

Bar. Casual attire. Reservations recommended. Outdoor seating. **$$$**

# Prineville (C-3)

*See also Bend, Madras, Redmond*

**Founded** 1868
**Population** 5,355
**Elevation** 2,864 ft
**Area Code** 541
**Zip** 97754
**Information** Prineville-Crook County Chamber of Commerce, 390 N Fairview; phone 541/447-6304

Two-thirds of the population of Crook County lives in or near Prineville. Livestock, alfalfa, wheat, mint, sugar beets, and lumbering are important in this county. Hunting, fishing, and rockhounding are popular. The City of Prineville Railroad, 19 miles of main line connecting the Union Pacific and Oregon Trunk Railway, is one of the few municipally-owned railroads in the US. Two Ranger District offices and headquarters of the Ochoco National Forest are located here.

## What to See and Do

**Mineral collecting.** *Prineville. Phone 541/447-6304.* Agates of various types, obsidian, petrified wood, geodes and other stones. More than 1,000 acres of digging space in Eagle Rock, Maury Mountain, White Rock Springs and other areas. Obtain info from Chamber of Commerce.

**Ochoco Lake Campground.** *Prineville. 7 miles E on Hwy 26. Phone 541/447-1209.* A 10-acre juniper-covered promontory on the N shore of Ochoco Reservoir. Fishing; boating (ramp). Hiking. Picnicking. Improved tent and trailer sites.

**Ochoco National Forest.** *Prineville. E on Hwy 26. Phone 541/416-6500. www.fs.fed.us/r6/centraloregon/.* An approximately 848,000-acre forest, plus the 111,000-acre **Crooked River National Grassland.** Central Oregon high desert, thunderegg deposits, and stands of ponderosa pine. Fishing in streams, Walton and Delintment lakes, Haystack and Antelope reservoirs; also hunting. Hiking trails. Winter sports. Picnicking. Camping (fee).

# Redmond (C-3)

*See also Bend, Madras, Prineville*

**Population** 7,163
**Elevation** 2,997 ft
**Area Code** 541
**Zip** 97756
**Information** Chamber of Commerce, 446 SW 7th St; phone 541/923-5191 or toll-free 800/574-1325
**Web Site** www.visitredmondoregon.com

Popular with sports enthusiasts and tourists, this is also the agricultural, lumbering, and industrial center of central Oregon. A Ranger District office of the Deschutes National Forest is located here. The US Forest Service Redmond Regional Air Center is located at Roberts Field.

## What to See and Do

**Cline Falls.** *Redmond. 4 miles W on Hwy 126. Phone 541/388-6055.* A 9-acre park on the banks of the Deschutes River. Fishing. Picnicking.

**Firemen's Lake.** *Lake Rd and Sisters Ave, Redmond (97756). Phone 541/548-6068.* Children's fishing pond. Three-acre lake stocked with bass and bluegill. Children under 14 and disabled persons only. (Mid-Apr-mid-Oct, daily) **FREE**

**Peter Skene Ogden Wayside.** *9241 NE Crooked River Rd, Terrebonne (97760). 9 miles N on Hwy 97. Phone 541/548-7501.* A 98-acre park with canyon 400 feet wide, 304 feet deep. Picnicking. Observation point.

**Petersen Rock Gardens.** *7930 SW 77th St, Redmond (97756). 7 miles S on Hwy 97, then 2 1/2 miles W. Phone 541/382-5574.* Model castles and bridges built with rock specimens; lagoons and flower beds; picnicking, fireplaces; museum. (Daily) **$$**

**Smith Rock.** *9241 NE Crooked River Rd, Terrebonne (97760). 9 miles NE off Hwy 97. Phone 541/548-7501.* A 623-acre park with views of unusual multicolored volcanic and sedimentary rock formations and the Crooked River Canyon. The Crooked River Gorge (403 feet deep) is 3 miles north. Fishing. Hiking, rock climbing. Picnicking.

## Special Event

**Deschutes County Fair and Rodeo.** *3800 SW Airport Way, Redmond (97756). Phone 541/548-2711.* First week in Aug.

## Limited-Service Hotel

**★ COMFORT SUITES AIRPORT.** *2243 SW Yew Ave, Redmond (97756). Phone 541/504-8900; fax 541/504-1316. www.choicehotels.com.* 92 rooms. Complimentary continental breakfast. Check-in 3 pm, check-out noon. Fitness room. **$**

## Full-Service Resort

**★ ★ INN AT EAGLE CREST RESORT.** *1522 Cline Falls Rd, Redmond (97756). Phone 541/923-2453; toll-free 800/682-4786; fax 541/923-1720. www.eagle-crest.com.* This central Oregon getaway is a haven for golfers with its two 18-hole championship courses, par-63 challenge course, and an 18-hole live-turf putting course. Its low elevation means that one of the courses can be kept open year-round, and an average of 300 days of sunshine makes it likely that you'll enjoy nice weather during your round. Some guest rooms have views of the 16th green and 17th tee. The resort also features an equestrian center offering guided rides and lessons. Sizable conference facilities make this a great choice for active-minded business travelers. 100 rooms, 2 story. Check-in 4 pm, check-out noon. Restaurant, bar. Children's activity center. Outdoor pool, whirlpool. Golf, 36 holes. Tennis. Airport transportation available. **$**

## Restaurant

**★ ★ MRS. BEASLEY'S.** *1555 S Hwy 97, Redmond (97756). Phone 541/548-4023.* American menu. Breakfast, lunch, dinner, Sun brunch. Closed Dec 25. Bar. Children's menu. **$**

# Reedsport (D-1)

*See also Coos Bay, Florence, North Bend*

**Population** 4,796
**Elevation** 10 ft
**Area Code** 541
**Zip** 97467
**Information** Chamber of Commerce, PO Box 11; phone 541/271-3495 or toll-free 800/247-2155
**Web Site** www.reedsportcc.org

Surrounded by rivers, lakes, and the ocean, the area has an abundance and variety of fish, particularly striped bass, steelhead, and salmon. Two of the best bass fishing lakes in Oregon are nearby. Reedsport was originally marshland subject to flooding at high tides, so the earliest buildings and sidewalks were built 3-8 feet above ground. A dike was built after the destructive Christmastime flood of 1964 to shield the lower part of town.

## What to See and Do

**Dean Creek Elk Viewing Area.** *Reedsport. 3 miles E on Hwy 38. Phone 541/756-0100.* Area has 440 acres of pasture and bottomland where Roosevelt elk (Oregon's largest land mammal) and other wildlife can be viewed. Interpretive center. No hunting. Contact Bureau of Land Management, 1300 Airport Ln, North Bend 97459. (Daily) **FREE**

**Oregon Dunes National Recreation Area.** *855 Hwy 101, Reedsport (97467). W off Hwy 101. Phone 541/271-3611.* Large coastal sand dunes, forests and wetlands comprise this 32,000-acre area in Siuslaw National Forest (see CORVALLIS). Beachcombing; fishing; boating. Hiking, horseback riding, off-road vehicle areas. Picnicking. Camping (fee; some campgrounds closed Oct-May). Visitors center and headquarters in Reedsport at Hwy 101 and Hwy 38 (Daily).

**Salmon Harbor.** *100 Ork Rock Rd, Winchester Bay (97495). Phone 541/271-3407.* Excellent boat basin for charter boats and pleasure and fishing craft. Fishing for silver and chinook salmon in the ocean, a short run from the mouth of the Umpqua River (May-Sept: daily; rest of year: Mon-Fri).

**Umpqua Discovery Center.** *409 Riverfront Way, Reedsport (97467). Phone 541/271-4816. www.umpquadiscoverycenter.com.* Interpretive displays centering on cultural and natural history of area. (Daily; closed Jan 1, Thanksgiving, Dec 25) **$$**

**Umpqua Lighthouse State Park.** *460 Lighthouse Rd, Reedsport (97467). 6 miles S off Hwy 101. Phone 541/271-4118.* This 450-acre park touches the mouth of the Umpqua River, borders the Umpqua Lighthouse Reservation, and skirts the ocean shore for more than 2 miles, with sand dunes rising 500 feet (highest in US). Noted for its marvelous, seasonal display of rhododendrons. Swimming; fishing. Hiking; trail to beach and around Lake Marie. Picnicking. Tent and trailer sites. Whale watching area.

**William M. Tugman State Park.** *Hwy 101 N, Lakeside. 8 miles S on Hwy 101. Phone 541/759-3604.* A 560-acre park in scenic coastal lake region. Swimming, bathhouse; fishing; boating (ramp to Eel Lake). Picnicking. Improved tent and trailer sites (dump station).

# Rockaway Beach (B-2)

*See also Cannon Beach, Seaside, Tillamook*

**Population** 970
**Elevation** 16 ft
**Area Code** 503
**Zip** 97136
**Information** Rockaway Beach Chamber of Commerce, Little Red Caboose at the Wayside, Hwy 101 downtown, PO Box 198; phone 503/355-8108
**Web Site** www.rockawaybeach.net

Once an extremely popular resort town for Portland residents, Rockaway Beach is quieter now, although its 7-mile stretch of sandy beach still attracts a crowd on summer weekends. It's not uncommon to see a cluster of colorful kites darting and diving in the sky above the shoreline. The town hosts a kite-flying festival each spring. Rockaway Beach is located on Highway 101, a short drive north of Tillamook.

## Limited-Service Hotel

★ **SURFSIDE MOTEL.** *101 NW 11th Ave, Rockaway Beach (97136). Phone 503/355-2312; toll-free 800/243-7786.* 79 rooms, 2 story. Pets accepted, some restrictions; fee. Check-out noon. Indoor pool. **$**

# Roseburg (D-2)

*See also Cannon Beach, Seaside, Tillamook*

**Settled** 1853
**Population** 17,032
**Elevation** 459 ft
**Area Code** 541
**Zip** 97470
**Information** Visitors and Convention Bureau, 410 Spruce St, PO Box 1262; phone 541/672-9731 or toll-free 800/444-9584
**Web Site** www.visitroseburg.com

Roseburg is in one of Oregon's big stands of virgin timber that supports lumbermills and plywood plants. Although roses were the local pride, the town's name came not from the flower but from Aaron Rose, an early settler. This is the seat of Douglas County and headquarters for Umpqua National Forest.

## What to See and Do

**Callahan Ridge Winery.** *340 Busenbark Ln, Roseburg (97470). W of I-5; Garden Valley exit 125, 2 miles W to Melrose then 1 mile S to Busenbark Ln, then right. Phone 541/673-7901; toll-free 888/946-3487.* Tasting room. (Apr-Oct, daily; other times call for appointment) **FREE**

**Douglas County Museum of History and Natural History.** *1020 Lighthouse Rd, Roseburg (97467). 1 mile S via I-5, exit 123 at fairgrounds. Phone 541/440-4507.* Exhibits include early history and natural history displays of the region; photographic collection; research library. Also Regional Tourist Information. (Daily) **$$**

**Henry Estate Winery.** *687 Hubbard Creek Rd, Umpqua (97486). 13 miles NW via I-5, 1 mile W of Umpqua on County 6. Phone 541/459-5120; toll-free 800/782-2686. www.henryestate.com.* Tours, tasting room; picnic area. (Daily; closed holidays) **FREE**

**Hillcrest Vineyard.** *240 Vineyard Ln, Roseburg (97470). Approximately 10 miles W; I-5 exit 125, W on Garden Valley Rd, Melrose Rd, Doerner Rd then N on Elgarose and follow signs. Phone 541/673-3709; toll-free 800/736-3709.* Wine tastings; tours. (Daily; closed holidays) **FREE**

**Umpqua National Forest.** *2900 NW Stewart Pkwy, Roseburg (97470). Direct access from Hwy 138, along North Umpqua River. Phone 541/672-6601.* Paved scenic byway takes visitors through magnificent scenery to Diamond Lake, which offers fishing (rainbow, steelhead trout) and forest camps. Mount Thielsen (9,182 feet) and Mount Bailey (8,363 feet) tower above the lake. The Colliding Rivers Visitor Information Center (daily) is located along Highway 138 in Glide; the Diamond Lake Visitor Center (summer) is located opposite the entrance to Diamond Lake Campground. The forest (nearly 1 million acres), named for Native Americans who once fished in the rivers, includes three wilderness areas: Boulder Creek, 19,100 acres; Mount Thielsen, 22,700 acres; and Roque-Umpqua Divide, 29,000 acres. Also the Oregon Cascades Recreation Area, 35,500 acres. Picnicking, lodging, hiking, camping (fee).

**Wildlife Safari.** *1790 Safari Rd, Winston (97496). 6 miles S on I-5, exit 119 to Hwy 42 for 4 miles. Phone 541/679-6761; toll-free 800/355-4848.* A 600-acre drive-through animal park; 600 exotic specimens of African, Asian and North American wildlife in natural habitats; petting zoo; elephant and train rides (seasonal); guided and walk-through tours by reservation; restaurant. (Daily) **$$$$**

## Special Events

**Douglas County Fair.** *2110 Frear St, Roseburg (97470). Phone 541/957-7010.* Early Aug.

**Greatest of the Grape.** *Roseburg. Phone 541/672-9731.* Mid-Feb.

**Roseburg Graffiti Week.** *Roseburg. Phone 541/672-9731.* 1950s car show and activities. First week in July.

**Spring Craft Fair.** *2110 Frear St, Roseburg (97470). Phone 541/672-9731.* Late Mar.

**Umpqua Valley Roundup.** *2110 Frear St, Roseburg (97470). Phone 541/672-5777.* Weekend in mid-June.

**Wildlife Safari Wildlights.** *Roseburg. Phone 541/679-6761.* Dec.

## Limited-Service Hotels

**★ QUALITY INN.** *427 NW Garden Valley Blvd, Roseburg (97470). Phone 541/673-5561; fax 541/957-0318.* 70 rooms, 2 story. Pets accepted, some restrictions; fee. Complimentary continental breakfast. Check-in 2 pm, check-out 11 am. Fitness room. Outdoor pool. **$**

**★ ★ WINDMILL INN OF ROSEBURG.** *1450 NW Mulholland Dr, Roseburg (97470). Phone 541/673-0901; toll-free 800/547-4747. www.windmillinns.com.* 128 rooms, 2 story. Pets accepted. Complimentary continental breakfast. Check-in 4 pm, check-out 11 am. Restaurant, bar. Fitness room. Outdoor pool, whirlpool. Business center. **$**

## Specialty Lodgings

**STEAMBOAT INN.** *42705 N Umpqua Hwy, Steamboat (97447). Phone 541/498-2230; toll-free 800/840-8825. www.thesteamboatinn.com.* Located inside the Umpqua National Forest along the banks of the North Umpqua River, this inn offers spectacular views of the local scenery. 3 rooms, 2 story. **$$**

**STEELHEAD RUN BED & BREAKFAST.** *23049 N Umpqua Hwy, Glide (97443). Phone 541/496-0563; toll-free 800/348-0563. www.steelheadrun.com.* Located on a bluff overlooking the North Umpqua River with private beach, picnic area, trails, and fishing.6 rooms, 2 story. Pets accepted. Complimentary full breakfast. Check-in 1 pm, check-out 11 am. **$**

## Restaurant

**★ ★ MCMENAMINS ROSEBURG STATION.** *700 SE Sheridan St, Roseburg (97470). Phone 541/672-1934. www.mcmenamins.com.* Situated in an 87-year-old railway station, this restaurant offers a fine selection of local specialties and microbrews. American menu. Lunch, dinner. **$**

# Salem (B-2)

*See also Albany, Corvallis, McMinnville, Newberg, Oregon City, Portland, Silverton*

**Settled** 1840
**Population** 107,786
**Elevation** 154 ft
**Area Code** 503
**Information** Convention & Visitors Association, 1313 Mill St SE, 97301; phone 503/581-4325 or toll-free 800/874-7012
**Web Site** www.travelsalem.com

The state capital and the third largest city in Oregon, Salem's economy is based on the state government, food processing, light manufacturing, agriculture, and wood products. Salem shares Oregon's sports attractions with other cities of the Willamette Valley.

## What to See and Do

**A.C. Gilbert's Discovery Village.** *116 Marion St, Salem (97301). Phone 503/371-3631. www.acgilbert.org.* Hands-on exhibits related to art, drama, music, science and nature. (Mon-Sat, also Sun afternoons) **$$**

**Bush House.** *Bush's Pasture Park, 600 Mission St SE, Salem (97302). 6 blocks S of capitol. Phone 503/363-4714.* Victorian mansion (1878) with authentic furnishings. (Tues-Sun; closed holidays) **$$** Also here is

> **Bush Barn Art Center.** *600 Mission St SE, Salem (97302). Phone 503/581-2228.* Remodeled barn houses two exhibit galleries with monthly shows and a sales gallery featuring Northwest artists. (Tues-Sun; closed holidays) **FREE**

**Enchanted Forest.** *8462 Enchanted Way SE, Turner (97392). 7 miles S, off I-5 Sunnyside-Turner exit 248. Phone 503/371-4242. www.enchantedforest.com.* Features storybook theme. Other exhibits include reproduction of early mining town, haunted house (fee), log flume ride (fee), ice mountain bobsled ride (fee), kiddie bumper boats and kiddie ferris wheel (fee), old world village, theater featuring live comedy and children's shows, water and light show. Picnic area; refreshments; gift stores. (Mid-Mar-Mar 31, May 1-Labor Day: daily; Apr and Sept: weekends only) **$$$**

**Historic Deepwood Estate.** *1116 Mission St SE, Salem (97302). Phone 503/363-1825.* (1894) Queen Anne-style house and carriage house designed by W. C. Knighton. Povey Brothers stained-glass windows, golden oak woodwork; solarium; Lord and Schryver gardens with wrought-iron gazebo from 1905, boxwood gardens, perennial garden with English teahouse; nature trail. House (May-Sept: Mon-Fri, Sun; rest of year: Tues-Sat; closed holidays). **$$**

**Honeywood Winery.** *1350 Hines St SE, Salem (97302). Phone 503/362-4111.* Oregon's oldest producing winery. Tours, tasting room, gift shop. (Daily; closed Thanksgiving, Dec 25) **FREE**

**Mission Mill Museum.** *1313 Mill St SE, Salem (97301). Phone 503/585-7012. www.missionmill.org.* Thomas Kay Woolen Mill Museum (1889) shows process of processing fleece into fabric. Jason Lee House (1841), John D. Boon House (1847), Methodist Parsonage (1841) and Pleasant Grove-Presbyterian Church (1858) help interpret missionary family life. Shops, park, picnicking. Tours of woolen mill, historic houses (Mon-Sat; closed Jan 1, Thanksgiving, Dec 25). **$$$**

**State Capitol.** *900 Court St NE, Salem (97301). Phone 503/986-1388.* (1938). Marble, of modern Greek design. Atop the capitol is a fluted tower topped by a bronze, gold-leafed statue symbolic of the pioneers who carved Oregon out of the wilderness. Tours of capitol (June-Aug: daily; rest of year: by appointment). Video; gift shop. Capitol building (Daily; closed Thanksgiving, Dec 25). **FREE** North of here is the

> **Capitol Mall.** *900 State St, Salem (97301). Phone 503/986-1388.* Flanked by four state buildings in modern Greek style, including the Public Service, Transportation, Labor and Industries and State Library buildings. The grounds are an arboretum with historical statuary and monuments.

**Willamette University.** *900 State St, Salem (97301). Between 12th and Winter sts. Phone 503/370-6300. www.willamette.edu.* (1842) (2,500 students) Oldest institution of higher learning west of Missouri River, with several historic buildings on campus including Waller Hall (1867) and the Art Building (1905) with the Hallie Brown Ford Art Gallery. The Mark O. Hatfield Library has a special area for research and viewing of Senator Hatfield's public papers. Campus tours; picnic area.

## Special Events

**Oregon State Fair.** *State Fairgrounds, 2330 17th St NE, Salem (97303). Phone 503/947-3247. www.oregonstatefair.org.* Horse racing, wine competition and tasting, agricultural exhibits, horse show, livestock, food, carnival, entertainment. Late Aug-early Sept.

**Salem Art Fair and Festival.** *Bush's Pasture Park, 600 Mission St SE, Salem (97302). Phone 503/581-2228. www.salemartassociation.com.* Arts and crafts booths and demonstrations, children's art activities and parade, ethnic folk arts, performing arts, street painting, 5K run, food; tours of historic Bush House. Late July.

**West Salem Waterfront Parade.** *Salem. Phone 503/362-3601.* Mid-Aug.

## Limited-Service Hotels

**★ BEST WESTERN NEW KINGS INN.** *1600 Motor Court NE, Salem (97301). Phone 503/581-1559; fax 503/364-4272. www.bestwestern.com.* 101 rooms, 2 story. Pets accepted, some restrictions; fee. Check-out noon. Fitness room. Indoor pool, whirlpool. Tennis. **$**

**★ ★ RED LION.** *3301 Market St, Salem (97301). Phone 503/370-7888; toll-free 800/248-6273; fax 503/370-6305. www.redlion.com.* 150 rooms, 4 story. Pets accepted; fee. Check-out 11 am. Restaurant, bar. Fitness room. Indoor pool, whirlpool. **$**

## Specialty Lodging

**A CREEKSIDE INN THE MARQUEE HOUSE.** *33 Wyatt Ct NE, Salem (97301). Phone 503/391-0837; toll-free 800/949-0837; fax 503/391-1713. www.marqueehouse.com.* 5 rooms. Children over 14 years only. Check-in 4-6 pm, check-out 11 am. Airport transportation available. **$**

## Restaurants

**★ ★ ★ ALESSANDRO'S.** *120 NE Commercial St, Salem (97301). Phone 503/370-9951; fax 503/375-3412.*

*www.alessandros120.com.* This family-owned northern Italian restaurant and bar has been in business for over 22 years, serving specialties such as baked salmon, various veal dishes, and a splendid tiramisu. Staff is friendly and attentive, and the historic storefront location is a simple, quiet retreat. Italian menu. Lunch, dinner. Closed Sun. Bar. Children's menu. Casual attire. **$$**

★ ★ **KWAN ORIGINAL CUISINE.** *835 Commerical St SE, Salem (97302). Phone 503/362-7711; fax 503/373-5818. www.kwanscuisine.com.* Chinese menu. Lunch, dinner. Closed holidays. Bar. Children's menu. **$$**

# Seaside (A-1)

*See also Astoria, Cannon Beach, Rockaway Beach*

**Population** 5,359
**Elevation** 13 ft
**Area Code** 503
**Zip** 97138
**Information** Chamber of Commerce, 7 N Roosevelt, PO Box 7; phone 503/738-6391 or toll-free 800/444-6740
**Web Site** www.seasideor.com

Seaside is the largest and oldest seashore town in Oregon. It has a concrete promenade 2 miles long; ocean beaches provide clam digging, surfing, surf fishing, and beachcombing.

## What to See and Do

**Saddle Mountain State Park.** *Seaside. 13 miles SE on Hwy 26, then 9 miles N. Phone 503/368-5154. www.oregonstateparks.org/park_197.php.* A 2,922-acre park with a 2 1/2-mile trail to the 3,283-foot summit of Saddle Mountain, one of the highest peaks in the Coastal Range. Hiking, picnicking. Ten primitive campsites (Mar-Nov). **FREE**

**Seaside Aquarium.** *200 N Promenade, Seaside (97138). On the beach at the end of Second Ave and N Promenade, two blocks N of the Seaside Turnaround. Phone 503/738-6211. www.seasideaquarium.com.* Deep-sea life and trained seals; seal feeding (fee); (Mar-Nov: daily at 9 am; rest of year: Wed-Sun; closed Thanksgiving, Dec 24-25) **$$$**

## Limited-Service Hotels

★ ★ **BEST WESTERN OCEAN VIEW RESORT.** *414 N Prom, Seaside (97138). Phone 503/738-3334; toll-free 800/234-8439; fax 503/738-3264. www.oceanviewresort.com.* 104 rooms, 5 story. Pets accepted, some restrictions; fee. Check-out 11 am. Restaurant, bar. Beach. Indoor pool, whirlpool. **$**

★ ★ **GEARHART BY THE SEA RESORT.** *1157 N Marion Ave, Gearhart (97138). Phone 503/738-8331; toll-free 800/547-0115; fax 503/738-0881. www.gearhartresort.com.* 80 rooms, 5 story. Pets accepted, some restrictions; fee. Check-out 11 am. Restaurant, bar. Indoor pool. Golf. **$**

★ ★ **SHILO INN.** *30 N Prom, Seaside (97138). Phone 503/738-9571; toll-free 800/222-2244; fax 503/738-0674. www.shiloinns.com.* 112 rooms, 5 story. Check-out noon. Restaurant, bar. Indoor pool, whirlpool. Airport transportation available. **$**

## Specialty Lodgings

**CUSTER HOUSE BED & BREAKFAST.** *811 1st Ave, Seaside (97138). Phone 503/738-7825; toll-free 800/738-7852; fax 503/738-4324. www.clatsop.com/custer.* 6 rooms, 2 story. Complimentary full breakfast. Check-in 3 pm, check-out 11 am.**$**

**GILBERT INN BED & BREAKFAST.** *341 Beach Dr, Seaside (97138). Phone 503/738-9770; toll-free 800/410-9770; fax 503/717-1070. www.gilbertinn.com.* This Queen Anne Victorian home, built in 1892, features a large fireplace in the parlor and a rich and warm atmosphere. It is located near shops, restaurants, beaches and other attractions of the Northwest coast. 10 rooms, 3 story. Closed Jan. Complimentary full breakfast. Check-in 3-11 pm, check-out 11 am. Airport transportation available. **$**

## Restaurants

★ **CAMP 18.** *42362 Hwy 26, Seaside (97138). Phone 503/755-1818.* American menu. Breakfast, lunch, dinner, Sun brunch. Closed Dec 25. Bar. Children's menu. **$$**

★ ★ **DOOGER'S SEAFOOD & GRILL.** *505 Broadway, Seaside (97138). Phone 503/738-3773.* Seafood, steak menu. Lunch, dinner. Children's menu. **$$**

# Silverton (B-2)

*See also Newberg, Oregon City, Salem*

**Population** 5,635
**Elevation** 249 ft
**Area Code** 503
**Zip** 97381
**Information** Chamber of Commerce, City Hall, 421 S Water St, PO Box 257; phone 503/873-5615
**Web Site** www.silverton.or.us

## What to See and Do

**Cooley's Gardens.** *11553 Silverton Rd NE, Silverton (97381). Phone 503/873-5463.* Largest producer of bearded iris in the world. Display gardens feature many varieties; over 1 million blossom in fields (Mid-May-early June). **FREE**

**Country Museum/Restored Train Station.** *428 S Water St, Silverton (97381).* Ames-Warnock House (1908) contains local historical items dating from 1846. Southern Pacific Station (1906) contains larger items. Contact Chamber of Commerce. (Mar-Dec, Thurs and Sun) **DONATION**

**Silver Falls State Park.** *Silverton. 15 miles SE on Hwy 214. Phone 503/873-8681. www.oregonstateparks.org/park_211.php.* Oregon's largest state park, at 8,706 acres, has ten waterfalls, five of which are more than 100 feet high; four may be viewed from road, the others from a forested canyon hiking trail. Swimming. Bridle, bicycle trails. Picnicking. Tent and improved sites (dump station), cabins. Pets allowed on leash only.

# Sweet Home (C-2)

*See also Albany*

**Population** 6,850
**Elevation** 525 ft
**Area Code** 541
**Zip** 97386
**Information** Chamber of Commerce, 1575 Main St; phone 541/367-6186
**Web Site** www.sweet-home.or.us

Gateway to Santiam Pass and the rugged Oregon Cascades, the area around Sweet Home is popular for fishing, boating, skiing, hiking, and rock hounding. A Ranger District office of Willamette National Forest is located here.

## What to See and Do

**East Linn Museum.** *746 Long St, Sweet Home (97386). At junction Hwy 228, Hwy 20. Phone 541/367-4580.* Nearly 5,000 artifacts of pioneer life in the area (1847). Period rooms; rock collection and mining equipment; logging tools; maps, photos, portraits; guns, dolls, bottles; saddlery and blacksmith shop. (May-Sept: Tues-Sun; rest of year: Thurs-Sun; also by appointment; closed holidays) **DONATION**

**Foster Lake.** *Hwy 20 and Foster, Foster (97345). 2 miles E on Hwy 20 at Foster. Phone 541/367-5124.* Swimming, water sports; fishing; boating.

## Special Events

**Oregon Jamboree.** *1314 Long St, Sweet Home (97386). Phone 541/367-8800.* Three-day country music and camping festival. Second weekend in Aug.

**Sweet Home Rodeo.** *1575 Main St, Sweet Home (97386). Phone 541/367-6186.* Bull riding, barrel racing, bronc riding, mutton bustin'. Second weekend in July.

# Tillamook (B-1)

*See also Lincoln City, Rockaway Beach*

**Founded** 1851
**Population** 4,001
**Elevation** 16 ft
**Area Code** 503
**Zip** 97141
**Information** Tillamook Chamber of Commerce, 3705 Hwy 101 N; phone 503/842-7525
**Web Site** www.tillamookchamber.org

Located at the southern end of Tillamook Bay, this is the county seat. Dairying, cheese and butter making, timber, and fishing are the main industries. There are many beaches for swimming, crabbing, clamming, and beachcombing; boat landings, camping, picnicking, and fishing sites are also in the area.

## What to See and Do

**Cape Lookout State Park.** *13000 Whiskey Creek Rd, Tillamook (97141). 12 miles SW off Hwy 101 on Whiskey Creek Rd. Phone 503/842-4981.* A 1,974-acre park with virgin spruce forest and an observation point; it's one of most primitive ocean shore areas in the state. Hiking trail to the end of the cape. Picnicking. Tent and trailer sites (dump station). **$**

**Capes Scenic Loop Drive to Cape Meares and Oceanside.** *Tillamook.* (Approximately 10 miles) West on 3rd Street, northwest on Bay Ocean Road to Cape Meares; go south on Loop Road to Cape Meares State Park. See Tillamook Bay County Boat Landing, Cape Meares Lake, beach with beachcombing; also Cape Meares Lighthouse; Native American burial Sitka spruce tree known as "Octopus Tree." Continue south to Oceanside, site of Three Arch Rocks Federal Sea Lion and Migratory Bird Refuge, and beach area with beachcombing and agates. Continue south to Netarts; see Netarts Bay Boat Landing and Whiskey Creek Fish Hatchery. Go south on Cape Lookout Road to Pacific City and Cape Kiwanda, then back to Highway 101 S. (Or take Whiskey Creek Rd from Netarts boat launching site, continue over Cape Lookout Mountain through Sandlake, Tierra Del Mar to Pacific City. Exceptionally scenic, it also avoids traffic on Highway 101.)

**Tillamook County Pioneer Museum.** *2106 2nd St, Tillamook (97141). At Pacific Ave. Phone 503/842-4553. www.tcpm.org.* Possessions of early settlers, replica of pioneer home and barn; blacksmith shop; logging displays, war relics; relics from Tillamook Naval Air Station and Blimp Base; minerals, guns, books, vehicles, natural history and wildlife exhibits including nine dioramas; "great grandma's kitchen." (Daily; closed Thanksgiving, Dec 25) **$$**

## Special Events

**Tillamook County Fair.** *Fairgrounds, 4603 3rd St, Tillamook (97141). Phone 503/842-2272.* First full week in Aug.

**Tillamook Dairy Parade and Rodeo.** *Fairgrounds, 4603 3rd St, Tillamook (97141). Phone 503/842-7525.* Fourth weekend in June.

## Limited-Service Hotels

**★ BEST WESTERN INN & SUITES.** *1722 N Makinster Rd, Tillamook (97141). Phone 503/842-7599; toll-free 800/780-7234; fax 503/842-7930. www.bestwestern.com.* 52 rooms. Check-in 3 pm, check-out noon. Fitness room. Indoor pool, whirlpool. **$**

**★★ SHILO INN.** *2515 N Main St, Tillamook (97141). Phone 503/842-7971; toll-free 800/222-2244; fax 503/842-7960. www.shiloinns.com.* 101 rooms, 2 story. Pets accepted; fee. Check-out noon. Restaurant, bar. Fitness room. Indoor pool, whirlpool.

## Specialty Lodging

**SANDLAKE COUNTRY INN.** *8505 Galloway Rd, Cloverdale (97112). Phone 503/965-6745; fax 503/965-7425. www.sandlakecountryinn.com.* Farmhouse built of timbers washed ashore from a shipwreck in 1890. 4 rooms, 2 story. Complimentary full breakfast. Check-in 3 pm. Check-out 11 am. **$**

# Troutdale (B-2)

*See also Lincoln City, Rockaway Beach*

## What to See and Do

**Columbia Gorge Premium Outlets.** *450 NW 257th Way, Troutdale (97060). Phone 503/669-8060. www.premiumoutlets.com/columbiagorge.* More than 40 factory outlet stores, including Adidas, Gap, and Samsonite.

## Restaurant

**★★ BLACK RABBIT.** *2126 SW Halsey, Troutdale (97060). Phone 503/492-3086. www.mcmenamins.com.* American menu. Breakfast, lunch, dinner. Bar. Children's menu. Outdoor seating. **$$**

# Umatilla (A-4)

*See also Hermiston, Pendleton*

**Founded** 1863
**Population** 3,046
**Elevation** 296 ft
**Area Code** 541
**Zip** 97882
**Information** Chamber of Commerce, PO Box 67; phone 541/922-4825 or toll-free 800/542-4944
**Web Site** www.umatilla.org

## What to See and Do

**Hat Rock State Park.** *Hat Rock, Hermiston. 9 miles E off Hwy 730 near junction Hwy 207. Phone 541/567-5032. www.oregonstateparks.org/park_19.php.* A 735-acre park on a lake formed by the McNary Dam. Hat Rock is a large monolith that looks like a man's top hat; this landmark is often referred to in the diaries of early explorers and travelers. Swimming beach, fishing (pond stocked with rainbow trout); boat ramp to the Columbia River. Hiking, picnicking. **FREE**

**McNary Lock and Dam.** *3rd St, Umatilla. 2 miles E on Hwy 730. Phone 541/922-4388.* Single lift navigation lock. Dam is 7,365 feet long, 92 feet high. The Columbia River forms Lake Wallula, a 61-mile waterway partly in Washington. Swimming, waterskiing; fishing, hunting; boating (marinas). Picnicking. Primitive camping (two areas; free). Tours of power, navigation and fish passage facilities (June-Sept, daily). **FREE**

**Umatilla Marina Park.** *1710 Quincy Ave, Umatilla (97882). NE edge of town on Columbia River. Phone 541/922-3939.* Swimming beach; boating (launch, storage, gas, oil). Picnicking. RV trailer camping (fee). (Daily)

## Special Event

**Sage Riders Rodeo.** *Umatilla. Phone 541/922-4825.* NRA sanctioned, Second weekend in June.

# Yachats (C-2)

*See also Florence, Newport*

**Population** 533
**Elevation** 15 ft
**Area Code** 541
**Zip** 97498
**Information** Yachats Area Chamber of Commerce, US 101; PO Box 728; phone 541/547-3530
**Web Site** www.yachats.org

Yachats (YA-hots) is a resort area on the central Oregon coast, west of Siuslaw National Forest. Derived from a Native American phrase meaning "waters at the foot of the mountain," Yachats is along a rocky shore with a fine sandy beach.

## What to See and Do

**Cape Perpetua Campground.** *2400 Hwy 101 S, Yachats (97498). 3 miles S on Hwy 101. Phone 541/563-3211.* Beachcombing; fishing. Hiking. Camping. Summer campfire programs (Sat, Sun). **$$$** Nearby is

> **Cape Perpetua Visitor Center.** *2400 Hwy 101 S, Yachats (97498). In Suislaw National Forest. Phone 541/547-3289.* Interpretive displays of oceanography, natural history of coastal area, movies. Nature trails, auto tour. (May: Wed-Sun; Memorial Day-Labor Day: daily; closed winter) **$$**

**Neptune State Scenic Viewpoint.** *Yachats. 3 miles S on Hwy 101. Phone 541/547-3416. www.oregonstateparks.org/park_126.php.* This 302-acre park features Cook's Chasm (near the north end), a long, narrow, deep fissure where the sea falls in with a spectacular fury; wind-depressed forest trees (near the north end); and slopes covered with huckleberry shrubs. A community of harbor seals makes its home on the rocks below Strawberry Hill; whales are also spotted here. Birdwatching. Surf fishing, windsurfing. Hiking, picnicking. Observation point. **FREE**

**Tillicum Beach Campground.** *8199 Hwy 101 N, Yachats (97498). 3 1/2 miles N on Hwy 101. Phone 541/563-3211.* Ocean view, beachcombing. Camping. Summer evening campfire programs Sat and Sun. Camping **$$$**

**Yachats State Recreation Area.** *Yachats. On Hwy 101. Phone 541/997-3851.* A 93-acre day-use park bordering the Yachats River, in the shadow of Cape Perpetua. Small picnic area. Observation point.

## Limited-Service Hotel

**★ OVERLEAF LODGE.** *2055 Hwy 101 N, Yachats (97498). Phone 541/547-4880; toll-free 800/338-0507. www.overleaflodge.com.* The Overleaf Lodge is situated alongside central Oregon's rugged coast. All rooms have ocean views. Select rooms have fireplaces, whirlpool tubs, and private balconies. The property's location is ideal for exploring the states coastline; nearby, you'll find great hiking trails at Cape Perpetua Recreation Area, wildlife at Sea Lion Caves, and dramatic scenery at Heceta Head Lighthouse, the most photographed lighthouse in the US. 39 rooms. Complimentary continental breakfast. Check-in 3 pm, check-out noon. Fitness room. **$$**

## Specialty Lodging

**SEA QUEST BED & BREAKFAST.** *95354 Hwy 101 S, Yachats (97498). Phone 541/547-3782; toll-free 800/341-4878; fax 541/547-3719. www.seaquestinn.com.* 5 rooms, 2 story. Children over 14 years only. Complimentary full breakfast. Check-in 3 pm, check-out 11 am. **$$**

# Washington

The Stillaguamish, Steilacoom and Hoh, Puyallup, Tulalip and La Push, the Duckabush, the Dosewallips and the Queets, the Skookumchuck, the Sol Duc and the Pysht—all these are Washington towns and rivers. There are many more like them, named by Native Americans.

**Population:** 5,894,121
**Area:** 70,637 square miles
**Elevation:** 0-14,410 feet
**Peak:** Mount Rainier (Pierce County)
**Entered Union:** November 11, 1889 (42nd state)
**Capital:** Olympia
**Motto:** *Al-ki* (By and by)
**Nickname:** Evergreen State
**Flower:** Rhododendron
**Bird:** Willow Goldfinch
**Tree:** Western Hemlock
**Time Zone:** Pacific
**Web Site:** www.tourism.wa.gov
**Fun Facts:**

- Washington has more glaciers than the other 47 contiguous states combined.
- More than half of all apples grown in the United States for fresh eating come from orchards in Washington.

Ruggedly handsome Washington is like a bank in which nature has deposited some of her greatest resources. In addition to dramatic mountain ranges, expansive forests, and inviting harbors, it is a cornerstone of American hydroelectric technology. Here are the majestic spectacles of mighty Mount Rainier—revered as a god by the Native American—sand the Olympic Peninsula, where one of the wettest and one of the driest parts of the country are only a mountain away from each other; also here is Puget Sound, a giant inland sea where 2,000 miles of shoreline bend into jewel-like bays.

Although British and Spanish navigators were the first Europeans to explore Washington's serrated shoreline, the first major discoveries were made in 1792, when an American, Captain Robert Gray, gave his name to Grays Harbor and the name of his ship, *Columbia*, to the great river. An Englishman, Captain George Vancouver, explored and named Puget Sound and christened Mount Baker and Mount Rainier, which he could see far inland. Fort Vancouver was the keystone of the British fur industry, dominating a Northwest empire. After conflicting US and British claims were resolved, Americans surged into this area by ship and wagon train.

Part of the Oregon Territory until separated in 1853, the state's eastern boundary was established in 1863, when Idaho became a territory. Entering the last decade of the 19th century as a state of the Union, Washington found itself no longer America's last territorial frontier.

Civilization has not dissipated Washington's natural wealth. On the contrary, after more than a century of logging operations, Washington retains 24 million acres of superb forests, and miracles of modern engineering have almost completely erased the wastelands through which the wagon trains of the pioneers passed on their way to the sea.

The mighty but capricious Columbia River meanders through the heart of northeast and central Washington, then runs for 300 miles along the Oregon-Washington border. Through a series of dams and the Grand Coulee Reclamation Project, the energies of the Columbia have been harnessed and converted into what is presently one of the world's great sources of water power. Irrigation and a vast supply of inexpensive power gave a tremen-

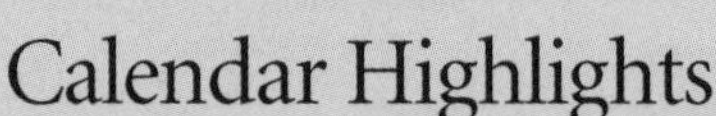

## Calendar Highlights

### March

**Chocolate Fantasy** *(Yakima). Phone 509/966-6309.* Chocolate manufacturers from across the nation showcase candy, cookies, and pies; sampling, "chocolate bingo."

### April

**Daffodil Festival** *(Tacoma). In Tacoma and Puyallup Valley. Phone 253/627-6176.* Flower show, coronation, four-city floral parade of floats, marine regatta, and bowling tournament.

### May

**Ski to Sea Festival** *(Bellingham). Phone 360/734-1330.* Parades, carnival, art show, and special events. Ski to Sea race; starts on Mount Baker, ends in Bellingham Bay and involves skiers, runners, canoeists, bicyclists, and kayakers. Memorial Day weekend.

**Wooden Boat Festival** *(Olympia). Percival Landing in Harbor. Phone 360/943-5404.* Wooden boats on display, some open for public viewing. Wooden crafts fair.

### July

**San Juan Island Jazz Festival** *(San Juan Islands). Friday Harbor. Phone 360/378-5509.* Indoor/outdoor jazz festival featuring Dixieland, swing, zydeco, and blues/jazz.

### August

**Seafair** *(Seattle). Phone 206/728-0123; www.seafair.com.* Citywide marine festival. Regattas, speedboat races, shows at Aqua Theater, parades, sports events, exhibits.

**Stampede and Suicide Race** *(Omak). Phone 509/826-1002.* Rodeo events; horses and riders race down a cliff and across the Okanogan River. Western art show. Native American dance contests. Encampment with more than 100 teepees.

**Southwest Washington Fair** *(Centralia). Phone 360/736-6072.* First held in 1909, this is the state's second oldest fair and one of the largest.

**Central Washington State Fair and Rodeo** *(Yakima). Fairgrounds. Phone 509/248-7160.* Thoroughbred racing. Pari-mutuel wagering.

### September

**Northeast Washington Fair** *(Colville). Stevens County Fairgrounds. Phone 509/684-2585.* Parade, livestock and horse shows, arts and crafts exhibits, and carnival.

**Western Washington Fair** *(Puyallup). Phone 253/841-5045.* The Pacific Northwest's largest fair; includes three statewide youth fairs, livestock shows, agricultural and commercial exhibits, free entertainment, midway, rodeo, and top-name grandstand acts.

dous push to Washington's economy, sparking new industries and making possible the state's production of huge crops of grains, vegetables, and fruit.

Central Washington is the apple barrel of the country; dairying is a big industry in the western valleys. Forestry and wood products as well as the production of paper and allied products are of major importance in the western and northern sections of the state; one-third of the state is covered by commercial forests. In recent years, Washington wines have enjoyed great popularity around the nation.

Since 1965, more than 25 percent of Washington's total manufacturing effort has been devoted to the production of transportation equipment, of which a large portion is involved in commercial jet aircraft. Along Puget Sound, industry means canning plants, lumber mills, and pulp and paper plants; but even here there is a new economic dimension: petroleum refineries of four major companies have a daily capacity of 366,500 barrels of crude oil and gasoline; biotechnology and software development are growing industries. Tourism is the state's fourth largest industry, amounting to more than $8.8 billion a year.

## When to Go/Climate

Moist air off the Pacific Ocean and Puget Sound creates rainy conditions in western Washington and heavy snowfall in the Cascades. While the western slopes of the Cascades and Olympic Mountains are soaked with moisture, the eastern slopes and, indeed, the entire eastern part of the state are almost desert dry. Temperatures are seasonally mild except for high in the mountains.

### AVERAGE HIGH/LOW TEMPERATURES (° F)

**Seattle**

| | | |
|---|---|---|
| **Jan** 46/36 | **May** 64/48 | **Sep** 69/53 |
| **Feb** 51/38 | **Jun** 70/53 | **Oct** 60/47 |
| **Mar** 54/40 | **Jul** 74/56 | **Nov** 52/41 |
| **Apr** 58/43 | **Aug** 74/57 | **Dec** 46/37 |

**Spokane**

| | | |
|---|---|---|
| **Jan** 33/21 | **May** 66/42 | **Sep** 72/46 |
| **Feb** 41/26 | **Jun** 75/49 | **Oct** 59/36 |
| **Mar** 48/30 | **Jul** 83/54 | **Nov** 41/29 |
| **Apr** 57/35 | **Aug** 83/54 | **Dec** 34/22 |

## Parks and Recreation

Water-related activities, hiking, riding, various other sports, picnicking, and visitor centers, as well as camping, are available in many of Washington's state parks. The 248,882 acres owned or managed by the Washington State Parks & Recreation Commission provide unusually good camping and trailer facilities at most locations, with a camping fee of $15 per site; hookups $21; ten-day limit in summer; 20 days rest of year. Most parks are open daily: April-mid-October, 6:30 am-dusk; some are closed the rest of the year. Pets are allowed on leash only. For further information, contact the Washington State Parks & Recreation Commission, 7150 Cleanwater Ln, PO Box 42650, Olympia 98504-2650, phone 360/902-8844 or toll-free 888/226-7688.

### FISHING AND HUNTING

With 10,000 miles of bay and Pacific shoreline, 8,000 lakes, and rivers that stretch from Oregon to Canada, Washington provides something for every angler's whim. Fish hatcheries dot the state, stocking nature's waterways and those artificially created by irrigation and navigation dams. If you like salmon and steelhead, Washington is the state to try your luck.

Nonresident freshwater fishing license $40; two-day license $6. A food fish license is required for salmon and saltwater bottomfish; nonresident food fish license, $20; nonresident saltwater fish license, $36; nonresident combination fresh water/saltwater fish license, $72. A shellfish/seaweed license is required for shellfish; nonresident license, $20. Razor clam season varies; contact the Department of Fish & Wildlife for season dates, phone 360/902-2200. Nonresident small-game hunting license $165; three-day $50; big game, $200-$725. Get hunting and freshwater fishing regulations and a complete list of license fees from the Department of Fish & Wildlife, 500 Capitol Way N, Olympia 98504. Fishing and hunting regulation pamphlets are available at local sporting goods stores.

## Driving Information

Safety belts are mandatory for all persons anywhere in a vehicle. Children under 40 pounds in weight must be in approved safety seats anywhere in a vehicle. For more information, phone 360/753-6197.

### INTERSTATE HIGHWAY SYSTEM

The following alphabetical listing of Washington towns in this book shows that these cities are within 10 miles of the indicated interstate highways. Check a highway map for the nearest exit.

| Highway Number | Cities/Towns within 10 Miles |
|---|---|
| Interstate 5 | Bellingham, Blaine, Centralia, Chehalis, Everett, Kelso, Longview, Marysville, Mount Vernon, Olympia, Puyallup, Seattle, Sedro Woolley, Snohomish, Tacoma, Vancouver. |
| Interstate 82 | Ellensburg, Kennewick, Pasco, Richland, Sunnyside, Toppenish, Yakima. |
| Interstate 90 | Bellevue, Ellensburg, Issaquah, Moses Lake, North Bend, Ritzville, Seattle, Spokane. |
| Interstate 182 | Pasco, Richland. |

## MOUNTAIN WATERWAYS IN THE CASCADES

This route passes through spectacular mountain scenery in one of the West's most rugged national parks. Starting on the moist Pacific side of the Cascade range at Sedro-Woolley, Highway 20 follows the increasingly narrow Skagit River valley inland through dripping fir and cedar forests. Near Rockport, the landscape becomes wilder and steeper; this is a major wintering area for bald eagles, which come here to dine on migrating salmon. As the route enters the park near Marblemount, the Skagit is dammed in quick succession in a precipitous canyon by three early-20th-century hydrodams (this is where Seattle gets its power). Tours of the largest dam are the most popular activity in the park; getting up to the dam itself involves riding an incline railroad up a sheer cliff face. Around the dams are hikes to waterfalls and mist gardens. After climbing Rainy Pass, which has incredible views of tooth-edged mountain ranges and volcanoes in good weather, Highway 20 drops onto the dry side of the Cascades, where the forests are suddenly dominated by ponderosa pines and juniper. The highway follows the Methow River, a lovely semiarid valley that was once the province of cattle ranches but is now lined with resort homes and golf courses. The town of Winthrop, which just 20 years ago was filled with feed stores and tractor dealerships, now epitomizes the wealthy New West culture with its art galleries, fine restaurants, and home dcor boutiques. From the delightfully named town of Twisp, follow Highway 153 through ranch land, which slowly gives way to apple orchards as the route joins Highway 97 and the Columbia River at Pateros. **(Approximately 168 miles)**

## MOUNT RAINIER AND NORTHWEST WILDLIFE

A popular day trip from Seattle, this route rounds the imposing volcanic cone of Mount Rainier, the centerpiece of Mount Rainier National Park. Take Highway 410 east and climb along the White River with the towering white cone of 14,412-foot Mount Rainier rising above the forest. The park itself has a number of different viewpoints for taking in the peak, and each has its own personalities. Sunrise–the highest point reached by road in the park–is on the drier, east side of the peak; there are hikes to wildflower meadows and glacial overlooks, and mountain goats are often seen in the area. The aptly named Paradise area–on the southern side of the mountain atop a broad timberline shoulder–shares postcard views of the peak with the Paradise Inn, a vast historic stone-and-log lodge built in classic Arts-and-Crafts style. An extensive trail system explores flower-filled meadows and tumbling waterfalls. Other highlights of this route are Ohanapecosh, a riparian wetland with a stand of massive old-growth cedar trees, and Longmire, the original park headquarters with several turn-of-the-20th-century structures and another heritage hotel. A highlight of the return trip near Eatonville (on Highway 161) is the Northwest Trek Wildlife Park, a private refuge that rehabilitates wolves, cougars, and other wildlife native to the area that have been injured or must be removed from the wild for other reasons. **(Approximately 142 miles)**

## Additional Visitor Information

Washington travel information and brochures are available from the Washington State Tourism Department of Community, Trade, and Economic Development, 101 General Administration Building, PO Box 42500, Olympia 98504-2500. Phone toll-free 800/544-1800 for a copy of *Washington State Lodging and Travel Guide*; phone 360/586-2088 or toll-free 800/638-8474 for tourism information.

There are 180 visitor information centers in Washington; most are open May-September. Visitors who stop by will find information and brochures helpful in planning stops at points of interest. The locations for the official state visitor centers at points of entry are as follows: 7 miles south of Blaine, near the Canadian border; east of Spokane at the Idaho/Washington border, I-90 exit 299 westbound; 404 E 15th St, Vancouver; in Oroville on Hwy 97, near the

Canadian border; at the Oregon border on Hwy 97, near Maryhill State Park and Sam Hill Bridge; and on Hwy 401 near the Astoria Bridge.

# Aberdeen (C-1)

*See also Hoquiam, Ocean Shores, Westport*

**Settled** 1878
**Population** 16,461
**Elevation** 19 ft
**Area Code** 360
**Zip** 98520
**Information** Grays Harbor Chamber of Commerce, 506 Duffy St; phone 360/532-1924 or toll-free 800/321-1924
**Web Site** www.graysharbor.org

Aberdeen and Hoquiam (see) are twin cities on the eastern tip of Grays Harbor. Born as a cannery named for the city in Scotland, Aberdeen later blossomed as a lumber town, with one of the greatest stands of Douglas fir ever found in the Pacific Northwest at its back. Many Harbor residents are descendants of Midwestern Scandinavians who came here to fell the forests. Today, the town's commerce consists of wood processing, fishing, and shipbuilding. The Port of Grays Harbor is located along the waterfront of the two towns.

## What to See and Do

**Aberdeen Museum of History.** *111 E 3rd St, Aberdeen (98520). Phone 360/533-1976.* Special exhibits with 1880s-1940s furnishings and implements include kitchen and bed, general mercantile store, one-room school; farm and logging equipment and displays; blacksmith shop; pioneer church; fire trucks. Slide show, photographs. (June-Labor Day: Wed-Sun; rest of year: weekends) **DONATION**

**Grays Harbor Historical Seaport.** *813 E Heron St, Aberdeen (98520). Phone 360/532-8611. www.graysharbor.org.* Historical interpretive center; classes in long boat building. Includes a museum with informational and active exhibits on the history of sailing in the Pacific Northwest. Also a replica of Robert Gray's tall ship *Lady Washington* (seasonal; fee). (Daily; closed holidays) **FREE**

**Lake Sylvia State Park.** *1812 Lake Sylvia Rd N, Montesano (98563). 10 miles E on Hwy 12, then 1 mile N on an unnumbered road. Phone 360/249-3621. www.parks.wa.gov.* An old logging camp, this park contains approximately 233 acres of protected timber on the freshwater shoreline of Lake Sylvia. Activities include boating (non-motorized), swimming, fishing, hiking (5 miles of trails), mountain biking, and bird-watching. Camping (Mar-Oct). Picnicking, concession. (Daily 8 am-dusk)

**Samuel Benn Park.** *E 9th and N I sts, Aberdeen (98520). Phone 360/537-3230. www.aberdeenparksandrec.com.* Named for pioneer settler. Rose and rhododendron gardens; picnic facilities, playground, tennis. (Daily) **FREE**

**Schafer State Park.** *Aberdeen. 13 miles E on Hwy 12, then 10 miles N on an unnumbered road. Phone 360/482-3852. www.parks.wa.gov.* Approximately 120 acres on the Satsop River. Activities include swimming, fishing (steelhead, cutthroat trout, and salmon), hiking (2 miles of trails), and bird-watching. Abundant wildlife. Picnicking, camping (hookups; dump station; late Apr-Oct). (Daily 8 am-dusk)

## Limited-Service Hotel

**★ RED LION HOTEL.** *521 W Wishkah St, Aberdeen (98520). Phone 360/532-5210; fax 360/533-8483.* This motel is located just off Highway 101 near the tall ship *Lady Washington*, just five blocks from the city center. 67 rooms, 2 story. Pets accepted. Complimentary continental breakfast. Check-out noon. **$**

## Specialty Lodging

**ABERDEEN MANSION BED AND BREAKFAST.** *807 N M St, Aberdeen (98520). Phone 360/533-7079; toll-free 888/533-7079. www.aberdeenmansionbb.com.* This sunny yellow Victorian furnished with antiques was built in 1905 for a local lumber baron. Two libraries and a large wraparound porch encourage reading, conversation, or quiet contemplation; the game room contains a pool table and board games for guests' use. All five guest rooms have king-size beds and TVs, and the carriage house also has two twin beds and a small kitchen. 5 rooms, 2 story. Children over 12 years only. Complimentary full breakfast. Check-in 4-7 pm, check-out 11 am. **$**

## Restaurants

**★★ BILLY'S RESTAURANT.** *322 E Heron, Aberdeen (98520). Phone 360/533-7144.* American menu. Lunch, dinner. Closed Thanksgiving, Dec 25. Bar. Children's menu. In 1904 building with antique furnishings. **$$**

★★ **BRIDGES RESTAURANT.** *112 N G St, Aberdeen (98520). Phone 360/532-6563; fax 360/532-5490.* American menu. Lunch, dinner. Bar. Children's menu. **$$**

# Anacortes (A-2)

*See also Coupeville, La Conner, Mount Vernon, Oak Harbor, Sedro-Woolley*

**Settled** 1860
**Population** 14,557
**Elevation** 24 ft
**Area Code** 360
**Zip** 98221
**Information** Visitor Information Center at the Chamber of Commerce, 819 Commercial Ave; phone 360/293-3832
**Web Site** www.anacortes.org

Anacortes, at the northwest tip of Fidalgo Island, houses the San Juan Islands ferries. The town's name honors Anna Curtis, the wife of one of its founders.

## What to See and Do

**Deception Pass State Park.** *41229 Hwy 20, Anacortes (98277). 9 miles S on Hwy 20. Phone 360/675-2417. www.parks.wa.gov.* More than 4,100 acres of sheltered bays and deep old-growth forests with fjordlike shoreline. Four lakes provide ample opportunities for swimming (lifeguards in summer), scuba diving, fishing, clamming, boating (eight ramps, saltwater and freshwater dock). More than 170 varieties of birds make this a popular bird-watching spot. You'll also find 38 miles of hiking trails, some accessible for the disabled. Picnicking, camping (with showers). Pets on leash only. (Summer: 6:30 am-dusk; winter: 8 am-dusk)

**San Juan Islands trip.** *Anacortes. Phone 360/293-3832.* Ferry boats leave several times daily for Lopez Island, Shaw Island, Orcas Island, Friday Harbor, and Sidney, British Columbia. Either leave your car at the dock in Anacortes or take your vehicle with you, disembark at any point, and explore from paved roads. For schedules and fares, contact Washington State Ferries, phone 206/464-6400 or toll-free 888/808-7977 (in state), www.wsdot.wa.gov/ferries.

**Swinomish Northern Lights Casino.** *12885 Casino Dr, Anacortes (98221). Phone 360/293-2691. www.swinomishcasino.com.* The largest Washington casino north of Seattle has tables, machines, off-track betting, and a large poker room. Lower-key gamblers can hit the bingo hall or keno lounge. The Starlight Lounge features live comedy; you'll also find pro boxing, musical entertainment, and a family-style restaurant with both buffets and table service. (Daily)

**Washington Park.** *End of Sunset Ave, Anacortes (98221). 4 miles W on 12th St (Oakes Ave). Phone 360/293-1927. www.anacortes.org.* With more than 100 species of birds, this 220-acre park is popular with bird-watchers; it also draws whale-watchers in season. Sunset Beach; saltwater fishing, boating (ramps); picnicking, camping (14-day limit; electricity and water; showers).

## Special Events

**Anacortes Jazz Festival.** *Anacortes.* Some of the best jazz artisits from around the Pacific Northwest will converge on Curtis Warf and in the Port Wharehouse, overlooking the waters of Guemes Channel, for three days of great live jazz music. Mid-Sept.

**Barbershop Concert and Salmon Barbecue.** *Anacortes. Phone 360/293-1282.* Last weekend in July.

**Peace Arch Celebration.** *International Peace Arch, I-5, exit 276, Anacortes (98230). Phone 360/332-4544.* Ceremony celebrates the relationship between the United States and Canada; scouts and veterans from both nations. Second Sun in June.

**Shipwreck Day.** *819 Commercial Ave, Anacortes (98221). Phone 360/293-7911.* Shipwreck Day flea market is a fun annual event featuring eight city blocks in downtown Anacortes packed full of good junk, antiques, collectibles, tools and all kinds of treasures for today's bargain hunter or urban pirate. There is also food and merchant sidewalk sales to plunder. Mid-July.

**Waterfront Festival.** *1019 Q Ave, Anacortes (98221). Phone 360/293-7911.* Fidalgo Island is the place to be for this traditional celebration of Anacortes' maritime heritage. It's a great family festival, with activities and entertainment, food and displays. Mid-May.

## Limited-Service Hotel

★ **SHIP HARBOR INN.** *5316 Ferry Terminal Rd, Anacortes (98221). Phone 360/293-5177; toll-free 800/852-8568; fax 360/299-2412. www.shipharborinn.com.* 16 rooms, 2 story. Pets accepted, some restrictions; fee. Complimentary continental breakfast. Check-out 11 am. Bar. **$**

# Arlington (B-3)

## What to See and Do

**Possession Point Fishing Charters.** *2807 Freestad Rd, Arlington (28223). Phone 360/652-3797. www.possessionpointfishing.com.* Based out of the Port of Everett marina—about 30 miles north of downtown Seattle—Possession Point Fishing Charters offers a variety of seven-hour trips. Most expeditions focus on King, Coho, and silver salmon or bottom fish, but the company also offers crabbing tours. Tackle, bait, and fishing licenses are all available on board.

# Ashford (C-3)

## Specialty Lodging

**ALEXANDER'S COUNTRY INN.** *37515 Hwy 706 E, Ashford (98304). Phone 360/569-2300; toll-free 800/654-7615. www.alexanderscountryinn.com.* 14 rooms, 3 story. Complimentary full breakfast. Check-in 3 pm, check-out 11 am. Restaurant. **$**

# Auburn (C-2)

*See also Seattle, Tacoma*

**Founded** 1891
**Population** 40,314
**Web Site** www.ci.auburn.wa.us

## What to See and Do

**Auburn Golf Course.** *29630 Green River Rd, Auburn (98092). Phone 253/833-2350.* This excellent 18-hole public course abuts the Green River in Auburn, about 25 miles southeast of downtown Seattle. Well known for its lush vegetation and challenging greens, the course is alternately flat (the front nine) and hilly (after the turn). It is widely regarded as one of the best golf values in the state, and is accordingly crowded on weekends. **$$$$**

**Emerald Downs.** *2300 Emerald Downs Dr, Auburn (98001). Phone 253/288-7000. www.emdowns.com.* The only live thoroughbred horse racing venue in the Seattle area, Emerald Downs features a full slate of races from spring to late summer. The esteemed Longacres Mile, an area tradition since the 1930s with an ever-growing purse ($250,000 in 2003), is the schedule's highlight, held in August. Built in 1996, the grandstand is thoroughly modern, with a wide range of seating on six levels and numerous food stands, restaurants, and bars. The 1-mile oval track hosts a number of special events and concerts (including an Independence Day celebration with fireworks). Sundays bring "family fun days," with clowns, face painting, pony rides, and other kid-friendly diversions. **$**

**Muckleshoot Casino.** *2402 Auburn Way S, Auburn (98002). Phone toll-free 800/804-4944. www.muckleshootcasino.com.* Located between Seattle and Tacoma in Auburn, Muckleshoot Casino sports a tropical theme and more than 2,000 gaming machines, as well as the usual array of Vegas-style tables. The distinguishing features here are a piano lounge/cigar bar and a sushi bar. Entertainment includes a "Legends" show (with impersonators aping Elvis, Madonna, and other stars) and pro boxing matches on Saturday nights. (Sat-Tues 24 hours, Wed-Fri 10 am-5:45 am)

# Bellevue (B-3)

*See also Issaquah, Seattle*

**Population** 109,569
**Elevation** 125 ft
**Information** Bellevue Chamber of Commerce, 10500 NE 8th St #212, 98004; phone 425/454-2464
**Web Site** www.bellevuechamber.org

Incorporated in 1953, Bellevue has rapidly become the state's fourth largest city. It is linked across Lake Washington to Seattle by the Evergreen Floating Bridge.

## What to See and Do

**Bellevue Botanical Garden.** *12001 Main St, Bellevue (98005). Phone 425/452-2749. www.bellevuebotanical.org.* Features 36 acres of woodlands, meadows, and display gardens including Waterwise Garden, Japanese Gardens, and Fuchsia Display. Garden shop. Visitor Center. (Daily) **FREE**

**Bellevue Square.** *575 Bellevue Sq, Bellevue (98004). Phone 425/454-2431. www.bellevuesquare.com.* One of the biggest and most posh shopping centers in metro Seattle, Bellevue Square is located 8 miles east of the city in suburban Bellevue, on the eastern shore of Lake Washington. Well-heeled locals love the place for its eye-catching design, climate-controlled corridors, and 200 high-end stores: anchors such as Nordstrom and the Bon March, specialty stores like Pottery Barn and Williams-Sonoma, and upscale eateries including P.F. Chang's China Bistro and Ruth's Chris Steak House. This is not to mention the non-shopping facilities and services, which are head and shoulders above that of the typical mall, with a concierge, valet parking, a local shuttle bus, and a pair of kids play areas. An Eastside institution since the 1940s, Bellevue Square underwent a major redevelopment in the 1990s that transformed it into the shoppers paradise it is today.

**Rosalie Whyel Museum of Doll Art.** *1116 108th Ave NE, Bellevue (98004). Phone 425/455-1116. www.dollart.com.* Features curated collection of dolls, teddy bears, toys, and miniatures. Museum shop. (Daily; closed holidays) **$$$**

## Special Event

**Pacific Northwest Arts Fair.** *Bellevue. 4 miles E. Phone 206/363-2048.* Art exhibits, handicrafts. Late July.

## Limited-Service Hotels

**★ ★ HILTON BELLEVUE.** *300 112th Ave, Bellevue (98004). Phone 425/455-1300; fax 425/455-0466. www.hilton.com.* Convenient to downtown and numerous shopping and dining choices, this hotel caters equally well to business travelers—with up-to-date amenities and an executive level—and families, although you probably wouldn't choose it for a romantic getaway. The guest rooms surround a dramatic seven-story atrium. Open-air balconies let guests get a feel for the great outdoors. 353 rooms, 10 story. Pets accepted, some restrictions. Check-in 3 pm, check-out noon. High-speed Internet access. Restaurant, bar. Fitness room, spa. Outdoor pool, whirlpool. Business center. **$$**

**★ ★ RED LION BELLEVUE INN.** *11211 Main St, Bellevue (98004). Phone 425/455-5240; toll-free 800/421-8193; fax 425/455-0654. www.redlion.com.* Located just six blocks from Bellevue Square Mall, and convenient to the city's attractions, the hotel has a warm, lodge-like feel with overstuffed furniture and comforters on the extra-long double or king-size beds. It's a car-friendly place, with ample free parking and rental cars available on the premises. 181 rooms, 2 story. Pets accepted, some restrictions; fee. Check-in 4 pm, check-out noon. High-speed Internet access. Restaurant, bar. Fitness room. Outdoor pool. **$**

**★ SILVER CLOUD INN BELLEVUE.** *10621 NE 12th St, Bellevue (98004). Phone 425/637-7000; toll-free 800/205-6937; fax 425/455-0531. www.scinns.com.* Found on the outskirts of downtown Bellevue, The Silver Cloud Inn is within walking distance of many attractions, including Bellevue Square Mall, the Meydenbauer Convention Center, and the Rosalie Whyel Museum of Doll Art. Perhaps the best attraction nearby is the small park across the street, where you can jog before a day of meetings or relax afterward. The lobby is warmly appointed with a fireplace, cozy sofas and chairs, and warm earth tones, and guest rooms have refrigerators and microwaves. 97 rooms, 4 story. Pets accepted, some restrictions. Complimentary full breakfast. Check-in 3 pm, check-out noon. High-speed Internet access. Fitness room. Outdoor pool, whirlpool. **$**

## Full-Service Hotels

**★ ★ ★ BELLEVUE CLUB HOTEL.** *11200 SE 6th St, Bellevue (98004). Phone 425/454-4424; toll-free 800/579-1110; fax 425/688-3101. www.bellevueclub.com.* You instantly feel the hush of the Bellevue Club Hotel when you walk through the vine-covered entrance to this exquisite hotel. Visitors are instantly welcomed to this temple of serenity and contemporary elegance set on 9 acres in the center of Bellevue. While the Bellevue Club feels very private and exclusive, hotel guests are warmly greeted with thoughtful touches and deluxe amenities. Each room has an inviting atmosphere, complete with luxurious bedding and baths crafted of marble, limestone, or granite. Stone fireplaces, oversized baths, or private balconies set each room apart from another. An Olympic-size pool, state-of-the-art equipment, racquet courts, and spa make the fitness facility a true sanctuary. Quick bites are provided at two other establishments for those on the go. 67 rooms, 4 story. Pets accepted, some restrictions. Check-in 3 pm, check-out 1 pm. High-speed Internet access, wireless Internet access. Restaurant, bar. Children's activity center. Fitness room, fitness classes available. Spa. Indoor pool, outdoor pool, whirlpool. Tennis. Business center. **$$**

**★ ★ ★ HYATT REGENCY BELLEVUE.** *900 Bellevue Way NE, Bellevue (98004). Phone 425/462-1234; toll-free 800/233-1234; fax 425/646-7567. www.bellevue.hyatt.com.* Located in the fashionable Eastside area and directly across from Bellevue Square Mall, this hotel is situated within Bellevue Place, a mixed-use development that includes retail stores, a fitness center, and plenty of dining options. The hotel makes the most of its location and, instead of maintaining its own fitness facilities, encourages guests to use the Bellevue Place Club (for a fee). When it comes to mealtime, guests need not venture too far; the hotel's own Eques Restaurant offers plenty of options for breakfast, lunch, and dinner, and more than 30 restaurants are found within a one-block radius. 382 rooms, 24 story. Pets accepted, some restrictions. Check-in 3 pm, check-out noon. High-speed Internet access, wireless Internet access. Restaurant, bar. Business center. **$$**

## Restaurant

**★★ SEASTAR RESTAURANT AND RAW BAR.** *205 108th Ave NE, Bellevue (98004). Phone 425/456-0010; fax 425/456-0020. www.seastarrestaurant.com.* Downtown Bellvue is the location of this seafood gem, which has been receiving accolades since opening in 2002. Fresh seafood, steaks, poultry, and pasta dishes are served in surroundings so beautiful—with light wood tones, caramel and terra cotta accents, and high ceilings—you'll forget that the restaurant is located an office building. Seafood menu. Dinner. Bar. Children's menu. Casual attire. Reservations recommended. Valet parking. **$$$**

# Bellingham (A-2)

*See also Blaine, Sedro-Woolley, Vancouver; see also Vancouver, BC; Victoria, BC*

**Founded** 1853
**Population** 67,171
**Elevation** 68 ft
**Area Code** 360
**Information** Bellingham/Whatcom County Convention & Visitors Bureau, 904 Potter St, 98226; phone 360/671-3990 or toll-free 800/487-2032 (order Information). The Bureau operates a Visitor Information Center off I-5 exit 253 (daily; closed holidays).
**Web Site** www.bellingham.org

This small city, located on Bellingham Bay, has the impressive Mount Baker as its backdrop and is the last major city before the Washington coastline meets the Canadian border. The broad curve of the bay was charted in 1792 by Captain George Vancouver, who named it in honor of Sir William Bellingham. When the first settlers arrived here, forests stretched to the edge of the high bluffs along the shoreline. Timber and coal played major roles in the town's early economy.

Today, Bellingham has an active waterfront port, which supports fishing, cold storage, boat building, shipping, paper processing, and marina operations. Squalicum Harbor's commercial and pleasure boat marina accommodates more than 1,800 vessels, making it the second largest marina on Puget Sound. The marina is a pleasant area to dine, picnic, and watch the fishermen at work. Fairhaven, the downtown area, contains a mix of restaurants, art galleries, and specialty shops. Bellingham is also home to Western Washington University, located on Sehome Hill, which affords a scenic view of the city and bay.

## What to See and Do

**Chuckanut Drive.** *Bellingham. S from Fairhaven Park on Hwy 11 along Chuckanut Bay to Larrabee State Park.* A 10-mile drive, mostly along highway cut into mountain sides; beautiful vistas of Puget Sound and San Juan Islands.

**City recreation areas.** *3424 Mindian, Bellingham (98225). Phone 360/676-6985.* More than 2,000 acres of parkland offer a wide variety of activities. Fee for some activities. (Daily) Areas include

**Arroyo Park.** *Chuckanut Dr and Old Samish Rd, Bellingham.* Approximately 40 acres of dense, second-growth forest in a canyon setting. Creek fishing. Hiking, nature, and bridle trails.

**Bloedel Donovan Park.** *2214 Electric Ave, Bellingham (98229). NW area of Lake Whatcom.* Swimming beach, fishing, boat launch (fee); picnicking, playground, concession (summer). Community center with gym.

**Boulevard Park.** *S State St and Bayview Dr, Bellingham.* Fishing, boat dock; bicycle paths, picnicking, playground. Craft studio.

**Civic Field Athletic Complex.** *Lakeway Dr and Orleans St, Bellingham. Phone 360/676-6976.* Contains multiple athletic fields and indoor community pool.

**Cornwall Park.** *2800 Cornwall Ave, Bellingham (98225).* Approximately 65 acres. Wading pool, steelhead fishing in Squalicum Creek; fitness trail, tennis, other game courts and fields, picnicking, playground. Extensive rose garden in park.

**Fairhaven Park.** *107 Chuckanut Dr, Bellingham (98229).* Wading pool; hiking trails, tennis, picnicking, playground.

**Lake Padden Park.** *4882 Samish Way, Bellingham (98229).* Approximately 1,000 acres with a 152-acre lake. Swimming beach, fishing, boat launch (no motors), hiking and bridle trails, 18-hole golf course (fee), tennis, athletic fields, picnicking, playground.

**Sehome Hill Arboretum.** *25th St and McDonald Pkwy, Bellingham.* The 165-acre native plant preserve contains hiking and interpretive trails; scenic views of city, Puget Sound, San Juan Islands, and mountains from observation tower atop hill.

**Whatcom Falls Park.** *1401 Electric Ave, Bellingham (98229). Near Lake Whatcom.* Approximately 240 acres. Children's fishing pond, state fish hatchery; hiking trails, tennis, athletic fields, picnicking, playground.

★ **Fairhaven District.** *107 Chuckanut Dr, Bellingham (98229).* In the late 1800s, this area was a separate city that had hopes of becoming the next Chicago. The 1890s buildings are now restaurants and shops. Brass plaques detail the history of the area. Walking tour brochures at the information gazebo, 12th and Harris.

**Ferndale.** *Bellingham. Approximately 9 miles NW off I-5, exit 262. Phone 360/384-3444.* Community founded in mid-1800s, with several preserved areas. **Hovander Homestead,** on Neilson Road, is a county park with working farm and museum; interpretive center with nature trails and observation tower. **$$**

**Larrabee State Park.** *425 Chuckanut Dr, Bellingham (98226). 7 miles S on Hwy 11. Phone 360/676-2093.* Approximately 2,000 acres. Scuba diving, fishing, clamming, crabbing, tide pools, boating (ramp); hiking, picnicking, camping (hookups). Mountain viewpoints.

**Lynden Pioneer Museum.** *217 Front St, Lynden (98264). Approximately 12 miles N via Hwy 539. Phone 360/354-3675.* Exhibits on history of this Dutch community; antique car and buggy, farm equipment. (Mon-Sat) **$**

**Maritime Heritage Center.** *1600 C St, Bellingham (98225). Phone 360/715-8352.* Salmon life-cycle facility and learning center. Outdoor rearing tanks; indoor displays detail development from egg to adult. Park (daily). Learning Center (Mon-Fri; closed holidays). **FREE**

**Mount Baker Ski Area.** *Bellingham. 55 miles E on Hwy 542. Phone 360/734-6771. www.mtbakerskiarea.com.* Four quad, three double chairlifts, rope tow; patrol, school, rentals; restaurant, cafeteria, bar; lodge. Longest run 1 1/2 miles; vertical drop 1,500 feet. Also cross-country trails. Half-day rates (weekends, holidays). (Nov-Mar: daily; Apr: Fri-Sun; closed Dec 25)

**Mount Baker-Snoqualmie National Forest.** *21965 64th Ave W, Mountlake Terrace (98043). Phone 425/775-9702; toll-free 800/627-0062. www.fs.fed.us/r6/mbs.* The Mount Baker and Snoqualmie national forests were combined under a single forest supervisor in July 1974. Divided into five ranger districts, the combined forest encompasses nearly 2 million acres. The Snoqualmie section lies east and southeast of Seattle; the Mount Baker section lies east on Highway 542 and includes the Mount Baker Ski Area. The forest extends from the Canadian border south to Mount Rainier National Park and includes rugged mountains and woodlands on the western slopes of the Cascades, the western portions of the Glacier Peak and Alpine Lakes, Henry M. Jackson, Noisy-Diobsud, Boulder River, Jackson, Clearwater, and Norse Peak wildernesses; seven commercial ski areas; 1,440 miles of hiking trails; and picnic areas and campsites. Mount Baker rises 10,778 feet in the north, forming a center for recreation all year, famous for deep-powder snow skiing and snowboarding. Snoqualmie Pass (via I-90) and Stevens Pass (via Hwy 2) provide year-round access to popular scenic destinations; Baker Lake provides excellent boating and fishing. East of the forest is

**North Cascades National Park.** *Sedro-Woolley.* (See SEDRO WOOLLEY)

**Western Washington University.** *516 High St, Bellingham (98225). Phone 360/650-3963.* (1893) (11,500 students) A 189-acre campus; internationally acclaimed outdoor sculpture collection; contemporary art at Western Gallery.

**Whatcom Museum of History and Art.** *121 Prospect St, Bellingham (98225). Phone 360/676-6981.* Regional and historic displays; also changing art exhibits; in former city hall (1892) and three adjacent buildings. Fee for special exhibitions. (Tues-Sun; closed holidays) **FREE**

## Special Events

**Deming Logging Show.** *3295 Cedarville Rd, Bellingham (98226). Log show grounds, in Deming. Phone 360/592-3051. www.demingloggingshow.com.* Log chopping, tree climbing, logger rodeo, salmon barbecue. Second weekend in June.

**Lummi Stommish.** *Bellingham. Lummi Reservation, 15 miles NW via I-5, exit 260 to Hwy 540. Phone 360/384-1489.* Water carnival with war canoe races, arts and crafts; salmon bake, Native American dancing. June.

**Ski to Sea Festival.** *1435 Railroad Ave, Bellingham (98225). Phone 360/734-1330.* Parades, carnival, art show, special events. Ski to Sea race starts on Mt. Baker, ends in Bellingham Bay and involves skiers, runners, canoeists, bicyclists, and kayakers. Memorial Day weekend.

## Limited-Service Hotels

**★ ★ BEST WESTERN HERITAGE INN.** *151 E Mcleod Rd, Bellingham (98226). Phone 360/647-1912; toll-free 800/780-7234; fax 360/671-3878. www.bestwestern.com.* 90 rooms, 3 story. Complimentary continental breakfast. Check-out noon. Restaurant. Outdoor pool, whirlpool. Airport transportation available. **$**

**★ ★ BEST WESTERN LAKEWAY INN.** *714 Lakeway Dr, Bellingham (98226). Phone 360/671-1011; toll-free 888/671-1011; fax 360/676-8519. www.bellingham-hotel.com.* Just off I-5 at the south end of Bellingham, the Best Western Lakeway Inn is a great base from which to explore this lovely area. Golf and ski packages are available. It's also a nice place to host a meeting, with ample meeting space, a grand ballroom, and a 24-hour business center. Restaurants and shops are nearby, although you'll need to drive to the city's historic Fairhaven District. 132 rooms, 4 story. Pets accepted, some restrictions; fee. Check-in 3 pm, check-out noon. Two restaurants, bar. Fitness room. Indoor pool, whirlpool. Business center. **$**

**★ HAMPTON INN BELLINGHAM AIRPORT.** *3985 Bennett Dr, Bellingham (98225). Phone 360/676-7700; toll-free 800/426-7866; fax 360/671-7557. www.hamptoninn.com.* If you need to stay near the airport, this is your best option. This well-maintained hotel has a nice pool area and a sunken atrium dining room, where breakfast is served each morning. 132 rooms, 4 story. Complimentary full breakfast. Check-in 3 pm, check-out noon. Fitness room. Outdoor pool. **$**

**★ QUALITY INN.** *100 E Kellogg Rd, Bellingham (98226). Phone 360/647-8000; toll-free 800/900-4661; fax 360/647-8094. www.qualityinn.com.* 85 rooms, 3 story. Pets accepted; fee. Complimentary continental breakfast. Check-in 3 pm, check-out noon. Fitness room. Outdoor pool, whirlpool. **$**

## Full-Service Hotel

**★ ★ ★ HOTEL BELLWETHER.** *1 Bellwether Way, Bellingham (98225). Phone 877/411-1200; toll-free 877/411-1200; fax 360/392-3101. www.hotelbellwether.com.* 68 rooms. Pets accepted; fee. Check-in 3 pm, check-out noon. High-speed Internet access. Restaurant, bar. Fitness room. Airport transportation available. Business center. **$$**

## Full-Service Inn

**★ ★ ★ THE CHRYSALIS INN & SPA.** *804 10th St, Bellingham (98225). Phone 360/756-1005; toll-free 888/808-0005. www.thechrysalisinn.com.* 43 rooms. Check-in 4 pm, check-out noon. Restaurant, bar. **$$**

## Specialty Lodging

**FAIRHAVEN VILLAGE INN.** *1200 10th St, Bellingham (98225). Phone toll-free 877/733-1100. www.fairhavenvillageinn.com.* 22 rooms. Complimentary continental breakfast. Check-in 3 pm, check-out 11 am. High-speed Internet access. Business center. **$$**

## Restaurant

**★ ★ CHUCKANUT MANOR.** *3056 Chuckanut Dr, Bow (98232). Phone 360/766-6191. www.chuckanutmanor.com.* Seafood, steak menu. Lunch, dinner, Sun brunch. Closed Mon. Bar. Children's menu. Valet parking. **$$**

# Blaine (A-2)

*See also Bellingham*

**Population** 3,770
**Elevation** 41 ft

**Area Code** 360
**Zip** 98231
**Information** Visitor Information Center, 215 Marine Dr, PO Box 4680; phone 360/332-4544 or toll-free 800/487-2032
**Web Site** www.blaine.net

Blaine sits just south of the Canadian border on I-5.

## What to See and Do

**Birch Bay State Park.** *5105 Helwig Rd, Blaine (98230). 10 miles SW via I-5, exit 266, then 7 miles W via Grandview Rd, N via Jackson Rd to Helwig Rd. Phone 360/371-2800.* Approximately 190 acres. Swimming, scuba diving, fishing, crabbing, clamming, picnicking, camping (hookups; dump station). (Daily, reservations advised Memorial Day-Labor Day)

**International Peace Arch.** *Blaine. N at point where I-5 reaches Canadian border.* (1921) The 67-foot-high arch is on the boundary line between the US and Canada and marks more than a century of peace and friendship between the two countries. The surrounding park is maintained by the state of Washington and Province of British Columbia; gardens, picnicking, playground.

**Semiahmoo Park.** *9565 Semiahmoo Pkwy, Blaine (98230). Off I-5, exit 274, on Semiahmoo Sandspit, Drayton Harbor. Phone 360/371-2000.* A cannery once located on this 1 1/2-mile-long spit was the last port of call for Alaskan fishing boats on Puget Sound. Restored buildings now house museum, gallery, and gift shop (June-mid-Sept, Sat and Sun afternoons). Park offers clam digging, picnicking, bird watching. (Daily) **$$**

## Special Event

**Peace Arch Celebration.** *International Peace Arch, I-5, exit 276, Anacortes (98230). Phone 360/332-4544.* Ceremony celebrates the relationship between the United States and Canada; scouts and veterans from both nations. Second Sun in June.

## Full-Service Resort

**★ ★ ★ RESORT SEMIAHMOO.** *9565 Semiahmoo Pkwy, Blaine (98230). Phone 360/318-2000; toll-free 800/770-7992; fax 360/318-2087. www.semiahmoo.com.* Spellbinding views are the calling card of Resort Semiahmoo. This cottage-style resort, located on a wildlife preserve at the tip of a peninsula stretching into Puget Sound, enjoys one of the most scenic spots in the state. Wherever the eye looks, views of snow-capped peaks, the Gulf Islands, Drayton Harbor, or Semiahmoo Bay captivate and enchant. Blond woods and clean lines create an uncluttered look throughout the resort, while fireplaces, patios, and balconies enhance the exceedingly comfortable guest rooms and suites. Relaxation is the order of the day here, where golf, water activities, and a terrific spa compete for attention. Dining is especially memorable, with creative and artfully presented cuisine tempting even the most demanding taste buds. 261 rooms, 4 story. Pets accepted, some restrictions; fee. Check-in 4 pm, check-out noon. Restaurant, bar. Fitness room, spa. Indoor pool, outdoor pool, whirlpool. Golf. Tennis. **$**

# Bow (A-2)

## What to See and Do

**Skagit Valley Casino Resort.** *5984 N Darrk Ln, Bow (98232). Phone 360/724-7777. www.svcasinoresort.com.* Positioned midway between Seattle and Vancouver, British Columbia, the Skagit Valley Casino Resort is swank and full of facilities. Beyond the casino (with 600 machines and numerous tables), there are 103 hotel rooms, a pool, and three restaurants (a fine dining room, a buffet, and a deli). The entertainment is varied, with country stars, dance troupes, and tribute acts among the performers gracing the Pacific Showrooms stage. (Daily)

# Bremerton (B-2)

*See also Seattle, Union*

**Founded** 1891
**Population** 37,259
**Elevation** 60 ft
**Information** Bremerton Chamber of Commerce, 301 Pacific Ave, Port Gamble, 98364; phone 360/479-3579
**Web Site** www.bremertonwa.com

The tempo of the Puget Sound Naval Shipyard is the heartbeat of Bremerton, a community surrounded on three sides by water. The six dry docks of the Naval Shipyard make Bremerton a home port for the Pacific fleet.

## What to See and Do

**Belfair.** *3151 NE Hwy 300, Belfair (98529). 15 miles SW via Hwy 3. Phone 360/275-0668.* Approximately 80 acres. Swimming; picnicking, camping (hookups). (Reservations Memorial Day-Labor Day, by mail only)

**Blake Island.** *Bremerton. 6 miles SE, accessible only by boat. Phone 360/731-8330.* More than 475 acres. Salt-water swimming beach, scuba diving, fishing, boating (dock); hiking, picnicking, primitive camping.

★ **Bremerton Naval Museum.** *130 Washington Ave, Bremerton (98337). Phone 360/479-7447.* Ship models, pictures, display of navy and shipyard history. Naval artifacts. (Mon-Sun; closed holidays) **FREE**

**Illahee.** *Bremerton. 3 miles NE off Hwy 306. Phone 360/478-6460.* Approximately 75 acres. Swimming, scuba diving; fishing, clamming; boating (ramp, dock). Hiking. Picnicking. Primitive camping.

**Kitsap County Historical Society Museum.** *280 4th St, Bremerton (98337). Phone 360/479-6226. www.kitsaphistory.org.* Re-creation of 1800s pioneer settlements. Photos and documents of history to World War II era. (Tues-Sat; closed holidays) **$**

**Scenic Beach.** *Bremerton. 12 miles NW on Hwy 3. Phone 360/830-5079.* Approximately 90 acres. Swimming, scuba diving; limited fishing, oysters in season. Nature trail. Picnicking. Primitive camping.

**USS *Turner Joy*.** *300 Washington Beach Ave, Bremerton (98337). Phone 360/792-2457.* Tours of Vietnam War-era US Navy destroyer. (May-Sept: daily; rest of year: Mon, Thurs-Sun; closed Dec 25)

## Special Events

**Armed Forces Day Parade.** *301 Pacific, Bremerton (98337). Phone 360/479-3579.* Bremerton's Armed Forces Day parade is the longest continually running Armed Forces Day event in the nation. It is one of only seven Armed Forces Day events to be officially recognized by the Department of Defense. Over a hundred floats, bands and dance teams, from military and non-military organizations participate in the parade. Mid-May.

**Blackberry Festival.** *2nd and Washington, Bremerton (98337). Phone 360/479-3579.* One can stop and sample the best blackberry jams, jellies, pies and cobblers as they walk down Main Street. The beer garden has blackberry cider, blackberry wine, and over hundred vendors offer a vast array of foods, drinks and art. Early Sept.

**Kitsap County Fair and Stampede.** *Fairgrounds, 1200 Fairgrounds Rd, Tracyton (98311). Phone 360/337-5376.* Late Aug.

**Mountaineers' Forest Theater.** *Bremerton. 8 miles W via Hwy 3, Kitsap Way, Seabeck Hwy, watch for signs. Phone 206/284-6310.* Oldest outdoor theater in the Pacific Northwest. Natural amphitheater surrounded by hundreds of rhododendrons beneath old-growth Douglas fir and hemlock. Log terraced seats. Family-oriented play. The 1/3-mile walk to the theater is difficult for the physically disabled or elderly (assistance available). Picnicking; concession. Contact 300 Third Ave W, Seattle 98119. Late May-early June.

## Limited-Service Hotels

**★ BEST WESTERN BREMERTON INN.** *4303 Kitsap Way, Bremerton (98312). Phone 360/405-1111; toll-free 800/780-7234; fax 360/377-0597. www.bestwestern.com.* 103 rooms, 3 story. Complimentary continental breakfast. Check-out 11 am. Fitness room. Outdoor pool, whirlpool. **$**

**★ ★ RED LION.** *3073 NW Bucklin Hill Rd, Silverdale (98383). Phone 360/698-1000; fax 360/682-0932. www.redlion.com.* 150 rooms, 3 story. Check-out noon. Restaurant, bar. Fitness room. Indoor pool, whirlpool. Tennis. **$**

**★ ★ YACHT CLUB BROILER.** *9226 Bay Shore Dr, Silverdale (98383). Phone 360/698-1601; fax 360/692-1348.* Seafood, steak menu. Breakfast, lunch, dinner, Sun brunch. Bar. Children's menu. Valet parking. Outdoor seating. **$$$**

# Cashmere (B-4)

*See also Leavenworth, Wenatchee*

**Founded** 1881
**Population** 2,965
**Elevation** 853 ft
**Area Code** 509
**Zip** 98815
**Information** Chamber of Commerce, PO Box 834; phone 509/782-7404
**Web Site** www.visitcashmere.com

Cashmere's history dates to the 1860s, when a Catholic missionary came to the area to set up a school for Native Americans. The town is located in the Wenatchee Valley in the center of the state on the North Cascade Loop. It has strong timber and fruit industries.

## What to See and Do

**Cashmere Museum.** *600 Cotlets Way, Cashmere (98815). E edge of town. Phone 509/782-3230. www.cashmeremuseum.com.* Pioneer relics, Native American artifacts; Columbia River archaeology exhibit; water wheel (1891); mineral exhibit; "pioneer village" with 21 cabins, mining displays. Great Northern Railroad depot, passenger car and caboose. (Mar-Nov: daily; rest of year: by appointment) **$$**

**Liberty Orchards Company, Inc.** *117 Mission Ave, Cashmere (98815). Off Hwy 2. Phone 509/782-2191.* Makes fruit-nut confections known as "aplets," "cotlets," "grapelets," and "fruit festives." Tour, samples. Children with adult only. (May-Dec: daily; rest of year: Mon-Fri; closed holidays)

## Special Events

**Apple Days.** *Chelan County Historical Museum, 600 Cotlets Way, Cashmere (98815). Phone 509/782-3230.* Apple pie contest, old-time crafts, Pioneer Village in operation, cider making. First weekend in Oct.

**Chelan County Fair.** *5700 Westcott Dr, Cashmere (98815). Phone 509/782-0708.* First weekend after Labor Day.

**Founders' Day.** *Chelan County Historical Museum, 600 Cotlets Way, Cashmere (98815). Phone 509/782-3230.* Everyone's eyes will be on the sky as they wait in anxious anticipation for 5,000 Ping-Pong balls to be dropped from a hovering helicopter on to the fields at Riverside Park. The Ping-Pong ball drop is one of the most popular events during Cashmere's Founders' Days celebration. Last weekend in June.

# Centralia (C-2)

*See also Chehalis, Olympia*

**Founded** 1875
**Population** 14,742
**Elevation** 189 ft
**Area Code** 360
**Zip** 98531
**Information** The Centralia, Chehalis, and Greater Lewis County Chamber of Commerce, 500 NW Chamber of Commerce Way, Chehalis 98532; phone 360/748-8885 or toll-free 800/525-3323
**Web Site** www.chamberway.com

Centralia was founded by a former slave named George Washington. The town's George Washington Park is named for the founder, not for the country's first president.

## What to See and Do

**Schaefer County Park.** *822 Hwy 507, Centralia (98531). 1/2 mile N on Hwy 507. Phone 360/740-1135.* Swimming in the Skookumchuck River; fishing; hiking trails, picnicking (shelter), playground, horseshoe pits, volleyball. **FREE**

## Special Event

**Southwest Washington Fair.** *2555 N National Ave, Chehalis (98532). 1 mile S on I-5. Phone 360/736-6072.* First held in 1909, this is the state's second-oldest fair and one of the largest. Third week in Aug.

## Limited-Service Hotel

**★ HOLIDAY INN EXPRESS.** *1233 Alder St, Centralia (98531). Phone 360/330-9441; toll-free 800/465-4329; fax 360/330-1467. www.holiday-inn.com.* 75 rooms. Complimentary continental breakfast. Check-in 3 pm, check-out noon. Indoor pool, whirlpool. **$**

# Chehalis (C-2)

*See also Centralia, Longview*

**Settled** 1873
**Population** 7,057
**Elevation** 226 ft
**Area Code** 360
**Zip** 98532
**Information** The Centralia, Chehalis, and Greater Lewis County Chamber of Commerce, 500 NW Chamber of Commerce Way; phone 360/748-8885 or toll-free 800/525-3323
**Web Site** www.chamberway.com

First called Saundersville, this city takes its present name, Native American for "shifting sands," from its position at the point where the Newaukum and Chehalis rivers meet. Farms and an industrial park give economic sustenance to Chehalis and neighboring Centralia (see).

## What to See and Do

**Historic Claquato Church.** *125 Water St, Chehalis (98532). 3 miles W on Hwy 6, on Claquato Hill. Phone 360/748-4551.* (1858) Oldest church in state, original building on original site; handmade pews, pulpit. (Schedule varies)

**Lewis County Historical Museum.** *599 NW Front Way, Chehalis (98532). Phone 360/748-0831.* Restored railroad depot (1912). Pioneer displays; Native American exhibits. Cemetery, genealogical history; artifacts, newspapers, books, photographs, written family histories, oral histories of pioneers. (Tues-Sun; closed holidays) **$**

**Rainbow Falls State Park.** *Chehalis. 18 miles W on Hwy 6. Phone 360/291-3767.* Approximately 125 acres of woodland. Fishing; hiking trails, picnicking, camping (dump station).

## Special Events

**Music and Art Festival.** *Chehalis. Phone 360/748-8885.* Arts and craft vendors, food. Late July.

**Southwest Washington Fair.** *2555 N National Ave, Chehalis (98532). 1 mile S on I-5. Phone 360/736-6072.* First held in 1909, this is the state's second-oldest fair and one of the largest. Third week in Aug.

## Restaurant

**★ MARY MC CRANK'S DINNER HOUSE.** *2923 Jackson Hwy, Chehalis (98532). Phone 360/748-3662; fax 360/740-9222. www.marymccranks.com.* American menu. Lunch, dinner. Closed Mon, children's menu. **$$**

# Chelan (B-4)

*See also Wenatchee*

**Settled** 1885
**Population** 3,552
**Elevation** 1,208 ft
**Area Code** 509
**Zip** 98816
**Information** Lake Chelan Chamber of Commerce, 102 E Johnson; phone 509/682-3503 or toll-free 800/424-3526
**Web Site** www.lakechelan.com

Located in an apple-growing region, Chelan is a gateway to Lake Chelan and the spectacular northern Cascade Mountains. A Ranger District office of the Wenatchee National Forest is located here.

## What to See and Do

**Alta Lake.** *191 Alta Lake Rd, Chelan (98846). 20 miles N on Hwy 97, then 2 miles W on Hwy 153. Phone 509/923-2473.*More than 180 acres. Swimming, fishing, boating (ramps); hiking, snowmobiling, ice skating, camping (hook-ups).

**Lake Chelan.** *Chelan. Phone 360/902-8844.* This fjord-like lake, the largest and deepest in the state, stretches northwest for approximately 55 miles through the Cascade Mountains to the community of Stehekin in the North Cascades National Park; the lake is nearly 1,500 feet deep in some areas. There are two state parks and several recreation areas along the lake.

> **Lake cruises.** *1418 W Woodin Ave, Chelan (98816). Phone 509/682-4584; toll-free 888/424-3526.* The passenger boats *Lady of the Lake II* and *Lady Express* and the High-Speed *Lady Cat* make daily cruises on Lake Chelan to Stehekin, Holden Village, and North Cascades National Park. (Call or visit Web site for schedule) **$$$$**

**Lake Chelan State Park.** *7544 S Lakeshore Dr, Chelan (98816). 9 1/2 miles W via Hwy 97 and South Shore Dr or Navarre Coulee Rd. Phone toll-free 800/452-5687.* Approximately 130 lakefront acres. Swimming, fishing, boating (ramps, dock); picnicking, camping (hookups; reservations required late May-Aug). (Apr-Oct: daily; rest of year: weekends and holidays)

**Twenty-Five Mile Creek.** *20530 S Lakeshore, Chelan (20530). 18 miles NW on S Shore Dr. Phone toll-free 800/452-5687.* Approximately 65 acres. Fishing, boating (launch, mooring, gas); hiking, concession, camping (hook-ups).

## Special Event

**Lake Chelan Rodeo.** *5700 Wescott Dr, Chelan (98815). Phone 509/682-4061.* Last weekend in July.

## Limited-Service Hotels

**★ BEST WESTERN LAKESIDE LODGE AND SUITES.** *2312 W Woodin Ave, Chelan (98816). Phone 509/682-4396; toll-free 800/468-2781; fax 509/682-3278. www.lakesidelodge.net.* Although the in-season rates can be high for a limited-service hotel, this is the place to stay in Chelan. With a private beach and boat dock, accessing lovely Lake Chelan is easy, and the heated outdoor pool has a truly majestic view. Small pets are allowed, but access is very restricted, so call ahead for details if you plan to bring your pet along. 67 rooms. Pets accepted, some restrictions; fee. Complimentary continental breakfast. Check-in 3 pm, check-out 11 am. Indoor pool, outdoor pool, whirlpool. **$**

★ ★ **CAMPBELL'S RESORT AND CONFERENCE CENTER.** *104 W Woodin Ave, Chelan (98816). Phone 509/682-2561; toll-free 800/553-8225; fax 509/682-2177. www.campbellsresort.com.* Lovely Lake Chelan is the centerpiece at this 8-acre resort in central Washington, where families and groups come to work and play. Every guest room is on the water, and private balconies enable guests to enjoy the stunning views of the Cascades looming beyond the lake. Summer brings all kinds of activities, from drawing and fishing classes to outdoor barbecues to magicians and jugglers on weekend evenings. The resort's meeting facilities can accommodate groups of up to 325 people, making this a popular spot for weddings and business meetings. 170 rooms, 4 story. Check-in 3 pm, check-out 11 am. High-speed Internet access. Two restaurants, bar. Fitness room, spa. Two outdoor pools, two whirlpools. Business center. **$$**

# Cheney (B-6)

*See also Centralia, Longview*

**Population** 8,832
**Elevation** 2,350 ft
**Area Code** 509
**Zip** 99004
**Information** Chamber of Commerce, 201 First St; phone 509/235-8480
**Web Site** www.westplainschamber.org

Cheney, on a rise of land that gives it one of the highest elevations of any municipality in the state, has been a university town since 1882. It is also a farm distribution and servicing center.

## What to See and Do

**Cheney Historical Museum.** *614 3rd St, Cheney (99004). Phone 509/235-4343.* Features pioneer artifacts. (Mar-Nov, Tues and Sat afternoons) **FREE**

**Eastern Washington University.** *Cheney. Phone 509/359-2397.* (1882) (9,000 students) Tours of campus. On campus are a theater, recital hall, and

> **Gallery of Art.** *526 Fifth St, Cheney (99004). Phone 509/359-2493.* Changing exhibits. (Academic year, Mon-Fri; closed holidays) **FREE**
>
> **Museum of Anthropology.** *Cheney. Phone 509/359-2433.* Teaching-research facility concerning Native Americans of North America. **FREE**

**Turnbull National Wildlife Refuge.** *Cheney. 4 miles S on Cheney-Plaza Rd, then 2 miles E. Phone 509/235-4723.* Located on the Pacific Flyway; more than 200 species of birds have been observed in the area; also a habitat for deer, elk, coyotes, beaver, mink, chipmunks, red squirrels, and Columbia ground squirrels. Refuge named after Cyrus Turnbull, an early settler. A 2,200-acre public use area (daily).

## Special Event

**Rodeo Days.** *Cheney. Phone 509/235-4848.* Rodeo, parade. Second weekend in July.

# Clarkston (D-6)

*See also Pullman; see also Lewiston, ID*

**Founded** 1896
**Population** 7,337
**Elevation** 736 ft
**Area Code** 509
**Zip** 99403
**Information** Chamber of Commerce, 502 Bridge St; phone 509/758-7712 or toll-free 800/933-2128
**Web Site** www.clarkstonchamber.org

Clarkston is located on the Washington-Idaho boundary at the confluence of the Clearwater and Snake rivers. The town became a shipping center when the construction of four dams on the lower Snake River brought barge transportation here. Many recreation areas are located near Clarkston, especially along the Snake River and in the Umatilla National Forest. River trips are available into Hell's Canyon.

## What to See and Do

**Asotin County Museum.** *215 Filmore St, Asotin (99402). Approximately 6 miles S on Hwy 129. Phone 509/243-4659.* Main museum contains sculptures, pioneer equiptment, pictures, and clothing. On the grounds are a furnished pioneer house, shepherd's cabin, one-room schoolhouse, 1882 log cabin, blacksmith shop, a windmill, and Salmon River barge. (Tues-Sat; closed holidays) **FREE**

**Fields Spring State Park.** *Clarkston. 30 miles S on Hwy 129. Phone 509/256-3332.* Approximately 800 forested acres in the Blue Mountains. A 1-mile uphill hike from parking lot to Puffer Butte gives view of three states. Wide variety of wildflowers and birdlife. Picnicking, primitive camping.

**Petroglyphs.** *Asotin. Phone toll-free 800/933-2128.* Ancient writings inscribed in cliffs of Snake River near Buffalo Eddy. Near town of Asotin.

**Umatilla National Forest.** *Clarkston. S of Hwy 12, access near Pomeroy. Phone 877/958-9663. www.fs.fed.us/r6/uma.* Approximately 319,000 acres of heavily forested mountain area extending into Oregon. Many recreation areas offer fishing, hunting, hiking, camping, and downhill skiing. For further information, contact the Supervisor, 2517 SW Hailey Ave, Pendleton, OR 97801.

**Valley Art Center.** *842 6th St, Clarkston (99403). Phone 509/758-8331.* Various types of art and crafts; changing monthly exhibits with featured artists and special showings. Northwest Heritage Show is held for two months in summer. (Mon-Fri, closed holidays) **FREE**

## Special Events

**Asotin County Fair.** *Clarkston. Phone 509/758-7712.* Includes cowboy breakfast, barbecue, parade. Last Thurs-Sun in Apr.

**Sunflower Days.** *Clarkston. Phone 509/758-7712.* Second Fri-Sat in Aug.

## Limited-Service Hotels

**★ BEST WESTERN RIVERTREE INN.** *1257 Bridge St, Clarkston (99403). Phone 509/758-9551; toll-free 800/597-3621; fax 509/758-9551. www.bestwestern.com.* Many rooms with spiral staircase to loft. 61 rooms, 2 story. Check-out noon. Fitness room. Outdoor pool, whirlpool. **$**

**★ ★ QUALITY INN.** *700 Port Dr, Clarkston (99403). Phone 509/758-9500; toll-free 800/228-5151; fax 509/758-5580. www.qualityinn.com.* 75 rooms, 3 story. Check-out noon. Restaurant, bar. Fitness room. Outdoor pool. **$**

## Restaurant

**★ ROOSTER'S LANDING.** *1550 Port Dr, Clarkston (99403). Phone 509/751-0155; fax 509/751-8706. www.roosterslanding.com.* American menu. Lunch, dinner. Bar. Children's menu. Outdoor seating. **$$**

# Colville (A-6)

*See also Spokane*

**Population** 4,988
**Elevation** 1,635 ft
**Area Code** 509
**Zip** 99114
**Information** Chamber of Commerce, 121 E Astor; phone 509/684-5973
**Web Site** www.colville.com

Once a brawling frontier town, Colville, the seat of Stevens County, has quieted down and now reflects the peacefulness of the surrounding hills and mountains. Many towns flourished and died in this area—orchards, mills, and mines all had their day. The portage at Kettle Falls, a fort, and the crossing of several trails made Colville a thriving center.

## What to See and Do

**Colville National Forest.** *765 S Main St, Colville (99114). Phone 509/684-7000.* This million-acre forest is located in the northeast corner of Washington, bordering Canada. The forest extends along its western boundary from the Canadian border south to the Colville Reservation and east across the Columbia River to Idaho. Comprising conifer forest types, small lakes, and winding valleys bounded by slopes leading to higher mountainous areas, the forest offers good hunting and fishing and full-service camping. Also here is Sullivan Lake, offering such recreational opportunities as boating, fishing, swimming, and hiking trails, and developed and dispersed campground settings. The bighorn sheep that inhabit adjacent Hall Mountain can be viewed at a feeding station near the lake, which is cooperatively managed by the forest and the Washington Department of Wildlife. Also located here are a Ranger District office and

**Lake Gillette Recreation Area.** *2430 Hwy 20 E, Colville (99114). E via Tiger Hwy (Hwy 20). Phone 509/684-5657.* Boating, swimming, fishing; picnicking, amphitheater with programs, camping (fee). (Mid-May-Sept) **FREE**

**Keller Heritage Center.** *700 N Wynne St, Colville (99114). Phone 509/684-5968.* Site of three-story Keller home (1910), carriage house; blacksmith shop; farmstead cabin; gardens; museum; schoolhouse; machinery building; lookout tower. Local records, Native American artifacts. (May-Sept, daily) **DONATION**

**St. Paul's Mission.** *Colville. 12 miles NW, near intersection of Columbia River and Hwy 395. Phone 509/738-6266.* A chapel was built by Jesuit Priests assisted by Native Americans near here in 1845, followed by the hand-hewn log church in 1847. It fell into disuse in the 1870s and in 1939 was restored to its original state. Self-guided tour. Located at Kettle Falls in Lake Roosevelt National Recreation Area. (All year)

## Special Events

**Colville PRCA Rodeo.** *Colville. Phone 509/684-4849.* Father's Day weekend.

**Northeast Washington Fair.** *Colville. Stevens County Fairgrounds. Phone 509/684-2585.* Parade, livestock and horse shows; arts and crafts exhibits; carnival. Aug.

**Rendezvous.** *Colville. Phone 509/684-5973.* Arts and crafts, entertainment. First weekend in Aug.

# Coulee Dam (B-5)

*See also Soap Lake*

**Founded** 1934
**Population** 1,044
**Elevation** 1,145 ft
**Area Code** 509
**Zip** 99116
**Information** Grand Coulee Dam Area Chamber of Commerce, 306 Midway Ave, PO Box 760, Grand Coulee, 99133-0760; phone 509/633-3074 or toll-free 800/268-5332
**Web Site** www.grandcouleedam.org

Established as a construction community for workers on the Grand Coulee Dam project, this town is now the home of service and maintenance employees of the dam and the headquarters for the Lake Roosevelt National Recreation Area.

## What to See and Do

**Colville Tribal Museum.** *512 Mead Way, Coulee Dam (99116). Phone 509/633-0751.* More than 8,000 years of history on 11 tribes. (Late May-Sept: Mon-Sat; rest of year: schedule varies) **FREE**

★ **Grand Coulee Dam.** *306 Midway Ave, Grand Coulee (99116). Near jct Hwys 155, 174. Phone 509/633-9265; toll-free 800/268-5332. www.grandcouleedam.org.* This is the major structure of the multipurpose Columbia Basin Project, built by the Bureau of Reclamation to bring water to the dry farms in central Washington. Water is diverted from the Columbia River to what in prehistoric days was its temporary course down the Grand Coulee (a deep water-carved ravine). The project will reclaim more than a million acres through irrigation and already provides a vast reservoir of electric power. One of the largest concrete structures in the world, the dam towers 550 feet high and has a 500-foot-wide base and a 5,223-foot-long crest. Power plants contain some of world's largest hydro-generators. In summer, a nightly laser light show tells the story of the dam using the concrete spillway as a backdrop. **FREE**

**Lake Roosevelt National Recreation Area.** *1008 Crest Dr, Coulee Dam (99116). Phone 509/633-9441. www.nps.gov/laro.* Totals 100,059 acres, including Franklin D. Roosevelt Lake. The lake, formed by the Grand Coulee Dam, serves as a storage reservoir with a 630-mile shoreline and extends 151 miles northeast, reaching the Canadian border. The southern part is semi-arid; the northern part is mountainous, forested with ponderosa pine, fir, and tamarack. Excellent for all sizes of motorboats with a 151-mile waterway along the reservoir and 200 miles of cruising water in Canada provided by Arrow Lakes, reached from Lake Roosevelt by the Columbia River. Thirty-eight areas have been specially developed; most provide camping (fee), picnicking; swimming, boating and launching sites (fee). Visitors can fish all year in Roosevelt Lake. Within the area is

> **Fort Spokane.** *Coulee Dam. Phone 509/725-2715.* One of the last frontier military outposts of the 1800s. Four of 45 buildings remain; brick guardhouse is now a visitor center and small museum. Built to maintain peace between the settlers and Native Americans; no shot was ever fired. Self-guided trail around old parade grounds; interpretive displays. Living history programs performed on weekends in summer. Nearby are beach and camping (fee). (Mid-June-Labor Day, daily)

**Steamboat Rock State Park.** *Hwy 155, Electric City. 11 miles S. Phone 509/633-1304; toll-free 800/452-5687.* Approximately 900 acres. Swimming, fishing, boating (launch); hiking, picnicking, camping (hookups; reservations recommended Memorial Day-Labor Day weekends).

## Special Events

**Colorama Festival & PWRA Rodeo.** *306 Midway Ave, Coulee Dam (99133). Phone 509/633-3074; toll-free 800/268-5332. www.grandcouleedam.org/colorama/.* Second weekend in May.

**Laser Light Festival.** *Coulee Dam. Phone 509/633-9265.* Memorial Day weekend.

## Limited-Service Hotel

**★ COLUMBIA RIVER INN.** *10 Lincoln Ave, Coulee Dam (99116). Phone 509/633-2100; toll-free 800/633-6421. www.columbiariverinn.com.* View of dam. 34 rooms, 2 story. Check-out 11 am. Outdoor pool, whirlpool. **$**

# Coupeville (B-2)

*See also Anacortes, Oak Harbor, Port Townsend*

**Population** 1,723
**Elevation** 80 ft
**Area Code** 360
**Zip** 98239
**Information** Visitor Information Center, 107 S Main St; phone 360/678-5434

One of the oldest towns in the state, Coupeville was named for Thomas Coupe, a sea captain and early settler, the only man ever to sail a full-rigged ship through Deception Pass. Fortified to protect the settlers and for the defense of Puget Sound, Coupeville was once the home of the only seat of higher education north of Seattle, the Puget Sound Academy. Today it is near Whidbey Island Naval Air Station, home of naval aviation for the Pacific Northwest.

## What to See and Do

**Alexander Blockhouse.** *Coupeville. Near Front St, on waterfront. Phone 360/678-5434.* (1855) One of four such buildings built on Whidbey Island to protect settlers' homes from Native Americans during the White River Massacre.

**Fort Casey State Park.** *Coupeville. 3 miles S. Phone 360/678-4519.* Approximately 140 acres. Scuba diving, saltwater fishing, boating (launch); picnicking, camping. Museum (early May-mid-Sept).

## Full-Service Inn

**★ ★ ★ INN AT LANGLEY.** *400 First St, Langley (98260). Phone 360/221-3033; fax 360/221-3033. www.innatlangley.com.* A tranquil retreat awaits guests at this exquisitely designed inn. Guest rooms are luxurious with water views, an outdoor porch, and an oversized whirlpool jet tub. 24 rooms, 4 story. Children over 12 years only. Complimentary continental breakfast. Check-in 3 pm, check-out noon. Restaurant. **$$**

## Specialty Lodgings

**CAPTAIN WHIDBEY INN.** *2072 W Captain Whidbey Inn Rd, Coupeville (98239). Phone 360/678-4097; toll-free 800/366-4097. www.captainwhidbey.com.* This turn-of-the-century log inn (1907) is situated on a sheltered cove. 32 rooms. Complimentary full breakfast. Check-in 4 pm, check-out noon. Bar. **$**

**GUEST HOUSE BED & BREAKFAST COTTAGES.** *24371 Hwy 525, Greenbank (98253). Phone 360/678-3115. www.guesthouselogcottages.com.* This inn is located on 25 acres of forest and features a scenic wildlife pond and marine and mountain views. 6 rooms, 2 story. No children allowed. Complimentary full breakfast. Check-in 4 pm, check-out 11 am. Fitness room. Outdoor pool. **$$**

# Dayton (D-6)

*See also Walla Walla*

**Settled** 1859
**Population** 2,655
**Elevation** 1,613 ft
**Area Code** 509
**Zip** 99328
**Information** Chamber of Commerce, 166 E Main St; phone 509/382-4825 or toll-free 800/882-6299
**Web Site** www.historicdayton.com

Once an important stagecoach depot and stopping-off place for miners, Dayton is now the center of a farm area in which sheep, cattle, wheat, apples, peas, asparagus, and hay are raised. Little Goose Lock and Dam, a multipurpose federal project and one of four such developments on the Snake River, is about 35 miles north of town. Vegetable canning and lumbering are key local industries.

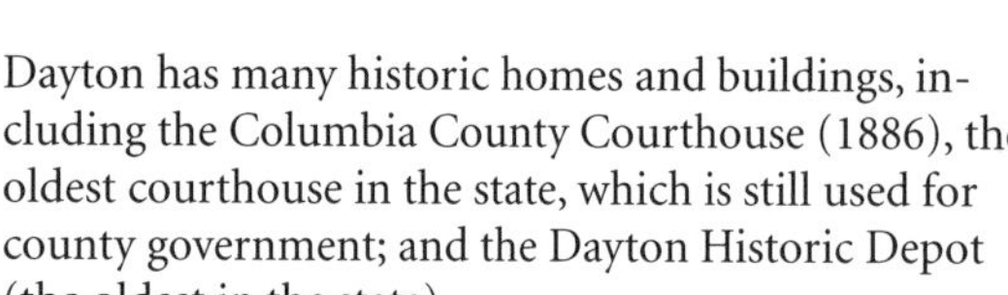

Dayton has many historic homes and buildings, including the Columbia County Courthouse (1886), the oldest courthouse in the state, which is still used for county government; and the Dayton Historic Depot (the oldest in the state).

## What to See and Do

**Kendall Skyline Drive.** *Dayton. South of town.* Scenic route through the Blue Mountains and Umatilla National Forest. Usually open by July. Contact Chamber of Commerce for details.

**Lewis and Clark Trail State Park.** *36149 Hwy 12, Dayton (Columbia Co) (99328). 5 miles SW on Hwy 12. Phone 509/337-6457.* Approximately 40 acres. Swimming, fishing; hiking, picnicking, camping.

**Palouse River Canyon.** *Dayton. 18 miles N on Hwy 12, then 22 miles NW on unnumbered roads.* Deeply eroded gorge pierces wheatlands of region; cliffs rise hundreds of feet above river. At Palouse Falls, river roars over 198-foot cliff into deep ravine of basaltic rock, continues south to join Snake River. Nearby are Lyons Ferry and Palouse Falls state parks.

**Ski Bluewood.** *262 E Main, Dayton (99328). 22 miles S via 4th St (North Touchet Rd), in Umatilla National Forest. Phone 509/382-4725. www.bluewood.com.* Two triple chairlifts, platter pull, half pipe; patrol, school, rentals; cafeteria, bar. Longest run 2 1/4 miles; vertical drop 1,125 feet. Snowboarding. Half-day rates. (Jan-Feb: daily; mid-Nov-Dec and Feb-Apr: Tues-Sun) **$$$$**

## Special Events

**Columbia County Fair.** *Dayton. Dayton Fairgrounds. Phone toll-free 800/882-6299.* Second weekend in Sept.

**Dayton Depot Festival.** *222 E Commercial St, Dayton (Columbia Co) (99328). Phone 509/382-2026.* Third weekend in July.

# Ellensburg (C-4)

*See also Quincy, Yakima*

**Settled** 1867
**Population** 12,361
**Elevation** 1,508 ft
**Area Code** 509
**Zip** 98926
**Information** Chamber of Commerce, 609 N Main; phone 509/925-3137 or toll-free 888/925-2204
**Web Site** www.ellensburg-chamber.com

Although this community has long abandoned its first name, Robber's Roost, it cherishes the tradition and style of the West, both as a center for dude ranches and as the scene of one of the country's best annual rodeos. At the geographic center of the state, Ellensburg processes beef and dairy products. The county ranges from lakes and crags in the west through irrigated farmlands to sagebrush prairie along the Columbia River to the east.

A Ranger District office of the Wenatchee National Forest is located here.

## What to See and Do

**Central Washington University.** *262 E Main, Dayton (Columbia Co) (99328). 8th Ave and Walnut St. Phone 509/963-1111. www.cwu.edu.* (1890) (7,000 students) Liberal arts and sciences, business, technology, education.

> **CWU Library.** *14th Ave and D St, Ellensburg (98926). Phone 509/963-3682.* Regional depository for federal documents; collection of microforms, maps, general materials. (Daily) **FREE**

> **Sarah Spurgeon Art Gallery.** *400 E University Way, Ellensburg (98926). In Randall Hall. Phone 509/963-2665.* Features national, regional, and advanced students' art exhibits in all media. (Sept-June, Mon-Fri; closed school holidays) **FREE**

**Clymer Museum of Art.** *416 N Pearl, Ellensburg (98926). Phone 509/962-6416.* Changing gallery exhibits; local artists. (Daily; Sat-Sun afternoons) **$$**

**Ginkgo/Wanapum State Park.** *4511 Huntzinger Rd, Vantage (98950). 28 miles E on I-90 exit 136. Phone 509/856-2700.* One of world's largest petrified forests (7,600 acres), with more than 200 species of petrified wood, including a prehistoric ginkgo tree. Waterskiing, fishing, boating; hiking, picnicking, camping (hook-ups). **FREE**

**★ Olmstead Place State Park-Heritage Site.** *Ellensburg. 4 miles E via Kittitas Hwy on Squaw Creek Trail Rd. Phone 509/925-1943.* This turn-of-the-century Kittitas Valley farm, originally homesteaded in 1875, is being converted to a living historical farm. Eight buildings; wildlife, flowers and trees; 1/2-mile interpretive trail. Farm machinery. Tours. (June-Sept: weekends; rest of year: by appointment). **FREE**

**Thorp Grist Mill.** *Ellensburg. From I-90, take exit 101, turn N, and go 3 miles to Thorp to reach the mill at the far edge of town. Phone 509/964-9640. www.thorp.org.* This flour mill, built in 1883, is the only one in the country with its machinery completely intact. **FREE**

**Wanapum Dam Heritage Center.** *15655 Wanapum Village Ln SW, Ellensburg (99321). 29 miles E on I-90, then 3 miles S on Hwy 243. Phone 509/754-3541.* Self-guided tour of center; fish-viewing; petroglyph rubbings; exhibits detail life of the Wanapum, fur traders, ranchers, miners. (Daily) **FREE**

## Special Events

**Kittitas County Fair & Rodeo.** *512 N Poplar, Ellensburg (98926). Phone 509/962-7639.* Carnival, exhibits, livestock, crafts, contests, entertainment. Labor Day weekend.

**National Western Art Show and Auction.** *Ellensburg. Phone 509/962-2934. www.westernartassociation.org.* Third weekend in May.

**Threshing Bee and Antique Equipment Show.** *Ellensburg. Olmstead Place State Park. Phone 509/925-1943. www.kveic.org/.* Steam and gas threshing, blacksmithing demonstrations, horse-drawn equipment, old-time plowing. Third weekend in Sept.

## Limited-Service Hotel

**★★ ELLENSBURG INN.** *1700 Canyon Rd, Ellensburg (98926). Phone 509/925-9801; toll-free 800/321-8791; fax 509/925-2093. www.ellensburginn.com.* 105 rooms, 2 story. Pets accepted, some restrictions; fee. Check-in 4 pm, check-out noon. Restaurant, bar. Indoor pool, whirlpool. **$**

# Enumclaw (C-3)

*See also Puyallup, Tacoma*

**Population** 7,227
**Elevation** 750 ft
**Area Code** 360
**Zip** 98022
**Information** Chamber of Commerce/Visitor Information, 1421 Cole St; phone 360/825-7666
**Web Site** chamber.enumclaw.wa.us

At the northwest entrance of Mount Rainier National Park, Enumclaw (which means "loud rattling noise") prides itself on small-town hospitality. The six-block downtown area features shops, restaurants, and other tourist-friendly amenities. A Ranger District office of the Mount Baker-Snoqualmie National Forest is located here.

## What to See and Do

**Federation Forest State Park.** *49201 Hwy 410 E, Enumclaw (98022). 18 miles SE on Hwy 410. Phone 360/663-2207.* Approximately 620 acres of old-growth timber. Catherine Montgomery Interpretive Center has displays on the state's seven life zones. Three interpretive trails, hiking trails, and part of the Naches Trail, one of the first pioneer trails between eastern Washington and Puget Sound. Fishing; hiking, picnicking. **FREE**

**Green River Gorge Conservation Area.** *29500 SE Green River Gorge, Enumclaw (98022). 12 miles N on Hwy 169.* Protects a unique 12-mile corridor of the Green River, which cuts through unusual rock areas, many with fossils. Views of present-day forces of stream erosion through caves, smooth canyon walls. **FREE** One of the many areas in the gorge is

> **Flaming Geyser State Park.** *23700 SE Flaming Geyser Rd, Auburn (98002). Phone 253/931-3930.* Two geysers (actually old test holes for coal), one burning about 6 inches high and the other bubbling methane gas through a spring. Fishing, boating, rafting; hiking, picnicking, playground. Abundant wildlife, wildflowers. No camping. (Daily)

**Mud Mountain Dam.** *Enumclaw. 7 miles SE via Hwy 410. Phone 360/825-3211.* One of the world's highest earth core and rock-fill dams.

## Special Events

**King County Fair.** *Fairgrounds, 45224 284th Ave SE, Enumclaw (98022). Phone 360/825-7777.* Third week in July.

**Pacific NW Scottish Highland Games.** *Fairgrounds, 45224 284th Ave SE, Enumclaw (98022). Phone 360/825-7777.* Fourth weekend in July.

## Limited-Service Hotel

**★★ BEST WESTERN PARK CENTER HOTEL.** *1000 Griffin Ave, Enumclaw (98022). Phone 360/825-4490; fax 360/825-3686. www.bestwestern.com.* 40 rooms, 2 story. Pets accepted; fee. Check-out

11 am. Restaurant, bar. Fitness room. **$**

# Ephrata (C-4)

*See also Moses Lake, Quincy, Soap Lake*

**Settled** 1882
**Population** 5,349
**Elevation** 1,275 ft
**Area Code** 509
**Zip** 98823
**Information** Chamber of Commerce, 90 Alder NW; phone 509/754-4656
**Web Site** www.ephratawachamber.com

The growth of this area is the result of the development of surrounding farmland, originally irrigated by wells, now supplied by the Columbia Basin irrigation project. Ephrata is the center of an area containing a series of lakes that offer fishing and water sports. There is excellent upland game bird hunting as well.

## What to See and Do

**Grant County Historical Museum and Village.** *742 Basin St NW, Ephrata (98823). Phone 509/754-3334.* Displays trace natural history and early pioneer development of area. Native American artifacts. Pioneer homestead and country village with 31 buildings (some original, restored), including church, schoolhouse, saloon, barbershop, Krupp-Marlin Jail, photography studio, bank, firehouse, livery stable, blacksmith shop; farm machinery exhibit. Guided tour. (Early May-Sept: Mon-Tues, Thurs-Sun; rest of year: guided tour by appointment) **$**

**Oasis Park.** *2541 Basin St SW, Ephrata (98823). 1 1/2 miles SW on Hwy 28. Phone 509/754-5102.* Picnicking; nine-hole, par-three golf (fee); children's fishing pond; playground; miniature golf (fee). Camping (fee); swimming pool (free to campers). (Daily)

## Special Event

**Sage and Sun Festival.** *Ephrata. Phone 509/754-4656.* Parade, sports events, arts and crafts shows. Second weekend in June.

## Limited-Service Hotel

**★ BEST WESTERN RAMA INN.** *1818 Basin St SW, Ephrata (98823). Phone 509/754-7111; toll-free 888/726-2466; fax 509/754-7171. www.bestwestern.com.* 45 rooms. Complimentary continental breakfast. Check-in 3 pm, check-out noon. High-speed Internet access. Indoor pool, whirlpool. **$**

## Specialty Lodging

**IVY CHAPEL INN BED & BREAKFAST.** *164 D St SW, Ephrata (98823). Phone 509/754-0629.* Built in 1948; was first Presbyterian church in Ephrata. 6 rooms, 3 story. Children over 12 years only. Complimentary full breakfast. Check-in 3 pm, check-out 11 am. **$**

# Everett (B-3)

*See also Marysville, Oak Harbor, Port Townsend, Seattle, Snohomish*

**Founded** 1890
**Population** 91,488
**Elevation** 157 ft
**Area Code** 425
**Information** Everett/Snohomish County Convention and Visitor Bureau, 2000 Hewitt Ave, Suite 205; phone 425/257-3222
**Web Site** www.everettchamber.com

This lumber, aircraft, electronics, and shipping city is on a sheltered harbor where the Snohomish River empties into Port Gardner Bay. To the east is the snowcapped Cascade Mountain Range; to the west are the Olympic Mountains. Developed by Eastern industrial and railroad money, Everett serves as a major commercial fishing port and receives and dispatches a steady stream of cargo vessels. The Boeing 747 and 767 are assembled here.

Along the waterfront is an 1890s-style seaside marketplace, the Everett Marina Village.

## What to See and Do

**Boat tours.** *Everett. Phone 425/257-3222.* For information on companies offering sightseeing, dinner, and whale-watching cruises, contact the Convention and Visitors Bureau.

**Boeing Everett Facility.** *3003 W Casino, Everett (98203). I-5 exit 189, approximately 3 miles W on Hwy 526. ; toll-free 800/464-1476.* Audiovisual presentation;

bus tour of assembly facility. Gift shop. No children under 10. (Mon-Fri; closed holidays) **$$$**

**Harbour Pointe Golf Club.** *11817 Harbour Pointe Blvd, Mukilteo (98275). Phone toll-free 800/233-3128. www.harbourpointegolf.com.* Harbour Pointe is really a tale of two nines, with the front a very flat, target-oriented layout and the back lined with tall evergreen trees and narrower fairways, which force players to work their way around each hole for the best approach to each green. Opened in 1991, Harbour Pointe has won awards as one of America's best public courses. It's better to play on a day when it hasn't rained for at least a week; otherwise, the course plays considerably longer due to the moisture. **$$$$**

**Mukilteo.** *Phone 425/347-1456.* This town, just west of Everett, is the major ferry point from the mainland to the southern tip of Whidbey Island. Its name means "good camping ground." A lighthouse built in 1905 is open for tours (Sat).

**Recreation areas.** *802 Mukilteo Blvd, Everett (98203). Phone 425/257-8300.* There are many recreation areas in and near the city that offer swimming (fee), fishing, boat launch; hiking, picnicking, camping, nature centers, tennis, golf (fee). **FREE**

**Totem Pole.** *Rucker Ave and 44th St, Everett.* 80 feet high, carved by Tulalip Chief William Shelton.

## Special Events

**Auto racing.** *Evergreen Speedway, 17901 Hwy 2, Monroe (98272). 15 miles SE via Hwy 2, exit 194 off I-5. Phone 360/805-6100.* NASCAR super and mini stocks, SVRA modifieds, hobby stocks, figure eights; demolition events. Apr-Sept.

**Salty Sea Days.** *2520 Colby Ave, Everett (98201).* Festival, parade, displays, food and carnival. Early June.

## Limited-Service Hotel

**★ BEST WESTERN CASCADIA INN.** *2800 Pacific Ave, Everett (98201). Phone 425/258-4141; toll-free 800/822-5876; fax 425/258-4755. www.bestwestern.com.* 134 rooms, 3 story. Pets accepted, some restrictions. Complimentary continental breakfast. Check-in 3 pm, check-out noon. Outdoor pool, whirlpool. **$**

# Forks (B-1)

*See also Olympic National Park*

**Population** 3,120
**Elevation** 375 ft
**Area Code** 360
**Zip** 98331
**Information** Chamber of Commerce, 1411 S Forks Ave; phone 360/374-2531 or toll-free 800/443-6757

The major town in the northwest section of the Olympic Peninsula, Forks takes its name from the nearby junction of the Soleduck, Bogachiel, and Dickey rivers. Timber processing is a major industry. A Ranger District office of the Olympic National Forest is located here.

## What to See and Do

**Bogachiel State Park.** *185983 Hwy 101, Forks (98331). 6 miles S on Hwy 101. Phone 360/374-6356.* Approximately 120 acres, on the shores of the Bogachiel River with swimming, fishing; hiking, camping (hook-ups, dump station). (Daily)

## Limited-Service Hotel

**★ FORKS MOTEL.** *351 S Forks Ave, Forks (98331). Phone 360/374-6243; toll-free 800/544-3416; fax 360/374-6760. www.forksmotel.com.* 73 rooms, 2 story. Check-out 11 am. Outdoor pool, children's pool. **$**

# Goldendale (D-4)

**Settled** 1863
**Population** 3,760
**Elevation** 1,633 ft
**Area Code** 509
**Zip** 98620
**Information** Greater Goldendale Area Chamber of Commerce, Box 524; phone 509/773-3400

Agriculture, aluminum smelting, and an assortment of small industries comprise the major business of Goldendale, named for John J. Golden, a pioneer settler.

## What to See and Do

**Brooks Memorial State Park.** *2465 Hwy 97, Goldendale (98620). 12 miles N on Hwy 97. Phone 509/773-4611.*

More than 700 acres. Fishing; hiking, picnicking, camping (hook-ups).

**Goldendale Observatory.** *1602 Observatory Dr, Goldendale (98620). Phone 509/773-3141.* Nation's largest amateur-built Cassegrain telescope for public use; tours, demonstrations, displays, audiovisual programs. (Apr-Sept: Wed-Sun; rest of year: schedule varies) **FREE**

**Klickitat County Historical Museum.** *127 W Broadway, Goldendale (98620). Phone 509/773-4303.* Furniture and exhibits from early days of Klickitat County, in 20-room restored mansion. Gift shop. (Apr-Oct: daily; rest of year: by appointment) **$$**

**Maryhill Museum of Art.** *35 Maryhill Museum Dr, Goldendale (98620). 11 miles S on Hwy 97, then 2 miles W on Hwy 14. Phone 509/773-3733.* Constructed by Samuel Hill. Permanent exhibits include a Rodin sculpture, European and American paintings, Russian icons, chess collection, French fashion mannequins, Native American baskets and artifacts. (Mid-Mar-mid-Nov, daily) **$$**

**Mount Adams Recreation Area.** *Goldendale. NW of town.* Lakes, streams, forests; excellent fishing, bird hunting.

## Special Event

**Klickitat County Fair and Rodeo.** *228 W Main St, Goldendale (98620). Phone 509/773-3900.* Fourth weekend in Aug.

## Limited-Service Hotel

**★★ QUALITY INN.** *808 E Simcoe Dr, Goldendale (98620). Phone 509/773-5881; toll-free 800/358-5881. www.choicehotels.com.* 48 rooms, 2 story. Check-out 11 am. Restaurant, bar. Outdoor pool. Airport transportation available. **$**

# Hoquiam (C-1)

*See also Aberdeen, Ocean Shores, Westport*

**Settled** 1859
**Population** 9,097
**Elevation** 10 ft
**Area Code** 360
**Zip** 98550
**Information** Grays Harbor Chamber of Commerce, 506 Duffy St, Aberdeen 98520; phone 360/532-1924 or toll-free 800/321-1924
**Web Site** www.graysharbor.org

Twin city to Aberdeen (see), Hoquiam is the senior community of the two and the pioneer town of the Grays Harbor region. A deepwater port 12 miles from the Pacific, it docks cargo and fishing vessels, manufactures wood products and machine tools, and cans the harvest of the sea.

## What to See and Do

**Hoquiam's "Castle".** *515 Chenault Ave, Hoquiam (98550). Phone 360/533-2005.* A 20-room mansion built in 1897 by lumber tycoon Robert Lytle; antique furnishings; oak-columned entry hall; authentic Victorian atmosphere. (Summer, Mon-Fri) **$**

**Polson Park and Museum.** *1611 Riverside Ave, Hoquiam (98550). Phone 360/533-5862.* (1924) Restored 26-room mansion; antiques; rose garden. (June-Aug: Wed-Sun; rest of year: weekends)

# Issaquah (B-3)

*See also Bellevue, North Bend, Seattle*

**Population** 11,212
**Elevation** 100 ft
**Area Code** 425
**Zip** 98027
**Information** Chamber of Commerce, 155 NW Gilman Blvd; phone 425/392-7024
**Web Site** www.issaquahchamber.com

Historic buildings and homes of Issaquah have been renovated and moved to a 7-acre farm site, called Gilman Village, where they now serve as specialty shops.

## What to See and Do

**Boehm's Chocolate Factory.** *255 NE Gilman Blvd, Issaquah (98027). Phone 425/392-6652.* The home of Boehm's Candies was built here in 1956 by Julius Boehm. The candy-making process and the Edelweiss Chalet, filled with artifacts, paintings, and statues, can be toured. The Luis Trenker Kirch'l, a replica of a 12th-century Swiss chapel, was also built by Boehm. Tours by appointment (July-Aug). **FREE**

**Lake Sammamish State Park.** *20606 SE 56th St, Issaquah (98027). 2 miles W off I-90. Phone 425/455-*

*7010.* Approximately 430 acres. Swimming, fishing, boating (launch); hiking, picnicking. Standard fees.

## Special Event

**Salmon Days Festival.** *155 NW Gilman Blvd, Issaquah (98027). Phone 425/392-0661.* Welcomes return of Northwest salmon to original home. First full weekend in Oct.

## Limited-Service Hotel

**★ ★ HOLIDAY INN.** *1801 12th Ave NW, Issaquah (98027). Phone 425/392-6421; toll-free 800/465-4329; fax 425/391-4650. www.holiday-inn.com/sea-issaquah.* 100 rooms, 2 story. Check-in 2 pm, check-out noon. Restaurant, bar. Outdoor pool, whirlpool. **$**

# Kelso (D-2)

*See also Bellevue, North Bend, Seattle*

**Founded** 1847
**Population** 11,895
**Elevation** 40 ft
**Information** Chamber of Commerce, 105 Minor Rd; phone 360/577-8058
**Web Site** www.kelso.gov

Kelso straddles the Cowlitz River and is an artery for the lumber industry. The river also yields a variety of fish from giant salmon to tiny smelt.

## What to See and Do

**Cowlitz County Historical Museum.** *405 Allen St, Kelso (98626). Phone 360/577-3119.* Exhibits depict history of the area. (Tues-Sun; closed holidays) **DONATION**

**Seaquest State Park.** *3030 Spirit Lake Hwy, Kelso (98611). 10 miles N on I-5 exit 49, then 5 miles E on Hwy 504. Phone 360/274-8633.* Approximately 300 acres. Hiking, picnicking, camping (hookups). Nearby is Silver Lake with fishing (about 10,000 fish are caught here every summer).

**Volcano Information Center.** *105 Minor Rd, Kelso (98626). Off I-5 exit 39. Phone 360/577-8058.* Pictorial and scientific exhibits on the eruption of Mount St. Helens; 3-D narrated topographical display of the devastation. Also visitor information on surrounding area. (Daily) **FREE**

## Limited-Service Hotels

**★ COMFORT INN.** *440 Three Rivers Dr, Kelso (98626). Phone 360/425-4600; toll-free 800/252-7466; fax 360/423-0762. www.choicehotels.com.* 57 rooms, 2 story. Complimentary continental breakfast. Check-out noon. Indoor pool, whirlpool. **$**

**★ MT. ST. HELENS MOTEL.** *1340 Mount Saint Helens Way, Castle Rock (98611). Phone 360/274-7721; fax 360/274-7721. www.mtsthelensmotel.com.* 32 rooms, 2 story. Check-in 3 pm, check-out 11 am. **$**

**★ ★ RED LION.** *510 Kelso Dr, Kelso (98626). Phone 360/636-4400; toll-free 800/733-5466; fax 360/425-3296. www.redlion.com.* 162 rooms, 2 story. Pets accepted; fee. Check-out noon. Restaurant, bar. Fitness room. Outdoor pool, children's pool, whirlpool. **$**

# Kennewick (D-5)

*See also Pasco, Richland*

**Founded** 1892
**Population** 54,693
**Elevation** 380 ft
**Area Code** 509
**Information** Chamber of Commerce, 3180 W Clearwater Ave, Suite F, 99336; phone 509/736-0510
**Web Site** www.ci.kennewick.wa.us/home/

Huge hydroelectric dams harnessing the lower stem of the Columbia River have brought economic vitality to the "Tri-Cities" of Kennewick, Pasco, and Richland (see both). On the south bank of Lake Wallula and near the confluence of the Columbia, Snake, and Yakima rivers, Kennewick has chemical and agricultural processing plants. Irrigation of the 20,500-acre Kennewick Highland project has converted sagebrush into thousands of farms, producing three cuttings of alfalfa annually, plus corn and beans. Appropriately enough, this city with the Native American name meaning "winter paradise" enjoys a brief winter and is the center of the state's grape industry.

## What to See and Do

**Columbia Park.** *6515 Columbia Dr Trail, Kennewick (99336). 2 1/2 miles W on Hwy 12 on Lake Wallula, formed by McNary Dam. Phone 509/585-4529.* Approximately 300 acres. Waterskiing, fishing, boating (ramps)l 18-hole golf, driving range (fee), tennis, picnicking, camping (hookups; fee). Park open all year (daily). **FREE**

**Two Rivers Park.** *213316 E Finley Rd, Kennewick (99337). 5 miles E, off Finley Rd. Phone 509/783-3118.* Picnicking; boating (ramp), swimming, fishing. Park open all year (daily). **FREE**

## Limited-Service Hotel

**★ QUALITY INN KENNEWICK.** *7901 W Quinault Ave, Kennewick (99336). Phone 509/735-6100; toll-free 800/205-6938; fax 509/735-3084. www.choicehotels.com.* 125 rooms, 4 story. Complimentary continental breakfast. Check-in 3 pm, check-out noon. High-speed Internet access. Fitness room. Indoor pool, outdoor pool, whirlpool. Business center. **$**

## Full-Service Hotel

**★ ★ RED LION.** *1101 N Columbia Center Blvd, Kennewick (99336). Phone 509/783-0611; toll-free 800/733-5466; fax 509/735-3087. www.redlion.com.* 162 rooms, 2 story. Pets accepted. Check-in 3 pm, check-out noon. High-speed Internet access, wireless Internet access. Restaurant, bar. Fitness room. Outdoor pool. Airport transportation available. **$**

# Kirkland (B-2)

*See also Pasco, Richland*

## Full-Service Hotel

**★ ★ ★ THE WOODMARK HOTEL ON LAKE WASHINGTON.** *1200 Carillon Point, Kirkland (98033). Phone 425/822-3700; fax 425/822-3699.* With the blinking lights of Seattles skyline only 7 miles in the distance, the Woodmark Hotel gently rests on the shores of scenic Lake Washington. Convenient to Bellevue and Redmond, the Woodmark is an ideal stop for travelers to the pristine Pacific Northwest. Set within a complex of specialty shops, restaurants, and marina, the hotel is a true getaway enhanced by a marvelous destination spa. Characterized by the serenity and casual elegance of the region, the Woodmark instills a sense of belonging in its guests. From the friendly staff to the cozy furnishings, a relaxed, residential style pervades the hotel. The 100 rooms are luxurious without being pretentious and feature lake, marina, or creek views. The regions fresh, delicious cuisine is the highlight at Waters Lakeside Bistro, and the Library Bar serves a wonderful afternoon tea, complete with a special menu and china service for children. 100 rooms, 4 story. Pets accepted. Check-in 4 pm, check-out noon. Restaurant, bar. Fitness room, spa. Business center. **$$**

## Restaurants

**★ ★ ★ CAFE JUANITA.** *9702 120th Pl NE, Kirkland (98034). Phone 425/823-1505; fax 425/823-8500. www.cafejuanita.com.* The dining destination for the Puget Sound region since 1979, Cafe Juanita serves some of the best northern Italian food around. The wine list complements the café's chalkboard menu of well-executed cuisine, much of which is gathered from the restaurant's lush, peaceful herb garden. Northern Italian menu. Dinner. Closed Mon. Bar. Children's menu. Business casual attire. Valet parking. **$$$**

**★ ★ THIRD FLOOR FISH CAFE.** *205 Lake St S, Kirkland (98033). Phone 425/822-3553; fax 425/827-1364. www.fishcafe.com.* Breathtaking views of Lake Washington and the Seattle skyline are found at this third floor restaurant, where fresh seafood like crab, calamari, clams, and tuna are beautifully prepared and presented in an elegant atmosphere. Seafood menu. Dinner. Bar. Children's menu. Casual attire. Reservations recommended. Valet parking. **$$$**

# La Conner (A-2)

*See also Anacortes, Mount Vernon*

**Population** 761
**Area Code** 360
**Zip** 98257
**Information** Chamber of Commerce, PO Box 1610; phone 360/466-4778 or toll-free 888/642-9284
**Web Site** www.laconnerchamber.com

A picturesque town along the Swinomish Channel, La Conner is a popular destination for weekend travelers. Many of the town's homes and businesses are housed in the clapboarded structures built by its founders around the turn of the century. Numerous boutiques, galleries, and antique shops, some containing the works of local artists and craftspeople, line its streets.

## What to See and Do

**Museum of Northwest Art.** *121 S 1st St, La Conner (98257). Phone 360/466-4446. www.museumofnwart.org.* Exhibits artist of the "Northwest School." (Tues-Sun; closed Jan 1, Thanksgiving, Dec 25) **$$**

**Skagit County Historical Museum.** *501 S 4th St, La Conner (98257). Phone 360/466-3365.* Exhibits depicting history of Skagit County. (Tues-Sun afternoons; closed Jan 1, Thanksgiving, Dec 25) **$**

## Specialty Lodgings

**THE HERON.** *117 Maple Ave, La Conner (98257). Phone 360/466-4626; toll-free 877/883-8899; fax 360/466-3254. www.theheron.com.* Country-style inn. 12 rooms, 3 story. Children over 12 years only. Complimentary full breakfast. Check-in 3-6 pm, check-out 11 am. Spa. **$**

**LACONNER COUNTRY INN.** *107 S Second St, La Conner (98257). Phone 360/466-3101; toll-free 888/466-4113; fax 360/466-0199. www.laconnerlodging.com.* 28 rooms, 2 story. Pets accepted; fee. Complimentary continental breakfast. Check-in 3 pm, check-out noon. High-speed Internet access. Restaurant, bar. **$**

# Langley (B-2)

## Restaurant

**★ ★ CAFE LANGLEY.** *113 1st St, Langley (98260). Phone 360/221-3090; fax 360/221-8542. www.langley-wa.com/cl.* Mediterranean menu. Lunch, dinner. Daily. Bar. Children's menu. Casual attire. Reservations recommended. **$$**

# Leavenworth (B-4)

*See also Cashmere, Wenatchee*

**Founded** 1892
**Population** 2,074
**Elevation** 1,165 ft
**Area Code** 509
**Zip** 98826
**Information** Chamber of Commerce, PO Box 327; phone 509/548-5807
**Web Site** www.leavenworth.org

Surrounded by the Cascade Mountains, Leavenworth has an old-world charm enhanced by authentic Bavarian architecture. Less than three hours from Seattle, the village is a favorite stop for people who enjoy river rafting, hiking, bicycling, fishing, golf, and skiing. Two Ranger District offices of the Wenatchee National Forest are located here.

## What to See and Do

**Leavenworth Nutcracker Museum.** *735 Front St, Leavenworth (98826). Phone 509/548-4573; toll-free 800/892-3989. www.nutcrackermuseum.com.* Spanning the wall and floor space of a beautiful Bavarian-style house is the Nutcracker Museum, born out of Arlene Wagner's love of the Tchaikovsky ballet of the same name. Wagner now has more than 4,000 nutcrackers in her museum, having traveled the world over in search of the most exotic specimens she and her husband could find. Some of the examples housed in the museum date as far back as the 15th century and detail the history of these very functional, yet ornamental items. (May-Oct: daily 2-5 pm; rest of year: weekends only; also by appointment) **$**

**National Fish Hatchery.** *Leavenworth. 3 1/2 miles S on Icicle Creek Rd. Phone 509/548-7641.* Raises chinook salmon and steelhead. Educational exhibits. Fishing, boat ramp; hiking, interpretive trails, picnicking, cross-country skiing. (Daily; closed Dec 25)

**Stevens Pass Ski Area.** *Summit Stevens Pass, Hwy 2, Leavenworth (98288). 36 miles NW on Hwy 2. Phone 206/812-4510. www.stevenspass.com.* Quad, four triple, six double chairlifts; patrol, school, rentals; snowboarding; tubing; restaurant, cafeteria, bar; nursery. (Late Nov-mid-Apr, daily) **$$$$**

## Special Events

**Autumn Leaf Festival.** *Front and 8th sts, Leavenworth (98826). Phone 509/548-6348.* Late Sept and Early Oct.

**Bavarian Ice Fest.** *Leavenworth. Phone 509/548-5807.* Snowshoe races, dogsled rides. Fireworks. Mid-Jan.

**Bavarian Maifest.** *Leavenworth. Phone 509/548-5807.* Bandstand music, grand march, Maypole dance, art, chuck wagon breakfast. Early May.

**Chamber Music Festival.** *Icicle Creek Music Center, 9286 Icicle Rd, Leavenworth (98826). Phone 877/265-6026. www.iciclearts.org.* Professional chamber music festival featuring classical, jazz, bluegrass. Kayak and raft races. Tours, booths, and more. May.

**Christmas Lighting.** *Leavenworth. Phone 509/548-5807.* Sleigh rides, sledding. Early and mid-Dec.

## Limited-Service Hotels

★★ **BEST WESTERN ICICLE INN.** *505 Hwy 2, Leavenworth (98826). Phone 509/548-7000; toll-free 800/558-2438; fax 509/548-7050. www.bestwestern.com.* Set right on the main highway through town, this hotel has been a landmark property in Leavenworth. As expected in a city that celebrates its German heritage, a Bavarian theme dominates the hotel, especially the lobby. Next door is the Icicle Junction Family Fun Center, with miniature golf, bumper boats, arcade, and movie theater, making the Icicle Inn a great choice for families. 93 rooms, 3 story. Pets accepted, some restrictions; fee. Complimentary full breakfast. Check-in 3 pm, check-out 11 am. High-speed Internet access. Restaurant. Fitness room, spa. Outdoor pool, whirlpool. **$**

★ **ENZIAN INN.** *590 Hwy 2, Leavenworth (98826). Phone 509/548-5269; toll-free 800/223-8511; fax 509/548-9319. www.enzianinn.com.* 104 rooms, 4 story. Complimentary full breakfast. Check-in 3 pm, check-out 11 am. Fitness room. Indoor pool, outdoor pool, whirlpool. **$**

## Full-Service Inn

★★★ **MOUNTAIN HOME LODGE.** *8201 Mountain Home Rd, Leavenworth (98826). Phone 509/548-7077; toll-free 800/414-2378; fax 509/548-5008. www.mthome.com.* In a picturesque, serene setting, this great escape is a wonderful mix of luxury, comfort, and style. Some guests come for relaxation and seclusion while others enjoy the activities. 12 rooms, 4 story. No children allowed. Complimentary full breakfast. Check-in 3 pm, check-out noon. Restaurant. Outdoor pool, whirlpool. Tennis. **$$$**

## Specialty Lodgings

**ALL SEASONS RIVER INN.** *8751 Icicle Rd, Leavenworth (98826). Phone 509/548-1425; toll-free 800/254-0555. www.allseasonsriverinn.com.* Located 80 feet above the Wenatchee River, this serene bed-and-breakfast feels more like a private home than a hotel. Guest rooms lack TVs and telephones, but lovely water views and Jacuzzi tubs provide their own form of entertainment. Passionate about antiques, the innkeeper has meticulously furnished each room with unique pieces. The inn makes bicycles available for the 1/2-mile ride to downtown Leavenworth. 6 rooms, 2 story. No children allowed. Complimentary full breakfast. Check-in 3 pm, check-out 11 am. **$$**

**BOSCH GARTEN.** *9846 Dye Rd, Leavenworth (98826). Phone 509/548-6900; toll-free 800/535-0069. www.boschgarten.com.* 3 rooms. Children over 12 years only. Complimentary full breakfast. Check-in 3 pm, check-out 11 am. Whirlpool. **$**

**RUN OF THE RIVER BED & BREAKFAST.** *9308 E Leavenworth Rd, Leavenworth (98826). Phone 509/548-7171; toll-free 800/288-6491; fax 509/548-7547. www.runoftheriver.com.* This small, quiet inn on the Icicle River is tucked among the towering Cascade Mountains. Visitors will enjoy hiking, walking, or mountain biking through forest trails. 6 rooms. No children allowed. Complimentary full breakfast. Check-in 3 pm, check-out 11 am. Whirlpool. **$$**

# Long Beach (D-1)

**Population** 1,283
**Elevation** 10 ft
**Area Code** 360
**Zip** 98631
**Information** Peninsula Visitors Bureau, PO Box 562; phone 360/642-2400 or toll-free 800/451-2542
**Web Site** www.funbeach.com

This seashore resort is on one of the longest hard-sand beaches in the world, stretching 28 miles along a narrow peninsula just north of where the Columbia River empties into the Pacific Ocean.

## What to See and Do

**Cape Disappointment.** *Ilwaco. 2 miles S on Hwy 100. Phone 360/642-3078; toll-free 800/452-5687. www.parks.wa.gov.* (1864) More than 1,880 acres overlooking mouth of Columbia River. Strategic base from pioneer days through World War II. The Lewis and Clark Interpretive Center, built near an artillery bunker on a hillside, has exhibits depicting the historic expedition and the contributions made by Native American tribes; also multimedia presentations (daily). Fishing; hiking, picnicking, camping (hookups). (Daily)

**Fort Columbia.** *Long Beach. 11 miles SE on Hwy 101. Phone 360/902-8844.* More than 580 acres. Site of former coastal artillery corps post with Endicott-period fortifications that protected mouth of Columbia River. Interpretive center in former barracks (Apr-Sept, daily) Also here is Columbia House, a former commander's residence. Hiking, picnicking. Grounds (daily).

**Oysterville.** *Hwy 101 and 103, Seaview. 15 miles N via Sandridge Rd. Phone toll-free 800/451-2542.* Community founded in 1854; original settlers were lured by oysters found on tidal flats of Willapa Bay. Many original homes remain, as well as church and schoolhouse.

**Seascape scenic drive.** *Long Beach. 14 miles N from Seaview on Hwy 103, through Long Beach to Ocean Park.*

## Limited-Service Hotels

**★ CHAUTAUQUA LODGE.** *304 14th St NW, Long Beach (98631). Phone 360/642-4401; toll-free 800/869-8401; fax 360/642-2340. www.chautauqualodge.com.* 180 rooms, 3 story. Pets accepted; fee. Check-out 11 am. Bar. Indoor pool, whirlpool. **$**

**★ ★ EDGEWATER INN.** *409 10th St, Long Beach (98631). Phone 360/642-2311; toll-free 800/561-2456; fax 360/642-8018.* 84 rooms, 3 story. Pets accepted, some restrictions; fee. Check-out 11 am. Restaurant, bar. **$**

**★ SUPER 8.** *500 Ocean Beach Blvd, Long Beach (98631). Phone 360/642-8988; toll-free 888/478-3297; fax 360/642-8986. www.super8.com.* 50 rooms, 3 story. Complimentary continental breakfast. Check-out noon. **$**

## Specialty Lodgings

**BOREAS BED & BREAKFAST.** *607 Ocean Beach Blvd N, Long Beach (98631). Phone 360/642-8069; toll-free 888/642-8069. www.boreasinn.com.* This scenic oceanfront bed-and-breakfast comes well equipped with many personal touches. Each of the suites is designed to reflect the style and fun-loving personalities at the inn. 5 rooms, 2 story. Complimentary full breakfast. Check-in 4 pm, check-out 11 am. **$**

**SCANDINAVIAN GARDENS INN BED & BREAKFAST.** *1610 California Ave SW, Long Beach (98631). Phone 360/642-8877; toll-free 800/988-9277; fax 360/642-8764. www.rendezvousplace.com.* Each room decorated to theme of different Scandinavian country. 5 rooms, 2 story. Children over 6 years only. Complimentary full breakfast. Check-in 3-6 pm. Check-out 11 am. **$**

# Longview (D-2)

*See also Chehalis, Kelso*

**Settled** 1923
**Population** 34,660
**Elevation** 21 ft
**Area Code** 360
**Zip** 98632
**Information** Longview Area Chamber of Commerce, 1563 Olympia Way; phone 360/423-8400
**Web Site** www.ci.longview.wa.us

Situated between Seattle, Washington and Portland, Oregon, Longview is the home of one of the largest forest products mills in the world. Factories produce pulp, fine and kraft papers, paper boxes, plywood, glassine, pig aluminum, concrete paint, caustic soda, and chlorine. The first planned city in the West, Longview is a deepwater port fed by six railroad systems and several highways. Fishing for steelhead, smelt, and salmon is excellent.

## What to See and Do

**Lake Sacajawea Park.** *Longview. Between Kessler and Nichols blvds, Hwy 30 and Hwy 432.* A 120-acre park with 60-acre lake; picnic areas, playgrounds; gardens, jogging, bike and fitness trail. Fishing, wildlife refuge. (Daily)

**Monticello Convention Site.** *Olympia Way and Maple St, Longview.* Here residents of Washington met to petition the federal government to separate Washington Territory from Oregon.

**Mount St. Helens Visitor Center.** *Castle Rock. 10 miles N on I-5 to Castle Rock, then 5 miles E on Hwy 504.*

## Special Events

**Cowlitz County Fair.** *Cowlitz County Expo Center, 430 Washington St, Longview (98632). Phone 360/577-3121.* Exhibits, entertainment, carnival, pro rodeo. Early Aug.

**Rain Fest.** *Cowlitz County Expo Center, 430 Washington St, Longview (98632). Phone 360/577-3121.* Wine tasting, exhibit booths, music. Early Oct.

# Marysville (B-3)

*See also Everett, Snohomish*

**Settled** 1872
**Population** 25,315
**Area Code** 360
**Information** The Greater Marysville Tulalip Chamber of Commerce, 4411 76th St NE, 98270; phone 360/659-7700

Natural surroundings, including lakes, rivers, and wooded countryside, make Marysville a popular spot for outdoor recreation.

## What to See and Do

**Tulalip Casino.** *6410 33rd Ave NE, Marysville (98271). Phone 360/651-1111. www.tulalipcasino.com.* Just off I-5 about 35 miles north of downtown Seattle is the Tulalip Casino, with an array of Vegas-style tables, a bingo parlor, and more than 1,000 gaming machines. Hunger is sated at three eateries (a steak and seafood restaurant and two delis), and the waters of Puget Sound—just a stones throw away—beckon non-gamblers outdoors. (Mon-Tues 10-6 am, Wed-Sun 24 hours)

**Tulalip Reservation.** *6700 Totem Beach Rd, Marysville (98271). 6 miles NW via Hwy 506. Phone 360/651-4000.* Within the community are St. Anne's Church (1904) with old mission bell, the Native American Shaker Church, and tribal community center.

**Wenberg State Park.** *15430 Lake Goodwin Rd, Stanwood (98292). N via I-5 exit 206, 2 miles W to Lakewood Rd, then 3 miles N to E Lake Goodwin Rd, then S. Phone 360/652-7417.* A 46-acre park. Swimming, fishing, boating (launch); picnicking, concession (summer), camping (some hook-ups).

## Special Events

**Home-Grown Festival.** *3rd and State sts, Marysville. Phone 360/659-4997.* Open-air market, arts and crafts booths, street fair. Early Aug.

**Merrysville for the Holidays.** *Marysville. Phone 360/651-5085.* Water-tower lighting, lighted holiday parade. Early Dec.

**Strawberry Festival.** *1624 Grove St, Marysville (98270). Phone 360/659-7664.* Parade, art show, races. Third week in June.

## Limited-Service Hotel

**★★ BEST WESTERN TULALIP INN.** *3228 Marine Dr NE, Marysville (98271). Phone 360/659-4488; toll-free 800/780-7234; fax 360/659-5688. www.bestwestern.com.* 69 rooms. Check-in 3 pm, check-out noon. Restaurant, bar. Indoor pool, whirlpool. **$**

## Restaurant

**★ VILLAGE.** *220 Ash Ave, Marysville (98270). Phone 360/659-2305; fax 360/659-6661.* American menu. Breakfast, lunch, dinner. Closed Dec 25. Bar. Children's menu. Casual attire. **$**

# Moses Lake (C-5)

*See also Ephrata, Othello, Ritzville*

**Settled** 1910
**Population** 14,953
**Elevation** 1,060 ft
**Area Code** 509
**Zip** 98837
**Information** Chamber of Commerce, 324 S Pioneer Way; phone 509/765-7888
**Web Site** www.moses-lake.com

Because of the water impounded by Grand Coulee Dam, the recreational and agricultural resources of this area have blossomed. Swimming, fishing, and hunting abound within a 25-mile radius. The city is also an important shipping and processing point for agricultural products.

## What to See and Do

**Moses Lake Museum and Art Center.** *122 W 3rd Ave, Moses Lake (98837). Phone 509/766-9395.* Native American artifacts; regional artwork; local history. (Tues-Sat afternoons; closed holidays) **FREE**

**Moses Lake Recreation Area.** *401 S Balsam St, Moses Lake (98837). Phone 509/766-9240.* South and west of city. **FREE** Includes

**Cascade Park.** *Valley Rd and Cascade Valley, Moses Lake (98837). Phone 509/766-9240.* Swimming, boating (launch), fishing, waterskiing; camping (fee). Park (May-Sept, daily).

**Moses Lake.** *401 S Balsam St, Moses Lake (98837). NW off I-90, Hwy 17. Phone 509/766-9240.* 18 miles long.

**Moses Lake State Park.** *111 W Shore, Moses Lake (98837). 2 miles W on I-90. Phone 509/766-9240.* A 78-acre park with swimming, fishing, boating (launch); picnicking. (Daily)

**Potholes Reservoir.** *Moses Lake. 14 miles SW off Hwy 17, I-90 on Hwy 170.* Formed by O'Sullivan Dam (10 miles S). Swimming, boating, waterskiing, fishing.

**Potholes State Park.** *Moses Lake. 14 miles SW on Hwy 17 to Hwy 170.* Approximately 2,500 acres. Water sports, fishing, boat launch; hiking, picnicking, camping (hook-ups).

## Special Events

**Grant County Fair.** *Fairgrounds, 3953 Airway Dr NE, Moses Lake (98837). Phone 509/765-3581.* Rodeo. Five days in mid-Aug.

**Spring Festival.** *Moses Lake. Phone 509/765-8248.* Memorial Day weekend.

## Limited-Service Hotels

**★ BEST VALUE INN.** *1214 S Pioneer Way, Moses Lake (98837). Phone 509/765-9173; toll-free 888/315-2378; fax 509/765-1137. www.bestvalueinn.com.* 20 rooms. Pets accepted, some restrictions. Check-out 11 am. Outdoor pool. **$**

**★ ★ BEST WESTERN HALLMARK INN & CONFERENCE CENTER.** *3000 Marina Dr, Moses Lake (98837). Phone 509/765-9211; toll-free 800/235-4255; fax 509/766-0493. www.hallmarkinns.com.* 161 rooms, 3 story. Pets accepted, some restrictions; fee. Check-in 3 pm, check-out noon. Restaurant, bar. Fitness room. Outdoor pool, whirlpool. Airport transportation available. **$**

**★ SHILO INN.** *1819 E Kittleson, Moses Lake (98837). Phone 509/765-9317; fax 509/765-5058. www.shiloinn.com.* 100 rooms, 2 story. Pets accepted, some restrictions; fee. Check-in 3 pm, check-out noon. Fitness room. Indoor pool, whirlpool. Airport transportation available. **$**

# Mount Rainier National Park (C-3)

*See also Ephrata, Othello, Ritzville*

**Web Site** www.nps.gov/mora/

Majestic Mount Rainier, towering 14,411 feet above sea level and 8,000 feet above the Cascade Range of western Washington, is one of America's outstanding tourist attractions. More than 2 million people visit this 378-square-mile park each year to picnic, hike, camp, climb mountains, or simply admire the spectacular scenery along the many miles of roadways.

The park's various "life zones," which change at different elevations, support a wide array of plant and animal life. Douglas fir, red cedar, and western hemlock, some rising 200 feet into the air, thrive in the old-growth forests. In the summer, the subalpine meadows come alive with brilliant, multicolored wildflowers. These areas are home to more than 130 species of birds and 50 species of mammals. Mountain goats, chipmunks, and marmots are favorites among visitors, but deer, elk, bears, mountain lions, and other animals can also be seen here.

Mount Rainier is the largest volcano in the Cascade Range, which extends from Mount Garibaldi in southwestern British Columbia to Lassen Peak in northern California. The eruption of Mount St. Helens in 1980 gives a clue to the violent history of these volcanoes. Eruptions occurred at Mount Rainier as recently as the mid-1800s. Even today, steam emissions often form caves in the summit ice cap and usually melt the snow along the rims of the twin craters.

A young volcano by geologic standards, Mount Rainier was once a fairly symmetrical mountain rising about 16,000 feet above sea level. But glaciers and further volcanic activity shaped the mountain into an irregular mass of rock. The sculpting action of the

ice gave each face of the mountain its own distinctive profile. The glaciation continues today, as Mount Rainier supports the largest glacier system in the contiguous United States , with 35 square miles of ice and 26 named glaciers.

Much of the park's beauty can be attributed to the glaciers, which at one time extended far beyond the park boundaries. The moving masses of ice carved deep valleys separated by high, sharp ridges or broad plateaus. From certain vantages, the valleys accentuate the mountain's height. The glaciers are the source of the many streams in the park, as well as several rivers in the Pacific Northwest. The meltwaters also nourish the various plants and animals throughout the region.

Winters at Mount Rainier are legendary. Moist air masses moving eastward across the Pacific Ocean are intercepted by the mountain. As a result, some areas on the mountain commonly receive 50 or more feet of snow each winter. At 5,400 feet in elevation, Paradise made history in 1971-1972, when it received 93 feet of snow, the heaviest snowfall ever recorded in this country; the three-story Paradise Inn is often buried up to its roof in snow. Because the mountain's summit is usually above the storm clouds, the snowfall there is not as great.

The park's transformation from winter wonderland to summer playground is almost magical. Beginning in June or July, the weather becomes warm and clear, although the mountain is occasionally shrouded in clouds. The snow at the lower elevations then disappears; meltwaters fill stream valleys and cascade over cliffs; wildflowers blanket the meadows; and visitors descend on the park for its many recreational activities.

There are several entrances to the park. The roads from the Nisqually entrance to Paradise and from the southeast boundary to Ohanapecosh are usually open year-round but may be closed temporarily during the winter. Following the first heavy snow, around November 1, all other roads are closed until May or June. The entrance fee is $10 per vehicle. For further information, contact Mount Rainier National Park, Tahoma Woods, Star Rte, Ashford 98304; phone 360/569-2211.

## What to See and Do

**Camping.** *Tahoma Woods, Ashford. Phone toll-free 800/365-2267.* Major campgrounds are located at Cougar Rock, Ohanapecosh, and White River, and have fireplaces, tables, water, and sanitary facilities. Smaller campgrounds are at Sunshine Point and Ipsut Creek. No hook-ups; dump stations at Cougar Rock and Ohanapecosh only. All areas closed during winter except Sunshine Point. **$$$$**

**Carbon River.** Located on the Pacific side of Mount Rainier, the Carbon River area receives the most rainfall and contains the most luxurious forests. In fact, much of the woodland here is considered temperate rainforest. The main road into the Carbon River and the northwestern corner of the park leads from Carbonado into Ipsut Creek, a seasonal ranger station and campground.

**Crystal Mountain Resort.** *33914 Crystal Mountain Blvd, Crystal Mountain (98022). E via Hwy 410, then 6 miles E, on NE boundary of Mount Rainier National Park, in Mount Baker-Snoqualmie National Forest. Phone 360/663-2265. www.crystalmt.com.* Located 75 miles south of Seattle in the shadows of Mount Rainier, Crystal Mountain is a ski resort with an impressive 3,100-foot vertical drop and equally impressive 340 inches of average annual snowfall. During the December-to-April ski season, ten lifts service 1,300 acres of skiable terrain on Silver King Mountain, a nice balance of beginner, intermediate, and advanced trails; there are an additional 1,000 acres of backcountry terrain for diehards. The place is known for its family-friendly perks, such as free children's passes with an adult purchase and a Kids Club that offers supervision, skiing classes, and lunch while parents enjoy the slopes. The resort also encompasses several hotels (ranging from a basic room to a slope-side honeymoon cabin) and restaurants, as well as a rental shop, skiing and snowboarding school, and a day spa.

**Fishing.** No license required. Fishing season is open in lakes and ponds late April-October, in rivers and streams late May-November. Heavy snowfall restricts access to all water November-May. Most lakes are usually not ice-free until early July; ice-fishing not permitted. Specific regulations and details on special closure areas are available at ranger stations.

**Hiking.** More than 250 miles of trails wind throughout the park, offering unspoiled views of Mount Rainier, glaciers, meadows, lakes, waterfalls, and deep valleys; many trails converge at Paradise and Sunrise; trails vary in degree of difficulty. The **Wonderland Trail,** a 93-mile trail that circles the mountain, is linked with several other trails in the park. A *Pictorial Map* (1986) of the park's topography and *50 Hikes in Mount Rainier National Park,* an illustrated book with maps and hiking details, are available for purchase. Hiking information centers (summer, daily) are located at Longmire and White River. Permit is required year-round for overnight backpacking; available at ranger stations and visitor centers (fee).

**Interpretive programs and walks.** Programs, including nature walks and evening slide shows, are offered at several locations. Schedules are posted in visitor centers and at other locations. (Late June-Labor Day)

**Longmire.** *Near the Nisqually entrance, in SW corner of park.* Longmire is often the first stop for visitors in this area of the park. Visitor center; lodging; cafe, limited groceries. Facilities usually open year-round.

**Mountain climbing-Mount Rainier.** *Phone 360/569-2211. www.nps.gov/mora.* The park has many opportunities for climbers; one of the most popular climbs is the two-day trek to the summit of Mount Rainier. The guide service at Paradise conducts various programs for new and experienced climbers. Climbs should be attempted only by persons who are in good physical condition and have the proper equipment; deep crevasses and unstable ridges of lava are dangerous. All climbers must register with a park ranger (fee).

**Ohanapecosh.** *SE corner of park. Phone 360/569-2211.* A preserve of rushing waters and dense old growth forest. Some of the largest trees in the park—many over 1,000 years old—are here. The Grove of the Patriarchs, a cluster of massive conifers on an island in the Ohanapecosh River, is reached by bridge along a popular trail that starts near the Steven's Canyon Entrance Station. At the Ohanapecosh Visitor Center, exhibits tell the story of the lowland forest ecosystem, where Douglas fir, western hemlock, and red cedar trees reign supreme.

**Paradise.** *Accessible from Nisqually entrance at SW corner of park, and from Stevens Canyon entrance at SE corner of park (summer only). Phone 360/569-2211.* This is the most visited area of the park, featuring subalpine meadows covered with wildflowers, and hiking trails that provide views of Nisqually, Paradise, and Stevens glaciers. Visitor center with slide programs and films (May-mid-Oct: daily; rest of year: weekends only); lodging (see LIMITED-SERVICE HOTELS); café (summer, daily); snack bar (summer, daily; winter, weekends and holidays only). The nearby Narada Falls drop 168 feet to Paradise River Canyon; viewpoints along stairway.

**Paradise area.** *Phone 360/569-2211.* Cross-country skiing is popular here; equipment rentals and lessons available at Longmire. For further information contact park headquarters.

**Sunrise.** On northeast side of mountain; accessible only July-mid-September. This is the highest point reached by a paved road within Washington (6,400 feet). The drive to Sunrise is worth the time; the crowds are smaller, and this area offers spectacular views of the mountain and Emmons Glacier, the largest in the United States outside Alaska. Visitor center, snack bar, picnic area.

★ **Visitor centers.** Located at Longmire; at Paradise; at Sunrise (summer only); and at Ohanapecosh (summer only), near the Stevens Canyon entrance, in southeastern corner of park. All offer exhibits and publications.

**White Pass Village.** *Naches. On Hwy 12, 12 miles E of Stevens Canyon (SE) entrance to the park. Phone 509/672-3101. www.skiwhitepass.com.* Quad, triple, two double chairlifts, Pomalift, rope tow; patrol, school, rentals; accommodations, restaurant, bar, daycare, general store, service station. Longest run 2 1/2 miles; vertical drop 1,500 feet. Cross-country trails. (Mid-Nov-mid-Apr, daily) **$$$$**

## Limited-Service Hotels

**★★ THE NISQUALLY LODGE.** *31609 Hwy 706, Ashford (98304). Phone 360/569-8804; toll-free 888/674-3554; fax 360/569-2435. www.escapetothemountains.com.* This chalet-style lodge is near the entrance to Mount Rainier National Park, making it a great place from which to explore the outdoors. The accommodations are simple but do provide telephones and TVs; laundry facilities, an outdoor hot tub, and a great room with fireplace round out the amenities. 24 rooms, 2 story. Complimentary continental breakfast. Check-out 11 am. Restaurant. Whirlpool. **$**

**★★ PARADISE INN.** *PO Box 108, Ashford (98304). Phone 360/569-2275; fax 360/569-2770.* This shake-shingle mountain lodge, part of the Mount Rainier National Park system, was built with onsite timber in 1917. The decorative woodwork inside, including the rustic piano and 14-foot grandfather clock, was added shortly thereafter. But the real reason to come here is the outdoors, as attested by the lack of telephones and TVs in the guest rooms. In the shadow of majestic Mount Rainier, guests enjoy miles of hiking trails, flowering meadows, and the many other activities afforded by the nearby national park. Fuel up after a busy day at the Paradise Inn Dining Room,

which serves classic American cuisine with a Pacific Northwest twist. If you'd like to visit the park between mid-October and mid-May, when the inn is closed, try its sister property, the National Park Inn, which is open year-round. (Their contact information is the same.) 117 rooms, 4 story. Closed mid-Oct-mid-May. Check-out 11 am. Restaurant, bar. **$**

# Mount St. Helens National Volcanic Monument

*See also Ephrata, Othello, Ritzville*

*(From I-5 exit 68: 48 miles E on Hwy 12 to Randle, then S on Forest Service Rd 25; from I-5 exit 21: approximately 35 miles NE on Hwy 503, Forest Service rds 90, 25)*

**Web Site** www.fs.fed.us/gpnf/mshnvm

In 1978, two geologists who had been studying Mount St. Helens warned that this youngest volcano in the Cascade Range could erupt again by the end of the century. On March 27, 1980, the volcano did just that, ending 123 years of inactivity. Less than two months later, on May 18, a massive eruption transformed this beautiful snow-capped mountain and the surrounding forest into an eerie, desolate landscape with few signs of life.

The eruption sent a lateral blast of hot ash and gases out across the land at speeds up to 670 miles per hour, flattening 150 square miles of forest north of the volcano. An ash plume rising 13 miles into the atmosphere was spread eastward by the wind, coating many cities in Washington, Idaho, and Montana with a fine grit. Rivers were choked with logs and mud, huge logging trucks were toppled like small toys, and the mountain, having lost 1,300 feet of its summit, was left with a gaping crater 2,000 feet deep, 1/2 mile wide, and a mile long.

Among the 57 people missing or killed by the eruption was 83-year-old Harry Truman, who for many years owned a lodge on Spirit Lake, just north of the mountain. Truman refused to heed evacuation warnings, believing his "beloved mountain" would not harm him; he and his lodge are now beneath hundreds of feet of mud and water.

The Monument, established in 1982, covers 110,000 acres within the Gifford Pinchot National Forest and provides a rare, natural laboratory in which scientists and visitors can view the effects of a volcanic eruption. Despite the destruction, the return of vegetation and wildlife to the blast zone has been relatively rapid. Within just weeks of the eruption, small plants and insects had begun to make their way through the ash. Today, herds of elk and other animals, as well as fir trees and wildflowers, have taken a strong foothold here.

Forest Service Road 25, which runs north-south near the eastern boundary, provides access to views of the volcano. The roads are usually closed from approximately November-May because of snow; some roads are narrow and winding.

Visitors are advised to phone ahead for current road conditions. Although volcanic activity at Mount St. Helens has decreased greatly in the last few years, some roads into the Monument could be closed if weather conditions dictate.

For further information, including a map with the locations of various facilities and attractions, contact the Monument Headquarters, 42218 NE Yale Bridge Rd, Amboy 98601; phone 360/247-3900.

## What to See and Do

**Ape Cave.** *Amboy. On Forest Service Rd 8303, in southern part of monument. Phone 360/247-3900.* At 12,810 feet in length, the cave is said to be one of the longest intact lava tubes in the continental United States. Downslope portion of cave, extending approximately 4,000 feet, is the most easily traveled. Upslope portion, extending nearly 7,000 feet, is recommended only for visitors carrying the proper equipment. All visitors are advised to carry three sources of light and wear sturdy shoes or boots and warm clothing; cave is a constant 42° F. An information station is also here; lantern rentals available seasonally.

**Camping.** There are no campgrounds within the Monument, but many public and private campgrounds are located nearby. Primitive camping is usually allowed throughout the Gifford Pinchot National Forest (see VANCOUVER).

**Coldwater Ridge Visitor Center.** *3029 Spirits Lake Hwy, Mount St. Helens National Volcanic Monument (98611). 45 miles E of Castle Rock. Phone 360/274-*

*2131. www.fs.fed.us/gpnf/mshnvm.* Major interpretive center at 3,100 feet offers views directly into mouth of crater. Lodgelike building overlooks Coldwater Lake created by eruption landslide. Films and viewing area; displays focus on rebirth of nature. Bookstore, cafeteria, interpretive hikes. (Daily)

**Hiking.** An extensive system of trails offers hikers impressive views of the volcano and surrounding devastated areas. Trails vary in degree of difficulty. Some trails are accessible to wheelchairs. Temperatures can be very warm along the trails due to a lack of shade; hikers are advised to carry water.

**Interpretive walks and programs.** Presented at several locations. Details are available at the information stations, Monument headquarters, or visitor centers.

**Johnston Ridge Observatory.** *3029 Spirit Lake Hwy, Mount St. Helens National Volcanic Monument (98611). 52 miles E of Castle Rock. Phone 360/274-2131.* At 4,200 feet. State-of-the-art interpretive displays focus on sequence of geological events that drastically altered the landscape and opened up a new era in the science of monitoring an active volcano and forecasting eruptions. Wide-screen theater presentation, interpretive exhibits, staffed information desk, bookstore. Views of the lava dome, crater, pumice plain, and landslide deposit. Visitors can take a 1/2-mile walk on Eruption Trail. Interpretive talks and hikes in summer. (Daily) **$**

★ **Mount St. Helens Visitor Center.** *Outside the Monument, off I-5 exit 49, 5 miles east of Castle Rock on Hwy 504. Phone 360/274-2100.* (Center cannot be reached directly from the northeast side Monument.) The center houses exhibits that include a walk-through model of the volcano, displays on the history of the mountain and the 1980 eruption, and volcano monitoring equipment. A 10-minute slide program and a 22-minute movie are shown several times daily, and special programs are held throughout the year. Also here are volcano viewpoints and a nature trail along Silver Lake. Contact 3029 Spirit Lake Hwy, Castle Rock 98611. (Daily; closed holidays) **$**

**Summit climb.** *Phone 360/247-3961.* Climbers are allowed to hike to the summit; free climbing permits are issued on a limited basis. Climb should be attempted only by persons in good physical condition. For climbing information contact the headquarters.

**Visitor information stations.** Located at Pine Creek, on Forest Service Rd 90 near the southeast side of the Monument; at Woods Creek, at the junction of Forest Service roads 25 and 76 near the northeast side of the Monument; and at Ape Cave. (Summer, daily; may remain open until Labor Day)

**Volcano viewpoints.** *Off Forest Service Rd 99.* There are several viewpoints throughout the eastern side of the Monument, particularly along Forest Service Road 99; this road leads to Windy Ridge, with a spectacular view of the volcano and Spirit Lake. Lahar Viewpoint, on Forest Service Road 83, provides an excellent view of mud flow activity on the south side of the mountain.

# Mount Vernon (A-2)

*See also Anacortes, La Conner, Sedro-Woolley*

**Settled** 1870
**Population** 26,232
**Elevation** 31 ft
**Area Code** 360
**Zip** 98273
**Information** Chamber of Commerce, 105 E Kincade; phone 360/428-8547
**Web Site** www.mountvernonchamber.com

Developed by farmers and loggers, Mount Vernon is a major commercial center. Centrally located between Puget Sound and the North Cascades, the Skagit Delta's deep alluvial soil grows 125 varieties of produce, including flowers and bulbs, fruit, and vegetables. Spring brings fields of daffodils, tulips, and irises to the country; a map of the fields is available at the Chamber of Commerce. The city is named for George Washington's plantation in Virginia.

## What to See and Do

**Bay View State Park.** *10905 Bay View Edison Rd, Mount Vernon (98273). 7 miles W via Hwy 20, then right on Bay View Edison Rd. Phone 360/757-0227.* Approximately 25 acres. Sand beach (no swimming), picnicking, camping (hookups). Interpretive center nearby.

**Hillcrest Park.** *1717 S 13th St, Mount Vernon (98274). Phone 360/336-6213.* Approximately 30 acres with playgrounds, tennis and basketball courts, hiking trails, covered and open picnic facilities, barbecue pits. **FREE**

**Little Mountain.** *Mount Vernon. SE of city on Blackburn Rd W. Phone 360/336-6213.* Observation area atop 934-foot mountain, providing view of Skagit Valley, Olympic Mountains, Mount Rainier, and San Juan Islands; surrounded by 480-acre forested park. Hiking, picnicking. (Daily)

**Prime Outlets at Burlington.** *448 Fashion Way, Burlington (98233). I-5 to exit 229. Phone 360/757-3549.* If you're a bargain shopper who wants to take a drive out of the city, the Prime Outlets at Burlington is your place. Just about 65 miles north of Seattle, this shopper's paradise houses nearly 50 stores, like Tommy Hilfiger, Gap, Reebok, Farberware, and Samsonite. On the drive here, you'll be able to enjoy some of the Northwest's breathtaking scenery.

## Special Events

**Awesome Autumn Festival.** *Mount Vernon. Phone 360/428-8547.* Six weeks of events including a 4-acre corn maze, arts and crafts fair, pumpkin festival. Sept-Oct.

**Skagit County Fair.** *1410 Virginia St, Mount Vernon (98273). Phone 360/336-9453.* Second week in Aug.

**Skagit Valley Tulip Festival.** *Mount Vernon. Phone 360/428-5959. www.tulipfestival.org.* This annual festival gives the county's two primary tulip growers, the Skagit Valley Bulb Farm and the Washington Bulb Company, a chance to display their beautiful blooms at sites throughout the county. Each grower invites visitors to tour its gardens, which feature hundreds of thousands of bulbs and more than 60 varieties of the famous Dutch export. But this month-long festival is about more than just flowers: the many events include the Anacortes Quilt Walk, Art in a Pickle Barn, and a bald eagle and birding float trip. Apr.

## Full-Service Hotel

**★ ★ BEST WESTERN COTTONTREE INN.** *2300 Market St, Mount Vernon (98273). Phone 360/428-5678; toll-free 800/662-6886; fax 360/428-1844. www.bwcottontreeinn.com.* Just off I-5 and near Mount Vernon College, this hotel is close to a variety of restaurants, making it a convenient stopover. Recently renovated guest rooms have refrigerators and microwaves, and wireless Internet access is availble throughout the property. The hotel doesn't have its own fitness room, but guests receive complimentary privileges at the nearby Riverside Health Club. 120 rooms, 3 story. Pets accepted, some restrictions; fee. Complimentary full breakfast. Check-in 3 pm, check-out noon. Wireless Internet access. Restaurant, bar. Outdoor pool. **$**

## Specialty Lodging

**THE WHITE SWAN GUEST HOUSE.** *15872 Moore Rd, Mount Vernon (98273). Phone 360/445-6805. www.thewhiteswan.com.* Queen Anne-style farmhouse (circa 1890). 3 rooms. Complimentary continental breakfast. Check-in 3-6 pm, check-out 11 am. **$$**

# Neah Bay (A-1)

*See also Port Angeles, Sequim*

**Settled** 1791
**Population** 794
**Elevation** 0 ft
**Area Code** 360
**Zip** 98357
**Web Site** www.olympicpeninsula.com/index.htm

## What to See and Do

**Makah Cultural and Research Center.** *Hwy 112 and Bay View Ave, Neah Bay. Hwy 112, 1 mile E. Phone 360/645-2711.* Exhibits on Makah and Northwest Coast Native Americans; 500-year-old artifacts uncovered at the Ozette archaeological site, a Makah village dating back 2,000 years. Craft shop; dioramas; canoes; complete longhouse. (Memorial Day-mid-Sept: daily; rest of year: Wed-Sun; closed Jan 1, Thanksgiving, Dec 25) **$**

## Specialty Lodgings

**CHITO BEACH RESORT.** *7639 Hwy 112, Clallam Bay (98326). Phone 360/963-2581. www.chitobeach.com.* Long regarded as one of the state's best waterfront accommodations, Chito Beach is home to an amazingly beautiful stretch of Washington State's rugged coastline. 4 rooms, 2 story. **$**

**KING FISHER INN.** *1562 Hwy 112, Neah Bay (98357). Phone toll-free 888/622-8216. www.kingfisherenterprises.com.* Overlooking the Straight of San Juan de Fuca and international shipping lanes with views of Vancouver Island in the background, this inn is perfect for year-round hiking, surfing, and kayaking. 4 rooms, 3 story. **$$**

**STRAITSIDE RESORT.** *241 Front St, Sekiu (98381). Phone 360/963-2100.* Located on the Strait of Juan de Fuca with waterfront views, full kitchens, and plenty of outdoor excursions available. 7 rooms, 2 story. **$**

# Newport (A-6)

*See also Spokane*

**Settled** 1890
**Population** 1,921
**Area Code** 509
**Zip** 99156
**Information** Chamber of Commerce, 325 W 4th St; phone 509/447-5812
**Web Site** www.newportoldtownchamber.org

A shopping, distribution, and lumbering center, Newport was born in Idaho. For a while, there was a Newport on both sides of the state line, but the US Post Office interceded on behalf of the Washington community, which was the county seat of Pend Oreille County. Newport is known as "the city of flags"; flags from around the world are displayed on the main streets. A Ranger District office of the Colville National Forest is located here.

## What to See and Do

**Historical Society Museum.** *402 S Washington Ave, Newport (99156). Phone 509/447-5388.* In old railroad depot; houses historical artifacts of Pend Oreille County; two reconstructed log cabins. (Mid-May-Sept, daily) **DONATION**

**Big Wheel.** *Centennial Plaza. Phone 509/447-5812.* Giant Corliss steam engine that for years powered the town's foremost sawmill. Flag display. A visitor information center is located here.

# North Bend (B-3)

*See also Issaquah, Seattle*

**Founded** 1889
**Population** 4,746
**Elevation** 442 ft
**Area Code** 425
**Zip** 98045
**Information** The Upper Snoqualmie Valley Chamber of Commerce, PO Box 357, 98045; phone 425/888-4440
**Web Site** www.ci.north-bend.wa.us

A gateway to Mount Baker-Snoqualmie National Forest—Snoqualmie section—and a popular winter sports area, North Bend also serves as a shipping town for this logging, farming, and dairy region. A Ranger District office of the Mount Baker-Snoqualmie National Forest is located here.

## What to See and Do

**Alpental.** *1001 Hwy 906, North Bend (98068). 17 miles SE on I-90, then 1 mile N on Alpental Rd. Phone 425/434-7669.* Three double chairlifts, quad, three rope tows, platter pull; patrol, school, rentals; cafeteria, bar. Longest run 1 1/2 miles; vertical drop 2,200 feet. (Hours, fees same as Summit West) Shuttle bus to Summit West, Summit East, and Summit Central (Fri nights, weekends and holidays); tickets interchangeable. (Mid Nov-Apr, daily) **$$$$**

**North Bend Outlet Stores.** *461 S Fork Ave SW, North Bend (98045). 31 miles E of Seattle; I-90 to exit 31. Phone 425/888-4505. www.factorystoresatnorthbend.com.* Located just 40 minutes from Seattle, this complex of outlet stores offers amazing bargains from names such as Eddie Bauer, Gap, the Naturalizer, KB Toys, and many more. The mall, itself, doesn't have many choices for satiating the appetite you're sure to work up after power shopping, (just a lone Subway), but there are many options across the street.

**Snoqualmie Falls.** *North Bend. 4 miles NW via Hwy 202. www.snoqualmiefalls.com.* Perpetual snow in the Cascade Mountains feeds the 268-foot falls. Power plant; park area; trail to bottom of falls. Salish Lodge (see RESORT) overlooks falls.

**Snoqualmie Valley Historical Museum.** *320 Bendigo Blvd S, North Bend (98045). Phone 425/888-3200.* Displays, room settings of early pioneer life from 1890s; photos, Native American artifacts; logging exhibits; farm shed; reference material. Slide shows; changing exhibits. (Apr-mid-Dec, Thurs-Sun; tours by appointment) **DONATION**

**Summit Central.** *1001 Hwy 906, North Bend (98068). 18 miles SE on I-90 at Snoqualmie Pass. Phone 425/434-7669.* Two triple, six double chairlifts, five rope tows; patrol, school, rentals; cross-country center; cafeteria, bar; day care center. Vertical drop 1,020 feet. Shuttle bus to Summit West, Summit East, and Alpental (Fri nights, weekends, and holidays); tickets interchangeable. (Mid-Nov-Apr, daily) **$$$$**

**Summit East.** *1001 Hwy 906, North Bend (98068). 19 miles SE on I-90, at Snoqualmie Pass. Phone 425/434-7669.*Two double chairlifts; patrol, school, rentals; cafeteria, bar. Vertical drop 1,055 feet. Shuttle bus to

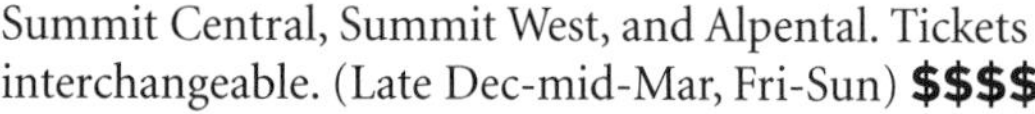

Summit Central, Summit West, and Alpental. Tickets interchangeable. (Late Dec-mid-Mar, Fri-Sun) **$$$$**

**Summit West.** *1001 Hwy 906, North Bend (98068). 17 miles SE on I-90. Phone 425/434-7669. www.summit-at-snoqualmie.com.* Six double, two triple, quad chairlifts; two rope tows; 15 slopes and trails. Patrol, school, rentals; bar, restaurant, cafeteria; day care center. Vertical drop 900 feet. Intermediate chairs; half-day and evening rates. (Mid-Nov-Apr, daily) **$$$$**

## Full-Service Resort

**★ ★ ★ SALISH LODGE & SPA.** *6501 Railroad Ave, Snoqualmie (98065). Phone 425/888-2556; toll-free 800/272-5474; fax 425/888-2420. www.salishlodge.com.* Just 30 miles east of Seattle, the Salish Lodge & Spa is a celebration of the rugged beauty of the Pacific Northwest. Nestled in the foothills of the Cascade Mountains, this understated lodge enjoys a majestic setting amid lush evergreen forests and the roaring whitewater of the Snoqualmie Falls. World-weary travelers quickly adopt a gentle pace here, whether hiking the serene mountain trails or enjoying a hot rock massage in the Asian-inspired spa. A rustic simplicity pervades the accommodations, while luxurious details such as wood-burning fireplaces, whirlpool tubs, and pillow menus ensure maximum comfort and large windows focus attention on the serene views. Three exceptional restaurants delight the palates of discriminating diners with a focus on fresh, regional cuisine. 91 rooms, 4 story. Check-in 4 pm, check-out noon. Restaurant, bar. Fitness room, spa. Whirlpool. **$$$**

# Oak Harbor (A-2)

*See also Anacortes, Coupeville, Everett, Port Townsend*

**Settled** 1849
**Population** 19,795
**Elevation** 115 ft
**Area Code** 360
**Zip** 98277
**Information** Chamber of Commerce Visitor Information Center, 32630 Hwy 20; phone 360/675-3535
**Web Site** www.oakharborchamber.org

This trading center on Whidbey Island was first Settled by sea captains and adventurers and then in the 1890s by immigrants from the Netherlands who developed the rich countryside. The town's name was inspired by the oak trees that cloaked the area when the first settlers arrived, which have been preserved. Side roads lead to secluded beaches and excellent boating and fishing, with marinas nearby.

## What to See and Do

**Holland Gardens.** *SE 6th Ave W and Ireland St, Oak Harbor.* Gardens of flowers and shrubs surround blue and white windmill; Dutch provincial flags, tulips, and daffodils decorate gardens during Holland Happening. (Daily) **FREE**

**Oak Harbor Beach Park.** *Oak Harbor. Phone 360/679-5551. www.oakharbor.org.* Authentic Dutch windmill; picnicking, barbecue pit; 1,800-foot sand beach, lagoon swimming, bathhouse, wading pools; tennis, baseball diamonds, playground; illuminated trails. Camping (hookups, dump station; fee). (Daily) **FREE**

**Whidbey Island Naval Air Station.** *1170 W Lexington Ave, Oak Harbor (98278). Approximately 5 miles N on Hwy 20. Phone 360/257-2286.* Only active naval air station in the Northwest. Guided group tours (minimum ten persons); reservations required several months in advance. **FREE**

## Special Events

**Anacortes Jazz Festival.** *Anacortes.* Some of the best jazz artisits from around the Pacific Northwest will converge on Curtis Warf and in the Port Wharehouse, overlooking the waters of Guemes Channel, for three days of great live jazz music. Mid-Sept.

**Holland Happening.** *Oak Harbor. Phone 360/675-3755.* Tulip show, arts and crafts, Dutch buffet, carnival, culture foodfest, square dance exhibition, parade. Late Apr.

## Limited-Service Hotel

**★ ★ BEST WESTERN HARBOR PLAZA.** *33175 Hwy 20, Oak Harbor (98277). Phone 360/679-4567; toll-free 800/927-5478; fax 360/675-2543. www.bestwestern.com/harborplaza.* 80 rooms, 3 story. Pets accepted; fee. Complimentary continental breakfast. Check-in 4 pm, check-out noon. Restaurant, bar. Fitness room. Outdoor pool. **$**

# Ocean Shores (C-1)

*See also Aberdeen, Hoquiam, Westport*

**Population** 3,836
**Elevation** 21 ft
**Area Code** 360
**Zip** 98569
**Information** Chamber of Commerce, Box 382; phone 360/289-2451 or toll-free 800/762-3224
**Web Site** www.oceanshores.org

This 6,000-acre area at the southern end of the Olympic Peninsula is a seaside resort community with 6 miles of ocean beaches, 23 miles of lakes and canals, and 12 miles of bay front. Clamming, crabbing, and trout and bass fishing are popular.

## What to See and Do

**Pacific Paradise Family Fun Center.** *767 Minard Ave, Ocean Shores (98569). Phone 360/289-9537; fax 360/289-9566.* 36-hole miniature golf (fee); entertainment center; Paradise Lake (fee).

## Limited-Service Hotels

**★ CANTERBURY INN.** *643 Ocean Shores Blvd, Ocean Shores (98569). Phone 360/289-3317; toll-free 800/562-6678; fax 360/289-3420. www.canterburyinn.com.* 44 rooms, 3 story. Check-out noon. Indoor pool, whirlpool. **$**

**★ ★ SHILO INN.** *707 Ocean Shores Blvd NW, Ocean Shores (98569). Phone 360/289-4600; toll-free 800/222-2244; fax 360/289-0355. www.shiloinns.com.* 113 rooms, 4 story. Check-out noon. Restaurant, bar. Fitness room. Indoor pool, whirlpool. **$**

# Olympia (C-2)

*See also Centralia, Tacoma*

**Founded** 1850
**Population** 42,514
**Elevation** 100 ft
**Area Code** 360
**Information** Olympia/Thurston County Chamber of Commerce, 809 Legion Way SE, 98507-1427; phone 360/357-3362
**Web Site** www.thurstonchamber.com

As though inspired by the natural beauty that surrounds it—Mount Rainier and the Olympic Mountains on the skyline and Puget Sound at its doorstep—Washington's capital city is a carefully groomed, parklike community. Although concentrating on the business of government, Olympia also serves tourists and the needs of nearby military installations. It is a deep-sea port and a manufacturer of wood products, plastics, and mobile homes. The tiny village of Smithfield was chosen in 1851 as the site for a customhouse. The US Collector of Customs prevailed on the citizens to rename the community for the Olympic Mountains. Shortly afterward, agitation to separate the land north of the Columbia from Oregon began. In 1853, the new territory was proclaimed, with Olympia as territorial capital. The first legislature convened here in 1854, despite Native American unrest that forced construction of a stockade ringing the town. (The 15-foot wall was later dismantled and used to plank the capital's streets.) The Olympia metropolitan area also includes the communities of Lacey and Tumwater, the oldest settlement in the state (1845) north of the Columbia River. The city today has a compact 20-square-block business section and a variety of stores that attract shoppers from a wide area.

## What to See and Do

**Capitol Group.** *Capitol Way and 11th Ave, Olympia. On Capitol Way between 11th and 14th aves. Phone 360/586-3460.* In 35-acre park overlooking Capitol Lake and Budd Inlet of Puget Sound are

**Capitol grounds.** *Olympia.* Grounds lined with Japanese cherry trees attract hundreds of visitors in the spring; plantings are changed seasonally. Also here is a replica of Tivoli Gardens Fountain in Copenhagen, Denmark; sunken gardens, state conservatory (Memorial Day-Labor Day, daily); World War I and Vietnam memorials. Grounds (daily).

**Legislative Building.** *Cherry Ln and 14th Ave, Olympia. Phone 360/586-3460.* A 287-foot dome with 47-foot lantern; Neoclassical architecture; lavishly detailed interior.

**Library Building.** Houses rare books; murals, mosaics. (Mon-Fri; closed holidays)

**Temple of Justice.** *Cherry Ln and 12th Ave, Olympia.* Houses State Supreme Court. (Mon-Fri; closed holidays)

**Capitol Lake.** *14th and Capitol Way, Olympia (98409). Phone 360/586-3460.* Formed by a dam at the point where fresh water of the Deschutes River empties into salt water of Budd Inlet. From the top of the dam, thousands of salmon can be seen making their way upstream during spawning season starting in mid-Aug. Boating, bicycle and running trails, playground and picnic tables. (Daily) **FREE**

**Millersylvania State Park.** *12245 Tilley Rd S, Olympia (98512). 10 miles S off I-5. Phone 360/753-1519.* More than 800 acres along Deep Lake. Swimming, fishing, boating; hiking, picnicking, camping (hook-ups).

**Mima Mounds Natural Area.** *1405 Rush Rd, Olympia (98506). I-5 S to exit 95 toward Littlerock (Hwy 121), then 128th Ave SW 1 mile to t-jct with Waddell Creek Rd. Turn N 1 mile to preserve. Phone toll-free 800/527-3305. www.dnr.wa.gov.* Mounds 8 to 10 feet high and 20 to 30 feet in diameter spread across miles of meadows west of Olympia. Once thought to be ancient burial chambers, they are now believed to be the result of Ice Age freeze-thaw patterns. Trails wind through 500-acre site. Information kiosk, picnic area. Contact Washington Department of Natural Resources. **FREE**

**Olympic National Forest.** *1835 Black Lake Blvd SW, Olympia (98502). NW of city, reached via Hwy 101, exit 104. Phone 360/956-2400. www.fs.fed.us/r6/olympic.* More than 632,000 acres. Picturesque streams and rivers, winding ridges, rugged peaks, deep canyons, tree-covered slopes; rain forest, the world's largest stand of Douglas fir, public-owned oyster beds; populous herd of Roosevelt elk. Swimming, fishing; hiking, hunting, picnicking, camping (May-Sept).

**Oyster beds.** *Olympia.* Big Skookum, Little Skookum, Mud, Oyster bays. Beds of rare Olympia oyster found only in South Puget Sound.

**Percival Landing Park.** *Waterfront, Olympia. Between Thurston St and 4th Ave.* Pleasant 1/2-mile walk along marina filled with pleasure crafts and seals. Observation tower; at south end is statue of *The Kiss.* Also Heritage Fountain, popular with children on summer days. **FREE**

**Priest Point Park.** *Olympia. E Bay Dr, overlooks Budd Inlet.* Playgrounds, hiking trails, picnic facilities in heavily wooded area with view of Olympic Mountains. (Daily) **FREE**

**State Capital Museum.** *212 21st Ave SW, Olympia (98501). Phone 360/753-2580.* A 1920 Spanish-style stucco mansion houses art gallery; Native American art and culture exhibits; pioneer exhibits. (Tues-Sun; closed holidays) **$**

**State Capitol Campus.** *14 Capitol Way, Olympia (98409). On Capitol Way between 11th and 14th aves. Phone 360/753-5000.*

**Tumwater Falls Park.** *Olympia. S of city off I-5, 15 acres. Phone 360/943-2550. www.olytumfoundation.org.* Gentle walk (1 mile) follows spectacular falls of the Deschutes River. Landscaped grounds, picnicking, playground. Good view of fall salmon run on man-made fish ladder. (Daily) Adjacent is

**Tumwater Valley Athletic Club.** *4833 Tumwater Valley Dr, Tumwater (98501). Phone 360/943-9500.* Indoor swimming pools. Tennis and racquetball courts. 18-hole golf course. Fee for activities. (All year)

**Wolf Haven International.** *3111 Offut Lake Rd, Tenino (98589). Phone 360/264-4695.* Wolf Sanctuary center on 75 acres; also home to 40 wolves no longer able to live in the wild. Interpretive center, tours, and ecology center. (May-Sept: daily; rest of year: Wed-Sun; closed Jan-Feb) **$$**

**Yahiro Gardens.** *Plum St and Union Ave, Olympia.* A cooperative project between Olympia and its sister city, Yashiro, Japan. The gardens include a pagoda, bamboo grove, pond, and waterfall. (Daily during daylight hours) **FREE**

## Special Events

**Capital City Marathon and Relay.** *2139 Lakemoor Dr SW, Olympia (98512). Phone 360/786-1786.* Features an 8-kilometer run, children's run, 5-10-kilometer walk, wheelchair division. Weekend before Memorial Day weekend.

**Lakefair.** *612 5th Ave, Olympia (98501). Capitol Lake. Phone 360/943-7344.* Parade, carnival midway, boating and swimming competition, naval vessel tours, flower shows. Mid-July.

**Olympia Farmers Market.** *700 Capitol Way N, Olympia (98501). Phone 360/352-9096.* Includes fresh produce, baked goods, food booths, seafood, crafts. First weekend in Apr through Dec; weekends only in Apr, Nov, and Dec.

**Super Saturday.** *Evergreen State College, 2700 Evergreen Pkwy, Olympia (98505). Phone 360/867-6000.* Arts, crafts, food fair. Early June.

**Thurston County Fair.** *Fairgrounds, 3054 Carpenter Rd SE, Lacey (98503). Phone 360/786-5453.* Early Aug.

## Limited-Service Hotels

**★ BEST WESTERN TUMWATER INN.** *5188 Capitol Blvd, Tumwater (98501). Phone 360/956-1235; fax 360/357-6025. www.bestwestern.com.* 89 rooms, 2 story. Pets accepted; fee. Complimentary continental breakfast. Check-out 11 am. Fitness room. **$**

**★ ★ RED LION.** *2300 Evergreen Park Dr, Olympia (98502). Phone 360/943-4000; toll-free 800/733-5466; fax 360/357-6604. www.redlion.com.* This state capital property is near the beautiful Cascade Mountains and many recreational activities. 190 rooms, 3 story. Pets accepted; fee. Complimentary continental breakfast. Check-in 3 pm, check-out noon. High-speed Internet access. Restaurant, bar. Fitness room. Outdoor pool, whirlpool. Business center. **$**

## Full-Service Hotel

**★ ★ RAMADA INN GOVERNOR HOUSE.** *621 S Capitol Way, Olympia (98501). Phone 360/352-7700; toll-free 800/272-6232; fax 360/943-9349. www.ramada.com.* 125 rooms, 8 story. Pets accepted; fee. Complimentary full breakfast. Check-in 3 pm, check-out noon. Restaurant, bar. Fitness room. Outdoor pool, whirlpool. **$**

## Restaurant

**★ ★ BUDD BAY CAFE.** *525 N Columbia St, Olympia (98501). Phone 360/357-6963. www.buddbaycafe.com.* Seafood menu. Lunch, dinner, Sun brunch. Closed Jan 1, Dec 25. Bar. Children's menu. Casual attire. Reservations recommended. Outdoor seating. **$$**

# Olympic National Park (B-1)

*See also Forks, Port Angeles, Sequim*

*Heart o the Hills Rd, Port Angeles. 119 miles NW of Olympia on Hwy 101. Phone 360/565-3130. www.nps.gov/olym.*

In these 1,442 square miles of rugged wilderness are such contrasts as the wettest climate in the contiguous United States (averaging 140-167 inches of precipitation a year) and one of the driest, seascapes and snow-cloaked peaks, glaciers and rain forests, elk and seals. With Olympic National Forest, State Sustained Yield Forest No. 1, much private land, and several American Indian reservations, the national park occupies the Olympic Peninsula, due west of Seattle and Puget Sound.

The Spanish explorer Juan Perez was the first European explorer to spot the Olympic Mountains in 1774. However, the first major western land exploration did not take place until more than a century later. Since then, generations of adventurous tourists have rediscovered Mount Olympus, the highest peak (7,965 feet); several other 7,000-foot peaks; and hundreds of ridges and crests between 5,000 and 6,000 feet high. The architects of these ruggedly contoured mountains are glaciers, which have etched these heights for thousands of years. About 60 glaciers are still actively eroding these mountains; the largest three are on Mount Olympus.

From approximately November through March, the west side of the park is soaked with rain and mist, while the northeast side is the driest area on the West Coast except southern California. The yearly deluge creates a rain forest in the western valleys of the park. Here Sitka spruce, western hemlock, Douglas fir, and western red cedar grow to heights of 250 feet with 8-foot diameters. Mosses carpet the forest floor and climb tree trunks. Club moss drips from the branches.

Some 50 species of mammals inhabit this wilderness, including several thousand elk, Olympic marmots, black-tailed deer, and black bears. On the park's 60-mile strip of Pacific coastline wilderness, deer, bears, raccoons, and skunks can be seen; seals sun on the

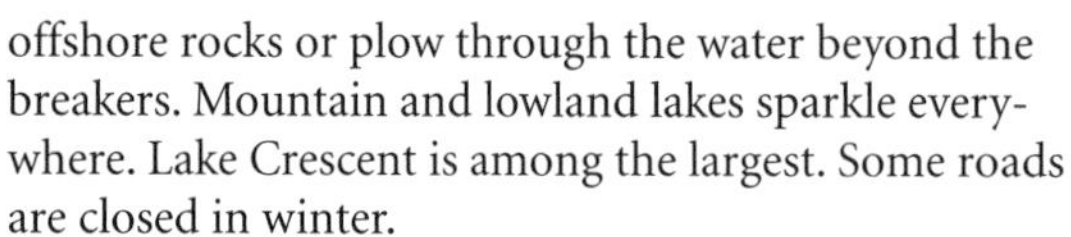



offshore rocks or plow through the water beyond the breakers. Mountain and lowland lakes sparkle everywhere. Lake Crescent is among the largest. Some roads are closed in winter.

## What to See and Do

**Fishing.** *3002 Mount Angeles Rd, Olympic National Park (98362). Phone 360/565-3130.* Streams and lakes have game fish including salmon, rainbow, Dolly Varden, eastern brook trout, steelhead, and cutthroat. No license required in the park; permit or punch card is necessary for steelhead and salmon. Contact Park Headquarters for restrictions.

**Hiking.** Over 600 miles of trails. Obtain maps and trail guides in the park. Guided walks conducted July and Aug.

**Mountain climbing.** Something for everyone, from the novice to the experienced climber. Climbing parties must register at a ranger station.

**Rain forests.** Along Hoh, Queets, and Quinault river roads. Hall of Mosses and Spruce Nature Trails and trail to Mount Olympus start at end of Hoh River Road.

**★Visitor Center.** *3002 Mount Angeles Rd, Olympic National Park (98362).* Has information, natural history exhibits, displays of American Indian culture, orientation slideshow. (Daily) 3002 Mt Angeles Rd. From here, one can enter the park on Heart O' the Hills Pkwy to Hurricane Ridge (there is limited access Nov-Apr). 600 E Park Ave in Port Angeles. **$$$** Here is

> **Hurricane Ridge Winter Use Area.** Pomalift, intermediate, and beginner's runs; school, rentals; snack bar. (Late Dec-late Mar, Sat-Sun) Also snowshoeing and cross-country ski trails.

## Full-Service Resorts

**★ ★ KALALOCH LODGE.** *157151 Hwy 101, Forks (98331). Phone 360/962-2271; fax 360/962-3391. www.visitkalaloch.com.* No room phones. 65 rooms, 2 story. Pets accepted, some restrictions; fee. Check-in 4 pm, check-out 11 am. Restaurant. Beach. **$**

**★ ★ SOL DUC HOT SPRINGS RESORT.** *Sol Duc Rd and Hwy 101, Port Angeles (98362). Phone 360/327-3583; fax 360/327-3593. www.northolympic.com/solduc.* Originally conceived as a European-style health spa (circa 1912), the Sol Duc Resort is a haven for nature lovers. The natural mineral pools for which the resort is named range in temperature from 98° F to 106° F. Rates include use of the pools. At the northern end of Olympic National Park, next to the Sol Duc River, the resort is the perfect place from which to explore the area's rain forests and waterfalls. Studio cabins, some with kitchens, house those guests who choose not to rough it in tents. In addition to The Springs, a casual but upscale restaurant, you'll find a deli and a grocery store. 32 rooms. Closed Oct-late Mar. Check-in 4 pm, check-out 11 am. Restaurant. Outdoor pool, mineral pools, children's pool. **$**

# Omak (A-4)

*See also Winthrop*

**Settled** 1900
**Population** 4,721
**Elevation** 837 ft
**Area Code** 509
**Zip** 98841
**Information** Tourist **Information** Center, 401 Omak Ave; phone 509/826-4218 or toll-free 800/225-6625
**Web Site** www.omakchronicle.com/omakvic/

This lumber town is the largest in the north-central part of Washington and is also known for its production of apples and its many orchards. The name of the town and nearby lake and mountain is derived from a Native American word meaning "good medicine." Omak is the "baby's breath capital of the world," a flower much used by florists.

## What to See and Do

**Conconully State Park.** *Omak. 5 miles N on Hwy 97, then 10 miles NW on Conconully Hwy (unnumbered road). Phone 509/826-7408.*Approximately 80 acres along Conconully Reservoir; swimming, fishing, boating; picnicking, snowmobiling, camping. (Daily)

**Okanogan National Forest.** *1240 Second Ave S, Okanogan (98840). NE and NW of town, reached via Hwy 97, Hwy 20. Phone 509/826-3275. www.fs.fed.us/r6/oka.* Nearly 1.75 million acres. In the northern part of the forest is the 530,031-acre Pasayten Wilderness. In the southwestern part is the 95,976-acre Lake Chelan-Sawtooth Wilderness. Hunting and fishing are plentiful; picnicking and camping at 41 sites, most of which have trailer spaces; eight boating sites. 38 miles west of town at

Methow Valley Airport, between Winthrop and Twisp, is the North Cascades Smokejumper Base; visitors are welcome. There is a 1-mile paved wheelchair trail to Rainy Lake at Rainy Pass.

## Special Event

**Stampede and Suicide Race.** *Omak. Phone 509/826-1002.* Rodeo events; horses and riders race down a cliff and across the Okanogan River. Western art show. Native American dance contests. Encampment with more than 100 teepees. Second weekend in Aug.

## Limited-Service Hotel

★ ★ **OKANOGAN INN.** *1 Apple Way, Okanogan (98840). Phone 509/422-6431; fax 509/422-4214. www.okanoganinn.com.* 78 rooms, 3 story. Pets accepted; fee. Check-out 11 am. Restaurant, bar. Outdoor pool. **$**

# Othello (C-5)

*See also Moses Lake*

**Population** 5,847
**Area Code** 509
**Zip** 99344
**Information** Chamber of Commerce, 33 E Larch; phone 509/488-2683 or toll-free 800/684-2556
**Web Site** www.televar.com/chambers/othello

Another beneficiary of the Grand Coulee project, Othello had a population of only 526 in 1950. The Potholes Canal runs by the town, linking the Potholes Reservoir and the smaller Scooteney Reservoir.

## Special Events

**Adams County Fair.** *831 S Reynolds, Othello (99344). Phone 509/488-2871.* Carnival, entertainment, tractor pull, exhibits. Mid-Sept.

**Sandhill Crane Festival.** *735 E Main St, Othello (99344). Phone 509/488-2668.* Wildlife Refuge. View migrating birds. Guided tours, wildlife workshops. Late Mar-early Apr.

## Limited-Service Hotel

★ ★ **BEST WESTERN LINCOLN INN.** *1020 E Cedar, Othello (99344). Phone 509/488-5671; toll-free 800/240-7865; fax 509/488-5084. www.bestwestern.com.* 50 rooms, 2 story. Pets accepted; fee. Complimentary continental breakfast. Check-out 11 am. Restaurant. Fitness room. Outdoor pool. **$**

# Packwood (C-3)

*See also Forks, Mount Rainier National Park*

**Population** 950
**Elevation** 1,051 ft
**Area Code** 360
**Zip** 98361

Named for William Packwood, a colorful explorer who helped open this region, this town is a provisioning point for modern-day explorers of Mount Rainier National Park and Snoqualmie and Gifford Pinchot national forests. A Ranger District office of the Gifford Pinchot National Forest is located here. The area abounds in edible wild berries and mushrooms; no permit is needed for picking. Winter and spring are popular with game-watchers; elk, deer, bears, and goats can be spotted in the local cemetery as well as in nearby parks.

## What to See and Do

**Goat Rocks Wilderness.** *Packwood. E and S of town, in Gifford Pinchot National Forest.* 105,600 acres of alpine beauty with elevations from 3,000-8,200 feet. Jagged pinnacles rising above snowfields, cascading streams, mountain meadows with wildflowers; this is the home of the pika and mountain goat.

## Limited-Service Hotels

★ **COWLITZ RIVER LODGE.** *13069 Hwy 12, Packwood (98361). Phone 360/494-4444; toll-free 888/305-2185; fax 360/494-2075. www.escapetothemountains.com.* If you plan to explore Mount St. Helens, this simple lodge will put you right in the heart of the action, providing a clean, simple place from which to set off on hikes and nature tours. Mount Rainier National Park is also close by. 32 rooms, 2 story. Complimentary continental breakfast. Check-out 11 am. Whirlpool. **$**

★**CREST TRAIL LODGE.** *12729 Hwy 12, Packwood (98361). Phone 360/494-4944; toll-free 800/477-5339; fax 360/494-6629. www.cresttriallodge.com.* 27 rooms, 2 story. Complimentary continental breakfast. Check-out 11 am. Airport transportation available. **$**

# Pasco (D-5)

*See also Kennewick, Richland*

**Founded** 1880
**Population** 32,066
**Elevation** 381 ft
**Area Code** 509
**Zip** 99301
**Information** Greater Pasco Area Chamber of Commerce, 2705 St. Andrew's Loop, Suite C; phone 509/547-9755
**Web Site** www.pascochamber.org

One of the "tri-cities" (see KENNEWICK and RICHLAND), Pasco has been nurtured by transportation throughout its history. Still a rail, air, highway, and waterway crossroads, Pasco is enjoying increased farm and industrial commerce thanks to the Columbia Basin project.

## What to See and Do

**Kahlotus.** *42 miles NE via Hwy 395 and Hwy 260.* Town redone in Old West atmosphere. Many of the businesses and buildings are museums in themselves. Near Palouse Falls and Lower Monumental Dam.

**McNary Lock and Dam.** *Umatilla. 3 miles S of Hwy 14 in Umatilla, OR. Phone 541/922-4388.* Single-lift navigation lock. Dam is 7,365 feet long, 92 feet high, and is the easternmost of four multipurpose dams on the lower Columbia River between Portland, OR, and Pasco. The Columbia River forms Lake Wallula here. The 61-mile-long lake reaches beyond the tri-cities up to Ice Harbor Dam on Snake River. Developed parks with boating, marinas, water-skiing, swimming, fishing; picnicking and camping nearby. For information contact Park Ranger, PO Box 1441, Umatilla, OR 97882. (Daily)

**Preston Premium Wines.** *502 E Vineyard Dr, Pasco (99301). 5 miles N via Hwy 395, watch for road sign. Phone 509/545-1990.* Self-guided tour of tasting room, oak aging casks, storage tanks, and bottling line; park with picnic and play area, amphitheater, gazebo, pond. (Daily; closed holidays) **FREE**

**Sacajawea State Park.** *2501 Sacajawea Park Rd, Pasco (99301). 2 miles SE off Hwy 12. Phone 509/545-2361.* Site where Lewis and Clark camped in 1805. Approximately 280 acres. Swimming, fishing, boating (launch, dock); picnicking. (Daily)

## Special Events

**Fiery Food Festival.** *Pasco. Phone 509/545-0738.* The Festival provides two fun-filled days with wonderful food, great arts and crafts, fresh fruits and vegetables, entertainment on two stages. Weekend after Labor Day.

**Jazz Unlimited.** *Columbia Basin Community College, 2600 N 20th Ave, Pasco (99301). Phone 509/547-0511.* Usually the second and third weekend in Apr.

**Tri-Cities Water Follies.** *1313 W Clark St, Pasco (99301). Phone 509/547-5563.* Events scheduled throughout month of July leading to hydroplane races on Columbia River on last weekend of month. July.

## Limited-Service Hotel

**★ ★ RED LION.** *2525 N 20th Ave, Pasco (99301). Phone 509/547-0701; toll-free 800/733-5466; fax 509/547-4278. www.redlion.com.* Located in the heart of Washington State wine country, this hotel is close to plenty of shopping and many attractions. 279 rooms, 3 story. Pets accepted. Check-in 3 pm, check-out noon. High-speed Internet access, wireless Internet access. Two restaurants, bar. Fitness room. Outdoor pool, whirlpool. Airport transportation available. Business center. **$**

# Port Angeles (B-2)

*See also Neah Bay, Olympic National Park , Sequim*

**Population** 18,397
**Elevation** 32 ft
**Area Code** 360
**Zip** 98362
**Information** Chamber of Commerce, 121 E Railroad; phone 360/452-2363
**Web Site** www.portangeles.org

Sitting atop the Olympic Peninsula, Port Angeles has the Olympic Mountains at its back and the Juan de Fuca Strait at its shoreline; just 17 miles across the strait is Victoria, British Columbia. Ediz Hook, a sandspit, protects the harbor and helps make it the first American port of entry for ships coming to Puget Sound from all parts of the Pacific; there is a US Coast Guard Air Rescue Station here. A Spanish captain who entered the harbor in 1791 named the village he found here Port of Our Lady of the Angels, a name that has survived in abbreviated form. The fishing fleet; pulp, paper and lumber mills; and tourism are its economic mainstays today.

Port Angeles is the headquarters for Olympic National Park. It is an excellent starting point for expeditions to explore the many faces of the peninsula.

## What to See and Do

**Ferry service to Victoria, BC, Canada.** *Port Angeles. Phone 360/457-4491. www.cohoferry.com.* A 90-minute trip; departs from Coho ferry terminal to Victoria's Inner Harbour. Contact Black Ball Transport Inc, 10777 Main St, Suite 106, Bellevue 98004. (Daily; summer, four trips; spring and fall, two trips; rest of year, one trip) **$$$$**

**Joyce Depot Museum.** *Joyce. www.joycewa.com/museum.htm.* The museum is located in a former railroad station. Visitors can browse through general store items from the 1920s through the 1940s, logging equipment, and historical railroad equipment. Old photos of the area have been preserved, as well as articles from the former *City of Port Crescent* newspaper. Stop for a short trip back to the early days of this area.

**Joyce General Store.** *50883 Hwy 112, Port Angeles. Phone 360/928-3568. www.joycewa.com.* Built in the early 1900s, the Joyce General Store still has the same false front, beaded ceiling, oiled wood floors, and original fixtures. Much of the interior came from the Markham House Hotel, which stood in the now-extinct town of Port Crescent. Joyce's namesake, Joe Joyce, transported much of what was used to build the store from Port Crescent (now Crescent Bay) to its present location. The store has been in the same family for more than 48 years.

**Merrill and Ring Tree Farm Interpretive Tour.** *Hwy 112, Port Angeles (98363). Phone 800/998-2382. www.nps.gov/olym/.* Merrill and Ring Tree Farm and Forestry Trail offers self-guided tours of the Pysht Forestry Trail. Along the trail are interpretive resources explaining resource management and reforestation, providing an opportunity to educate visitors about the clear-cuts along the SR 112 corridor. The Merrill and Ring Tree Farm also offers a bit of history, as the site still has the original cabins built by Merril and Ring to house its loggers in the early 1900s.

**Olympic Raft and Guide Service.** *123 Lake Aldwell Rd, Port Angeles (98363). Phone 360/452-1443. www.raftandkayak.com.* River rafting in Olympic National Park.

**Olympic Van Tours, Inc.** *731 W 4th St, Port Angeles (98363). Phone 360/457-3545.* Unique, interpretive sightseeing tours into Olympic National Park (eight hours). Reservations required. For schedule and fees contact PO Box 2201.

## Special Events

**Clallam County Fair.** *1608 W 16th St, Port Angeles (98363). Phone 360/417-2551.* Mid-Aug.

**Dungeness Crab & Seafood Festival.** *Port Angeles. Phone 360/457-6110. www.crabfestival.org.* The annual festival celebrates the region's diverse bounty of seafood, agriculture and maritime traditions. Mid-Oct.

## Limited-Service Hotels

**★ PORT ANGELES INN.** *111 E 2nd St, Port Angeles (98362). Phone 360/452-9285; toll-free 800/421-0706; fax 360/452-7935. www.portangelesinn.com.* 23 rooms, 3 story. Check-out 11 am. **$**

**★ ★ RED LION HOTEL.** *221 N Lincoln, Port Angeles (98362). Phone 360/452-9215; toll-free 800/733-5466; fax 360/452-4734. www.redlion.com.* Overlooks harbor. 186 rooms, 2 story. Pets accepted, some restrictions; fee. Check-out noon. Restaurant. Outdoor pool, whirlpool. **$**

## Specialty Lodgings

**DOMAINE MADELEINE.** *146 Wildflower Ln, Port Angeles (98362). Phone 360/457-4174; toll-free 888/811-8376; fax 360/457-3037. www.domainemadeleine.com.* The guest rooms at this intimate bed-and-breakfast are individually decorated. The views of Victoria, British Columbia, and the San Juan Islands are magnificent. 5 rooms, 2 story. Children over 12 years only. Complimentary full breakfast. Check-in 4-6 pm, check-out 11 am. Airport transportation available. **$$**

**FIVE SEASUNS BED & BREAKFAST.** *1006 S Lincoln St, Port Angeles (98362). Phone 360/452-8248; toll-free 800/708-0777; fax 360/417-0465. www.seasuns.com.* 5 rooms, 2 story. Children over 12 years only. Complimentary full breakfast. Check-in 4-6 pm. Check-out 11 am. Restored Dutch Colonial inn built in 1920s; pond, waterfall. **$**

**TUDOR INN BED & BREAKFAST.** *1108 S Oak St, Port Angeles (98362). Phone 360/452-3138; fax 360/457-9360. www.tudorinn.com.* This European, Tudor-style bed-and-breakfast offers guests a historical location from which to enjoy the Pacific Northwest. Visitors can relax in the living room, the library, or the inn's natural surroundings while enjoying the view of the Strait of Juan de Fuca. 5 rooms, 2 story. Children over 12 years only. Complimentary full breakfast. Check-in 4-6 pm, check-out 11 am. **$**

## Restaurants

★ ★ **BELLA ITALIA.** *118 E 1st St, Port Angeles (98362). Phone 360/457-5442. www.bellaitaliapa.com.* Italian menu. Dinner. Closed Thanksgiving, Dec 25. Bar. Children's menu. Casual attire. Reservations recommended. **$$**

★ ★ **BUSHWHACKER.** *1527 E 1st St, Port Angeles (98362). Phone 360/457-4113.* Seafood menu. Dinner. Closed Dec 25. Bar. Children's menu. Casual attire. **$$**

★ ★ ★ **C'EST SI BON.** *23 Cedar Park Dr, Port Angeles (98362). Phone 360/452-8888. www.cestsibon-frenchcuisine.com.* Elaborate paintings and floral wall coverings and fabrics give this restaurant its classic French feel. A gracious host and talented chef deliver a delightful dining experience. French menu. Dinner. Closed Mon. Bar. Casual attire. Reservations recommended. Outdoor seating. **$$$**

★ **LANDINGS.** *115 E Railroad Ave (Hwy 101), Port Angeles (98362). Phone 360/457-6768.* Seafood menu. Breakfast, lunch, dinner. Children's menu. Casual attire. Outdoor seating. **$**

★ ★ ★ **TOGA'S INTERNATIONAL CUISINE.** *122 W Lauridsen Blvd, Port Angeles (98362). Phone 360/452-1952.* The menu at this quaint, intimate restaurant shows influences from all over Europe and highlights Northwest ingredients. The dining room is located in a remodeled, 1943 home and boasts beautiful Olympic Mountain Range views from its back window. International menu. Dinner. Closed Sun-Mon; holidays; also Sept. Children's menu. Reservations recommended. Outdoor seating. **$$**

# Port Gamble (B-2)

*See also Port Ludlow, Seattle*

**Settled** 1853
**Area Code** 360
**Zip** 98364

Captain William Talbot, a native of Maine, discovered the vast Puget Sound timberlands and located what has become the oldest continuously operating sawmill in North America here. Spars for the ships of the world were a specialty. The community, built by the company and still owned by it, gradually developed a distinctive appearance because of its unusual (to this part of the country) New England-style architecture.

The company, realizing an opportunity to preserve a bit of the past, has rebuilt and restored more than 30 homes, commercial buildings, and St. Paul's Episcopal Church. Replicas of gas lamps and underground wiring have replaced street lighting. The entire town has been declared a historic district.

## What to See and Do

**Hood Canal Nursery.** *4110 Carver Dr, Port Gamble (98364). W edge of town. Phone 360/297-7555.* Self-guided tour covers storage and maintenance building, soil mixing, pump house, and chemical storage, water reservoir, greenhouses with a capacity of 3 1/2 million seedlings. (Mon-Fri) **FREE**

**Kitsap Memorial State Park.** *202 NE Park St, Port Gamble (98370). 4 miles S on Hwy 3. Phone 360/779-3205.* Over 50 acres. Saltwater swimming, scuba diving, fishing, boating (mooring); hiking, picnicking, shelters, camping (dump station).

**Of Sea and Shore Museum.** *General Store Building, 3 Rainier Ave, Port Gamble (98364). Phone 360/297-7636. www.ofseaandshore.com.* One of the largest shell collections in the country. Gift, book shop. (Daily; closed Jan 1, Thanksgiving, Dec 25) **FREE**

**Port Gamble Historic Museum.** *32400 Rainier NE, Port Gamble (98364). Downhill side of the General Store. Phone 360/297-8074.* Exhibits trace the history of the area and the timber company. Displays arranged in order of time: replica of old saw filing room; San Francisco office, captain's cabin from ship; individual rooms from hotels and houses; Forest of the Future exhibit. (May-Oct, daily) **$$**

# Port Ludlow (B-2)

*See also Port Gamble, Sequim*

**Settled** 1878
**Population** 1,968
**Elevation** 0-30 ft
**Area Code** 360
**Zip** 98365
**Information** Port Ludlow Olympic Peninsula Gateway Visitor Center, 93 Beaver Valley Rd; phone 360/437-0120
**Web Site** www.portludlowchamber.org

## Full-Service Inn

★★★ **INN AT PORT LUDLOW.** *1 Heron Rd, Port Ludlow (98365). Phone 360/437-7000; toll-free 877/805-0868; fax 360/437-0310. www.heronbeachinn.com.* This inn, resting on the shores of the Olympic Peninsula, offers its own brand of charm. Built to resemble an estate in Maine, the inn features rooms with exquisite views, comfortable amenities, and tasteful touches. 39 rooms, 3 story. Complimentary continental breakfast. Check-in 4 pm, check-out noon. Restaurant. **$$**

## Restaurant

★★★ **THE FIRESIDE.** *1 Heron Rd, Port Ludlow (98365). Phone 360/437-7000; toll-free 800/702-1239; fax 360/437-7410. www.ludlowbayresort.com.* Reminiscent of the East Coast's charming summer homes, this veranda-wrapped inn provides a serene setting for waterfront dining at its best. Seafood menu. Dinner. Bar. Children's menu. Casual attire. Reservations recommended. Outdoor seating. **$$**

# Port Townsend (B-2)

*See also Coupeville, Everett, Oak Harbor, Sequim*

**Settled** 1851
**Population** 8,334
**Elevation** 100 ft
**Area Code** 360
**Zip** 98368
**Information** Tourist Information Center, 2437 E Sims Way; phone 360/385-2722
**Web Site** www.ptchamber.org

Located on the Quimper Peninsula at the northeast corner of the Olympic Peninsula, this was once a busy port city served by sailing vessels and sternwheelers. Captain George Vancouver came ashore in 1792 and named the spot Port Townshend, after an English nobleman. Port Townsend is a papermill town with boat building and farming.

## What to See and Do

**Fort Flagler.** *Marrowstone Island. 20 miles SE on Marrowstone Island. Phone 360/385-3701.* More than 780 acres. Saltwater swimming, scuba diving, fishing, boating (launch, mooring); hiking, picnicking, camping (reservations required Memorial Day-Labor Day). Nature study; forested areas, some military areas.

**Fort Worden.** *200 Battery Way, Port Townsend (98368). 1 mile N. Phone 360/344-4431. www.parks.wa.gov.* Approximately 430 acres. Home of Centrum Foundation, with poetry and visual arts symposiums; fiction writer's workshop; fiddletune, jazz, and folk dance festivals. **FREE**

**Old Fort Townsend.** *Port Townsend. 3 miles S on Hwy 20. Phone 360/385-3595. www.parks.wa.gov.* Approximately 380 acres. Posted site of a fort established in 1856, abandoned in 1895. Swimming, scuba diving, bank fishing; hiking, picnicking, camping. (Mid-Apr-mid-Sept)

**Rothschild House.** *Franklin and Taylor sts, Port Townsend. Phone 360/379-8076.* (1868) Furnished in original style; flower and herb gardens. (May-Sept: daily; rest of year: Sat-Sun and holidays only) **$**

## Special Events

**House Tours.** *2437 E Sims Way, Port Townsend (98368). Phone 360/385-2722.* Third weekend in Sept.

**Jefferson County Fair.** *4907 Landes St, Port Townsend (98368). Phone 360/385-1013.* Agricultural and 4-H displays, livestock shows. Weekend in mid-Aug.

**Wooden Boat Festival.** *103 Hudson St, Port Townsend (98368). Phone 360/385-3628.* Displays, classes, and lectures. First weekend after Labor Day.

## Limited-Service Hotel

★★ **INN AT PORT HADLOCK.** *310 Alcohol Loop Rd, Port Hadlock (98339). Phone 360/385-7030; toll-free 800/785-7030; fax 360/385-6955. www.innat-porthadlock.com.* A former alcohol plant built in 1910, the Inn at Port Hadlock is a half-hour drive or ferry ride from Seattle. If you're bringing your own boat, the inn has a 164-slip marina to accommodate it. 33 rooms, 3 story. Pets accepted, some restrictions; fee. Check-in 3 pm, check-out 11 am. Wireless Internet access. Restaurant, bar. **$**

## Specialty Lodgings

**ANN STARRETT MANSION VICTORIAN BED & BREAKFAST.** *744 Clay St, Port Townsend (98368). Phone 360/385-3205; toll-free 800/321-0644; fax 360/385-2976. www.starrettmansion.com.* Overlooking the mountains and waters of Puget Sound, this bed-and-breakfast was built in 1889 using Victorian architecture. It is furnished with antiques and decorated with carvings and fine art work, and features a winding staircase and frescoed ceilings. 11 rooms, 4 story. Complimentary full breakfast. Check-in 3-8 pm, check-out 11 am. **$$**

**BISHOP VICTORIAN GUEST SUITES.** *714 Washington St, Port Townsend (98368). Phone 360/385-6122; toll-free 800/824-4738; fax 360/379-1840. www.bishopvictorian.com.* Built in 1890 as an office/warehouse; converted to English inn. 15 rooms, 3 story, all suites. Pets accepted, some restrictions; fee. Complimentary continental breakfast. Check-in 3 pm, check-out 11 am. **$**

**F. W. HASTINGS HOUSE OLD CONSULATE.** *313 Walker St, Port Townsend (98368). Phone 360/385-6753; toll-free 800/300-6753; fax 360/385-2097. www.oldconsulateinn.com.* This is an elegant and tastefully stylish inn with the feel of an old Victorian Manor home. Attention to all details have been taken care of by the staff. 8 rooms, 3 story. Children over 12 years only. Complimentary full breakfast. Check-in 3-6 pm, check-out 11 am. Airport transportation available. **$$**

**HOLLY HILL HOUSE B&B.** *611 Polk St, Port Townsend (98368). Phone 360/385-5619; toll-free 800/435-1454; fax 360/385-4610. www.hollyhillhouse.com.* This guest house is located only a short walk from downtown, antique shops, museums, art galleries, and restaurants. Some rooms offer a view of the water. 5 rooms. Children over 12 years only. Complimentary full breakfast. Check-in 3-6 pm, check-out 10:30 am. **$**

**JAMES HOUSE.** *1238 Washington St, Port Townsend (98368). Phone 360/385-1238; toll-free 800/385-1238; fax 360/379-5551. www.jameshouse.com.* Built in 1889, this grand Victorian mansion sits on a bluff overlooking Puget Sound and mountains. Featuring fine woodwork, furnishings, and well-kept gardens, this bed-and-breakfast is a perfect place for a getaway. 12 rooms, 4 story. Children over 12 years only. Complimentary full breakfast. Check-in 3 pm, check-out 11 am. **$**

**PALACE.** *1004 Water St, Port Townsend (98368). Phone 360/385-0773; toll-free 800/962-0741; fax 360/385-0780. www.palacehotelpt.com.* 17 rooms, 2 story. Pets accepted; fee. Complimentary continental breakfast. Check-in 3 pm, check-out 11 am. **$$**

## Restaurants

**★ ★ FINS COASTAL CUISINE.** *1019 Water St, Port Townsend (98368). Phone 360/379-3474; fax 360/385-0946. www.finscoastalcuisine.com.* Seafood menu. Lunch, dinner. Bar. Casual attire. Reservations recommended. **$$**

**★ ★ MANRESA CASTLE.** *7th and Sheridan sts, Port Townsend (98368). Phone 360/385-5750. www.manresacastle.com.* This century-old, European-inspired castle is the home of an elegant yet casual dining room with spectacular views of the Olympic and Cascade Mountains. American menu. Dinner. Closed Sun-Tues; Jan 1, Dec 25. Bar. Casual attire. **$$**

**★ ★ SILVERWATER CAFE.** *237 Taylor St, Port Townsend (98368). Phone 360/385-6448. www.silverwatercafe.com.* Seafood menu. Lunch, dinner. Bar. Children's menu. Casual attire. Reservations recommended. **$$**

# Pullman (C-6)

*See also Clarkston*

**Settled** 1881
**Population** 24,675
**Elevation** 2,351 ft
**Area Code** 509
**Zip** 99163

**Information** Chamber of Commerce, 415 N Grand Ave; phone 509/334-3565 or toll-free 800/365-6948
**Web Site** www.pullmanchamber.com

A university town and an agricultural storage and shipping center in the fertile Palouse Hills, this community is named for George M. Pullman, the inventor/tycoon who gave his name to the railroad sleeping car.

## What to See and Do

**Kamiak Butte County Park.** *Pullman. 10 miles N on Hwy 27. Phone 509/397-6238.* A timbered area with a rocky butte rising 3,641 feet high, trails leading to the summit. Approximately 300 acres. Picnicking, hiking, interpretive programs (summer). Camping (Apr-Oct; fee). Park (all year). **FREE**

**Washington State University.** *Pullman. E of town center. Guided tours at admission office, Lighty Building, Room 370 (afternoon, daily). Phone 509/335-8633. www.wsu.edu.* (1890) (17,000 students) On campus is

**Museum of Art.** *Pullman. Fine Arts Center. Phone 509/335-1910.* Exhibitions, lectures, films. (Sept-July, daily, hours vary) **FREE**

**Wawawai County Park.** *Pullman. 11 miles N on Hwy 27.* Boating, fishing; picnicking, hiking. Earth-sheltered home (afternoon tours, call for dates). Camping (Apr-Oct; fee). Park (all year).

## Special Event

**National Lentil Festival.** *Pullman. Phone 509/334-3565.* Food booths, arts and crafts, musical entertainment, parade. Late Aug.

## Limited-Service Hotels

**★ HOLIDAY INN EXPRESS HOTEL & SUITES PULLMAN.** *SE 1190 Bishop Blvd, Pullman (99163). Phone 509/334-4437; toll-free 800/465-4329; fax 509/334-4447. www.hiexpress.com/pullmanwa.* **$**

**★ QUALITY INN.** *SE 1400 Bishop Blvd, Pullman (99163). Phone 509/332-0500; toll-free 800/228-5151; fax 509/334-4271. www.choicehotels.com.* 66 rooms, 2 story. Pets accepted, some restrictions; fee. Check-out noon. Outdoor pool, whirlpool. Airport transportation available. **$**

# Puyallup (C-2)

*See also Enumclaw, Tacoma*

**Founded** 1877
**Population** 33,011
**Elevation** 40 ft
**Area Code** 253
**Information** Chamber of Eastern Pierce County, 417 E Pioneer, 98371; phone 253/845-6755
**Web Site** www.eastpiercechamber.com

Puyallup freezes the farm produce from the fertile soil and mild climate of the valley between Mount Rainier and Tacoma. A $2 million bulb industry (irises, daffodils, and tulips) was born in 1923, when it was discovered that the valley was ideal for growing. Ezra Meeker crossed the plains by covered wagon and named this city Puyallup (meaning "generous people") after a tribe that lived in the valley; Puyallups still live in the area.

## What to See and Do

**Ezra Meeker Mansion.** *312 Spring St, Puyallup (98372). Phone 253/848-1770.* (1890) The 17-room Victorian house of Ezra Meeker, pioneer, farmer, first town mayor, author, and preserver of the Oregon Trail. Six fireplaces, period furnishings, stained-glass windows, and hand-carved woodwork. (Mar-mid-Dec, Wed-Sun; closed Easter, Thanksgiving) **$**

**Pioneer Park.** *324 S Meridian, Puyallup (98371). Phone 253/841-5457.* Life-size statue of Ezra Meeker. Playground; wading pool (summer). **FREE**

## Special Events

**Ezra Meeker Community Festival.** *312 Spring St, Puyallup (98372). Phone 253/848-1770.* Fine arts show, arts and crafts, entertainment; ice cream social at Meeker Mansion. Late June.

**Pierce County Fair.** *21802 Meridian Ave E, Graham (98338). 6 miles S. Phone 253/847-4754.* Early Aug.

**Puyallup Fair.** *110 9th Ave SW, Puyallup (98371). Phone 253/841-5045. www.thefair.com.* An annual tradition every September since 1900, the Puyallup Fair is held on fairgrounds about 40 miles south of downtown Seattle for a period of nearly three weeks. The event includes all sorts of entertainment (including racing pigs, hypnotists, and local and national musical acts), as well as rodeo competitions, a full carnival with thrill rides and a midway, and a petting farm. There is also a three-day Spring Fair held here in April. Seventeen days in Sept.

**Sumner Summer Festival.** *Puyallup. Phone 253/845-3182.* Early Aug.

# Quinault (B-1)

**Population** 350
**Elevation** 221 ft
**Area Code** 360
**Zip** 98575
**Information** Grays Harbor Chamber of Commerce, 506 Duffy St, Aberdeen 98520; phone 360/532-1924 or toll-free 800/321-1924
**Web Site** www.graysharbor.org

Quinault, on the shore of Lake Quinault, is the south entrance to Olympic National Park. In the heart of the Olympic National Forest, it is the gateway to any of three valleys—the Hoh, Queets, and Quinault—that make up the rain forest, a lush green ecological phenomenon. It also provides an entrance to the Enchanted Valley area of the park. The Quinault Reservation is 2 miles west.

A Ranger District office of the Olympic National Forest is located here.

## Limited-Service Hotel

**★ ★ LAKE QUINAULT LODGE.** *345 South Shore Rd, Quinault (98525). Phone 360/288-2900; toll-free 800/562-6672; fax 360/288-2901. www.visitlake-quinault.com.* 92 rooms, 3 story. Check-out 11 am. Restaurant, bar. Beach. Indoor pool. **$**

# Quincy (C-4)

*See also Ellensburg, Ephrata, Wenatchee*

**Settled** 1892
**Population** 5,044
**Elevation** 1,301 ft
**Area Code** 509
**Zip** 98848
**Information** Quincy Valley Chamber of Commerce, 119 F St SE; phone 509/787-2140
**Web Site** www.quincyvalley.org

Although this area gets only about 8 inches of rain a year, irrigation has turned the surrounding countryside green. Quincy processes and markets farm produce; more than 80 crops are grown in the area. Deposits of diatomaceous earth (soft, chalky material used for fertilizers, mineral aids, and filters) are mined in the area and refined in Quincy. Fishing and game-bird hunting are good in the surrounding area.

## What to See and Do

**Crescent Bar Park.** *Quincy. 8 miles W off Hwy 28. On Wanapum Reservoir in the Columbia River.* Swimming, bathhouse, beaches, waterskiing, boating, fishing, marina; playground, picnicking, camping (Apr-Oct; hookups; fee), restaurants, putting green, shops, pro shop, grocery, nine-hole golf (fee), four tennis courts (fee). Park (all year).

## Special Event

**Farmer Consumer Awareness Day.** *Quincy High School, 16 Sixth Ave SE, Quincy (98848). Phone 509/787-3501.* Free tours to dairies, processing plants, packing houses, farms, harvesting operations. Exhibits, food booths, arts and crafts, petting zoo, antique autos, farm equipment, games, parade, 2K and 5K run, entertainment. Second Sat in Sept.

## Limited-Service Hotel

**★ TRADITIONAL INNS.** *500 F St SW, Quincy (98848). Phone 509/787-3525; fax 509/787-3528. www.traditionalinns.com.* 24 rooms, 2 story. Pets accepted, some restrictions; fee. Check-out 11 am. **$**

# Redmond (B-3)

*See also Ellensburg, Ephrata, Wenatchee*

**Settled** 1871
**Population** 45,256
**Elevation** 50 ft
**Area Code** 425
**Information** Redmond Chamber of Commerce, 16210 NE 80th St, 98073; phone 425/885-4014
**Web Site** www.redmondchamber.org

Redmond experienced dramatic change over the course of the 20th century, evolving from a sleepy logging town to a high-tech hub, a transformation driven by the exponential growth of Microsoft, which is headquartered here. Situated at the northern tip of Lake Sammamish, Redmond boasts safe neighborhoods, excellent schools, and a public park system that covers 1,350 acres and more than 25 miles of trails. A wide variety of shops and restaurants can be found at Redmond Town Center. The city is a short drive east of Seattle on Highway 520.

## What to See and Do

**Celtic Bayou Brewpub.** *7281 W Lake Sammamish Pkwy NE, Redmond (98052). Phone 425/869-5933. www.celticbayou.com.* An Irish pub with a laid-back vibe, a Cajun menu, and an in-house brewery, Celtic Bayou is a pleasant place to unwind, with walls clad in mellow-toned wood, booths and tables, and an outdoor beer garden. Located east of Seattle in suburban Redmond, the place attracts its fair share of Microsoft employees and other high-tech types. Live music is featured on Saturday nights. (Sun-Mon 11:30 am-10 pm, Tues-Thurs 11:30 am-midnight, Fri-Sat 11:30 am-1 am)

**Marymoor Park.** *6046 W Lake Sammamish Pkwy, Redmond (98052). Phone 206/205-3661.* Located in Redmond in Seattle's Eastside suburbs, Marymoor Park is the largest, and likely the busiest, park in metro Seattle. With 640 acres of parkland around a historic farmhouse, it is home to the area's only velodrome, as well as a climbing rock, a model airplane field, and numerous sports fields. Marymoor is also home to a very popular off-leash dog park, about 100 acres of forest and meadow on the shores of a slow-moving river.

**Redmond Town Center.** *16495 NE 74th St, Redmond (98052). Phone 425/867-0808. www.shopredmondtowncenter.com.* This 120-acre, open-air shopping and entertainment hub is in Redmond, the Eastside home of Microsoft and numerous other high-tech companies. National chains such as Gap, REI, Borders, and Eddie Bauer dominate the retail landscape, and there are also a number of restaurants (including national chains) and an eight-screen movie theater. Every Saturday from May though October, a farmers' market offers fresh produce and flowers, and on Tuesday evenings in summer, live music can be enjoyed. There are also a number of events for children on the Redmond Town Center calendar. (Mon-Sat 10 am-8 pm, Sun 11 am-6 pm)

**Sammamish River Trail.** *Bothell.* A 10-mile paved trail running southeast from Bothell to Redmond, the Sammamish River Trail connects with the Burke-Gilman Trail, forming a 27-mile route that leads to Gas Works Park in Seattle. This peaceful, mostly level trail follows alongside the gentle current of the Sammamish River, passing through Woodinville, with its two wineries and the Redhook Ale Brewery a short jaunt off the trail. The trail is popular with joggers, walkers, cyclists, and in-line skaters. At the north end of the trail, start your journey at Bothell Landing Park (9919 NE 180th St). Down south in Redmond, begin your trek at Marymoor Park (6046 W Lake Sammamish Parkway NE).

**Willows Run Golf Club.** *10402 Willows Rd NE, Redmond (98052). Phone 425/883-1200. www.willowsrun.com.* Willows Run offers an intriguing mix of golf getaway and closeness to civilization during your round. Much of the back nine is built next to an industrial park, but the course has few trees and resembles British Open layouts. There are two 18-hole tracks and a 9-hole par-three course as well. The holes are closely packed, but they are challenging, with plenty of water along either 18. The facility's signature hole is the 17th on the Eagle's Talon course, a long hole with a nearly island green that slopes to the front, assuring those who do not hit the ball far enough will go fishing. **$$$$**

# Renton (B-2)

*See also Ellensburg, Ephrata, Wenatchee*

## What to See and Do

**Spirit of Washington Dinner Train Tour.** *626 S 4th St, Renton (98055). Phone 425/227-7245; toll-free 800/876-7245. www.spiritofwashingtondinnertrain.com.* All aboard for breathtaking scenery, gourmet dining, and a winery tour! The Spirit of Washington Dinner Train takes passengers back in time to an era when railway travel was considered a luxury. Riders aboard the Spirit of Washington's vintage train cars are treated to a three-course gourmet meal, feasting on such delicacies as cherry smoke roasted salmon and crab enchiladas, during a 3 1/4-hour excursion that begins and ends in the city of Renton. The views are often spectacular, particularly in the cars offering glass dome ceilings, as the train winds along the shores of Lake Washington and passes through the Sammamish River Valley. A highlight of the trip is when it passes over the 102-foot-high Wilburton Trestle, a local landmark since its construction in 1891. The ride includes a 45-minute stop in Woodinville at the Columbia Winery, where guests tour the cellar and enjoy a wine tasting. The Spirit of Washington operates year-round, with daily trips during the summer months. **$$$$**

## Limited-Service Hotel

★ **QUALITY INN.** *1850 Maple Valley Hwy, Renton (98055). Phone 425/226-7600; fax 425/271-1296. www.choicehotels.com.* 105 rooms. Complimentary continental breakfast. Check-in 3 pm, check-out noon. High-speed Internet access. Fitness room. Whirlpool. Business center. **$**

# Richland (D-5)

*See also Kennewick, Pasco, Sunnyside*

**Population** 38,708
**Elevation** 360 ft
**Area Code** 509
**Zip** 99352
**Information** Chamber of Commerce, 710A George Washington Way; phone 509/946-1651
**Web Site** www.ci.richland.wa.us

Although it's one of the "tri-cities" (see KENNEWICK and PASCO), Richland has an entirely different personality due to the 560-square-mile Hanford Works of the Department of Energy (DOE)—formerly the US Atomic Energy Commission. In 1943, Richland was a village of 250, dedicated to fruit cultivation. A year later, Hanford was established by the government as one of four main development points for the atomic bomb, along with Oak Ridge, Tennessee; Los Alamos, New Mexico; and the Argonne Laboratory, near Chicago. Hanford no longer is involved in the production of plutonium, and the more than 16,000 employees are now dedicated to environmental cleanup and safe disposal of nuclear and hazardous wastes.

Once largely desert area, Richland today is surrounded by vineyards and orchards thanks to irrigation from the Grand Coulee Dam and the Yakima River Irrigation Projects. The city is at the hub of an area of spectacular scenery and outdoor activities within a short drive in any direction.

## What to See and Do

**CRESHT Museum.** *95 Lee Blvd, Richland (99352). Phone 509/943-9000.* Displays, models, computer exhibits relating to US energy, science, and environmental topics. (Mon-Sat, Sun afternoon; closed holidays) **$**

## Special Events

**Benton-Franklin Fair and Rodeo.** *Franklin County Fairgrounds. Phone 509/586-9211.* Fair, parade, carnival. Aug.

**Columbia Cup.** *5111 Columbia Dr SE, Richland (99336). Phone 509/547-2203.* Hydroplane races. July.

**Cool Desert Nights Car Show.** *515 Lee Blvd, Richland (99352). Phone 509/697-5898.* June.

**NASCAR Auto Racing.** *Richland.* June-Sept.

## Limited-Service Hotels

★ **HAMPTON INN RICHLAND-TRI CITIES, WA.** *486 Bradley Blvd, Richland (99352). Phone 509/943-4400; toll-free 800/426-7866; fax 509/943-1797. www.hamptoninn.com.* 100 rooms. Pets accepted, some restrictions. Complimentary continental breakfast. Check-in 3 pm, check-out noon. High-speed Internet access, wireless Internet access. Fitness room. Indoor pool, whirlpool. Airport transportation available. **$**

★ ★ **RED LION.** *802 George Washington Way, Richland (99352). Phone 509/946-7611; toll-free 800/733-5466; fax 509/943-8564. www.redlion.com.* 149 rooms, 2 story. Pets accepted; fee. Check-in 3 pm, check-out 1 pm. High-speed Internet access, wireless Internet access. Restaurant, bar. Fitness room. Outdoor pool, whirlpool. Airport transportation available. Business center. **$**

# Ritzville (C-5)

*See also Moses Lake*

**Settled** 1878
**Population** 1,736
**Elevation** 1,815 ft
**Area Code** 509
**Zip** 99169
**Information** Chamber of Commerce, 201 W Railroad; phone 509/659-1936

## Special Events

**Ritzville Blues Festival.** *Ritzville. Phone 509/659-1936.* Second Sat in July.

**Wheat Land Communities Fair.** *Ritzville. Phone 509/659-0141.* Parade, rodeo. Labor Day weekend.

## Limited-Service Hotel

★ **BEST WESTERN BRONCO INN.** *105 W. Galbreath Way, Ritzville (99169). Phone 509/659-5000; fax 509/659-5002. www.bestwesternritzville.com.* 64 rooms. Pets accepted. Complimentary continental breakfast. Check-in 4 pm, check-out noon. Fitness room. Indoor pool, whirlpool. Business center. **$**

## Restaurant

★ ★ **CIRCLE T INN.** *214 W Main Ave, Ritzville (99169). Phone 509/659-0922.* American menu. Breakfast, lunch, dinner. Bar. **$$**

# San Juan Islands (A-2)

*See also Anacortes; also see Vancouver, BC*

**Area Code** 360
**Information** San Juan Islands Visitor Information Service, PO Box 65, Lopez Island, 98261; phone 360/468-4664 or toll-free 888/468-3701
**Web Site** www.guidetosanjuans.com

These 172 islands nestled between the northwest corner of Washington and Vancouver Island, British Columbia, Canada, compose a beautiful and historic area. Secluded coves, giant trees, freshwater lakes, fishing camps, modest motels, numerous bed-and-breakfasts, and plush resorts characterize the four major islands. Over 500 miles of paved or gravel roads swing through virgin woodlands and along lovely shorelines. The islands are accessible by ferry from Anacortes.

San Juan Island gave birth in 1845 to the expansionist slogan "fifty-four forty or fight" and was the setting for the "pig war" of 1859, in which a British pig uprooted an American potato patch. The subsequent hostilities between the islands' 7 British and 14 American inhabitants reached such proportions that eventually Kaiser Wilhelm I of Germany was called in to act as arbiter and settle the boundaries. During the 13 years of controversy, the pig was the only casualty. This island was the last place the British flag flew within the territorial United States. Friday Harbor, most westerly stop in the United States on San Juan Islands ferry tour, is county seat of San Juan.

## What to See and Do

★ **San Juan Island.** *Anacortes.* Friday Harbor on eastern shore serves as base for salmon fleet; major commercial center of islands. Fishing lakes; camping facilities, golf, International Seaplane Base, and two airstrips are here. Also on San Juan is

> **San Juan Island National Historical Park.** *Anacortes. Phone 360/378-2240.* Commemorates the settlement of the boundary issue between the United States and Great Britain. English Camp, 10 miles northwest of Friday Harbor on Garrison Bay, has a restored blockhouse, commissary, hospital, formal garden, and barracks built during the British occupation. American Camp, 6 miles southeast of Friday Harbor, has remains of redoubt, the American defensive earthwork; laundresses' and officers' quarters. Picnicking; information specialist at both camps (June-Sept: daily; rest of year: Thurs-Sun). Office and information center in Friday Harbor, 1st and Spring sts (June-Aug: daily; May and Sept: Mon-Fri; closed rest of year; closed holidays)

**Whale Museum.** *62 1st St N, Friday Harbor (98250). Phone 360/378-4710.* Art and science exhibits document the lives of whales and porpoises in this area. (Daily; closed holidays) **$$**

## Special Event

**San Juan Jazz Festival.** *Friday Harbor. Friday Harbor and Roche Harbor.* Last weekend in July.

## Limited-Service Hotel

★ **HOTEL DE HARO AT ROCHE HARBOR SEASIDE VILLAGE.** *248 Reuben Memorial Dr, Roche Harbor (98250). Phone 360/378-2155; toll-free 800/451-8910; fax 360/378-6809. www.rocheharbor.com.* 29 rooms, 3 story. Check-in 3 pm, check-out 11 am. Bar. Outdoor pool. Tennis. Business center. **$**

## Full-Service Resort

★ ★ ★ **ROSARIO RESORT.** *1400 Rosario Rd, Eastsound (98245). Phone 360/376-2222; toll-free 800/562-8820; fax 360/376-2289. www.rosarioresort.com.* Few places induce an adrenalin rush upon arrival, yet Rosario Resort is one spot that bears that distinction. Located at the tip of Orcas Island in Washington's picturesque San Juan Islands, visitors land directly in front of the resort via a thrilling and scenic seaplane ride (less adventurous types may opt for the ferry). This resort is a veritable Eden for outdoor enthusiasts, with a variety of recreational opportunities available both on- and off-resort. From whale-watching and sea kayaking to nature hikes in Moran State Park, Rosarios backdrop serves as a playground for visitors. Back at the resort, the Avanyu Spa soothes frayed nerves and four restaurants satisfy hearty appetites. Fanning out across Cascade Bay, the welcoming guest accommodations reflect the resorts dedication to casual elegance. 116 rooms, 2 story. Check-in 4 pm, check-out 11 am. Three restaurants, bar. Children's activity center. Fitness room, fitness classes available, spa. Indoor pool, two outdoor pools, children's pool, whirlpool. Tennis. Airport transportation available. **$$**

## Specialty Lodgings

**ARGYLE HOUSE BED & BREAKFAST.** *685 Argyle Ave, Friday Harbor (98250). Phone 360/378-4084; toll-free 800/624-3459. www.argylehouse.net.* Built in 1910; country setting, gardens. 4 rooms, 2 story. Children over 10 years only. Complimentary full breakfast. Check-in 3 pm, check-out 11 am. **$**

**FRIDAY'S HISTORIC INN.** *35 First St, San Juan Island (98250). Phone 360/378-5848; toll-free 800/352-2632; fax 360/378-2881. www.friday-harbor.com.* Found only a short walk from this bed-and-breakfast are Friday Harbor's waterfront, town shops, and restaurants. The property features limited-edition wildlife art, soundproof rooms, and a large parlor. 15 rooms, 3 story. Complimentary continental breakfast. Check-in 3:30 pm, check-out 11 am. **$$**

**HILLSIDE HOUSE BED AND BREAKFAST.** *365 Carter Ave, Friday Harbor (98250). Phone 360/378-4730; toll-free 800/232-4730; fax 360/378-4715. www.hillsidehouse.com.* A contemporary home among acres of fir and pine trees. Some rooms overlook the atrium; others have a view of the harbor. 7 rooms, 3 story. Complimentary full breakfast. Check-in 3 pm, check-out 11 am. **$**

**INN AT SWIFTS BAY.** *856 Port Stanley Rd, Lopez Island (98261). Phone 360/468-3636; toll-free 888/903-9536; fax 360/468-3637. www.swiftsbay.com.* Incredible comfort and unsurpassed amenities are on the top of the list at this Tudor-style bed-and-breakfast. It lies in the San Juan Islands away from busy city life and offers amazing bedrooms and a great living area, dining room, and library. 5 rooms, 2 story. Complimentary full breakfast. Check-in 3-7 pm, check-out 11 am. Fitness room. **$$**

**TUCKER HOUSE BED & BREAKFAST.** *260 B St, Friday Harbor (98250). Phone 360/378-2783; toll-free 800/965-0123; fax 360/378-8775. www.tuckerhouse.com.* Victorian home built in 1898. 6 rooms, 2 story. Pets accepted; fee. Complimentary full breakfast. Check-in 3 pm. Check-out 11 am. **$**

**TURTLEBACK FARM INN.** *1981 Crow Valley Rd, Eastsound (98245). Phone 360/376-4914; toll-free 800/376-4914; fax 360/376-5329. www.turtlebackfarminn.com.* The inn is a country farmhouse located on Orcas Island overlooking the clear waters of the Puget Sound. It features spacious guest rooms decorated with antiques and contemporary pieces. Fine dining and unique shopping are nearby. 11 rooms, 2 story. Complimentary full breakfast. Check-in 2 pm, check-out 11 am. **$$**

## Restaurants

**★★★ CHRISTINA'S.** *310 Main, East Sound (98245). Phone 360/376-4904. www.christinas.net.* Christina's is one of the most highly regarded establishments in the Northwest. Photos of the owners' Hollywood connections adorn the wall of the small bar. The innovative treatments of meat, fresh Northwest seafood, and fowl keep devotees returning. Seafood menu. Dinner. Closed Dec 25; first 3 weeks in Jan and Nov. Bar. Children's menu. Outdoor seating. **$$**

**★★ DOWNRIGGERS.** *10 Front St, San Juan Islands (98250). Phone 360/378-2700; fax 360/378-3026. www.downriggerssanjuan.com.* Seafood, steak menu. Breakfast, lunch, dinner. Bar. Outdoor seating. **$$**

**★★ MANSION DINING ROOM.** *1400 Rosario Rd, East Sound (98245). Phone toll-free 800/562-8820 ext 400. www.rosariorockresorts.com.* Seafood, steak menu. Breakfast, lunch, dinner. Bar. Children's menu. Casual attire. Reservations recommended. **$$**

# Seattle

*See also Auburn, Bellevue, Bremerton, Everett, Issaquah, North Bend*

**Founded** 1852
**Population** 563,374
**Elevation** 125 ft
**Area Code** 206
**Information** Seattle-King County Convention & Visitors Bureau, 701 Pike St, Suite 1300, 98101; phone 206/461-5840
**Web Site** www.seeseattle.org

**Suburbs** Bellevue, Bremerton, Everett, Federal Way, Issaquah, Marysville, Port Gamble, Tacoma. (See individual alphabetical listings.)

Seattle has prospered from the products of its surrounding forests, farms, and waterways, serving as a provisioner to Alaska and the Orient. Since the 1950s, it has acquired a new dimension from the manufacture of jet airplanes, missiles, and space vehicles—which, along with tourism, comprise the city's most important industries.

The Space Needle, which dominated Seattle's boldly futuristic 1962 World's Fair, still stands, symbolic of the city's forward-looking character. The site of the fair is now the Seattle Center. Many features of the fair have been made permanent.

Seattle is on Elliott Bay, nestled between Puget Sound, an inland-probing arm of the Pacific Ocean, and Lake Washington, a 24-mile stretch of fresh water. The city sprawls across hills and ridges, some of them 500 feet high, but all are dwarfed by the Olympic Mountains to the west and the Cascades to the east. Elliott Bay, Seattle's natural harbor, welcomes about 2,000 commercial deep-sea cargo vessels a year. From Seattle's piers, ships wind their way 125 nautical miles through Puget Sound and the Strait of Juan de Fuca, two-thirds of them Orient-bound, the others destined for European, Alaskan, and Eastern ports.

On the same latitude as Newfoundland, Seattle is warmed by the Japan Current, shielded by the Olympics from excessive winter rains, and protected by the Cascades from midcontinent winter blasts. Only twice has the temperature been recorded at 100F; there isn't a zero on record.

Five families pioneered here and named the town for a friendly Native American chief. The great harbor and the timber surrounding it made an inviting combination; shortly thereafter, a sawmill and a salmon-canning plant were in operation. Soon wagon trains were rolling to Seattle through Snoqualmie Pass, a tempting 3,022 feet, lower than any other in the Northwest.

Isolated at the fringe of the continent by the vast expanse of America, Seattle enjoyed great expectations but few women, an obvious threat to the community's growth and serenity. Asa Mercer, a civic leader and the first president of the Territorial University, went east and persuaded 11 proper young women from New England to sail with him around the Horn to Seattle to take husbands among the pioneers. This venture in long-distance matchmaking proved so successful that Mercer returned east and recruited 100 Civil War widows. Today, many of Seattle's families proudly trace their lineage to these women.

When a ship arrived from Alaska with a "ton of gold" in 1897, the great Klondike Gold Rush was on, converting Seattle into a boomtown—the beginning of the trail to fortune. Since then, Seattle has been the natural gateway to Alaska because of the protected Inside Passage; the commercial interests of the two remain tightly knit. Another major event for Seattle was the opening of the Panama Canal in 1914, a tremendous stimulant for the city's commerce.

## Additional Visitor Information

For additional accommodations, see SEATTLE-TACOMA INTERNATIONAL AIRPORT AREA, which follows SEATTLE.

## Public Transportation

**Metro Transit System** Phone 206/553-3000. Web transit.metrokc.gov

## What to See and Do

**5th Avenue Theater.** *1305 5th Ave, Seattle (98101). Phone 206/625-1418. www.fifthavenuetheater.org.* This historic theater, which opened as a vaudeville house in 1926, now features musicals, concerts, films, and lectures. Its ornate interior, modeled after some of China's architectural treasures, may well distract you from whatever's taking place onstage.

## The Buzz on Seattle's Caffeine Culture

Seattle is known worldwide for its eclectic and innumerable mix of coffee establishments, ranging from chic espresso bars in trendy downtown hotels to tin-roofed java huts in grocery store parking lots. But for most of the 20th century, Seattle was regarded as a great place to partake in fresh fish, not fresh coffee. The emergence of Seattles coffee scene corresponded with the spectacular success of a local company bearing a now familiar name, **Starbucks.** Founded in 1971, Starbucks first coffeehouse opened in the citys Pike Place Market. It wasnt until the mid-1980s—when Starbucks employee Howard Schultz convinced the company's founders to develop a coffee bar culture similar to that found in Milan's espresso bars—that Starbuck's fortunes took off. At that time, it became a cultural and commercial phenomenon in Seattle and around the globe. Attempting to take advantage of the coffee craze, the likes of **Seattle's Best Coffee** and **Tully's** opened numerous Seattle locations, and now it's almost impossible to walk a city block without passing a franchise coffeehouse.

To fully appreciate Seattle's coffee culture, you should visit a few of the city's many independent coffee shops, one of the best being **Espresso Vivace Roasteria** (901 E Denny Way). Situated on Capitol Hill near the Seattle Center, Espresso Vivace has taken espresso preparation to an art form, having spent 15 years perfecting the roasting process for their signature beverage. Espresso Vivace even offers an intensive three-day espresso preparation course.

Artists like to gather downtown at the stylish and hip **Zeitgeist Coffee** (171 S Jackson St). Zeitgeist is particularly crowded on the first Thursday of each month, when the art galleries in and around Pioneer Square stay open late and hundreds of art lovers congregate in the area. Coffee is not the only thing on the menu; Zeitgeist also serves fresh pastries and grilled sandwiches.

Visitors to the Queen Anne neighborhood should stop by **Uptown Espresso** (525 Queen Anne Ave N). Weekends are particularly crowded at this casual coffeehouse situated at the bottom of Queen Anne Hill. Uptown Espresso's "velvet foam lattes" are a local favorite. The coffeehouse features vintage décor and the artwork of local painters.

Before you venture into one of the city's hundreds of coffee shops, it behooves you to study up on your coffee lexicon, which means that, if you dont want to sound like an instant-coffee drinker while ordering a small decaf espresso to go, you should know to request a short harmless espresso on a leash. At the very least, you should know these key terms:

*Americano:* An espresso mixed with hot water.

*Barista:* An individual who makes coffee drinks.

*Cappuccino:* An espresso with foamed milk on top.

*Espresso:* A roughly 1-ounce shot of espresso. Espresso is made from Arabica beans rather than the Robusta beans used to make regular coffee.

*Latte:* An espresso mixed with steamed milk, then topped by foamed milk.

*Mochaccino:* A cappuccino flavored with chocolate.

*Ristretto:* The strongest espresso; it is made using less water and more coffee.

**ACT Theatre.** *700 Union St, Seattle (98101). Phone 206/292-7660. www.acttheatre.org.* ACT Theatre presents contemporary (read: edgy and daring) pieces as well as classic plays and musicals. Performances are held in two main theaters in Kreielsheimer Place, a renovation of the historic Eagles Auditorium completed in 1996. The Allen, a theater in the round, was carved out of the old auditorium's floor; the top row of seats is actually at ground level. The Falls features a restored Joshua Green Foundation Vault, used by the Eagles as a bank vault.

**Alderwood Mall.** *3000 184th St, Lynwood (98037). Phone 425/771-1211. www.alderwoodmall.com.* The largest shopping center in north Seattle, the Alderwood Mall is undergoing a major redevelopment slated for completion in November 2004. The goal is to transform the mall into an upscale retail and entertainment destination with shops in an indoor "village" and on outdoor "terraces," as well as a 16-screen movie theater. Of the 120-plus stores, Alderwoods anchors include Nordstrom and the Bon Marché. (Mon-Sat 10 am-9:30 pm, Sun 11 am-7 pm)

**Alki Beach.** *1100 Alki Ave SW, Seattle (98116). Phone 206/684-4075.* Skirting the northwestern waterfront of the South Seattle neighborhood, the 2.5-mile Alki Beach is a Mecca for outdoor types of all kinds—joggers, divers, bicyclists, beach volleyball players, sunbathers, and rollerbladers. The beach, administered by the Seattle Parks Department, runs from Duwamish Head to Alki Point on Elliot Bay and offers stunning views of Puget Sound and the city skyline. Facilities are a notch above the norm, with scads of picnic tables, a playground, small boat access, and a wide, multi-use path. At Alki Point (the southern end of the beach), there is a bathhouse/art studio and a plaque commemorating the landing of the first settlers here in 1851. At Duwamish Head (the northern tip of the beach) are the sea-walled site of a former amusement park and a miniature version of the Statue of Liberty.

**Argosy Harbor Cruise.** *Pier 56, Alaskan Way, Seattle (98101). From Pier 55, at the foot of Seneca St. Phone 206/623-1445. www.argosycruises.com.* Boasting a 50-year history in Seattle's harbors, the family-owned Argosy Cruises is in proud possession of a fleet of nine cruise ships, ranging in size from the 77-foot *Champagne Lady* to the 180-foot *Royal Argosy*. The company operates from piers at the Seattle waterfront, Lake Union, and suburban Kirkland (on the eastern shore of Lake Washington). The most basic Argosy outing is a one-hour Harbor Cruise, which explores Seattle's downtown shoreline and offers some nice skyline views. Longer options include the Locks Cruise, which meanders from the salty waters of Puget Sound to Lake Union via the Ballard Locks, and a pair of lake cruises that explore Lake Union and Lake Washington. Snacks and beverages are offered on every Argosy cruise, but food is not included in the ticket price—the exceptions being ritzy lunch and dinner trips on the *Royal Argosy*. (Daily) **$$$$**

**Bainbridge Island.** *Seattle. www.bainbridgeisland.org.* A half-hour ferry trip from downtown Seattle (ferries depart regularly throughout the day), Bainbridge Island is the size of Manhattan but a world apart. In the late 1800s, the island boasted the worlds largest sawmill and a substantial shipbuilding industry, but its economy stumbled. It has recently regained footing as a tourist destination. With about 20,000 residents, the city of Bainbridge Island is now known for its delightful Victorian architecture and abundant shops and galleries. Densely wooded and lush with greenery, the island also attracts outdoor enthusiasts of all stripes—kayaking, golfing, fishing, and hiking are all popular—and boasts an active arts and entertainment scene. The Bainbridge Island Historical Museum is a great starting point, presenting displays on the islands geology, history, and industry in a converted 1908 schoolhouse.

**Ballard Locks.** *3015 NW 54th St, Seattle (98107). Phone 206/783-7059.* Popularly known as the Ballard Locks because of their location in Seattle's Ballard neighborhood, the Hiram M. Chittenden Locks are a marvel of engineering. Built in the early 20th century by the US Army Corps of Engineers, the locks are part of the canal system that connects salty Puget Sound (and, by extension, the Pacific Ocean) to Seattle's freshwater, providing a link for safe passage of watercraft. Salmon use a manmade "fish ladder" here to navigate their annual spawn through the locks. Underwater observation windows afford visitors a firsthand look at the migrating fish (and the seals and sea lions that feast on them, which workers struggle to keep out), but only at certain times of the year; the coho and chinook runs peak in midsummer. A visitor center presents exhibits that detail the locks history and ecology, and an impressively vibrant botanical garden is also onsite. (May-Sept: daily 7 am-9 pm; Oct-Apr: Thurs-Mon 7 am-8 pm) **FREE**

**★ Boeing Field–King County International Airport.** *7277 Perimeter Rd S, Seattle (98108). Phone 206/296-7380.* Observation Park has viewing, picnicking facilities. Southeast Side. Also here is

> **Museum of Flight.** *9404 E Marginal Way S, Seattle (98108). Phone 206/764-5700.* As a major hub for plane-maker Boeing—even since the aviation giant's headquarters bolted for Chicago in 2001Seattle is the ideal location for this impressive air and space museum. The facility is highlighted by the soaring Great Gallery, home of more than 50 vintage aircraft, many of which are suspended in formation six stories above the ground. On display here are the original presidential *Air Force One* and a replica of the Wright Brother's biplane from Kitty Hawk, North Carolina, alongside mint-condition models of the first fighter jet (a 1914 Caproni Ca 20) and the first jumbo jet (a prototype Boeing 747); many planes are open for visitors to sit in the cockpit or explore the hold. Located near Seattle-Tacoma International Airport in southern Seattle, the museum is also

## Under and Above Ground in Downtown Seattle

Begin in Seattle's Pioneer Square district, the city's original downtown, which was built in the 1890s (after a disastrous fire) as money from the Yukon Gold Rush started pouring in. The architecture is amazingly harmonious (one architect was responsible for nearly 60 major buildings in a ten-block radius) and graciously restored. The area also features the underground tour and many galleries, cafes, and antique shops. A collection of totem poles can be found in tree-lined Occidental Park and in Pioneer Square itself.

Continue across Alaskan Way (or take Waterfront Trolley, a vintage street car that runs from Pioneer Square to the waterfront to Pike Place Market) to the waterfront. Walk along the harbor, watching ferries dart to and fro, or take a boat tour (see FERRY TRIPS AND CRUISES). Stop at the Seattle Aquarium, located in Waterfront Park at Pier 59, then stop for clam chowder at Ivar's, located at Pier 54.

Continue north, recrossing Alaskan Way, and climb to Pike Place Market, eight stories above the harbor on a bluff. There are two ways to do this: there's an elevator hidden at the base of the market, or you can take the Harbor Stairs, a new cascade of steps flanked by shops and gardens. The Pike Place Market is Seattle's most interesting destination, an old-fashioned public market (built around 1910) in a warrenlike building with three floors of food, baked goods, ethnic shops, fresh fish, and crafts. You could spend hours here. Also in the Market are some of Seattles best-loved restaurants; many of them have great views over the harbor to the islands and Olympic Mountains to the west. Just down the street is the new Seattle Art Museum, with its excellent collection of Northwest Native Art.

home to the restored "Red Barn" where the Boeing Company was founded nearly a century ago and several space-themed exhibits. (Daily 10 am-5 pm; closed Thanksgiving, Dec 25) **$$$**

**Capitol Hill.** *12th Ave and E Madison St, Seattle. 12th Ave to Boren Ave and E Madison St to Denny Way.* Melding metropolitan chic, Victorian elegance, and urban grunge just east of downtown, Capitol Hill is one of Seattle's oldest and grandest neighborhoods and, today, is the nexus of the city's youth culture and gay scene. Broadway, the heart of Capitol Hill and one of the city's liveliest thoroughfares, has hip nightclubs, eateries, and tattoo parlors to spare. The neighborhood also features an eclectic mix of stores that cater to fashion plates, tattooed punks, antique lovers, and everyone in between. The primary shopping areas here are on Broadway (home to a bevy of youth fashion and resale shops, music retailers, and unusual bookstores), 15th Street (plenty of home and garden stores with a more upscale slant than Broadway), and Pike and Pine streets (a mix of antique stores, florists, coffee shops, and funky specialty retailers).

**Carkeek Park.** *950 NW Carkeek Park Rd, Seattle (98177).* Approximately 190 acres on Puget Sound. Beach, picnic area; model airplane meadow, hiking trail (1 mile). (Daily) **FREE**

★ **Center for Wooden Boats.** *1010 Valley St, Seattle (98109). Phone 206/382-2628. www.cwb.org.* Located north of downtown on the southern tip of Lake Union, this is a "hands-on maritime heritage museum" where the focus is squarely set on historic wooden sailboats, kayaks, and canoes. Visitors can learn time-tested boat-building skills from master craftsmen, take sailing lessons, or rent a classic sailboat for a spin around the lake. The center also provides the setting for numerous annual festivals and boat shows. (Winter: daily 11 am-5 pm; Spring and Fall: daily 10 am-6 pm; Summer: daily 10 am-8 pm) **FREE**

**Central Library.** *1000 Fourth Ave, Seattle (98104). Phone 206/386-4100. www.spl.org.* The new Central Library opened to much acclaim in 2004. The library was designed by famed Dutch architect Rem Koolhaas, winner of the 2000 Pritzker Prize, his profession's highest honor. With a transparent exterior of diamond-shaped panes of glass, the library stands as a marvel of contemporary architecture. The interior is equally amazing, highlighted by the Books Spiral, a series of tiers and ramps winding through four floors of book stacks. The library features more than 400 public computers, and wireless Internet access is available throughout the facility. Built at a cost of $165.5 million, the 11-level library exemplifies Seattles passion for books and learning. **FREE**

**Century Ballroom.** *915 E Pine, 2nd Floor, Seattle (98122). Phone 206/324-7263. www.centuryballroom.com.* Home to one of Seattles largest dance floors (2,000 square feet of refinished wood), the stylishly restored Century Ballroom is the place to go for swing and salsa dancing in the Emerald City. Many nights are themed (tango night, salsa night, and swing night). For those with two left feet, lessons are offered; while most are multi-week endeavors, there are occasional one-shot workshops. With a full bar, seating at comfortable tables, and a cavernous downtown location, the venue also hosts a number of concerts every month, with the talent tending to be jazz acts and singer/songwriters. There is also a popular restaurant here serving lunch, dinner, and Sunday brunch. The cuisine is eclectic, with a menu that melds the Far East with the Deep South (i.e. potpies and Vietnamese noodle bowls). (Daily) **$$$**

**Charles and Emma Frye Art Museum.** *704 Terry Ave, Seattle (98104). At Cherry St, downtown. Phone 206/622-9250. www.fryeart.org.* In a city where abstract and postmodern art are the norm, the conservative Frye Art Museum bucks the trend by focusing solely on representational art: contemporary and classic landscapes and portraits. The works are both dark and bright (in both tint and theme), and are all bathed in natural light in simple, classic settings. Among the artists represented here are Winslow Homer and Andrew Wyeth. The café and the bookstore here are both excellent, and worth a visit. (Tues-Wed, Fri-Sat 10 am-5 pm, Thurs to 8 pm, Sun noon-5 pm; closed holidays) **FREE**

**Crocodile Café.** *2200 2nd Ave, Seattle (98121). Phone 206/441-5611. www.thecrocodile.com.* Established just as the Seattle rock scene was exploding onto the national scene in 1991, a concert at the Crocodile Café is a feast for both the ears and the eyes. Beyond the varnished driftwood tables and psychedelic décor, the Belltown venue doubles as a gallery, with rotating exhibits by local artists. As Seattle has been the center of the grunge scene for more than a decade, most of the performers who take the Crocodile's stage are up and coming rock bands (including past shows by homegrown acts like Pearl Jam and Nirvana), but some nights feature electronic acts and lighter pop bands. There is also a café here that serves a menu of burgers and other pub grub, and is an especially popular breakfast destination for eggs and a Crocodile Mary ("a bloody Mary with a bite"). (Tues-Sat 11-2 am, Sun 9 am-2 pm; Sun 9 am-3pm)

**Dimitriou's Jazz Alley.** *2033 6th Ave, Seattle (98121). Phone 206/441-9729. www.jazzalley.com.* Jazz aficionados descend on Dimitriou's Jazz Alley in droves on a near-nightly basis to enjoy top musicians in an intimate setting. Widely considered the best jazz club in Seattle, the downtown venue originally opened in the University District in 1979, then moved downtown in 1985, and has seen performances by such big names as Taj Mahal and Eartha Kitt in the time since. The atmosphere is refined, with chairs and tables surrounding the circular stage and a mezzanine overlooking it. A renovation in 2002 expanded Jazz Alley's capacity and bolstered the sound system while retaining the heralded ambiance. A restaurant here serves a varied menu with an Italian thrust, with options ranging from calamari and salmon to manicotti and rib eye steak. (Tues-Sun; doors open Tues-Sat 5:30 pm, Sun 4:30 pm)

**Discovery Park.** *3801 W Government Way, Seattle (98119). Phone 206/386-4236. www.discoverypark.org.* An in-city wildlife sanctuary and nature preserve, the 534-acre Discovery Park is the largest park in Seattle, located on the western shores of the swanky Magnolia neighborhood. It is centered on a tall bluff that formerly served as a post for the US Army, making for great views of the Olympic Mountains to the west and the Cascades to the east, with waterfront access to the north and west. An extensive trail system lures joggers, bikers, and other fitness buffs from all over the city, but the educational program is at the heart of the parks mission, hence the Discovery tag. School buses and day campers frequent the park year-round, but the events calendar has something for every age and interest. A diverse population of flora and fauna—including wildflowers, owls, hummingbirds, and crustaceanscalls the parks dunes, thickets, forests, and tide pools home.(Tues-Sun) **FREE**

**Downtown Shopping District.** *1st Ave and Madison St, Seattle. 1st Ave to 7th Ave, Madison St to Pine St. www.downtownseattle.com.* Downtown is undoubtedly the heart of Seattle's vibrant shopping scene, with a who's who of national department stores alongside fun and funky retailers of all stripes. Prime window-shopping corridors include First and Second avenues, populated by fashionable boutiques, upscale galleries, and a few quirky curiosities to boot; and Fifth and Sixth avenues, brimming with jewelers, kitchen stores, and clothing stores ranging from small boutiques to mega-sized versions of national staples. There ia also a pair of malls on Pine Street: Westlake (between Fourth and Fifth avenues), a fairly typical enclosed shopping

center; and the ritzy Pacific Place Mall, downtown Seattles newest (and most stylish) retail destination. The centerpiece of the whole shopping district is Nordstrom (500 Pine St), the flagship store for the Seattle-based department store chain.

**Druids Glen Golf Course.** *29925 207th Ave SE, Covington (98042). Phone 253/638-1200. www.druidsglengolf.com.* Completed in June 2003, Druids Glen offers affordable prices and the backdrop of Mount Rainier on a sparkling new course. The second hole offers a view of the majestic mountain from the tee box, and several holes require difficult shots over water right off the tee or on the approach to the green. Four different pros are available for private lessons, and the practice facility is unblemished. **$$$$**

**Evergreen Floating Bridge.** *Seattle. On Hwy 520, near Montlake Pl, SE Side.* Almost 1 1/2 miles long; connects downtown Seattle with Bellevue (see).

**Experience Music Project.** *325 5th Ave, Seattle (98109). Phone 206/770-2700. www.emplive.com.* More than 30 years after his death, legendary rock guitarist Jimi Hendrix remains Seattle's favorite native son, and this thoroughly modern museum is a tribute to the huge impact of his short life. Financed by Microsoft co-founder and Hendrix fanatic Paul Allen, the $200 million museum opened in 2000 as an archive of rock and roll memorabilia and a tribute to musical innovation. The striking architecture, all sharp angles, contrasting textures, and bright hues, intentionally evokes the image of a smashed guitar and the rhythms of rock and roll. The facilities within are similarly cutting-edge, from the grand hall/musical venue dubbed the "Sky Church" to Crossroads, an exhibit space that meshes historical artifacts with multimedia to present the history of American music, to Sound Lab, a recording studio that's as high-tech as it gets. Food and drink (and live music) are available at the highly stylized Turntable Restaurant and Liquid Lounge. (Memorial Day-Labor Day: daily 10 am-8 pm; closed Dec 25) **$$$$**

**Ferry trips.** *Seattle. Seattle Ferry Terminal, Colman Dock, foot of Madison St. Phone 206/464-6400; toll-free 800/843-3779.* Access to Olympic Peninsula; a number of interesting ferry trips. Contact Washington State Ferries, Colman Dock, 98104. **$$$$**

**Freeway Park.** *6th and Seneca, Seattle. Downtown.* This 5-acre park features dramatic water displays. Free concerts (summer, Mon). (Daily)

**Fremont District.** *Fremont Ave and 34th St, Seattle.* Undoubtedly Seattle's funkiest neighborhood, Fremont wears its eccentricity like a badge: the self-proclaimed "Center of the Universe" went as far as to declare facetious independence from Seattle in 1994. North of downtown and the Lake Washington Ship Canal, the former lumber-mill center is now an artists paradise, well known for such public sculptures as a towering statue of Vladimir Lenin, a post-Cold War import from the former Soviet Union; the Fremont Troll, gobbling a VW Beetle under Aurora Bridge; and "Waiting for Interurban," six cast aluminum figures waiting for the bus. The area is also home to an unusually high concentration of brewpubs, coffee shops, and secondhand stores. In an afternoon, shoppers can comb vintage stores for Space Age décor, browse unusual galleries, try on all kind of interesting clothing, and shop for bulk foods. Atypical shopping strips line Fremont Avenue, Fremont Place, and 34th and 35th streets.

**Gas Works Park.** *2101 N Northlake Way, Seattle (98103). Phone 206/684-4075.* A former gas-processing plant on the north side of Lake Union, the 20-acre Gas Works Park is a model for urban renewal and a magnet for kite-flyers. The plant's facilities have been nicely converted for recreational use: the boiler house is now a picnic area and the exhauster-compressor building is now the "Play Barn," a brightly painted playground for kids. The 12.5-mile Burke-Gilman trail begins here, offering a paved route north to suburban Kirkland for joggers and bikers. (Daily) **FREE**

**Golden Gardens.** *8499 Seaview Pl NW, Seattle (98117). Phone 206/684-4075.* Nestled on the bluffs that front Puget Sound in Seattle's Ballard neighborhood, Golden Gardens Park attracts sunbathers and fishermen to its beach and pier, and all sorts of outdoor buffs to its myriad of recreational opportunities. The park's trail system connects the beach with the forested bluffs above, with a leash-optional dog park at the summit. A teen center called the "Brick House" is on the beach, which features concerts and other events year-round. **FREE**

**Golf Club at Newcastle.** *15500 Six Penny Ln, Newcastle (98059). Phone 425/793-4653. www.newcastlegolf.com.* Some of the best views in the Seattle area can be found at Newcastle, which includes sightlines of the city's skyline and nearby Mount Rainier. There are two courses, the Coal Creek and the China Creek, with the latter the more difficult of the two. There is a putting course and a practice facility for warming up before your round and an excellent restaurant and bar for afterwards. **$$$$**

**Gray Line bus tours.** *4500 W Marginal Way SW, Seattle (98106). Phone 206/624-5077; toll-free 800/426-7505. www.graylineofseattle.com.* Tours include City Sights, Double Decker Tour, Boeing Tour, and Mount Rainier Tour.

**Green Lake Park.** *7201 E Green Lake Dr N, Seattle (98103). Phone 206/684-0870.* Ground zero for jogging in fitness-crazy Seattle, Green Lake is the heart of a bustling 320-acre park of the same name. Two paved trails encircle the lake and see a good deal of use from a cross-section of ages and speeds. Each trail is about 3 miles around the lake, and there are separate lanes for bikers, walkers, and runners. The trails aside, the lake itself is a recreation destination: a private company provides boat rentals, and the Green Lake Small Craft Center offers rowing, sailing, and canoe classes, and organizes several annual regattas. The lush park surrounding Green Lake is home to a "Pitch and Putt" golf course (with nine par-three holes) and an indoor pool, as well as a community center, tennis courts, picnic tables, and a children's playground. **FREE**

**International District.** *4th Ave and Yesler Way, Seattle. SE of Downtown, 4th Ave to I-5 and Yesler to S Dearborn sts. www.internationaldistrict.org.* Southeast of downtown, the colorful International District is home to one of the largest and most vibrant Asian communities in the US. Its roots took seed in the late 19th century, and the neighborhood is now one of the most diverse ethnic populations in the world. Asian markets and eateries of all kinds dot the streets; top attractions include the Wing Luke Asian Museum, the Nippon Kan Theatre, and Uwajimaya, a huge food market and cooking school.

**Jefferson Park Golf Club.** *4101 Beacon Ave S, Seattle (98108). Phone 206/762-4513. www.jeffersonparkgolf.com.* Seattle's Jefferson Park offers a shorter par-70 layout, but at least it doesn't cost quite as much as some of the other courses in the area. There is also a par-three course on the grounds, but its the big course people come for, with a hilly layout that is challenging at times but still playable for just about any golfer. Go for the views as much as the golf. Bring your camera to take pictures of the long putt you made and then smile in front of Mount Rainier for the subsequent photo. **$$$$**

**Klondike Gold Rush National Historical Park.** *319 2nd Ave S, Seattle (98104). Phone 206/220-4240.* The 1897 gold strike in the Canadian Yukon triggered an influx of tens of thousands of prospectors to Seattle and its commercial district, Pioneer Square. Motivated by dreams of riches, they arrived here to purchase food, equipment, and pack animals in preparation for the arduous six-month trip to the frozen wilderness of the Klondike Gold Fields. While the gold rush provided an economic boost to the city, it was an economic failure for nearly all of the prospectors. Only a handful struck it rich. Most discovered no gold, and many lost their lives during the trek across the steep, snow-covered trail leading to the Klondike. The stampede of prospectors spurred commercial development in Pioneer Square, where the Klondike Gold Rush National Historical Park is located. The National Historical Park offers exhibits, audiovisuals, and ranger programs that document the gold rush and its impact on Seattle. (Daily 9 am-5 pm; closed Jan 1, Thanksgiving, Dec 25)

**Lake Union.** *Seattle. Seen from George Washington Memorial Bridge, NW side.* There are boatyards, seaplane moorages, and houseboat colonies on the lake.

**Lake Washington Canal.** *Seattle. Can be seen from Seaview Ave NW or NW 54th St, NW side.* Chittenden Locks raise and lower boats to link saltwater and freshwater anchorages. More than 400,000 passengers and 6 million tons of freight pass through annually. Commodore Park and a salmon ladder with viewing windows are on the south side.

**Lake Washington Floating Bridge.** *Lake Washington Blvd and Lakeside Ave, Seattle.* Connects downtown Seattle with Mercer Island via I-90.

**Lincoln Park.** *8011 Fauntleroy Way SW, Seattle (98102). SW Side.* Trails, picnic areas, tennis; beach, bathhouse, saltwater pool (Mid-June-early Sept, daily; fee), wading pool (June-Sept, daily); fitness trail. (Daily) **FREE**

**Mount Baker-Snoqualmie National Forest.** *Outdoor Recreation Information Center, 222 Yale Ave N, Seattle (98174). Phone 206/470-4060.* Snoqualmie section. Includes several ski areas; eight wilderness areas; picnic and campsites, fishing, hunting. More than 1 million acres. East and south of city, reached via I-90.

**Museum of History and Industry.** *2700 24th Ave E, Seattle. On N side of Hwy 520, just S of Husky Stadium, SE side. Phone 206/324-1126. www.seattlehistory.org.* The showcase of the Seattle Historical Society, this excellent facility (popularly known as MOHAI) tracks the people and events that have shaped Seattle over the course of its 150-year history. With a collection of more than a million photographs and historical artifacts, MOHAI is a treasure trove for history buffs, giving visitors a comprehensive look into the social and economic roots of the Puget Sound area. The Great Seattle Fire is documented by an exhibit complete with a historic fire engine, murals, and other relics of the disaster that razed the city in 1889; a mock-up of an 1880s street scene gives visitors a glimpse into the pre-fire Emerald City. Another highlight is the comprehensive collection of souvenirs from the 1962 World's Fair. (Daily 10 am-5 pm; closed Thanksgiving, Dec 25) **$$**

**Myrtle Edwards/Elliott Bay.** *Seattle. North of Pier 70, NW Side.* One mile of shoreline; paved bike trail; views of Puget Sound, the Olympic Peninsula, and oceangoing vessels; Seamen's Memorial and a granite and concrete sculpture.

**Nordic Heritage Museum.** *3014 NW 67th St, Seattle (98117). NW Side. Phone 206/789-5707. www.nordicmuseum.org.* Center for Scandinavian community in Pacific Northwest. Represents all five Scandinavian countries. Historical exhibits; art gallery; performing arts. (Tues-Sat 10 am-4 pm, Sun from noon) **$$**

**Northwest Outdoor Center.** *2100 Westlake Ave N, Suite 1, Seattle (98109). Phone 206/281-9694.* A 20-year-old Seattle institution on the docks of Lake Union, the Northwest Outdoor Center is a major hub for the Pacific Northwest's paddling community. A combination school/store/guide service, the place has over 100 kayaks available for rental (starting at $10 for an hour on Lake Union) and a full slate of whitewater and sea kayaking classes, ranging from a 2.5-hour session to a 6-day immersion. The center's guided tours include day trips spent sea kayaking in Puget Sound and multi-day wildlife-watching adventures that take participants to the San Juan Islands and beyond. A bit off the beaten path, sunset and nighttime excursions explore Lake Union and—via the Lake Washington Ship Canal and the water elevator known as the Ballard Locks—Puget Sound. The Northwest Outdoor Center is also the best source of paddling information and advice in the city. **$$$$**

**Paramount Theatre.** *911 Pine St, Seattle (98101). Phone 206/682-1414. www.theparamount.com.* This 75-year-old theater brings a wide range of entertainment to Seattle: Broadway plays and musicals, ballet and modern dance performances, jazz and rock-and-roll concerts, and comedy acts. It also shows silent films and hosts family-oriented entertainment. Check out the Publix theater organ, one of only three remaining, which has been magnificently restored.

★ **Pike Place Market.** *85 Pike St, Seattle (98101). First Ave and Pike St, in 9-acre historical district, downtown. Phone 206/587-0351. www.pikeplacemarket.org.* Area that farmers established the Pike Place Market in 1907 because they were tired of middlemen taking more than their fair share. Today, the indoor/outdoor market is a Seattle landmark and a cornucopia for the senses, with burly guys tossing fresh fish back and forth at the fish market, bin after bin of fresh, colorful fruits, vegetables, and flowers, the sounds and sights of street performers, and the wares of hundreds of artists on display. But it doesn't stop there: the astoundingly comprehensive Pike Place Market has dozens of restaurants and food stands, a day spa, a barbershop, a tattoo parlor, and a dating service onsite. Just two blocks east of the waterfront, the market is a quick walk from the center of downtown and surrounded by eateries and bars. Guided tours are available Wednesday to Sunday year-round, but there is a fee ($7 adults, $5 seniors and children). (Mon-Sat 10 am-6 pm, Sun 11 am-5 pm; closed holidays) **FREE**

**Pioneer Square.** *James St and Yesler Way, Seattle. Bounded by 1st Ave, James St, and Yesler Way.* Seattle's oldest neighborhood, the original Pioneer Square saw its beginnings in the early 1850s but soon met a blazing fate in the Great Seattle Fire of 1889. Today's Pioneer Square was built atop the scorched remains, resulting in a ghostlike underground beneath the city streets. (The Underground Tour allows visitors to explore this buried history.) The area boomed again after the lure of gold began attracting miners during the following decade, and a seedy underbelly (that remains to this day) followed in their wake. Now dominated by stately (and inflammable) Victorian and Romanesque redbricks above cobblestone squares, the neighborhood is a commercial and social hub: a melting pot of offices, stores, galleries, restaurants, and nightclubs wedged between downtown and a pair of major stadiums, SAFECO Field (baseball) and Seahawks Stadium (football).

**Queen Anne Neighborhood.** *Seattle. Queen Anne Hill.* Named for its predominant architectural style, the Queen Anne neighborhood dates from the 1880s and is one of Seattle's most scenic spots. Built on the 456-foot slope of Queen Anne Hill, the ritzy area is dotted with overlooks that are perfect perches for views of the Space Needle, downtown, and Mount Rainier. The neighborhoods top attraction is the Seattle Center, with the Space Needle, the Experience Music Project, and KeyArena, the pyramidal home court of the National Basketball Associations Seattle SuperSonics.

**Rock Bottom Brewery.** *1333 Fifth Ave, Seattle (98101). Phone 206/623-3070. www.rockbottom.com.* This brewpub in the heart of downtown Seattle is one of the flagships of the Rock Bottom chain, which consists of about 30 breweries in the US. At any given time, at least six beers are on tap, all of which are brewed onsite with Washington-grown hops. The menu is varied, with burgers, pizzas, salads, and steaks, served inside in an upstairs dining room and a downstairs bar/poolroom or outside on a breezy patio.

**SAFECO Field.** *1250 1st Ave S, Seattle (98134). Phone 206/346-4000. www.mariners.mlb.com.* First opening in 1999, SAFECO Field replaced the much-maligned Kingdome as the home of Major League Baseball's Seattle Mariners. It's easy to see why the $517 million ballpark quickly won the hearts of the Emerald City's sports fans, based on nostalgic architecture, stunning views of the Seattle skyline and the Puget Sound sunset, and a one-of-a-kind umbrella for the city's infamous rainstorms: a retractable roof that weighs 22 million pounds and covers nine acres. Hour-long tours of the facility are available on a near-daily basis (except Mondays during baseball's off-season and day game days during the season), and cover a walking distance of about 1 mile. Aside from the roof and old-time ironwork, some of SAFECO's can't-miss features are the works of public art integrated into its design, a playground for kids, and the official Mariners team store.

**Schmitz Park.** *Admiral Way SW and SW Stevens St, Seattle.* Section of forest as it was when first settlers arrived. **FREE**

**Seattle Aquarium.** *1483 Alaskan Way, Seattle (98101). Pier 59, Waterfront Park, downtown. Phone 206/386-4300. www.seattleaquarium.org.* A Waterfront mainstay at Pier 59 since 1977, the Seattle Aquarium is an engrossing educational experience for curious minds of all ages. The top facility of its kind in the region, the aquarium is home to nearly 400 species of fish, birds, marine mammals, and other sea life. Staff here have celebrated several breakthroughs over the years, including the first live births of sea otters in North American captivity, which has happened six times here, and the rearing of a giant Pacific octopus to adulthood, another first. (The 50-pound octopus, "Dudley," is still an aquarium resident and visitor favorite.) Another highlight is the underwater dome, which allows guests to immerse themselves in a transparent bubble on the bottom of a fish-filled, 400,000-gallon tank. An IMAX theater is adjacent, charging separate entry fees. Plans are in the works to build a new aquarium on the Waterfront in coming years. (Daily) **$$$**

**Seattle Art Museum.** *100 University St, Seattle (98101). Downtown. Phone 206/654-3255. www.seattleartmuseum.org.* Its entrance guarded by an animated, 48-foot-tall sculpture named "Hammering Man," the Seattle Art Museum (known locally as SAM) is the premiere facility of its kind in the Pacific Northwest. There is something for everybody here, from ancient Greek sculpture to modern Russian decorative art. Held in particularly high regard are the collections of contemporary art (with pieces by Andy Warhol, Jackson Pollock, and Roy Lichtenstein) and Northwest Coast Native American art (comprised of nearly 200 masks, sculptures and household items). SAMs temporary exhibitions are similarly diverse. A dynamic events calendar helps distinguish the museum, offering up a bevy of concerts, films, lectures, demonstrations, family programs, and classes. Admission is waived on the first Thursday of every month, and a restaurant and two gift shops are onsite. (Tues-Wed and Fri-Sun 10 am-5 pm, Thurs 10 am-9 pm; closed holidays) **$$**

★ **Seattle Center.** *305 Harrison St, Seattle (98109). Phone 206/684-7200; fax 206/684-7366.*Site of 1962 World's Fair. Its 74 acres include

**Center House.** *305 Harrison St, Seattle (98109). Phone 206/684-7200.* Three floors of specialty shops, restaurants, conference facilities, administrative offices. (Daily)

**Fun Forest Amusement Park.** *305 Harrison, Seattle (98109). Phone 206/728-1585.* Rides (fees), games in parklike setting. (June-Labor Day: daily; Mar-June and early Sept-Nov: Fri-Sun) **FREE**

**International Fountain.** *305 Harrison St, Seattle (98109). Phone 206/684-7200.* Like the Space Needle, the International Fountain is a remnant of the 1962 Worlds Fair, but unlike that other Seattle icon, it was demolished and rebuilt in 1995. More inviting than its rocky, sunflower-inspired predecessor, the new fountain is interactive: visitors can play aside its sleek silver globe in the path of splashing arcs of water, which go off hourly and shoot up to 150 feet in the air. The spot is the site of several festival events. (Daily 11 am-8 pm)

**Marion Oliver McCaw Hall.** *321 Mercer St, Seattle (98109). Phone 206/443-2222.* The Opera House is home of the Seattle Opera Association, Pacific Northwest Ballet, and Seattle Symphony. Bagley Wright Theatre is home of Seattle Repertory Theatre.

**Monorail.** *305 Harrison St, Seattle (98109).* Provides a scenic 90-second ride between Center House and Westlake Center, Downtown. Legacy of 1962 World's Fair, the Swedish-built train makes frequent runs throughout the day. (Daily, closed Jan 1, Thanksgiving, Dec 25) **$$**

**Pacific Science Center.** *200 2nd Ave N, Seattle (98109). Phone 206/443-2001.* This educational museum in downtown Seattle is aimed at young minds, but the exhibits tend to engage every age group. With subject matter that balances cutting-edge technology and natural history, the center features such permanent exhibits as an indoor butterfly house, a room-sized model of Puget Sound, and "Dinosaurs: A Journey through Time," complete with seven robotic dinosaurs; on the other side of the science spectrum is "Tech Zone," where visitors can challenge a robot to a game of tic-tac-toe or create art on a computer. Beyond the permanent and seasonal exhibits, there are movies on a pair of giant-sized IMAX screens (one of which is coupled with a 3-D projector), astronomy demonstrations in the onsite planetarium, and dazzling light displays with rock and roll soundtracks in the Adobe Laser Dome. (Daily 10 am-5 pm; Sat-Sun to 6 pm) **$$$$**

**Space Needle.** *400 Broad St, Seattle (98109). Phone toll-free 800/937-9582.* First a sketch on a placemat, then the centerpiece of the 1962 World's Fair, and now Seattle's face to the world, the Space Needle is one of the most distinctive structures in the US. Capping the 605-foot tower, the flying saucer-inspired dome is symbolic of both the Seattle Worlds Fair's theme—Century 21—and the coinciding national push into space. The dome houses an observation deck (with stunning city views) and SkyCity, a revolving restaurant that goes full circle every 48 minutes. There is also a banquet facility 100 feet above street level and a gift shop at the tower's base, where visitors board an elevator for the 43-second journey to the top. The Space Needle is the setting for one of the West Coasts premiere New Years Eve celebrations every Dec 31. **$$$**

**Seattle Mariners (MLB).** *1250 1st Ave S, Seattle (98134). Phone 206/346-4000. www.seattlemariners.com.* The city's Major League Baseball franchise has been a Seattle sports stalwart since 1977, its inaugural season playing in the American League. The Mariners played home games at the now-demolished (and often criticized) Kingdome, but the team got new digs in 1999the state-of-the-art SAFECO Field (with a retractable roof to thwart Seattle's notorious rainstorms), located just south of downtown. In recent years, the Mariners have enjoyed a nice resurgence in fan support, thanks to the new ballpark, a competitive team, and a fitting Asian flairthanks to Japanese stars like Ichiro Suzuki and a sushi bar just beyond SAFECOs outfield fences. The season runs from March to October; the team's schedule includes 81 home games every year.

**Seattle Opera.** *321 Mercer St, Seattle (98109). Phone 206/389-7676. www.seattleopera.org.* This renowned company presents five operas per season (Aug-May). After a year and a half of renovation of the historic Opera House, performances return to their old home, now called Marian Oliver McCaw Hall. **$$$$**

**Seattle Seahawks (NFL).** *800 Occidental Ave S, Seattle (98134). Phone 425/827-9777; toll-free 888/635-4295; fax 425/893-5066. www.seahawks.com.* The Seattle Seahawks have been competing in the National Football League since the franchises inaugural season of 1976. The team takes to the gridiron at 67,000-seat Seahawks Stadium, a state-of-the-art facility that opened for play in 2002. Seventy percent of the seats are covered by a pair of arcing roofs that shield spectators from the rain—and also serve to amplify crowd noise. The stadiums Ring of Honor celebrates the on-field accomplishments of Seahawk greats such as wide receiver Steve Largent and running back Curt Warner. The Seahawks were originally owned by department-store giant John Nordstrom, but today the franchise is owned by billionaire Paul Allen, who co-founded Microsoft with Bill Gates.

**Seattle Sounders (USL).** *S Royal Bourgham Way, Seattle (98055). Phone 206/622-3415. www.seattlesounders.net.* The Seattle Sounders play professional soccer in the United Soccer League's A-League and have had many players go on to play in Major League Soccer. The team has had a successful run, winning the league championship during the 1990s. The 28-game schedule runs from May to September, with the Sounders playing 14 home games at Seahawks Stadium, just south of downtown Seattle.

**Seattle Storm (WNBA).** *300 1st Ave, Seattle (98109). Phone 206/684-7200. www.wnba.com/storm.* The Emerald City's entry in the Women's National Basketball Association, the Storm plays 16 home games at KeyArena between May and August. The teams inaugural season was in 2000, making it the newest professional sports franchise in Seattle. After floundering for the first two years of its existence, the Storm made the playoffs in 2002 behind rookie phenomenon Sue Bird.

**Seattle SuperSonics (NBA).** *KeyArena, 305 Harrison St, Seattle (98109). First Ave N between Thomas and Republican. Phone 206/283-3865. www.supersonics.com.* Longtime Seattleites still wax nostalgic about the 1979 SuperSonics. Guided by legendary coach Lenny Wilkens and featuring balanced scoring from the likes of Gus Williams and "Downtown" Freddie Brown, the Sonics, as theyre better known, won the NBA Championship, upsetting a talented Washington Bullets squad. Unfortunately for Seattle hoops fans, the franchise has never repeated its 1979 championship performance. Nonetheless, the citys support for the team remains strong. The Sonics play home games at KeyArena, a 17,000-seat facility on the grounds of the Seattle Center. In 2004, the team was shuffled into the newly created Northwest Division of the NBA's Western Conference.

**Seattle University.** *901 12th St, Seattle (98122). Phone 206/296-6000. www.seattleu.edu.* (1891) (4,800 students) Landscaped urban campus with more than 1,000 varieties of exotic flowers, trees and shrubs; water fountain sculpture by George Tsutakawa. Tours of campus.

**Seward Park.** *Lake Washington Blvd S and S Orcas St, Seattle. Occupies peninsula off Lake Washington Blvd S and S Orcas St, SE Side.* Swimming beach (Mid-June-early Sept, daily), bathhouse; picnic and play areas, tennis; amphitheater; Japanese lantern and *torii* (Japanese arch); fish hatchery. (Daily) **FREE**

**Shilshole Bay Marina.** *7001 Seaview Ave NW, Seattle (98117). NW Side. Phone 206/728-3385.* Moorage for 1,500 boats, fuel, repairs, launching ramp, marine supplies; restaurants.

**Six Arms.** *300 E Pike St, Seattle (98122). Phone 206/223-1698.* McMenamins, the tycoons of Portland, Oregons bar scene, have also dipped their toes in the Seattle waters with this brewpub on the western slope of Capitol Hill. It's a pleasant space, the décor blending Seattle's ever-present grunge with a pseudo-European feel and a Hindu motif. The oversized wooden booths are a bonus, as is the menu of international pub standards. McMenamins also owns Dad Watsons in Fremont and McMenamins Queen Anne Hill in Queen Anne. (Mon-Thurs 11-1 am, Fri-Sat to 2 am; Sun noon-midnight)

**Smith Cove.** *Elliott Ave and W Garfield St, Seattle.* Navy ships at anchor; Seattle Annex, Naval Supply Center along north side of West Garfield Street.

**Sur La Table.** *84 Pine St, Seattle (98101). Phone 206/448-2244. www.surlatable.com.* In the 1970s, Seattle spawned this clearinghouse for hard-to-find kitchen gear, and it soon became known as a source for cookware, small appliances, cutlery, kitchen tools, linens, tableware, gadgets, and specialty foods. Sur La Table has since expanded to include cooking classes (**$$$$**), chef demonstrations, and cookbook author signings, as well as a catalog and online presence. Cooking connoisseurs discover such finds as cool oven mitts, zest graters, copper whisks, onion soup bowls, and inspired TV dinner trays. (Daily)

**Teatro ZinZanni.** *2301 6th Ave, Seattle (98121). Phone 206/802-0015. www.teatrozinzanni.org.* An avant-garde dinner theater with a sister facility in San Francisco, Teatro ZinZanni offers entertainment like nothing else in town: a hyper-imaginative circus/nightclub act hybrid of music, comedy, trapeze, Kabuki, and magic. The food is similarly enchanting—an eclectic fusion of culinary traditions—as is the venue itself, a beautifully restored antique circular pavilion with a hazy, opulent vibe, complete with reams of velvet, crystal chandeliers, and hand-carved wooden columns. **$$$$**

**Tillicum Village.** *Blake Island State Park, 2992 SW Avalon Way, Seattle (98126). Excursion from Pier 55/56, foot of Seneca St. Phone toll-free 800/426-1205. www.tillicumvillage.com.* Narrated harbor cruise; baked salmon dinner; stage show. Reservations advised. (May-mid-Oct: daily; rest of year: hours vary) **$$$$**

**Underground Tour.** *608 First Ave, Seattle (98104). Phone 206/682-4646; toll-free 888/608-6337. www.undergroundtour.com.* A fun and funny look at Seattle's colorful past, Bill Speidel's Underground Tour takes guests on a journey under the streets of Pioneer Square, where remnants of the frontier town that met its fiery end here in 1889 still remain. The tour begins in a bar (Doc Maynard's Public House) and lasts about an hour and a half, with Speidel dishing enough humorous insight into Seattles history to fill a book. (Daily; closed holidays; advance reservations recommended) **$$$**

**University of Washington.** *17th Ave NE and NE 45th St, Seattle. 17th Ave NE and NE 45th St, NE side. Phone 206/543-9198.* (1861) (34,400 students) Visitor Information Center, 4014 University Way NE. A 694-acre campus with 128 major buildings and a stadium. Special exhibits in Henry Art Gallery (daily except Mon; closed holidays; fee); Henry Suzzallo Library. Meany Hall for the Performing Arts, three theaters; health sciences research center and teaching hospital; Waterfront Activities Center; Washington Park Arboretum. Parking fee. Located here are

**Burke Museum of Natural History and Culture.** *University of Washington, 17th Ave NE and NE 45th St, Seattle (98195). Phone 206/543-5590.* Located on the campus of the University of Washington, the Burke Museum is Washington State's official museum of natural and cultural history, and a research hub for the entire Pacific Northwest. Between its collections in four areas—anthropology, geology, zoology and botany—the museum is in possession of 5 million specimens in all. The facility houses a pair of notable permanent exhibits (in addition to a number of rotating temporary displays each year): "The Life and Times of Washington State," a look at the last 500 million years of the states geology and biology (with fossils and skeletons galore), and "Pacific Voices," which delves into the rich melting pot of cultures present in the Pacific Northwest. Also on site is the Erna Gunther Ethnobotanical Garden, alive with hundreds of plants used by the region's natives, as well as a café and a gift shop. (Daily 10 am-5 pm, Thurs to 8 pm; closed Thanksgiving, Dec 25) **$$**

**University of Washington Huskies.** *3807 Montlake Blvd, Seattle (98195). Phone 206/543-2200.* During the school year, the University of Washington Huskies play NCAA Division I-A schedules in a wide variety of men's and women's sports, including football, basketball, track and field, swimming, baseball, and swimming. The school's teams play in the Pac-10 conference, competing against the likes of UCLA and Arizona, as well as cross-state rival Washington State. The University of Washington football team plays its home games at picturesque Husky Stadium, situated on the western shores of Lake Washington. Because of the stadium's lakefront location, many fans travel to and from games by boat, and traditionally throw tailgate parties in the water prior to kickoff. The men's and women's basketball teams play on a home court at the 10,000-seat Clarence S. "Hec" Edmundson Pavilion. Most venues for other UW sports are also on the Seattle campus.

**University Village Shopping.** *45th St, Seattle (98105). Phone 206/523-0622. www.uvillage.com.* Located near the University of Washington campus in northeast Seattle, University Village has a rare balance of national and local establishments. Chains are well represented here, with Abercrombie & Fitch, Pottery Barn, and Restoration Hardware, but there is also a nice sampling of homegrown retailers and eateries—about 50 in all. The area also has banking, insurance, childcare centers, and day spa services on-site.

**Victoria Clipper Charters.** *2701 Alaskan Way, Pier 69, Seattle (98121). Phone 206/448-5000. www.victoriaclipper.com.* This tour company operates a fleet of high-speed, passenger-only ferries on routes between Seattle, the San Juan Islands in Puget Sound, and Victoria, Canada. The trip to Victoria takes about two hours, and VCC offers many packages that integrate hotel stays, recreational excursions and other transportation. There are also narrated whale-watching cruises, and the clippers have basic cafés and duty-free shops on board. **$$$$**

**Volunteer Park.** *1247 15th Ave E, Seattle (98112). NE Side.* Tennis, play area, wading pool (June-Sept, daily), picnic area; conservatory (daily), formal gardens; observation deck in water tower (520 feet) with view of mountains, city, Puget Sound (daily). **FREE**

**Warren G. Magnuson Park.** *NE 65th and Sand Point Way NE, Seattle. NE Side.* Approximately 200 acres; 1-mile shoreline. Swimming beach (Mid-July-early Sept, daily); picnicking, playfield, small boat launch ramp, concessions. Fee for some activities. (Daily)

**Washington Park Arboretum.** *2300 Arboretum Dr E, Seattle (98112). On both sides of Lake Washington Blvd, between E Madison and Montlake, SE Side. Phone 206/543-8800.*Arboretum Drive East winds over 200 acres containing more than 5,000 species of trees and shrubs from all parts of world. Rhododendrons, cherries, azaleas (Apr-June). Arboretum open daily all year. Tours (Jan-Nov, 1st and 3rd Sun). **FREE** Within is

**Japanese Garden.** *1075 Lake Washington Blvd E, Seattle (98122). Phone 206/684-4725.* Ornamental plants, glassy pools, 12-tier pagoda, and teahouse. Tea ceremony. **$$**

**Waterfront.** *Seattle.* The most tourist-trafficked spot in all of Seattle, the downtown Waterfront bustles with activity year-round. Abutting Puget Sound on the western fringe of downtown, such landmarks as the Pike Place Market and the Seattle Aquarium reel in visitors by the thousands. Then there are the crowds drawn in by the boats—including the ferry to Bainbridge Island and Victoria Clipper Charters—that depart from the piers, encrusted with touristy shops, seafood restaurants, and oyster bars. One particularly kitschy retailer that's worth a peek is Ye Olde Curiosity

Shop on Pier 54, with a circus-meets-harbor atmosphere accentuated by the mummies and jar-encased, two-headed calves on display. As for recreation, some people fish here; others engage in a pursuit that is distinctly Seattle: jigging for squid.

★ **Waterfront Drive.** *Alaskan Way, Seattle.* Follow Alaskan Way along Elliott Bay to see ships of many nations docked at piers. Or take higher level Alaskan Way Viaduct along a parallel route to view the harbor, sound, and mountains. A trolley runs the length of the waterfront and continues into Pioneer Square and the International District.

**West Seattle Golf Course.** *4470 35th Ave SW, Seattle (98126). Phone 206/935-5187. www.westseattlegolf.com.* This public course, designed by course architect H. Chandler Eagan and opened in 1940, has drawn good reviews over the years. You can usually get on for less than $30, and early-bird specials make it even cheaper. With a recent change in ownership, the course has undergone a resurgence in popularity and is now one of the more heavily played courses in the area. Still, it's a good course on which to learn, something the course staff realizes and is willing and able to help with. **$$$$**

**Wing Luke Asian Museum.** *407 7th Ave S, Seattle (98104). Phone 206/623-5124. www.wingluke.org.* An apt counterpart to the Seattle Asian Art Museum, the Wing Luke Asian Museum in Seattle's busy International District illuminates the Asian American experience in a historical and cultural light. A collection of diverse artifacts details the 200-year history of Asians in the Pacific Northwest. Another permanent exhibit, the Densho Project, allows visitors to access oral histories recorded by Japanese Americans who were detained in Word War II-era internment camps. (Tue-Fri 11 am-4:30 pm, Sat-Sun noon-4 pm) **$**

**Woodland Park Zoo.** *5500 Phinney Ave N, Seattle (98103). Phone 206/684-4800. www.zoo.org.* One of the biggest and best zoos in the country sits in the park of the same name in north Seattle. The exhibits focus on ecosystems instead of single species: the Alaska enclosure is home to Kodiak bears that catch live trout out of a stream; "Tropical Asia" inhabitants include elephants, tapirs, and orangutans; and the African Savannah features giraffes, hippos, and zebras—as well as a plaque dedicated to Seattle native son Jimi Hendrix. There is also a Komodo dragon display, a petting zoo, "Bug World" (with such spine-chilling denizens as millipedes, scorpions, and tarantulas), and an enclosed aviary housing hawks, falcons, and owls. The special events calendar is dense and varied, with breakfasts and overnighters for kids, as well as lectures, festivals, and holiday happenings. (Daily) **$$$**

## Special Events

**A Contemporary Theatre (ACT).** *700 Union St, Seattle (98101). Phone 206/292-7676. www.acttheatre.org.* One of the major resident theaters in the country, ACT is a professional (Equity) theater. Tues-Sun, May-Nov. Shows *A Christmas Carol* in Dec.

**Bumbershoot.** *305 Harrison St, Seattle (98109). Phone 206/281-7788. www.bumbershoot.com.* This annual 4-day music fest is the largest of its kind on the West Coast. Legendary artists and rising stars alike perform in more than 30 different indoor and outdoor venues, stages, and galleries. Bumbershoot also features poetry, dance, comedy, and contemporary art exhibits. Labor Day weekend. **$$$$**

**Chilly Hilly Bicycle Classic.** *Seattle (98115). Phone 206/522-3222. www.cascade.org.* One of *Bicycle Magazine*'s top four recreational bike rides in the United States, this 33-mile course on Bainbridge Island attracts thousands of riders for a one-day organized ride in February. The course starts at the ferry dock and makes many gains and losses in elevation (with 2,700 feet of elevation change in all) before skidding to a stop at a finish line festival with a huge chili feast. Late Feb.

**Fremont Oktoberfest.** *Fremont District, 35th and Fremont Ave N, Seattle (98103). Phone 206/633-0422. www.fremontoktoberfest.org.* The eccentric Fremont neighborhood puts its own stamp on the traditional Bavarian beer-drinking festival, with a rambunctious chainsaw pumpkin-carving contest, a street dance, polka-dancing lessons, and live bands that run the gamut from mainstream to bizarre. Held in the shadows of the Aurora Avenue Bridge, this street fair is considered one of the top Oktoberfest festivals outside of Germany, taking place over the course of the third weekend in September. The rowdy beer garden here is quite a sight, serving up a wide variety of beers (including root beer for kids), with an emphasis on local microbrews. The street fair is free and open to the public, but admission is charged to enter the beer garden; six beer tokens and a souvenir cup are included. Late Sept. **FREE**

**Opening Day Regatta.** *1807 E Humlin St, Seattle (98112). Phone 206/325-1000. www.seattleyachtclub.org.* A Seattle tradition since the 1910s, the opening day of yachting season takes place every year on the first Saturday in May, with such featured events as a boat parade and a rowing regatta. Most of the action is centered on the Montlake Cut that links Lake Washington and Lake Union, and there are a number of great viewpoints on and near the campus of the University of Washington. May.

**Pacific Northwest Arts Fair.** *Bellevue. 4 miles E. Phone 206/363-2048.* Art exhibits, handicrafts. Late July.

**Seafair.** *Seattle (98121). Phone 206/728-0123.* Citywide marine festival. Regattas, speedboat races, shows at Aqua Theater, parades, sports events, exhibits. Early July-early Aug.

**Seattle International Film Festival.** *600 Pine St, Seattle (98101). Phone 206/324-9997. www.seattlefilm.com.* Held annually from late May to mid-June, Seattle's top-notch film fest is one of the largest cinema showcases in the US, and perhaps the preeminent event of its kind held in a major city. While the content tends toward documentaries and international independent films, Hollywood is also well represented. **$$**

**Seattle Marathon.** *Downtown. Seattle (98103). Phone 206/729-3660. www.seattlemarathon.org.* Held annually in late November, the Seattle Marathon is open to runners and walkers of all skill levels and registers more than 10,000 entrants each year. Much of the hilly, scenic route runs along the Lake Washington shoreline, taking entrants from the Seattle Center to Seward Park in southeast Seattle, and back again. A kids marathon, a half marathon, and a marathon walk are also held. Late Nov. **$$$$**

**Seattle Rep.** *155 Mercer St, Seattle (98109). Phone 206/443-2222. www.seattlerep.org.* Short for Seattle Repertory Theatre, the award-winning Seattle Rep is one of the top regional non-profit theatre companies in the US. Two stages host six to ten productions a year, with the emphasis on challenging dramatic works and time-tested classics injected with fresh perspectives. Recent performances staged by the Rep include *Romeo and Juliet*, *Wit*, and *The Search for Signs of Intelligent Life in the Universe*. Sept-June.

**Seattle to Portland Bicycle Classic.** *74th St, Seattle (98115). Phone 206/522-3222. www.cascade.org.* This 200-mile road race draws up to 8,000 riders each year for a one- or two-day tour through Washington and Oregon's forests and farmlands. Early July. **$$$$**

**Summer Nights at the Pier.** *1901 Alaskan Way, Seattle (98101). Phone 206/281-8111. www.summernights.org.* The location of this music venu—eat Pier 62/63 on the downtown Seattle waterfront—is exceedingly picturesque, rivaling the Gorge Amphitheater with great views of the downtown skyline, ferries cruising Puget Sound, and sunsets over the looming Olympic Mountains to the west. Owned by the citys Parks Department, the 3,800-seat amphitheater hosts touring rock and rhythm and blues acts during its summer season, with such performers as the Flaming Lips, Billy Idol, and the Roots taking its stage in recent years. Many locals moor their sailboats around the pier at show time—and take in the concert without buying a ticket in the process. Beer, wine, fast food, and coffee are all available on the premises; visitors can also bring their own outside food and non-alcoholic beverages. June-Aug.

## Limited-Service Hotels

**★ ★ COURTYARD BY MARRIOTT.** *925 Westlake Ave N, Seattle (98109). Phone 206/213-0100; fax 206/213-0101. www.courtyard.com.* That glass elevator at this modern Courtyard hotel affords some of the best views of Lake Union, located across the street. The hotel offers a complimentary shuttle to take guests to many nearby attractions, including the Space Needle, Woodland Park Zoo, and the Seattle Waterfront. 250 rooms, 7 story. Check-in 3 pm, check-out noon. High-speed Internet access. Restaurant, bar. Fitness room. Indoor pool, whirlpool. Business center. **$$**

**★ HAMPTON INN & SUITES.** *700 Fifth Ave N, Seattle (98109). Phone 206/282-7700; toll-free 800/426-7866; fax 206/282-0899. www.hamptoninn.com.* Great for families or guests seeking a larger space in which to unwind, the Hampton Inn features suites with full kitchens, fireplaces, and balconies. Its location near the Seattle Center puts guests close to restaurants, shopping, the opera, ballet, and theater, as well as the Space Needle. 198 rooms, 6 story. Pets accepted, some restrictions; fee. Complimentary continental breakfast. Check-in 3 pm, check-out noon. High-speed Internet access. Fitness room. Business center. **$**

**★ HOMEWOOD SUITES DOWNTOWN SEATTLE.** *206 Western Ave W, Seattle (98119). Phone 206/281-9393; toll-free 800/225-5466; fax 206/283-5022. www.homewoodsuites.com.* Both business travelers and families enjoy the spacious suites at this downtown Seattle hotel, which feature sleeper sofas and fully-equipped kitchens with microwaves and dishwashers. The Space Needle and Seattle Center attractions are just a short distance away, as are the Seattle Waterfront and a host of local businesses. 161 rooms. Pets accepted, some restrictions; fee. Complimentary full breakfast. Check-in 3 pm, check-out noon. High-speed Internet access, wireless Internet access. Fitness room. Business center. **$$**

★ ★ ★ **MARRIOTT SEA-TAC AIRPORT.** *3201 S 176th St, Seattle (98188). Phone 206/241-2000; toll-free 800/228-9290; fax 206/248-0789. www.marriotthotels.com.* The Marriott Sea-Tac offers a convenient location across from the airport. The indoor pool under an atrium is a nice touch, with screening plants to give swimmers a sense of privacy. The business center caters to every need of business travelers, and the small spa offers opportunities for pampering. Try the concierge level for services beyond the ordinary. 459 rooms, 7 story. Pets accepted, some restrictions. Check-in 3 pm, check-out 1 pm. High-speed Internet access. Restaurant, bar. Children's activity center. Fitness room. Spa. Indoor pool, whirlpool. Airport transportation available. Business center. **$$**

★ ★ **UNIVERSITY TOWER HOTEL.** *4507 Brooklyn Ave NE, Seattle (98105). Phone 206/634-2000; toll-free 800/899-0251; fax 206/545-2103. www.universitytowerhotel.com.* This boutique hotel offers beautiful panoramic views of the University of Washington campus, the Seattle skyline, Mount Rainier, and the Olympic and Cascade mountains. Guests will feel right at home in the stylish and comfortable rooms which have down blankets, down pillows, high-loft comforters, and rich color palettes. Guests are always welcome at the in-house restaurant, the District Lounge, which features a Northwestern eclectic, globally inspired menu. 158 rooms, 16 story. Complimentary continental breakfast. Check-in 3 pm, check-out noon. High-speed Internet access, wireless Internet access. Restaurant, two bars. Fitness room. Credit cards accepted. **$$**

## Full-Service Hotels

★ ★ ★ **ALEXIS.** *1007 First Ave, Seattle (98104). Phone 206/624-4844; toll-free 888/850-1155; fax 206/621-9009. www.alexishotel.com.* This luxury boutique hotel has been in operation since the turn of the 20th century, making it as much a Seattle landmark as the famous Space Needle. Warm color tones and antiques fill the elegantly appointed rooms, which feature Aveda bath amenities, private bars, plush terrycloth bath robes, and soft Egyptian cotton bed linens. A friendly staff complements these luxurious accommodations with services like evening turndown with chocolates, complementary morning coffee, a complementary evening wine reception, and a Concierge that assists guests with every aspect of their Seattle trip. The Library Bistro, a 1940s-style supper club, offers contemporary American cuisine in a cozy, bookstore-like setting, while The Bookstore Bar is the perfect spot to unwind with a cocktail at the end of the day. 109 rooms, 6 story.Check-in 3 pm, check-out noon. High-speed Internet access, wireless Internet access. Restaurant, bar. Fitness room. Spa. Business center. **$$**

★ ★ ★ ★ **THE FAIRMONT OLYMPIC HOTEL.** *411 University St, Seattle (98101). Phone 206/621-1700; toll-free 800/441-1414; fax 206/682-9633. www.fairmont.com.* The Fairmont Olympic Hotel brings grand tradition and pampering service to downtown Seattle. Carefully blending its 1920s Italian Renaissance heritage with 21st-century hospitality, The Fairmont is a premier destination. The hotel is conveniently located in Rainier Square, only minutes from the city's top attractions. The guest rooms and suites are tasteful retreats with floral draperies, soft pastel colors, and period furnishings, while fresh fruit and flowers make guests feel at home. Guests are cosseted throughout the hotel whether enjoying room service or visiting the full-service salon and spa. The bounty of the Pacific Northwest is the focus at The Georgian (see), where pale yellow walls and crystal chandeliers set a refined tone. Shuckers is a popular oyster bar at which Seattles famous microbrews are savored, and a selection of cocktails is available at The Terrace. Traditional high tea service is a treat worth making time for. 450 rooms, 13 story. Pets accepted, some restrictions; fee. Check-in 3 pm, check-out noon. High-speed Internet access. Three restaurants, two bars. Fitness room, spa. Indoor pool, whirlpool. Business center. Credit cards accepted. **$$$**

★ ★ ★ **GRAND HYATT SEATTLE.** *721 Pine St, Seattle (98101). Phone 206/774-1234; toll-free 800/233-1234; fax 206/774-6311. www.grandseattle.hyatt.com.* The Grand Hyatt Seattle brings contemporary dash to Seattle's bustling financial and business district. From the wired public spaces ideal for meetings and conferences to the fantastic in-room digital concierges, this hotel is a technology aficionado's paradise. Earth tones and Asian inspiration create a sanctuary-like ambience in the guest rooms and suites, where well-defined workspaces are a boon to business travelers. Large windows frame striking city or Puget Sound views, while oversized bathrooms implore guests to enjoy some quiet time soaking in the tub. The Grand Hyatt Seattle understands the needs of modern travelers, with a comprehensive fitness center and a variety of dining options. Starbucks appeals to those on the go, while others enjoy comfort food at the Cheesecake Factory or linger over gourmet fare at 727 Pine. 425 rooms, 30 story. Check-in 4 pm, check-out noon. High-speed Internet access, wireless Internet access. Restaurant, bar. Fitness room. Spa. Whirlpool. Business center. **$$$**

**★ ★ ★ HOTEL ANDRA.** *2000 Fourth Ave, Seattle (98121). Phone 206/448-8600; toll-free 800/448-8601; fax 206/441-7140. www.hotelandra.com.* The Hotel Andra combines Northwest and Scandinavian design influences, creating a warm and inviting retreat in Seattle's vibrant Belltown neighborhood. Situated near art galleries, boutiques, and restaurants, the hotel appeals to travelers who like to be out and about, getting a taste for the local scene. Guests are greeted by a dramatic lobby fireplace built from split-grain granite and bookended by a pair of golden maple bookcases. Above the fireplace, a plasma screen projects a collection of electronic fine art. Rooms include such luxuries as 300-thread-count cotton linens, goose down pillows, and alpaca headboards as well as Frette bath towels, spa bath robes, and Face Stockholm bath amenities. 119 rooms. Pets accepted; fee. Check-in 3 pm, check-out 1 pm. High-speed Internet access, wireless Internet access. Restaurant, bar. Fitness room. Airport transportation available. **$$$**

**★ ★ ★ HOTEL MONACO.** *1101 Fourth Ave, Seattle (98101). Phone 206/621-1770; toll-free 800/945-2240; fax 206/621-7779. www.monaco-seattle.com.* This hip hotel is centrally located near the waterfront, Pikes Market, the Seattle Art Museum, convention centers, and shops. Guests will enjoy the intimate feel here—palettes of reds, yellows, and blues; wrought iron chandeliers; and comfortable furnishings. The complimentary evening wine reception in the two-story lobby is the perfect place for guests to relax in front of the fireplace or mingle with other guests. Pets are accepted, and the hotel offers (upon request) a temporary pet goldfish for lonely pet owners. Both leisure and business travelers will enjoy the Southern-inspired restaurant, Sazerac. 189 rooms, 11 story. Pets accepted, some restrictions. Check-in 3 pm, check-out noon. High-speed Internet access, wireless Internet access. Restaurant, bar. Fitness room. Business center. Credit cards accepted. **$$$**

**★ ★ ★ HOTEL VINTAGE PARK.** *1100 Fifth Ave, Seattle (98101). Phone 206/624-8000; toll-free 800/624-4433; fax 206/623-0568. www.vintagepark.com.* This renovated hotel, built in 1922, offers well-appointed and finely furnished (rich fabrics and cherry furniture) guest rooms, each named after a local winery or vineyard. Popular with business travelers, it is centrally located in the heart of the city and is just steps from shops, theaters, and restaurants. Visitors will enjoy the comfortable lobby while sitting by the fireplace and tasting local wines and microbeers—a complimentary reception is held every night. After the reception, Tulio Ristorante, the in-house Italian cuisine restaurant and a local favorite, is the perfect place to grab some dinner. 126 rooms, 11 story.Pets accepted. Check-in 3 pm, check-out noon. High-speed Internet access, wireless Internet access. Restaurant, bar. Credit cards accepted. **$$$**

**★ ★ ★ INN AT THE MARKET.** *86 Pine St, Seattle (98101). Phone 206/443-3600; toll-free 800/446-4484; fax 206/448-0631. www.innatthemarket.com.* Seattle's renowned creative spirit is perhaps best felt at the delightful Inn at the Market. This boutique hotel enjoys a prime location at the vibrant Pike Place Market, overlooking the pristine waters of Elliott Bay. Picturesque views and cultural attractions are just outside the door at this country chic home-away-from-home. The spacious and stylish accommodations are the last word in comfort, with in-room massages and special Tempur-Pedic mattresses ensuring restful sleep. The rooftop garden provides the perfect place to daydream or keep watch on the goings-on at the market below. From guest privileges at the Seattle Clubs state-of-the-art fitness facility to in-room dining provided by two restaurants, guests reap the rewards of the inns market location. 70 rooms, 8 story. Pets accepted, some restrictions. Check-in noon, check-out 4 pm. High-speed Internet access, wireless Internet access. Three restaurants, bar. **$$$**

**★ ★ ★ MAYFLOWER PARK HOTEL.** *405 Olive Way, Seattle (98101). Phone 206/623-8700; toll-free 800/426-5100; fax 206/382-6996. www.mayflowerpark.com.* The historic Mayflower Park Hotel offers a much-sought-after location in the heart of Seattle, near the Monorail system, many eclectic shops, and attractions like Pike Place Market and Seattle Center. But even if it weren't located in the city's center, this beautiful hotel would still be a destination on its own. First opened in 1927 as The Bergonian, the Mayflower has since been renovated to recapture the grandeur and classic style of days gone by. Guest rooms are luxuriously appointed with beautiful furnishings, rich fabrics, large-screen televisions, fluffy bath robes, and pampering Baudelaire bath amenities, while everyone from the Concierge to room service staff provides friendly and gracious service. The hotel's bar, Oliver's, consistently comes out on top in Seattle's annual Martini Classic Challenge. 171 rooms, 12 story. Check-in 4 pm, check-out noon. High-speed Internet access, wireless Internet access. Two restaurants, two bars. Fitness room. Business center. **$$**

**★ ★ ★ THE PARAMOUNT.** *724 Pine St, Seattle (98101). Phone 206/292-9500; fax 206/292-8610. www.paramounthotelseattle.com.* This European-style hotel is located near the Washington State Convention Center, Trade Center, Paramount Theater, and great shopping and entertainment. Inside, a cozy fireplace warms the lobby like a small English cottage, and guest rooms are elegant and spacious. 146 rooms, 11 story. Pets accepted, some restrictions; fee. Check-in 3 pm, check-out noon. High-speed Internet access, wireless Internet access. Restaurant, bar. Fitness room. Business center. **$$**

**★ ★ ★ RENAISSANCE SEATTLE HOTEL.** *515 Madison St, Seattle (98104). Phone 206/583-0300; toll-free 800/278-4159; fax 206/447-0992. www.renaissancehotels.com.* Located in the heart of Seattle, this hotel combines contemporary décor of marble and glass with earth-toned colors that convey a warm, rich ambience. Guests have magnificent city views from the 25th floor, where the indoor pool is located. Nearly everything that defines Seattle is less than a mile away—Pike Place Market and the waterfront, Pioneer Square, Safeco Field (home of the Mariners), and Seahawks Stadium. 553 rooms, 28 story. Check-in 3 pm, check-out noon. High-speed Internet access. Two restaurants, bar. Fitness room. Indoor pool, whirlpool. Business center. **$$**

**★ ★ ★ SEATTLE MARRIOTT WATERFRONT.** *2100 Alaskan Way, Seattle (98121). Phone 206/443-5000; toll-free 800/228-9290; fax 206/256-1100. www.seattlemarriottwaterfront.com.* This waterfront hotel affords fantastic views of the city skyline, the Olympic Mountains, Mt. Rainier, and Elliott Bay. Common areas feature modern touches like colorful blown glass displays and eclectic mosaic tile floors, while guest rooms feature CD players, luxurious bedding with down comforters and pillows, and complimentary Starbucks coffee service. 358 rooms. Check-in 4 pm, check-out noon. High-speed Internet access. Restaurant, bar. Fitness room. Indoor pool, outdoor pool, whirlpool. Airport transportation available. **$$$**

**★ ★ ★ THE SHERATON SEATTLE HOTEL.** *1400 Sixth Ave, Seattle (98101). Phone 206/621-9000; toll-free 800/325-3535; fax 206/621-8441. www.sheraton.com/seattle.* Located in the heart of Seattle's vibrant downtown area, The Sheraton Seattle Hotel offers a great location near many of the city's attractions, including Key Arena and Seattle Center, as well as close proximity to world-class shopping and fantastic dining. Guest rooms feature a host of amenities to make a stay here pleasant and comfortable, including Sheraton's signature "Sweet Sleeper Bed." 840 rooms, 35 story. Pets accepted, some restrictions. Check-in 3 pm, check-out noon. High-speed Internet access, wireless Internet access. Restaurant, bar. Fitness room. Indoor pool. Business center. **$$**

**★ ★ ★ SORRENTO HOTEL.** *900 Madison St, Seattle (98104). Phone 206/622-6400; fax 206/343-6155. www.hotelsorrento.com.* Drawing on its namesake Italian village for inspiration, the Sorrento Hotel is a classic Mediterranean masterpiece. This historic Seattle hotel remains close to the attractions of downtown while maintaining an unparalleled intimacy. Jewel tones, stunning fabrics, and rich mahogany furnishings set a regal ambience throughout this traditional hotel. The guest accommodations are the very definition of elegance, with tones of red and gold, brocade fabrics, marble baths, plush amenities, and distinctive artwork. From knowledgeable concierges to shiatsu massage therapists, the hotel's seamless service makes it a perfect place for business and leisure travelers alike. Home to the Hunt Club (see), one of Seattles revered landmarks, the Sorrento whets the appetite of its visitors with two other dining establishments, including the cozy Fireside Room and the seasonal outdoor Piazza Capri. 76 rooms, 7 story. Pets accepted, some restrictions; fee. Check-in 4 pm, check-out noon. High-speed Internet access, wireless Internet access. Restaurant, bar. Fitness room. Airport transportation available. Business center. **$$$**

**★ ★ ★ W SEATTLE HOTEL.** *1112 Fourth Ave, Seattle (98101). Phone 206/264-6000; toll-free 888/625-5144; fax 206/264-6100. www.whotels.com.* The W Seattle Hotel combines cutting-edge style with top-notch comfort and cute and quirky touches—like a candy necklace in the in-room munchies box. Since this hotel is designed for tech-savvy business travelers, rooms offer CD players, high-speed Ethernet access, and cordless phones at well-equipped workstations. Young children may not be the best fit for the decidedly upscale atmosphere, but if you want your every business need catered to or are looking for a romantic getaway, look no further than the bright colors and cool leather of W Seattle. The lobby, adjacent bar, and dining room are contenders in the "now" scene of Seattle. 426 rooms, 26 story. Pets accepted, some restrictions; fee. Check-in 3 pm, check-out noon. High-speed Internet access. Restaurant, bar. Fitness room. Business center. Credit cards accepted. **$$$**

## Full-Service Inns

**★ ★ ★ INN AT HARBOR STEPS.** *1221 First Ave, Seattle (98101). Phone 206/748-0973; toll-free 888/728-8910; fax 206/748-0533. www.innatharborsteps.com.* Guests of this inn on Seattle's waterfront will find themselves near all of the city's best attractions, including shops, galleries, cafés, Harbor Steps Park, Woodland Park Zoo, and the world-famous Pike Place Market. Rooms are elegant yet urban, with floral-patterned bed spreads and furniture, fireplaces, garden views, and sitting areas, as well as wet bars, refrigerators, and high-speed Internet access. 28 rooms, 2 story. Complimentary full breakfast. Check-in 3 pm, check-out noon. High-speed Internet access. Fitness room. Indoor pool, whirlpool. Business center. **$$**

**★ ★ ★ THE INN AT EL GAUCHO.** *2502 First Ave, Seattle (98121). Phone 206/728-1337.elgaucho.com.* Seattle's hip Belltown district is the setting for the ultra-swank Inn at El Gaucho. Guests will find rooms to be equipped with many luxurious amenities, including pillow-top beds with soft Egyptian cotton linens, rainfall showerheads, L'Occitane bath amenities, oversized Egyptian cotton towels, plasma TVs, and CD players. The inn understands that guests may find it hard to break away from the magnificent rooms, so in-room dining—with bedside preparation—is provided by the downstairs El Gaucho steakhouse. 18 rooms. Check-in 3 pm, check-out noon. High-speed Internet access, wireless Internet access. Restaurant, bar. **$$**

## Specialty Lodgings

**ACE HOTEL.** *2423 First Ave, Seattle (98121). Phone 206/448-4721; fax 206/374-0745. www.acehotel.com.* The ultra-hip Ace Hotel bills itself as "the ultimate lodging for the urban nomad on a mission of experience." Modeled after European hotels, Ace presents a stylish décor, with modern furnishings and clean white walls throughout. Rooms feature exposed brick walls, lofted ceilings, and hardwood floors. Half of the hotel's accommodations have private bathrooms, while the other half utilize shared facilities. Each private bathroom is entered through a revolving door that's hidden in the wall. All rooms include a sink and vanity. 28 rooms. Pets accepted. Check-in 3 pm, check-out noon. Wireless Internet access. **$$**

**CHAMBERED NAUTILUS BED & BREAKFAST.** *5005 22nd Ave NE, Seattle (98105). Phone 206/522-2536; toll-free 800/545-8459; fax 206/528-0898. www.chamberednautilus.com.* Built in 1912 by a professor at the University of Washington, this quaint Georgian colonial B&B offers cozy and distinctive rooms just a short walk from campus. Each antique-filled guest room offers a private bath and phone as well as its own resident teddy bear; there's also a library/sitting room with a fireplace and a sundeck. The plentiful steps make the Chambered Nautilus inappropriate for those in wheelchairs and those who have trouble climbing. 10 rooms, 3 story. Children over 8 years only. Complimentary full breakfast. Check-in 4 pm, check-out 11 am. Wireless Internet access. **$**

**GASLIGHT INN.** *1727 15th Ave, Seattle (98122). Phone 206/325-3654; fax 206/328-4803. www.gaslight-inn.com.* A charming bed-and-breakfast housed in a restored mansion, the Gaslight Inn offers turn-of-the-century ambience along with many modern amenities that make a stay here comfortable and relaxing. Rooms are lovingly appointed with antiques and Northwest Indian art pieces, and feature double or queen-size beds, refrigerators, televisions, fireplaces, and private decks, or gardens. 8 rooms, 3 story. Complimentary continental breakfast. Check-in 3-6 pm, check-out 11 am. Wireless Internet access. Outdoor pool. **$**

**HILL HOUSE BED & BREAKFAST.** *1113 E John St, Seattle (98102). Phone 206/720-7161; toll-free 800/720-7161; fax 206/323-0772. www.seattlebnb.com.* Restored 1903 Victorian inn. 9 rooms, 3 story. Children over 12 years only. Complimentary full breakfast. Check-in by appointment, check-out 11 am. **$**

**SALISBURY HOUSE BED & BREAKFAST.** *750 16th Ave E, Seattle (98112). Phone 206/328-8682; fax 206/720-1019. www.salisburyhouse.com.* This 1904 house has been carefully renovated to preserve its charm, yet features many modern conveniences. Be aware that these conveniences don't extend to a TV in every room, though—only the Suite has one. Each of the five rooms has at least one distinctive feature: the Blue Room has a private deck, the Suite a private entrance and fireplace, the Rose Room a bay window and window seat, the Lavender Room a 6-foot-long soaking tub, and the Garden Room a country French and wicker décor. 5 rooms, 4 story. Children over 12 years only. Complimentary continental breakfast. Check-in 4 pm, check-out 11 am. High-speed Internet access, wireless Internet access. **$**

## Restaurants

**★ ★ ★ AL BOCCALINO.** *1 Yesler Way, Seattle (98104). Phone 206/622-7688; fax 206/622-1788. www.alboccalino.com.* This intimate Italian restaurant in Pioneer Square features soft antique lighting and candlelit tables that set the stage for many marriage proposals or other special-occasion celebrations. The owner, Carlos Tager, is a nightly fixture and warmly greets each guest. The menu features dishes from northern and southern Italy, but diners in the know come Sunday through Thursday to endulge in the five-course dinner for two offering. Italian menu. Lunch, dinner. Closed Mon; holidays. Business casual attire. Reservations recommended. Credit cards accepted. **$$**

**★ ★ ★ ANDALUCA.** *407 Olive Way, Seattle (98101). Phone 206/382-6999; fax 206/382-6997. www.andaluca.com.* With an intimate atmosphere and a James Beard Award-winning chef, Andaluca has had no problem maintaining its reputation as a favorite place to dine in Seattle. Mediterranean-influenced fare such as chilled green gazpacho with Dungeness crab and grilled double cut lamb chops with almond and current couscous keep both locals and tourists coming back time and time again. Mediterranean menu. Breakfast, lunch, dinner. Bar. Children's menu. Casual attire. Reservations recommended. Valet parking. **$$**

**★ ★ ★ ASSAGGIO RISTORANTE.** *2010 Fourth Ave, Seattle (98121). Phone 206/441-1399; fax 206/441-0603. www.assaggioseattle.com.* Diners feel like family when they enter this Italian Belltown restaurant. The executive chef/owner, Mauro Golmarvi, meets and greets every person. The atmosphere is friendly and the décor is Renaissance style, with Michaelangelo replica murals, wood booths, soft sconce lighting, and intimate tables. The restaurant's authentic Italian cuisine emphasizes the North Central Adriatic region of Italy, and Mauro takes numerous trips to Italy each year to replenish his wine offerings. Italian menu. Lunch, dinner. Closed Sun. Children's menu. Casual attire. Reservations recommended. Valet parking. Outdoor seating. **$$$**

**★ ATLAS FOODS.** *2820 NE University Village, Seattle (98105). Phone 206/522-6025; fax 206/988-8763. www.chowfoods.com.* International menu. Breakfast, lunch, dinner, brunch. Bar. Children's menu. Business casual attire. Reservations recommended. **$$**

**★ ★ BANDOLEONE.** *703 N 34th St, Seattle (98102). Phone 206/329-7559; fax 206/583-0133. www.bandoleone.net.* The L-shaped bar is the focal point of this very hip and happening dining spot. Located in the Fremont area of Seattle, the restaurant is small and intimate and decorated with light woods, yellow walls, high ceilings and windows, and unique sconces. The exterior brickwork is quite appealing and really draws you in. Portuguese, Spanish menu. Lunch, dinner, late-night. Bar. Children's menu. Casual attire. Reservations recommended. Outdoor seating. **$$**

**★ BLUWATER BISTRO.** *1001 Fairview Ave N, Seattle (98109). Phone 206/447-0769; fax 206/447-6977. www.bluwaterbistro.com.* BluWater Bistro's friendly and welcoming vibe makes it a favorite with everyone from families taking a break from sightseeing to groups of friends meeting for a drink. With menu items like house-made meatloaf and roasted stuffed pork chops; an extensive cocktail menu; and spectacular views of Lake Union and the marina, this charming spot sets the standard for casual dining in Seattle. American, seafood menu. Lunch, dinner. Bar. Children's menu. Business casual attire. Reservations recommended. Valet parking. Outdoor seating. **$$**

**★ ★ ★ BRASA.** *2107 Third Ave, Seattle (98121). Phone 206/728-4220; fax 206/728-8067. www.brasa.com.* Seattle's trendy residents gather at Brasa on a regular basis to indulge in this hotspots robust, Mediterranean-inspired fare. While the crowd at the bar tends to be young and hip, the folks filling the rustic but sleek dining room, decorated with terrazzo floors, black- and tan-accented wood, and wrought-iron railings, are a stylish set of thirty- and forty-somethings. No matter what your age, however, the vibrant cuisine at Brasa is easy for all to love. Two of the signature dishes show off the kitchens culinary brilliance: the roast suckling pig and the mussels and clams served oven-steamed in a *cataplana* (a double-domed copper pot that's used to cook stews in Portugal). All dishes are dishes layered with the bold flavors of Spain, Portugal, France, and Brazil. Brasa serves wonderful food that dazzles the palate and the eye and expertly balances the rustic and the sophisticated. Mediterranean menu. Dinner. Closed holidays. Bar. Business casual attire. Reservations recommended. Valet parking. Credit cards accepted. **$$$**

★ ★ ★ **BRASSERIE MARGAUX.** *Fourth and Lenora, Seattle (98121). Phone 206/777-1990. www.margauxseattle.com.* This French brasserie is adjacent to the beautiful Warwick Seattle Hotel and offers breathtaking views of the Seattle skyline, making it a great choice for special-occasion meals. The intimate dining room is decorated with warm dark woods, upholstered chairs, and candlelit tables. The menu specializes in Northwest cuisine with French influences, and Brasserie Margaux is the only dining room in Seattle which carves prime rib tableside. For a special dining experience, try the wine pairing dinner—a delicious and educational choice. American, French menu. Breakfast, lunch, dinner. Bar. Children's menu. Business casual attire. Reservations recommended. Valet parking. **$$**

★ ★ **BROOKLYN SEAFOOD, STEAK & OYSTER HOUSE.** *1212 Second Ave, Seattle (98101). Phone 206/224-7000; fax 206/224-7088.* This traditional steak and chophouse is a local favorite. The interior is decorated with old-fashioned chandeliers; black and cream tiles; and booths with a very private feel. The central focus is the energizing bar, offering cocktails and oysters. Seafood, steak menu. Lunch, dinner. Closed Thanksgiving, Dec 25. Bar. Children's menu. Business casual attire. Reservations recommended. Valet parking. Outdoor seating. **$$$**

★ ★ **CAFE CAMPAGNE.** *1600 Post Alley, Seattle (98101). Phone 206/728-2233. www.campagnerestaurant.com.* With its no-fuss French cuisine, this restaurant proves to be a popular jaunt for casual dining. Its comfortable décor features warm yellow walls, velvet curtains, large mirrors and posters, and a wooden bar for seating. Visitors come in droves for the Sunday brunch, which includes French toast made with brioche. French bistro menu. Breakfast, lunch, dinner, brunch. Bar. Casual attire. Reservations recommended. Outdoor seating. Credit cards accepted. **$$**

★ ★ ★ **CAFE FLORA.** *2901 E Madison, Seattle (98112). Phone 206/325-9100; fax 206/324-9783. www.cafeflora.com.* There are people who believe that the words "delicious" and "innovative" could never be used to describe vegetarian cuisine, but Café Flora proves them wrong. Since 1991, this Seattle gem has been turning out perfect plates of fresh and nutritious fare that consistently receives raves from both vegetarians and carnivores alike. Herbs from the restaurant's own garden are used in seasonal dishes like mushroom asparagus risotto with artichoke bottoms, pine nuts, scallions, mascarpone, and parsley oil; and coconut-breaded tofu with basil, cilantro, and sweet chili dipping sauce. Vegetarian menu. Lunch, dinner, brunch. Closed holidays. Children's menu. **$$**

★ ★ **CAFE LAGO.** *2305 24th Ave E, Seattle (98112). Phone 206/329-8005.*A hotspot among locals, this casual Italian eatery has great food and a welcoming atmosphere. Italian menu. Dinner. Closed holidays. Bar. Children's menu. Casual attire. **$$$**

★ ★ ★ **CAMPAGNE.** *86 Pine St, Seattle (98101). Phone 206/728-2800. www.campagnerestaurant.com.* This charming French restaurant is located at Inn at the Market in the popular Pike Place Market. Its delicious menu focuses on regions of Southern France and features entrees such as boneless rib-eye steak with red wine shallot sauce, spinach and pommes frtes ' la canard'; roasted leg of lamb with chick pea pure and red pepper, artichoke and red wine relish; and guinea hen breast roasted with garlic confit and carrots, served with sautéed escargots. A majority of its ingredients are supplied from the local farmers' market. Guests will feel as if they're in a restaurant in France when they enter this establishment, with its beautiful woodwork, warm yellow walls, and large posters. French menu. Dinner. Bar. Casual attire. Reservations recommended. Outdoor seating. Credit cards accepted. **$$$**

★ ★ ★ **CANLIS RESTAURANT.** *2576 Aurora Ave N, Seattle (98109). Phone 206/283-3313; fax 206/283-1766. www.canlis.com.* This spot is definitley worth findingit's located away from the downtown core of hotels and restaurants, in an extremely desirable location. The interior is decorated with neutral touches and offers many intimate dining areas. Guests come for the serene and spectacular views of Lake Union and the Cascade Mountains, but the ever-attentive service keeps them coming back.Menu offerings include Alaskan halibut, Muscovy duck breast, Peter Canlis prawns, and white corn risotto. A pianist performs nightly. American, Pacific Northwest menu. Dinner. Closed Sun; holidays. Bar. Jacket required. Reservations recommended. Valet parking. **$$$$**

★ ★ **CARMELITA.** *7314 Greenwood Ave N, Seattle (98103). Phone 206/706-7703. www.carmelita.net.* Vegan, vegetarian menu. Dinner. Closed Mon; Jan 1, Dec 24-25. Bar. Children's menu. Outdoor seating. **$$**

★ ★ ★ **CASCADIA.** *2328 First Ave, Seattle (98121). Phone 206/448-8884; fax 206/448-2242. www.cascadiarestaurant.com.* Situated in the hip Belltown neighborhood of Seattle, this sleek and sophisticated restaurant welcomes diners to endulge in chef-owner Kerry Sear's creative International menu. Hardwood floors, impressive floral displays, warm cherrywood walls, high ceilings, a cozy fireplace, and modern, upbeat music create a comfortable setting for tasting such dishes as summer vegetable flan with a stuffed Spanish pepper, Columbia River sturgeon, and green curry-rubbed rack of lamb. During warm weather months, the outdoor patio is also open. International menu. Dinner. Closed Sun; holidays. Bar. Children's menu. Business casual attire. Reservations recommended. Outdoor seating. Credit cards accepted. **$$$**

★ ★ ★ **CHEZ SHEA.** *94 Pike St, Seattle (98101). Phone 206/467-9990; fax 206/467-9990. www.chezshea.com.* Tucked into Pike Place Market, you'll discover Chez Shea, an old-world charmer featuring the finest ingredients of the Northwest prepared with French technique and regional gusto. The intimate, candlelit dining room boasts picture-perfect views of the sun setting over the Puget Sound and is usually filled with couples well versed in the art of cross-table handholding, lingering stares, and soft whispers. But locals in the know about cuisine dine here as much for the food as for the cozy ambience. The four-course prix fixe menu features hearty, home-style regional fare that makes beautiful use of local produce as the seasons dictate. A simple salad ends the meal; dessert comes at an extra charge. The chocolate torte and the ginger-steeped bread pudding are worth the splurge. An eight-course chef's tasting menu is also available. French bistro menu. Dinner, late-night. Closed Mon. Bar. Casual attire. Reservations recommended. Valet parking. Credit cards accepted. **$$$**

★ ★ ★ **DAHLIA LOUNGE.** *2001 Fourth Ave, Seattle (98121). Phone 206/682-4142; fax 206/467-0568. www.tomdouglas.com.* Chef/owner Tom Douglas (previous James Beard Award winner) and his wife Jackie Cross (both also of Palace Kitchen and Etta's Seafood) oversee this artsy eatery in the heart of downtown. Red walls, yellow pillars, glass sconces and chandeliers, and upholstered booths create a colorful, playful backdrop for boldly flavored Pacific Northwest cuisine.The daily changing meny offers diners a variety of inventive beef, seafood, and poultry dishes. Diners with a sweet tooth can visit the Dahlia Bakery next door for take-home treats. American, Pacific Northwest menu. Lunch, dinner. Closed holidays. Bar. Children's menu. Business casual attire. Reservations recommended. Credit cards accepted. **$$$**

★ ★ **DULCES LATIN BISTRO.** *1430 34th Ave, Seattle (98122). Phone 206/322-5453; fax 206/322-5275. www.dulceslatinbistro.com.* This neighborhood favorite also has a strong following outside it boundaries. The setting is romantic, with red walls, dark woods, white tablecloths, lots of greenery, and intimate lighting. Many bottles of wine line the restaurant, and a wine case serves as a large centerpiece at one end. Enjoy relaxing piano music every Tuesday and Wednesday evening from 7-9 pm. Mediterranean, Spanish menu. Dinner. Closed Mon. Bar. Children's menu. Casual attire. Reservations recommended. **$$**

★ ★ ★ **EARTH AND OCEAN.** *1112 Fourth Ave, Seattle (98101). Phone 206/260-6060; fax 206/264-6070. www.earthocean.net.* A trendy, chic clientele matches the restaurant's New York-inspired scene, with its ultrahip décor and fusion cuisine. Artfully prepared and creatively named dishes make up the tasting-style menu.Located in the W Seattle hotel (see), this downtown restaurant is also a great people-watching spot. American, Pacific Northwest menu. Breakfast, lunch, dinner, late-night, brunch. Bar. Casual attire. Reservations recommended. Valet parking. Credit cards accepted. **$$$**

★ ★ ★ **EL GAUCHO.** *2505 First Ave, Seattle (98121). Phone 206/728-1337; fax 206/728-7744. www.elgaucho.com.* Located just a few minutes from the center of downtown, this swanky, nostalgic restaurant—a former union hall for merchant seamen—is known mainly for its martinis and meat.However, diners will also enjoy tableside preparations of Caesar salad, chateaubriand, and bananas Foster. Nightly piano music sets the mood for an enjoyable meal, and the lively lounge area is the perfect place for a before- or after-dinner cocktail. Steak menu. Dinner, late-night. Closed holidays. Bar. Business casual attire. Reservations recommended. Valet parking. Credit cards accepted. **$$$**

★ ★ ★ **ETTA'S SEAFOOD.** *2020 Western Ave, Seattle (98121). Phone 206/443-6000. www.tomdouglas.com.* With an atmosphere as colorful as the food, Etta's brings in droves of hungry patrons both day and night.The casual seafood house, owned and operated by Seattle's renowned chef, Tom Douglas, and his wife, Jackie, is located just half a block from the popular Pikes Peak Market and is named after the owners' daughter, Loretta. Its large windows overlook the bustling farmers' market which supplies a majority of the fresh ingredients on the menu. There's something on the menu for everyone, from fish and chips to juicy crab cakes to Oregon country beef rib eye steak. Seafood menu. Lunch, dinner, brunch. Bar. Children's menu. Casual attire. Reservations recommended. Credit cards accepted. **$$$**

★ ★ **F.X. MCRORY'S STEAK, CHOP & OYSTER HOUSE.** *419 Occidental Ave S, Seattle (98104). Phone 206/623-4800; fax 206/613-3105. www.mickmchughs.com.* Located on the cusp of Pioneer Square, this popular steakhouse is just a walk across the street from Qwest Field—so expect a sports-fan crowd. The masculine décor of crown molding, dark walls, and historic photos of Seattle are the perfect complement to the heavy menu of steaks, chops, burgers, and seafood. The belt will need to be loosened after a meal here. Steak menu. Lunch, dinner. Closed Thanksgiving, Dec 25. Bar. Children's menu. Casual attire. Reservations recommended. Outdoor seating. Credit cards accepted. **$$$**

★ ★ ★ **FLYING FISH.** *2234 First Ave, Seattle (98121). Phone 206/728-8595; fax 206/728-1551. www.flyingfishseattle.com.* At this hip Belltown seafood house, guests will find Asian-influenced fish dishes that are artfully presented in a fun and casual environment. The décor is eclectic with glass chandelier "tubes" hanging from a "popcorn" ceiling with exposed pipes, burnt orange walls, and various fish sculptures dot the room. Chef/owner Christine Keff is committed to using fresh organic ingredients, so the fish served here comes directly from Puget Sound, and the organic produce is supplied by a farm in the Green River Valley—resulting in a wonderfully tasty dining experience. Seafood menu. Lunch, dinner, late-night. Closed holidays. Bar. Casual attire. Reservations recommended. Outdoor seating. **$$**

★ ★ ★ **GENEVA.** *1106 Eighth Ave, Seattle (98101). Phone 206/624-2222; fax 206/624-2519. www.genevarestaurant.com.* Possibly the best kept secret in Seattle, this romantic restaurant is decorated with European style and elegance. The magnificient floral arrangement is the focal point in the dining room. Tables are perfectly set, and the subdued walls are dotted with beautiful works of art. The chef, Hanspeter Aebersold, creates his continental masterpieces using fresh, Northwest ingredients. With dishes such as jaeger schnitzel with mushrooms, bacon, and onions; linguini with pan-seared sea scallops topped with roasted hazelnuts; and almond-crusted baked salmon, diners will have a difficult time choosing their meal. Continental menu with Northwest influence. Dinner. Closed Sun-Mon. Bar. Business casual attire. Reservations recommended. Outdoor seating. Credit cards accepted. **$$$**

★ ★ ★ ★ **THE GEORGIAN.** *411 University St, Seattle (98101). Phone 206/621-1700; fax 206/623-2271. www.fairmont.com.* Don't even think of wearing tattered flannel to The Georgian. Unless, of course, the soft fabric takes the form of a handkerchief, neatly tucked into a dapper dinner jacket àla Jay Gatsby. That's because The Georgian, the flagship restaurant of the stately Fairmont Olympic Hotel (see), is like a pocket of rarefied, old-world elegance in a city that's perhaps better known for grunge rock, computer nerds, and corporate coffee. Although jackets are not technically required, the sartorial set won't feel out of place amidst the French furnishings and soaring ceilings of the main dining room. The cuisine is equally rich, like salmon accented by red wine marmalade and summer truffles, and American Kobe beef with marrow shallot butter. There's even afternoon tea, a tradition that the staff presents without pretension—a quality that exemplifies the service at every meal. American, French, Northwest menu. Breakfast, lunch, dinner. Bar. Children's menu. Business casual attire. Reservations recommended. Valet parking. Credit cards accepted. **$$$**

★ ★ ★ **HUNT CLUB.** *900 Madison St, Seattle (98104). Phone 206/343-6156. www.hotelsorrento.com.* Nestled in the Hotel Sorreno, this clubby restaurant is the epitome of elegance. Guests are treated to beautiful surrounds that feature deep, lush colors with dark overtones and tables topped with crisp, white linens.

Chef Brian Scheesher delivers sensational plates of regional American cuisine using fresh, organic produce from his 2-acre garden, which includes heirloom tomatoes, winter squash, potatoes, pumpkins, and four honey-producing beehives. Pacific Northwest menu. Breakfast, lunch, dinner, brunch. Bar. Children's menu. Business casual attire. Reservations recommended. Valet parking. Outdoor seating. **$$$**

★ ★ **IL BISTRO.** *93A Pike St, Seattle (98101). Phone 206/682-3049. www.ilbistro.net.* Located down a quiet cobblestone street and looking out to the commotion of Pike Place Market above, this intimate hideaway, with its low ceilings, ivory curtain-framed black wood windows, and arched doorways, is dimly lit and cozy—perfect for a romantic dinner.The relaxed atmosphere sets the mood for a traditional Italian dinner, featuring local produce and stellar wine selections. Italian menu. Dinner, late-night. Bar. Casual attire. Reservations recommended. Outdoor seating. Credit cards accepted. **$$$**

★ ★ ★ **IL TERRAZZO CARMINE.** *411 First Ave S, Seattle (98104). Phone 206/467-7797; fax 206/447-5716. www.ilterrazzocarmine.com.* High standards and a faithful clientele make this the darling of Italian restaurants in Seattle. While guests enjoy relaxing in the beautifully designed dining area, it's the fresh fare, well-selected wine list, and impeccable service that is truly appreciated here. Surprisingly, this classic Itallian restaurant is located within an office building, but this is quickly forgotten as guests enter the dining room. Carmine's personal artwork graces the walls, the ceiling is accented with wood beams, and the outdoor patio gives diners the option to enjoy their meal alfresco. Only the freshest ingredients are used in Chef Smeraldo's distinctive pasta, veal, beef, and chicken dishes. Italian menu. Lunch, dinner. Closed Sun; holidays. Bar. Business casual attire. Reservations recommended. Valet parking. Outdoor seating. Credit cards accepted. **$$$**

★ ★ ★ ★ **LAMPREIA RESTAURANT.** *2400 First Ave, Seattle (98121). Phone 206/443-3301. www.lampreiarestaurant.com.* You can taste the fresh ingredients in chef Scott Carsberg's International cuisine in everything from the fresh pasta to the hearty game dishes. A few of his delicious dishes include poached veal fillet with shaved purple asparagus, morel mushrooms with zucchini flowers, and blue fin tuna belly with citrus accents. The dining room is sleek and elegant, and the service is friendly and helpful.Dining here is a truly delightful experience. International menu. Dinner. Closed Sun-Mon; Thanksgiving, Dec 25. Business casual attire. Reservations recommended. Valet parking. Credit cards accepted. **$$$**

★ ★ ★ **LE GOURMAND.** *425 NW Market St, Seattle (98107). Phone 206/784-3463.* It's no wonder this is one of the best French restaurants in town, with delectable cuisine and magnificent desserts. Each dish is prepared with fresh ingredients and imagination.A three-course menu and a seven-course tasting menu are offered to guests. Murals of scenery, brick walls, white-clothed tables, and a patio with silver wrought-iron chairs and tables all add to the charming French ambience. Le Gourmand is located at the edge of Ballard, on the way to the Fremont area of Seattle. French menu. Dinner. Closed Sun-Tues. Bar. Business casual attire. Reservations recommended. Outdoor seating. **$$$**

★ ★ ★ **LOLA.** *2000 Fourth Ave, Seattle (98121). Phone 206/441-1430. www.tomdouglas.com.* Located in Belltown and adjacent to the Hotel Andra, this Greek/Mediterranean cuisine restaurant is the most recent addition to Tom and Jackie Douglas' restaurant group (Dahlia Lounge is just across the street). The modern dining room is welcoming with warm brown colors, floor-to-ceiling windows, high-backed booths, and hand-painted chandeliers. For dinner, the kabobs are a must, and the lamb and fish dishes are delicious. Breakfast offerings include favorites such as buttermilk pancakes with blueberries. During warm weather, grab a seat outside. Greek, Mediterranean menu. Breakfast, lunch, dinner, late-night. Bar. Children's menu. Casual attire. Reservations recommended. Valet parking. Outdoor seating. **$$**

★ ★ ★ **MADISON PARK CAFE.** *1807 42nd Ave E, Seattle (98112). Phone 206/324-2626; fax 206/328-0432. www.madisonparkcafe.citysearch.com.* This intimate French bistro is located in a charming residential neighborhood across the street from a beautiful park—making guests feel as if they've been transported to Paris. The interior space has a warm, cozy feeling with its toasty fireplace and works from local artists hang on the warm, sunny yellow walls. On nice summer nights, the outdoor patio is the perfect place to dine. The dinner menu offers French favorites such as onion soup, cassoulet, and steak au poivre. There are no reservations taken for brunch, so come early. French bistro menu. Dinner, brunch. Closed

Mon. Bar. Casual attire. Reservations recommended. Outdoor seating. Credit cards accepted. **$$**

★ ★ **MAXIMILIEN FRENCH CAFE.** *81A Pike St, Seattle (98101). Phone 206/682-7270. www.maximilienrestaurant.com.* Located at Seattle's popular Pike Place Market, this quaint French restaurant will make guests feel as if they've been whisked away to Paris. The restaurant's panoramic windows offer breathtaking views of Elliott Bay, Puget Sound, and the Olympic Mountains. French menu. Breakfast, lunch, dinner. Bar. Children's menu. Business casual attire. Reservations recommended. Credit cards accepted. **$$$**

★ ★ **METROPOLITAN GRILL.** *820 2nd Ave, Seattle (98104). Phone 206/624-3287; fax 206/340-1152. www.themetropolitangrill.com.* Located in a historic 1903 building, this popular steakhouse is a throwback to the 1930s, with tall mahogany doors, tuxedo-clad maitre d's, columns trimmed with original moldings, oversized booths, and mahogany- and brass-trimmed tables and railings. Hearty steaks are the main draw here, and they are dramatically showcased in glass cases for diners to choose their meal. Steak menu. Lunch, dinner, late-night. Closed Thanksgiving, Dec 25. Bar. Casual attire. Valet parking. Credit cards accepted. **$$$**

★ ★ **NISHINO.** *3130 E Madison, Seattle (98112). Phone 206/322-5800. www.nishinorestaurant.com.* Heralded as one of Seattle's best and most popular, Nishino is known for having the freshest fish around. The restaurant is set in an impeccably refined space and decorated with elaborate Japanese screens and paintings. The kitchen serves perfectly prepared sashimi and sushi; however, eat omakase (chef's choice) style for a delicious dining experience. Japanese, sushi menu. Dinner. Children's menu. Casual attire. Reservations recommended. Credit cards accepted. **$$$**

★ ★ ★ **THE OCEANAIRE SEAFOOD ROOM.** *1700 Seventh Ave, Seattle (98101). Phone 206/267-2277; fax 206/267-2156. www.theoceanaire.com.* Seafood menu. Lunch, dinner. Bar. Casual attire. Reservations recommended. Valet parking. **$$$**

★ ★ ★ **PALACE KITCHEN.** *2030 5th Ave, Seattle (98121). Phone 206/448-2001; fax 206/448-1979. www.tomdouglas.com.* Located under the monorail at 5th and Lenora in Belltown, this theatrical restaurant/saloon, owned and operated by Tom and Jackie Douglas, caters to a drinking crowd in search of imaginative rustic food. A horseshoe-shaped wood bar is the focal point of the space, just beating out the spectacular "Palace Feast" mural. The atmosphere is comfortable with Italian chandeliers, velvet drapes, wood booths and tables, and gilded mirrors. Although the American-cuisine menu changes daily, there is always a delicious rotisserie dish (prepared over an applewood grill) available. And a slice of Douglas' legendary coconut-cream pie is the perfect ending to a great meal. American menu. Dinner, late-night. Bar. Casual attire. Reservations recommended. Valet parking. **$$$**

★ ★ ★ **PALISADE.** *2601 W Marina Pl, Seattle (98199). Phone 206/285-5865; fax 206/298-4879. www.palisaderestaurant.com.* Palisade is set on the Magnolia Marina, with incredible waterfront views of the Seattle skyline and yachts galore! Guests cross over a bridge and large pond, filled with fish. The appealing interior features unusual brown weave chairs and unique blown glass artwork. Menu options include dishes such as passion fruit-glazed duck breast, rotisserie rack of lamb, and wood oven-roasted prawns. Guest can also enjoy the views from the bar. American, seafood menu. Lunch, dinner. Bar. Children's menu. Casual attire. Reservations recommended. Valet parking. Outdoor seating. **$$$**

★ ★ ★ **PALOMINO.** *1420 Fifth Ave, Seattle (98101). Phone 206/623-1300; fax 206/467-1386. www.palomino.com.* This attractive restaurant is located on the third floor of the City Centre Mall—a great spot for people-watching. High ceilings, chandeliers and sconces, and an open kitchen add to ambience. Guests can dine at booths or large round tables. Italian, Mediterranean menu. Lunch, dinner. Bar. Children's menu. Casual attire. Reservations recommended. Credit cards accepted. **$$$**

★ ★ **PIATTI RESTAURANT.** *2695 NE University Village Ln, Seattle (98105). Phone 206/524-9088; fax 206/524-3116. www.piatti.com.* Situated within University Village—an upscale, open-air shopping mall—Piatti Restaurant serves up Italian dishes in a warm, sunny atmosphere. An inviting bar area provides a great place to relax, enjoy the menu, or wait for a table. Italian menu. Lunch, dinner. Bar. Children's menu. Casual attire. Reservations recommended. Outdoor seating. Credit cards accepted. **$$**

★ ★ **THE PINK DOOR.** *1919 Post Alley, Seattle (98101). Phone 206/443-3241. www.thepinkdoor.net.* To find this lively Italian-American restaurant, walk down "Post Alley," look for the pink door, open it and go downstairs. A warm, eclectic experience awaits! Live entertainment such as tap dancing, jazz ensembles, and a trapeze act are featured nightly. The outdoor patio offers incredible views of Elliott Bay and the Olympic Mountains. American, Italian menu. Lunch, dinner, late-night. Bar. Casual attire. Reservations recommended. Outdoor seating. Credit cards accepted. **$$**

★ ★ ★ **PLACE PIGALLE.** *81 Pike St, Seattle (98101). Phone 206/624-1756.* Hidden in a back corner of the popular Pikes Place Market, this local favorite serves American cuisine with a regional Northwest specialties. The crisp linens and a black-and-white parquet floor create a truly romantic setting alongside the bustling Puget Sound.Diners enjoy views of Elliott Bay and the San Juan Mountains while enjoying a delicious meal. This restaurant is a great choice for any celebration. American, Northwest Regional menu. Lunch, dinner. Closed Sun. Bar. Casual attire. Reservations recommended. Outdoor seating. Credit cards accepted. **$$$**

★ ★ ★ **PONTI SEAFOOD GRILL.** *3014 3rd Ave N, Seattle (98109). Phone 206/284-3000; fax 206/284-4768. www.pontiseafoodgrill.com.* A charming courtyard with a terra-cotta lion fountain is located at the entrance of Ponti Seafood Grill. Inside, there are beautiful yellow walls with windows, allowing the brilliance of the waterway to be the focus. Guests can dine on the outside patio while taking in the views of Lake Union. Menu offerings include house-smoked Alaskan black cod, Ponti shellfish paella, and Parmesan and spinach-stuffed chicken. Seafood menu. Dinner. Bar. Children's menu. Casual attire. Reservations recommended. Valet parking. Outdoor seating. **$$**

★ ★ **QUEEN CITY GRILL.** *2201 First Ave, Seattle (98121). Phone 206/443-0975. www.queencitygrill.com.* One of Belltown's longest-running and most popular restaurants, the Queen City Grill stays young with a hip atmosphere and delicious grilled fresh seafood and dry-aged steaks.Housed in a nearly century-old brick building, the décor features high-backed wooden booths (each with window views), triangular wall lamps, yellow walls, and a magnificent bar area. Seafood, steak menu. Dinner. Closed holidays. Bar. Casual attire. Reservations recommended. Outdoor seating. Credit cards accepted. **$$**

★ ★ ★ **RAY'S BOATHOUSE.** *6049 Seaview Ave NW, Seattle (98107). Phone 206/789-3770; fax 206/781-1960. www.rays.com.* Located in quaint Ballard, this upscale, casual seafood house is a true Seattle landmark, approximately 20 minutes from downtown. Many people find the best part of Ray's to be the café and deck upstairs. The main restaurant's woodwork is very shiplike and has an appealing charm. Numerous old black-and-white photos line the walls. The deck on top is truly outstandingguests can sit on the benches (with warm blankets provided by Ray's) and watch the boats pass by as they come out of the Ballard Locks to Elliott Bay and the Pacific Ocean. For fresh Northwest seafood, this favorite on the water is a sure bet. American, seafood menu. Dinner. Bar. Children's menu. Casual attire. Reservations recommended. Valet parking. Outdoor seating. **$$$**

★ ★ ★ ★ **ROVER'S.** *2808 E Madison St, Seattle (98112). Phone 206/325-7442. www.rovers-seattle.com.* A small white clapboard cottage located in the upscale Madison Park neighborhood houses Rover's, an intimate restaurant serving innovative and amazing contemporary cuisine. Thierry Rautureau, the chef and owner, stays true to the regional ingredients of the Northwest while paying homage to impeccable French technique, perhaps because he hails from France. The restaurant's modest but lovely décor does little to tip you off to the extraordinary culinary masterpieces that await you. Presented like precious little works of art, the portions are perfect in size, taste, and appearance. The miraculous part of Rautureau's menu is that as soon as you finish the course in front of you, you are ready and salivating for the next. (The restaurant offers five-course and eight-course tasting menus in addition to a five-course vegetarian menu. Lunch is served on Friday.) Not only is Rautureau a gifted chef, but he is also a gregarious and witty host who makes a point of visiting and welcoming every guest personally. American, Pacific Northwest menu. Lunch, dinner. Closed Sun-Mon; holidays. Business casual attire. Reservations recommended. Outdoor seating. Credit cards accepted. **$$$$**

★ ★ ★ **RUTH'S CHRIS STEAK HOUSE.** *727 Pine St, Seattle (98104). Phone 206/624-8524; fax 206/624-6268. www.ruthschris.com.* Born from a single New Orleans restaurant that Ruth Fertel bought in 1965 for $22,000, the Ruths Chris Steak House chain has made it to the top of every steak lovers list. Aged prime Midwestern beef is broiled to your liking and served on a heated plate, sizzling in butter, a staple ingredient used generously in most entrées; even healthier alternatives like chicken arrive at your table drenched in the savory substance. Sides like creamed spinach and fresh asparagus with hollandaise are not to be missed, and are the perfect companion to any entre. And who can forget the potatoes? Choose from seven different preparations, from a 1-pound baked potato with everything to au gratin potatoes with cream sauce and topped with cheese. Steak menu. Lunch, dinner. Closed holidays. Bar. Children's menu. Casual attire. Reservations recommended. Valet parking. **$$$**

★ ★ ★ **SAZERAC.** *1101 Fourth Ave, Seattle (98101). Phone 206/624-7755; fax 206/621-7779. www.sazeracrestaurant.com.* Sazerac serves reliably satisfying, Southern-inspired food. The interior features a vibrant, eclectic décor, and the fun atmosphere makes it a hit with the happy-hour crowd.The restaurant is located adjacent to the Hotel Monaco. Guests can dine at the counter seating of the rotisserie grill and pizza oven or at tables or booths. American menu. Breakfast, lunch, dinner, late-night. Bar. Children's menu. Casual attire. Reservations recommended. Valet parking. Outdoor seating. Credit cards accepted. **$$**

★ ★ **SERAFINA.** *2043 Eastlake Ave E, Seattle (98102). Phone 206/323-0807; fax 206/325-2766. www.serafinaseattle.com.* Concrete-distressed floors, unique murals, chandeliers covered with fabric, and a "European courtyard," all add to the Italian atmopsphere at Serafina. Located just around the bend of Lake Union in the Eastlake area, it is approximately ten minutes from downtown. The atmosphere at this bistro is casual and intimate. Jazz is featured on Friday and Saturday evenings, and at Sunday brunch. Italian menu. Lunch, dinner, late-night, Sun brunch. Bar. Children's menu. Casual attire. Reservations recommended. Outdoor seating. **$$**

★ ★ **SHIRO'S.** *2401 Second Ave, Seattle (98121). Phone 206/443-9844; fax 206/443-9974. www.shiros.com.* Chef-owner Shiro Kashiba, a two-time James Beard nominee, presents delicious Japanese dishes with Pacific Northwest influences at his modestly sized Belltown property. The dcor is modern with black lacquer chairs, wood accents, a sushi counter, and a comfortable outdoor patio. Japanese menu. Dinner. Closed holidays. Casual attire. Reservations recommended. Outdoor seating. Credit cards accepted. **$$**

★ ★ ★ **SHUCKERS.** *411 University St, Seattle (98101). Phone 206/621-1700; fax 206/623-2271. www.fairmont.com.* An upscale yet inviting ambience will be found at Shuckers, located on the lower level of the Fairmont Olympic Hotel (see). Deep rich woods and lots of leather add to the décor of this traditional oyster bar setting. Locals and tourists alike head to this true "Seattle institution." Seafood menu. Lunch, dinner. Bar. Children's menu. Casual attire. Reservations recommended. Valet parking. Credit cards accepted. **$$**

★ ★ ★ **SZMANIA'S MAGNOLIA.** *3321 W McGraw, Seattle (98199). Phone 206/284-7305; fax 206/283-7303. www.szmanias.com.* Guests at this favorite neighborhood hangout can always see the German chef at work in the open kitchen, which features counter seating. A unique, one-of-a-kind glass mural is located at the front of the restaurant, and vibrant paintings by a local artist hang throughout. The setting is intimate, eclectic, and luxurious, with cozy booths and fireplaces. Szmania's Magnolia is located just ten minutes from downtown Seattle. German menu. Lunch, dinner. Closed Mon; holidays. Bar. Children's menu. Casual attire. Reservations recommended. **$$**

★ **TRATTORIA MITCHELLI.** *84 Yesler Way, Seattle (98104). Phone 206/623-3883; fax 206/682-5029.* Located in the Pioneer Square area and just minutes from Seattle's football and baseball fields, this kitschy Italian trattoria is the perfect spot for breakfast. Italian menu. Breakfast, lunch, dinner. Closed Dec 25. Bar. Children's menu. Casual attire. Reservations recommended. Outdoor seating. Credit cards accepted. **$$**

★ ★ ★ **TULIO RISTORANTE.** *1100 Fifth Ave, Seattle (98101). Phone 206/624-5500; toll-free 800/624-4433; fax 206/623-0568. www.tulio.com.* An intimate dining room with dark wood paneling and dim chandeliers creates a cozy setting for a classic Tuscan trattoria. The food is inventive yet unpretentious and highlighted by ample tomatoes, cheeses, and fresh pasta. A knowledgeable and gracious staff completes the inviting experience. Italian menu. Breakfast, lunch, dinner, brunch. Closed Thanksgiving, Dec 25. Bar. Children's menu. Casual attire. Reservations recommended. Valet parking. Outdoor seating. Credit cards accepted. **$$$**

★ ★ ★ **UNION BAY CAFE.** *3515 NE 45th St, Seattle (98105). Phone 206/527-8364. www.unionbaycafe.com.* Eclectic artwork by a local artist adorns the yellow walls at Union Bay Café, a small, intimate restaurant located just 15 minutes from downtown. This long-standing bistro was "one of the first" to concentrate on local organic ingredients. A very well-known wine collection is featured here, and, often, there are special wine events. The outdoor dining area is particularly appealing. American menu. Dinner. Closed Mon. Bar. Casual attire. Reservations recommended. Outdoor seating. **$$**

**★ ★ ★ UNION SQUARE GRILL.** *621 Union St, Seattle (98101). Phone 206/224-4321. www.unionsquaregrill.com.* Comfortable booth seating a busy, vibrant, Art Deco-inspired design; and quick service make this eatery, with a bistrolike menu, a popular stop for business lunches and pre-theater meals. American menu. Lunch, dinner. Closed Dec 25. Bar. Children's menu. Business casual attire. Reservations recommended. **$$$**

**★ ★ ★ WILD GINGER ASIAN RESTAURANT & SATAY BAR.** *1401 Third Ave, Seattle (98101). Phone 206/623-4450; fax 206/623-8265. www.wildginger.net.* One of downtown Seattle's premier restaurants, Wild Ginger is a hot spot for celebrities who sometimes come for Monday night jazz sessions. Decorated in black, tan, and gold hues, the dining room offers intimate seating arrangements and features large, round tables. Pan-Asian menu. Lunch, dinner, late-night. Bar. Casual attire. Reservations recommended. Credit cards accepted. **$$$**

# Seattle-Tacoma International Airport Area (B-2)

**Airport** Seattle-Tacoma International Airport

**Web Site** www.portseattle.org/seatac

**Information** Phone 206/433-5388

**Lost and Found** Phone 206/433-5312

**Airlines** Aeroflot Airlines, Air Canada, Alaska Airlines, America West, American Airlines, American Trans Air, Asiana Airlines, Big Sky, British Airways, Continental Airlines, Delta Air Lines, EVA Air, Frontier Airlines, Hawaiian Airlines, Horizon Air, Iberia Airlines, jetBlue Airways, KLM Royal Dutch, Lufthansa, Mesa Airlines, Northwest Airlines, Scandinavian Airlines (SAS), Skywest Airlines, Sun Country Airlines, United Airlines, United Express, United States Airways

## Limited-Service Hotels

**★ ★ BEST WESTERN FEDERAL WAY EXECUTEL.** *31611 20th Ave S, Federal Way (98003). Phone 253/941-6000; toll-free 800/648-3311; fax 253/941-9500. www.bestwestern.com.* Just half a mile from Sea-Tac Mall, this hotel sits amid a wide variety of dining and shopping options. Business travelers appreciate the high-speed Internet access in every room and the ample meeting facilities. Vacation travelers find themselves within easy reach of Wild Waves Enchanted Village water park and other area attractions, and the hotel provides shuttle service to and from Sea-Tac Airport as well as area business headquarters and attractions. 112 rooms, 3 story. Complimentary continental breakfast. Check-in 3 pm, check-out noon. High-speed Internet access. Restaurant, bar. Outdoor pool, whirlpool. Airport transportation available. Business center. **$**

**★ ★ ★ MARRIOTT SEA-TAC AIRPORT.** *3201 S 176th St, Seattle (98188). Phone 206/241-2000; toll-free 800/228-9290; fax 206/248-0789. www.marriotthotels.com.* This large Marriott is located across from the airport. The indoor pool under an atrium is a nice touch, with screening plants to give swimmers a sense of privacy. The business center caters to every need of business travelers, and the small spa offers opportunities for pampering. Try the concierge level for services beyond the ordinary. 459 rooms, 7 story. Check-in 3 pm, check-out 1 pm. High-speed Internet access. Restaurant, bar. Children's activity center. Fitness room, spa. Indoor pool, whirlpool. Airport transportation available. **$**

## Restaurant

**★ ★ SEAPORTS.** *18740 Pacific Hwy S, Seattle (98188). Phone 206/246-8600.* Seafood menu. Dinner. Closed Dec 25. Bar. Children's menu. Casual attire. Valet parking. **$$**

# Sedro-Woolley (A-2)

*See also Anacortes, Bellingham, Mount Vernon*

**Founded** 1889
**Population** 8,658
**Elevation** 509 ft
**Area Code** 360
**Zip** 98284
**Information** Chamber of Commerce, 714-B Metcalf St; phone 360/855-1841 or toll-free 888/225-8365
**Web Site** www.sedro-woolley.com

A thick growth of cedar once cloaked the Skagit River Valley, but it has been replaced with fertile farms, for which Sedro-Woolley is the commercial center. Lumbering is still one of the main industries. The town represents the merger of the town of Sedro (Spanish for "cedar") and its onetime rival, Woolley, named for its founder.

A Ranger District station of the Mount Baker-Snoqualmie National Forest is located here.

## What to See and Do

**Lake Whatcom Railway.** *4180 S Bay Dr, Wickersham (98284). 11 miles N on Hwy 9. Phone 360/595-2218.* A 7-mile, round-trip steam train ride in antique Northern Pacific passenger cars through countryside. (July-Aug: Sat and Tues; Dec: Sat only; rest of year: charter trips) **$$$**

**North Cascades National Park.** *Sedro-Woolley. 50 miles E on Hwy 20 (portions of this road are closed in winter). Phone 360/856-5700. www.nps.gov/noca.* Authorized in 1968, this 504,781-acre area has beautiful alpine scenery, deep glaciated canyons, more than 300 active glaciers, and hundreds of jagged peaks and mountain lakes. It is adjacent to the 576,865-acre Glacier Peak Wilderness dominated by 10,541-foot-high Glacier Peak and to Ross Lake and Lake Chelan National Recreation Areas. Camping along WA 20 in Ross Lake area (June-Sept, fee); fishing; climbing, hiking, backpacking (by permit).

**Seattle City Light Skagit Hydroelectric Project.** *500 Newhalem St, Diablo (98283). 62 miles E of I-5/Mt Vernon on Hwy 20 (North Cascades Hwy), in Ross Lake National Recreation Area. Phone 206/684-3030.* The 4 1/2-hour tours includes a 560-foot ride up the mountain on an incline lift, a 4 1/2-mile boat ride to Ross Dam and Powerhouse (tour) and return by boat to Diablo; family-style dinner. (Late June-Labor Day, Mon, Thurs-Sun) Reservations and advance payment required. Single 90-minute tour also available. Contact Skagit Tours, Seattle City Light, 1015 3rd Ave, Seattle 98104. (July-Labor Day, Thurs-Mon) **$$$$** Self-guided mini-tours at Ross Lake National Recreation Area include

> **Gorge Powerhouse/Ladder Creek Falls and Rock Gardens.** *Newhalem.* Begins at Gorge Powerhouse, Newhalem; self-guided tour of powerhouse, walk through Gorge Rock Gardens to Ladder Creek Falls. Gardens lighted at night. (Late June-Labor Day, daily) **FREE**
>
> **Newhalem Visitor Information Center.** *Sedro-Woolley.* Information on Skagit Project and National Park/Recreation Area. (Mid-June-Labor day, daily) **FREE**
>
> **Trail of the Cedars.** *Newhalem. Begins at end of Main St.* (45 minutes) Informative nature walk on south bank of Skagit River. **FREE**

**Swimming, hiking, camping, boating, fishing, windsurfing.** *Sedro-Woolley. Clear Lake. 3 miles S on Hwy 9. RV sites in town.* Also fishing in Skagit River.

## Special Events

**Loggerodeo.** *Sedro-Woolley. Phone 360/770-8452. www.loggerodeo.com.* Logging contests, rodeos, parades. One week in late June-early July.

**Santa's City of Lights.** *Sedro-Woolley. Phone 360/855-1841.* Parade, tree lighting. First weekend in Dec.

**Woodfest.** *1235 3rd St, Sedro-Woolley (98284). Phone 360/855-1841.* Woodcarvers displaying their craft. Second weekend in May.

# Sequim (B-2)

*See also Neah Bay, Olympic National Park, Port Angeles, Port Ludlow, Port Townsend*

**Population** 4,334
**Elevation** 183 ft
**Area Code** 360
**Zip** 98382
**Information** Sequim-Dungeness Valley Chamber of Commerce, 1192 E Washington St; phone 360/683-6197 or toll-free 800/737-8462
**Web Site** www.cityofsequim.com

Sequim (pronounced SKWIM) is a Native American name meaning "quiet water."

## What to See and Do

**Dungeness Recreation Area.** *Clallam County Park, 554 Voice of America W, Sequim (98382). 6 miles NW. Phone 360/683-5847.* Approximately 200 acres. Camping (Feb-Oct; fee). Access to Dungeness National Wildlife Refuge. (Daily)

**Olympic Game Farm.** *1423 Word Rd, Sequim (98382). 6 miles NW. Phone 360/683-4295.* Wild animals; guided walking tour (summer; drive-through rest of year). Endangered species breeding program. (Daily)

**Sequim Bay State Park.** *269035 Hwy 101, Sequim (98382). 4 miles SE on Hwy 101. Phone 360/683-4235.* Along Sequim Bay. Swimming, scuba diving, fishing, clamming, boating (dock); hiking, tennis, ballpark, picnicking, camping (hook-ups).

## Special Event

**Irrigation Festival.** *1192 E Washington, Sequim (98382). Phone 360/683-6197. www.irrigationfestival.com.* Irrigation may not sound like a very exciting reason to hold a festival, but the city of Sequim has been celebrating the gift of water for more than 100 years. The bringing of water to the parched Sequim Prarie enabled pioneer settlers to build a farming community here, and today's citizens remain thankful for the efforts that brought their hometown into existence. Festival events include parades, carnivals, flower shows, contests, and an arts and crafts street fair. First full week in May.

## Limited-Service Hotel

**★ ECONO LODGE.** *801 E Washington St, Sequim (98382). Phone 360/683-7113; toll-free 800/553-2666; fax 360/683-7343. www.econolodge.com.* 43 rooms, 2 story. Pets accepted; fee. Complimentary continental breakfast. Check-out 11 am. **$**

## Specialty Lodgings

**GREYWOLF INN.** *395 Keeler Rd, Sequim (98382). Phone 360/683-5889; toll-free 800/914-9653; fax 360/683-1487. www.greywolfinn.com.* This is a perfect inn for a romantic getaway. This bed-and-breakfast has a secluded location near Olympic National Park, the Pacific Ocean, and great beaches. 5 rooms, 2 story. Children over 12 years only. Complimentary full breakfast. Check-in 4 pm, check-out 11:30 am. Fitness room. **$**

**GROVELAND COTTAGE BED & BREAKFAST.** *4861 Sequim Dungeness Way, Sequim (98382). Phone 360/683-3565; toll-free 800/879-8859; fax 360/683-5181.* 4 rooms, 2 story. Pets accepted, some restrictions; fee. Children over 12 years only. Complimentary full breakfast. Check-in 3 pm, check-out noon. **$**

# Snohomish (B-3)

*See also Everett, Marysville*

**Settled** 1853
**Population** 8,494
**Elevation** 64 ft
**Area Code** 360
**Zip** 98290
**Information** Chamber of Commerce, 127 Ave A, Waltz Building, 98291; phone 360/568-2526
**Web Site** www.cityofsnohomish.com

Snohomish is sustained by dairy farms, tourism, and retail trade. The Boeing plant that manufactures 747s and 767s is nearby. Snohomish claims to be the antique capital of the Pacific Northwest, boasting 450 dealers and many specialty shops.

## What to See and Do

**Blackman Museum.** *118 Ave B, Snohomish (98290). Phone 360/568-5235.* Restored 1878 Victorian house; vintage furnishings. (June-Sept: daily; Mar-May and Oct-Dec: Wed-Sun afternoons; closed rest of year) **$**

**Old Snohomish Village.** *2nd and Pine sts, Snohomish (98290). Phone 360/568-5235.* Six authentic pioneer buildings moved here including the general store (circa 1910) and weaver's shop, which displays antique looms. (June-Sept: daily; rest of year: by appointment) **$**

**Star Center Antique Mall.** *829 2nd St, Snohomish (98290). Phone 360/568-2131.* More than 165 antique shops housed in a former armory. Restaurant, children's play area. (Daily)

**Stevens Pass Ski Area.** *Snohomish. 53 miles E on Hwy 2.* Road goes past Eagle Falls. Downhill, cross-country skiing; snowboarding, tubing. **$$$$**

**Walking tour of historical houses.** *116 Ave B, Snohomish (98290). Phone 360/568-2526.* Contact Chamber of Commerce Waltz Building, for brochure. **FREE**

# Snoqualmie (B-3)

## What to See and Do

**Meadowbrook Farm.** *Snoqualmie. From eastbound I-90, take exit 27, turn left, turn left again onto Meadowbrook Ave, and turn right onto Meadowbrook-North*

*Bend Rd. From westbound I-90, take exit 31, turn north, follow the curve onto State Rte 202, and turn right onto Boalch Ave. The farm lies on 450 acres in the heart of Snoqualmie Valley.* This preserved farm was the site of a Native American village and, later, the world's largest hop ranch.

**Mount Si Golf Course.** *9010 Boalch Ave SE, Snoqualmie (98065).Phone 425/391-4926. www.mtsigolf.com.* Mount Si used to be the world's largest field for growing hops for beer before being turned into an 18-hole course in the 1930s. Since then, it has undergone several renovations, most recently in 1994, when eight of the holes were completely changed. The change upped the length of the course to more than 6,300 yards, as well moving or adding more than 100 trees. The course has several leagues and sessions for younger golfers to learn the game, making it one of the better organized courses in the Seattle area. **$$$$**

**Summit at Snoqualmie.** *1001 State Rd 906, Snoqualmie Pass (98068). Phone 425/434-7669. www.summitatsnoqualmie.com.* About an hours drive east of downtown Seattle, the Summit at Snoqualmie is the top winter sports destination for the city's skiers and snowboarders. The mountain has four distinct base areas—Summit West, Central, and East, as well as the daunting Alpental—each with its own amenities and lifts. Between the four, the resort has varied terrain with ample acreage for every skill level. Of special note: the snowboarding paradise called the Nissan Terrain Park and Halfpipe at Summit West and the Nordic Center at Summit East, the starting point for more than 30 miles of groomed trails. Restaurant and ski rental services are at all four base areas; the repair shop is at Summit Central. Lodging is available in the area at hotels, motels, and vacation home rentals.

## Full-Service Resort

**★★★ SALISH LODGE & SPA.** *6501 Railroad Ave, Snoqualmie (98065). Phone 425/888-2556; toll-free 800/272-5474; fax 425/888-2420. www.salishlodge.com.* Just 30 miles east of Seattle, the Salish Lodge & Spa is a celebration of the rugged beauty of the Pacific Northwest. Nestled in the foothills of the Cascade Mountains, this understated lodge enjoys a majestic setting amid lush evergreen forests and the roaring whitewater of the Snoqualmie Falls. World-weary travelers quickly adopt a gentle pace here, whether hiking the serene mountain trails or enjoying a hot rock massage in the Asian-inspired spa. A rustic simplicity pervades the accommodations, while luxurious details such as wood-burning fireplaces, whirlpool tubs, and pillow menus ensure maximum comfort and large windows focus attention on the serene views. Three exceptional restaurants delight the palates of discriminating diners with a focus on fresh, regional cuisine. 91 rooms, 4 story. Check-in 4 pm, check-out noon. Restaurant, bar. Fitness room, spa. Whirlpool. **$$$**

## Restaurant

**★★★ SALISH LODGE & SPA DINING ROOM.** *6501 Railroad Ave, Snoqualmie (98065). Phone 425/888-2556; toll-free 800/272-5474; fax 425/888-2420. www.salishlodge.com.* The views overlooking the magnificent Snoqualmie Falls most certainly makes dining at this rustic lodge restaurant a unique experience, but it's the impressive menu that is truly unforgettable. Artfully presented dishes of regional Pacific Northwest fare dazzle the eyes, while their fresh, organic ingredients create a harmony of flavors that amaze the palate. Fig glazed Sonoma duck breast; herb-infused open ravioli with tomato fondue; and the signature Snoqualmie "Hot Rocks" seafood dish are just a few of the choices on the dinner menu, all perfect accompaniments to a selection from the extensive wine list. Pacific Northwest menu. Breakfast, lunch, dinner. Bar. Children's menu. Business casual attire. Reservations recommended. Valet parking. Outdoor seating. **$$$**

# Soap Lake (C-5)

*See also Coulee Dam, Ephrata*

**Population** 1,733
**Elevation** 1,075 ft
**Area Code** 509
**Zip** 98851
**Information** Soap Lake Chamber of Commerce, PO Box 433; phone 509/246-1821
**Web Site** www.soaplakecoc.org

The minerals and salts in Soap Lake (from the Native American name *Smokiam,* which means "healing waters") give the community status as a health resort. They also whip into a soaplike foam that lines the shore on windy days. This is the south entrance to the Grand Coulee, the 50-mile channel of the prehistoric Columbia River.

## Limited-Service Hotel

★ ★ **NOTARAS LODGE.** *13 Canna St, Soap Lake (98851). Phone 509/246-0462; fax 509/246-1054. www.notaraslodge.com.* Four log buildings make up this historic lodge, the original of which was destroyed by fire in 1998. Each guest room has a different theme, but all feature rustic furnishings, kitchenettes, and dual plumbing systems that allow visitors to choose between regular and Soap Lake mineral water. Five of the rooms have whirlpool tubs. 15 rooms, 2 story. Pets accepted; fee. Check-out 11 am. Restaurant. **$**

## Restaurant

★ ★ **DON'S.** *14 Canna St, Soap Lake (98851). Phone 509/246-1217; fax 509/246-1054.* Greek, seafood, steak menu. Lunch, dinner. Closed Dec 25. Bar. **$$**

# Spokane (B-6)

*See also Cheney, Colville, Newport; also see Coeur d'Alene, ID, Sandpoint, ID*

**Settled** 1871
**Population** 195,629
**Elevation** 1,898 ft
**Area Code** 509
**Information** Spokane Area Visitor Information Center, 801 W Riverside, #301, 99201; phone 509/624-1341
**Web Site** www.visitspokane.com

Spokane (spo-KAN) is the booming center of the vast, rich "Inland Northwest," an area that includes eastern Washington, northern Idaho, northeastern Oregon, western Montana, and southern British Columbia. A large rail center, the Spokane area also produces wheat, apples, hops, silver, gold, zinc, and lead. Thanks to the surrounding mountain ranges, Spokane enjoys what it likes to term New Mexico's climate in the winter and Maine's in the summer. The city itself is in a saucerlike setting amid pine-green hills, with the Spokane River running through its 52 square miles.

Long a favorite Native American hunting and fishing ground, Spokane began as a sawmill, powered by Spokane Falls. This village, the name meaning "children of the sun," was the only point in a 400-mile-long north-south range of mountains where railroads could cross the Rockies and reach the Columbia Basin. Railroading sparked the city's early growth. The Coeur d'Alene gold fields in Idaho helped finance Spokane's continuing development and helped it survive an 1889 fire that nearly leveled the city. Farming, lumbering, mining, and railroading aided Spokane's growth during the first decade of the century.

In 1974, the Havermale and Cannon islands in the Spokane River were the site of EXPO 74. The area has since been developed as Riverfront Park.

## Public Transportation

**Spokane Transit Authority** Phone 509/328-7433. www.spokanetransit.com

**Airport** **Spokane International Airport.** SW of the city off Hwy 2. Phone 509/455-6455

**Airlines** Air Canada, Alaska Airlines, America West Airlines, Big Sky Airlines, Delta Air Lines, Horizon Air, Northwest Airlines, Southwest Airlines, United Airlines

## What to See and Do

**Cathedral of St. John the Evangelist.** *127 E 12th Ave, Spokane (99202). Phone 509/838-4277.* (Episcopal) Magnificent sandstone Gothic structure; stained-glass windows by Boston's Connick Studios; wood and stone carvings. Tours (Mon-Sat; Sun after services). Recitals on 49-bell carillon (Thurs, Sun); also recitals on Aeolian-Skinner organ (schedule varies).

**Cheney Cowles Museum.** *2316 W 1st Ave, Spokane (99204). Phone 509/456-3931.* Houses collections of regional history and Native American culture. Fine Arts Gallery has changing art exhibits. Adjacent is **Campbell House** (1898), a restored mansion of Spokane's "age of elegance." **$$**

**Cliff Park.** *13th Ave and Grove St, Spokane (99204).* Built around old volcanic island; Review Rock, half acre at base, offers highest point in city for viewing. (Daily) **FREE**

**Comstock Park.** *29th Ave and Howard St, Spokane (99203).* Picnicking, tennis courts. Pool (Mid-June-Aug, daily; fee). Park (daily). **FREE**

**Finch Arboretum.** *3404 W Woodland Blvd, Spokane (99224). Off Sunset Blvd. Phone 509/624-4832.* Approximately 70 acres; includes Corey Glen Rhododendron Gardens, creek, 2,000 specimen plantings of ornamental trees and shrubs. (Daily) **FREE**

**Flour Mill.** *621 W Mallon, Spokane (99201). Adjacent to Riverfront Park N entrance.* (1890) When it was built it was the most modern mill west of the Mississippi River. Today it is the home of boutiques, designer shops, galleries, and restaurants. Overlooks Spokane River. (Daily) **FREE**

**Gonzaga University.** *Boone Ave and Addison St, Spokane (99201). Phone 509/328-4220.* (1887) (4,700 students) Rodin sculptures on display. In center of campus is Bing Crosby's gift to his *alma mater,* the Crosby Student Center; Academy Award Oscar, gold records, certificates, trophies on display in Crosbyana Room (daily). Tours of campus (including Crosby Center and St. Aloyisius Church; by appointment).

★ **Loop drive.** *Sprague Ave and Stevens St, Spokane (99201).* A 33-mile city drive to major points of interest; route, marked with "city drive" signs, begins at Sprague Ave and Stevens St.

**Manito Park.** *Grand Blvd and 18th Ave, Spokane (99203). Phone 509/625-6622.* Duncan Formal Gardens (May-Sept, daily); conservatory (Daily; closed Jan 1, Dec 25). Davenport Memorial Fountain with changing formations in 10-minute cycle (May-Sept, daily); Japanese, lilac, and rose gardens (Apr-Oct, daily). Duck pond; picnicking. **FREE**

**Mobius Kids.** *808 W Main, Spokane (99201). Phone 509/624-5437. www.mobiusspokane.org/.* Children are permitted to touch, encouraged to make noise, and create. Weather exhibit; hydroelectric power station; music, art; regional and cultural history. (Daily) **$$**

**Mount Spokane State Park.** *Spokane. 25 miles NE on Hwy 206. Phone 509/456-4169.* More than 13,000 acres; includes Mount Spokane (5,881 feet), with excellent view from summit, and Mount Kit Carson (5,306 feet). Hiking and bridle trails, downhill skiing, cross-country skiing, snowmobiling (special parking permit required), picnicking, camping. In park is

> **Mount Spokane.** *Spokane. 30 miles NE on Hwy 206, in Mount Spokane State Park. Phone 509/238-2220. www.mtspokane.com.* Five double chairlifts; patrol, school, rentals; cafeteria, bar; lodge, daycare. Longest run 1 1/2 miles; vertical drop 2,000 feet. (Dec-mid-Apr, Wed-Sun)

**Riverfront Park.** *Spokane Falls Blvd and Howard St, Spokane (99201). Phone 509/625-6600. www.spokaneriverfront.com.* A 100-acre recreational park features outdoor amphitheater, IMAX theater, opera house, game room. Spokane River runs through park; suspension bridges over Spokane River; foot bridges; skyride over falls. Miniature golf; roller coaster, carousel. Children's petting zoo. Ponds; ice rink. Restaurant, vending carts, picnicking. Fees for some activities. **FREE**

**Riverside State Park.** *Rutter Pkwy, Spokane. 6 miles NW via Downriver Dr. Phone 509/465-5064. www.riversidestatepark.org.* Approximately 7,300 acres along the Spokane River. Fishing, boating (launch); hiking, equestrian area, snowmobiling, picnicking, camping. Also 600-acre off-road vehicle area; outdoor stoves; interpretive center.

**Spokane Falls.** *Spokane.* Viewed from Bridge Avenue at Monroe Street or foot of Lincoln Street. Spokane River roars over rocks in series of cascades; illuminated at night.

## Special Events

**Ag Expo.** *Convention Center, 334 W Spokane Falls Blvd, Spokane (99201). Phone 509/459-4114. www.agshow.org.* Agricultural fair. Mid-Jan.

**Spokane Civic Theatre.** *1020 N Howard St, Spokane (99201). Phone 509/325-1413.* Live productions. Thurs-Sun, Sept-mid-June.

**Spokane Interstate Fair.** *Spokane County Fair and Expo Center, 404 N Havana St, Spokane (99202). Broadway and Havana sts. Phone 509/477-1766. www.spokanecounty.org/fair.* Livestock, arts and crafts, food, carnival. Nine days in mid-Sept.

## Limited-Service Hotels

**★ COMFORT INN.** *905 N Sullivan Rd, Veradale (99037). Phone 509/924-3838; toll-free 800/252-7466; fax 509/921-6976. www.choicehotels.com.* 76 rooms, 2 story. Pets accepted, some restrictions; fee. Complimentary continental breakfast. Check-out 11 am. Outdoor pool, whirlpool. **$**

**★ ★ COURTYARD BY MARRIOTT SPOKANE.** *N 401 Riverpoint Blvd, Spokane (99202). Phone 509/456-7600; toll-free 800/321-2211; fax 509/456-0969. www.courtyard.com.* Conveniently located in downtown Spokane, this property is 1/2 mile from Gonzaga University and one block from the Eastern Washington University and Washington State University campuses. The spacious guest rooms feature in-room coffee, free high-speed Internet access, and large work desks. Guest rooms overlook either the hotel courtyard (with indoor pool and whirlpool) or the

Spokane River. The business library in the lobby offers cellular telephone chargers, fax machine and printer, Internet access, laptop workstations, and small meeting table. The Market is available 24 hours and offers food and beverage items for those all-night work sessions. 149 rooms, 3 story. Check-in 3 pm, check-out noon. High-speed Internet access. Restaurant, bar. Fitness room. Indoor pool, whirlpool. Business center. Credit cards accepted. **$**

**★ ★ DOUBLETREE HOTEL SPOKANE-CITY CENTER.** *322 N Spokane Falls Ct, Spokane (99201). Phone 509/455-9600; toll-free 800/222-8733; fax 509/455-6285. www.doubletree.com.* Located on the Spokane River in Riverfront Park, this hotel is convenient to the convention center and arena, making it a popular choice of business travelers. Shopping, restaurants, and entertainment are also nearby, as is the Centennial Trail. The Doubletree's restaurant, Spencer's, is a steakhouse that appeals to locals as well as hotel guests. 375 rooms, 15 story. Pets accepted; fee. Check-in 4 pm, check-out noon. High-speed Internet access, wireless Internet access. Two restaurants, bar. Fitness room. Outdoor pool, whirlpool. Airport transportation available. Business center. Credit cards accepted. **$**

**★ ★ HAMPTON INN.** *2010 S Assembly Rd, Spokane (99224). Phone 509/747-1100; toll-free 800/426-7866; fax 509/747-8722. www.hamptoninn.com.* This cozy hotel is conveniently located near downtown, the Spokane International Airport, and local attractions such as the Finch Arboretum, Indian Canyon Golf Course, and Riverfront Park. Some of its amenities include fresh baked cookies and coffee every evening, complimentary breakfast, in-room refrigerators, and a complimentary airport shuttle. Guests can enjoy a nice meal at the in-house restaurant, Garden Springs Pantry. 129 rooms. Pets accepted. Complimentary full breakfast. Check-in 4 pm, check-out noon. High-speed Internet access. Restaurant, bar. Fitness room. Indoor pool, whirlpool. Airport transportation available. Business center. Credit cards accepted. **$**

**★ QUALITY INN VALLEY SUITES.** *8923 E Mission Ave, Spokane (99212). Phone 509/928-5218; toll-free 800/777-7355; fax 509/928-5211. www.spokanequalityinn.com.* Conveniently located just off the interstate between Spokane and Coeur d'Alene, this hotel is near a mall, numerous restaurants, and a grocery store. A full hot breakfast every morning and a complimentary wine reception Monday through Friday are offered to guests. If you don't feel like venturing out for dinner, in-room kitchen facilities—microwave, refrigerator, and bar sink—allow you to prepare your own meals. Add to this a handsome Mediterranean décor, a 24-hour business center, and exceptional cleanliness, and you get real value from this property. 128 rooms, 4 story, all suites. Pets accepted, some restrictions. Complimentary full breakfast. Check-in 3 pm, check-out 11 am. High-speed Internet access, wireless Internet access. Fitness room. Indoor pool, whirlpool. Business center. Credit cards accepted. **$**

**★ ★ RED LION HOTEL AT THE PARK.** *303 W North River Dr, Spokane (99201). Phone 503/268-000; toll-free 800/733-5466; fax 509/325-7329. www.redlion.com.* This warm and friendly hotel is located at the edge of Riverfront Park, the site of the 1974 World's Fair, and along the banks of the river. Families will enjoy the indoor pool, whirlpool, and outdoor swimming lagoon,complete with waterslide and waterfall. Business travelers will appreciate the business center, fitness room, and high-speed Internet access. 400 rooms. Pets accepted. Check-in 3 pm, check-out 11 am. High-speed Internet access, wireless Internet access. Three restaurants, bar. Fitness room. Indoor pool, outdoor pool, whirlpool. Airport transportation available. Business center. Credit cards accepted. **$**

**★ ★ RED LION RIVER INN.** *700 N Division St, Spokane (99202). Phone 509/326-5577; toll-free 800/733-5466; fax 509/326-1120. redlion.rdln.com.* This quaint resort is located along the banks of the Spokane River and is within walking distance of downtown shopping, entertainment, Riverfront Park, the Spokane Opera House, convention center, and Gonzaga University. Its numerous amenities include tennis courts, an outdoor pool and whirlpool, high-speed Internet access, and a fitness room. Guests can also enjoy the on-site restaurant and bar. 245 rooms, 2 story. Pets accepted; fee. Check-in 3 pm, check-out noon. High-speed Internet access, wireless Internet access. Restaurant, bar. Fitness room. Outdoor pool, whirlpool. Tennis. Airport transportation available. Credit cards accepted. **$**

## Full-Service Hotels

**★ ★ ★ THE DAVENPORT HOTEL AND**

**TOWER.** *10 S Post St, Spokane (99201). Phone 509/455-8888; toll-free 800/899-1482; fax 509/624-4455. www.thedavenporthotel.com.* Step back in time at this grand downtown hotel that opened in 1914 and has been restored it to its original grandeur. As soon as you step into the soaring two-story lobby, you can see the attention to detail that has been put into this property. The guest rooms feature hand-carved mahogany furniture, imported Irish linens (made by the same company that supplied the hotel when it first opened), and travertine marble bathrooms with spacious walk-in showers. Some suites and deluxe rooms have fireplaces, wet bars, and jetted tubs for extra comfort and luxury. Exquisite ballrooms provide magical settings for special events, making the Davenport a popular site for weddings and other important celebrations. The upscale Palm Court restaurant serves Euro-Asian cuisine, while the Peacock Room serves cocktails and a light menu. The hotel also offers a cigar bar, espresso bar, candy shop (which supplies the peanut brittle served at nightly turndown), flower shop, art gallery, and an impressive spa. 283 rooms, 14 story. Pets accepted, some restrictions. Check-in 4 pm, check-out noon. High-speed Internet access, wireless Internet access. Two restaurants, bar. Fitness room, spa. Indoor pool, whirlpool. Airport transportation available. Business center. Credit cards accepted. **$$**

★ ★ ★ **HOTEL LUSSO.** *N 1 Post, Spokane (99201). Phone 509/747-9750; fax 509/747-9751. www.slh.com/lusso.* Lusso means "luxury" in Italian, and that's exactly what you see when you stay here. This Italian Renaissance building is located in the business section of downtown Spokane, and the Cascade and the Rocky mountains are nearby. It's also conveniently located next to a skywalk which provides access to shops, restaurants, and entertainment. The interior is decorated with marble, hardwood, and warm Mediterranean colors. Guest rooms are comfortably decorated, and there is a variety of leisure activities for guests. The Cavallino Lounge is the perfect place for an after-dinner drink. 48 rooms. Pets accepted, some restrictions; fee. Check-in 3 pm, check-out noon. High-speed Internet access, wireless Internet access. Restaurant, bar. Airport transportation available. Credit cards accepted. **$$**

## Specialty Lodgings

**FOTHERINGHAM HOUSE.** *2128 W 2nd Ave, Spokane (99204). Phone 509/838-1891; fax 509/838-1807. www.fotheringhamhouse.com.* Restored to its original grandeur, the charming 1891 Queen Anne-style bed-and-breakfast has a wraparound porch and stunning gardens. In the evening, guests can relax with Scottish tea and hazelnut truffles. It's simply a worthwhile stay. The house was built by the first mayor of Spokane and is located across the street from Coeur d'Alene Park and 2 miles from downtown. 4 rooms. Children over 16 years only. Complimentary full breakfast. Check-in 4 pm, check-out noon. Credit cards accepted. **$**

**MARIANNA STOLTZ HOUSE BED & BREAKFAST.** *427 E Indiana Ave, Spokane (99207). Phone 509/483-4316; toll-free 800/978-6587; fax 509/483-6773. www.mariannastoltzhouse.com.* Built in 1908, this homey bed-and-breakfast reflects the era's tradition of craftsmanship. Each guest suite is unique and handsomely decorated, and the house is filled with antiques, dolls, and wood toys. Guests awake to scents from the kitchen, where puffy Dutch pancakes or peach Melba parfait are served up. After breakfast, the wraparound porch is the perfect place to relax. The property is within walking distance of Gonzaga University and about 2 miles from downtown. 4 rooms, 2 story. No children allowed. Complimentary full breakfast. Check-in 4 pm, check-out noon. Credit cards accepted. **$**

## Restaurants

★ ★ ★ **CLINKERDAGGER.** *W 621 Mallon Ave, Spokane (99201). Phone 509/328-5965; fax 509/327-4653. www.clinkerdagger.com.* Steak menu. Lunch, dinner. Bar. Children's menu. Business casual attire. Reservations recommended. Outdoor seating. Credit cards accepted. **$$$**

★ ★ **FUGAZZI AT HOTEL LUSSO.** *N 1 Post, Spokane (99201). Phone 509/747-9750; fax 509/747-9751. www.slh.com/lusso.*Located in the Hotel Lusso in the heart of downtown, this was the first "hip" restaurant in Spokane. The décor is airy with windows throughout, and the stone and hardwood accents are appealing. The eclectic Pacific rim cuisine has locals and tourists coming back for more. Pacific-Rim menu. Lunch, dinner. Closed Sun-Mon. Bar. Children's menu. Casual attire. Reservations recommended. Valet parking. Credit cards accepted. **$$**

★ ★ ★ **THE PALM COURT GRILL.** *10 S Post St, Spokane (99201). Phone 509/455-8888; toll-free 800/899-1482; fax 509/624-4455. www.thedavenporthotel.com.* American, Pacific Northwest menu. Breakfast, lunch, dinner, brunch. Bar. Children's menu. Business casual attire. Reservations recommended. Valet parking. Credit cards accepted. **$$**

**★ ★ ★ LUNA.** *5620 S Perry St, Spokane (99223). Phone 509/448-2383; fax 509/448-9765. www.lunaspokane.com.* Located on Spokane's South Hill and a 10-minute drive from downtown, this Mediterranean/International restaurant is worth the drive. Locals come for breakfast, lunch, dinner, and brunch, and are greeted in the foyer by a large, Hungarian crystal chandelier which sets the tone for the rest of the warm but eclectic interior. Diners enjoy the open kitchen, where they could watch their meal being made from scratch—everything here is, from the breads to the desserts. International, Mediterranean menu. Breakfast, lunch, dinner, brunch. Bar. Children's menu. Casual attire. Reservations recommended. Outdoor seating. Credit cards accepted. **$$$**

**★ ★ SPENCER'S.** *322 N Spokane Falls Ct, Spokane (99201). Phone 509/744-2372; fax 509/744-2396. www.spencersforsteaksandchops.com/spokane/.* Conveniently located for business or leisure guests inside the Doubletree Spokane, this steakhouse is great for business lunches or romantic dinners. The décor is cozy and dark with half-moon booths and wood and leather accents throughout. The restaurant also features an extensive wine list to complement the delicious steaks and chops. Steak menu. Lunch, dinner. Bar. Children's menu. Casual attire. Reservations recommended. Valet parking. Outdoor seating. Credit cards accepted. **$$$**

# Sunnyside (D-4)

*See also Richland, Toppenish*

**Founded** 1893
**Population** 13,905
**Elevation** 743 ft
**Area Code** 509
**Zip** 98944
**Information** Chamber of Commerce, 520 S 7th St; phone 509/837-5939 or toll-free 800/457-8089
**Web Site** www.sunnysidechamber.com

This is the home of one of the first irrigation projects of more than 100,000 acres in the state. Its selection as a site for a large settlement of the Christian Cooperative movement brought growth and prosperity to this community. Irrigation continues to bring rich crops to the fields that circle the city.

The town is aptly named. Sunnyside averages over 300 days of sunshine every year, with mild winters and dry summers.

## What to See and Do

**Apex Cellar.** *111 E Lincoln, Sunnyside (98944). Phone 509/839-9463. www.apexcellars.com.* Wine tasting. (Daily)

**Darigold Dairy Fair.** *400 Alexander Rd, Sunnyside (98944). Phone 509/837-4321.* Tours of cheese-making plant. (Daily; closed holidays) **FREE**

**Tucker Cellars Winery.** *70 Ray Rd, Sunnyside (98944). Yakima Valley Hwy and Ray Rd. Phone 509/837-8701.* Wine tasting. (Daily)

# Tacoma (C-2)

*See also Auburn, Enumclaw, Olympia, Puyallup*

**Settled** 1868
**Population** 193,556
**Elevation** 250 ft
**Area Code** 253
**Information** Tacoma-Pierce County Visitor & Convention Bureau, 1119 Pacific Ave, 5th floor, PO Box 1754, 98402; phone 253/627-2836 or toll-free 800/272-2662
**Web Site** www.traveltacoma.com

In its gemlike setting on Puget Sound, midway between Seattle and Olympia, Tacoma maintains its wood and paper industries and its shipping traditions. Its harbor is a port of call for merchant vessels plying the oceans of the world. Backed by timber, shipping facilities, and low-cost water and power, more than 500 industries produce lumber, plywood, paper, millwork, furniture, foodstuffs, beverages, chemicals, and clothing. Major railroad and shipbuilding yards are also located here. Healthcare is a major employer, and the high-tech industry continues to grow rapidly. The nearest metropolitan center to Mount Rainier National Park, Tacoma is a base for trips to Olympic National Park and Puget Sound. Mild weather keeps parks and gardens green throughout the year.

In 1833, the Hudson's Bay Company built its second post (Fort Nisqually) on the North Pacific Coast in the forest, 18 miles south of the present site of Tacoma. In 1841, Charles Wilkes, commander of a US expedition, began a survey of Puget Sound from this point and named the bay around which Tacoma is built Com-

# Point Defiance Park

One of Tacoma's preeminent attractions, this 700-acre park, flanked by the waters of Puget Sound, contains a wealth of gardens, the city zoo and aquarium, and a number of recreational and historical sites. The park includes 14 miles of hiking trails, which wind through groves of old-growth forests and lead to sheltered beaches. The main paved road through the park is called Five Mile Drive; on Saturdays this scenic road remains closed to motor vehicles until 1 pm, though it's open to cyclists, joggers, and inline skaters.

Enter the park at Pearl Street and follow signs to the parking area at the Vashon Island Ferry. From here, watch as the ferries cross to and from Vashon Island, an agricultural island in the misty distance. Walk past the tennis courts, and follow the path to the garden area.

Formal gardens are abundant at Point Defiance Park and are maintained cooperatively by members of local garden clubs, with help from Tacomas Metropolitan Park District. Park gardens include the Japanese Garden, with a Torii Gate and Shinto Shrine received as a gift from Kitakyushu, Tacoma's sister city in Japan. Also found here are iris gardens, dahlia test gardens, herb gardens, and a rhododendron garden that is a blaze of color in May. Just past the zoo entrance on Five Mile Drive is the civic Rose Garden, established in 1895, with more than an acre of bushes, many of heirloom varieties. The Northwest Native Garden, located near the Pearl Street entrance, presents a collection of indigenous plants ranging from trees to grasses.

Just past the main garden area is the Point Defiance Zoo & Aquarium. Often considered one of the best in the United States, the Point Defiance Zoo is unusual in that it focuses primarily on species from the Pacific Rim, including polar bears, musk ox, and Arctic fox. Peer at coastline mammals through the underwater windows at Rocky Shores. No less than 30 huge sharks swim among tropical fish and eels in the lagoon at Discovery Reef Aquarium. Elephants and apes and other zoo favorites are housed in the Southeast Asia complex.

From the zoo, follow trails north into the wild heart of the park. Point Defiance has been a public park for almost 125 years, and vast sections of it preserve old-growth forest and virgin meadowlands. Heading north, stop at Owens Beach to explore the shoreline or take in the sun along the sandy strand. Farther west, past a viewpoint onto Vashon Island, is Mountaineer Tree, a massive fir tree nearly 450 years old. The western edge of the park is at Gig Harbor Viewpoint, which overlooks the Tacoma Narrows, a constricted, surging strait between Point Defiance and the Kitsap Peninsula.

Round the cap and walk south along the western flank of the park. From here, watch for vistas onto the Tacoma Narrows Bridge. At a mile in length, it is the fifth longest span in North America. The present bridge replaced the infamous "Galloping Gertie" bridge that collapsed at this site during a wind storm in 1940.

At the southwest corner of the park are a number of attractions. If you have kids in tow, they may enjoy Never Never Land, a 10-acre, storyland theme park in an outdoor forest setting. Wooded paths lead to oversized sculpted figures of nursery-rhyme characters. On summer weekends, kids can meet real costumed characters.

Adjacent is Fort Nisqually Historic Site. In 1833, the Hudsons Bay Company trading post at Fort Nisqually was established 17 miles south of Tacoma, near DuPont. This restoration of the original fort includes the factor's house, granary, trade store, blacksmith shop, laborer

s quarters, and stockade, all furnished to reflect life on the frontier in the 1850s. Docents in period clothing demonstrate blacksmithing, spinning, beadwork, and black powder.

Walk back toward the main park entrance, stopping by Camp 6 Logging Museum, an open-air logging museum and reconstruction of a pioneer logging camp. On spring and summer weekends, hitch a ride on a logging train with a steam locomotive.

Back at the ferry terminal, refresh yourself with a stop at the Boathouse Grill, located above the marina with views over Vashon Island and the Olympic mountain peaks.

mencement Bay. When the rails of the Northern Pacific reached tidewater here late in 1873, they sparked the industrial growth of the city.

## What to See and Do

**Emerald Queen Casino.** *2024 E 29th St, Tacoma (98421). Phone toll-free 888/831-7655. www.emeraldqueen.com.* A Cajun-themed, Native American-owned riverboat in the Port of Tacoma with 180,000 square feet of gaming space, the Emerald Queen Casino is big and bright, brimming with antiques and Vegas-style tables (including blackjack, Caribbean stud poker, roulette, craps, and others), as well as 1,500 slots and video poker machines. (The place has some nice touches: a smoke-free gaming floor on the first deck and dealers in period costumes.) The stage here regularly attracts national rock and country acts, some of them household names. In addition to the requisite casino buffet, the boat has a pair of restaurants, one a casual café and the other an Asian eatery with regular surf-and-turf specials. A second, newer location in Tacoma nixes the riverboat and Deep South themes, operating from a landlocked building near I-5 (2024 E 29th St). (Daily)

**Enchanted Village.** *36201 Enchanted Pkwy S, Tacoma. S in Federal Way. Phone 253/661-8000; fax 253/661-8065. www.sixflags.com.* Family entertainment park with rides for all ages; wax museum, antique toy and doll museum. Live entertainment. Concessions. (Mid-May-Labor Day: daily; early Apr-mid-May and Sept after Labor Day: weekends) **$$$$** Also here is

> **Wild Waves Water Park.** *36201 Enchanted Pkwy S, Federal Way (98003). Phone 253/661-8000; fax 253/661-8065.* A 24,000-square-foot wave pool with body and mat surfing in ocean-size waves; raging river ride; adult activity pool; four giant water slides with flashing lights and music, two speed slides; spas; children's pool. Game room; raft rentals. Admission includes entry to Enchanted Village. (Memorial Day weekend-Labor Day weekend, daily) **$$$$**

**Ferry.** *Tacoma. Phone 206/464-6400.* Point Defiance to Vashon Island. Contact Washington State Ferries, Seattle Ferry Terminal, Colman Dock, Seattle 98104. **$$$**

**Fort Lewis.** *Tacoma. 11 miles SW on I-5. Phone 253/967-7206.* Army center of the Northwest, home of I Corps, the Seventh Infantry Division, and associated support units. Approximately 86,000 acres with military buildings and living quarters. Museum with exhibits on Northwest military history (Wed-Sun).

**McChord AFB.** *Tacoma. 8 miles SW on I-5. Phone 253/982-2485.* The 62nd Airlift Wing and 446th Aircraft Wing (Reserves) are based here. Tours (Tues and Thurs; reservations required one month in advance). Museum (Wed-Sat, afternoons).

**Mount Rainier National Park.** *Tacoma. Nisqually entrance, approximately 56 miles SE on Hwy 7. www.nps.gov/mora/.*

**Narrows Bridge.** *Tacoma. W on Olympic Blvd; Hwy 16.* Fifth-longest span for a suspension bridge in US (2,800 feet). Total length: 5,450 feet between anchorages. Successor to "Galloping Gertie," which collapsed in 1940, four months and seven days after it had officially opened.

**Northwest Trek.** *Tacoma. 32 miles SE via I-5, Hwy 512, 161. Phone 360/832-6117. www.nwtrek.org.* One-hour naturalist-guided and narrated tram tour takes visitors on a 5 1/2-mile ride through a 600-acre wilderness and wildlife preserve, where native Northwest animals may be seen roaming free in their natural habitat; self-guided nature walks through wetlands and forest animal exhibits; nature trails include barrier-free trail; children's discovery center. Theater with 14-minute film on history of facility. (Mar-Oct: daily; rest of year: Fri-Sun and selected holidays) **$$$**

**Pacific Lutheran University.** *Tacoma. 11 miles SW on I-5. Off I-5, exit 127. Phone 253/535-7430. www.plu.edu.* (1890) (3,500 students) Swimming pool. Nine-hole golf course open to public; On campus are

> **Robert Mortvedt Library.** *S 121st and Park, Tacoma (98447). Phone 253/535-7500.* African tribal art. (Mon-Sat) **FREE**
>
> **University Gallery.** *Tacoma. Ingram Hall. Phone 253/535-7573.* Changing art exhibits (Mon-Fri). Rune stones sculpture on campus mall.

**Pioneer Farm.** *7716 Ohop Valley Rd E, Tacoma (98328). 35 miles SE via Hwy 7, in the Ohop Valley. Phone 360/832-6300.* Replica of an 1887 homestead with animals; log cabin, barn, trading post, and other outbuildings; furnished with turn-of-the-century antiques. "Hands on" program; guided tours. (Mid-June-Labor Day: daily; Mar-mid-June and after Labor Day-Thanksgiving: Sat and Sun only)

★ **Point Defiance Park.** *54th and Pearl sts, Tacoma (98407). 6 miles N.* Approximately 700 acres of dense forest, clay cliffs, driftwood-covered gravel beaches, and formal gardens. On bold promontory, nearly surrounded by water. Boating, fishing, swimming; hiking, picnicking. Park (daily). **FREE** In the park are

**Boathouse Marina.** *5912 N Waterfront Dr, Tacoma (98407). Phone 253/591-5325.* Bait and tackle shop. Boat and motor rentals. Moorage. Restaurant. Gift shop. (Daily; closed Thanksgiving, Dec 25)

**Camp Six Logging Exhibit (Western Forest Industries Museum).** *54th and Pearl sts, Tacoma. Phone 253/752-0047.* Reconstructed steam logging camp set amid virgin timber. Dolbeer Donkey steam engine (one of two in existence), 110-foot spar pole, restored water wagon, bunkhouses. Logging train ride (Apr-Sept, Sat-Sun, and holidays). A 90-ton shay steam locomotive operates in summer (weekends and holidays). Santa train (three weekends in Dec). (Jan-Oct, Wed-Sun) **$**

**Five Mile Drive.** *54th and Pearl sts, Tacoma.* Around Point Defiance Park. Contains old growth forest with some 200-foot-high Douglas firs, variety of other evergreens, deciduous trees, shrubs. Scenic views of Puget Sound, Olympic and Cascade mountains, Narrows Bridge. Drive closed to motor vehicles Saturday mornings for cycling and walking.

**Fort Nisqually.** *54th and Pearl sts, Tacoma. Phone 253/591-5339.* (1833) Restored fur-trading outpost of Hudson's Bay Company reflects period of English control when fur pelts were used as currency. Purchased by the United States in 1869, moved to this site in 1937. Two remaining buildings of original outpost are the Factor's House (1853) and the Granary (1843), oldest existing building in state; eight other buildings reconstructed according to original specifications using handmade hardware, lumber. Living history presentations. Fee for some special events. (Memorial Day-Labor Day: daily; rest of year: Wed-Sun) **$**

**Gardens.** *54th and Pearl sts, Tacoma.* Formal gardens in park include an AARS rose garden, Japanese Garden, Northwest Native garden, Pacific Northwest dahlia trial garden, rhododendron garden, and seasonal annual displays. **FREE**

**Point Defiance Zoo & Aquarium.** *5400 N Pearl St, Ruston (98407). Phone 253/591-5337.* The zoo has a polar bear complex, a musk ox habitat, tundra waterfowl, elephants, beluga whales, walrus, seals, and otters. The 38 perimeter displays show off hundreds of Pacific Northwest marine specimens, and 2003 brings a special showing called "Project Seahorse" to the aquarium. The Reef Aquarium features sharks and other South Pacific sea life, and the Simpson lab shows how humans can affect the ecosystem of animals like sea urchins and hermit crabs. (Jan-Mar and Oct-Dec: daily 9:30 am-4 pm; Apr-late May: daily 9:30 am-5 pm; mid-May-early Sept: 9:30 am-6 pm; early-late Sept: 9:30 am-5 pm; closed July 16, Thanksgiving, Dec 25) **$$**

**Seattle Museum of Glass.** *1801 E Dock St, Tacoma (98402). Phone 253/396-1768. www.museumofglass.org.* The only museum in the US focusing on contemporary glass art, the Museum of Glass first opened its doors at the waterfront in downtown Tacoma (35 miles south of Seattle) in 2001. The collection includes works by some of the best-known glass artists in the world, including Dale Chiluly, whose 500-foot Chiluly Bridge of Glass here is one of the largest outdoor glass installations in existence anywhere. Visitors can watch glass artists ply their trade at an amphitheater on-site. (Memorial Day-Labor Day: daily; rest of year: Wed-Sun; closed holidays) **$$$**

**St. Peter's Church.** *2910 Starr St, Tacoma (98403). At N 29th St. Phone 253/272-4406.* (1873) (Episcopal) Oldest church in the city; the organ came around Cape Horn in 1874; half-ton bell, also shipped around the Horn, is mounted on tower beside church. (Sun; also by appointment)

**Tacoma Art Museum.** *1701 Pacific Ave, Tacoma (98402). 12th St and Pacific Ave. Phone 253/272-4258. www.tacomaartmuseum.org.* Permanent collection; changing exhibits; children's gallery with hands-on art activities. (Tues-Sun; closed Jan 1, Dec 25) **$$**

**Tacoma Nature Center.** *1919 S Tyler St, Tacoma (98405). Phone 253/591-6439.* Approximately 50 acres of marshland, forest, thickets, and ponds providing a wildlife haven in heart of urbanized Tacoma. Nature trails, observation shelters; natural science library. Interpretive center; lectures and workshops. Park (daily). **FREE**

**Totem Pole.** *9th and A sts, Tacoma (98401).* One of the tallest in the United States, carved from 105-foot cedar tree by Alaskan Native Americans; located in Firemen's Park with view of Commencement Bay and the Port of Tacoma.

**University of Puget Sound.** *1500 N Warner St, Tacoma (98416). Phone 253/879-3100. www.ups.edu.* (1888)

(2,800 students) Includes 37 Tudor Gothic buildings on a 72-acre campus. Many free cultural events, art gallery, theater, recital hall. University is older than state. Also here is

**James R. Slater Museum of Natural History.** *Tacoma.Thompson Hall.* Displays research specimens, particularly of Pacific Northwest flora and fauna; more than 11,000 birds, 4,600 egg sets; reptiles, amphibians, mammals, and pressed plants. (Mon-Fri by appointment; closed holidays) **FREE**

**Washington State History Museum.** *1911 Pacific Ave, Tacoma (98402). Phone toll-free 888/238-4373. www.wshs.org.* Exhibits include collections of pioneer, Native American, and Alaskan artifacts, and detail the history of the state and its people. Interactive, introductory, and changing exhibits. Indoor and outdoor theaters. Museum café and shop. (Memorial Day-Labor Day: daily; rest of year: Tues-Sun; closed holidays) **$$** Adjacent is

**Union Station.** *Tacoma. Phone 253/863-5173.* Built in 1911 by Northern Pacific Railroad, the station, with its 98-foot-high dome, has been restored. Now home to the federal courthouse. The rotunda houses the largest single exhibit of sculptured glass by Tacoma native Dale Chihuly. (Mon-Fri; closed holidays) **FREE**

**White River Valley Museum.** *918 H St SE, Auburn (98002). Phone 253/288-7433. www.wrvmuseum.org.* Situated in Les Gove Park, this historically rich museum celebrates the settlement of the White River Valley during the early part of the 20th century. Visitors can explore a Japanese-American farmhouse, climb aboard a Northern Pacific caboose, and tour a replica of downtown Auburn complete with public market, drugstore, and hat shop. Admission is free on Wednesdays. (Wed-Sun noon-4 pm) **$**

**Wright Park.** *316 S G St, Tacoma (98405). 6th Ave and I St. Phone 253/591-5330.* More than 800 trees of 100 varieties in one of finest arboretums in the Pacific Northwest. W. W. Seymour Botanical Conservatory, located in the park at S 4th and G streets, contains tropical plants, seasonal displays, and a botanical gift shop. Lawn bowling and horseshoe courts; playground, wading community center pool. (Tues-Sun) **FREE**

## Special Events

**Daffodil Festival.** *741 Saint Helens Ave, Tacoma (98402). In Tacoma and Puyallup Valley. Phone 253/863-9524.* Flower show, coronation, four-city floral parade of floats, marine regatta, bowling tournament. Two weeks in Apr.

**Tacoma Little Theater.** *210 N I St, Tacoma (98403). Phone 253/272-2281.* Five shows, including comedies, dramas, and musicals. Sept-June.

**Tacoma Symphony Orchestra.** *738 Broadway #301, Tacoma (98402). Phone 253/272-7264.* Late Sept-early Apr.

**Taste of Tacoma.** *Point Defiance Park, 5400 N Pearl St, Tacoma (98407). Phone 206/232-2982.* Entertainment, arts and crafts. Early July.

## Limited-Service Hotels

**★ ★ HOWARD JOHNSON INN TACOMA.** *8726 S Hosmer St, Tacoma (98444). Phone 253/535-2880; fax 253/537-8379.*Just off the interstate, this 149-room hotel offers comfortable, reliable lodgings for families and budget-minded travelers. Guests enjoy an extensive complimentary breakfast, and there's a large restaurant and sports bar in the adjacent building, with live music on weekends. In the small, cozy lobby with fireplace, computer access and fax service are available. 149 rooms, 2 story. Pets accepted; fee. Complimentary continental breakfast. Check-in 2 pm, check-out noon. Restaurant, bar. Outdoor pool. **$**

**★ ★ LA QUINTA INN.** *1425 E 27th St, Tacoma (98421). Phone 253/383-0146; toll-free 800/531-5900; fax 253/627-3280. www.laquinta.com.* 155 rooms, 7 story. Pets accepted. Complimentary continental breakfast. Check-in 3 pm, check-out noon. High-speed Internet access. Restaurant, bar. Fitness room. Indoor pool, whirlpool. Business center. View of both Mount Rainier and Commencement Bay. **$**

**★ SHILO INN.** *7414 S Hosmer, Tacoma (98408). Phone 253/475-4020; toll-free 800/222-2244; fax 253/475-1236. www.shiloinns.com.* Retaining a bit of 1970s ambience with the lobby's tile floor and overstuffed furniture, this motel is nonetheless well maintained and inviting. Although there's no on-site restaurant, you can get to-your-room delivery from a nearby restaurant or reserve a guest room with a refrigerator and microwave oven so. The sauna, steam rooms, and indoor pool are available 24 hours. 132 rooms, 4 story. Pets accepted. Complimentary continental breakfast. Check-in 3 pm, check-out noon. Fitness room. Indoor pool, whirlpool. **$**

## Full-Service Hotel

**★ ★ ★ SHERATON TACOMA HOTEL.** *1320 Broadway Plz, Tacoma (98402). Phone 253/572-3200; toll-free 800/325-3535; fax 253/591-4105. www.sheratontacoma.com.* The restaurant level overlooks the three-story, skylight-lit lobby, decorated with glass work by world-renowned local artist Dale Chihuly. At the very top of the hotel is Altezzo, the hotel's rooftop restaurant, where you can enjoy fine Italian cuisine and check out views of Mount Rainier and Commencement Bay. Make use of the fitness facilities at the YMCA next door for free. The hotel welcomes your small pet (under 30 pounds) and provides a doggie bed if desired. 319 rooms, 26 story. Pets accepted, some restrictions. Check-in 3 pm, check-out noon. High-speed Internet access. Two restaurants, two bars. Spa. Business center. **$**

## Specialty Lodgings

**CHINABERRY HILL.** *302 Tacoma Ave N, Tacoma (98403). Phone 253/272- 1282; fax 253/272-1335. www.chinaberryhill.com.* Nestled among century-old trees on a steep hill overlooking Puget Sound, this quaint 1889 Victorian mansion oozes old-world charm. Convenient to nearby shops, restaurants, theaters, and galleries, as well as the university and the Tacoma Dome, this inn has lovely multiroom suites furnished with antiques and an inviting wraparound porch. In addition to five standard rooms, the two-story carriage house sleeps six to seven guests, with two full baths and a private Jacuzzi. 6 rooms, 3 story. Complimentary full breakfast. Check-in 4-6 pm, check-out 11 am. **$**

**VILLA BED & BREAKFAST.** *705 N 5th St, Tacoma (98403). Phone 253/572-1157; toll-free 888/572-1157; fax 253/572-1157. www.villabb.com.* Stunning décor and sumptuous hospitality are only two reasons to check out this Italianate Villa, built in 1925. Each guest room offers distinctive décor and some special feature, ranging from a private veranda to a spa or claw-foot tub large enough for two to a gas fireplace. Relax in the beautifully landscaped and maintained gardens next to the gentle burble of a fountain. The full breakfast includes scrumptious gourmet offerings. 6 rooms, 2 story. Children over 10 years only. Complimentary full breakfast. Check-in 3 pm, check-out 11 am. High-speed Internet access. Whirlpool. **$**

## Restaurants

**★ ★ ★ ALTEZZO RISTORANTE.** *1320 Broadway Plz, Tacoma (98402). Phone 253/591-4155. www.sheratontacoma.com.* This restaurant offers breathtaking panoramic views of Puget Sound, Commencement Bay, and Mount Rainier. Italian menu. Dinner. Bar. Business casual attire. Reservations recommended. Valet parking. **$$$**

**★ ★ ★ CLIFF HOUSE.** *6300 Marine View Dr, Tacoma (98422). Phone 253/927-0400. www.cliffhouserestaurant.com.* Visitors will find Northwest-influenced cuisine at this dusty rose and floral-accented dining room. Northwest menu. Lunch, dinner. Closed Jan 1, Dec 25. Bar. Casual attire. Reservations recommended. **$$$**

**★ ★ HARBOR LIGHTS.** *2761 Ruston Way, Tacoma (98402). Phone 253/752-8600.* Seafood menu. Lunch, dinner, brunch. Closed holidays. Bar. Children's menu. Casual attire. Reservations recommended. **$$**

**★ ★ JOHNNY'S DOCK.** *1900 E D St, Tacoma (98421). Phone 253/627-3186. www.johnnysdock.com.* Seafood menu. Lunch, dinner, brunch. Bar. Children's menu. Casual attire. Reservations recommended. Outdoor seating. **$**

**★ ★ ★ LOBSTER SHOP SOUTH.** *4015 Ruston Way, Tacoma (98402). Phone 253/759-2165. www.lobstershop.com.* This Commencement Bay restaurant has a bright look, boat moorage, and outdoor dining (during spring and summer). The coastline location affords beautiful views. Seafood, steak menu. Lunch, dinner, Sun brunch. Closed Dec 25. Bar. Children's menu. Casual attire. Outdoor seating. **$$$**

# Toppenish (D-4)

*See also Sunnyside, Yakima*

**Population** 8,946
**Elevation** 755 ft
**Area Code** 509
**Zip** 98948
**Information** Chamber of Commerce, PO Box 28; phone 509/865-3262
**Web Site** www.toppenish.net

Toppenish is a Native American word meaning "people from the foot of the hills." The Yakama Indian Agency is here, and the nearby million-acre Yakama Reservation is an important tourist attraction. The cultural differences offer good opportunities for sightseeing and dining. The Toppenish area produces hops, fruits, vegetables, and dairy products. Average rainfall is only about 8 inches a year, but irrigation makes the countryside bloom.

### What to See and Do

**Fort Simcoe Historical State Park.** *Toppenish. 28 miles W on Hwy 220, Fort Rd. Phone 509/874-2372.* 200 acres. A restoration of a fort established in 1856 to protect treaty lands from land-hungry settlers and to guard military roads. Five original buildings have been restored; the interpretive center displays army and Native American relics. Picnicking, hiking. (Apr-Sept: daily; rest of year: weekends and holidays)

**Historical Murals.** *5 S Toppenniski Ave, Toppenish (98948). Phone 509/865-6516.* Painted on downtown buildings. For map or guided tour contact Mural Society.

**Yakama Nation Cultural Center.** *Hwy 97, Toppenish (98948). S on Hwy 97. Phone 509/865-2800.* Located on ancestral grounds of the Yakamas. Includes a museum depicting history of the Yakama Nation, library, theater, and restaurant. (Daily; closed Dec 25) **$$**

### Special Events

**Native American Celebrations.** *Toppenish. Phone 509/865-2800.* Most at Yakama Reservation in White Swan, 23 miles W on Hwy 220. Call for details and locations. **Yakama Nation Treaty Day, Powwow Rodeo.** Early June at fairgrounds. **Bull-O-Rama.** Early July.

**Old-Fashioned Melodrama.** *Yakama Nation Cultural Center Theatre, 280 Buster Rd, Toppenish (98948). Phone 509/865-5719.* Boo and hiss at the villain, cheer the hero. Late July-early Aug.

**Silver Spur PRCA Rodeo.** *Toppenish. Phone 509/248-7160.* Early July.

**Western Art Show.** *Toppenish. Downtown. Phone toll-free 800/569-3982.* Three-day art show, cowboy poetry. Late Aug.

## Tukwila (B-2)

### What to See and Do

**Southcenter Mall.** *633 Southcenter, Tukwila (98188). Phone 206/246-7400.* The nexus of a same-named office/retail/residential development in south suburban Tukwila (about a 15-minute drive from downtown Seattle), the Southcenter Mall opened in 1968 and continues to lure hordes of shoppers to its mix of national department stores and specialty shops. With more than 150 stores and restaurants in the mall—and countless more in the surrounding area—this is a retail destination that is entering middle age quite gracefully.

## Union (C-2)

*See also Bremerton*

**Settled** 1858
**Population** 600
**Elevation** 10 ft
**Area Code** 360
**Zip** 98592

This resort town at the curve of the Hood Canal almost became the saltwater terminus of the Union Pacific Railroad, but the failure of a British bank was a blow to Union's commercial future. There are public beaches, a marina, free launching sites, and a golf course in town.

### What to See and Do

**Lake Cushman State Park.** *7211 N Lake Cushman Rd, Hoodsport (98548). 5 miles SW via Hwy 106, 5 miles N via Hwy 101 to Hoodsport, then 7 miles NW via Lake Cushman Rd. Phone 360/877-5491; toll-free 800/233-0321.* Approximately 600 acres. Swimming, fishing, boating (launch, fee); hiking trails, picnicking, camping (Apr-Nov; hook-ups). Standard fees.

**Tollie Shay Engine and Caboose #7.** *230 W Railroad One, Shelton (98584). 5 miles W on Hwy 106, 10 miles S on Hwy 101. Phone 360/426-2021.* Refurbished three-cylinder locomotive and Simpson logging caboose with coal-burning stove and unique side-door design. Caboose is used by Shelton-Mason County Chamber of Commerce as an office and tourist information center. (Daily; closed holidays) **FREE**

**Twanoh State Park.** *12190 E Hwy 106, Union (98592). 12 miles E on Hwy 106, off Hwy 101. Phone 360/275-2222.*182 acres along Hood Canal. Swimming, scuba diving, boating (launch, dock), fishing, clamming; hiking, picnicking, camping (hook-ups). Standard fees.

# Vancouver (E-2)

*See also Bellingham; also see Victoria, BC*

**Founded** 1824
**Population** 143,560
**Elevation** 89 ft
**Area Code** 360
**Information** Greater Vancouver Chamber of Commerce, 1101 Broadway, Suite 120, 98660; phone 360/694-2588
**Web Site** www.vancouverusa.com

Vancouver treasures a national historic site, Fort Vancouver, now completely encircled by the city. The fort served as a commercial bastion for the Hudson's Bay Company, whose vast enterprises stretched far to the north and across the sea to Hawaii, bringing furs from Utah and California and dominating coastal trade well up the shoreline to Alaska. Around the stockaded fort, the company's cultivated fields and pastures extended for miles; drying sheds, mills, forges, and shops made it a pioneer metropolis. This community was a major stake in Britain's claim for all the territory north of the Columbia River, but by the treaty of 1846, Fort Vancouver became American. Settlers began to take over the Hudson's Bay Company lands, and an Army post was established here in 1849, continuing to the present day. In 1860, all of Fort Vancouver was turned over to the US Army.

The city is on the Columbia River, just north of Portland, Oregon. Vancouver has a diversified industrial climate, which includes electronics, paper products, fruit packing, malt production, and the manufacture of textiles, furniture, and machinery. The Port of Vancouver, one of the largest on the West Coast, is a deepwater seaport handling a wide range of commodities.

## What to See and Do

**Clark County Historical Museum.** *1511 Main St, Vancouver (98660). Phone 360/993-5679. www.cchmuseum.org.* Exhibits include 1890s store, doctor's office, printing press, doll collection, dioramas of area history, Native American artifacts; railroad exhibit; genealogical and historical research libraries. (Tues-Sat; closed holidays) **FREE**

**Fort Vancouver National Historic Site.** *1501 E Reserve, Vancouver (98661). Phone 360/816-6200. www.nps.gov/fova.* Over 150 acres. After extensive research and excavation, the fort has been partially reconstructed by the National Park Service. Now at the fort site are Chief Factor's house, a kitchen, wash house, stockade wall, gates, bastion, bake house, blacksmith shop, and trade shop-dispensary. The visitor center has a museum exhibiting artifacts, an information desk, and video presentations. Tours, interpretive talks, and living history programs are also offered. (Daily, hours vary by season; closed holidays)

**Gifford Pinchot National Forest.** *10600 NE 51st Cir, Vancouver (98682). NE of the city, reached via Hwys 14, 25, 503. Phone 360/891-5000. www.fs.fed.us/gpnf.* The forest's 1,379,000 acres include the 12,326-foot Mount Adams; the 8,400-foot Mount St. Helens; and 180,600 acres distributed among seven wilderness areas. Picnicking, hiking, swimming, fishing, boating; camping, hunting.

**Officers' Row.** *Vancouver.* Self-guided walking tour of 21 turn-of-the-century houses; two open to public.

**Pearson Air Museum.** *1115 E 5th St, Vancouver (98661). Phone 360/694-7026.* At M. J. Murdock Aviation Center, one of the oldest operating airfields in the nation. Vintage aircraft and flying memorabilia. (Tues-Sun; closed holidays) **$**

## Limited-Service Hotels

**★ COMFORT INN.** *4714 NE 94th Ave, Vancouver (98662). Phone 360/253-3100; toll-free 800/252-7466; fax 360/253-7998.* 68 rooms, 2 story. Complimentary continental breakfast. Check-in 3 pm, check-out noon. Indoor pool, whirlpool. **$**

**★ RAMADA VANCOUVER.** *9107 NE Vancouver Mall Dr, Vancouver (98662). Phone 360/253-5000; fax 360/253-3137. www.ramada.com.* 56 rooms, 2 story. Complimentary continental breakfast. Check-in 2 pm, check-out noon. Indoor pool, whirlpool. **$**

## Full-Service Resort

**★ ★ ★ THE HEATHMAN LODGE.** *7801 NE Greenwood Dr, Vancouver (98662). Phone 360/254-3100; toll-free 888/475-3100; fax 360/254-6100. www.heathmanlodge.com.* For travelers who like a little sophistication when retreating to the woods, the Heathman Lodge is just the place. This restful resort is just 15 minutes from downtown Vancouver and only a short distance from Portland, Oregon, yet it maintains a peaceful, mountain-retreat ambience. Part woodsy, part elegant, the guest rooms and suites have an inimitable charm with Pendleton blankets and leather lampshades. Guests never leave behind the conveniences of the 21st century when visiting this property; a complete fitness center and business center are among the many amenities offered here. Hudsons elevates simple comfort food to a new level with its delightful riffs on favorite dishes, and the casual setting perfectly complements the laid-back attitude of this resort. 143 rooms, 4 story. Check-out noon. Restaurant, bar. Fitness room. Indoor pool, whirlpool. Business center. **$**

# Walla Walla (D-5)

*See also Dayton*

**Founded** 1859
**Population** 29,686
**Elevation** 949 ft
**Area Code** 509
**Zip** 99362
**Information** Chamber of Commerce, 29 E Sumach, PO Box 644; phone 509/525-0850 or toll-free 877/998-4748
**Web Site** www.wwvchamber.com

Walla Walla Valley was first the site of a Native American trail and then an avenue for exploration and settlement of the West. Lewis and Clark passed through the area in 1805. Fur traders followed, and Fort Walla Walla was established in 1818 as a trading post at the point where the Walla Walla and Columbia rivers meet. One of the key figures in the area's history was Dr. Marcus Whitman, a medical missionary, who in 1836 founded the first settler's home in the Northwest—a mission 7 miles west of present-day Walla Walla. The Whitmans were killed by Native Americans in 1847. No successful settlement was made until after the Indian Wars of 1855-1858.

In 1859, the city became the seat of Walla Walla County, which then included half of present-day Washington, all of Idaho, and a quarter of Montana. It also had the first railroad in the Northwest, the first bank in the state, the first meat market and packing plant, and the first institution of higher learning.

Walla Walla means "many waters," but local enthusiasts will tell you that this is "the city they liked so much they named it twice." Agriculture is the major industry, with wheat the most important crop and green peas the second. Industries concentrate chiefly on food processing. The Walla Walla onion is known nationwide for its sweetness; a festival is held each July to honor the important crop. A Ranger District office of the Umatilla National Forest is located here.

## What to See and Do

**Fort Walla Walla Park.** *Walla Walla. Dalles Military Rd. 1 mile W of Hwy 125, W edge of town. Phone 509/527-4527.* Camping (dump station; fee). (Apr-Sept, daily; limited facilities rest of year) Also in park is Audubon Society Nature Walk, outdoor amphitheater, and

> **Fort Walla Walla Museum.** *755 Myra Rd, Walla Walla (99362). Phone 509/525-7703.* The largest horse-era agricultural museum in the West. Twelve original and replica buildings from the mid-1800s, including a schoolhouse, homestead cabin, railroad depot, blockhouse, doctor's office, and blacksmith shop. Living history programs by more than 40 characters make the period come alive on summer weekends. (Apr-Oct, daily 10 am-5 pm) **$$**

**Pioneer Park.** *Division and Alder sts, Walla Walla (99362). Phone 509/527-4527.* A 58-acre park with horticultural displays, including a rose garden; exotic bird aviary; playground; tennis courts and ball fields; and picnic tables and shelter. **FREE**

**Whitman Mission National Historic Site.** *328 Whitman Mission Rd, Walla Walla (99362). 7 miles W, just off Hwy 12. Phone 509/522-6360. www.nps.gov/whmi.* The memorial shaft, erected in 1897, overlooks the site of the mission established by Dr. Marcus and Narcissa Whitman in 1836. A self-guided trail with audio stations leads to the mission grounds, Old Oregon Trail, memorial shaft, and grave. The visitor center has a ten-minute slide presentation and a museum. In summer, there are cultural demonstrations Sat-Sun 1-4 pm. (Daily; summer: 8 am-6 pm, rest of year: 8 am-4:30 pm; closed Jan 1, Thanksgiving, Dec 25) **$**

## Limited-Service Hotel

**★ BEST WESTERN WALLA WALLA INN & SUITES.** *7 E Oak St, Walla Walla (99362). Phone 509/525-4700; toll-free 800/780-7234; fax 509/525-*

*2457. www.bestwestern.com.* 78 rooms. Complimentary continental breakfast. Check-in 3 pm, check-out noon. Fitnss room. Indoor pool, whirlpool. **$**

## Specialty Lodging

**GREEN GABLES INN.** *922 Bonsella St, Walla Walla (99362). Phone 509/525-5501; toll-free 888/525-5501. www.greengablesinn.com.* Built in 1909; period antiques. 5 rooms. Children over 11 years only. Complimentary full breakfast. Check-in 3 pm, check-out 11 am. High-speed Internet access. **$**

# Wenatchee (B-4)

*See also Cashmere, Chelan, Leavenworth, Quincy*

**Founded** 1888
**Population** 27,856
**Elevation** 727 ft
**Area Code** 509
**Information** Wenatchee Chamber of Commerce, 300 S Columbia, 98807; phone 509/662-2116 or toll-free 800/572-7753
**Web Site** www.wenatchee.org

The apple blossoms in the spring and the sturdy red of grown fruit in the fall are the symbols of this community. Nestled among towering mountains are fertile irrigated valleys where residents care for orchards. Cherries, pears, peaches, and apricots are also grown here. With the establishment in 1952 of a huge aluminum smelter and casting plant, Wenatchee no longer has an economy based only on agriculture. The headquarters of the Wenatchee National Forest is located here.

## What to See and Do

**Mission Ridge Ski Area.** *7500 Mission Ridge Rd, Wenatchee (98801). Phone 509/663-6543. www.missionridge.com.* Four double chairlifts, two rope tows; patrol, school, rentals; snowmaking; cafeteria; childcare. Vertical drop 2,200 feet. Half-day rates. Limited cross-country trails. (Dec-mid-Apr) **$$$$**

**Rocky Reach Dam.** *Wenatchee. 7 miles N on Hwy 97A, on the Columbia River. Phone 509/663-7522.* The Visitor Center has an underwater fish viewing gallery and a theater. The Powerhouse has the Gallery of the Columbia and the Gallery of Electricity, plus changing art exhibits. Landscaped grounds; picnic and play areas. (Daily; closed Dec 25, also Jan-mid-Feb) **FREE**

**Squilchuck State Park.** *Wenatchee. 9 miles SW on Hwy 297. Phone 509/664-6373. www.parks.wa.gov.* This 287-acre park at an elevation of 4,000 feet offers day use and group camping, 10 miles of hiking and biking trails, and ample opportunities for winter sports like skiing and snowshoeing. (May-late Sept, 6:30 am-dusk)

**Wenatchee National Forest.** *Forest Headquarters, 215 Melody Ln, Wenatchee (98801). N, S, and W of town. Phone 509/664-9200. www.fs.fed.us/r6/wenatchee.* Approximately 2 million forested, mountainous acres lying west of Columbia River. A trail system leads to jagged peaks, mountain meadows, and sparkling lakes. Fishing, hunting, horseback riding, winter sports, many developed campsites (some fees). A forest map is available (fee).

**Wenatchee Valley Museum & Cultural Center.** *127 S Mission St, Wenatchee (98801). Phone 509/664-3340. www.wenatcheevalleymuseum.com.* This regional history museum includes a restored, operational 1919 Wurlitzer pipe organ; a Great Northern Railway model; a fine-art gallery; an apple industry exhibit; an exhibit on the first trans-Pacific flight (Japan to Wenatchee); and archaeological and Native American exhibits. (Tues-Sat 10 am-4 pm; closed holidays) **$**

## Special Events

**Apple Blossom Festival.** *516 Washington St, Wenatchee (98801). 8 miles W via Hwy 150. Phone 509/662-3616. www.appleblossom.org.* The Apple Blossom Festival celebrates the area's apple production and is the oldest festival in the state. Second weekend in May.

**Washington State Apple Blossom Festival.** *516 Washington St, Wenatchee (98801). Phone 509/662-3616. www.appleblossom.org.* Parades, carnival, arts and crafts, and musical productions; Ridge to River Relay. Last weekend in Apr-first weekend in May.

## Limited-Service Hotels

**★ ★ BEST WESTERN CHIEFTAIN INN.** *1017 N Wenatchee Ave, Wenatchee (98801). Phone 509/665-8585; fax 509/665-9745.* 74 rooms. Complimentary continental breakfast. Check-in 3 pm, check-out noon. Restaurant, bar. Fitness room. Outdoor pool. Business center. **$**

**★★ RED LION.** *1225 N Wenatchee Ave, Wenatchee (98801). Phone 509/663-0711; toll-free 800/733-5466; fax 509/662-8175. www.redlion.com.* 149 rooms, 3 story. Pets accepted. Check-in 3 pm, check-out noon. High-speed Internet access. Restaurant, bar. Fitness room. Outdoor pool, whirlpool. Airport transportation available. **$**

## Specialty Lodging

**APPLE COUNTRY BED & BREAKFAST.** *524 Okanagon Ave, Wenatchee (98801). Phone 509/664-0400. www.applecountryinn.com.* One of the first homes built in 1920 in the 'Okanogan Heights' addition in Wenatchee. 5 rooms, 2 story. **$**

# Westport (C-1)

*See also Aberdeen, Hoquiam, Ocean Shores*

**Settled** 1858
**Population** 2,137
**Elevation** 12 ft
**Area Code** 360
**Zip** 98595
**Information** Westport-Grayland Chamber of Commerce, 2985 S Montesano St, 98595-0306; phone 360/268-9422 or toll-free 800/345-6223
**Web Site** www.ci.westport.wa.us

Near the tip of a sandy strip of land separating Grays Harbor from the Pacific, Westport is home to probably the largest sports fishing fleet in the Northwest. Pleasure and charter boats take novice and experienced anglers alike across Grays Harbor Bay into the Pacific for salmon fishing in the summer and deep-sea fishing nearly all year. In the winter, commercial fleets set their pots for crab and have their catch processed at one of Westport's large canneries. Whale-watching excursions operate from March to May.

## What to See and Do

**Grays Harbor Lighthouse.** *Ocean Ave, Westport.* (1898) At 107 feet, this is the tallest lighthouse on the West Coast.

**Twin Harbors State Park.** *3120 State Hwy 105, Westport (98595). 3 miles S on Hwy 105. Phone 360/268-9717. www.parks.wa.gov.* 172 acres. Surf fishing, clamming, bird- and whale-watching; hiking, picnicking, camping (hookups; reservations advised Memorial Day-Labor Day). Ocean swimming is permitted, but hazardous. (Daily; summer 6:30 am-10 pm, winter 8 am-5 pm)

**Westport Aquarium.** *321 E Harbor St, Westport (98595). Phone 360/268-0471.* This small aquarium has large tank aquariums and performing seals. (Feb-Oct: daily; Nov: weekends; closed holidays) **$$**

**Westport Maritime Museum.** *2201 Westhaven Dr, Westport (98595). Phone 360/268-0078. www.westportmuseum.org.* This museum complex features exhibits on the Coast Guard, shipwrecks and rescue operations, whales, and the area's cranberry and logging industries. The Children's Room has educational games and displays designed for elementary students. Also on the grounds are two Whale Houses, which exhibit sea mammal skeletons and other items, and the Lens Building, which contains a 100-year-old, 18-foot-high rotating lens with 1,176 glass prisms. (Memorial Day-Labor Day: daily 10 am-4 pm; rest of year: Thurs-Mon noon-4 pm) **$**

# Winthrop (A-4)

*See also Omak*

**Population** 349
**Elevation** 1,760 ft
**Area Code** 509
**Zip** 98862
**Information** Chamber of Commerce, Information Office, 202 Hwy 20; phone 509/996-2125 or toll-free 888/463-8469
**Web Site** www.winthropwashington.com

Redesigning the entire town on an Old West theme has transformed it into the "Old Western town of Winthrop," complete with annual events in the same vein.

Fifty-five miles west on the North Cascades Highway (Hwy 20) is North Cascades National Park. A Ranger District office of the Okanogan National Forest is located here.

## What to See and Do

**Shafer Museum.** *285 Castle Ave, Winthrop (98862). Phone 509/996-2712. www.winthropwashington.com/winthrop/shafer/.* This log house built in 1897 by the town's founder, Guy Waring, has been redecorated as a turn-of-the-century pioneer home and includes early farming and mining implements from the nearby gold and silver mines. Also on site are a schoolhouse, stagecoach, and early print shop. (Memorial Day-Labor Day, Wed-Mon 10 am-5 pm) **FREE**

## Limited-Service Hotel

**★ AMERICAS BEST VALUE INN.** *960 Hwy 20, Winthrop (98862). Phone 509/996-3100; fax 509/996-3317. www.bestvalueinn.com.* 30 rooms, 2 story. Pets accepted, some restrictions; fee. Check-out 11 am. Outdoor pool, whirlpool. **$**

## Full-Service Resort

**★ ★ ★ SUN MOUNTAIN LODGE.** *604 Patterson Lake Rd, Winthrop (98862). Phone 509/996-2211; toll-free 800/572-0493; fax 509/996-3133. www.sunmountainlodge.com.* Whether carpeted in wildflowers or blanketed in snow, Sun Mountain Lodge is a perfect year-round destination. Active families take advantage of the endless opportunities for recreation on the resorts 3,000 acres, located east of Seattle. During the summer months, hiking, biking, and fly fishing are popular pursuits, while winter months draw cross-country skiers, ice skaters, and sleigh riders. Antler chandeliers, wood beams, and massive stone fireplaces lend a sense of place to the interiors, and the guest rooms and suites continue the rustic theme with regional decorative objects and handcrafted furnishings. Firmly rooted in mountain traditions, yet forward-thinking, Sun Mountain Lodge is far from backwoods, with impressive dining complete with a 5,000-bottle wine cellar and a full-service spa. 102 rooms, 3 story. Check-in 4 pm, check-out noon. Restaurant, bar. Children's activity center. Fitness room. Two outdoor pools, whirlpool. **$$**

## Restaurant

**★ ★ ★ THE DINING ROOM.** *Patterson Lake Rd, Winthrop (98862). Phone 509/996-2211; fax 509/996-3133. www.sunmountainlodge.com.* A casual, rustic setting overlooking towering snow-capped mountains is the backdrop for a hearty meal of fresh regional cuisine. The kitchen skillfully combines fish, seafood and meat with a local blend of herbs and vegetables that accentuate the natural flavors. American menu. Breakfast, lunch, dinner, brunch. Bar. Children's menu. **$$$**

# Woodinville (B-2)

**Settled** 1871
**Population** 9,194
**Area Code** 425
**Zip** 98072
**Information** Woodinville Chamber of Commerce, 17301 133rd Ave NE; phone 425/481-8300.
**Web Site** www.woodinvillechamber.org

Woodinville sits at the northern end of the Sammamish River Valley, a short drive northeast of Seattle on either Highway 522 or Interstate 405. Woodinville's main artery, NE 175th Avenue, cuts through a downtown area occupied by shops and restaurants, as well as small offices. South of downtown, in the Tourist District, highlights include two wineries, a brewery, and romantic accommodations and lodging at the Willows Lodge and its two restaurants, The Herbfarm and Barking Frog. Once a community of loggers, the city retains much of its Pacific Northwest woodland charm, though today its residents are much more likely to work at the nearby Microsoft headquarters than at a sawmill.

## What to See and Do

**Chateau Ste. Michelle.** *14111 NE 145th St, Woodinville. Phone 425/415-3632; toll-free 800/267-6793. www.ste-michelle.com.* Washington State's oldest winery offers free tours and tastings at its 87-acre estate. The winery's grapes are grown east of the Cascade Mountains in the sunny and dry Columbia Valley. Chateau Ste. Michelle utilizes two distinct winemaking operations, one devoted to white wines and the other focusing exclusively on reds. During the busy summer season, arrive early to avoid the post-lunch throng of wine aficionados. The winery welcomes 250,000 visitors annually. Premium tastings are available for a nominal fee. (Daily 10 am-5 pm; closed holidays) **FREE**

**Columbia Winery.** *14030 NE 145th St, Woodinville (98072). Phone 425/488-2776; toll-free 800/488-2347. www.columbiawinery.com.* Columbia Winery's humble beginnings can be traced back to a garage in the Seattle neighborhood of Laurelhurst. It was in that garage in 1962 that the winery first began making wines. Founded by ten friends, the operation has grown steadily over the years, helping to launch Washington's wine industry, which now ranks behind only California in premium wine production. The winerys grapes are grown east of the Cascades, amid a climate of sunny days and cool nights in the Columbia and Yakima valleys of eastern Washington. On weekends, tours and tastings are available at the winerys Victorian-style manor in Woodinville. Group tours on weekdays are available by appointment. Retail shop (daily 10 am-6 pm). **FREE**

**Molbak's.** *13625 NE 175th St, Woodinville (98072). Phone 425/483-5000.* Each year more than a million green thumbs pay a visit to Molbaks, a garden shop located 20 miles northeast of Seattle. Egon and Laina Molbak emigrated from Denmark to Woodinville in 1956, purchasing a small greenhouse and becoming a wholesaler of cut flowers. Ten years later, the Molbak's expanded their business by opening a 700-square-foot retail shop. Their business has flourished ever since, and today Molbak's employs 200 people to oversee garden, gift, and floral shops, as well as a store selling Christmas items and patio furniture. (Sun-Fri 10 am-6 pm, Sat 9 am-9 pm)

**Redhook Ale Brewery.** *Suite 210,14300 NE 145th St, Woodinville (98072). Phone 425/483-3232. www.redhook.com.* In the early 1980s, Paul Shipman and Gordon Bowker identified two market trends: import beers were becoming increasingly popular, and the Pacific Northwest held the nation's highest per capita draft beer consumption rate. The pair responded by founding the Redhook Brewing Company, producing their ale at a brewery in the Ballard area of Seattle. They sold their first pint in 1982. Sales took off with the 1984 release of Ballard Bitter, and Redhook grew to become one of the most successful microbreweries in the US. To keep pace with demand, a brewery was built in Woodinville, opening in 1994. Here, for a mere $1, visitors can tour the brewery, sample several of Redhook's eight ales, receive a free tasting glass, and learn about the company's history. After the tour, sidle up to the bar in the Forecasters Public House and partake in pub-style food and, of course, fresh Redhook ale. (Daily) **$**

## Full-Service Hotel

**★ ★ ★ WILLOWS LODGE.** *14580 NE 145th St, Woodinville (98072). Phone 425/424-3900; toll-free 877/424-3930; fax 425/424-2585. www.willowslodge.com.* Bordering the Sammamish River in Washington's western wine country, The Willows Lodge is an exceptional getaway. Industrial chic meets Native American sensibilities at this former hunting lodge where guests rusticate in style. Stained concrete, slate, and sleek lines reveal a modern slant in the accommodations, while dynamic artwork crafted by Northwest Coast Native Americans showcases local pride. Luxuries are not lost on this country escape, where Frette linens and 300-thread-count bedding pamper guests. Lush, landscaped gardens complete with hidden courtyards create a veritable Eden, and the herb and edible plant gardens serve as the inspiration behind the excellent menus at The Herbfarm and Barking Frog restaurants (see). The resort's sanctuary-like atmosphere is enhanced by a full-service spa that offers a host of soothing and beautifying treatments. 86 rooms, 2 story. Pets accepted. Complimentary continental breakfast. Check-in 3 pm, check-out noon. High-speed Internet access, wireless Internet access. Two restaurants, two bars. Fitness room. Spa. Whirlpool. Business center. **$$$**

## Restaurants

**★ ★ ★ BARKING FROG.** *14580 NE 145th St, Woodinville (98072). Phone 425/424-2999; fax 425/424-2485. www.willowslodge.com.* After a busy day of touring nearby wineries, take a seat and relax at this cozy, lodgelike bistro located in the heart of Woodinville's Wine Country. A quaint and casual atmosphere of warm earth tones and exposed wood complements the rustic regional Northwest menu, which changes seasonally and features choices like organic chicken breast, Grand Marnier prawns, and grilled New York steak. Pacific Northwest menu. Breakfast, lunch, dinner. Bar. Children's menu. Casual attire. Reservations recommended. Valet parking. Outdoor seating. **$$$**

**★ ★ ★ ★ THE HERBFARM.** *14590 NE 145th St, Woodinville (98072). Phone 425/485-5300; fax 425/424-2925. www.theherbfarm.com.* A four-hour meal made up of nine unforgettable courses and five perfectly paired wines. A flamenco guitarist strumming in the half-light of flickering candles in an antique-filled dining room. A sun setting over a gracious, fragrant garden lying just outside your window. If this were real life in the rural world, America's cities would be empty. Obviously its not, but it does describe a typical dinner at The Herbfarm, a quaint country cottage that's home to an internationally renowned restaurant where reservations are rarer than forest truffles. Here, chef (and gentleman gardener) Jerry Traunfeld creates seasonal, themed meals—or more accurately, culinary events—based on the bounty of the restaurant's own gardens and farm, plus produce, meats, and artesian cheeses sourced from local growers, producers, ranchers, and fishermen. Don't want to leave? You don't have to—the restaurant sits on the grounds of the Willows Lodge, a charming hotel and spa. Pacific Northwest menu. Dinner. Closed Mon-Wed. Business casual attire. Reservations recommended. **$$$$**

# Yakima (C-4)

*See also Ellensburg, Toppenish*

**Settled** 1861
**Population** 71,845
**Elevation** 1,068 ft
**Area Code** 509
**Information** Yakima Valley Visitors & Convention Bureau, 10 N 9th St, 98901; phone 509/248-2021
**Web Site** www.yakima.org

Yakima (YAK-e-ma) County ranks first in the United States in production of apples, hops, sweet cherries, and winter pears. Irrigation was started as early as 1875, when early settlers dug crude canals. Orchards and farms replaced sagebrush and desert. The city takes its name from the Yakama Nation, whose reservation lies to the south. There are about 300 days of sunshine annually, with an average yearly rainfall of 8 inches.

## What to See and Do

**Ahtanum Mission.** *Yakima. 9 miles SW on unnumbered roads.* Founded in 1852, destroyed by fire in the Yakama Native American Wars, and rebuilt in 1867, the Ahtanum Mission was the site of the oldest irrigated apple orchards in the valley (1872).

**H. M. Gilbert Homeplace.** *2109 W Yakima Ave, Yakima (98902). Phone 509/248-0747. www.yakimavalleymuseum.org.* This late Victorian farmhouse, a restored orchard home, features period furnishings. (Apr-Dec, by appointment) **$**

**Historic North Front Street.** *Yakima.* Called "the birthplace of Yakima," this two-block section of downtown has restaurants and shopping.

**Painted Rocks.** *Yakima. 7 miles NW on Hwy 12.* Historic Yakima Nation pictographs.

**White Pass Village.** *Yakima. 55 miles NW on Hwy 12.* A ski area in Mount Baker-Snoqualmie National Forest. (See Mount Rainier National Park.)

**Yakima Interurban Trolley Lines.** *307 W Pine St, Yakima (98902). Phone 509/249-5656. www.yakimavalleytrolleys.org.* Trolley cars make trips around the city and the surrounding countryside on a historic railroad line. Board the trolley at the car barns at 3rd Avenue and W Pine Street. (Mid-May-mid-Oct, weekends at 10 am, noon, and 2 pm) **$**

**Yakima Sportsman State Park.** *904 Keys Rd, Yakima (98901). 3 miles E on Hwy 24. Phone 509/575-2774. www.parks.wa.gov.* Approximately 250 acres of "green zone" on the floodplain of the Yakima River. Birdwatching, fishing, picnicking, and camping (hookups; **$$$$**). (Daily; summer 6:30 am-10 pm, winter 8 am-5 pm)

**Yakima Valley Museum.** *2105 Tieton Dr, Yakima (98902). In Franklin Park. Phone 509/248-0747. yakimavalleymuseum.org.* Exhibits relate to the history of Yakima Valley, the Yakima Nation, pioneer life, and the area's fruit industry. The museum's collection of horse-drawn vehicles is a highlight. Children's Underground is an area designed just for kids ages 5 to 15, with a working replica of a 1930s soda fountain built from salvaged and restored parts. The Great Hall hosts concerts throughout the year. (Tues-Sun 11 am-5 pm; closed holidays) **$**

**Yakima Valley Wine Tours.** *Yakima. Phone toll-free 800/258-7270. www.wineyakimavalley.org.* The river-carved Yakima Valley, about 100 miles southeast of Seattle, has a climate that is nearly ideal for grape growing. The abundance of great wine is reminiscent of northern Californias Napa Valley, as is the requisite armada of B&Bs, but Yakima Valley is not nearly as exclusive or expensive. Almost all of the wineries here offer free tours and tasting, and the area draws big crowds for such annual traditions as the Red Wine and Chocolate festival over Presidents Day weekend and Merlotfest in May.

## Special Events

**Central Washington State Fair and Rodeo.** *Fairgrounds, Yakima. Phone 509/248-7160. www.fairfun.com.* Late Sept-early Oct.

**Spring Barrel Tasting.** *Various local wineries, Yakima. Phone toll-free 800/258-7270. www.yakimavalleywine.com/springbarrel.html.* Area wineries open their doors to visitors eager for a taste of the latest vintages. Last full weekend in Apr.

**Yakima Meadows Racetrack.** *Yakima. Phone 509/248-7160.* Fairgrounds. Thoroughbred racing. Pari-mutuel wagering.

## Limited-Service Hotels

★ ★ **CLARION HOTEL.** *1507 N First St, Yakima (98901). Phone 509/248-7850; toll-free 800/252-7466; fax 509/575-1694. www.choicehotels.com.* This hotel is located near the city center, wineries, the Yakima Mall, Sundome, and Mount Rainier National Park. 208 rooms, 2 story. Pets accepted; fee. Check-out noon. Restaurant, bar. Fitness room. Two outdoor pools, whirlpool. **$**

★ **OXFORD INN YAKIMA.** *1603 E Yakima Ave, Yakima (98901). Phone 509/457-4444; fax 509/453-7593. www.oxfordinnyakima.com.* 96 rooms, 4 story. Complimentary continental breakfast. Check-out noon. Bar. Outdoor pool, whirlpool. **$**

★ ★ **RED LION.** *607 E Yakima Ave, Yakima (98901). Phone 509/248-5900; fax 509/575-8975. www.redloin.com.* 153 rooms, 2 story. Pets accepted; fee. Check-out noon. Restaurant, bar. Two outdoor pools. Airport transportation available. Business center. **$**

# Vancouver (E-4)

*See also Nanaimo, Whistler, Vancouver Island, Victoria*

**Settled** 1886
**Population** 572,000
**Elevation** 38 ft (12 m)
**Area Code** 604
**Information** Tourism VancouverThe Greater Vancouver Convention and Visitors Bureau, 200 Burrard St, V6C 3L6; phone 604/682-2222
**Web Site** www.tourismvancouver.com

Surrounded by the blue waters of the Strait of Georgia and backed by the mile-high peaks of the Coast Range, Vancouver enjoys a natural setting surpassed by few other cities on this continent. The waters that wash the city's shores protect it from heat and cold, making it a pleasant place to visit year-round.

Captain George Vancouver, searching these waters for the Northwest Passage, sailed into Burrard Inlet and landed here in 1792. Fur traders, gold prospectors, and other settlers soon followed. In 1886, Vancouver was incorporated as a city, only to be destroyed by fire several months later. The city was rebuilt by the end of that same year. In the next four years, rail transportation from the east, along with the traffic of sailing vessels of the Canadian Pacific fleet, assured it's future growth. Today Vancouver is one of Canada's largest cities—a major seaport, cultural center, tourist spot, and gateway to Asia.

Vancouver's population is primarily English, but it's large number of ethnic groups—including Germans, French, Scandinavians, Dutch, Chinese, and Japanese—give the city an international flavor. Tourism, logging, mineral extraction equipment, marine supplies, chemical and petroleum products, and machine tools are among the city's major industries.

Vancouver is on the Canadian mainland, not on Vancouver Island as some people think. The downtown area, which includes many of the points of interest which follow, is a "peninsula on a peninsula": it juts out from the rest of Vancouver into Burrard Inlet, making it an especially attractive spot with beaches and marinas within easy walking distance of the city's busy heart. To the north across Burrard Inlet is North Vancouver; to the south is the mouth of the Fraser River and the island municipality of Richmond; to the east is Burnaby, and beyond that, the Canadian mainland.

For border crossing regulations, see MAKING THE MOST OF YOUR TRIP.

## Discovering Downtown Vancouver

Vancouver is one of the most cosmopolitan cities in the world, and part of it's considerable charm is the wonderful mix of people from all around the globe. Downtown Vancouver remains very dynamic, and a wander through the people-thronged streets is a great way to catch the energy of this city. Start at the Vancouver Art Gallery, which is the old City Hall. Walk up Robson Street, the city's primary boutique street, lined with all sorts of tiny shops, cafés, galleries, and food markets: this is a very busy place, and you'll hear dozens of languages in the bustle of the crowds. Grab a table at a coffee shop, and watch the world—literally—go by. Continue to Denman Street, and turn south (left). Denman is another busy commercial street, but less international. Here you'll find remnants of aging hippie Vancouver—bookstores, veggie restaurants, and little corner markets—rubbing shoulders with upscale 20-something cocktail bars and tattoo parlors for middle-class teenagers. Denman terminates at English Beach, where you can relax on the sand and enjoy the views of Vancouver's West Side across English Bay. Follow the seawall west (right) and, after a couple of blocks, enter Stanley Park, Vancouver's fantastic 1,000-acre (405-hectare) park filled with old-growth forests, winding paths, and a number of tourist destinations. Of these, Vancouver Aquarium, reached by a forest path from the southern part of the park, is a must-see. One of the best in North America, it features performing orcas and porpoises, as well as ecosystem tanks from waters around the world. Nearby is Vancouver's small zoo, mostly of interest to children; stop and watch the sea otters play.

## Public Transportation

**TransLink** Phone 604/953-3333, www.translink.bc.ca

**Airport** Vancouver International Airport (YVR). S of the city off Hwy 99.

**Information** Phone 604/207-7077

**Lost and Found** Phone 604/276-6104, toll-free 866/817-5243

**Airlines** Aeromexico, Air Canada, Air China, Air New Zealand, Air North, Air Pacific, Air Transat, Alaska Airlines, Alitalia, All Nippon Airways, Aloha Airlines, America West, American Airlines, Amigo Airways, ATA, Baxter Aviation, Belair, Britannia Airways, British Airways, British Midland, Canadian Western Airlines, Cathay Pacific Airways, Central Mountain Air, Champion Air, China Air, Condor Fuugdienst, Continental Airlines, Delta Air Lines, Delta Connector, EVA Air, Edelweiss Air, El Al, Finnair, HMY Airways, Harbor Airlines, Horizon Air, Japan Airlines, Jetsgo, KLM Royal Dutch, Korean Air, Lignum Air, Lufthansa, Martinair, Mexicana, Northwest Airlines, Philippine Airlines, Qantas Airways, Quikair, Regency North Vancouver Air, Scandinavian Airlines (SAS), Singapore Airlines, Skywest Airlines, Skyservice Airlines, Thai Airlines, Thomas Cook Airlines, Tofino Air, United Airlines, Varig Airlines, WestJet, Western Express Airlines, Whistler Air Services, Zip, Zoom

## Additional Visitor Information

There are many more interesting things to see and do in Vancouver and the suburbs of Burnaby and New Westminster to the east, Richmond to the south, North Vancouver, and West Vancouver. The Tourism Vancouver InfoCentre has pamphlets, maps, ferry schedules, and additional information at Plaza Level, Waterfront Centre, 200 Burrard St, V6C 3L6; phone 604/683-2000.

## What to See and Do

**Arts Club Theatre Company.** *1585 Johnston St, Vancouver (V6H 3R9). Phone 604/687-5315. www.artsclub.com.* Having helped launch the careers of actors Michael J. Fox and Brent Carver, The Arts Club Theatre steals the Vancouver stage spotlight. In addition to it's four annual mainstage productions at Stanley Theatre (Granville and 12th), the company mounts four productions at the Granville Island Stage. Bills range from musicals like *My Fair Lady* to contemporary dramas such as *Burn This.* The Revue Stage, adjacent to the Granville, presents popular musicals and comedies, including the likes of *A Closer Walk with Patsy Cline.* **$$$$**

**Ballet British Columbia.** *677 Davie St, Vancouver (V6B 2G6). Phone 604/732-5003. www.balletbc.com.* With a strong company of 14 dancers, Ballet BC reigns as Vancouver's top dance troupe. Directed by John Alleyne, former dancer with the Stuttgart Ballet and the National Ballet of Canada, the company's repertoire includes dances by famed choreographers like William Forsythe and John Cranko as well as commissioned works by Canadian talents. Ballet BC's home stage is the Queen Elizabeth Theatre (Hamilton at Dunsmuir). (Nov-May) **$$$$**

**Barbara Jo's Books to Cooks.** *1128 Mainland St, Vancouver (V6B 2T4). Phone 604/688-6755. www.bookstocooks.com.* Books to Cooks incarnates owner Barbara Jo McIntosh's passion for both food and books. A former restaurateur and cookbook author with many credits, McIntosh runs the Yaletown shop as bookstore-cum-cooking school. Beyond the stacks, which include both new releases and out-of-print finds, a demonstration kitchen enables a staff cooking teacher and visiting authors to whip up their favorites. Regularly scheduled two-hour classes on topics from slow roasting to Chinese food require pre-registration. (Mon-Fri 10 am-6 pm, Sat 10:30 am-5:30 pm, Sun 11:30 am-5 pm)

**BC Lions (CFL).** *777 Pacific Blvd, Vancouver (V6B 4Y8). Phone 604/589-7627. www.bclions.com.* The Canadian Football League's BC Lions, along with eight other CFL teams, contend for the season-winning Grey Cup. In contrast to American football, the Canadian game consists of only three downs per possession rather than four and takes place on a longer and wider field, which proponents say makes for more exciting, pass-driven games. Although the summer season may appeal to fair-weather fans, Vancouver's Lions play under the BC Place dome. (June-Nov)

**Bites-on Salmon Charters, Vancouver.** *200-1128 Hornby St, Vancouver (V6H 354). On Granville Island. Phone 604/688-2483. www.bites-on.com.* Coho, sockeye, and chinook salmon school in the waters around Vancouver, which is convenient for urban-bound fishing fans. Granville Islandbased Bites-On offers day trips of five or eight hours, during which you can sink a line into the Strait of Georgia on a yacht up to 40 feet (12 meters) long. The charters serve parties of 1 to 12 people. Peak fishing months are Apr-Oct, although charters operate year-round. Boat trips also acquaint fishermen with the region's abundant sea lion, porpoise, and whale populations. (Daily) **$$$$**

**Burnaby Village Museum.** *6501 Deer Lake Ave, Vancouver (V5G 3T6). Phone 604/293-6500. www.burnabyvillagemuseum.ca.*Living museum of the period before 1925 with costumed attendants; more than 30 full-scale buildings with displays and demonstrations. (Daily 11 am-4:30 pm; closed early Jan-early May) **$$$**

**Capilano Suspension Bridge.** *3735 Capilano Rd, Vancouver (V7R 4J1). Phone 604/985-7474. www.capbridge.com.* Want to get the kids to hold your hand again? Take them across the 400-foot-long (122 meters) Capilano Suspension Bridge strung some 230 feet (70 meters) above the Capilano River gorge. Originally constructed in 1889 and rebuilt in 1956, the wooden bridge is engineered of wire rope cemented at either end. In addition to the bridge, the surrounding park provides walking trails, gardens, a totem pole collection, and audiences with First Nations carvers at work. Arrive early in high season to best appreciate the thrill of the feat without the aggravation of the hordes. (Summer: daily 8:30 am-8 pm; spring-fall: daily 9 am-6 pm; winter: daily 9 am-5 pm; closed Dec 25) **$$$$**

**The Centre in Vancouver for Performing Arts.** *777 Homer St, Vancouver (V6B 2W1). Phone 604/602-0616. www.centreinvancouver.com.* Acclaimed Canadian architect Moshe Safdie designed the dramatic Centre in Vancouver with an arched glass facade and, punctuating the entry, a spiraling glass cone. Inside, polished marble floors and sweeping curved stairways heighten the pre-curtain lobby buzz. The auditorium seats 1,800, accommodating major Broadway tours including past productions of *Cabaret, Sunset Boulevard, The Phantom of the Opera, Joseph and the Amazing Technicolor Dreamcoat, Riverdance,* and *Ragtime.*

**Chan Centre for the Performing Arts.** *University of British Columbia,6265 Crescent Rd, Vancouver (V6T 1Z1). Phone 604/822-9197. www.chancentre.com.* In the University of British Columbia district, the Chan houses three venues for theater and music, all sharing the same light-flooded lobby. Built in 1997, the distinctive zinc-clad cylindrical building stands out amid the verdant campus. With superior acoustics, this is one of the best spots in town to hear concerts by touring soloists, UBC musicians, and the Vancouver Symphony.

**Chinatown.** *E Pender and Gore sts, Vancouver.* This downtown area is the nucleus of the third-largest Chinese community in North America (only those in San Francisco and New York are larger). At the heart lies the Chinese Market where 100-year-old duck eggs may be purchased; herbalists promise cures with roots and powdered bones. The Dr. Sun Yat-Sen Classical Chinese Garden (see) provides a beautiful centerpiece. Chinese shops display a variety of items ranging from cricket cages to cloisonné vases. Offices of three Chinese newspapers and one of the world's narrowest buildings are located within the community's borders. Resplendent Asian atmosphere offers fine examples of Chinese architecture, restaurants, and nightclubs. At the center is

> **Dr. Sun-Yat-Sen Classical Chinese Garden.** *578 Carrall St, Vancouver. Phone 604/662-3207.* Unique to the Western Hemisphere, this garden was originally built in China circa 1492 and transplanted to Vancouver for Expo '86. (Daily) **$$**

**CN IMAX Theatre.** *201-999 Canada Pl, Vancouver (V6A 3Z7). Phone 604/682-2384. www.imax.com/vancouver.* Under the white sails that distinguish waterfront Canada Place, CN IMAX screens wide-format documentary films on subjects ranging from space travel to wildlife conservation. Several shows are screened throughout the day, with a new film starting approximately every hour. A food court and shops join the cinema at Vancouver's convention center. (Daily noon-10 pm) **$$$**

**The Commodore Ballroom.** *868 Granville St, Vancouver (V6Z 1K3). Phone 604/739-4550. www.hob.com/venues/concerts/commodore.* Its been swinging since the big band era, and the Commodore flaunts it's age with brass chandeliers and polished wood stairs. A $3.5 million renovation in 1999 restored it's elegance (and kept the spring-loaded dance floor) while modernizing it's stage wizardry. US-based House of Blues now programs the acts that come through the ballroom, ranging primarily from rock to blues with a smattering of world talent. HOB also operates a kitchen on site, making food as well as drinks available.

**Cypress Mountain.** *Cypress Bowl and Hwy 1, Vancouver. 7 1/2 miles (12 kilometers) NW via BC 99, in Cypress Provincial Park. Phone 604/419-7669. www.cypressmountain.com.* Covering two mountains with 34 runs and five lifts, Cypress Mountain claims the regions biggest vertical drop at 1,750 feet (533 meters). But the ski areas bigger claim to fame is it's cross-country skiing facilities, which span 12 miles (19 kilometers) of groomed trails, nearly five of which are lit for night gliding. The region's most popular Nordic destination also offers private and group lessons as well as rental equipment. Snowshoers can tramp on designated trails solo or take a guided tour. (Winter: daily 9 am-10 pm) **$$$$**

**Dubrulle International Culinary & Hotel Institute of Canada.** *300 - 609 Granville St, Vancouver (V6J 4R8). Phone 604/738-3155; toll-free 800/667-7288. www.homechef.ca.* Graduates of Canada's largest private cooking school have gone on to work worldwide and at home, opening top-notch local restaurants like Lumiere (see also LUMIERE). For keen locals and visitors, it's "serious amateur" division offers evening and weekend training that ranges from stock prep to knife skills, Indian bread-making to do-it-yourself pasta. With a maximum enrollment of 16, courses are hands-on in a professional kitchen, capped by dining on the meal prepared in the prior three hours. (Call for class schedules) **$$$$**

**Ecomarine Ocean Kayak Centre.** *1668 Duranleau St, Vancouver (V6H 354). On Granville Island. Phone 604/689-7575. www.ecomarine.com.* To get the full impact of Vancouver's magnificent setting on the coast, troll the waterways under paddle power with a kayak from Ecomarine. The outfitter rents both single and double kayaks at it's Granville Island headquarters and at an outpost on Jericho Beach (Jericho Sailing Center, 1300 Discovery St), where first-timers can take a three-hour lesson before getting started. Navigate from placid False Creek to more rugged inlets up the shore. (Sept-May: daily 10 am-6 pm; June-Aug: Daily 9 am-6 pm, Thurs-Sat 9 am-9 pm; closed Jan 1, Dec 25) **$$$$**

**Exhibition Park.** *2901 E Hastings St, Vancouver. Between Renfrew and Cassiar sts. Phone 604/253-2311.* Approximately 165 acres (70 hectares). Concert, convention, entertainment facilities. Thoroughbred racing (late spring-early fall) and Playland Amusement Park (Apr-June: weekends; July-Oct: daily; also evenings).

**Gallery at Ceperley House.** *6344 Deer Lake Ave, Vancouver (V5G 2J3). Phone 604/205-7332. www.burnabyartgallery.ca.* Monthly exhibitions of local, national, and international artists. Collection of contemporary Canadian works on paper. Housed in Ceperley Mansion, overlooking Deer Lake and the surrounding gardens. (Tues-Fri 10 am-4:30 pm, to 8 pm first Thurs of month; Sat-Sun noon-5 pm; closed Mon) **DONATION**

**Gastown.** *Columbia and Alexander Sts, Vancouver. Roughly bounded by Burrard Inlet on the N, Dunsmuir St on the S, Carrall St to the E, and Richards St to the W. Phone 604/683-5650. www.gastown.org.* So gabby was the Brit-born barman Jack Deighton that patrons of his shoreside 1867 saloon called him Gassy. Thus, when the city started to grow around the joint south of the Burrard Inlet, the district came to be known as "Gassy's Town", hence "Gastown". Vancouver's historic nucleus consists of a series of Victorian buildings rehabbed to shelter an array of shops, clubs, and eateries. Among the highlights, the Gastown Steam Clock pipes up every 15 minutes and the Vancouver Police Centennial Museum covers the most notorious local crimes. To fully appreciate the neighborhood, show up for a free tour sponsored by the Gastown Business Improvement Society in Maple Tree Square at 2 pm daily in summer. **FREE** Adjacent is

> **Harbour Centre-The Lookout.** *555 W Hastings St, Vancouver. Phone 604/689-0421.* Glass elevators take you to a 360 viewing deck 553 feet (167 meters) above street level; multimedia presentation, historical displays, tour guides. (Daily; closed Dec 25) **$$$**

**Gordon Southam Observatory.** *Phone 604/738-7827.* Fri-Sat evenings and holidays, weather permitting **FREE**

**Granville Island.** *1661 Duranleau St, 2nd Fl, Vancouver (V6H 3S3). A 37-acre (15-hectare) area in the heart of the city, beneath the S end of Granville Bridge. Phone 604/666-5784. www.granvilleisland.bc.ca.* A former industrial isle, Granville Island is an urban renewal case study, fashioning markets, shops, homes, and entertainment out of decaying wharf warehouses beginning in the 1970s. Its hub is the Public Market, a prime picnic provisioner teeming with fishmongers, produce vendors, butchers, cheese shops, bakeries, and chef demonstrations. A specialized Kids Market and a free outdoor Water Park (May-Sept) appeal to children. The Maritime Market on the southwest shore serves as a dock for boat owners as well as those looking to hire a fishing charter, hop on a ferry, or rent a kayak. Three Granville Island museums showcase miniature trains, ship models, and sport fishing. Dozens of bars and restaurants, many with views back across the water to the downtown skyline, drive the after-dark trade. An art school, artists studios, and several galleries lend bohemian flare to the Granville, abetted by several theaters and a panoply of street musicians. (Daily) **FREE**

**Granville Island Kids Market.** *1496 Cartwright St, Vancouver (V6A 2S4). Phone 604/689-8447.* Vancouver's open food market turns it's third floor into something kids can enjoy—beyond pastries on the market floor, that is. Twenty-five children's shops, including eight selling toys and another seven selling clothes, take aim at junior consumers, many of whom, of course, prefer Kids Market's indoor play area. Strolling clowns and face-painters amplify the carnival-like setting. (Daily 10 am-6 pm) **FREE**

**Gray Line sightseeing tours.** *Vancouver. Phone 604/879-3363. www.graylinewest.com.* Pickup at all major Vancouver hotels; call for reservations.

**Great Canadian Casino.** *Holiday Inn Vancouver-Centre, 711 W Broadway, Vancouver (V6Z 3Y2). Phone 604/303-1000. www.greatcanadiancasino.com.* The Great Canadian Casino runs the two major gambling dens in town, one in the downtown financial district at the Renaissance Vancouver (1133 W Hastings) and the other on the south shore of False Creek, Holiday Inn Vancouver-Centre (711 W Broadway). Roulette and blackjack join many games popular in the Asian community, such as baccarat and pai gow poker, on the gaming floors (note that there are no slot machines at either casino). Dress is casual, and the minimum gambling age in Canada is 19. (Daily 24 hours) **FREE**

**Greater Vancouver Zoo.** *5048-264th St, Aldergrove (V4W 1N7). Phone 604/856-6825. www.greatervancouverzoo.com.* Explore 120 acres housing more than 700 animals. Miniature train ride; bus tour of North American Wild exhibit. (Apr-Sept: daily 9:30 am-7 pm; Oct-Mar: daily 9:30 am-4 pm; closed Dec 25) **$$$**

**Grouse Mountain.** *6400 Nancy Greene Way, Vancouver (V7R 4K9). Phone 604/984-0661. www.grousemountain.com.* For skiing in winter, hiking in summer, and sightseeing year-round, Grouse Mountain draws legions of visitors to Vancouver's North Shore. The area's first ski mountain is still it's most convenient, with ski and snowboard runs that overlook the metropolis, as well as a skating rink and sleigh rides available. Hikers have loads of trails to choose from, but the one to boast about is the Grouse Grind, a 1.8-mile (2.9 kilometers) hike straight up the 3,700-foot (1128 meter) peak, thus accounting for the "grind" ("grouse" is for "bird", not "complaint"). Look for mountain bike trails on the backside of the slopes. The Skyride gondola takes the easy route up in an eight-minute ride. At the top, seasonless attractions include Theater in the Sky, a high-definition aerial film, and several panoramic-view restaurants starring the Strait of Georgia and the twinkling lights of Vancouver. (Daily 10 am-10 pm) **$$$$**

**Harbour Cruises Ltd.** *#1 North Foot Denman St, Vancouver. Departures from northern foot of Denman St. Phone 604/688-7246. www.boatcruises.com.* Boat/train excursion (6 1/2 hours); also sunset dinner cruises; harbor tours, private charters. (Apr-Oct)

**Hastings Park Racecourse.** *Renfrew and Dundas sts, Vancouver (V5K 3N8). ; toll-free 800/677-7702. www.hastingspark.com.* Thoroughbreds run in Vancouver at Hastings Park on the city's east side. Although the lengthy racing season runs late Apr-Nov, most races are held on Sat and Sun, with extra meets scheduled for major holidays like Canada Day and Labour Day. Two-dollar-bet minimums encourage cheap dates, while self-service betting terminals patiently acquaint you with the track lingo. **$$**

**HR MacMillan Space Centre.** *1100 Chestnut St, Vancouver (V6J 3J9). Phone 604/738-7827. www.hrmacmillanspacecentre.com.* One of several museums in Vanier Park tucked between Kitsilano Beach and Granville Island, the MacMillan Space Centre appeals to would-be astronauts with a space flight simulator, planetarium, and interactive games. After hours, laser light shows depart from the scientific and delve into the psychedelic, dramatizing music by the likes of Pink Floyd and Led Zeppelin. (Tues-Sun 10 am-5 pm) **$$$**

**Inuit Gallery of Vancouver.** *206 Cambie St, Vancouver (V6B 2M9). Phone 604/688-7323. www.inuit.com.* From the moment you enter the gallery, Inuit immerses you in the rich artistic tradition of coastal natives with soapstone sculptures, native prints, ceremonial masks, and bentwood boxes. One of Vancouver's best sources for First Peoples art, Inuit represents tribes up and down the Pacific Northwest. Because many of it's pieces are large, including totem poles, the gallery ships worldwide. In the Gastown district, Inuit is a short walk from the convention center and cruise ship terminal. (Mon-Sat 10 am-6 pm, Sun 10 am-5 pm; closed Jan 1, Dec 25)

**Irving House Historic Centre.** *302 Royal Ave, Vancouver. Phone 604/527-4640.* (1864) Fourteen rooms of period furniture from 1864-1890. Adjacent is the **New Westminster Museum,** on the back of the property, which has displays on local history, household goods, and May Day memorabilia. (May-mid-Sept: Tues-Sun; rest of year: Sat-Sun; closed Jan 1, Dec 25-26) **DONATION**

**The Marine Building.** *355 Burrard St, Vancouver (V6C 2G8).* Vancouver's Art Deco gem, the ornate 25-story Marine Building was the tallest building in the British Empire when it was completed in 1929. But if the icon brought the international Deco style home to Canada, it also uniquely hailed the region. Exterior terra-cotta reliefs pay homage to the city's marine heritage in images of starfish, crabs, seashells, and snails as well as sail- and steam-powered boats. The office buildings lobby continues the motif in ornate coffered ceilings.

**Metrotown Centre.** *4700 Kingsway, Burnaby. Between Boundary Rd and Royal Oak. Phone 604/430-0501. www.metropolisatmetrotown.com.* Three connected shopping centers make up Metrotown, BC's largest shopping center, counting nearly 500 shops in the near suburb of Burnaby. Among it's tenants are well-known chains like menswear's Massimo, clothier Roots, outdoor outfitter Coast Mountain Sports, and Chapters bookstore. Several video game arcades and dozens of movie screens provide entertainment. (Mon-Fri 10 am-9 pm, Sat 9:30 am-6 pm, Sun 11 am-6 pm)

**Murchie's Tea.** *825 W Pender, Vancouver (V6Z 2E7). Phone 604/669-0783. www.murchies.com.* Gourmet coffee and high-grade tea are Murchie's considerable claims to fame. At it since 1894, the company blends it's own offerings with the care and sophistication normally associated with winemakers. In addition to the Robson Street shop, Murchie's operates five other stores in BC, as well as a mail-order business. Whether you're a fan of the drinks or not, the atmospheric shop makes it fun to peruse tea blends from Sri Lanka and Costa Rican Arabica whole beans. (Mon-Fri 8:30 am-6 pm, Sat 9 am-6 pm, Sun noon-5 pm; closed Jan 1, Dec 25)

**Oakridge Shopping Centre.** *650 W 41st Ave, Vancouver (V5Z 2M9). Phone 604/261-2511.oakridge.shopping.ca.* With 150 shops and services, a children's play area, movie theaters, and a walking club, Oakridge serves it's community with more than just sales. One of the city's original malls, built in 1959, Oakridge has grown to house magnet tenants such as The Bay department store, Eddie Bauer, Banana Republic, French Connection, MAC, MaxMara, and Swarovski. (Mon-Tues, Sat 9 am-6:00 pm, Wed-Fri 9:30 am-9 pm, Sun noon-6 pm; closed Jan 1, Dec 25)

**Old Hastings Mill.** *1575 Alma Rd, Vancouver. Phone 604/734-1212.* (circa 1865) One of the few buildings remaining after the fire of 1886, it now houses indigenous artifacts and memorabilia of Vancouver's first settlers. (Mid-June-mid-Sept: daily; rest of year: Sat and Sun afternoons) **FREE**

**Pacific Centre.** *550-700 W Georgia St, Vancouver (V7Y 1A1). Phone 604/688-7236. www.pacificcentre.ca.*Downtown Vancouver's major shopping destination, the three-block-long Pacific Centre runs a shopping arcade underground between Granville and Howe streets from Robson to Pender streets. National and international mid-range and upscale clothiers, including the Gap, Club Monaco, and Canada's trendsetter Holt Renfrew, dominate the tenant types. Its central locale makes it an easy pedestrian destination from many major hotels. (Mon-Wed 10 am-7 pm, Thurs-Fri to 9 pm, Sat 9:30 to 6 pm, Sun 11 am-6 pm; closed Jan 1, Dec 25)

**Pacific Institute of Culinary Arts.** *1505 W 2nd Ave, Vancouver (V6H 3Y4). Phone 604/734-4488. www.picularts.bc.ca.* In addition to offering culinary and baking degrees to professionals-in-training, the Pacific Institute customizes instruction for individuals and groups in evening and weekend sessions. Course topics are determined by arrangement with a staff chef and may include specialty sessions like cake decorating or the preparation of an entire gourmet meal. Full-time advanced students also staff the on-site restaurant and bakeshop serving lunch, tea, and dinner to the public. (Restaurant Mon-Fri 11 am-2 pm, 3-5 pm, 6-9 pm; Sat 6-9 pm; Bakeshop Mon-Fri 8 am-7 pm, Sat from noon)

**Park Royal Shopping Centre.** *2002 Park Royal S, West Vancouver (V7T 2W4). At the N end of the Lions Gate Bridge at Taylor Way and Marine Dr. Phone 604/925-9576. www.shopparkroyal.com.* A short hop over the Lion Gate Bridge lands shoppers at the Park Royal Shopping Centre, which reflects the affluence of the West Vancouver community in fashionable shops. Anchor department store The Bay joins other big-box retailers such as Linens 'n' Things, along with an interesting selection of specialty stores, including Aveda, Roots, the Disney Store, and Guess. (Mon-Wed 10 am-6 pm, Thurs-Fri to 9 pm, Sat 9:30 am-5:30 pm, Sun noon-6 pm; closed Jan 1, Dec 25)

**Queen Elizabeth Park.** *Cambie St and W 33rd Ave, Vancouver. Phone 604/257-8570.* Observation point affords a view of the city, harbor, and mountains; Bloedel Conservatory has more than 100 free-flying birds, plus tropical, desert, and seasonal displays. (Daily; closed Dec 25) **$$**

**Queen Elizabeth Theatre and Playhouse and Orpheum Theatre.** *Vancouver. Phone 604/683-2000.* A symphony orchestra, opera company, and many theater groups present productions around town, especially at the Queen Elizabeth Theatre and Playhouse and Orpheum Theatre. Consult the local paper for details.

**Robson Street.** *Robson Street Business Association,412-1155 Robson St, Vancouver (V6E 1B5). www.robsonstreet.ca.*The epicenter of Vancouver's street chic,

Robson makes a nice window-shopping stroll. A string of shops and sidewalk cafés runs several blocks in either direction from the intersection of Robson and Burrard streets. Retailers range from the tony Giorgio Armani and Salvatore Ferragamo to the playful Benetton on down to the bovine-mad T-shirt shop Cows. Jewelry stores, chocolatiers, and craft galleries round out the offerings.

***Royal City Star* Riverboat Casino.** *788 Quayside Dr, New Westminster. Docked on the Fraser River in downtown New Westminster, SW of Vancouver. Phone 604/519-3660. www.royalcity'star.bc.ca.* The late-model paddlewheeler *Queen of New Orleans*, once stationed on the Mississippi, now calls the Fraser River it's home port as the *Royal City Star*. On-board games of chance include pai gow poker, mini baccarat, blackjack, roulette, and Caribbean stud poker. Several bars, a deli, and a restaurant feed and water patrons. Between May and October, the boat schedules regular sailings. (Daily 10-4 am) **FREE**

***Samson V* Maritime Museum.** *Moored on the Fraser River at the Westminster Quay Market in New Westminster, 12 miles (19 kilometers) S via Hwy 1A. Phone 604/522-6894.* The last steam-powered paddlewheeler to operate on the Fraser River now functions as a floating museum. Displays focus on the various paddlewheelers and paddlewheeler captains that have worked the river, and on river-related activities. (May-June: Sat-Sun, holidays; July-Labor Day: daily; Labor Day-mid-Oct: Sat-Sun, holidays)

**Science World British Columbia.** *1455 Québec St, Vancouver (V6A 3Z7). Phone 604/443-7443. www.scienceworld.bc.ca.*The massive golf ball-shaped Science World attracts both architecture and museum fans. Modeled on the geodesic domes of F. Buckminster Fuller, the aluminum ball was erected for Expo '86 and now houses a science center devoted to interactive exhibits on nature, invention, ecology, and optical illusions. A play space with a water table and giant building blocks engages the 3-to-6 set, while the dome-projection Omnimax theater entertains the whole brood. (Mon-Fri 10 am-5 pm, Sat-Sun to 6 pm) **$$$**

**Shaughnessy.** *Vancouver. Between 16th and 41st aves, W of Granville St.* Originally developed by the Canadian Pacific Railway in 1907 for Vancouverites in search of urban escape, the elite Shaughnessy neighborhood housed (and still houses) the city's well-to-do in mansions of Tudor and colonial styles, among others. A prime neighborhood for biking or strolling, Shaughnessys quiet streets are curved, it's lots large, it's homes impressive, and it's gardens lush.

**Simon Fraser University.** *Gaglardi Way and University Dr W, Burnaby. 10 miles (16 kilometers) E off BC 7A (Hastings St). Phone 604/291-3210. www.sfu.ca.* (1965) (20,000 students) Located on Burnaby Mountain; architecturally outstanding buildings. Original campus was completed in only 18 months. Hourly guided tours (July-Aug, daily; free)

**Sinclair Centre.** *757 W Hastings St, Vancouver (V6C 1A1). www.sinclaircentre.com.* This one-square-block mall cobbles together four restored Victorian-era buildings into a shopping center with personality. Centered around a glass-topped atrium, the multilevel Sinclair preserves the limestone walls and archways of the original buildings retrofitted with contemporary retailers. Designer boutiques like Plaza Escada, Leone, and clothier A'Wear join several restaurants, including Morton's of Chicago, among the top shops. (Mon-Fri 9:30 am-6 pm, Sat to 5:30 pm, Sun noon-5 pm; closed Jan 1, Dec 25)

**Spokes Bicycle Rentals.** *1789 W Georgia St, Vancouver (V6G 2V7). Phone 604/688-5141. www.vancouver-bikerental.com.* For bike rides along the Stanley Park seawall and interior trails, Spokes couldnt be better located. Just across from the park entrance on Georgia St, the cycle shop rents from a vast fleet that includes cruisers, tandems, mountain bikes, and hybrid models. Spokes also offers bike tours of the Stanley Park perimeter (1 1/2 hours) and Granville Island (3 1/2 hours). (Daily) **$$$**

**Stanley Park.** *2099 Beach Ave, Vancouver (V6G 3E2). A peninsula between English Bay and Burrard Inlet at the foot of W George St. Phone 604/257-8400. www.seestanleypark.com.* One thousand acres of native British Columbia in the heart of the city, Stanley Park, the largest city park in Canada, is a green haven with few peers. Towering forests of cedar, hemlock, and fir spill onto sand beaches, immersing visitors and residents alike in the wild just minutes from the civilized. Come shod to explore. Park-goers recreate along forest hiking trails, on three beaches, and along the 5.5-mile(8.9-kilometers) 1920s vintage seawall, where in-line skaters, runners, and cyclists admire skyline and ocean views. Mans hand distinguishes the park in gardens devoted to roses and rhododendrons and in a vivid stand of First Nations totem poles. Providing an appeal for every interest, Stanley Park also hosts the Vancouver Aquarium (see also VANCOUVER AQUARIUM MARINE SCIENCE CENTRE), Children's Farmyard,

Miniature Railway, Theatre Under the Stars, and several worth-the-trip restaurants. (Daily)

**Vancouver Aquarium Marine Science Centre.** *845 Avison Way, Stanley Park, Vancouver (V6B 3X8). Phone 604/659-3474.* With inviting, hands-on exhibits, Vancouver Aquarium in sylvan Stanley Park explores the undersea world from Amazon to Arctic, assembling 300 species of fish, their invertebrate tank mates (sea stars, jellyfish, and octopuses), and food-chain-higher-ups (sea mammals). For all it's globetrotting interests, the aquarium is a top spot to study the local environment as well. In outdoor pools, graceful beluga whales, frisky sea lions, and playful otters prove comfortable with the changeable Pacific Northwest climate (private encounters with the belugas and dolphins run $125 to $175 per parent/child pair). Progeny of salmon released by the aquarium in 1998 from a park river return each winter, roughly November to February, illustrating BC's rich salmon spawning waterways. Behind-the-scenes tours with trainers (an extra $15 to $20) provide visitors a glimpse of the marine mammal rescue and rehab program for which the aquarium is lauded. (Sept-June: daily 10 am-5:30 pm; July-Aug: daily 9:30 am-7 pm) **$$$$**

**University of British Columbia.** *2329 West Mall, Vancouver. 8 miles (13 kilometers) SW via Burrard St, 4th Ave. Phone 604/822-2211. www.ubc.ca.*(1915) (34,869 students) The 990-acre (401-hectare) campus features museums, galleries (some fees), many spectacular gardens; almost 400 buildings complement the natural grandeur of the area. Free guided campus tours (May-Aug). Beautifully situated on scenic Point Grey. Includes

**Frederic Wood Theatre.** *6354 Crescent Rd, Vancouver. Phone 604/822-2678.* Summer stock and winter mainstage productions.

**Museum of Anthropology at the University of British Columbia.** *6393 NW Marine Dr, Vancouver (V6T 1Z2). Phone 604/822-3825.* Built to reference a First Nations longhouse, the glass and concrete Museum of Anthropology makes a fitting shrine for the art and artifacts of West Coast natives. The Great Hall surrounds visitors in immense totem poles, canoes, and feast dishes of the Kwakwakawakw, Nisgaa, Gitksan, and Haida peoples, among others. An outdoor sculpture garden sets tribal houses and totem poles, many carved by the best known contemporary artists, against a backdrop of sea and mountain views. In it's mission to explore all the cultures of the world, the Anthro also catalogs 600 ceramics works from 15th- to 19th-century Europe. (Winter: Wed-Sun 11 am-5 pm, Tues to 9 pm; Summer: daily 10 am-5 pm, Tues to 9 pm; closed Mon in winter, Dec 25-26) **$$**

**UBC Botanical Garden.** *6804 SW Marine Dr, Vancouver. Phone 604/822-3928.* Seven separate areas include Asian, Physick, BC Native, Alpine, and Food gardens. **Nitobe Garden,** authentic Japanese tea garden located behind Asian Centre (mid-Mar-early Oct: daily; rest of year: Mon-Fri). (Daily; closed Jan 1, Dec 25). **$$**

**Vancouver Art Gallery.** *750 Hornby St, Vancouver (V6Z 2H7). Phone 604/662-4700. www.vanartgallery.bc.ca.* Most visitors bound up to the Vancouver Art Gallery's fourth floor for a look at the largest collection of works by British Columbia's best known painter, Emily Carr. But the other galleries in western Canada's largest art museum, housed in an early 20th-century courthouse, warrant a poke around; subjects range from Group of Seven landscapes to photo conceptual art. A cozy caf, sculpture garden, and intriguing museum shop bid you to linger a bit longer. (Daily 10 am-5:30 pm, Thurs to 9 pm; closed Jan 1, Dec 25) **$$$**

**Vancouver Canadians.** *Nat Bailey Stadium in Queen Ellizabeth Park,4601 Ontario St, Vancouver (V5V 2H4). Phone 604/872-5232. www.canadiansbaseball.com.* In the 76-game short season, the single-A Minor League Baseball Canadians compete in the Northwest League. Most games start at 7 pm in order to draw the after-work crowd, although "nooners," or weekday afternoon starts, make popular ex-office outings. Team talent is often secondary to fans who come out for the low ticket prices, comic stadium antics, and park setting. The University of British Columbia's baseball team calls Nat Bailey it's home field as well. (Mid-June-early Sept) **$$$**

**Vancouver Canucks (NHL).** *800 Griffiths Way, Vancouver (V6B 6G1). Phone 604/820-4400. www.canucks.com.* Canada's love of hockey comes alive in black and blue at rowdy Vancouver Canucks matches, where joining the beer-fueled fans may be as close as you can get to feeling like a local. The National Hockey League franchise came to town in the mid-1970s, launching an industry of boosters and media wags. Having won the Stanley Cup in 1995, the Canucks are perennially in the hunt for the sports top prize. (Sept-Apr)

**Vancouver Giants.** *100 North Renfrew St, Vancouver (V5K 3N7). Phone 604/444-2687. www.vancouvergi-*

*ants.com.* As training grounds for National Hockey League hopefuls, the Western Hockey League vets young players, ages 15 to 20, in a hardscrabble league cheered on largely by the friends and families of players. The Giants, Vancouver's local boys new to the WHL in 2001, play 36 games at home at Pacific Coliseum (Hastings and Renfrew) and another 36 on the road against a 19-team field. (Sept-Mar) **$$$$**

**Vancouver Griffins.** *1st and 3rd aves, New Westminster. Phone 604/619-0726. www.vancouvergriffins.com.* One of the newest members of the National Women's Hockey League (NWHL), the Vancouver Griffins compete against nine other Canadian women's pro teams. Olympic silver medalist, five-time world champion, and seven-time national champion Nancy Drolet leads the Griffins on the ice in the 3,500-seat arena. Hockey is popular enough in the region that the Griffins often join the NHL Canucks, or at least their mascot, in promotional appearances. (Oct-Mar) **$$$**

**Vancouver Maritime Museum.** *1905 Ogden Ave, Vancouver (V6J 3J9). Phone 604/257-8300. www.vmm.bc.ca.* Built around the *St. Roch*, the first ship to navigate Canada's Inside Passage from west to east, Vanier Parks Maritime Museum lets seafaring fans explore the 1928 supply ship from wheelhouse to captains quarters. In addition to the series of historic model ships housed inside the museum, several historic craft are tethered outside it's waterfront Heritage Harbour, including two tugs, a rescue boat, and the 1927 seiner once featured on Canada's $5 bill. (Daily 10 am-5 pm; winter Tues-Sat 10 am-5 pm, Sun from noon; closed Mon in winter) **$$**

**Vancouver Museum.** *1100 Chestnut St, Vancouver (V6J 3J9). 1 1/2 miles (2 1/2 kilometers) SW via Burrard, Cypress sts. Phone 604/736-4431. www.vanmuseum.bc.ca.* Keeper of city history, and another Vanier Park attraction, Vancouver Museum takes a sweeping view of civilization, collecting everything from Egyptian mummies to local vintage swimming togs. In addition to the urban story, told in lifelike re-creations of an Edwardian parlor, ship's berth, and trading post, the museum examines First Nations artifacts, the contributions of Asian Rim cultures, and world history. (Tues-Wed, Fri-Sun 10 am-5 pm, Thurs to 9 pm; closed Mon, Dec 25) **$$$**

**Vancouver Opera.** *835 Cambie St, Vancouver (V6B 4Z9). Phone 604/683-0222. www.vanopera.bc.ca.* From the frolic of Mozart's Figaro! Figaro! Figaro! to the passion of *Carmen*, Vancouver Opera stages four productions annually. Established in 1958, the company has hosted a roster of greats, including guest singers Placido Domingo, Joan Sutherland, and Marilyn Horne. Performances take place at the Queen Elizabeth Theatre (Hamilton at Dunsmuir) with subtitles projected above the stage. (Oct-May, Tues, Thurs, Sat 8 pm) **$$$$**

**Vancouver Police Centennial Museum.** *240 E Cordova St, Vancouver (V6A 1L3). Phone 604/665-3346. www.city.vancouver.bc.ca/police/museum/.* For fans of the macabre, the Vancouver Police Centennial Museum in Gastown not only supplies the gruesome details of the city's most lurid crimes (such as bodies found in Stanley Park and the man who tried to murder his wife with arsenic-laced milkshakes) but also dramatizes them crime-scene style. Run by the city's police department, the museum tells the history of local law-keeping and ushers visitors into an eerie mock-forensics lab in the former city morgue. (Mon-Sat 9 am-5 pm; closed holidays) **$$**

**Vancouver Ravens.** *800 Griffiths Way, Vancouver (V6B 6G1). www.vancouverravens.com.* Vancouver's entry in the National Lacrosse League, the Ravens play a spirited four-month schedule at the indoor General Motors Place. The towns newest professional team, the Ravens franchise got the green light with the 2001/2002 season, competing in the Northern division against Toronto, Calgary, and Ottawa. Eight more US teams vie in the Eastern and Central divisions. (Dec-Apr) **$$$$**

**Vancouver Symphony Orchestra.** *601 Smithe St, Vancouver (V6B 5G1). Phone 604/684-9100. www.Vancouver'symphony.ca.* Canada's third largest orchestra, the Vancouver Symphony presents more than 140 concerts annually, most of them at the ornate 1927-built Orpheum Theatre (Granville at Smithe Street) downtown. Under the direction of Bramwell Tovey, the symphonys featured programs broadly encompass classical, light classical, pops, and children's works. Most of the concerts cluster around weekends (Fri-Mon) and include family-oriented matinees. (Sept-June)

**Vancouver Trolley Company Ltd.** *875 Terminal Ave, Vancouver. Phone 604/801-5515. www.vancouvertrolley.com.* Narrated trolley tours to top attractions and neighborhoods throughout the city. Get on and off at designated stops throughout the day. **$$$$**

**Vancouver Whitecaps.** *Kingsway and Boundary Rd, Burnaby (V3J 1A1). Phone 604/669-9283. www.whitecapssoccer.com.* Named for the whitecaps on the surrounding waters and mountains, the men's professional soccer team competes in the United Soccer League's A-League. In suburban Burnaby, Swangard Stadium entertains up to 6,500 fans with both on-field activity and a pine-forested backdrop. A Whitecaps-affiliated womens team, The Breakers, plays here in the USLs W-League. (May-Aug) **$$$$**

**VanDusen Botanical Garden.** *5251 Oak St, Vancouver. Phone 604/878-9274. www.vandusengarden.org.* Approximately 55 acres (22 hectares) of flowers and exotic plants. Seasonal displays, mountain views, restaurant. (Daily; closed Dec 25) **$$$**

**Vogue Theatre.** *918 Granville St, Vancouver (V6Z 1L2). Phone 604/331-7900. www.voguetheatre.com.* Following the soaring neon marquee to the well-preserved 1941 Art Deco Vogue Theatre. Updated sound and light systems enable the vintage stage to produce 1,200-seat shows that range from local rockers to percussion groups and stand-up comedy reviews. Though largely a concert venue, the Vogue also screens movies throughout the Vancouver International Film Festival held each Sept.

**Whale-watching tours.** *950 Wharf St, Victoria.* Whale-watching boats line both the Wharf St waterfront and Inner Harbour. Half-day tours display marine life, including orcas, sea lions, seals, and porpoises. Victoria Marine Adventures (phone 250/995-2211) and Prince of Whales (phone 250/383-4884) are two of the finer tour companies.

**Windsure Windsurfing School.** *1300 Discovery St, Vancouver (V6R 4L9). Phone 604/224-0615. www.windsure.com.* Head to Jericho Beach to catch the offshore drafts in English Bay aboard a windsurfer. Windsure Windsurfing School, operating out of the Jericho Sailing Center, rents both boards and wetsuits, including rigs suitable for children. Just starting out? Two-hour introductory group lessons go for $39, and three-hour semi-private tutorials (meaning no more than three students per teacher) cost $99. (May-Labor Day, 9 am-8 pm)

**The Yale Hotel.** *1300 Granville St, Vancouver. Phone 604/681-9253. www.theyale.ca.* Built in 1889 as a hotel for rough-and-tumble miners, fishermen, and loggers, The Yale, née The Colonial, prizes it's working-class roots and makes a fitting home for the city's best blues club. The mansard-roofed Yale stages nightly shows from a pool of local talent as well as touring acts. Past headliners include John Lee Hooker, Clarence "Gatemouth" Brown, Jeff Healey, and Jim Byrnes. (Nightly)

**Yaletown.** *Hamilton St, Vancouver. From False Creek to Burrard Inlet on the NW and Georgia St on the NE.* A former rail yard, Yaletown once held the world record for the most bars per acre. With time and prosperity, the warehouse district is now one of Vancouver's hippest, drawing urban dwellers with an arty bent. The former loading docks along Hamilton and Mainland teem with cafés disgorging umbrella-shaded tables onto concrete terraces. Tucked in between are a slew of shops, galleries, and clothiers.

## Special Events

**Alcan International Dragon Boat Festival.** *401-788 Beatty St,Festival Office, Vancouver (V6B 1A2). Phone 604/688-2382.* Vancouver's considerable Asian community imports an eastern rite in dragon boat racing, the traditional Chinese rain ceremony that is equal parts pageant and competition. But dont tell that to the 100 or so crews that enter the False Creek event paddling boats with dragon figureheads representing the Asian water deity. Bring loads of film to the colorful event, which, in addition to racing, features a Taoist blessing of the fleet and, on land, Asian entertainment, crafts, and food. Mid-June. **FREE**

**Bard on the Beach Shakespeare Festival.** *Vanier Park,Whyte Ave, Vancouver (V6J 3J9). Phone 604/739-0559. www.bardonthebeach.org.* The works of Shakespeare take the outdoor stage at Vanier Park's permanent seasonal theater, Bard on the Beach. Elizabethan-style tents cover the audience and actors, who play against an open backdrop of BC coastal landscape. The company mounts approximately three plays each summer, performed in repertory with several shows slated daily on two stages. June-Sept. **$$$$**

**Caribbean Days Festival.** *Waterfront Park, North Vancouver. Take the Seabus from Canada Place to Lonsdale Quay, which borders Waterfront Park. Phone 604/515-2400. www.caribbeandaysfestival.com.* The Trinidad and Tobago Cultural Society of BC throws the province's biggest island jump-up at this North Vancouver park. Its highlight parade kicks off Saturday morning with a slow, carnival-like promenade of bands and costumes, drawing crowds of pan-Caribbean expats. Head to the park festival grounds for calypso, steel drum, soca, and reggae music as well as island food and crafts. Late July. **FREE**

**Christmas events.** *Vancouver Tourism Infocenter,200 Burrard St, Vancouver. Phone 604/683-2000.* Christmas

Carol Ship and lighted ship parade; New Year's Day Polar Bear swim.

**HSBC Powersmart Celebration of Light.** *English Bay, Vancouver. Phone 604/641-1193. www.celebration-of-light.com.* On four nights spread over two weeks, pyrotechnic fans ooh and ah as the world's best fireworks designers compete for bragging rights in Vancouver's Celebration of Light. Teams from Italy, Canada, and Spain have competed on the basis of originality, rhythm, musical synchronization, and color, leading up to the grand finale night on which all competitors restage their shows. For best viewing, park your beach towel along English Bay at Stanley or Vanier parks, Kitsilano or Jericho beaches. Come prepared for very large crowds, especially for the finale. Late July-early Aug. **FREE**

**Hyack Festival.** *1st and 3rd aves, New Westminster. 12 miles (19 kilometers) S via Hwy 1A. Phone 604/522-6894. www.hyack.bc.ca.* Commemorates the birthday of Queen Victoria, held yearly since 1871; 21-gun salute; band concerts, parade, carnival, sports events. Ten days in mid-May.

**International Bathtub Race.** *Front St and Terminal Ave, Nanaimo.. Phone toll-free 800/663-7337.* Thirty-four-mile (55-kilometers) race from Nanaimo to Vancouver. Third or fourth Sun in July.

**Pacific National Exhibition Annual Fair.** *Exhibition Park, 2901 E Hastings St, Vancouver. — 604/253-2311. www.pne.bc.ca.* Second-largest fair in Canada. Hundreds of free exhibits, major theme event, concerts, thrill shows, world championship timber show; petting zoo, thoroughbred horse racing, commercial exhibits, roller coaster, agricultural shows, horse shows, livestock competitions, horticultural exhibits. Usually mid-Aug-early Sept.

**Theatre Under the Stars.** *Stanley Park, Malkin Bowl,2099 Beach Ave, Vancouver (V6G 3E2). Phone 604/687-0174.* Theatre Under the Stars puts the outdoors in outdoor theater. Towering forests of Douglas fir surround the 1,200-seat open-air Malkin Bowl theater in Stanley Park, binding art and nature in nightly performances. The short summer season generally presents two shows in every-other-night rotation, an annual repertory that hews to comedies and musicals. July-Aug.

**Vancouver Fringe Festival.** *1402 Anderson St, Vancouver (V6H 3R6). Phone 604/257-0350. www.vancouver-fringe.com.* From comedies to musical acts to full-on drama, Vancouver Fringe trains the spotlight on fledgling theater troupes who come from around the globe to participate in the 11-day annual arts festival. Modeled on the oft-copied fringe festival in Edinburgh, Scotland, the Canadian organization mounts about 100 productions in a variety of venues—theaters, yes, but also garages and even the Aquabus. Early-mid-Sept. **$$$$**

**Vancouver International Children's Festival.** *Vanier Park,1100 Chestnut St, Vancouver (V6J 3J9). Phone 604/708-5655. www.vancouverchildren'sfestival.com.* Although the 7-day slate of events programmed by the annual Children's Festival aims at school group audiences, it's talent warrants broader attention. In a program ranging from music to theater, the performance lineup for young audiences might include Japanese dancers, Australias teen troupe Flying Fruit Fly Circus, Aboriginal storytellers, and clown companies. Aside from showtime, the festival engages kids with more than two dozen hands-on arts activities. Mid-May. **$$$$**

**Vancouver International Jazz Festival.** *316 W 6th Ave,Coastal Jazz and Blues Society, Vancouver (V5Y 1K9). Phone 604/872-5200. www.jazzvancouver.com.* The Coastal Jazz and Blues Society runs this annual jazz festival over a ten-day span in several venues, climaxing in the headlining stage at the Orpheum Theatre. Past performers range from greats like Dizzy Gillespie to New Age interpreters like Pat Metheny to crooners such as Diana Krall. In addition to the main event, CJBS also sponsors 40 concerts between September and May each year (its 24-hour jazz hotline delivers a useful what's-on-now club report year-round). June. **$$$$**

## Limited-Service Hotels

**★ ★ BEST WESTERN SANDS.** *1755 Davie St, Vancouver (Z6G 1W5). Phone 604/682-1831; toll-free 800/663-9400; fax 604/682-3546. www.bestwestern.com.* 121 rooms, 5 story. Pets accepted; fee. Check-in 4 pm, check-out noon. Restaurant, bar. Fitness room. Beach. **$$**

**★ ★ DELTA TOWN AND COUNTRY INN.** *6005 Hwy 17 at Hwy 99, Delta (V4K 5B8). Phone 604/946-4404; fax 604/946-5916. www.deltainn.com.* 48 rooms, 2 story. Check-out 11 am. Restaurant. Fitness room. Tennis. **$**

★ ★ **GOLDEN TULIP GEORGIAN COURT HOTEL.** *773 Beatty St, Vancouver (V6B 2M4). Phone 604/682-5555; toll-free 800/663-1155; fax 604/682-8830. www.georgiancourt.com.* This hotel's handsome exterior, with it's overhead terraced brick garden boxes, leads guests into a lobby full of old-world charm. The grandfather clock is just one of several antique pieces amid the rich mahogany furnishings. Just steps away from many downtown attractions and dining options, the Georgian Court offers it's own appealing restaurants, including the well-known William Tell, open for dinner each evening.180 rooms, 12 story. Pets accepted; fee. Check-in 3 pm, check-out 1 pm. High-speed Internet access. Restaurant, bar. Fitness room. Whirlpool. **$$**

★ ★ **HAMPTON INN & SUITES.** *111 Robson St, Vancouver (V6B 2A8). Phone 604/602-1008; toll-free 877/602-1008; fax 604/602-1007. www.hamptoninnvancouver.com.* This high rise hotel is more upscale than a typical Hampton Inn & Suites. The décor is contemporary with sage spreads, patterned carpet, blond wood, and kitchenettes in the suites and microwaves and refrigerators in the regular rooms. It's located across the street from BC Place Stadium and GM Place in the theatre district of downtown. 132 rooms. Check-in 3 pm, check-out 11 am. High-speed Internet access. Restaurant, bar. Children's activity center. Fitness room. Whirlpool. **$$**

★ **HAMPTON INN VANCOUVER AIRPORT.** *8811 Bridgeport Rd, Richmond (V6X 1R9). Phone 104/232-5505; toll-free 800/426-7866; fax 604/232-5508. www.hamptoninn.com.* 111 rooms, 5 story. Complimentary continental breakfast. Check-in 3 pm, check-out noon. Fitness room. Golf. Business center. **$**

## Full-Service Hotels

★ ★ **BEST WESTERN DOWNTOWN VANCOUVER.** *718 Drake St at Granville, Vancouver (V6Z 2W6). Phone 604/669-9888; toll-free 800/780-7234; fax 604/669-3440.* A complimentary shuttle to the cruise ship terminal and BC Place Stadium is offered by this contemporary downtown property. Other services and amenities include guest laundry facilities, a fitness center with rooftop panoramic views of False Creek and English Bay, and indoor ping pong. 143 rooms. Pets accepted; fee. Check-in 3 pm, check-out 11 am. High-speed Internet access. Restaurant, bar. Children's activity center. Fitness room. Whirlpool. Business center. **$$**

★ ★ ★ **COAST PLAZA SUITE HOTEL.** *1763 Comox St, Vancouver (V6G 1P6). Phone 604/688-7711; toll-free 800/663-1144; fax 604/688-5934. www.coasthotels.com.* This tower hotel is located just blocks from Stanley Park in Vancouver's West End. It overlooks English Bay and is near other major attractions in the Vancouver area. Because of the range of amenities offered here, such as a fitness center, indoor pool, business center, Internet access, restaurants, and a bar, this hotel is a nice choice for the business or leisure traveler. The hotel also offers many suites with kitchenettes, and there is a mall on the lower floors of the building. 269 rooms, 35 story. Pets accepted; fee. Check-in 3 pm, check-out noon. High-speed Internet access, wireless Internet access. Two restaurants, bar. Fitness room, fitness classes available. Indoor pool. Business center. **$$$**

★ ★ **DAYS INN VANCOUVER DOWNTOWN.** *921 W Pender St, Vancouver (V6C 1M2). Phone 604/681-4335; fax 604/681-7808. www.daysinnvancouver.com.* The building this property is located in has been continuously operating as a hotel since 1918, and the Irish pub downstairs has been around since 1898—with the original chandeliers and wood work to prove it. The hotel is located in Vancouver's financial district and is just blocks from Canada Place and the cruise ship terminals (hotel offers a complimentary shuttle). The rooms are decorated in bright colors, with crown molding, refrigerators, safes, and umbrellas. 85 rooms. Check-in 3 pm, check-out 11 am. High-speed Internet access. Restaurant, Two bars. Business center. **$$**

★ ★ ★ **DELTA VANCOUVER SUITES.** *550 W Hastings St, Vancouver (V6B 1L6). Phone 877/814-7706; toll-free 888/663-8811; fax 604/605-8881. www.deltahotels.com.* 225 rooms, 22 story, all suites. Pets accepted. Check-in 3 pm, check-out noon. High-speed Internet access. Restaurant, bar. Fitness room, spa. Indoor pool, whirlpool. Business center. **$$$**

★ ★ ★ **THE FAIRMONT HOTEL VANCOUVER.** *900 W Georgia St, Vancouver (V6C 2W6). Phone 604/684-3131; toll-free 800/441-1414; fax 604/662-1929. www.fairmont.com.* The Fairmont Hotel echoes the vibrancy of it's home city. This gracious hotel offers guests the perfect blend of history and cosmopolitan panache. Grand and inviting, it has been a preeminent destination since 1939, when it opened to celebrate the royal visit of King George VI and Queen Elizabeth. The guest rooms employ rich jewel tones and sumptuous fabrics to create a wonderful English castle ambience. The décor gives a nod to the past, but the dining and entertainment venues are cutting edge and are hotspots on the local scene. Business and fitness centers keep guests focused on goals, while world-renowned boutiques, including Louis Vuitton and St. John, tempt shoppers.556 rooms, 14 story. Pets accepted; fee. Check-in 3 pm, check-out 11 am. High-speed Internet access. Restaurant, bar. Fitness room. Indoor pool, children's pool, whirlpool. Business center. **$$**

**★ ★ ★ THE FAIRMONT VANCOUVER AIRPORT.** *3111 Grant McConachie Way, Vancouver (V7B 1X9). Phone 604/207-5200; toll-free 800/676-8922; fax 604/248-3219. www.fairmont.com.* It doesn't get much more convenient than The Fairmont Vancouver Airport. Located right inside this international gateway, the stylish hotel is easily accessed by a quick escalator ride. Popular with those making connections, this hotel provides a gracious home-away-from-home for those visitors exploring Vancouver's cultural and natural treasures. The rooms and suites are the very definition of modern sophistication with elegant furnishings and thoughtful amenities. Airport dining is elevated to new levels at the Globe@YVR, where diners marvel at the soaring jets while enjoying cosmopolitan cuisine, and the Jetside Bar makes delayed departures seem like a godsend.392 rooms, 14 story. Pets accepted, some restrictions; fee. Check-in 3 pm, check-out noon. High-speed Internet access. Restaurant, bar. Fitness room, spa. Indoor pool, children's pool, whirlpool. Airport transportation available. Business center. **$$$**

**★ ★ ★ THE FAIRMONT WATERFRONT.** *900 Canada Way, Vancouver (V6C 3L5). Phone 604/691-1991; toll-free 800/441-1414; fax 604/691-1828. www.fairmont.com.* Guests stay at The Fairmont Waterfront for it's gracious accommodations, central location, and complete range of services, but they keep returning for it's views. This contemporary glass tower showcases the finest view in all of Vancouver. From it's superior harborfront location, this hotel gives guests a birds eye view of the city's renowned sparkling waters and majestic, misty mountains. The modern exterior belies it's warm interiors, where rooms and suites are outfitted with all the comforts of home. Room service is available throughout the day for those who prefer to remain in their elegant accommodations, while the Herons Restaurant and Lounge serves up more of the hotels signature views along with it's regionally influenced menu.489 rooms, 23 story. Pets accepted; fee. Check-in 4 pm, check-out noon. High-speed Internet access. Restaurant, bar. Fitness room, fitness classes available. Outdoor pool, whirlpool. Business center. **$$$**

**★ ★ ★ ★ FOUR SEASONS HOTEL VANCOUVER.** *791 W Georgia St, Vancouver (V6C 2T4). Phone 604/689-9333; toll-free 800/819-5053; fax 604/684-4555. www.fourseasons.com.* Impeccable service and an ideal location make the Four Seasons Hotel a natural choice in Vancouver. The city's vibrant arts and entertainment area is just a short walk from this hotel, situated above the shops of the Pacific Centre. The guest rooms are comfortably elegant. Moods are instantly brightened in the accommodations, where plaid and floral fabrics add a cheery feel. Unencumbered views of the city, mountains, and harbor delight visitors. Fitness and business centers assist travelers with their needs, and the indoor/outdoor pool is an urban oasis with it's flower-filled outdoor terrace. The signature restaurant, Chartwell, looked to Winston Churchill's favorite country home for it's design influences, and the walnut-paneled walls, clubby furnishings, and parquet floors capture that spirit perfectly. Blooming plants and large windows impart a greenhouse atmosphere at the Garden Terrace, where patrons enjoy informal dining. 376 rooms, 28 story. Pets accepted, some restrictions. Check-in 3 pm, check-out noon. High-speed Internet access. Two restaurants, bar. Fitness room, fitness classes available. Indoor pool, outdoor pool, whirlpool. Business center. **$$$**

**★ ★ ★ HILTON VANCOUVER METROTOWN.** *6083 McKay Ave, Burnaby (V5H 2W7). Phone 604/438-1200; toll-free 800/445-8667; fax 604/431-7782. www.hiltonvancouver.com.* The Hilton Vancouver Metrotown is the perfect property for a business or leisure traveler. It's located in suburban Burnaby, a 20-minute drive from downtown and the airport, in the Metrotown Shopping Mall complex. A skytrain light rail station is across the street and offers high-speed travel to downtown. After a busy day, head to the hotel's small outdoor area with an outdoor lap pool, children's pool, whirlpool, and sundeck for some relaxation. 283 rooms, 32 story. Pets accepted; fee. Check-in 4 pm, check-out noon. High-speed Internet

access. Restaurant, bar. Fitness room, spa. Outdoor pool, children's pool, whirlpool. Business center. **$$**

**★ ★ ★ HYATT REGENCY VANCOUVER.** *655 Burrard St, Vancouver (V6C 2R7). Phone 604/683-1234; toll-free 800/233-1234; fax 604/689-3707. www.vancouver.hyatt.com.* This hotel is located within the Royal Centre shopping complex, which also includes two levels of shops, restaurants, and a Skytrain station. It is near Pacific Centre, Robson Street, theaters, Granville Island, and is across the street from the cathedral. After checking in, take a dip in the indoor pool, work out in the fitness room, or get a bite to eat in one of the three restaurants. Then later, relax in one of the attractive guest rooms, which all feature pillow-top mattresses and flat-screen televisions. 644 rooms, 34 story. Check-in 4 pm, check-out noon. High-speed Internet access. Three restaurants, two bars. Fitness room. Indoor pool, whirlpool. Business center. **$$**

**★ ★ ★ LE SOLEIL HOTEL AND SUITES.** *567 Hornby St, Vancouver (V6C 2E8). Phone 604/632-3000; toll-free 877/632-3030; fax 604/632-3001. www.hotellesoleil.com.* In the heart of the city's financial and business districts sits this charming boutique hotel. The stunning lobby boasts 30-foot gilded ceilings, crystal chandeliers, and a Louis XVI-style collection of imported Italian furniture. Complimentary bottled water and fruit upon arrival are welcome surprises, and the property's restaurant, a cool hotspot, offers an eclectic Asian-Mediterranean cuisine. 119 rooms. Pets accepted; fee. Check-in 4 pm, check-out noon. High-speed Internet access. Restaurant, bar. Business center. **$$**

**★ ★ ★ METROPOLITAN HOTEL VANCOUVER.** *645 Howe St, Vancouver (V6C 2Y9). Phone 604/687-1122; toll-free 800/667-2300; fax 604/643-7267. www.metropolitan.com.* The Metropolitan Hotel Vancouver is the hotel of choice for executives, VIPs, and technology aficionados. This contemporary hotel makes it easy to stay in touch, with dual-line telephones and broadband Internet connections in all accommodations, even in public spaces. Contemporary artwork adorns the walls of the guest rooms. Light woods and neutral colors result in a soothing ambience in the private spaces, where luxurious bed linens ensure a good nights sleep. Guests enjoy views of this beautiful city from the privacy of their rooms, and many of the suites feature balconies. A fitness center, indoor pool, and squash court are available, and the hotels convenient location makes it popular with joggers and walkers who want to experience the city by foot. Diva at the Met earns bravos from diners who feast on sensational regional specialties. 197 rooms, 18 story. Pets accepted. Check-in 3 pm, check-out noon. High-speed Internet access. Restaurant, bar. Fitness room. Indoor pool, whirlpool. Airport transportation available. Business center. **$$$**

**★ ★ ★ OPUS HOTEL.** *322 Davie St, Vancouver (V6B 5Z6). Phone 604/642-6787; toll-free 866/642-6787; fax 604/642-6780.*96 rooms. Pets accepted. Check-in 3 pm, check-out noon. Restaurant, bar. Fitness room. Business center. **$**

**★ ★ ★ PACIFIC PALISADES HOTEL.** *1277 Robson St, Vancouver (V6E 1C4). Phone 604/688-0461; toll-free 800/663-1815; fax 604/688-4374. www.pacificpalisadeshotel.com.* So many attractions in the lobby alone! Look up in wonder at the striking Murano chandelier and gaze in awe at the stainless-steel floating fireplace. Relax in the courtyard that connects the two towers, or while away some time in the Art + Soul Gallery. This hotel underwent a total makeover in 2001 and is now among the trendiest locations on the very hip Robson Street with a lively, citrus-colored motif. Roomy guest accommodations owe their largesse to the fact that the building started life as an apartment complex. Fitness-minded guests enjoy complimentary yoga kits and a designated yoga channel on the TV; personal trainers are available for private yoga and Pilates sessions. Pets are welcomed here (the hotel even donates part of the pet deposit to the local Society for the Prevention of Cruelty to Animals), and dogs rate a special goodie bag. 233 rooms, 23 story. Pets accepted. Check-in 3 pm, check-out noon. High-speed Internet access, wireless Internet access. Restaurant, bar. Fitness room, fitness classes available, spa. Indoor pool, whirlpool. Business center. **$$$**

**★ ★ ★ PAN PACIFIC VANCOUVER.** *300-999 Canada Pl, Vancouver (V6C 3B5). Phone 604/662-8111; toll-free 800/937-1515; fax 604/685-8690. www.panpacific.com.* Awe-inspiring views take center stage at Vancouver's Pan Pacific Hotel, located on the waterfront. This contemporary hotel enjoys a serene setting on the harbour, yet is only minutes from the alluring shopping of Robson Street. The guest rooms are a testament to subtle luxury, with clean lines and neutral tones. Large windows look out over unobstructed, picture-perfect views of the mountains and sea, and many accommodations include private balconies for further enjoyment. Whether taking advantage of the fitness center or relaxing in the privacy of their accommodations, guests reap the rewards of the hotels commitment to the latest technology. Diners traverse the world in the four distinctive restaurants, where sushi, Italian, and other international dishes tantalize taste buds. 504 rooms, 23 story. Pets accepted, some restrictions; fee. Check-in 4 pm, check-out noon. High-speed Internet access, wireless Internet access. Three restaurants, bar. Fitness room, spa. Outdoor pool, whirlpool. Business center. **$$$**

**★ ★ ★ RENAISSANCE VANCOUVER HARBOURSIDE HOTEL.** *1133 W Hastings, Vancouver (V6E 3T3). Phone 604/689-9211; toll-free 800/905-8582; fax 604/689-4358. www.renaissancehotel.com.* This contemporary hotel, located on the waterfront overlooking Vancouver Harbor, Burrard Inlet, and the North Shore Mountains, is within easy walking distance to Robson Street and the Pacific Centre shopping area. The guest rooms are decorated with blue and yellow soft goods, a work desk, two comfortable armchairs, heated floors in the bathrooms, and beautiful mountain and Inlet views. Vistas, the revolving, twentieth-floor restaurant, is a great place to take in a delicious meal and a panoramic view. 437 rooms, 19 story. Pets accepted; fee. Check-in 3 pm, check-out noon. High-speed Internet access. Two restaurants, bar. Children's activity center. Fitness room. Indoor pool, whirlpool. Business center. **$$**

**★ ★ SHERATON GUILDFORD HOTEL.** *15269 104th Ave, Surrey (V3R 1N5). Phone 604/582-9288; fax 604/582-9712. www.sheraton.com.* 278 rooms, 18 story. Check-out noon. Restaurant. Fitness room. Business center. **$**

**★ ★ ★ ★ THE SUTTON PLACE HOTEL - VANCOUVER.** *845 Burrard St, Vancouver (V6Z 2K6). Phone 604/682-5511; toll-free 866/378-8866; fax 604/682-5513. www.suttonplace.com.* The Sutton Place Hotel is a little slice of Europe transplanted to Vancouver's city center. Located one block from Robson Conference Center and only a short distance from the energetic cultural scene, this hotel is ideal for business travelers or vacationers. Spacious and elegant, the guest rooms reflect the grace of the continent with unique decorative accents and traditional furnishings, yet all modern amenities are included to maximize guests comfort. This hotel epitomizes full service, from the intuitive personal attention to the complete business and fitness centers. A European-style spa features wonderful options, including the popular La Stone therapy. Patrons sink into the large club chairs and relax by the fire at the English-style Gerard Lounge, while diners relish French classics in the warm setting of Fleuri. 397 rooms, 21 story. Pets accepted, some restrictions; fee. Check-in 3 pm, check-out noon. High-speed Internet access. Two restaurants, bar. Fitness room, fitness classes available, spa. Indoor pool, whirlpool. Business center. **$$$**

**★ ★ ★ WEDGEWOOD HOTEL.** *845 Hornby St, Vancouver (V6Z 1V1). Phone 604/689-7777; toll-free 800/663-0666; fax 604/608-5348. ww.wedgewoodhotel.com.* Tradition abounds at this independent boutique hotel. The public areas are richly furnished and appointed with original artwork, handsome antiques, and fresh flower arrangements. The lobby boasts a large fireplace. Renovations completed in 2003 gave each bathroom separate shower and soaking-tub areas and added a small but full-service spa and an up-to-date business center. Bachus, the on-site restaurant, offers a full menu plus sumptuous weekend brunch menus and traditional high tea served from 2-4 pm daily. 83 rooms, 14 story. Check-in 3 pm, check-out noon. High-speed Internet access. Restaurant, bar. Fitness room, spa. Business center. **$$$**

**★ ★ ★ THE WESTIN GRAND.** *433 Robson St, Vancouver (V6B 6L9). Phone 604/602-1999; toll-free 888/680-9393; fax 604/647-2502. www.westingrand-vancouver.com.* All of Vancouver is within reach of the Westin Grand. This high-rise tower is perfectly located for business travelers conducting meetings or leisure visitors absorbing the local culture. Sleek and stylish, this property introduces visitors to the hip side of this western Canadian city. The accommodations define city chic with modern, polished-wood furnishings and floor-to-ceiling windows with skyline vistas. Guests never leave behind the comforts of home here, where all rooms feature well-stocked kitchenettes. The hotel caters to the sophisticated, and many services, including the fitness center, are offered 24 hours daily. Diners feast on Pacific Rim dishes at the Aria Restaurant & Lounge (see also) and dance the night away at the fashionable Club Voda. 207 rooms, 31 story. Pets accepted; fee. Check-in 4 pm, check-out noon. High-speed Internet access, wireless Internet access.

Restaurant, bar. Fitness room. Outdoor pool, whirlpool. Business center. **$$**

## Full-Service Resort

**★ ★ RAMADA PLAZA VANCOUVER AIRPORT CONFERENCE RESORT.** *10251 St. Edwards Dr, Richmond (V6X 2M9). Phone 000/000-0000; fax 000/000-0000.*438 rooms, 21 story. Pets accepted, some restrictions; fee. Check-out noon. Restaurant, bar. Children's activity center. Fitness room. Indoor pool, two outdoor pools, whirlpool. Tennis. Business center. **$$**

## Full-Service Inn

**★ ★ ★ RIVER RUN COTTAGES.** *4551 River Rd W, Ladner (V4K 1R9). Phone 604/946-7778; fax 604/940-1970. www.riverruncottages.com.* Kayaking, canoeing, and rowboats are available for guests to venture out to watch the eagles, seals, otters, and beavers in their natural environment. Guests can pack a picnic and enjoy a romantic getaway on No Name Island. 4 rooms, 1 story. Pets accepted; fee. Complimentary full breakfast. Check-in 4 pm. Check-out noon. **$**

## Specialty Lodgings

**BARCLAY HOUSE IN THE WEST END.** *1351 Barclay St, Vancouver (V6E 1H6). Phone 604/605-1351; toll-free 800/971-1351; fax 604/605-1382. www.barclay-house.com.* Guests staying in this restored 1904 late Victorian home sleep in large two-room suites complete with TV/VCRs and CD players. Videos and classical music CDs are on hand, as are four soaking tubs, hot three-course breakfasts, and private bathrooms. Vancouver attractions such as Stanley Park, Gastown, and Granville are close by. 5 rooms. Children over 12 only. Complimentary full breakfast. Check-in noon-3 pm, check-out 11 am. High-speed Internet access, wireless Internet access. **$$**

**★ ★ ★ ENGLISH BAY INN.** *1968 Comox St, Vancouver (V6G 1R4). Phone 604/683-8002; toll-free 866/683-8002; fax 604/683-8069. www.englishbayinn.com.* This relaxing, 20th-century Tudor-style escape is a short walk from the West End's Stanley Park, shops and restaurants on Denman Street, and the sea. All guest rooms feature Ralph Lauren linens, featherbeds, antiques, reproductions, and some rooms have fireplaces. After settling in, unwind with an afternoon sherry, visit the library for a great read, or take some time to lounge in the rear garden. 5 rooms. Complimentary full breakfast. Check-in 1 pm, check-out 11 am. **$$**

**O CANADA HOUSE.** *1114 Barclay St, Vancouver (V6E 1H1). Phone 604/688-0555; toll-free 877/688-1114; fax 604/488-0556. www.ocanadahouse.com.* Housed in a historic home built in 1897, this bed-and-breakfast gives guests personalized service with the convenience of a location close to attractions such as Stanley Park, Granville Island, and Gastown. This home is where owner Ewing Buchan and his brother penned the Canadian anthem "O Canada" in 1909. The wraparound porch and English garden give guests plenty of space to unwind outdoors. Inside, guests are treated to a three-course daily breakfast and have access to a 24-hour stocked pantry. Evening sherry in the front parlor and a video library and book collection make guests feel at home.7 rooms. Children over 11 only. Complimentary full breakfast. Check-out 11 am. Wireless Internet access. **$$**

**WEST END GUEST HOUSE.** *1362 Haro St, Vancouver (V6E 1G2). Phone 604/681-2889; toll-free 888/546-3327; fax 604/688-8812.westendguesthouse.com.* This beautifully restored 1906 late Victorian residence, located in the heart of downtown in a quiet neighborhood, is one block from trendy Robson Street and is within walking distance of Stanley Park, Canada Place, and other city centre sites. The pink with white trim property is decorated with period furnishings and equipped with modern conveniences such as feather mattresses, VCRs/TVs, and phones. The property also offers bicycles, a library, afternoon sherry, and a rear deck, patio, and porch for lounging.8 rooms, 3 story. Children over 11 years only. Complimentary full breakfast. Check-in 3 pm, check-out 11 am. **$$**

## Restaurants

**★ ★ AQUA RIVA.** *200 Granville St, Vancouver (V6C 1S4). Phone 604/683-5599; fax 604/680-7551. www.aquariva.com.* Located on Vancouver's waterfront, next to Canada Place and the cruise ship terminal, Aqua Riva affords diners an excellent water and mountain view. To get to the tables, diners first pass through the large display kitchen where the chef prepares an eclectic Pacific Northwest menu. The dining room features a large bar and lounge, floor-to-ceiling windows, and a wood grill. Don't miss this fun, upbeat restaurant. International menu. Lunch, dinner, Sun brunch. Closed Dec 24-25. Bar. Business casual attire. Reservations recommended. **$$$**

★ ★ ★ **BACCHUS.** *845 Hornby St, Vancouver (V6Z 1V1). Phone 604/608-5319; toll-free 800/663-0666; fax 604/608-5348. wedgewoodhotel.com.* This luxurious restaurant, tucked inside the Wedgewood Hotel, is adorned with richly upholstered furniture, light fixtures from Venice, and of course, a large canvas depicting Bacchus, Greek god of wine and revelry. French menu. Breakfast, lunch, dinner, late-night, brunch. Bar. Children's menu. Business casual attire. Reservations recommended. Valet parking. **$$$**

★ ★ ★ **THE BEACH HOUSE.** *150 25th St, West Vancouver (V7B 4H8). Phone 604/922-1414; fax 604/922-7971. www.atthebeachhouse.com.* Originally built in 1912, this multilevel, waterfront restaurant affords all diners beautiful views of Burrard Inlet. Pacific Northwest menu. Lunch, dinner, Sun brunch. Closed Dec 25. Bar. Business casual attire. Reservations recommended. Outdoor seating. **$$$**

★ ★ ★ ★ **BISHOP'S.** *2183 W 4th Ave, Vancouver (V6K 1N7). Phone 604/738-2025; fax 604/738-4622. www.bishopsonline.com.* If your radar is set for one of the most coveted tables in Vancouver, you will find it at Bishop's. Intimate, modern, and airy, with a lofty, homelike yet upscale feel, this chic duplex restaurant is known for West Coast continental cuisine—a menu that emphasizes seasonal, organic produce and British Columbia seafood. The kitchen serves high art in the form of food. It isn't uncommon to spy celebrities and VIPs nibbling on these delicious culinary wares. For those who like to sample lots of different wines with dinner, Bishop's offers a nice selection of wines by the glass and an outstanding range of wines by the half-bottle. In addition to being a visionary chef, owner John Bishop is a gracious host, which makes Bishops a hot spot, so call ahead to secure your very own coveted table. International menu. Dinner. Closed Dec 24-26; also first week in Jan. Bar. Business casual attire. Reservations recommended. Outdoor seating. **$$$**

★ ★ ★ **C RESTAURANT.** *1600 Howe St, Vancouver (V6O 2L9). Phone 604/681-1164; fax 604/605-8263. www.crestaurant.com.* Located at the foot of Howe Street, along the boardwalk running under the Granville Building and overlooking the marina sits this contemporary seafood house. Its décor features floor-to-ceiling windows, black-and-white tile and hardwood floors, and a display kitchen so you can watch the kitchen prepare your meal. C's offers a raw bar, an enclosed patio area, and more than 900 wines to choose from to complement your dinner. Seafood menu. Lunch, dinner. Closed Dec 25-26. Bar. Children's menu. Business casual attire. Reservations recommended. Valet parking. Outdoor seating. **$$$**

★ ★ **CAFÉE DE PARIS.** *761 Denman St, Vancouver (V6G 2L6). Phone 604/687-1418; fax 604/464-3359.* Café de Paris is the perfect choice for a wonderful gourmet meal in an authentic French bistro atmosphere. Located in the popular West End area of Vancouver, this charming restaurant is decorated with window awnings, lace curtains, copper cookware displays, antique plates, French posters and photos, and a traditional mahogany bar. The three-course table d'hote meal (menu changes daily) is a great bargain. French bistro menu. Lunch, dinner. Closed Dec 25. Bar. Casual attire. Reservations recommended. **$$$**

★ ★ **CANNERY.** *2205 Commissioner St, Vancouver (V5L 1A4). Phone 604/254-9606; toll-free 877/254-9606; fax 604/254-1820. www.cannerseafood.com.* Although this seafood restaurant is isolated and somewhat difficult to find (can be reached only through the Clark Drive and McGill Street gates on Port Vancouver), it is well worth the effort. Once you find it, you'll taste why this is an award-winning restaurant. The nautical décor includes nets, rope ladders, crab trappers, anchors, and a small ship's boiler converted to a fireplace. There is also a dock for diners who choose to travel by boat. Seafood menu. Lunch, dinner. Closed Dec 24-26. Bar. Children's menu. Children's menu. Casual attire. Reservations recommended. **$$$**

★ ★ ★ **CINCIN RISTORANTE.** *1154 Robson St, Vancouver (V6E 1V5). Phone 604/688-7338; fax 604/688-7339. www.cincin.net.* Located upstairs in a two-story building on trendy Robson Street, this Italian dining room has a mellow Tuscan atmosphere and décor. The room is decorated with Italian sculptures, attractive artwork, metal chandeliers, and leather furniture. An arched doorway leads to the heated balcony, and a wood-fired, brick oven emits a wonderful aroma throughout the restaurant. The extesive wine list offers the perfect complement to any meal. Italian menu. Lunch, dinner, late-night. Closed Jan 1, Dec 25. Bar. Business casual attire. Reservations recommended. Outdoor seating. **$$$**

★ ★ **CLOUD 9.** *1400 Robson St, Vancouver (V6G 1B9). Phone 604/687-0511; toll-free 800/830-6144; fax 604/687-7267. www.cloud9restaurant.ca.* Catch

360-degree views of Vancouver from this revolving steak and seafood restaurant. Located on popular Robson Street, the property is located atop the Empire Landmark Hotel. Cloud 9 completes a full revolution every 1 hour and 25 minutes, giving diners a remarkable view—a piano player adds to the atmosphere on Friday and Saturday nights. Seafood, steak menu. Dinner. Bar. Children's menu. Business casual attire. Reservations recommended. **$$$**

**★ ★ DELILAH'S.** *1789 Comox St, Vancouver (V6G 1P5). Phone 604/687-3424. www.delilahs.ca.* Continental, tapas menu. Dinner. Closed Dec 24-26. Bar. Business casual attire. Reservations recommended. **$$$**

**★ ★ DOCKSIDE BREWING COMPANY.** *1253 Johnston St, Vancouver (V6H 3R9). Phone 604/685-7070; fax 604/685-7079. www.docksidebrewing.com.* Located within the Granville Island Hotel and facing a yacht basin, this seafood restaurant has great views from it's many windows and French doors. The décor is simple—polished wood tables with inlaid tiles, blue drinking goblets, flower vases, and oil lamps—and the atmosphere is casual. The adjacent active brewery provides the property's beer supply. Seafood menu. Breakfast, lunch, dinner, brunch. Bar. Children's menu. Casual attire. Reservations recommended. Valet parking. Outdoor seating. **$$$**

**★ ★ ★ FISH HOUSE IN STANLEY PARK.** *8901 Stanley Park Dr, Vancouver (V6E 3E2). Phone 604/681-7275; toll-free 877/681-7275; fax 604/681-3137. www.fishhousestanleypark.com.* This Vancouver landmark seafood restaurant is visited by both locals and tourists. It's located in Vancouver's West End, opposite English Bay and at the south entrance to beautiful Stanley Park. And it's décor is reminiscent of a sports club/dining room with a dark green and red color scheme, hardwood floors, paintings of fish, and old tennis racquets hanging from the walls. Seafood menu. Lunch, dinner, brunch. Closed Dec 24-26. Bar. Children's menu. Business casual attire. Reservations recommended. Outdoor seating. **$$$**

**★ ★ ★ FIVE SAILS.** *300-999 Canada Pl, Vancouver (V6C 3B5). Phone 604/662-8111; toll-free 800/937-1515; fax 604/891-2864. www.dinepanpacific.com.* Exceptional views of the harbor and neighboring mountains, a talented kitchen that produces creative Northwest/Asian fusion food, and good service make this restaurant a favorite destination among locals. International menu. Dinner. Bar. Children's menu. Business casual attire. Reservations recommended. Valet parking. **$$$$**

**★ ★ ★ GOTHAM STEAKHOUSE AND COCKTAIL BAR.** *615 Seymour St, Vancouver (V6B 3K3). Phone 604/605-8282; fax 604/605-8285. www.gothamsteakhouse.com.* It's worth the splurge for truly excellent steaks, smooth, friendly service, and a sleek crowd at this downtown destination. The dining room, actually a converted bank, is modern and opulent with main floor and balcony dining and a large, comfortable bar. Steak menu. Dinner. Bar. Children's menu. Business casual attire. Reservations recommended. Valet parking. Outdoor seating. **$$$**

**★ ★ ★ HART HOUSE ON DEER LAKE.** *6664 Deer Lake Ave, Burnaby (V5E 4H3). Phone 604/298-4278; fax 604/298-0124. www.harthouserestaurant.com.* International/Fusion menu. Lunch, dinner. Closed Mon. Business casual attire. Reservations recommended. Outdoor seating. **$$**

**★ ★ ★ IL GIARDINO DI UMBERTO RISTORANTE.** *1382 Hornby St, Vancouver (V6Z 1W5). Phone 604/669-3732; fax 604/669-9723. www.umberto.com.* Part of Umberto Menghi's local restaurant empire, this rustic room, neighboring the original Umberto's, transports it's young, established clientele to a Tuscan villa. Italian menu. Lunch, dinner. Closed Sun; holidays. Bar. Business casual attire. Reservations recommended. Valet parking. Outdoor seating. **$$$**

**★ ★ IMPERIAL CHINESE SEAFOOD RESTAURANT.** *355 Burrard St, Vancouver (V6C 2G8). Phone 604/688-8191; fax 604/688-8466. www.imperialrest.com.* At this contemporary Cantonese/Chinese restaurant, floor-to-ceiling windows and balcony seating offer breathtaking views of the bay and mountains. The dining room features Asian décor, and there is a display wall with four fish tanks. Cantonese, Chinese menu. Lunch, dinner. Bar. Business casual attire. Reservations recommended. Valet parking. **$$$**

**★ ★ ★ ★ LA BELLE AUBERGE.** *4856 48th Ave, Ladner (V4K 1V2). Phone 604/946-7717; fax 604/276-2651. www.labelleauberge.com.* If a trip to Paris isn't on the horizon but you crave the glorious food of France's best kitchens, you can opt for a 30-minute drive from Vancouver to Ladner and settle in for dinner at La Belle Auberge. Set in a charming 1902 country inn, La Belle Auberge is an intimate restaurant made of up five antique-filled, salon-style dining rooms. Refined service adds to the restaurant's unbeatable charm. The kitchen, led by chef/owner Bruno Marti, offers spectacular, authentic French cuisine. Marti is a masterful culinary technician who serves impeccable classics that will please the most discerning Francophile. Close your eyes, and you will feel like you're dining along the Seine. Open them, and you won't care that you aren't. French menu. Dinner. Closed Mon; also two weeks in Jan. Business casual attire. Reservations recommended. Outdoor seating. **$$$**

**★ ★ ★ LA TERRAZZA.** *1088 Cambie St, Vancouver (V6B 6J5). Phone 604/899-4449; fax 604/899-9179. www.laterrazza.ca.* This impressive restaurant feels like a classical villa with burnt-sienna walls, murals, massive windows, and vaulted ceilings. The wine library, cellar and private dining room are signs of the owners' commitment to stocking many fine, unique bottles. Italian menu. Dinner. Bar. Business casual attire. Reservations recommended. Valet parking. Outdoor seating. **$$$**

**★ ★ LE BISTRO CHEZ MICHEL.** *1373 Marine Dr, Vancouver (V7T 1B6). Phone 604/926-4913. www.chezmichelvancouver.com.* French menu. Lunch, dinner. Closed Sun; holidays. Business casual attire. Reservations recommended. **$$**

**★ ★ ★ LE CROCODILE.** *909 Burrard St, Vancouver (V6Z 2N2). Phone 604/669-4298; fax 604/669-4207. www.lecrocodilerestaurant.com.* A wonderful dress-up place, this downtown French bistro is worth a trip for the food alone. However, the ambience is also something to experience—red walls with mahogany wainscoting, citron curtains, a mahogany bar, lamps, flowers—a wonderful choice for a special-occasion or romantic dinner. With a highly acclaimed chef preparing delicious meals, no wonder this bistro is one of Vancouver's favorites. French menu. Lunch, dinner. Closed Sun. Bar. Business casual attire. Reservations recommended. Valet parking. Outdoor seating. **$$$**

**★ ★ ★ ★ LUMIERE.** *2551 W Broadway, Vancouver (V6K 2E9). Phone 604/739-8185; fax 604/739-8139. www.lumiere.ca.* Lumiere is a glossy, stunning, and elegant restaurant that offers European-style dining of the most divine order. The inspired and innovative fare is French with Asian accents and a respect for regional ingredients. Plates are beautiful and balanced and come in eightsas in eight coursesand each of the eight-course chefs, signature, and vegetarian menus changes with the seasons. While eight courses could be overkill, each portion is perfectly sized so that you dont finish dinner feeling perilously inflated and exhausted from the exercise. Instead, you feel deliciously satiated and utterly pampered by the experience. The global wine list is in sync with the kitchens style, but attention should also be paid to the classic cocktails served at Lumieres slick and sexy bar. The bartenders here recall a pre-Prohibition era, where the craft of cocktail was taken as seriously as the mastery of the plate. French menu. Dinner. Closed Mon; Dec 25. Bar. Business casual attire. Reservations recommended. Valet parking. Outdoor seating. **$$$$**

**★ ★ MONK MCQUEENS.** *601 Stamps Landing, Vancouver (V5Z 3Z1). Phone 604/877-1351; fax 604/813-5816. www.monkmcqueens.com.* This nautical seafood restaurant is located on the south bank of False Creek, looking across at downtown Vancouver and the coastal mountains. The property can be reached by ferry from Yaletown, English Bay, and Kitsiland. Cool jazz is offered on Friday and Saturday nights. Seafood menu. Lunch, dinner, brunch. Closed Dec 25. Bar. Children's menu. Business casual attire. Reservations recommended. Valet parking. Outdoor seating. **$$$**

**★ ★ PROVENCE MEDITERRANEAN GRILL.** *4473 W 10th Ave, Vancouver (V6R 2H2). Phone 604/222-1980; fax 604/222-1908. www.provencevancouver.com.* This casual Mediterranean café bistro has a Southern France ambience, although it's located in Point Grey, a neighborhood of Vancouver. The restaurant is set amongst shops and eateries, near the University of British Columbia. It's a great choice for a reasonably priced meal. Mediterranean menu. Lunch, dinner, brunch. Closed holidays. Children's menu. Casual attire. Reservations recommended. Outdoor seating. **$$**

**★ ★ ★ QUATTRO ON FOURTH.** *2611 W 4th, Vancouver (V6K 1P8). Phone 604/734-4444; fax 604/734-4321. www.quattrorestaurants.com.* This popular suburban Italian restaurant is located a few miles from downtown Vancouver. The dinner-only menu has an excellent selection of Italian entrees, and the chef's menu is complemented with wine pairings. Italian, Mediterranean menu. Dinner. Closed Dec 24-26. Bar. Business casual attire. Reservations recommended. Outdoor seating. **$$$**

**★ ★ ★ RAINCITY GRILL.** *1193 Denman St, Vancouver (V6G 2N1). Phone 604/685-7337; fax 604/685-7362. www.raincitygrill.com.* Located in Vancouver's West End, this eclectic, fine dining restaurant has views across a small park to English Bay. The property's décor is smart and contemporary with splashes of modern art. There are three levels in the main dining room, and there is additional seating on a side patio. The delicious a la carte and chef's tasting menus draw almost exclusively on organic, regional sources. Don't miss brunch on Saturdays and Sundays. International menu. Dinner, brunch. Closed Dec 25-26. Business casual attire. Reservations recommended. Valet parking. Outdoor seating. **$$$**

**★ ★ ★ SAVEUR.** *850 Thurlow St, Vancouver (V6E 1W2). Phone 604/688-1633; fax 604/734-0547. www.saveurrestaurant.com.* Located a block off Robson in downtown Vancouver, this warm and intimate French restaurant is the perfect spot for a special-occasion celebration. The atmosphere is set with red-toned parquet flooring, contemporary silk dividers, lush burgundy banquettes, and candles on each communal-style table. A French West Coast menu is served for lunch and dinner. French menu. Lunch, dinner. Closed Sun. Business casual attire. Reservations recommended. **$$$**

**★ ★ ★ SEASONS HILL TOP BISTRO.** *33rd and Cambie, Vancouver (V6G 3E7). Phone 604/874-8008; toll-free 800/632-9422; fax 604/874-7101. www.seasonshilltopbistro.com.* This restaurant was the site of a Clinton-Yeltsin summit in 1993—so come for the history and stay for the incredible International menu—and the view. Located on top of a hill in beautiful Queen Elizabeth Park in suburban Vancouver, there are magnificent views from the tiered dining room and attractive heated terrace. And you can't go wrong with the extensive wine list. International menu. Lunch, dinner, brunch. Closed Dec 25. Bar. Children's menu. Business casual attire. Reservations recommended. Valet parking. Outdoor seating. **$$$**

**★ ★ SEQUOIA GRILL.** *7501 Stanley Park Dr, Vancouver (V6G 3E7). Phone 604/669-3281; fax 604/687-5662. www.sequoiarestaurants.com.* Formerly the historic Teahouse, this contemporary property has retained the much-loved glass-topped conservatory and flower garden patio. Located at the western end of Stanley Park, along the scenic park drive, the restaurant's three dining rooms feature views of the Strait of Georgia. The kitchen offers a West Coast eclectic menu, and there is a bar and lounge to relax in before or after dinner. International menu. Lunch, dinner. Bar. Children's menu. Business casual attire. Reservations recommended. Outdoor seating. **$$$**

**★ ★ SHIJO JAPANESE RESTAURANT.** *1926 W 4th Ave, Vancouver (V6J 1M5). Phone 604/732-4676.* At this popular Japanese/sushi restaurant, a line is usually formed before the restaurant opens for dinner—and this happens mid-week. The menu also features sashimi, robata-grill fare, and Japanese a la carte entrees. The restaurant is located in the Kitsilaro neighborhood of suburban Vancouver, across the Burrard Bridge from downtown. Japanese menu. Lunch, dinner. Closed Jan 1. Casual attire. Reservations recommended. **$$$**

**★ ★ STAR ANISE.** *1485 W 12th Ave, Vancouver (V6H 1M6). Phone 604/737-1485; fax 604/737-1489. www.staranise.ca.* This romantic, intimate property, located in the South Granville Theater and Art Gallery District, is just a short drive south of downtown Vancouver across the Granville Bridge. You know you've reached the right place when you spot the unique bronze sculpture of a man and a dog at a cafe table on the front sidewalk. Come for lunch or dinner to enjoy the West Coast/Pacific Northwest cuisine which has both French and Indian influences. The three-course pre-theater menu is a great bargain. International menu. Lunch, dinner. Closed Jan 1, Dec 25. Bar. Casual attire. Reservations recommended. **$$$**

**★ ★ SUN SUI WAH SEAFOOD RESTAURANT.** *3888 Main St, Vancouver (V5V 3N9). Phone 604/872-8822; toll-free 866/872-8822; fax 604/876-1638. www.sunsuiwah.com.* Grab an egg tart from the dim sum cart even if you're not ready for dessert; they sell out quickly at this huge, widely acclaimed chain restaurant. Chinese menu. Lunch, dinner. Casual attire. Reservations recommended. **$$**

**★ TAPASTREE.** *1829 Robson St, Vancouver (V6G 1E4). Phone 604/606-4680; fax 604/682-6509. www.tapastree.ca.* Vegetable, seafood, and meat tapas are offered in a European atmosphere at this West End tapas eatery. Since the food is served tapas-style, you can order a bit of everything and share with your tablemates. Spanish, tapas menu. Dinner. Closed holidays. Bar. Casual attire. Reservations recommended (Fri-Sat). Outdoor seating. **$$**

**★ ★ TOJO'S.** *777 W Broadway, Vancouver (V5Z 4J7). Phone 604/872-8050; fax 604/872-8060. www.tojos.com.* Frequented by entertainment industry insiders, this popular Japanese restaurant serves great food with friendly service. Menu items keep the hip and cool crowd coming back time and time again. Japanese menu. Dinner. Closed Sun; also mid-Jan. Children's menu. Casual attire. Reservations recommended. Outdoor seating. **$$**

**★ ★ TOP OF VANCOUVER.** *555 W Hastings St, Vancouver (V6B 4N6). Phone 604/669-2220; fax 604/683-4609. www.topofvancouver.com.* Located more than 500 feet above the city at the top of Harbour Centre Tower, this revolving fine dining restaurant offers a 360 degree view of the city, the ocean, the bay, and the mountains. Its International menu is complemented by the elegant, contemporary decor. International menu. Lunch, dinner. Bar. Casual attire. Reservations recommended. **$$$**

**★ TRUE CONFECTIONS.** *866 Denman St, Vancouver (V6G 2L8). Phone 604/682-1292; fax 604/682-6158. www.trueconfections.ca.* If you have a sweet tooth, this is the place for you! Located on Denman Street, among the trendy restaurants and shops, is this luscious dessert bar. The décor features red and black tables and funky hanging lamps—oh, and a large cake display case. Your favorite dessert can be washed down with one of the many beverages available including wine, specialty coffees, teas, soft drinks, or beer. Dessert menu. Lunch, dinner, late-night. Closed Dec 25. Casual attire. **$**

**★ ★ ★ VILLA DEL LUPO.** *869 Hamilton St, Vancouver (V6B 2R7). Phone 604/688-7436; fax 604/688-3058. www.villadellupo.com.* Tiny white lights and sparkling bay windows attract attention at this classic Italian restaurant housed in a charming, turn-of-the-century home. The menu highlights different regions of Italy using fresh, local ingredients in dishes such as osso bucco with risotto Milanese. Italian menu. Dinner. Closed Dec 25. Bar. Casual attire. Reservations recommended. Valet parking. **$$$**

**★ ★ ★ ★ WEST.** *2881 Granville St, Vancouver (V6H 3J4). Phone 604/738-8938; fax 604/738-5909. www.westrestaurant.com.* West is one of those sleek, heavenly spots that makes sipping cocktails for hours on end an easy task—they use fresh juices and know how to mix a serious drink. It is also one of those restaurants that makes the act of eating an art and a delight. It is an ideal choice for gourmets in search of an inventive, eclectic meal, as well as for simple eaters who crave local flavor and seasonal ingredients that are seamlessly married on the plate. Whatever your appetite and whatever the occasion—if you are entertaining colleagues, in need of a night out with friends, or just searching for a place to have dinner with your significant other—look no further than West, a restaurant with an inspiring menu and a stylish, contemporary urban setting. Located in Vancouver's chic South Granville neighborhood, West offers diners the chance to sample the vibrant cuisine of the Pacific Northwest region. Stunning, locally sourced ingredients are on display here, and the masterful kitchen staff offers a glorious show. International menu. Lunch, dinner. Closed Jan 1, Dec 25. Bar. Business casual attire. Reservations recommended. Valet parking. **$$$**

# Victoria (F-4)

*See also Vancouver, Nanaimo, Vancouver Island*

Founded 1843
**Population** 64,379
**Elevation** 211 ft (64 m)
**Area Code** 250
**Information** Tourism Victoria, 812 Wharf St, V8W 1T3; phone 250/953-2033 or toll-free 800/663-3883
**Web Site** www.tourismvictoria.com

Bordered by the Juan de Fuca Strait on one side, and majestic mountains on the other, Victoria is situated on the southeast tip of Vancouver Island. Established in 1843 as a trading post of the Hudson's Bay Company, the city was later called Fort Victoria. In the late 1850s, Victoria became the provisioning and outfitting base for miners on their way to British Columbia's goldfields. In 1866, Vancouver Island was administratively linked with the mainland; Victoria became the provincial capital in 1871.

A major port with two harbors—the outer for ocean shipping and cruising and the inner for coastal shipping, pleasure boats, ferries to the US mainland, amphibian aircraft, and fishing—Victoria has a distinctly British flavor with many Tudor-style buildings and a relaxed way of life. It is a center of Pacific Northwest indigenous culture.

Victoria is a city of parks and gardens; even the five-globed Victorian lampposts are decorated with baskets of flowers in summer. Visitors may take a horse-drawn carriage or double-decker bus tour through many historic and scenic landmarks; inquire locally for details. In winter, temperatures rarely go below 40° F (4° C). Victoria's climate is Canada's most moderate, making it a delightful place to visit any time of year.

## Public Transportation

**Lost and Found** Phone 250/953-7511

**Airlines** Air Canada, Air Canada Jazz, Helijet International, Horizon Air, Pacific Coastal Airlines, WestJet, Zip

## What to See and Do

**Art Gallery of Greater Victoria.** *1040 Moss St, Victoria (V8V 4P1). Phone 250/384-4101.aggv.bc.ca.* This gal-

## Cycling

Victorias mild climate and natural beauty inspire locals and visitors to get out and enjoy the great outdoors. Year-round outdoor adventure includes access to miles of scenic trails and sites that incorporate old growth rainforests, ocean shores, and mountains. In the Greater Victoria Region, cycling accounts for 6.2 percent of commuter travel—more than any other city in Canada. In Victoria, most people live within a 30-minute bike ride of their workplace and, from some neighborhoods, up to 20 percent of trips to work are made by bicycle. Bike lanes on many of Victoria's downtown streets and bike racks on city buses that travel to the suburban communities also promote cycling.

One of the best routes to cycle is the Galloping Goose Trail—a linear park that stretches 44 miles (70 kilometers) from Victoria to Sooke. Built on abandoned railway tracks and trestles, and named after a 1920's rail car, the Galloping Goose is part of the Trans Canada Trail. The Galloping Goose trail surface is wide, mostly flat, and leads through a wonderful diversity of landscapes. Many local cyclists use the Galloping Goose Trail to get around southern Vancouver Island. The Galloping Goose Trail connects with the Lochside Trail and Seaside Cycling Route to create the first bicycle touring route in the southern Vancouver Island region. For more information visit www.crd.bc.ca/parks/galloping_goose.htm.

lery is said to have the finest collection of Japanese art in Canada; it includes major holdings of Asian ceramics and paintings. Also housed here are collections of Canadian and European art, with a focus on prints and drawings, and decorative arts. The gallery is home to the only Shinto shrine outside of Japan and is the site of many lectures, film screenings, and concerts. (Mon-Sat 10 am-5 pm, Thurs to 9 pm, Sun 1-5 pm; closed Good Fri, Nov 11, Dec 25) **$$**

**BC Forest Museum.** *Hwy 1, Duncan. 40 miles (64 kilometers) N on Hwy 1, near Duncan. Phone 250/715-1113.* Logging museum; old logging machines and tools, hands-on exhibits, logging camp, 1 1/2 miles (2.4 kilometers) steam railway ride, sawmill, films, nature walk, picnic park, snack bar, gift shop. (May-Sept, daily)

**Beacon Hill Park.** *Douglas St and Dallas Rd, Victoria. From Douglas St to Cook St, between Superior St and waterfront. Phone 250/361-0370.* Approximately 180 acres (75 hectares) with lakes, wildfowl sanctuary, children's petting farm, walks and floral gardens, cricket pitch; world's second-tallest totem pole; beautiful view of the sea. For a list of additional recreational areas, contact Tourism Victoria. **FREE**

**Butchart Gardens.** *800 Benvenuto, Victoria. 13 miles (21 kilometers) N on Benvenuto Ave, near Brentwood Bay. Phone 250/652-4422. www.butchartgardens.com.* Approximately 50 acres (20 hectares). The Sunken Garden was created in the early 1900s by the Butcharts on the site of their depleted limestone quarry with topsoil brought in by horse-drawn cart. Already a tourist attraction by the 1920s, the gardens now include the Rose, Japanese, and Italian gardens; also Star Pond, Concert Lawn, Fireworks Basin, Ross Fountain, and Show Greenhouse. The gardens are subtly illuminated at night (mid-June-mid-Sept), and on Sat evenings in July and August, visitors enjoy fireworks displays. Restaurants; seed and gift store. Fees vary by season. **$$$$**

**Capital City Tally-Ho and Sightseeing Company.** *8615 Ebor Terrace, Victoria. Phone 250/383-5067.* English horse-drawn carriage sightseeing tours: of city highlights, departing from Inner Harbour beside Parliament Buildings; or past Victorian homes and through 200-acre (81-hectare) Beacon Hill Park and it's extensive flower gardens (departs from Menzies and Belleville sts). Fully narrated. (Apr-Sept, daily)

**Carr House.** *207 Government St, Victoria. Phone 250/383-5843.* (1863) Italianate birthplace of famous Canadian painter/author Emily Carr. Ground floor restored to period. (Mid-May-Oct: daily; rest of year: by appointment) **$$**

**Centennial Square.** *Douglas and Pandora sts, Victoria.* Includes fountain plaza; Elizabethan knot garden of herbs and flowers. Occasional noontime concerts.

**Chinatown.** *Victoria.* Chinese immigrants, used for railroad labor, established Canada's oldest Chinatown in 1858. Two key attractions are Fan Tan Alley, the narrowest street in North America and the Gate of Harmonious Interest, guarded by hand-carved stone lions from Szuchou, China. Visit shops with exotic merchandise and restaurants.

**Craigdarroch Castle.** *1050 Joan Crescent, Victoria. Phone 250/592-5323. www.craigdarrochcastle.com.* (1890) Historic house museum with beautifully crafted wood, stained glass; furnished with period furniture and artifacts. (Daily 10 am-4:30 pm; mid-June-Labor Day 9 am-7 pm; closed Jan 1, Dec 25-26) **$$$**

**Craigflower Farmhouse & Schoolhouse Historic Site.** *2709 Manor and Schoolhouse, Victoria (V9B 1M5). Phone 250/383-4627.*This farmhouse was built in 1856 in simple Georgian style. The adjoining 1854 schoolhouse is the oldest in western Canada. Some original furnishings. (Daily; guided tours June 10-Labour Day, Wed-Sun noon-4 pm) **$$**

**Crystal Garden.** *713 Douglas St, Victoria. Phone 250/953-8800. www.bcpcc.com/crystal.*Glass building formerly housed the largest saltwater pool in the British Empire. Tropical gardens, waterfall, fountain, aviary, monkeys, free-flying butterflies, exotic fish pool; restaurant, shops. (Daily) **$$$**

**Dominion Astrophysical Observatory.** *5071 W Saanich Rd, Victoria (V9E 2E7). Phone 250/363-0001. www.hia-iha.nrc-gc.ca.* The observatory contains three telescopes, two of which are used for research by professional astronomers. The 72-inch Plaskett Telescope is used for public viewing on Saturday nights during "Star Parties" (Apr-Oct 31, 7-11 pm). Interactive exhibits, film presentations, and other special programs are designed to entertain visitors while educating them about the universe. (Daily 10 am-6 pm; to 11 pm Fri, May 1-Aug 31, and Sun, July 1-Aug 31; closed Mon Nov-Apr) **$$$**

**Empress Hotel.** *721 Government St, Victoria.* This historically famous building was constructed by Canadian Pacific Railroad in 1908 and restored in 1989. Victorian in tradition, afternoon tea and crumpets are served in the lobby—an impressive, if expensive affair. Guests leave with a full stomach and a canister of tea as a souvenir.

**Ferry trips.** *430 Bellville St, Victoria.* **Black Ball Transport, Inc:** between Victoria, BC, and Port Angeles, WA, car ferry, phone 250/386-2202; **Washington State Ferries:** between Sidney, BC, and Anacortes, WA (see), phone 250/381-1551; **British Columbia Ferry Corp**: between Victoria and British Columbia mainland or smaller island destinations, car ferry, phone 250/386-3431 or 604/669-1211 (Vancouver).

**Fort Rodd Hill and Fisgard Lighthouse National Historic Site.** *603 Fort Rodd Hill Rd, Victoria. 8 miles (13 km) W, then 1/2 mile (1 km) S of BC 1A. Phone 250/478-5849. www.pc.gc.ca.* A coastal artillery fort from 1895 to 1956; casemated barracks, gun and searchlight positions, loopholed walls. Grounds (daily; closed Dec 25). Historic lighthouse (1860) adjacent. **$$**

**Gray Line bus tours.** *700 Douglas St, Victoria (V8W 2B3). Phone 250/388-5248.* Several bus tours of Victoria and vicinity are offered (all year). **$$$$**

**Hatley Castle.** *2005 Sooke Rd, Colwood. 6 miles (10 km) W via Trans-Canada Hwy 1 and 1A, Colwood exit, on Hwy 14 (Sooke Rd). Phone 250/391-2600. www.royalroads.ca.* (Royal Roads University, 1908) Once the private estate of James Dunsmuir, former Lieutenant Governor of British Columbia. Buildings are noted for their beauty, as are the grounds, with their Japanese, Italian, and rose gardens. Grounds (daily). **$$**

**Helmcken House.** *10 Elliot Sq, Victoria. Phone 250/356-7226.* (1852) Second-oldest house in British Columbia; most furnishings are original. Extensive 19th-century medical collection. (May-Oct: daily; rest of year: by appointment) **$$**

**Maritime Museum.** *28 Bastion Sq, Victoria. Phone 250/385-4222.* Located in Old Provincial Courthouse. Depicts rich maritime heritage of the Pacific Northwest from early explorers through age of sail and steam; Canadian naval wartime history; large collection of models of ships used throughout the history of British Columbia. The *Tilikum,* a converted dugout that sailed from Victoria to England during the years 1901 to 1904, is here. Captain James Cook display. (Daily; closed Jan 1, Dec 25) **$$**

**Miniature World.** *649 Humboldt St, Victoria. Phone 250/385-9731. www.miniatureworld.com.* More than 80 miniature, 3-D scenes of fact, fiction, and history. Two large doll houses; very large rail diorama; villages; world's smallest operational sawmill. (Daily; closed Dec 25) **$$$**

**Pacific Undersea Gardens.** *490 Belleville St, Victoria. Phone 250/382-5717.* Underwater windows for viewing of more than 5,000 marine specimens; scuba diver shows. (Daily; closed Dec 25) **$$$**

**Parliament Buildings.** *501 Belleville St, Victoria. Phone 250/387-3046.* Built from 1893 to 1897 mostly of native materials, beautifully illuminated at night; houses British Columbia's Legislative Assembly. Guided tours (mid-June-Labour Day, daily; rest of year, Mon-Fri;

closed holidays except summer). Foreign language tours. Advance notice suggested for group tours. **FREE**

**Point Ellice House Museum.** *2616 Pleasant St, Victoria. Phone 250/380-6506.* (1861) Original Victorian setting, furnishings. Afternoon tea served in restored garden. (May-mid-Sept; daily) **$$**

**Royal British Columbia Museum.** *675 Belleville St, Victoria (V8W 1A1). Phone 250/356-7226; toll-free 888/447-7977. www.royalbcmuseum.bc.ca.* Three-dimensional exhibits include natural and human history, indigenous history, and art; also a re-creation of a turn-of-the-century town. In the natural history gallery, the "Living Land-Living Sea" exhibit depicts the natural history of British Columbia from the Ice Age to the present. (Daily 9 am-5 pm; closed Jan 1, Dec 25) **$$$** While here, see

**Carillon.** *Government and Belleville sts, Victoria. Phone 250/387-1616.*Bells made in Holland; presented to the province by citizens of Dutch descent. Concerts; inquire locally for private tour.

**National Geographic IMAX Theatre.** *675 Belleville St, Victoria (V8W 9W2). Phone 250/480-4887.* A selection of acclaimed films on topics from nature to exotic destinations appears larger than life on this giant IMAX screen. Purchase tickets in the museum's lobby; combination tickets are available. (Shows daily 10 am-9 pm; closed Jan 1, Dec 25) **$$**

**Thunderbird Park.** *675 Belleville St, Victoria.* Collection of authentic totem poles and indigenous carvings, representing the work of the main Pacific Coastal tribes. Indigenous carvers may be seen at work in the Carving Shed. (May-Sept).

**Royal London Wax Museum.** *470 Belleville St, Victoria. Phone 250/388-4461. www.waxmuseum.bc.ca.* More than 250 figures in theatrical settings. (Daily; closed Dec 25) **$$$**

**Scenic Drives. North.** *Victoria.* Malahat Dr (Trans-Canada Hwy 1), a continuation of Victoria's Douglas St, through Goldstream Park over Malahat Dr to Mill Bay, Cowichan Bay, Duncan, and the BC Forest Museum. **North.** On the continuation of Victoria's Blanshard St (Hwys 17 and 17A) through rural communities, pastoral valleys known as the Saanich Peninsula where on 50 acres (20 hectares) of manicured lawns, ponds, fountains, and formal gardens bloom the world-famous Butchart Gardens. Around the seashore along Dallas Rd through beautiful, traditionally English residential areas to Beach Dr, Oak Bay, and beyond to Cordova Bay. Leave the city behind on Trans-Canada Hwy 1 to Hwy 14, which winds through rural communities to the village of Sooke, where the population is still engaged in fishing, clamming, and logging. Unspoiled beaches, hiking trails, rocky seashores are accessible from this West Coast road. Continuation on Hwy 14 will lead to Jordan River and to Port Renfrew, with it's beautiful Botanical Beach.

## Limited-Service Hotels

**★ ★ ★ ABIGAIL'S HOTEL.** *906 McClure St, Victoria (V8V 3E7). Phone 250/388-5363; toll-free 800/561-6565; fax 250/388-7787. www.abigailshotel.com.* This colorfully painted inn consists of an historic Tudor mansion and converted carriage house. The quiet setting belies the inn's location just three blocks from Victoria's Inner Harbour and main tourist attractions. Enjoy afternoon tea in the book-lined library while sinking into a leather armchair or sofa in front of a blazing fire. A full gourmet breakfast is served overlooking the patio and English-style gardens. The guest rooms are well appointed, with down-filled duvets and private baths, many with Jacuzzi tubs. 23 rooms, 4 story. Pets accepted, some restrictions; fee. Children over 10 only. Complimentary full breakfast. Check-in 3 pm, check-out 11 am. High-speed Internet access, wireless Internet access. Fitness classes available**. $$$**

**★ ★ BEDFORD REGENCY HOTEL.** *1140 Government St, Victoria (V8W 1Y2). Phone 250/384-6835; toll-free 800/665-6500; fax 250/386-8930. www.bedfordregency.com.* Built around 1910, this building started it's life as a bookstore and stationery shop. Today, it combines it's old-world ambience with modern conveniences—window boxes outside every room and high-speed Internet access within. Nestled in Victoria's business district, it's just a short walk to the Parliament Buildings, museums, and other attractions. No recent renovation has marred the traditional feel or the size of the guest rooms, although the bathrooms are a bit on the small side. 40 rooms, 6 story. Check-in 3 pm, check-out 11 am. Wireless Internet access. Restaurant, bar**. $$**

**★ ★ CHATEAU VICTORIA HOTEL AND SUITES.** *740 Burdett Ave, Victoria (V8W 1B2). Phone 250/382-4221; toll-free 800/663-5891; fax 250/380-1950. www.chateauvictoria.com.* Its location atop a hill, across the street from the Victoria Conference Centre, gives this hotel's Vista 18 restaurant on the top floor prime position for spectacular views of the city and the Inner Harbour. The fairly large lobby is a bright and comfortable place for meeting or relaxing. The hotel offers nearly twice as many suites as regular guest rooms; all the rooms boast recent-renovation touches such as duvets and writing desks. With it's secure storage area for bicycles, Chateau Victoria is a good choice for cyclists. 177 rooms, 19 story. Pets accepted, some restrictions; fee. Check-in 3 pm, check-out 11 am. Restaurant, bar. Fitness room. Indoor pool, whirlpool. **$$**

★ ★ **EXECUTIVE HOUSE HOTEL.** *777 Douglas St, Victoria (V8W 2B5). Phone 250/388-5111; toll-free 800/663-7001; fax 250/385-1323. www.executivehouse.com.* This family-owned hotel has an excellent location across from the Victoria Conference Centre and just one block from the Inner Harbour and it's many attractions. The original artwork in both public spaces and guest rooms is one of the advantages of staying at this independent hotel, as is a friendly staff. The guest accommodations are spacious and comfortable; executive suites boast a full kitchen. The Executive Club and Executive Level cater to business travelers, and pet-friendly policies let families feel at home away from home.181 rooms, 17 story. Pets accepted; fee. Check-in 3 pm, check-out noon. High-speed Internet access, wireless Internet access. Two restaurants, two bars. Fitness room. Whirlpool. **$$**

★ ★ ★ **MIRALOMA ON THE COVE.** *2308 Harbour Rd, Sidney (V8L 2P8). Phone 250/656-6622; toll-free 877/956-6622; fax 250/656-6212. www.shoalharbourinn.com.* Here, guests stay in either the Miraloma on the Cove suites or the historic Latch guest rooms. The Latch Mansion, built in the 1920s, was the summer residence for the lieutenant governor of British Columbia. It is located in Sidney, just 20 minutes from downtown Victoria and five minutes from ferries and the airport. Guest rooms are decorated with Canadian furnishings and artwork. Dine in the intimate small dining rooms in the Latch Mansion after watching the sun set over the harbor from the terrace. 26 rooms. Check-in 3 pm, check-out 11 am. High-speed Internet access. Restaurant, bar. Fitness room. Whirlpool. Business center. **$$**

★ ★ **ROYAL SCOT SUITE HOTEL.** *425 Quebéc St, Victoria (V8V 1W7). Phone 250/388-5463; toll-free 800/663-7315; fax 250/388-5452. www.royalscot.com.* Most of the guest rooms at this hotel—about 80 percent—are suites. but even the regular rooms are spacious and inviting. The inn has a billiards room with a full-size table as well as a game room stocked with board games, puzzles, playing cards, and a TV. Although the hotel is located on a street filled with commercial businesses, it backs up to a quiet residential area and takes on some of that ambience. The extensive and beautifully landscaped grounds help give guests the feeling of being in an oasis in the middle of the city.176 rooms, 4 story. Check-in 3 pm, check-out noon. Restaurant, bar. Children's activity center. Fitness room. Indoor pool, whirlpool. **$**

★ ★ **TRAVELODGE.** *229 Gorge Rd E, Victoria (V9A 1L1). Phone 250/388-6611; toll-free 800/565-3777; fax 250/388-4153. www.travelodgevictoria.com.* Both business and leisure travelers with find this property a great value. It's located about ten minutes from downtown in a quiet residential neighborhood and offers a number of amenities and services such as airport transportation, a business center, an indoor pool, a restaurant and bar, and a fitness room.73 rooms. Pets accepted; fee. Check-in 3 pm, check-out 11 am. Restaurant, bar. Fitness room. Indoor pool. Airport transportation available. Business center. **$**

## Full-Service Hotels

★ ★ **BEST WESTERN CARLTON PLAZA HOTEL.** *642 Johnson St, Victoria (V8W 1M6). Phone 250/388-5513; toll-free 800/663-7241; fax 250/388-5343. www.bestwesterncarlton.com.* Choose your entrance—from the street or through the Carlton Plaza shopping center, which shares this historic building. Although the building is heritage, the hotel is contemporary, with wireless Internet access in the lobby and complimentary bottled water in the guest rooms. Make use of the in-house fitness room or get a pass to the nearby YMCA/YWCA for a range of exercise and spa options. The onsite pancake house is open for breakfast and lunch. 103 rooms, 6 story. Pets accepted, some restrictions; fee. Check-in 3 pm, check-out 11 am. High-speed Internet access. Restaurant. Fitness room. Airport transportation available. **$$**

★ ★ ★ **COAST HARBOURSIDE HOTEL & MARINA.** *146 Kingston St, Victoria (V8V 1V4). Phone 250/360-1211; toll-free 800/663-1144; fax 250/360-1418. www.coasthotels.com.* A contemporary high-rise built in 1991, this hotel has it's own marina where you can dock overnight or stay for a month. Marine-life and whale-watching tours leave directly from the marina. Additional water-based attractions include the indoor/outdoor pool and whirlpool, both with views of the harbor. Take a shuttle, water taxi, or a scenic stroll into downtown and the attractions there. Well-appointed guest rooms provide large writing desks, Web TV, and two phone lines for business travelers, and the Blue Crab restaurant provides a full-service grill and fantastic views.132 rooms, 10 story. Pets accepted. Check-in 3 pm, check-out noon. High-speed Internet access. Restaurant, bar. Fitness room. Indoor pool, outdoor pool, whirlpool. Business center. **$$**

**★ ★ HARBOUR TOWERS HOTEL & SUITES.** *345 Quebéc St, Victoria (V8V 1W4). Phone 250/385-2405; toll-free 800/663-5896; fax 250/360-2313. www.harbourtowers.com.* Convenient to downtown, this hotel's comfortable contemporary décor includes solid dark woods and soothing neutral colors in the overstuffed sofas and chairs. You can relax in front of the fire in the lobby, swim laps in the indoor pool, or make use of the facilities at the independently operated spa. A full-service restaurant can take care of your dining needs, and a children's activity center and babysitting services are helpful for families.195 rooms, 12 story. Pets accepted, some restrictions; fee. Check-in 4 pm, check-out 11 am. High-speed Internet access. Restaurant, bar. Children's activity center. Fitness room, spa. Indoor pool, whirlpool. Business center. **$$**

**★ ★ ★ HOTEL GRAND PACIFIC.** *463 Belleville St, Victoria (V8V 1X3). Phone 250/386-0450; toll-free 800/663-7550; fax 250/380-4475. www.hotelgrandpacific.com.* Located at the southern tip of Vancouver Island, Victoria is a tiny slice of England on a ruggedly beautiful island. Its quaint downtown and beautiful Inner Harbour is home to the sophisticated Hotel Grand Pacific, one of the city's best hotels. Its location is superb, with serene water views and easy access to historic Old Town and area businesses. The rooms and suites are light and airy, with pastel colors rounding out the sun-filled spaces. Fine dining is one of Victorias hallmarks, and this hotel is no exception. The Pacific Northwest cuisine at The Pacific is a stand-out, while The Marks regionally influenced dishes are equally delicious. Extra calories aren't a worry here, where a large fitness center and spa help guests work off any dietary indiscretions. 304 rooms, 10 story. Pets accepted, some restrictions; fee. Check-in 3 pm, check-out 11 am. High-speed Internet access. Three restaurants, bar. Fitness room, fitness classes available, spa. Indoor pool, children's pool, whirlpool. Business center. **$$**

**★ ★ ★ LAUREL POINT INN.** *680 Montréal St, Victoria (V8V 1Z8). Phone 250/386-8721; toll-free 800/663-7667; fax 250/386-9547. www.laurelpoint.com.* Every room of this hotel has a balcony and a fabulous view of either the Inner Harbour or the Upper Harbour. Or you can check out the view as you stroll along the paved harbor walkway. The grounds include a Japanese-style garden, and the Asian influence is felt in the décor of the hotel's public rooms (which include 11 meeting rooms) and, to a lesser extent, it's guest rooms. Relax in the cozy piano lounge, the fragrant garden, or the outdoor patio.200 rooms, 3 story. Pets accepted, some restrictions; fee. Check-in 3 pm, check-out 11:30 am. High-speed Internet access. Restaurant, bar. Indoor pool, whirlpool. Business center. **$$$**

**★ ★ ★ MAGNOLIA HOTEL AND SPA.** *623 Courtney St, Victoria (V8W 1B8). Phone 250/381-0999; toll-free 877/624-6654; fax 250/381-0988. www.magnoliahotel.com.* This luxury boutique hotel one block from the Inner Harbour provides comfort and pampering throughout. The cherry-paneled walls and oversized chairs and sofas of blue, taupe, and gold tones in the lobby immerse guests in an old-world ambience and touch on the contemporary with excellent photographs of area landmarks. The cherry wood carries through into the spacious guest rooms, each with a large work desk and two armchairs. The spa offers a full range of beauty and relaxation regimens and prides it'self on using natural products from renewable resources.63 rooms, 7 story. Pets accepted; fee. Complimentary continental breakfast. Check-in 3 pm, check-out noon. High-speed Internet access. Two restaurants, two bars. Fitness room, spa. **$$$**

**★ ★ ★ SWANS SUITE HOTEL.** *506 Pandora Ave, Victoria (V8W 1N6). Phone 250/361-3310; toll-free 800/668-7926; fax 250/361-3491. www.swanshotel.com.* Built in 1913, this hotel holds 30 one- and two-bedroom suites that sleep up to six adults. It's a lively place with it's own brewery and two popular eating and drinking establishments that serve ales brewed in the British tradition. Most of the guest rooms have a loft that contributes a spacious feeling, and various rooms have a variety of features, including skylights and private patios. All room boast full kitchens, duvets, and original artwork. 29 rooms, 4 story, all suites. Complimentary continental breakfast. Check-in 4 pm, check-out noon. High-speed Internet access. Restaurant, bar. **$$**

**★ ★ ★ THE FAIRMONT EMPRESS.** *721 Government St, Victoria (V8W 1W5). Phone 250/384-8111; toll-free 800/441-1414; fax 250/389-2747. www.fairmont.com.* The Fairmont Empress is one of British Columbia's most cherished landmarks. Nearly a century old, this storybook castle resting on the banks of Victorias Inner Harbour enjoys a legendary past. Royals and celebrities have long favored this graceful hotel, where a walk through the doors returns guests to the grace of a bygone era. Classic and elegant, the public and private spaces reflect Victorian-era styling with mahogany furnishings and floral fabrics. Afternoon tea at The Fairmont Empress is a local institution and is a must for all visitors to Victoria. Additional dining options include the exotic Bengal Lounge, the sophisticated Empress Room (see), and the casual Kiplings. Steeped in tradition while embracing the 21st century, the hotel has recently added a spa to it's list of amenities. 477 rooms, 7 story. Pets accepted; fee. Check-in 4 pm, check-out 11 am. High-speed Internet access. Two restaurants, bar. Fitness room, spa. Indoor pool, children's pool, whirlpool. Business center. **$$$**

## Full-Service Resorts

**★ ★ ★ DELTA VICTORIA OCEAN POINTE RESORT AND SPA.** *45 Songhees Rd, Victoria (V9A 6T3). Phone 888/778-5050; toll-free 888/244-8666; fax 250/360-2999. www.deltahotels.com.* Located on a point between Victoria's Inner and Upper harbours, this elegant, modern hotel offers wonderful views of the waterfront, Parliament Buildings, and the Royal BC Museum—just choose a vantage point. Everything is prime, from the high-end amenities in the guest rooms to the full range of services in the European-style spa to the food served in the restaurants. Taking advantage of the full resort experience may include participating in water aerobics and other fitness classes, booking a tee time on a nearby golf course, and playing tennis on one of the hotel's two lighted courts.239 rooms, 8 story. Pets accepted; fee. Check-in 3 pm, check-out noon. High-speed Internet access. Restaurant, bar. Fitness room, spa. Indoor pool. Tennis. Business center. **$$**

**★ ★ OAK BAY BEACH AND MARINE RESORT.** *1175 Beach Dr, Victoria (V8S 2N2). Phone 250/598-4556; toll-free 800/668-7758; fax 250/598-6180. www.oakbaybeachhotel.com.* Almost all of this resort's individually decorated guest rooms have a spectacular view of Oak Bay and beyond to Mount Baker. The Tudor-style inn offers plenty of activities and amenities for the adventuresome, including the loan of a tennis racquet or mountain bike. Start the day with a continental breakfast and then pursue hiking, kayaking, golfing, or whale-watching activities. Or choose a day cruise to Roche Harbour or a rail ride to take in the magnificent scenery. You can choose pub fare for your meals or go the fine-dining route at Bentley's Seaside Patio. End the day by gathering around the fireplace for hot chocolate and cookies.49 rooms, 3 story. Pets accepted, some restrictions; fee. Complimentary continental breakfast. Check-in 2 pm, check-out noon. Restaurant, bar. Beach. **$$**

## Full-Service Inns

**★ ★ ★ ENGLISH INN & RESORT.** *429 Lampson St, Victoria (V9A 5Y9). Phone 250/388-4353; toll-free 866/388-4353; fax 250/382-8311. www.englishinnresort.com.* This unique resort was built to echo an English country village. The main manor is a replica of Anne Hathaway's cottage, and the names of the satellite houses continue the Shakespearean theme. The buildings are set amidst 5 acres of beautifully landscaped English-style gardensthe perfect setting for a wedding, the hosting of which is one of the resort's specialties. Renovations in 2003 gave the resort a more modern feel, with hardwood floors and contemporary colors, although plenty of antiques still grace the guest rooms and public spaces. The lack of elevators may dissuade some guests. 30 rooms, 3 story. Check-in 3 pm, check-out 11 am. High-speed Internet access, wireless Internet access. Restaurant, bar. **$$$**

**★ ★ ★ ★ HASTINGS HOUSE.** *160 Upper Ganges Rd, Salt Spring Island (V8K 2S2). Phone 250/537-2362; toll-free 800/661-9255; fax 250/537-5333. www.hastingshouse.com.* Snuggled on a sylvan knoll on Canada's Salt Spring Island, the Tudor-style Hastings House captures the essence of the English countryside. This charming country estate delights it's visitors, who retreat to this inn for a taste of the good life. Scattered throughout the lovely grounds, the rooms and suites are housed within ivy-covered garden cottages and the timber-framed barn. The accommodations are full of character and distinguished by wood-burning fireplaces, beamed ceilings, window seats, and overstuffed furnishings. All feature enchanting views of the estates verdant lawns or the sparkling harbor.

Guests don jackets for the formal setting and refined cuisine of the Dining Room, while the Verandah offers the same menu in a more casual garden setting. The Snug, adjacent to the wine cellar, provides an inviting spot for informal fare. While outdoor enthusiasts will find a bevy of athletic pursuits, many choose to remain within this storybook setting. 18 rooms. Closed mid-Nov-mid-Mar. Check-in 3 pm, check-out 11 am. Restaurant**. $$$$**

**★ ★ ★ SOOKE HARBOUR HOUSE.** *1528 Whiffen Spit Rd, Sooke (V0S 1N0). Phone 250/642-3421; toll-free 800/889-9688; fax 250/642-6988. www.sookeharbourhouse.com.* Located on Vancouver Island by the sea, this bed-and-breakfast features beautifully designed guest rooms with fireplaces and spectacular ocean views. Guests can enjoy such area activities as hiking, whale-watching and cross-country skiing. Ideal for a romantic getaway or honeymooners. 28 rooms, 4 story. Closed 3 weeks in Jan. Pets accepted; fee. Complimentary continental breakfast. Check-in 3 pm. Check-out noon. Restaurant**. $$$**

## Specialty Lodgings

**ANDERSEN HOUSE.** *301 Kingston St, Victoria (V8V 1V5). Phone 250/388-4565; toll-free 877/264-9988; fax 250/388-4563. www.andersenhouse.com.* This sprawling Queen Anne Victorian home successfully blends old-world charm with contemporary excitement. The guest rooms' hardwood floors are covered with Persian rugs, and the walls are decorated with lively modern artwork. Individual rooms may have a Jacuzzi for two, European stained-glass windows, a microwave and fridge, or a private sundeck; all rooms have feather beds, TVs, CD players, and Calvin Klein robes. Spotless cleanliness, a full breakfast, and several outdoor lounging areas make this inn worth checking into. 4 rooms, 3 story. Children over 11 years only. Complimentary full breakfast. Check-in 2-4 pm, check-out 11 am. High-speed Internet access, wireless Internet access**. $$**

**★ ★ ★ BEACONSFIELD INN.** *998 Humboldt St, Victoria (V8V 2Z8). Phone 250/384-4044; toll-free 888/884-4044; fax 250/384-4052. www.beaconsfieldinn.com.* Built around 1905 by a local financier, this three-story Edwardian mansion on Victoria's south side, not far from the water, is a Registered Heritage Property. The inn makes the most of it's British heritage both in appearance and attitude. Rich wood paneling is complimented by antique furnishings and period décor. The gardens are kept in the English style, and high tea and sherry are served each afternoon. Each guest room boasts unique décor and features, among them canopied beds, skylights, beamed ceilings, leaded and stained-glass windows, and wood-burning fireplaces.9 rooms, 3 story. Children over 11 only. Complimentary full breakfast. Check-in 3 pm, check-out 11 am. Wireless Internet access**. $$$**

**GATSBY MANSION B&B.** *309 Belleville St, Victoria (V8V 1X2). Phone 250/388-9191; toll-free 800/563-9656; fax 250/920-5651. www.gatsbymansion.com.* Soak up the sunshine off of Victorias Inner Harbour from the bay windows of the Gatsby Mansion. Victorian décor enhances the 20 guest suites. Chandeliers, stained-glass windows, and hand-frescoed ceilings in the public rooms take guests back in time. Rooms face the harbor, a rose garden, or the topiary.19 rooms. Complimentary full breakfast. Check-in 3 pm, check-out 11 am. Wireless Internet access. Restaurant. Spa**. $$**

**HATERLEIGH HERITAGE INN.** *243 Kingston St, Victoria (V8V 1V5). Phone 250/384-9995; toll-free 866/234-2244; fax 250/384-1935. www.haterleigh.com.* This six-room inn was converted from a private residence built in 1901. The city designated it a heritage property, and the neighborhood surrounding it and the antiques decorating itincluding remarkable leaded stained-glass windowstell you why. The innkeepers reflect traditional values by providing locally made soaps along with plush robes in the guest rooms and using local organic produce in preparing a full gourmet breakfast each morning. The afternoon social hour provides an opportunity to mingle, browse the Internet, or relax on the covered veranda. 6 rooms, 2 story, all suites. Children over 9 only. Complimentary full breakfast. Check-in 4 pm, check-out 11 am. High-speed Internet access, wireless Internet access**. $$$**

**PRIOR HOUSE B&B INN.** *620 St. Charles, Victoria (V8S 3N7). Phone 250/592-8847; toll-free 877/924-3300; fax 250/592-8223. www.priorhouse.com.* Set in a nice residential area close to Craigdarroch Castle and within walking distance of many historic sites and shops, this Edwardian English manor-style home features six formally decorated rooms filled with tasteful antiques, some with ocean and mountain views. Spacious accommodations range from 400 to 1,500 square feet, but be aware that guest must climb stairs to reach their rooms. The property's beautifully manicured gardens are a wonderful place to relax after a formal three-course breakfast or afternoon sherry or tea. 6 rooms, 3 story. Pets accepted, some restrictions.

Complimentary full breakfast. Check-in 3 pm, check-out 11 am. High-speed Internet access. **$$$**

**ROSEWOOD VICTORIA INN.** *595 Michigan St, Victoria (V8V 1S7). Phone 250/384-6644; toll-free 866/986-2222; fax 250/384-6117. www.rosewoodvictoria.com.* Each suite in this English-style inn boasts a distinctive decorating style. Some rooms are done up in traditional English floral patterns, while other rooms reflect contemporary colors and style. Most rooms have a fireplace, some have a patio or veranda, and all have a private bath and sitting room with TV and telephone. The quiet, residential location is a short walk to the Inner Harbour, restaurants and shopping, and ferry terminals. The grounds are beautifully landscaped, and the courtyard boasts a goldfish pond. 10 rooms, 3 story. Complimentary full breakfast. Check-in 4 pm, check-out 11 am. High-speed Internet access. **$$**

## Restaurants

**★ ★ BLUE CRAB BAR AND GRILL.** *146 Kingston, Victoria (V8V 1V4). Phone 250/360-1211; fax 250/360-1418. www.bluecrab.ca.*Facing the outer reaches of the Inner Harbor, this popular seafood restaurant is located on the main floor of the Coast Harbourside Hotel & Marina in Victoria's James Bay neighborhood. It's pictures windows highlight the harbor views, and the attractive bar is the perfect spot for a before- or after-dinner drink. Seafood menu. Breakfast, lunch, dinner. Bar. Children's menu. Casual attire. Reservations recommended. Valet parking. **$$$**

**★ ★ ★ CAFE BRIO.** *944 Fort St, Victoria (V8V 3K2). Phone 250/383-0009; fax 250/383-0063. www.cafe-brio.com.* This award-winning, eclectic restaurant is located in downtown Victoria. Its menu focuses on West Coast/Continental cuisine, and only fresh wild fish is served. The daily menu also offers local, seasonal, organic foods, and for an exceptional value come for the early prix fixe menu. The upbeat staff makes this a dining experience not to be missed. International menu. Dinner. Closed first two weeks in Jan. Bar. Business casual attire. Reservations recommended. Outdoor seating. **$$$**

**★ ★ CAMILLE'S.** *45 Bastion Sq, Victoria (V8W 1J1). Phone 250/381-3433; fax 250/381-3403. www.camillesrestaurant.com.* This romantic, eclectic restaurant is actually located below Bastion Square, a pedestrian-only area in historic old town Victoria. To find the restaurant, go down a set of stairs below the city's old law chamber building and proceed to it's cellar. The décor is exactly what you'd expect—brick walls, oil lamps, fine china, and modern art. International menu. Dinner. Closed Mon; Dec 24-25. Business casual attire. Reservations recommended. **$$$**

**★ ★ ★ DEEP COVE CHALET.** *11190 Chalet Rd, Sidney (V8L 4R4). Phone 250/656-3541; fax 250/656-2601. www.deepcovechalet.com.* This charming and historic country inn has a great view overlooking the waters of the inside passage. Built in 1914; originally a teahouse for a railroad station. French menu. Lunch, dinner. Closed Mon. Bar. Business casual attire. Reservations recommended. Outdoor seating. **$$$**

**★ ★ ★ EMPRESS ROOM.** *721 Government St, Victoria (V8W 1W5). Phone 250/384-8111; fax 250/381-5939. www.fairmont.com.* Dine on classic cuisine in this richly appointed room of tapestries, intricately carved ceilings, and live harp music. The 100-year-old hotel's waterfront location is full of European style, a great spot for a romantic meal. International menu. Dinner. Business casual attire. Reservations recommended. Valet parking. **$$$$**

**★ ★ GATSBY MANSION.** *309 Belleville St, Victoria (V8V 1X2). Phone 250/388-9191; toll-free 800/563-9656; fax 250/920-5651. www.gatsbymansion.com.* This Victorian-style, West Coast eclectic restaurant is housed in the historic Belleville Mansion. The mansion, located in Belleville Park, is on the west side of Victoria's Inner Harbor, which is a short walk from the downtown area. The restaurant's four dining rooms occupy most of the bottom floor of the mansion and are decorated with green carpeting, flowered drapes, crystal chandeliers, stained glass, oil lamps, and original art work. International menu. Lunch, dinner, Sun brunch. Children's menu. Casual attire. Reservations recommended. Outdoor seating. **$$$**

**★ ★ ★ HERALD STREET CAFFE.** *546 Herald St, Victoria (V8W 1S6). Phone 250/381-1441; fax 250/381-1093. www.heraldstreetcaffe.com.* This restaurant has a consistently great menu, served up in a casual, lively atmosphere, providing exceptionally good service. International menu. Lunch, dinner, brunch. Bar. Children's menu. Casual attire. Reservations recommended. Outdoor seating. **$$**

**★ ★ HUGO'S.** *619 Courtney St, Victoria (V8W 1B8). Phone 250/920-4844; fax 250/920-4842. www.hugoslounge.com.* Steak menu. Lunch, dinner. Closed Dec

25. Bar. Business casual attire. Reservations recommended. Valet parking. Outdoor seating. **$$$**

**★ ★ IL TERRAZZO.** *555 Johnson St, Victoria (V8W 1M2). Phone 250/361-0028; fax 250/360-2594. www.ilterrazzo.com.* This popular, active Italian restaurant, located in Waddington Alley behind Willie's Bakery, has received many awards for it's delicious cuisine. The comfortable décor features a bar at the entry, hardwood floors, exposed brick walls, six fireplaces, and a display kitchen with brick wood oven. Italian menu. Lunch, dinner. Closed Sun. Bar. Casual attire. Reservations recommended. Outdoor seating. **$$$**

**★ J & J WONTON NOODLE HOUSE.** *1012 Fort St, Victoria (V8V 3K4). Phone 250/383-0680. www.jjnoodlehouse.com.* Chinese menu. Lunch, dinner. Closed Sun-Mon; holidays; two weeks (time varies). Casual attire. **$$**

**★ ★ JAPANESE VILLAGE STEAK AND SEAFOOD HOUSE.** *734 Broughton St, Victoria (V8W 1E1). Phone 250/382-5165. www.japanesevillage.bc.ca.* Located between Blanchard and Douglas streets in downtown Victoria, this traditional Japanese restaurant features seven Teppan-grill cooking tables and a sushi bar in a side room. The décor and furnishings are distinctly Japanese—a small waterfall and traditional garden, Japanese artifacts, sculptures, and decorated room dividers. Japanese menu. Lunch, dinner. Closed holidays. Children's menu. Business casual attire. Reservations recommended. **$$**

**★ ★ ★ LURE.** *45 Songhees Rd, Victoria (V9A 6T3). Phone 250/360-5873; fax 250/360-2999. www.lureatoceanpointe.com.* This contemporary, sophisticated seafood restaurant is located inside the Delta Ocean Pointe Resort and offers excellent water and downtown views. The two-level dining room is decorated with floor-to-ceiling windows that overlook the Inner Harbour, dark wood tables, and small bamboo on each tabletop. The lounge, with it's leather chairs and sofas, is a perfect spot to relax before or after dinner. Seafood menu. Breakfast, lunch, dinner. Bar. Children's menu. Casual attire. Reservations recommended. Valet parking. Outdoor seating. **$$$**

**★ ★ ★ ★ RESTAURANT MATISSE.** *512 Yates St, Victoria (V8W 1K8). Phone 250/480-0883; fax 250/480-0886. www.restaurantmatisse.com.* Right smack in the heart of downtown Victoria, you will discover a delightful retreat for authentic French fare. Warmed with yellow brick walls, colorful floral arrangements, and country-style charm, Restaurant Matisse is a gem of a dining room that has become a destination for simple, traditional French fare among Vancouver's dining elite. Many dishes taste as though theyve been beamed over from a Parisian kitchen. House specialties include duck palette and Marseilles-style bouillabaisse. In addition to the la carte selections, the chef offers a nine-course prix fixe menu for those who have penciled excess and indulgence into the evening. While French wines dominate the list, a great selection of California bottles is also included. French menu. Dinner. Closed Mon-Tues; also two weeks in spring. Business casual attire. Reservations recommended. **$$$**

**★ ★ SPINNAKER'S BREW PUB.** *308 Catherine St, Victoria (V9A 3S8). Phone 250/386-2739; toll-free 877/838-2739; fax 250/384-3246. www.spinnakers.com.* Spinnaker's, Canada's oldest brewpub, is located in West Victoria across the Johnson Street bridge from downtown. This casual restaurant offers an eclectic menu, house-made artisan breads, smoked wild seafood, and their own dog biscuits, ales, lagers, and seasonal brews. International menu. Lunch, dinner, brunch. Bar. Children's menu. Casual attire. Reservations recommended. Outdoor seating. **$$**

**★ ★ THE MARINA.** *1327 Beach Dr, Victoria (V8S 2N4). Phone 250/598-8555; fax 250/598-3014. www.marinarestaurant.com.* This contemporary, eclectic restaurant is located just 15 minutes from downtown Victoria and offers 180 degree views of the marina and Oak Bay from it's floor-to-ceiling windows. Brunch, lunch, and dinner menus are offered. This restaurant is a great place for groups and families. International menu. Lunch, dinner, brunch. Bar. Children's menu. Business casual attire. Reservations recommended. **$$**

**★ WHITE HEATHER TEA ROOM.** *1885 Oak Bay Ave, Victoria (V8R 1C6). Phone 250/595-8020; fax 250/598-4667. www.whiteheathertearoom.com.* This delightful restaurant is located approximately 10-15 minutes from the Inner Harbour in the small Oak Bay area. The lunch menu is Scottish, but other offerings include afternoon tea and delicious baked goods. Don't forget to take home some Scottish shortbread. Scottish menu. Lunch. Closed Sun-Mon; also two weeks in Sept. Business casual attire. Reservations recommended. **$**

# Index

## C

## E

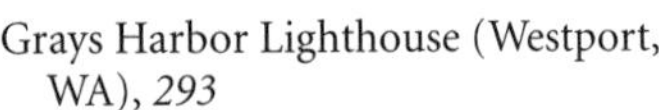

## I

## J



## K

## N

**P**

## S

**T**

**U**



**V**

# Chain Restaurants

## Alaska

### Anchorage

**Benihana,** 1100 W 8th Ave, Anchorage, AK, 99501, (907) 222-5212, 11:30 am-10 pm

**Black Angus Steakhouse,** 300 Tudor Rd, Anchorage, AK, 99503, (907) 562-2844, 11 am-10 pm

**Hooters,** 701 E Tudor Rd, Ste 119, Anchorage, AK, 99503, (907) 563-5653, 11 am-midnight

**Round Table Pizza,** 800 E Dimond Blvd Ste 3-125, Anchorage, AK, 99515, (907) 522-1007, 11:30 am-9 pm

**Sullivan's Steakhouse,** 20 W 5th Ave, Anchorage, AK, 99501, (907) 258-2882, 11 am-11 pm

**Village Inn,** 1130 E Northern Lights Blvd, Anchorage, AK, 99508, (907) 279-6012, 7 am-midnight

**Village Inn,** 720 W Dimond, Anchorage, AK, 99515, (907) 344-0010, 7 am-midnight

**Village Inn,** 4403 Spenard Rd, Anchorage, AK, 99517, (907) 243-6009, 7 am-midnight

### Elmendorf, AFB

**Godfather's Pizza,** 7176 Fighter Dr, Elmendorf, AFB, AK, 99506, (907) 753-7204

### Fort Richardson

**Godfather's Pizza,** 560 D St, Fort Richardson, AK, 99505, (907) 428-4005

### Ketchikan

**Godfather's Pizza,** 2050 Sea Level Dr, Ketchikan, AK, 99901, (907) 225-4444

**Godfather's Pizza,** 5 Salmon Landing, Ketchikan, AK, 99901, (907) 247-2151

## Idaho

### Boise

**Chili's,** 916 BRdway, Boise, ID, 83706, (208) 389-2200, 11 am-10 pm

**Chili's,** 7997 Franklin Rd, Boise, ID, 83709, (208) 327-0088, 11 am-10 pm

**Cracker Barrel,** 1733 S Cole Rd, Boise, ID, 83709, (208) 321-8280, 6 am-10 pm

**Fuddruckers,** 1666 S Entertainment Blvd, Boise, ID, 83709, 11 am-9 pm

**Golden Corral,** 8460 W Emerald St, Boise, ID, 83704, (208) 373-7101, 11 am-9 pm

**Hooters,** 8000 W Franklin Rd, Boise, ID, 83709, (208) 321-4668, 11 am-midnight

**Marie Callender's,** 8574 Fairview Ave, Boise, ID, 83704, (208) 375-7744, 11 am-10 pm

**Melting Pot,** 6th and Idaho St, Boise, ID, 83712, (208) 383-0900, 5 pm-10:30 pm

**On the Border,** 7802 Spectrum St, Boise, ID, 83709, (208) 322-8145, 11 am-10 pm

**P.F. Changs,** 391 S8th St, Boise, ID, 83702, (208) 342-8100, 11 am-10 pm

**Round Table Pizza,** 5120 Overland Rd, Boise, ID, 83705, (208) 331-7979, 11:30 am-9 pm

**Round Table Pizza,** 10412 Overland Rd, Boise, ID, 83709, (208) 672-7878, 11:30 am-9 pm

**Round Table Pizza,** 7072 S Eisenman Rd, Boise, ID, 83716, (208) 385-7900, 11:30 am-9 pm

**Sizzler,** 459 N Cole, Boise, ID, 86326, (208) 322-2930, 11 am-10 pm

### Coeur d'Alene

**Chili's,** 482 W Sunset Ave, Coeur d'Alene, ID, 83815, (208) 676-1826, 11 am-10 pm

### Eagle

**Round Table Pizza,** 395 W State St, Eagle, ID, 83616, (208) 939-2900, 11:30 am-9 pm

### Garden City

**Round Table Pizza,** 5865 Glenwood St, Ste D, Garden City, ID, 83714, (208) 658-7800, 11:30 am-9 pm

### Idaho Falls

**Chili's,** 620 N Utah Ave, Idaho Falls, ID, 83402, (208) 552-2577, 11 am-10 pm

**Godfather's Pizza,** 1680 1st St, Idaho Falls, ID, 83401, (208) 529-0553

**Sizzler,** 2380 E Seventeenth St, Idaho Falls, ID, 86001, (208) 525-2660, 11 am-10 pm

### Lewiston

**Old Country Buffet,** 2305 Nez Perce Dr, Lewiston, ID, 83501, (208) 746-5124, 11 am-9 pm

### Meridian

**Round Table Pizza,** 499 S Main St, Meridian, ID, 83642, (208) 887-1100, 11:30 am-9 pm

**Tony Roma's,** 790 S Progress Ave, Meridian, ID, 83642, (208) 895-8466, 11 am-10 pm

### Nampa

**Golden Corral,** 2122 N Cassia St, Nampa, ID, 83651, (208) 466-2883, 11 am-9 pm

**Round Table Pizza,** 2310 12th Ave Rd, Nampa, ID, 83686, (208) 468-7800, 11:30 am-9 pm

**Sizzler,** 501 Caldwell Blvd, Nampa, ID, 86004, (208) 466-8570, 11 am-10 pm

### Pocatello

**Golden Corral,** 850 Yellowstone Ave, Pocatello, ID, 83201, (208) 478-2057, 11 am-9 pm

**Sizzler,** 1000 Pocatello Creek Rd, Pocatello, ID, 86326, (208) 233-1547, 11 am-10 pm

### Twin Falls

**Chili's,** 1880 Blue Lakes Blvd N, Twin Falls, ID, 83301, (208) 734-1167, 11 am-10 pm

**Golden Corral,** 1823 Blue Lakes Blvd N, Twin Falls, ID, 83301, (208) 735-1820, 11 am-9 pm

**Sizzler,** 705 Blue Lakes Blvd N, Twin Falls, ID, 86326, (208) 733-8650, 11 am-10 pm

## Oregon

### Albany

**Sizzler,** 2148 Santiam Hwy, Albany, OR, 97320, (541) 926-6591, 11 am-10 pm

### Aloha

**Godfather's Pizza,** 17691 SW Farmington Mall, Aloha, OR, 97007, (503) 649-5600

### Beaverton

**Benihana,** 9205 SW Cascade Ave, Beaverton, OR, 97008, (503) 643-4016, 11:30 am-10 pm

**Hometown Buffet,** 3790 Sw Hall Blvd, Beaverton, OR, 97005, (503) 627-0337, 11 am-8:30 pm

**Hooters,** 11995 SW Be Averton-Hillsdale Hwy, Beaverton, OR, 97005, (503) 646-9464, 11 am-midnight

**Marie Callender's,** 16261 NW Cornell Rd, Beaverton, OR, 97006, (503) 439-8771, 11 am-10 pm

**Round Table Pizza,** 14342 SW Allen Blvd, Beaverton, OR, 97005, (503) 641-6821, 11:30 am-9 pm

**Round Table Pizza,** 10150 SW Be Averton Hillsdale, Beaverton, OR, 97005, (503) 646-6168, 11:30 am-9 pm

**Village Inn,** 10650 SW Be Averton-Hillsdale Hwy, Beaverton, OR, 97005, (503) 644-8848, 7 am-midnight

### Bend

**Round Table Pizza,** 1552 NE 3rd St, Bend, OR, 97701, (541) 389-2963, 11:30 am-9 pm

### Canby

**Godfather's Pizza,** 1477 SE First Ave, Ste 101, Canby, OR, 97013, (503) 263-2000

### Clackamas

**Chevy's,** 12520 SE 93rd Ave, Clackamas, OR, 97015, (503) 654-1333, 11 am-10 pm

**Godfather's Pizza,** 14682 SE Sunnyside Rd, Clackamas, OR, 97015, (503) 658-2200

### Eugene

**Marie Callender's,** 1300 Valley River Dr, Eugene, OR, 97401, (541) 484-7111, 11 am-10 pm

### Forest Grove

**Godfather's Pizza,** 2834-A Pacific Ave, Forest Grove, OR, 97116, (503) 359-5405

### Grants Pass

**Sizzler,** 1871 NE 7th St, Grants Pass, OR, 97526, (503) 479-1034, 11 am-10 pm

### Gresham

**Marie Callender's,** 305 NW Burnside St, Gresham, OR, 97030, (503) 669-8440, 11 am-10 pm

**Round Table Pizza,** 2009 NE Burnside Rd, Gresham, OR, 97030, (503) 661-6611, 11:30 am-9 pm

**Sizzler,** 105 NE Burnside Rd, Gresham, OR, 97030, (503) 465-8565, 11 am-10 pm

## Hillsboro

**Chevy's,** 1951 NW 185th Ave, Hillsboro, OR, 97124, (503) 690-4524, 11 am-10 pm

**Godfather's Pizza,** 7440 SW Baseline, Hillsboro, OR, 97123, (503) 848-0100

**P.F. Changs,** 19320 NW Emma Way, Hillsboro, OR, 97124, (503) 533-4580, 11 am-10 pm

**Round Table Pizza,** 2247 SE Tualatin Valley Hwy, Hillsboro, OR, 97123, (503) 693-1067, 11:30 am-9 pm

**Round Table Pizza,** 2473 NW 185th Ave, Hillsboro, OR, 97124, (503) 690-7712, 11:30 am-9 pm

## Klamath Falls

**Sizzler,** 2506 S 6th St, Klamath Falls, OR, 97601, (541) 884-1848, 11 am-10 pm

## Lake Oswego

**Chevy's,** 14991 Bangy Rd, Lake Oswego, OR, 97035, (503) 620-7700, 11 am-10 pm

**Fuddruckers,** 17815 S W 65th , Lake Oswego, OR, 97034, 11 am-9 pm

**Round Table Pizza,** 16444 Boones Ferry Rd, Lake Oswego, OR, 97035, (503) 636-3350, 11:30 am-9 pm

## Medford

**Hometown Buffet,** South Gateway Center, 1299 Center Dr, Medford, OR, 97501, (541) 770-6779, 11 am-8:30 pm

**Marie Callender's,** 1528 Biddle Rd, Medford, OR, 97504, (541) 772-5200, 11 am-10 pm

**Round Table Pizza,** 953 Medford Center, Medford, OR, 97504, (541) 773-3435, 11:30 am-9 pm

**Sizzler,** 700 Biddle, Medford, OR, 97501, (541) 772-2942, 11 am-10 pm

## Milwaukie

**Black Angus Steakhouse,** 16323 SE Mcloughlin Blvd, Milwaukie, OR, 97222, (503) 653-2700, 11 am-10 pm

**Round Table Pizza,** 16550 SE McLoughlin Blvd, Milwaukie, OR, 97267, (503) 653-6444, 11:30 am-9 pm

## Newport

**Sizzler,** 2426 N Pacific Coast Hwy, Newport, OR, 97365, (503) 265-7055, 11 am-10 pm

## North Bend

**Sizzler,** 3390 BRdway, North Bend, OR, 86326, (503) 756-7100, 11 am-10 pm

## Ontario

**Sizzler,** 830 S E First Ave, Ontario, OR, 86326, (541) 889-5005, 11 am-10 pm

## Portland

**Godfather's Pizza,** 4744 NW Bethany Blvd, Portland, OR, 97229, (503) 533-9777

**Godfather's Pizza,** 11140 SW Barnes Rd, Portland, OR, 97225, (503) 646-1100

**Hometown Buffet,** Clackamas Square, 11358 Se 82Nd Ave, Portland, OR, 97266, (503) 659-6335, 11 am-8:30 pm

**Hometown Buffet,** 205 Plz, 10542-A Se Washington St, Portland, OR, 97216, (503) 252-0741, 11 am-8:30 pm

**Hooters,** 9950 SE Stark St, Portland, OR, 97216, (503) 251-8400, 11 am-midnight

**Hooters,** 11875 N Jantzen Beach, Portland, OR, 97217, (503) 735-9464, 11 am-midnight

**Melting Pot,** SW Sixth Ave & Main St, Portland, OR, 97204, (503) 517-8960, 5 pm-10:30 pm

**P.F. Changs,** 1139 NW Couch St, Portland, OR, 97209, (503) 432-4000, 11 am-10 pm

**Rock Bottom,** 206 SW Morrison St, Portland, OR, 97204, (503) 796-2739, 11 am-Close

**Round Table Pizza,** 6250 S E Foster Rd, Portland, OR, 97206, (503) 777-1461, 11:30 am-9 pm

**Round Table Pizza,** 4831 NE Fremont St, Portland, OR, 97213, (503) 281-9592, 11:30 am-9 pm

**Round Table Pizza,** 4141 NE 122nd Ave, Portland, OR, 97230, (503) 253-3557, 11:30 am-9 pm

**Round Table Pizza,** 10389 SE 82nd St, Portland, OR, 97266, (503) 774-3129, 11:30 am-9 pm

**Round Table Pizza,** 10070 SW Barbur Blvd, Portland, OR, 97219, (503) 245-2211, 11:30 am-9 pm

**Round Table Pizza,** 13587 NW Cornell Rd, Portland, OR, 97229, (503) 646-9700, 11:30 am-9 pm

**Round Table Pizza,** 750 NE 181st Ave, Portland, OR, 97230, (503) 661-1011, 11:30 am-9 pm

**Sizzler,** 3737 S E 82nd St, Portland, OR, 97266, (503) 774-9865, 11 am-10 pm

**Todai,** 340 SW Morrison St, #4305, Portland, OR, 97204, (503) 294-0007, 11:30 am-9 pm

**Village Inn,** 1621 NE 10th Ave, Portland, OR, 97232, (503) 284-4141, 7 am-midnight

**Village Inn,** 10301 SE Stark St, Portland, OR, 97216, (503) 256-2380, 7 am-midnight

### Roseburg

**Round Table Pizza,** 2040 NW Stewart Pkwy, Roseburg, OR, 97470, (541) 673-2047, 11:30 am-9 pm

**Sizzler,** 1156 NW Garden Valley, Roseburg, OR, 97410, (503) 672-5443, 11 am-10 pm

### Salem

**Hometown Buffet,** Lancaster Center East, 636 Lancaster Dr NE, Salem, OR, 97301, (503) 585-8163, 11 am-8:30 pm

**Marie Callender's,** 2615 Lancaster Dr NE, Salem, OR, 97305, (503) 581-8421, 11 am-10 pm

**Sizzler,** 1151 Lancaster NE, Salem, OR, 97301, (503) 581-8658, 11 am-10 pm

### Sherwood

**Godfather's Pizza,** 15982 SW Tualatin-Sherwood Rd, Sherwood, OR, 97140, (503) 625-1600

### Springfield

**Hometown Buffet,** Gateway Mall, 3000 Gateway St, Springfield, OR, 97477, (541) 746-3220, 11 am-8:30 pm

**Round Table Pizza,** 5547 Main St, Springfield, OR, 97478, (541) 741-2165, 11:30 am-9 pm

**Sizzler,** 1010 Postal Way , Springfield, OR, 97477, (503) 726-9933, 11 am-10 pm

### Tigard

**Cheesecake Factory,** 9309 Washington Square Rd, Tigard, OR, 97223, (503) 620-1100, 11 am-11:30 pm

**Godfather's Pizza,** 14200 SW Barrows Rd, Tigard, OR, 97223, (503) 590-0900

**Hometown Buffet,** Tigard MarketPl, 13500 Sw Pacific Hwy, Tigard, OR, 97223, (503) 624-2794, 11 am-8:30 pm

**P.F. Changs,** 7463 SW Bridgeport Rd, Tigard, OR, 97224, (503) 430-3020, 11 am-10 pm

**Round Table Pizza,** 12085 SW Hall Blvd, , Tigard, OR, 97223, (503) 639-1545, 11:30 am-9 pm

**Village Inn,** 17070 SW 72nd Ave, Tigard, OR, 97224, (503) 620-2515, 7 am-midnight

### Troutdale

**Godfather's Pizza,** 2503 SW Cherry Park Rd, Troutdale, OR, 97060, (503) 492-3300

### West Linn

**Round Table Pizza,** 19121 Willamette Dr, West Linn, OR, 97068, (503) 635-6654, 11:30 am-9 pm

## Washington

### Auburn

**Godfather's Pizza,** 321 Auburn Way No, Auburn, WA, 98002, (253) 833-1772

**Round Table Pizza,** 4002 A St SE, Auburn, WA, 98002, (253) 735-4000, 11:30 am-9 pm

### Bellevue

**Black Angus Steakhouse,** 1411 156th NE, Bellevue, WA, 98007, (425) 746-1663, 11 am-10 pm

**Cheesecake Factory,** 401 Bellevue Sq, Bellevue, WA, 98004, (425) 450-6000, 11 am-11:30 pm

**Maggiano's,** 10455 NE 8th St, Bellevue, WA, 98004, (425) 519-6476, 11 am-10 pm

**Melting Pot,** 302 108th Ave NE, Bellevue, WA, 98004, (425) 646-2744, 5 pm-10:30 pm

**Old Country Buffet,** Factoria Mall, 4022 Factoria Mall Ne, Bellevue, WA, 98006, (425) 644-5499, 11 am-9 pm

**P.F. Changs,** 525 Bellevue Square, Bellevue Square, Bellevue, WA, 98004, (425) 637-3582, 11 am-10 pm

**Rock Bottom,** 550 106th Ave, Ste 103, Bellevue, WA, 98004, (425) 462-9300, 11 am-2 am

**Ztejas Southwestern Grill,** 535 Bellevue Sq , Bellevue, WA, 98004, (425) 467-5911, 11 am-10 pm

### Bellingham

**Black Angus Steakhouse,** 165 S Samish Way, Bellingham, WA, 98225, (360) 734-7600, 11 am-10 pm

**Old Country Buffet,** Plz At The Point, 1 Bellis Fair Pkwy #714, Bellingham, WA, 98226, (360) 715-8240, 11 am-9 pm

**Round Table Pizza,** 1145 E Sunset Dr #135, Bellingham, WA, 98226, (360) 671-6305, 11:30 am-9 pm

### Bonney Lake

**Godfather's Pizza,** 20625 Hwy 410 E, Bonney Lake, WA, 98390, (253) 826-9555

### Bremerton

**Sizzler,** 3558 Wheaton Way, Bremerton, WA, 98310, (360) 479-5748, 11 am-10 pm

### Burien

**Round Table Pizza,** 15730 First Ave S, Burien, WA, 98148, (206) 431-8600, 11:30 am-9 pm

### Centralia

**Godfather's Pizza,** 708 Harrison St, Centralia, WA, 98531, (360) 330-2051

## Covington

**Godfather's Pizza,** 27120 174th Pl SE, Covington, WA, 98042, (253) 630-3993

## Everett

**Round Table Pizza,** 305 SE Everett Mall Way #31, Everett, WA, 98208, (425) 267-0200, 11:30 am-9 pm

**Village Inn,** 8525 Evergreen Way, Everett, WA, 98204, (425) 355-2525, 7 am-midnight

## Federal Way

**Black Angus Steakhouse,** 2400 S 320th, Federal Way, WA, 98003, (253) 839-8370, 11 am-10 pm

**Coco's Bakery,** 32065 Pacific Hwy South, Federal Way, WA, 98003, (253) 839-1200, 6:30 am-10 pm

**Godfather's Pizza,** 2301 SW 336 St, Federal Way, WA, 98023, (253) 874-3313

**Marie Callender's,** 31920 Gateway Center Blvd, Federal Way, WA, 98003, (253) 839-8322, 11 am-10 pm

**Old Country Buffet,** Seatac Village Shopping Center, 1816 S 320Th St, Federal Way, WA, 98003, (253) 839-9207, 11 am-9 pm

**Round Table Pizza,** 1414 S 324th St, #213, Federal Way, WA, 98003, (253) 941-4000, 11:30 am-9 pm

**Village Inn,** 31711 Pacific Hwy S, Federal Way, WA, 98003, (253) 941-9860, 7 am-midnight

## Fort Lewis

**Godfather's Pizza,** 6029 41st Division Dr, Fort Lewis, WA, 98433, (253) 964-2267

## Gig Harbor

**Round Table Pizza,** 5500 Olympic Dr, #H101, Gig Harbor, WA, 98335, (253) 851-6250, 11:30 am-9 pm

## Issaquah

**Round Table Pizza,** 730 NW Gilman Blvd, Issaquah, WA, 98027, (425) 391-7117, 11:30 am-9 pm

## Kennewick

**Old Country Buffet,** 6821 W Canal Dr, Kennewick, WA, 99337, (509) 735-9887, 11 am-9 pm

**Old Country Buffet,** Columbia Shopping Center, 1321 N Columbia Center Blvd, Kennewick, WA, 99336, (509) 783-4880, 11 am-9 pm

**Round Table Pizza,** 3300 W Clearwater Ave, Kennewick, WA, 99336, (509) 783-2204, 11:30 am-9 pm

**Tony Roma's,** 8551 Gage Blvd, Kennewick, WA, 99336, (509) 783-7002, 11 am-10 pm

## Kent

**Old Country Buffet,** 25630 104Th Ave Se, Kent, WA, 98031, (253) 859-3224, 11 am-9 pm

**Round Table Pizza,** 13036 Kent Kangley Rd, Kent, WA, 98042, (253) 630-6900, 11:30 am-9 pm

## Kirkland

**Old Country Buffet,** Totem Lake Mall, 12618 Totem Lake Blvd, Kirkland, WA, 98034, (425) 823-2292, 11 am-9 pm

## Lacey

**Round Table Pizza,** 1401 Marvin Rd, Ste 310, Lacey, WA, 98516, (360) 438-8844, 11:30 am-9 pm

## Longview

**Sizzler,** 936 Ocean Beach Hwy, Longview, WA, 98632, (360) 577-0607, 11 am-10 pm

## Lynnwood

**Black Angus Steakhouse,** 20102 44th Ave West, Lynnwood, WA, 98036, (425) 774-6556, 11 am-10 pm

**Chevy's,** 19920 44th Ave W, Lynnwood, WA, 98036, (425) 776-2000, 11 am-10 pm

**Claim Jumper,** 18725 33rd Ave W, Lynnwood, WA, (425) 778-5700, 11 am-10 pm

**Hooters,** 19800 44th St, Lynnwood, WA, 98036, (425) 672-2900, 11 am-midnight

**Old Country Buffet,** Lynnwood Square, 4601 200Th St Sw, Lynnwood, WA, 98036, (425) 672-9731, 11 am-9 pm

**P.F. Changs,** 3000 184th St, Alderwood Mall , Lynnwood, WA, 98037, (425) 921-2100, 11 am-10 pm

**Tony Roma's,** 3828 196th St SW, Lynnwood, WA, 98036, (425) 771-3700, 11 am-10 pm

## Marysville

**Golden Corral,** 1065 State St, Marysville, WA, 98270, (360) 659-4035, 11 am-9 pm

## Mill Creek

**Round Table Pizza,** 16314 Bothell-Everett Hwy, Mill Creek, WA, 98012, (425) 745-4561, 11:30 am-9 pm

## Moses Lake

**Godfather's Pizza,** 517 S Pioneer Way, Moses Lake, WA, 98837, (509) 765-3900

**Golden Corral,** 930 N Stratford Rd, Moses Lake, WA, 98837, (509) 765-0565, 11 am-9 pm

## Mount Vernon

**Round Table Pizza,** 115 E College Way, Mount Vernon, WA, 98273, (360) 424-7979, 11:30 am-9 pm

## Olympia

**Sizzler,** 3315 Pacific Ave SE, Ste A, Olympia, WA, 98501, (360) 459-8657, 11 am-10 pm

Tony Roma's, 625 Black Lake Blvd SW, Olympia, WA, 98502, (360) 753-2911, 11 am-10 pm

## Pasco

**Round Table Pizza,** 3201 W Court St, Pasco, WA, 99301, (509) 545-1091, 11:30 am-9 pm

## Port Orchard

**Godfather's Pizza,** 1700 Hwy 160, Port Orchard, WA, 98366, (360) 876-9296

## Puyallup

**Black Angus Steakhouse,** 203 35th Ave SE, Puyallup, WA, 98374, (253) 841-1900, 11 am-10 pm

**Old Country Buffet,** South Hill Mall, 3500 S Meridan, Puyallup, WA, 98373, (253) 840-2895, 11 am-9 pm

**Round Table Pizza,** 16016 Meridian E, Puyallup, WA, 98375, (253) 840-5500, 11:30 am-9 pm

## Redmond

**Claim Jumper,** 7210 164th Ave NE, Redmond, WA, (425) 885-1273, 11 am-10 pm

**Round Table Pizza,** 15025 NE 24th St, Redmond, WA, 98052, (425) 644-7117, 11:30 am-9 pm

**Todai,** 7548 164th Ave NE, Redmond, WA, 98052, (425) 376-1922, 11:30 am-9 pm

## Renton

**Round Table Pizza,** 302 SW 43rd St, Renton, WA, 98055, (425) 251-0606, 11:30 am-9 pm

**Round Table Pizza,** 14020 SE Petrovitsky, Renton, WA, 98055, (425) 277-2100, 11:30 am-9 pm

## Richland

**Round Table Pizza,** 245 Torbett, Richland, WA, 99352, (509) 946-0667, 11:30 am-9 pm

**Round Table Pizza,** 1769 Leslie Rd, Richland, WA, 99352, (509) 946-9023, 11:30 am-9 pm

## Seattle

**Benihana,** 1200 Fifth Ave, Seattle, WA, 98101, (206) 682-4686, 11:30 am-10 pm

**Cheesecake Factory,** 700 Pike St, Seattle, WA, 98109, (206) 652-5400, 11 am-11:30 pm

**Hooters,** 901 Fairview Ave N #C-100, Seattle, WA, 98109, (206) 625-0555, 11 am-midnight

**Marie Callender's,** 9538 First Ave NE, Seattle, WA, 98115, (206) 526-5785, 11 am-10 pm

**Melting Pot,** 14 Mercer St, Seattle, WA, 98109, (206) 378-1208, 5 pm-10:30 pm

**P.F. Changs,** 400 Pine St, Westlake Center, Seattle, WA, 98101, (206) 393-0070, 11 am-10 pm

**Piatti Locali,** 2695 NE Village Ln, Seattle, WA, 98105, (206) 524-9088, 11 am-10 pm

**Rock Bottom,** 1333 Fifth Ave, Seattle, WA, 98101, (206) 623-3070

**Round Table Pizza,** 5111 - 25th Ave, NE, Seattle, WA, 98105, (206) 527-1550, 11:30 am-9 pm

**Todai,** 00 Pine St 4th Floor, Seattle, WA, 98101, (206) 749-5100, 11:30 am-9 pm

**Tony Roma's,** 543 NE Northgate Way, Seattle, WA, 98125, (206) 367-8384, 11 am-10 pm

## Shelton

**Godfather's Pizza,** 301 E Wallace Kneeland Blvd, Shelton, WA, 98584, (360) 426-3200

## Shoreline

**Old Country Buffet,** 16549 Aurora Ave N, Shoreline, WA, 98133, (206) 542-5665, 11 am-9 pm

## Silverdale

**Round Table Pizza,** 3276 NW Plz Rd, Ste 101, Silverdale, WA, 98383, (360) 698-4040, 11:30 am-9 pm

## Spokane

**Black Angus Steakhouse,** 14724 E Indiana, Spokane, WA, 99216, (509) 927-1177, 11 am-10 pm

**Chili's,** 207 w Spokane Falls Blvd, Spokane, WA, 99201, (509) 458-2345, 11 am-10 pm

**Chili's,** 4750 N Division St #1120, Spokane, WA, 99207, (509) 483-7000, 11 am-10 pm

**Golden Corral,** 7117 N Division St, Spokane, WA, 99208, (509) 468-1895, 11 am-9 pm

**Hooters,** 16208 E Indiana Ave, Spokane, WA, 99216, 11 am-midnight

**Marie Callender's,** N 2111 Argonne Rd, Spokane, WA, 99212, (509) 922-4123, 11 am-10 pm

**Old Country Buffet,** Franklin Park Mall, 5504 N Division St, Spokane, WA, 99207, (509) 484-5026, 11 am-9 pm

**Old Country Buffet,** Northpointe Plz, N 9606 Newport Hwy, Spokane, WA, 99218, (509) 467-3440, 11 am-9 pm

**Old Country Buffet,** Opportunity Center, 12209 E Sprague Ave, Spokane, WA, 99206, (509) 927-1002, 11 am-9 pm

**P.F. Changs,** 801 W Main, Spokane, WA, 99201, 11 am-10 pm

**Round Table Pizza,** 4510 S Regal St, Spokane, WA, 99223, (509) 448-2054, 11:30 am-9 pm

**Round Table Pizza,** 1908 W Francis Ave, Spokane, WA, 99205, (509) 324-2414, 11:30 am-9 pm

**Tony Roma's,** 14742 E Indiana, Spokane, WA, 99216, (509) 892-6944, 11 am-10 pm

**Tony Roma's,** N 7640 Division, Spokane, WA, 99207, (509) 482-7180, 11 am-10 pm

**Village Inn,** 518 W Francis Ave, Spokane, WA, 99208, (509) 467-5436, 7 am-midnight

## Tacoma

**Black Angus Steakhouse,** 9905 Bridgeport Way SW, Tacoma, WA, 98499, (253) 582-6900, 11 am-10 pm

**Chevy's,** 3702 S Fife St, Ste B-100-A, Tacoma, WA, 98409, (253) 472-5800, 11 am-10 pm

**Godfather's Pizza,** 15709 Pacific Ave, Pad 8, Tacoma, WA, 98444, (253) 536-0173

**Hooters,** 6812 Tacoma Mall Blvd, Tacoma, WA, 98409, (253) 476-9464, 11 am-midnight

**Melting Pot,** 2121 Pacific Ave, Tacoma, WA, 98402, (253) 535-3939, 5 pm-10:30 pm

**Old Country Buffet,** 5815 Lakewood Towne Center Blvd Sw, Tacoma, WA, 98499, (253) 584-0220, 11 am-9 pm

**Round Table Pizza,** 7901 S Hosmer, Ste A-1, Tacoma, WA, 98408, (253) 473-6121, 11:30 am-9 pm

**Round Table Pizza,** 2601 N Pearl, Tacoma, WA, 98407, (253) 756-5313, 11:30 am-9 pm

**Sizzler,** 10204 S Tacoma Way, Tacoma, WA, 98499, (253) 582-4001, 11 am-10 pm

**Tony Roma's,** 5221 Tacoma Mall Blvd, Tacoma, WA, 98409, (253) 473-7152, 11 am-10 pm

## Tukwila

**Claim Jumper,** 5901 S 180th St, Tukwila, WA, (206) 575-3918, 11 am-10 pm

**Sizzler,** 16615 S Center Pkwy, Tukwila, WA, 98188, (206) 575-0427, 11 am-10 pm

**Tony Roma's,** 17305 Southcenter Pkwy, Tukwila, WA, 98188, (206) 575-1050, 11 am-10 pm

## Union Gap

**Old Country Buffet,** Valley Mall, 2513 Main St, Union Gap, WA, 98903, (509) 457-8597, 11 am-9 pm

## University Place

**Round Table Pizza,** 7011 27th St W, University Place, WA, 98466, (253) 565-3000, 11:30 am-9 pm

## Vancouver

**Black Angus Steakhouse,** 415 E 13th St, Vancouver, WA, 98660, (360) 695-1506, 11 am-10 pm

**Chevy's,** 4315 NE Thurston Way, Vancouver, WA, 98662, (360) 256-6922, 11 am-10 pm

**Godfather's Pizza,** 6700 NE 162nd Ave, Ste E623, Vancouver, WA, 98682, (360) 254-5100

**Godfather's Pizza,** 2100 A SE 164th Ave, Ste 107, Vancouver, WA, 98684, (360) 256-0000

**Godfather's Pizza,** 1014 N Wenatchee Ave, Vancouver, WA, 98801, (509) 662-5255

**Hometown Buffet,** Vancouver Plz, 7809-B Ne Vancouver Plz Dr, Vancouver, WA, 98662, (360) 256-9420, 11 am-8:30 pm

**Round Table Pizza,** 13009 NE Hwy 99, Vancouver, WA, 98686, (360) 574-5755, 11:30 am-9 pm

**Round Table Pizza,** 616 NE 81st St, Ste A, Vancouver, WA, 98665, (360) 574-1666, 11:30 am-9 pm

**Round Table Pizza,** 13503 SE Mill Plain Blvd, Ste 1, Vancouver, WA, 98684, (360) 253-4921, 11:30 am-9 pm

**Round Table Pizza,** 5016 NE Thurston Way, Vancouver, WA, 98661, (360) 892-0450, 11:30 am-9 pm

## Woodinville

**Round Table Pizza,** 17600 140th Ave NE, Woodinville, WA, 98072, (425) 481-7117, 11:30 am-9 pm

## Yakima

**Black Angus Steakhouse,** 501 N Front St, Yakima, WA, 98901, (509) 248-4540, 11 am-10 pm

**Round Table Pizza,** 1300 N 40th Ave, Yakima, WA, 98908, (509) 248-7210, 11:30 am-9 pm

# Notes

# Notes

# Notes

# Notes